KILL ALL MONSTERS! ™

OMNIBUS—VOLUME 1

WRITTEN BY **MICHAEL MAY**

ILLUSTRATED BY **JASON COPLAND**

LETTERED BY **ED BRISSON, RYAN FERRIER, AND MICAH MYERS**

COVER COLORED BY **PAUL LITTLE**

LOGO CREATED BY **KEL NUTTALL**

EARLY STORY IDEAS BY **ALEX NESS**

ORIGINAL SERIES EDITED BY **JAMES W. POWELL**

PUBLISHER
MIKE RICHARDSON

EDITOR
DAVE MARSHALL

ASSISTANT EDITOR
RACHEL ROBERTS

DESIGNER
BRENNAN THOME

DIGITAL ART TECHNICIAN
CHRISTIANNE GOUDREAU

This volume collects *Kill All Monsters! Volume 1: Ruins of Paris*, originally serialized online, and "Kill All Monsters!: The Ministry of Robots," serialized in *Dark Horse Presents* (volume 3), #12–#14.

Published by
Dark Horse Books
A division of
Dark Horse Comics, Inc.
10956 SE Main Street
Milwaukie, OR 97222

DarkHorse.com
International Licensing: (503) 905-2377
Comic Shop Locator Service: (888) 266-4226

Library of Congress Cataloging-in-Publication Data

Names: May, Michael (Comic book writer), author. | Copland, Jason, illustrator. | Brisson, Ed, letterer. | Ferrier, Ryan, letterer. | Little, Paul John, colourist.
Title: Kill all monsters! omnibus / written by Michael May ; illustrated by Jason Copland ; lettered by Ed Brisson and Ryan Ferrier ; cover colored by Paul Little.
Description: First edition. | Milwaukie, OR : Dark Horse Books, 2017- | Volume 1: "This volume collects Kill All Monsters! Volume 1: Ruins of Paris, originally serialized online and Kill All Monsters! The Ministry of Robots, serialized in Dark Horse Presents volume 3, #12/#14."
Identifiers: LCCN 2017011220 | ISBN 9781616558277 (v. 1 : hardback)
Subjects: LCSH: Comic books, strips, etc. | BISAC: COMICS & GRAPHIC NOVELS / Science Fiction.
Classification: LCC PN6728.K54 M39 2017 | DDC 741.5/973–dc23
L C record available at https://lccn.loc.gov/2017011220
ISBN 978-1-61655-827-7

First edition: July 2017

10 9 8 7 6 5 4 3 2 1

Printed in China

Neil Hankerson Executive Vice President Tom Weddle Chief Financial Officer Randy Stradley Vice President of Publishing Matt Parkinson Vice President of Marketing David Scroggy Vice President of Product Development Dale LaFountain Vice President of Information Technology Cara Niece Vice President of Production and Scheduling Nick McWhorter Vice President of Media Licensing Mark Bernardi Vice President of Digital and Book Trade Sales Ken Lizzi General Counsel Dave Marshall Editor in Chief Davey Estrada Editorial Director Scott Allie Executive Senior Editor Chris Warner Senior Books Editor Cary Grazzini Director of Print and Development Lia Ribacchi Art Director Vanessa Todd Director of Print Purchasing Matt Dryer Director of Digital Art and Prepress Sarah Robertson Director of Product Sales Michael Gombos Director of International Publishing and Licensing

THE RUINS OF PARIS

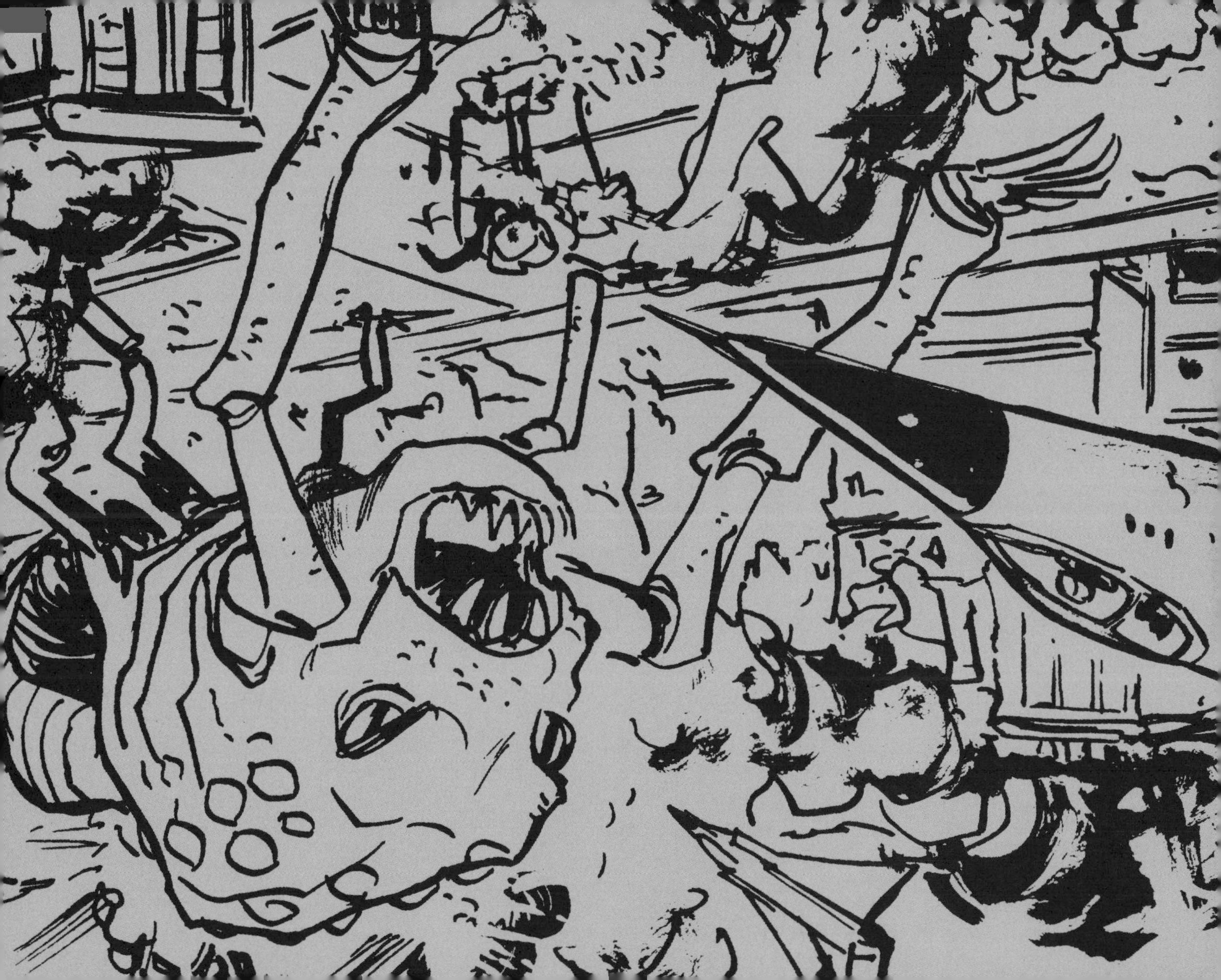

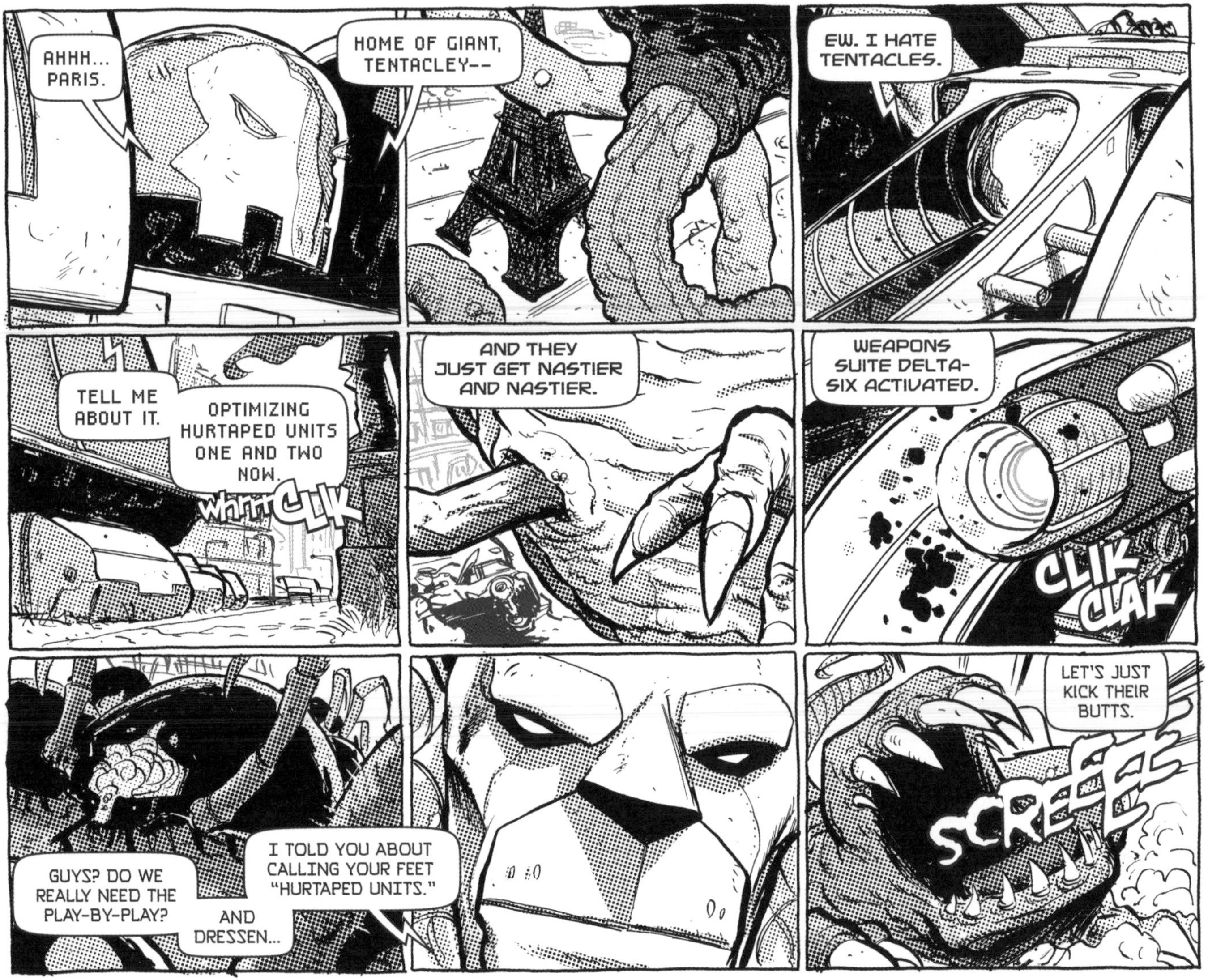
AHHH... PARIS.
HOME OF GIANT, TENTACLEY--
EW. I HATE TENTACLES.
TELL ME ABOUT IT.
OPTIMIZING HURTAPED UNITS ONE AND TWO NOW.
WHRRRCLIK
AND THEY JUST GET NASTIER AND NASTIER.
WEAPONS SUITE DELTA-SIX ACTIVATED.
CLIK CLAK
GUYS? DO WE REALLY NEED THE PLAY-BY-PLAY?
AND DRESSEN...
I TOLD YOU ABOUT CALLING YOUR FEET "HURTAPED UNITS."
LET'S JUST KICK THEIR BUTTS.
SCREEEE

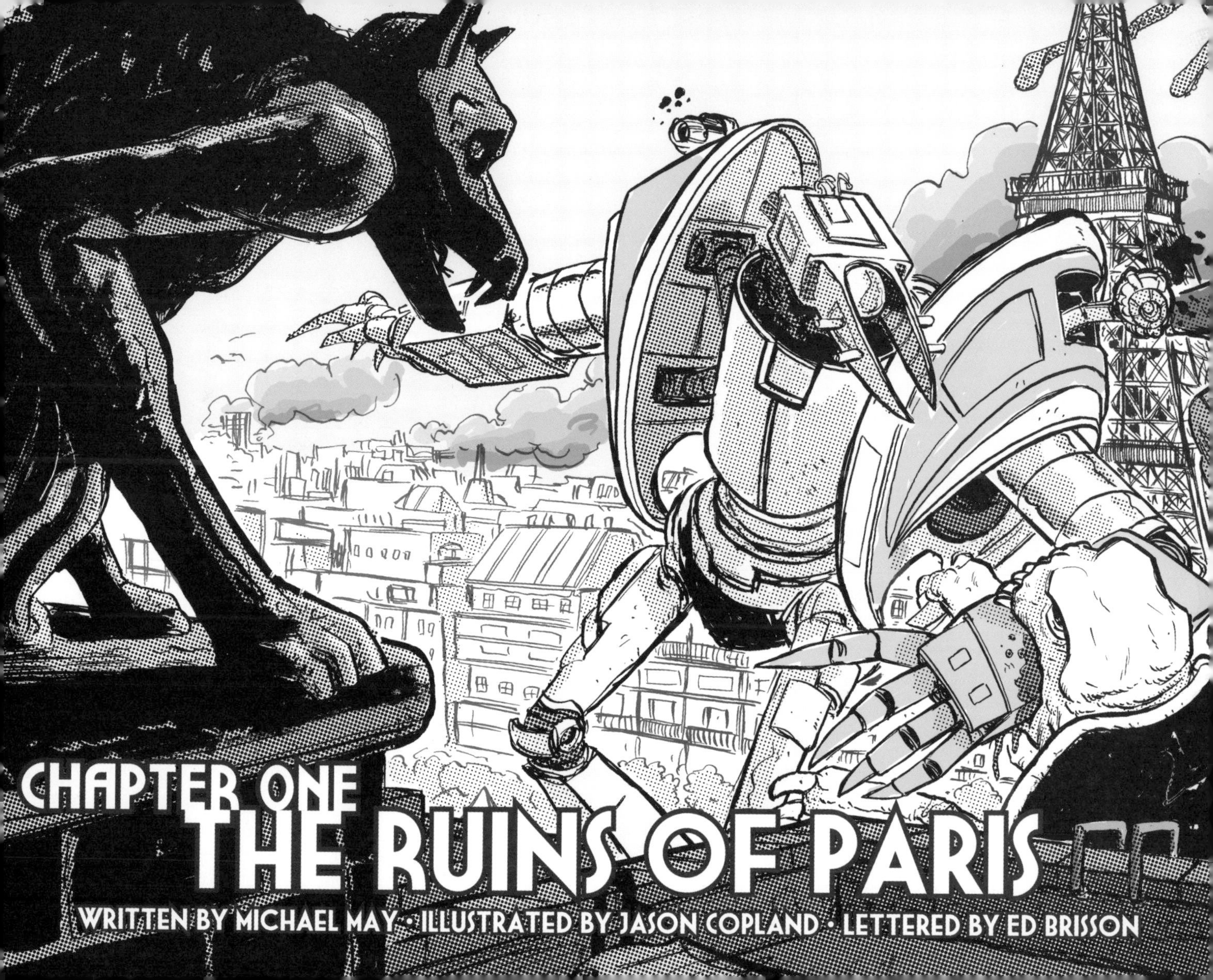
CHAPTER ONE
THE RUINS OF PARIS
WRITTEN BY MICHAEL MAY · ILLUSTRATED BY JASON COPLAND · LETTERED BY ED BRISSON

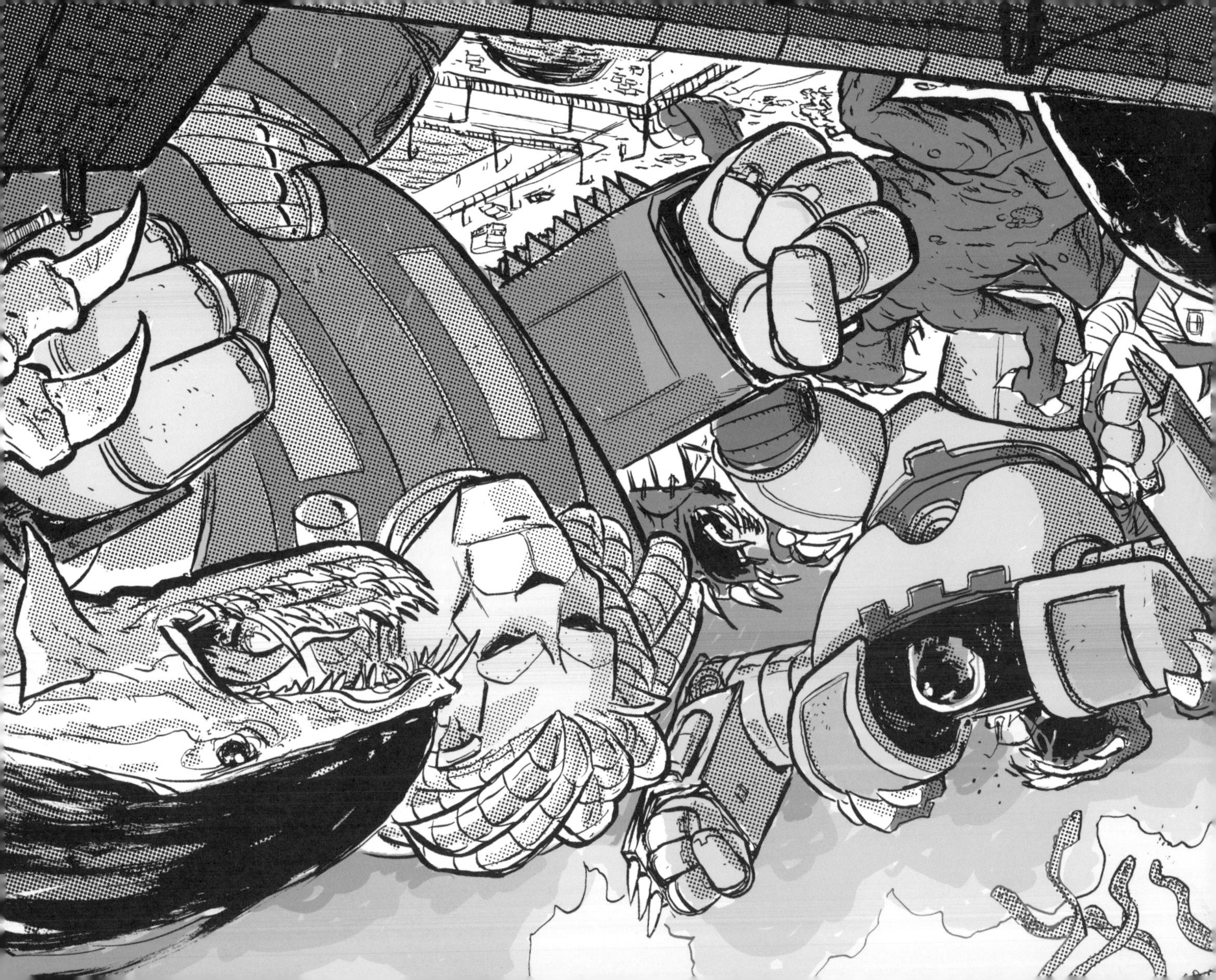

YIKES! WHERE'D ALL THESE COME FROM?
I KNOW! I'VE NEVER SEEN THIS MANY MONSTERS IN ONE PLACE BEFORE!
POW
WELCOME TO THE BIG CITY, SPENCE.

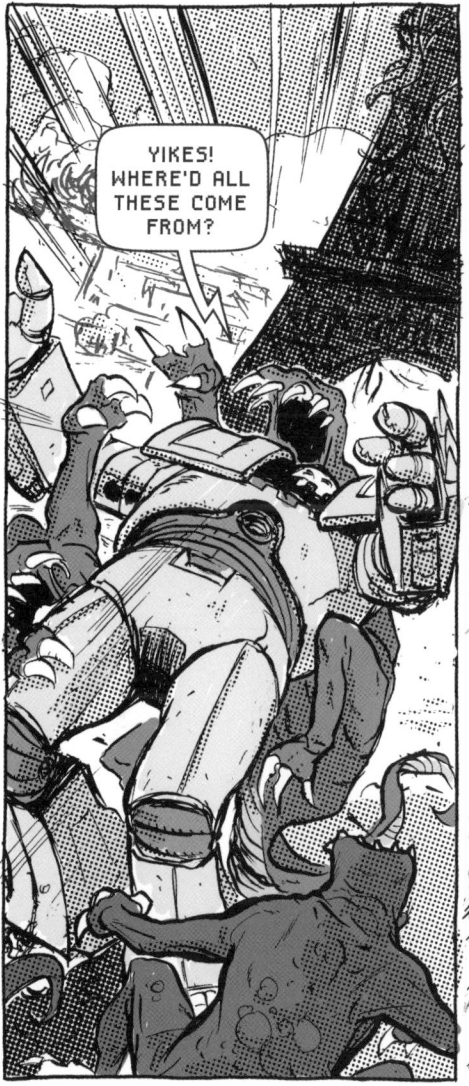

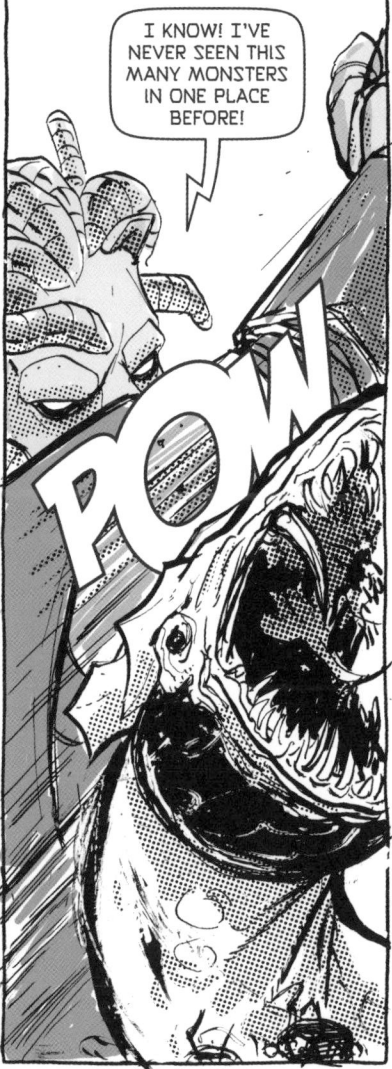

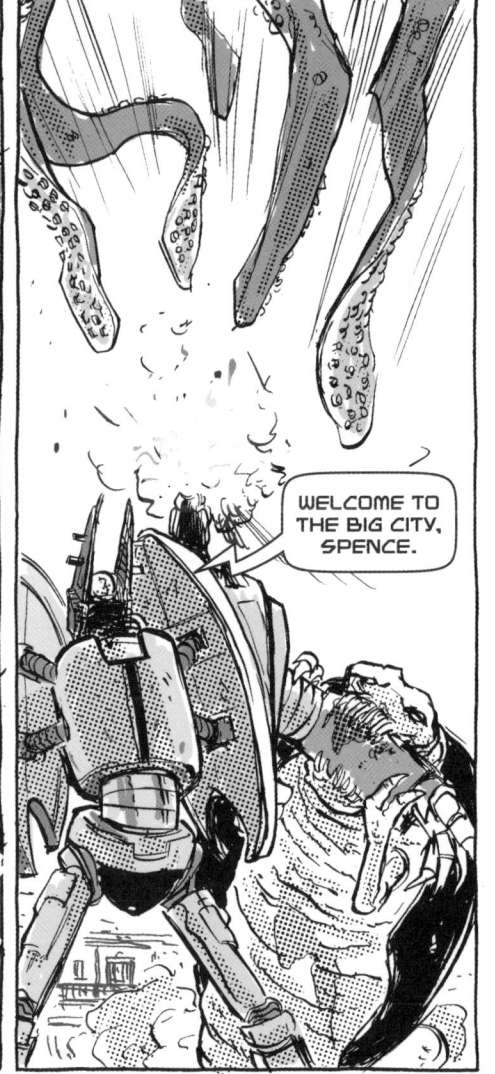

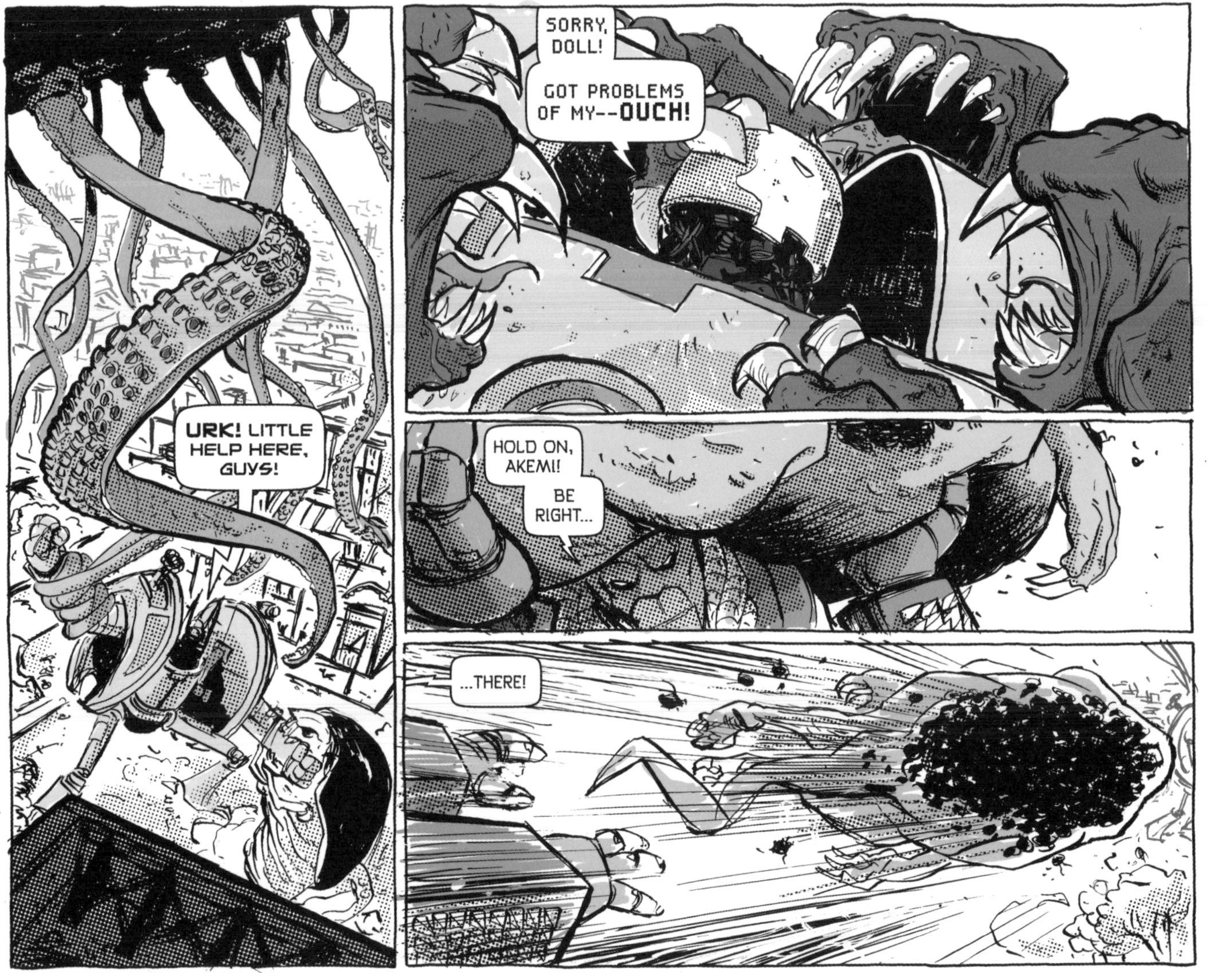
URK! LITTLE HELP HERE, GUYS!
SORRY, DOLL!
GOT PROBLEMS OF MY--OUCH!
HOLD ON, AKEMI!
BE RIGHT...
...THERE!

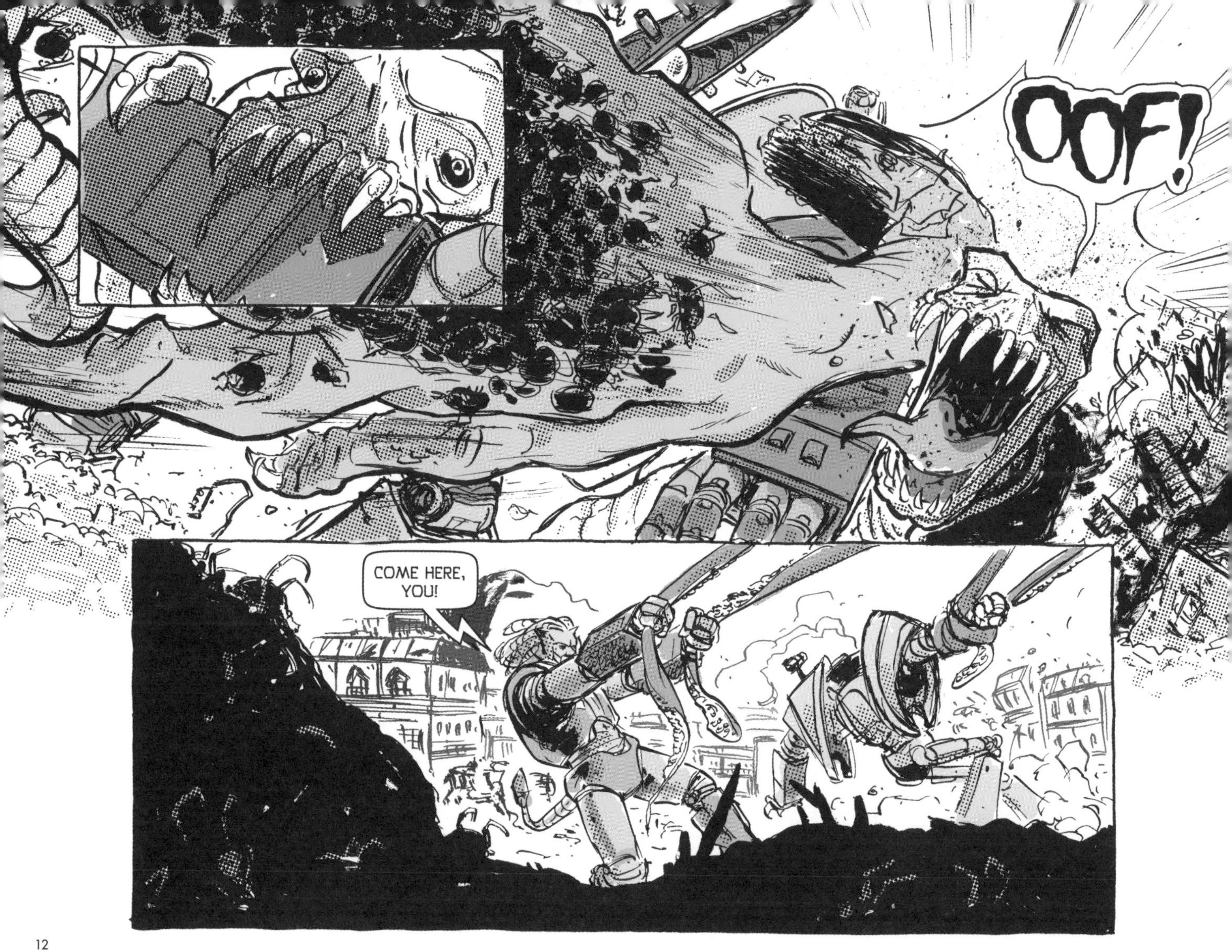
OOF!
COME HERE, YOU!

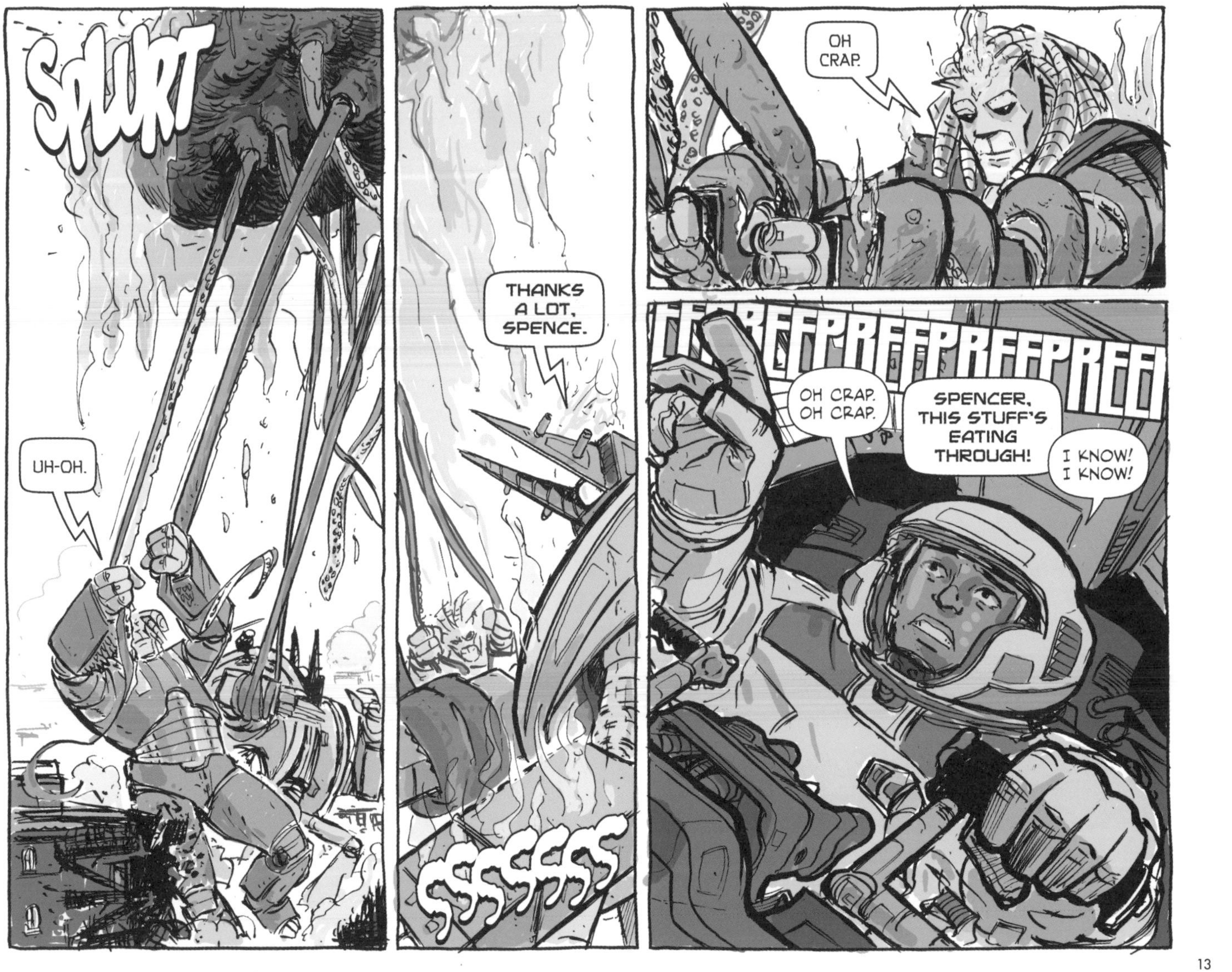
SPLURT
UH-OH.
THANKS A LOT, SPENCE.
SSSSSS
OH CRAP.
PREEPREEPREE
OH CRAP. OH CRAP.
SPENCER, THIS STUFF'S EATING THROUGH!
I KNOW! I KNOW!

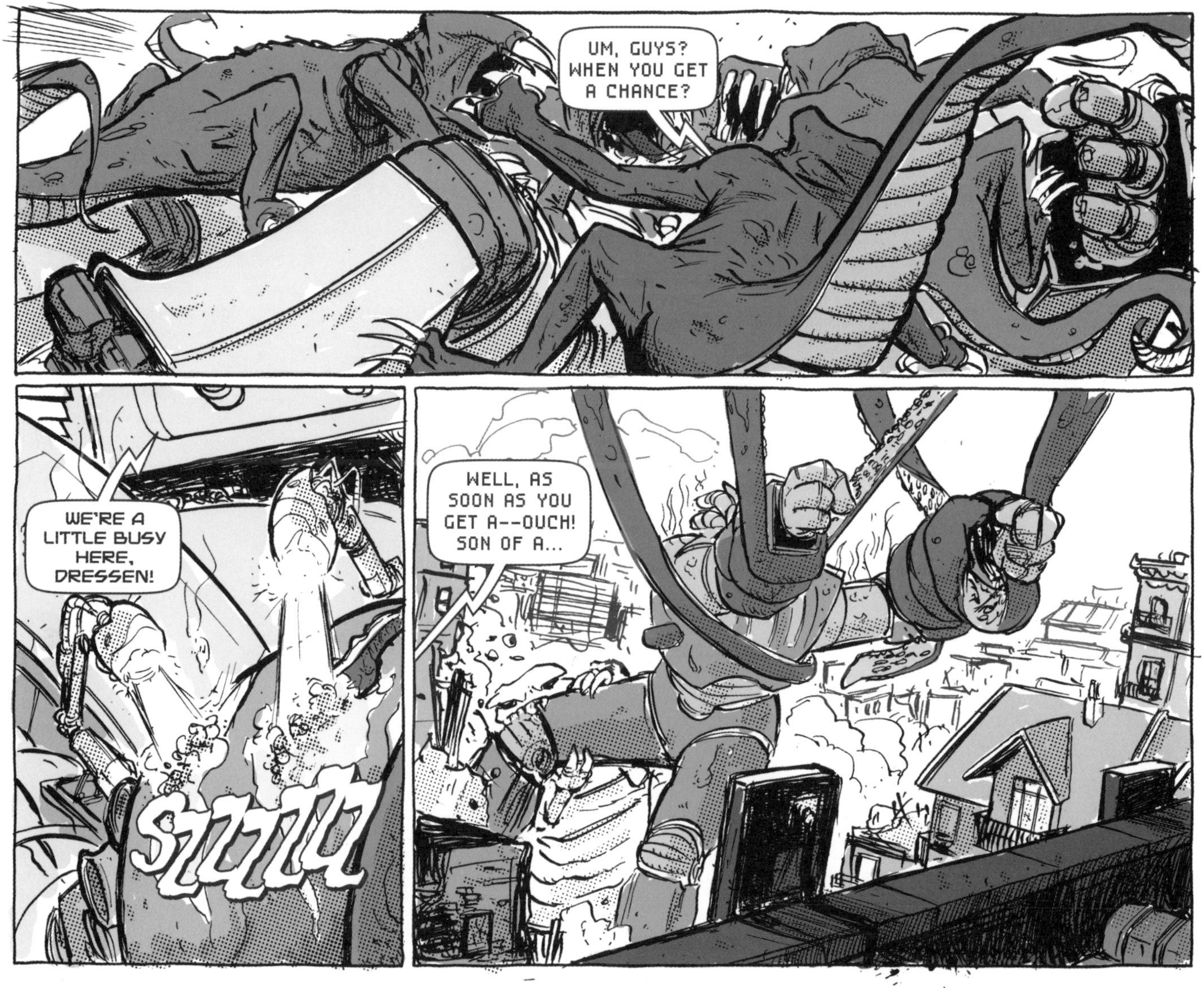
UM, GUYS? WHEN YOU GET A CHANCE?
WE'RE A LITTLE BUSY HERE, DRESSEN!
SSSSS
WELL, AS SOON AS YOU GET A--OUCH! SON OF A...

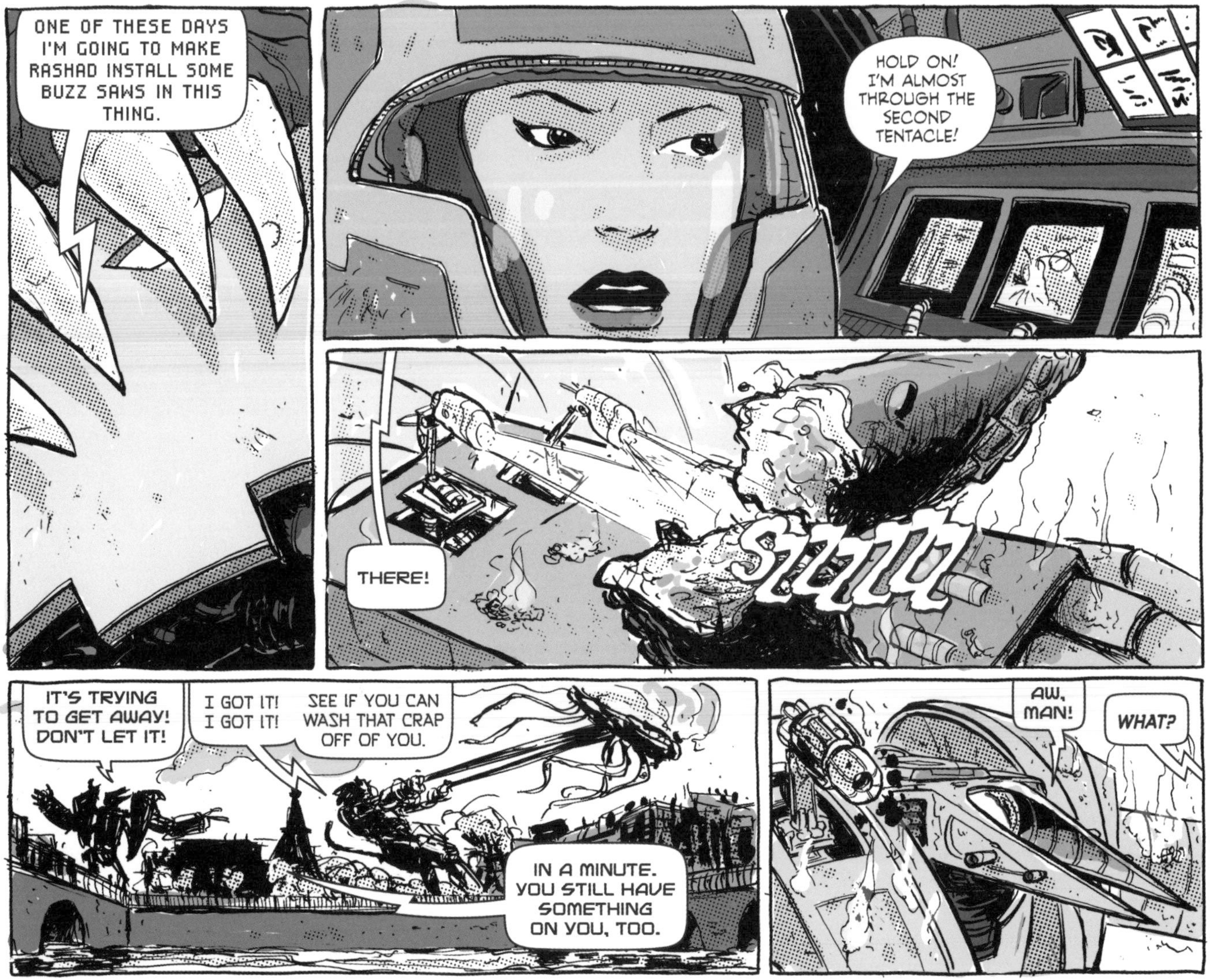
ONE OF THESE DAYS I'M GOING TO MAKE RASHAD INSTALL SOME BUZZ SAWS IN THIS THING.
HOLD ON! I'M ALMOST THROUGH THE SECOND TENTACLE!
THERE!
IT'S TRYING TO GET AWAY! DON'T LET IT!
I GOT IT! I GOT IT!
SEE IF YOU CAN WASH THAT CRAP OFF OF YOU.
IN A MINUTE. YOU STILL HAVE SOMETHING ON YOU, TOO.
AW, MAN!
WHAT?

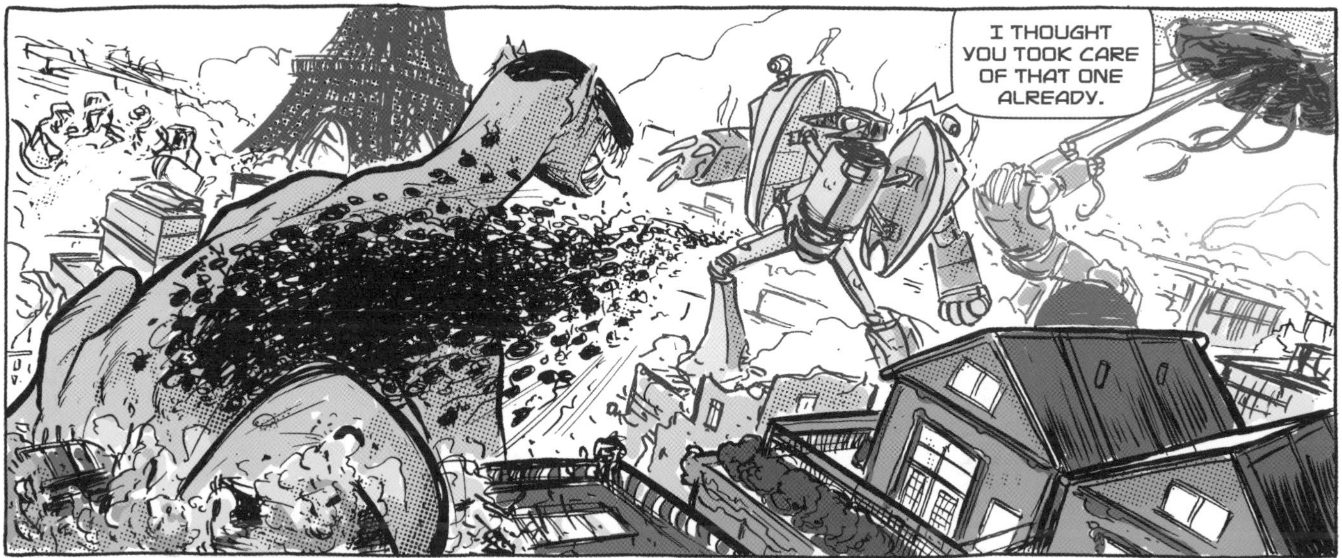
I THOUGHT YOU TOOK CARE OF THAT ONE ALREADY.

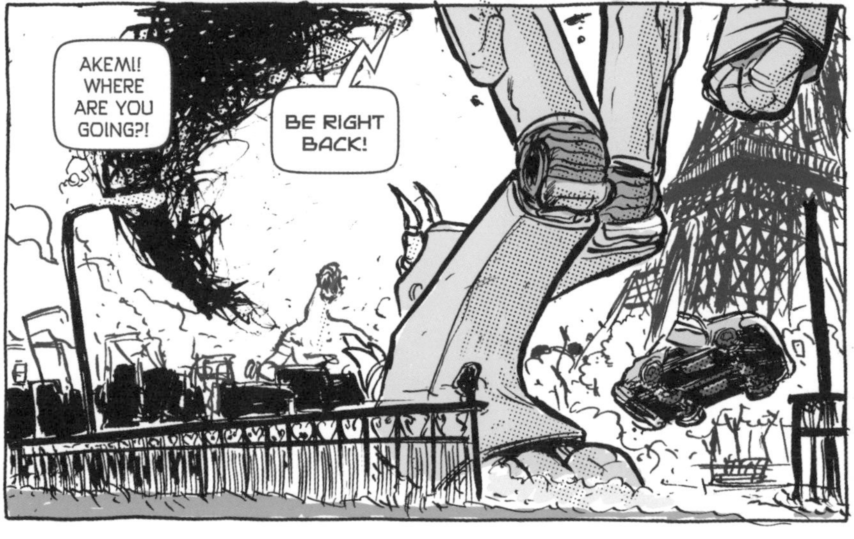
AKEMI! WHERE ARE YOU GOING?!
BE RIGHT BACK!

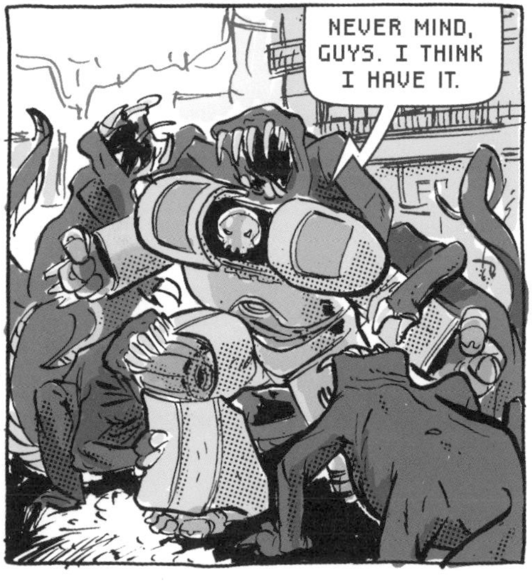
NEVER MIND, GUYS. I THINK I HAVE IT.

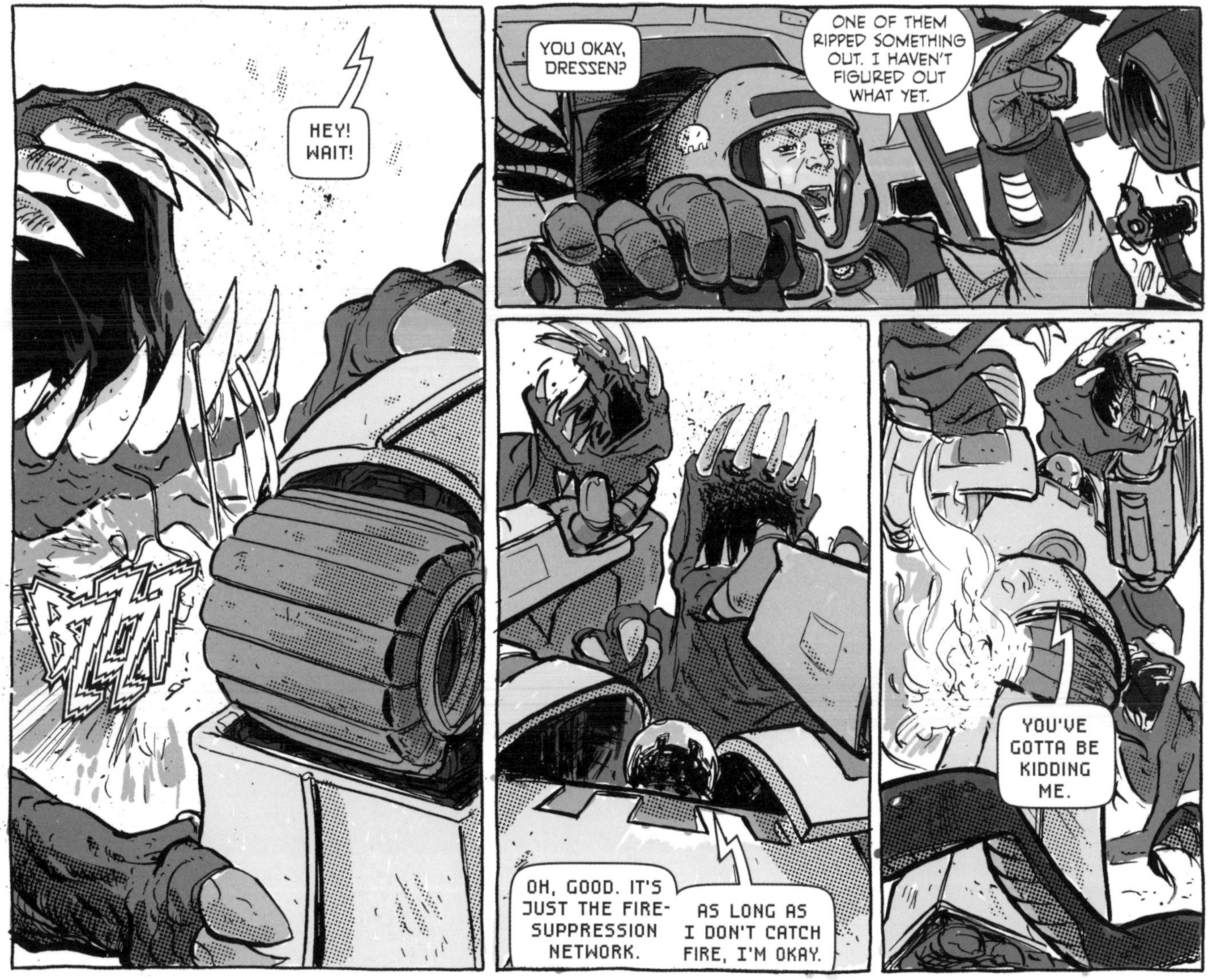
HEY! WAIT!
BZZT
YOU OKAY, DRESSEN?
ONE OF THEM RIPPED SOMETHING OUT. I HAVEN'T FIGURED OUT WHAT YET.
OH, GOOD. IT'S JUST THE FIRE-SUPPRESSION NETWORK.
AS LONG AS I DON'T CATCH FIRE, I'M OKAY.
YOU'VE GOTTA BE KIDDING ME.

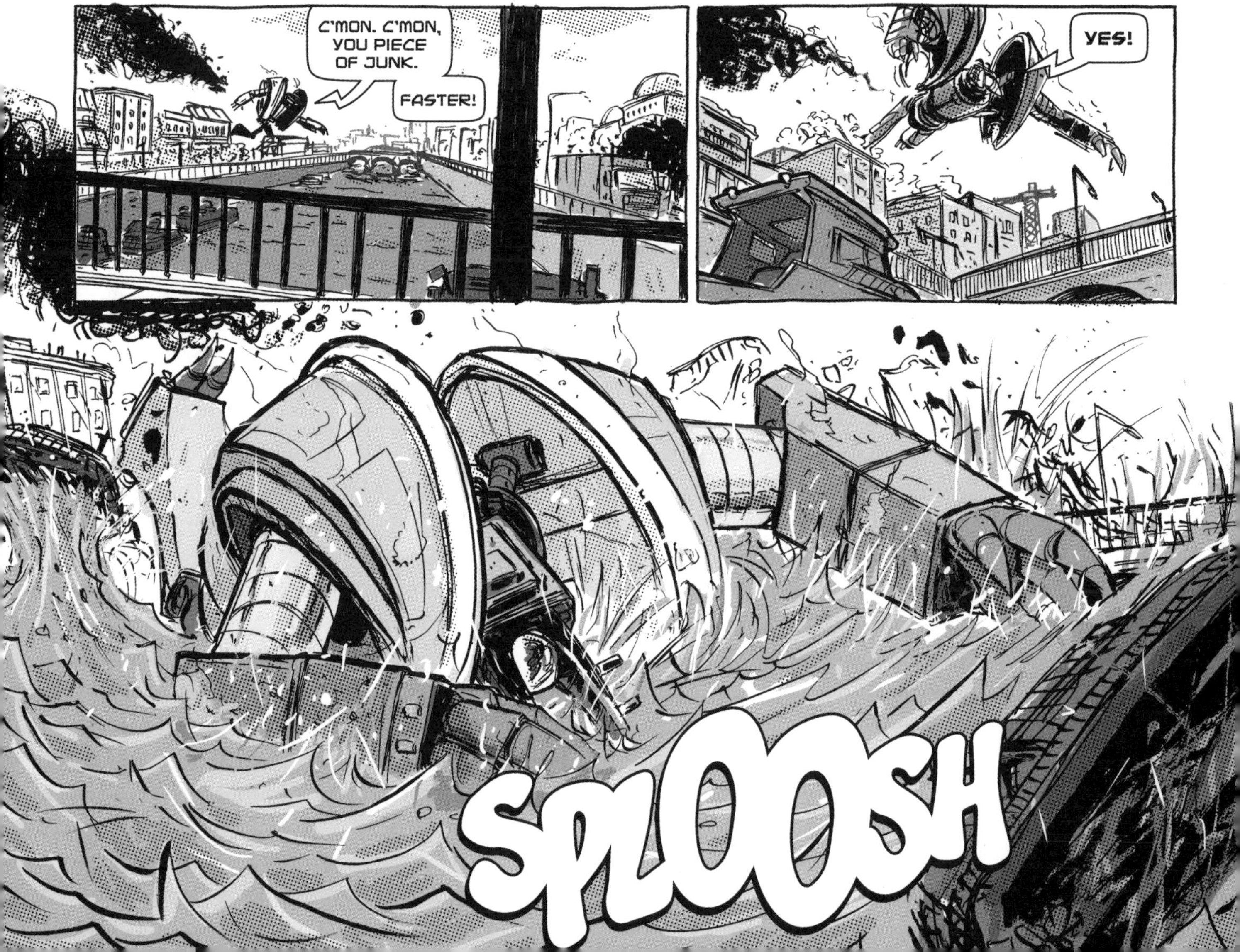
C'MON. C'MON, YOU PIECE OF JUNK.
FASTER!
YES!
SPLOOSH

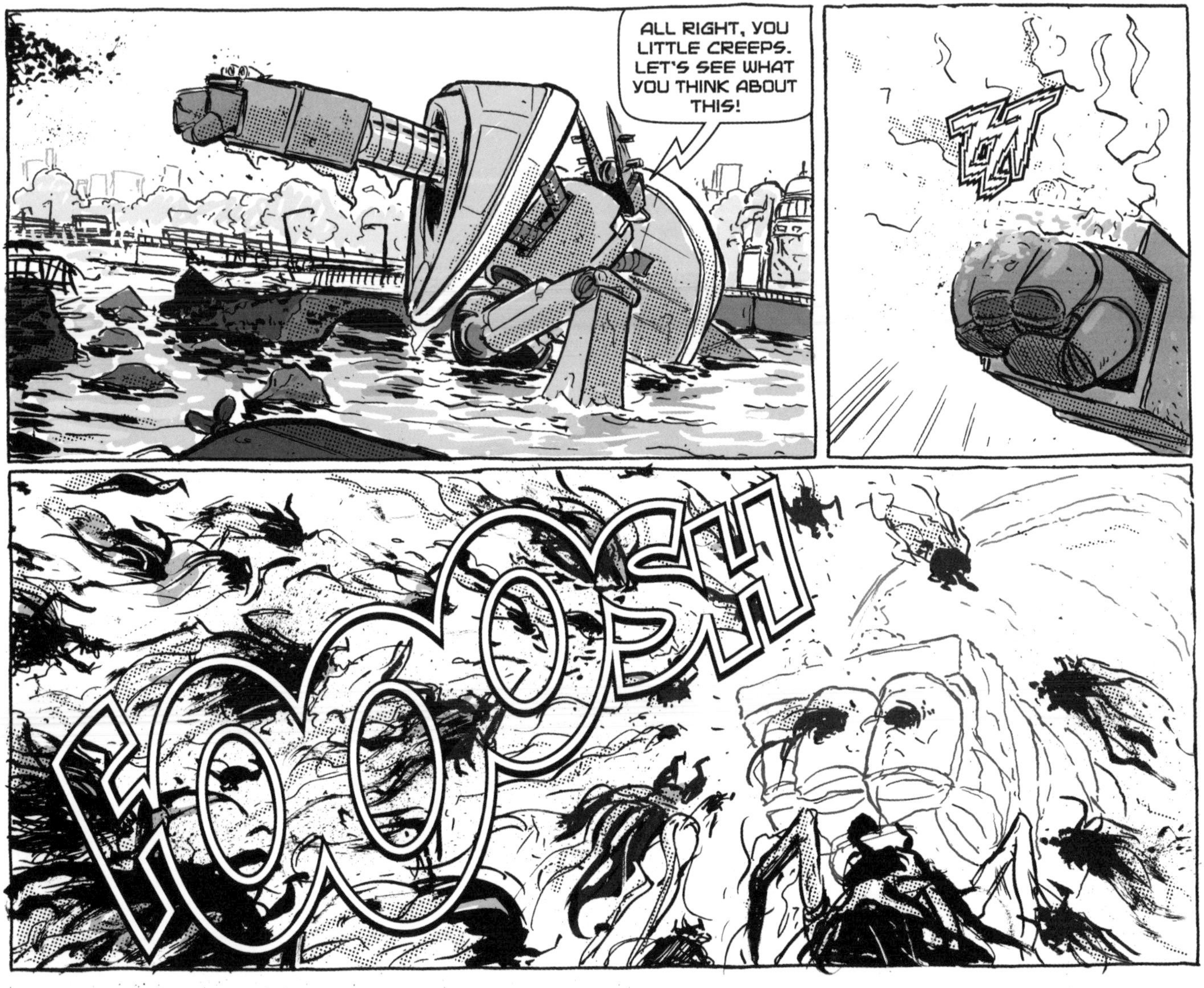
ALL RIGHT, YOU LITTLE CREEPS. LET'S SEE WHAT YOU THINK ABOUT THIS!
WHOOOOSH

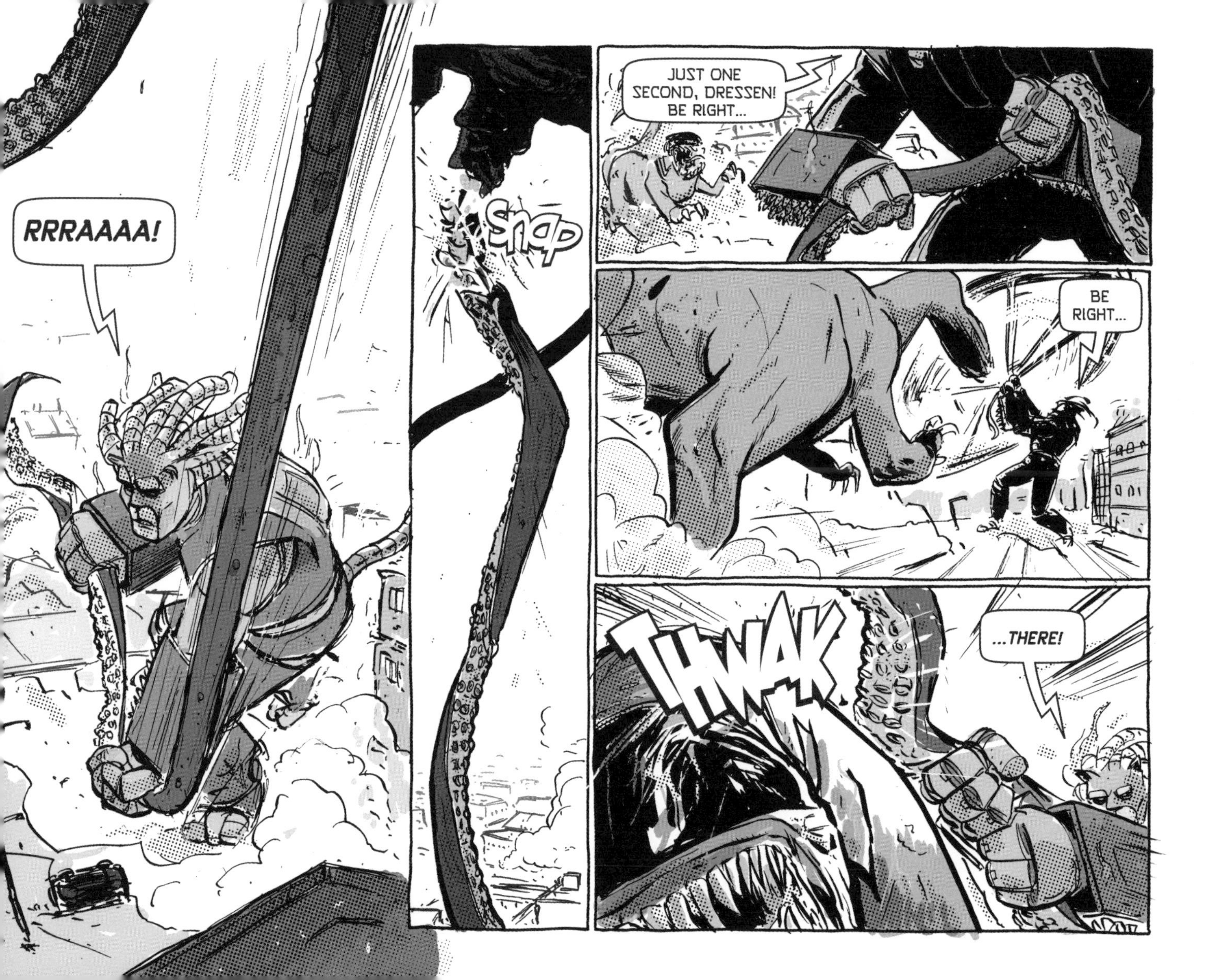
RRRAAAA!
SNAP
JUST ONE SECOND, DRESSEN! BE RIGHT...
BE RIGHT...
THWAK
...THERE!

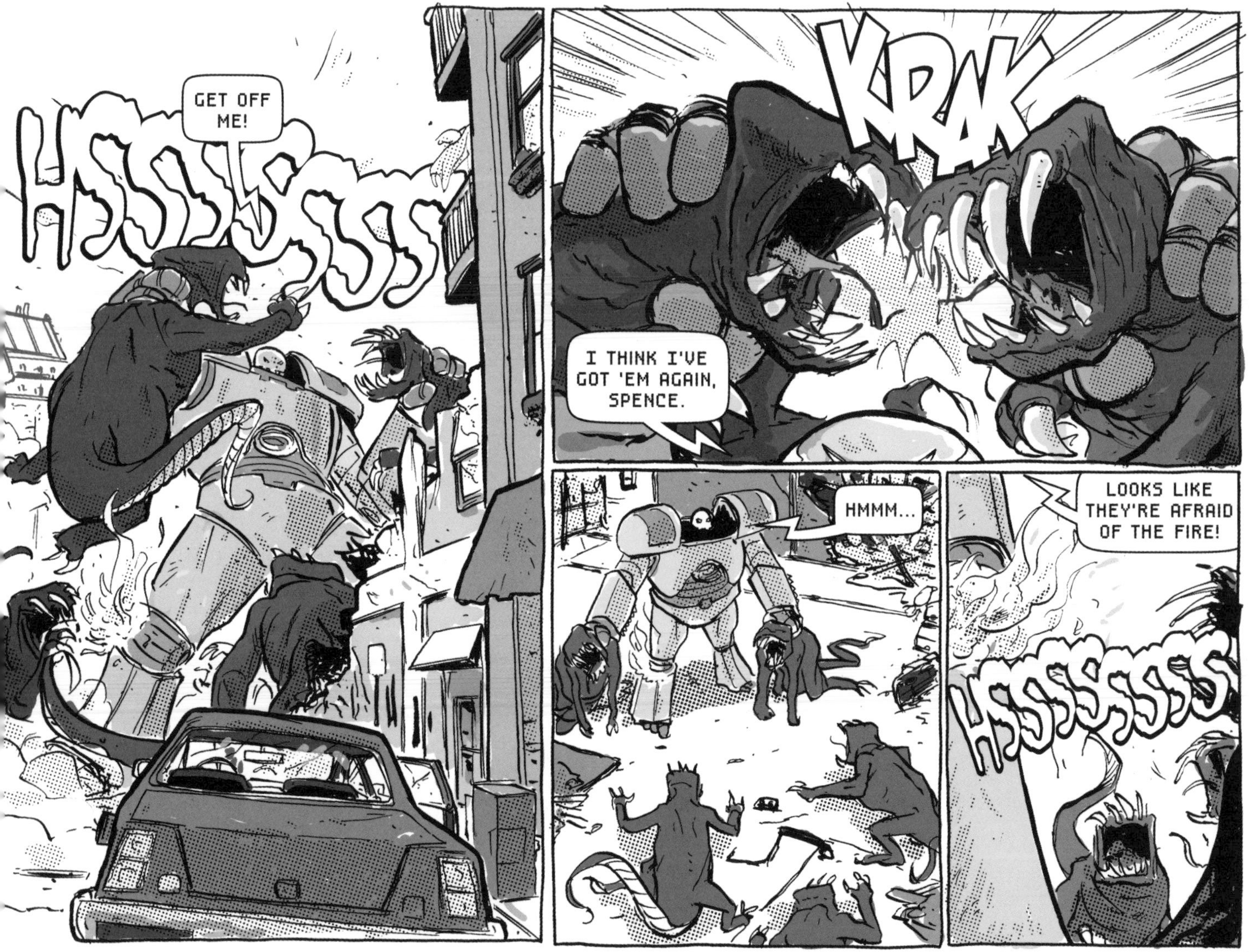
HSSSSSSSS
GET OFF ME!
KRAK
I THINK I'VE GOT 'EM AGAIN, SPENCE.
HMMM...
LOOKS LIKE THEY'RE AFRAID OF THE FIRE!
HSSSSSSSS

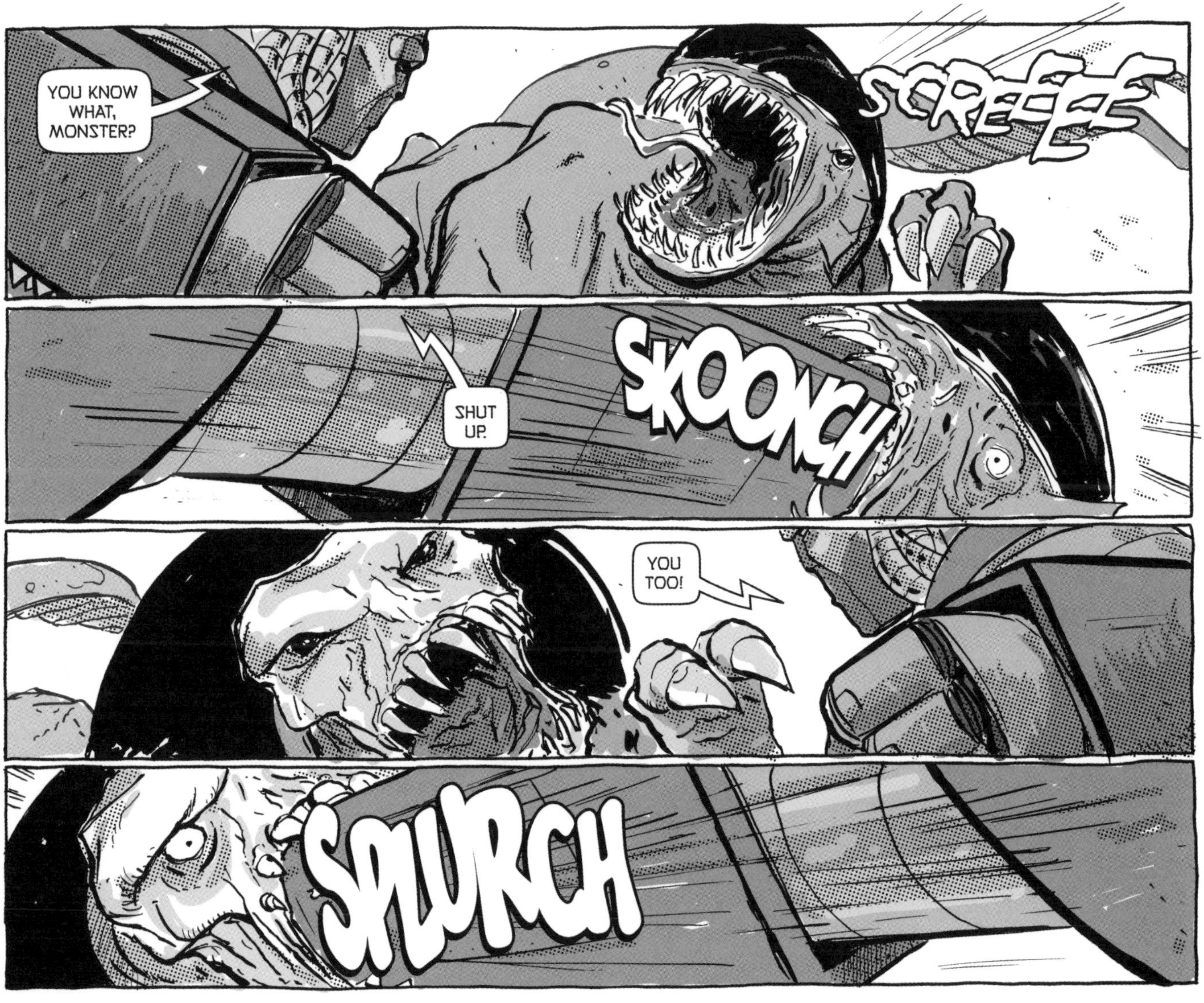
YOU KNOW WHAT, MONSTER?
SCREEEE
SHUT UP.
SKOONCH
YOU TOO!
SPLURCH

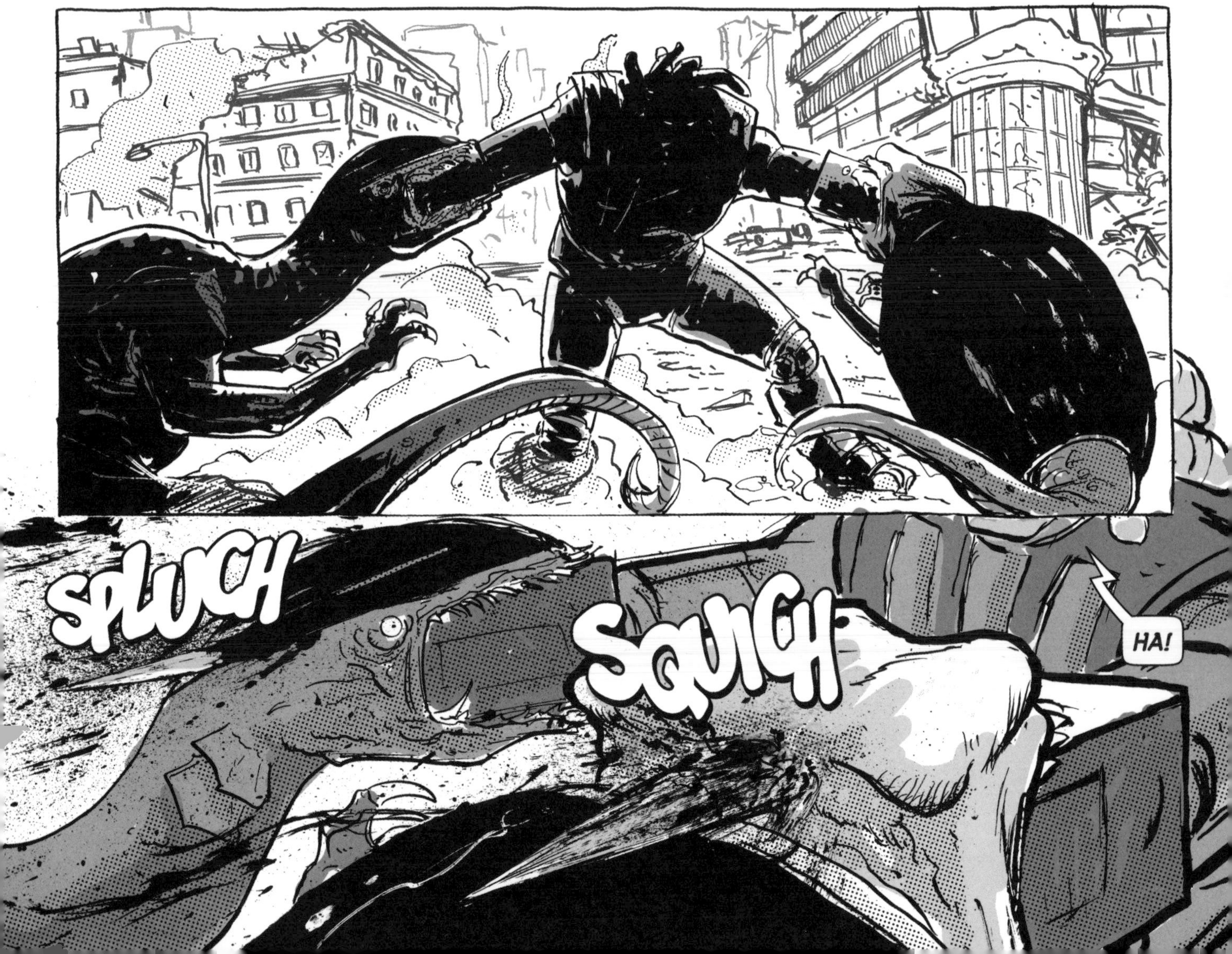
SPLUCH
SQUICH
HA!

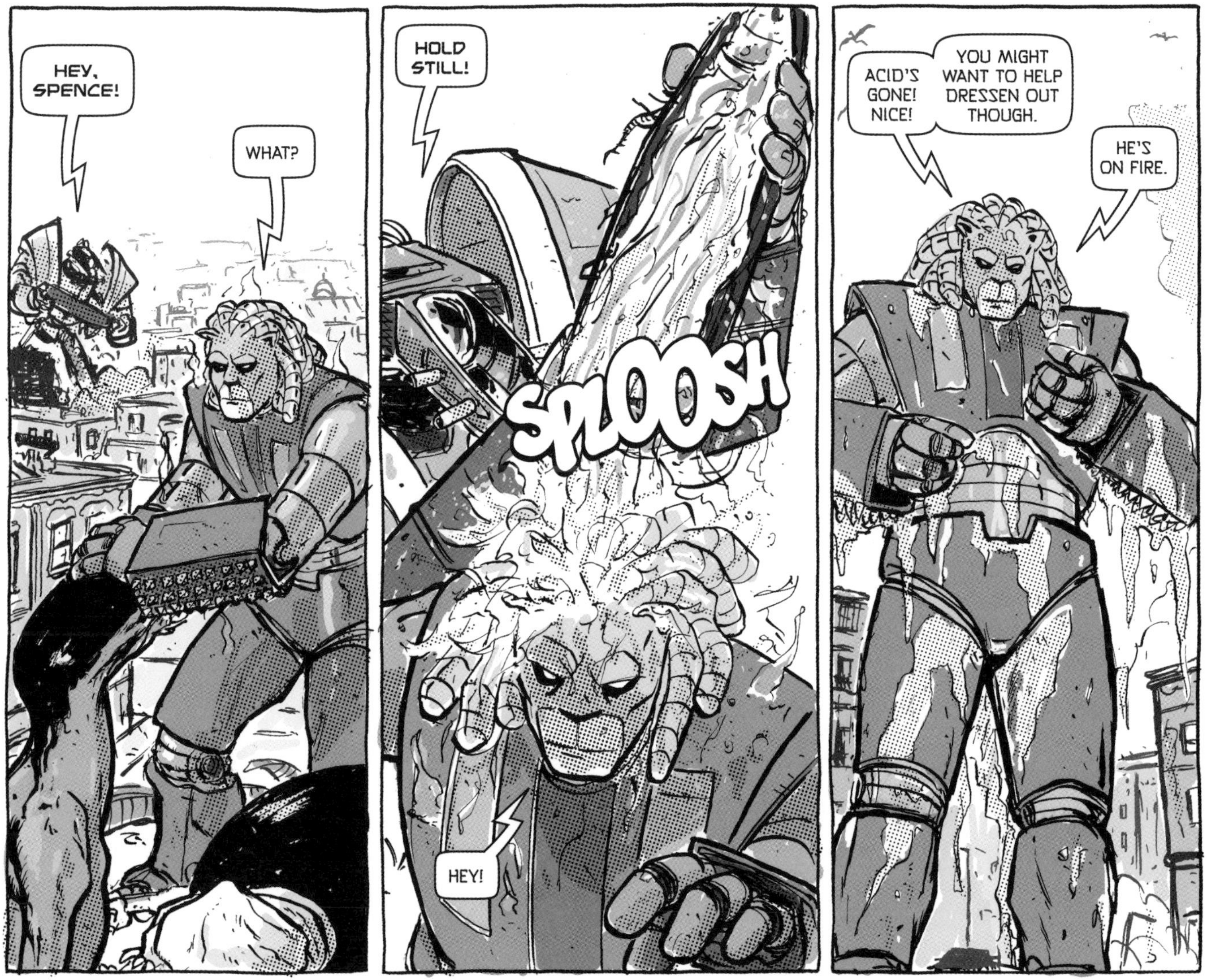
HEY, SPENCE!
WHAT?
HOLD STILL!
SPLOOSH
HEY!
ACID'S GONE! NICE!
YOU MIGHT WANT TO HELP DRESSEN OUT THOUGH.
HE'S ON FIRE.

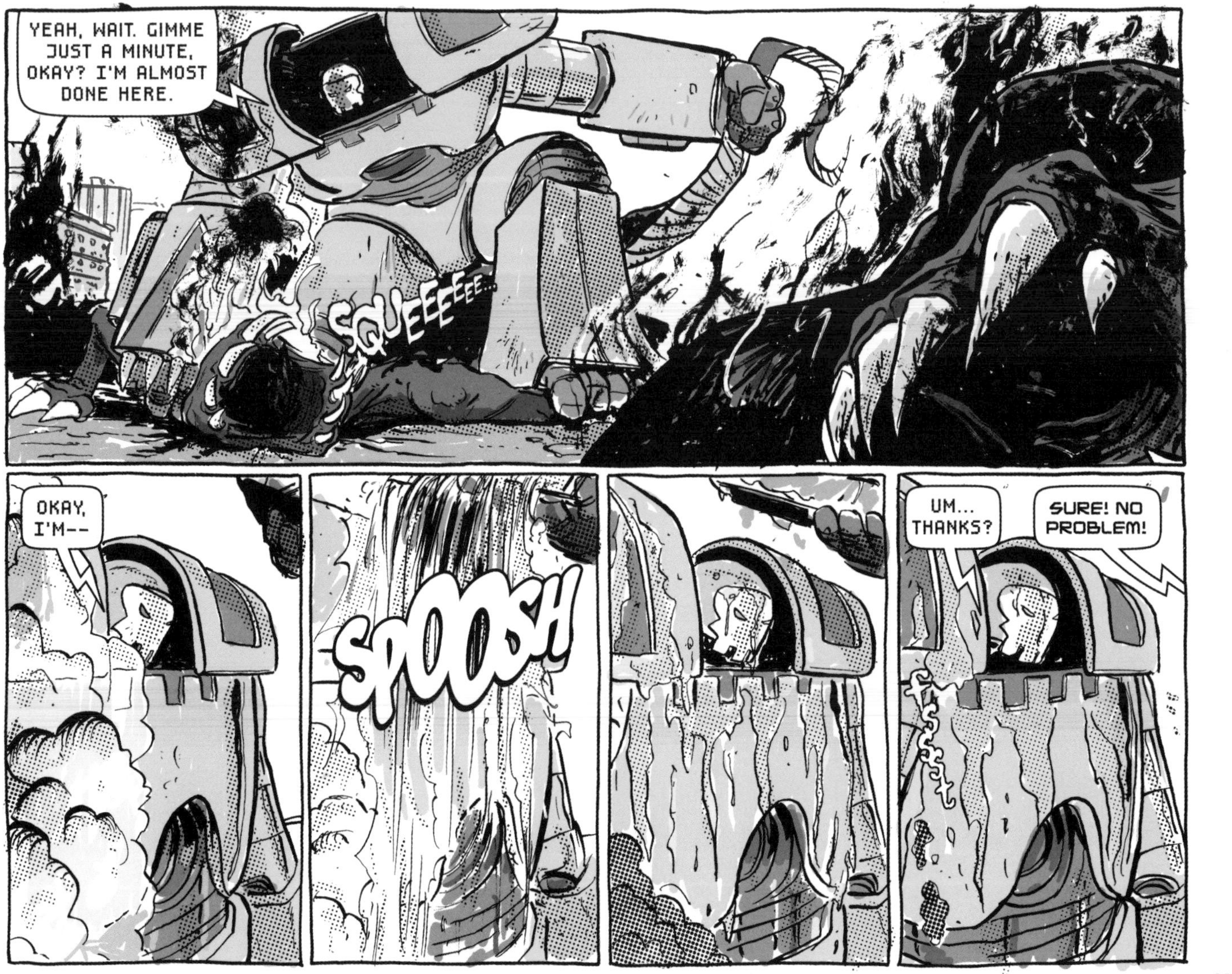
YEAH, WAIT. GIMME JUST A MINUTE, OKAY? I'M ALMOST DONE HERE.
SQUEEEEEE...
OKAY, I'M--
SPOOSH
UM... THANKS?
SURE! NO PROBLEM!
FSSST

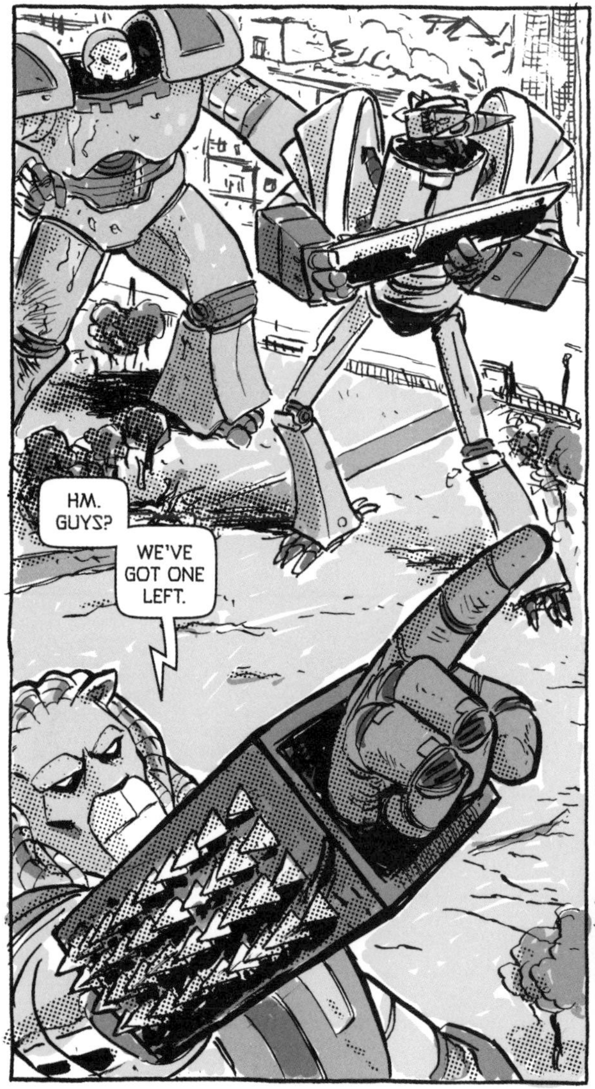
HM. GUYS?
WE'VE GOT ONE LEFT.
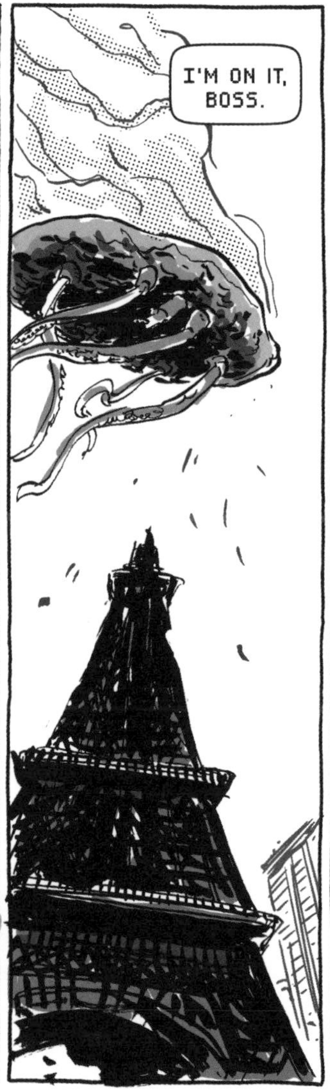
I'M ON IT, BOSS.
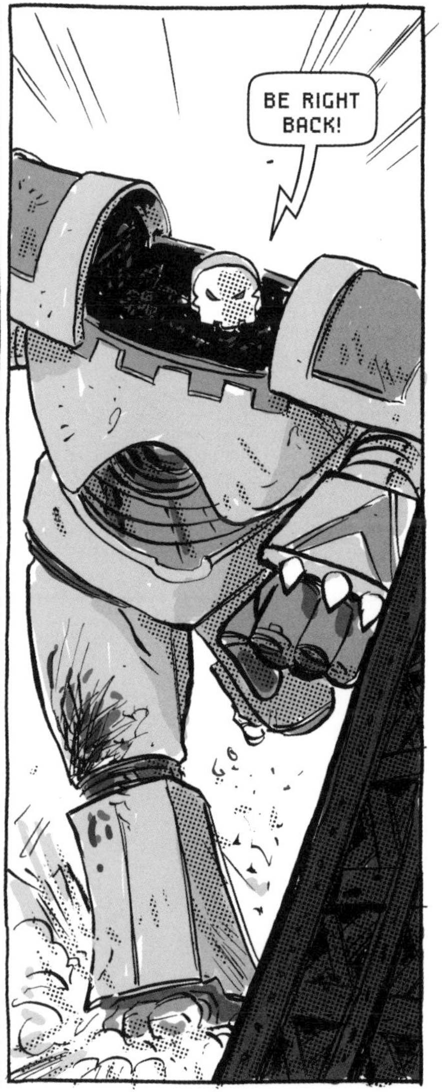
BE RIGHT BACK!

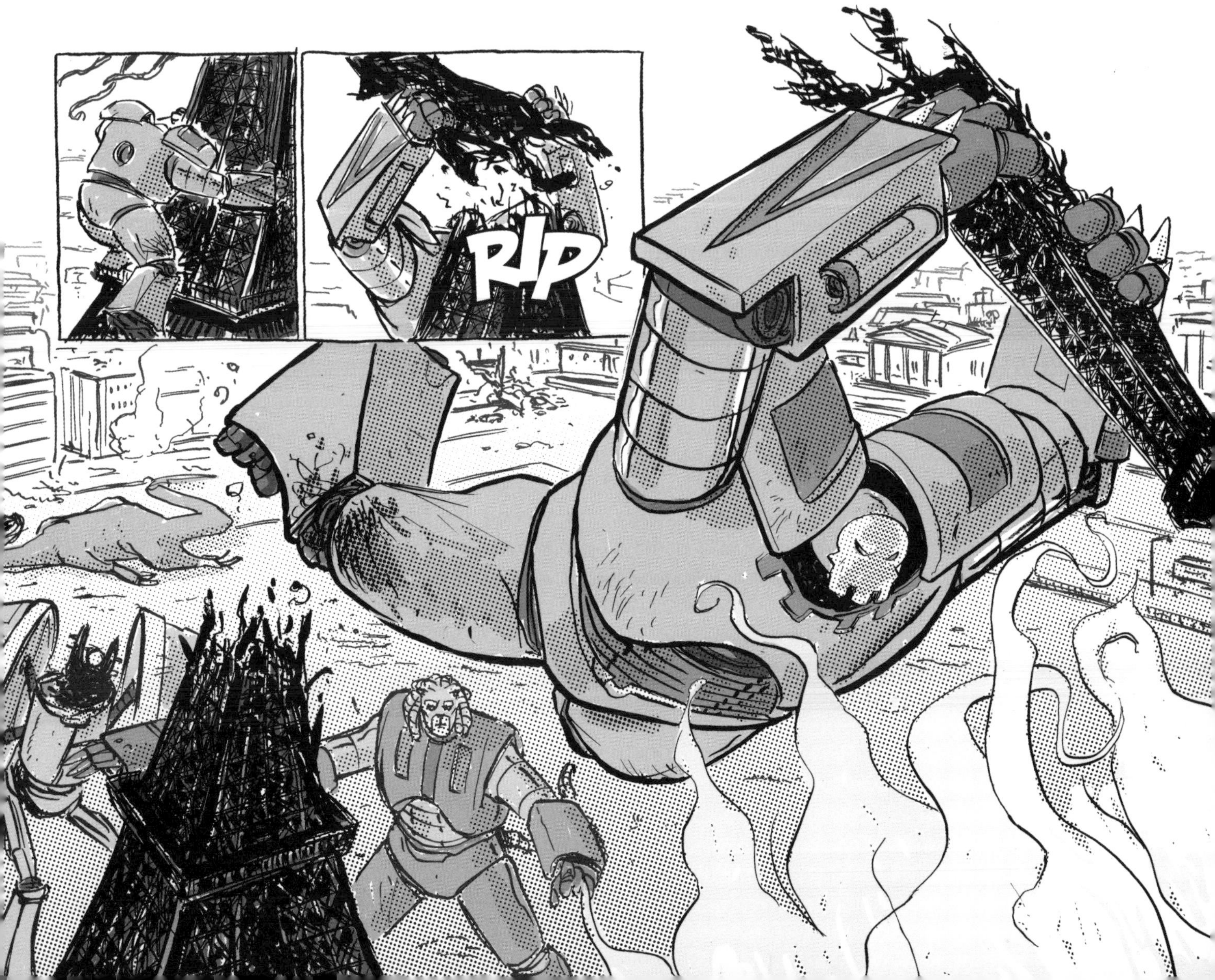
RIP

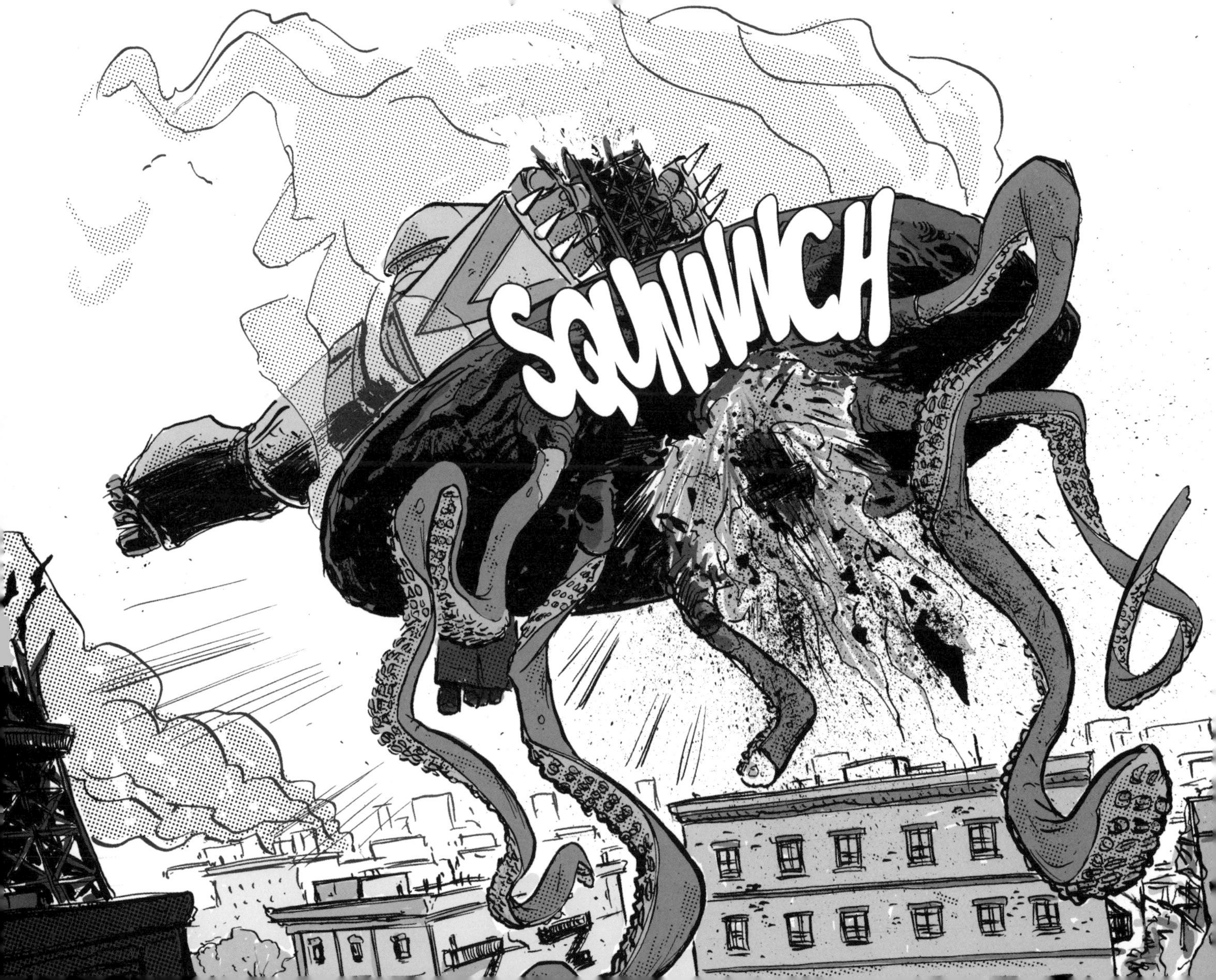
SQUNNNCH

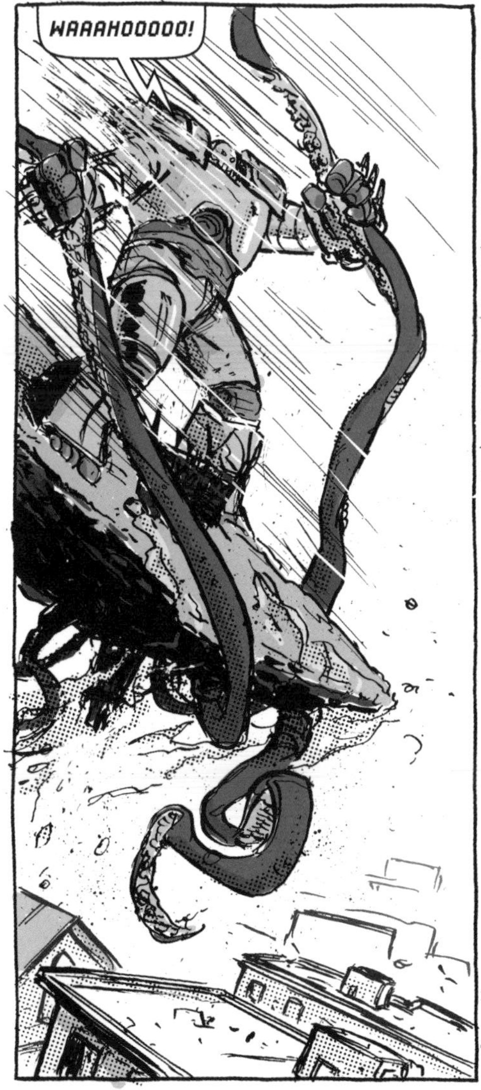
WAAAHOOOOO!

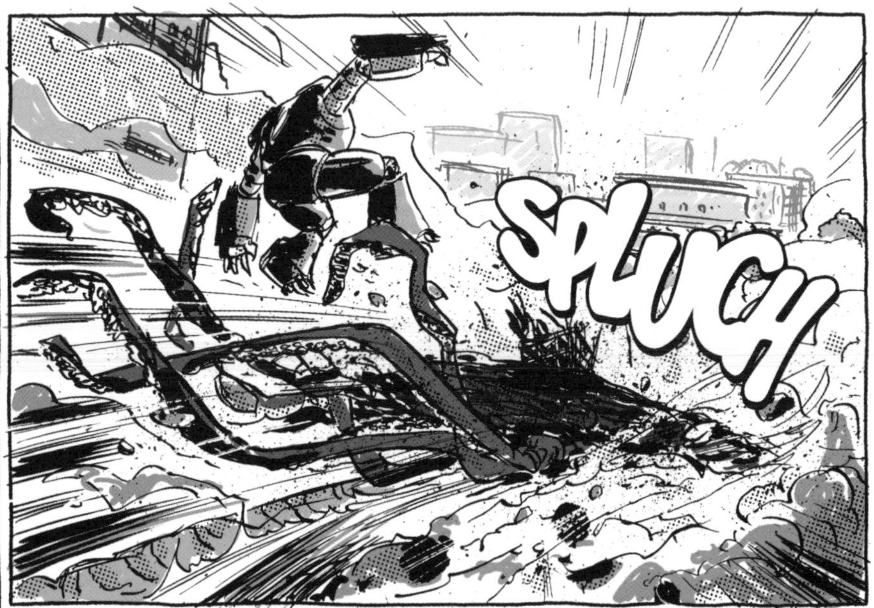
SPLUCH

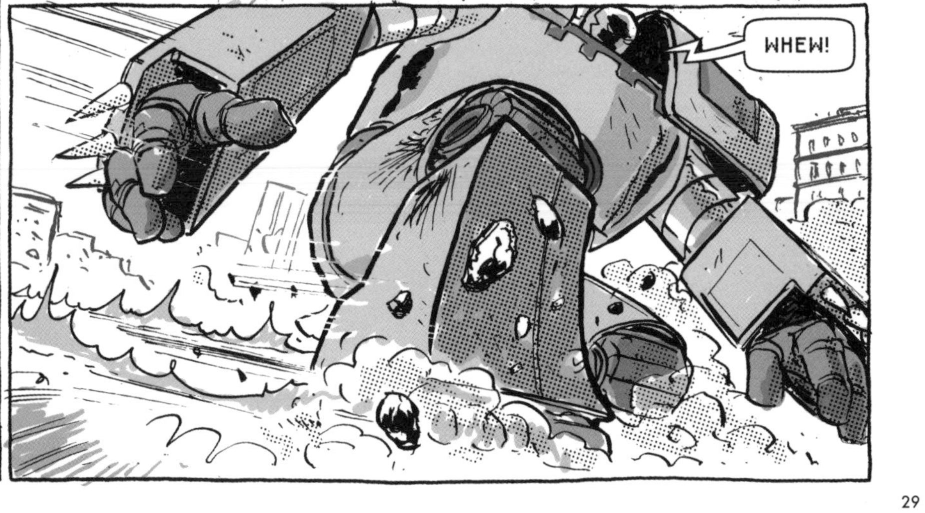
WHEW!

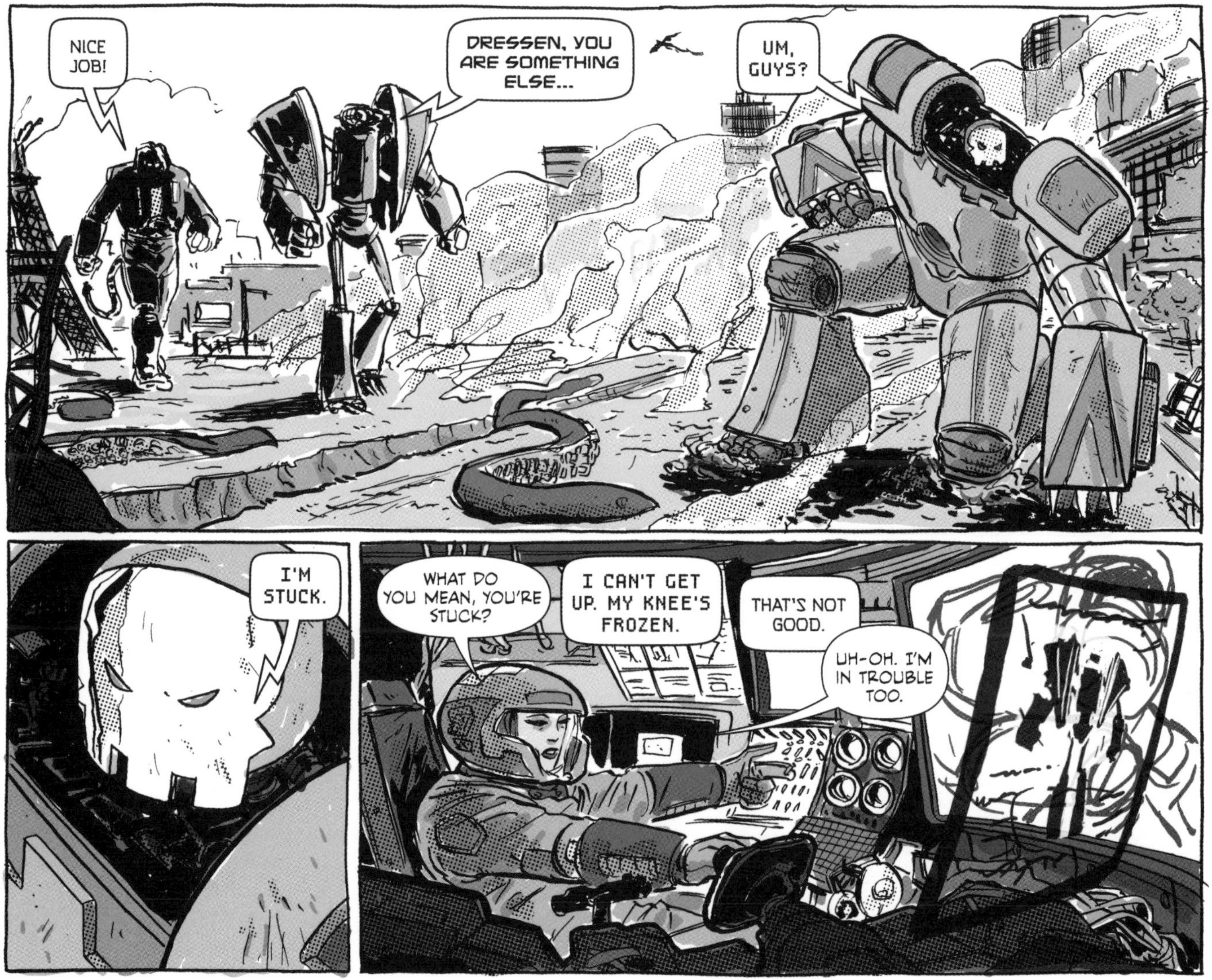
NICE JOB!
DRESSEN, YOU ARE SOMETHING ELSE...
UM, GUYS?
I'M STUCK.
WHAT DO YOU MEAN, YOU'RE STUCK?
I CAN'T GET UP. MY KNEE'S FROZEN.
THAT'S NOT GOOD.
UH-OH. I'M IN TROUBLE TOO.

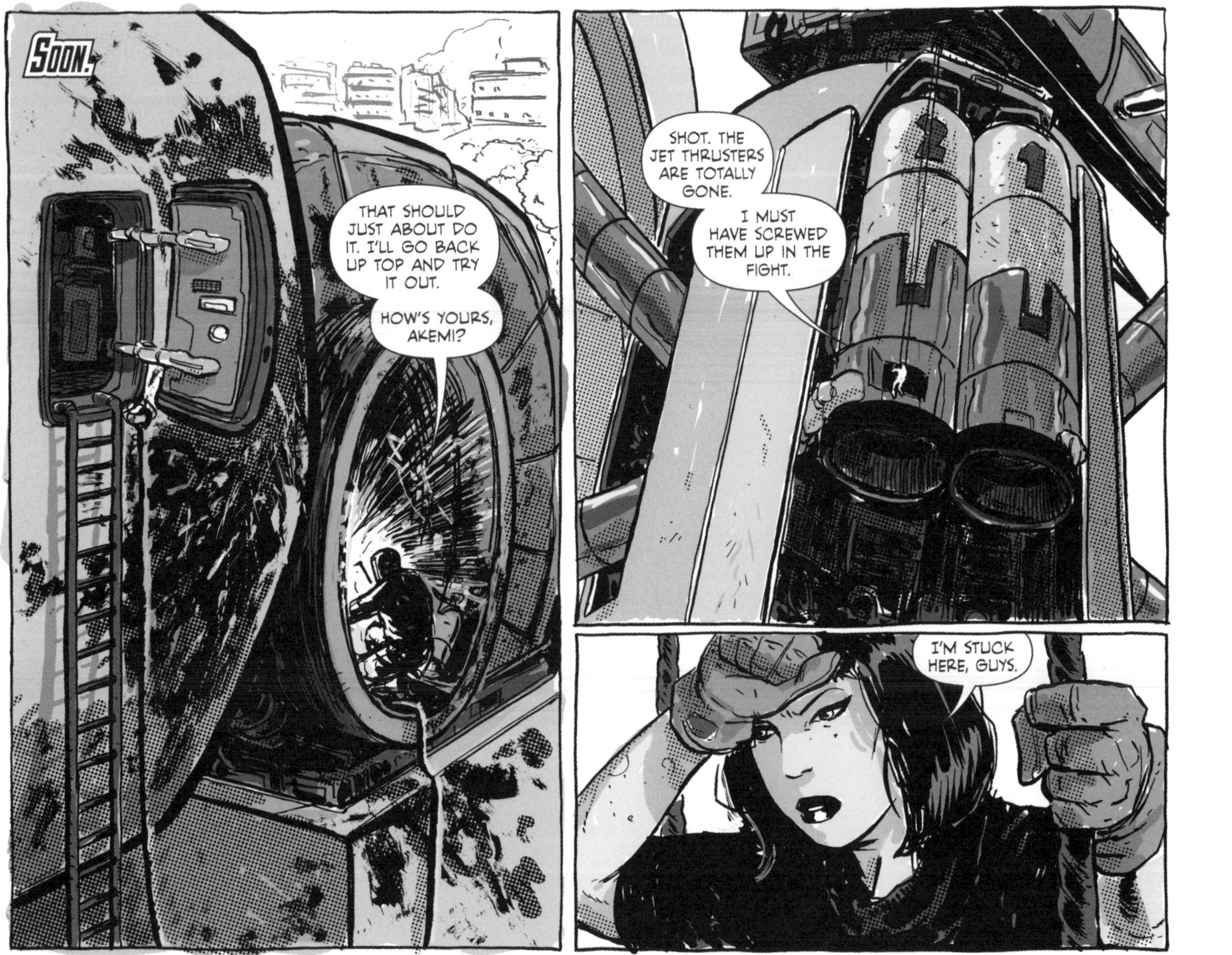
SOON.
THAT SHOULD JUST ABOUT DO IT. I'LL GO BACK UP TOP AND TRY IT OUT.
HOW'S YOURS, AKEMI?
SHOT. THE JET THRUSTERS ARE TOTALLY GONE.
I MUST HAVE SCREWED THEM UP IN THE FIGHT.
I'M STUCK HERE, GUYS.

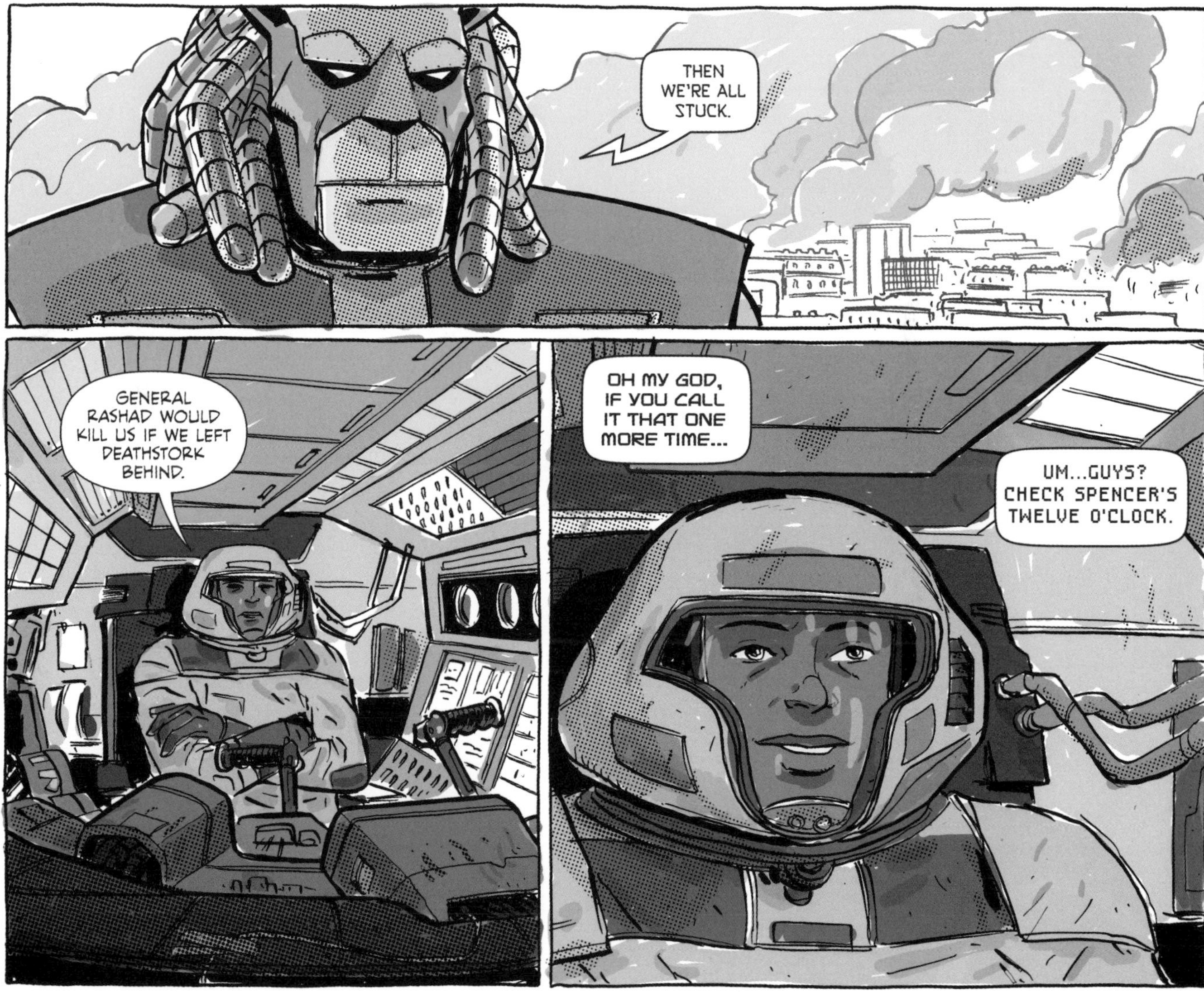
THEN WE'RE ALL STUCK.
GENERAL RASHAD WOULD KILL US IF WE LEFT DEATHSTORK BEHIND.
OH MY GOD, IF YOU CALL IT THAT ONE MORE TIME...
UM...GUYS? CHECK SPENCER'S TWELVE O'CLOCK.

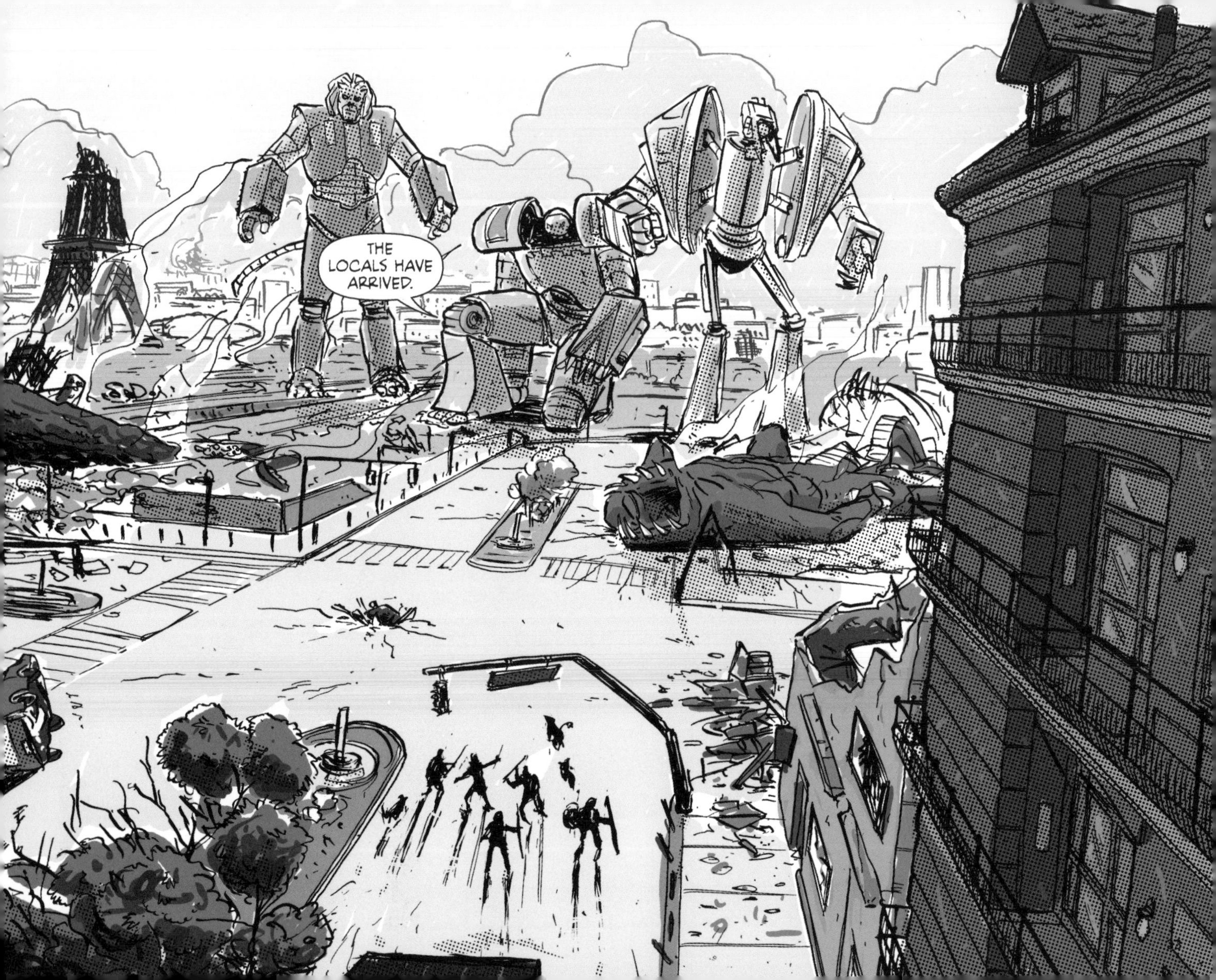
THE LOCALS HAVE ARRIVED.

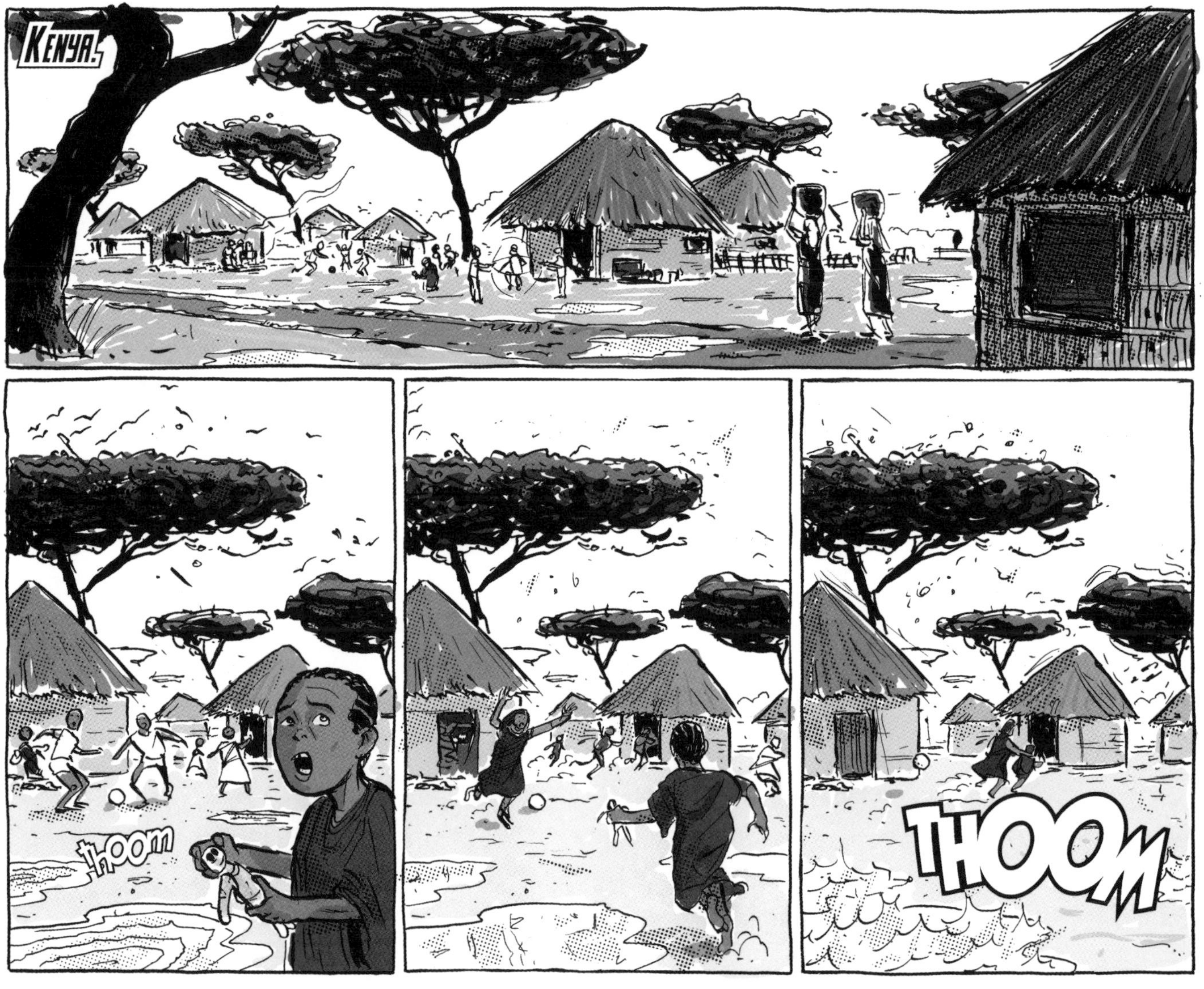
KENYA.
THOOM
THOOM

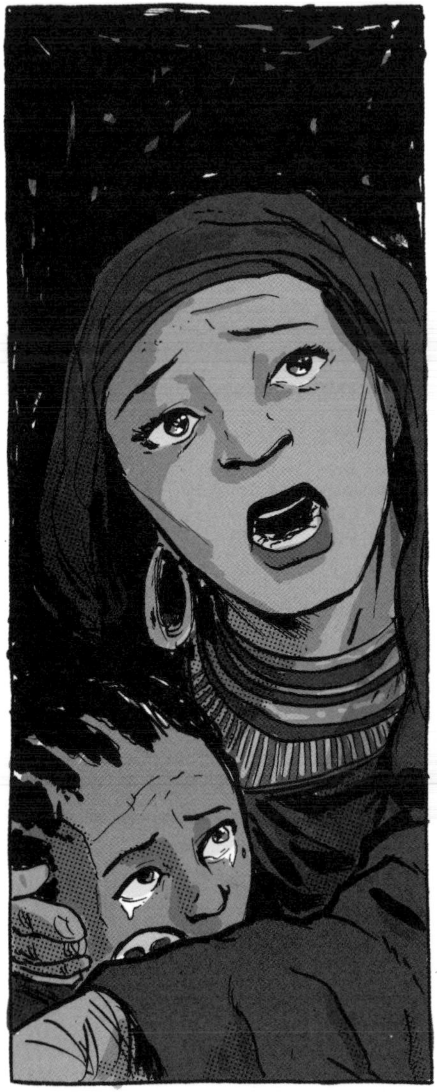

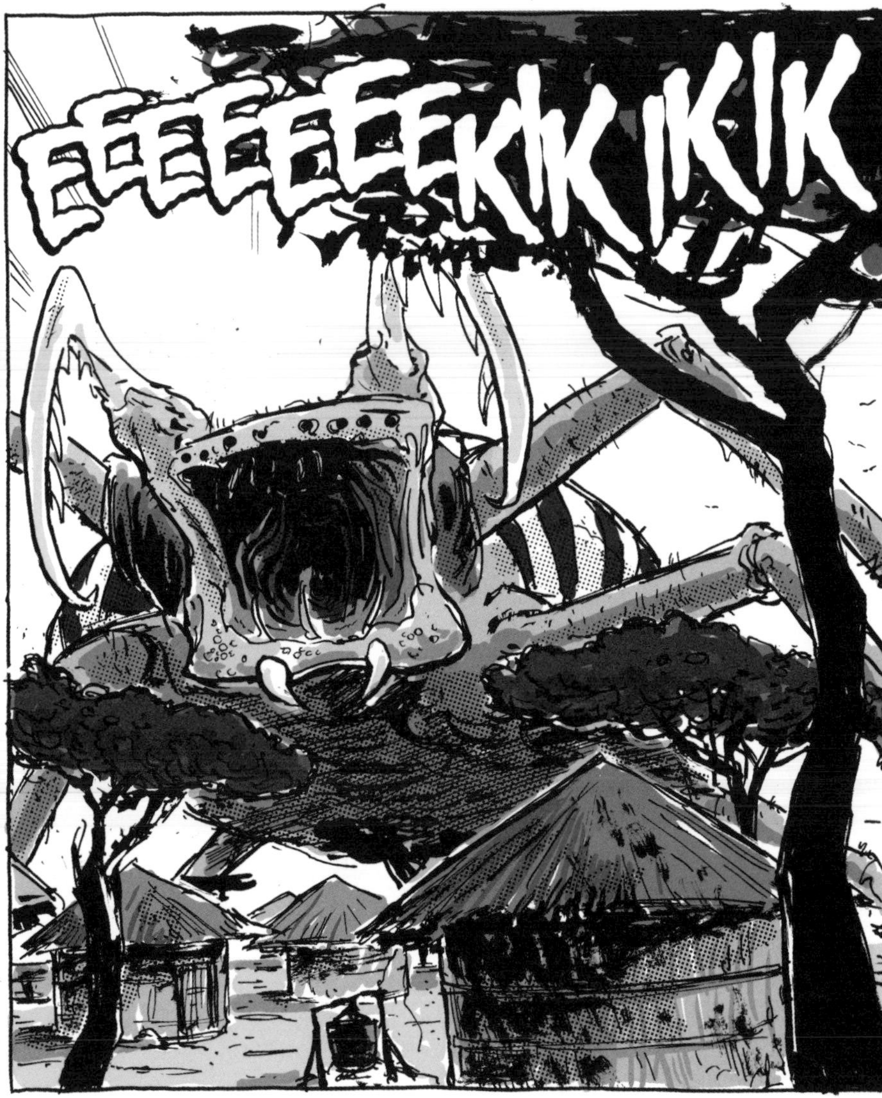
EEEEEEEEKIK IKIK

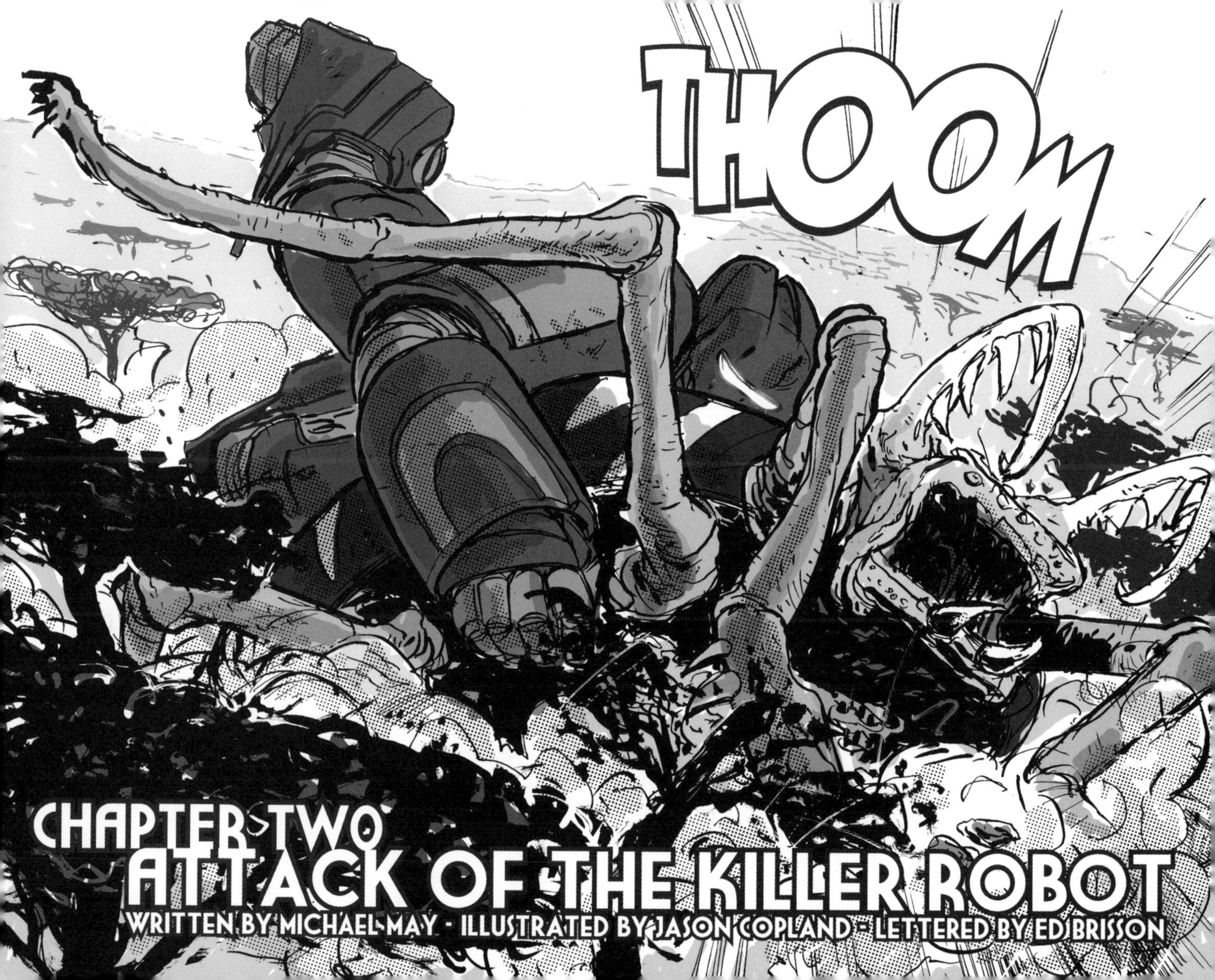
THOOM

CHAPTER TWO ATTACK OF THE KILLER ROBOT

WRITTEN BY MICHAEL MAY - ILLUSTRATED BY JASON COPLAND - LETTERED BY ED BRISSON

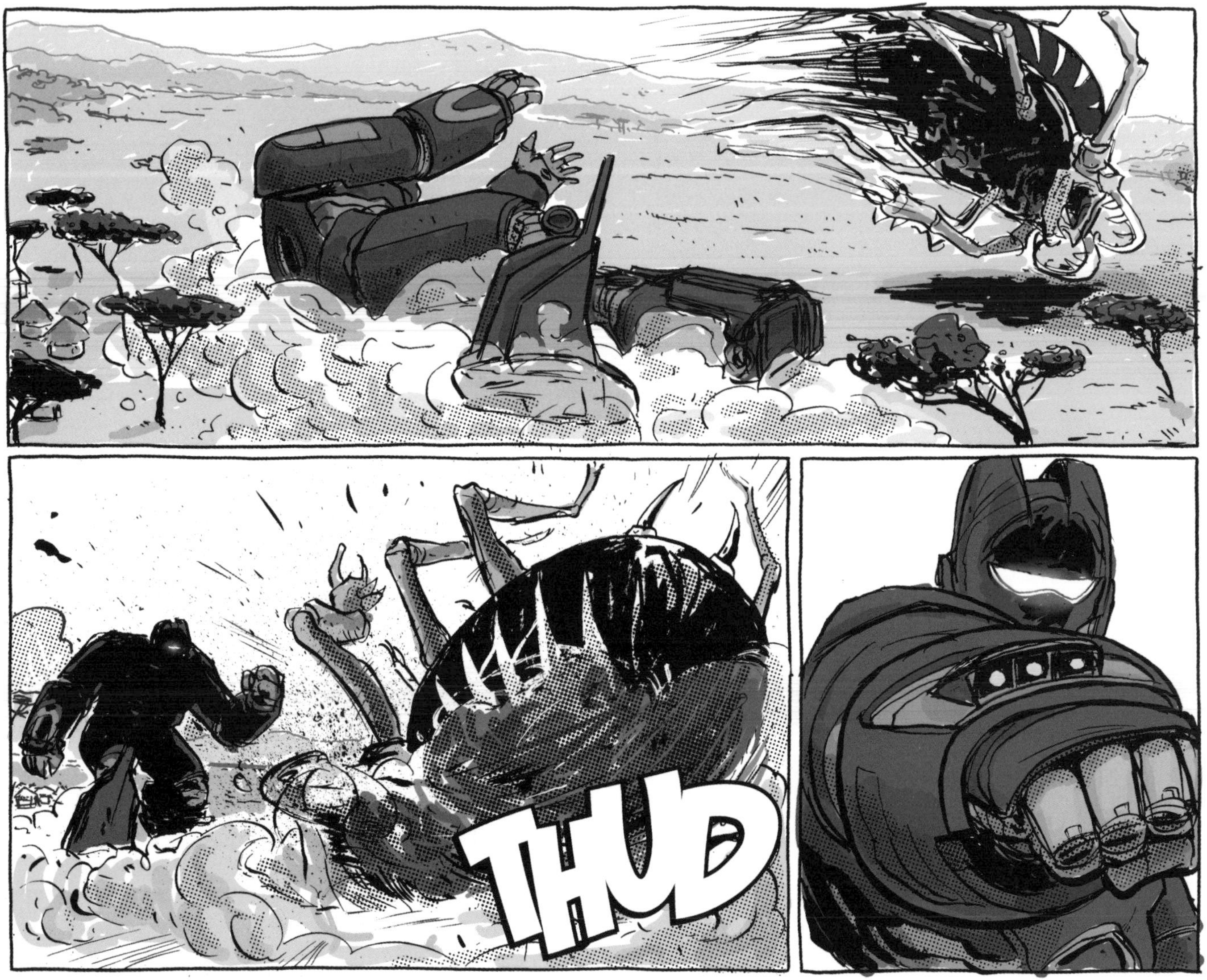
THUD

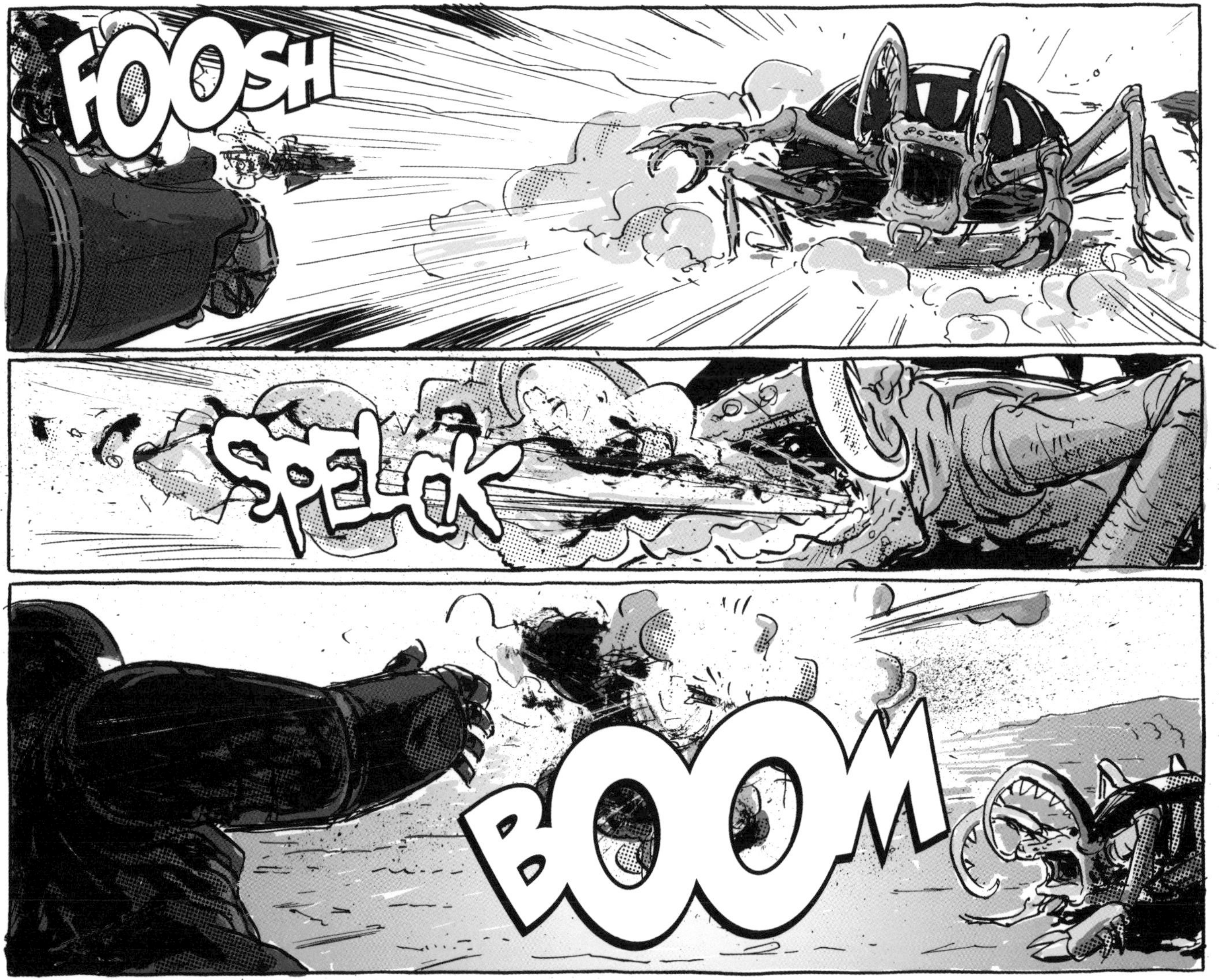
FOOSH
SPELCK
BOOM

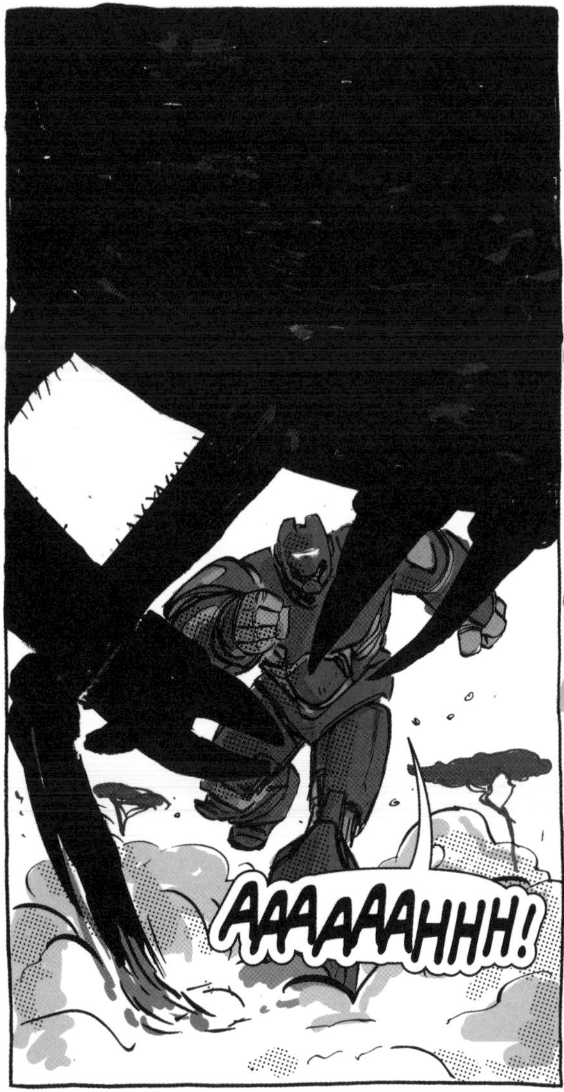
AAAAAAHHH!
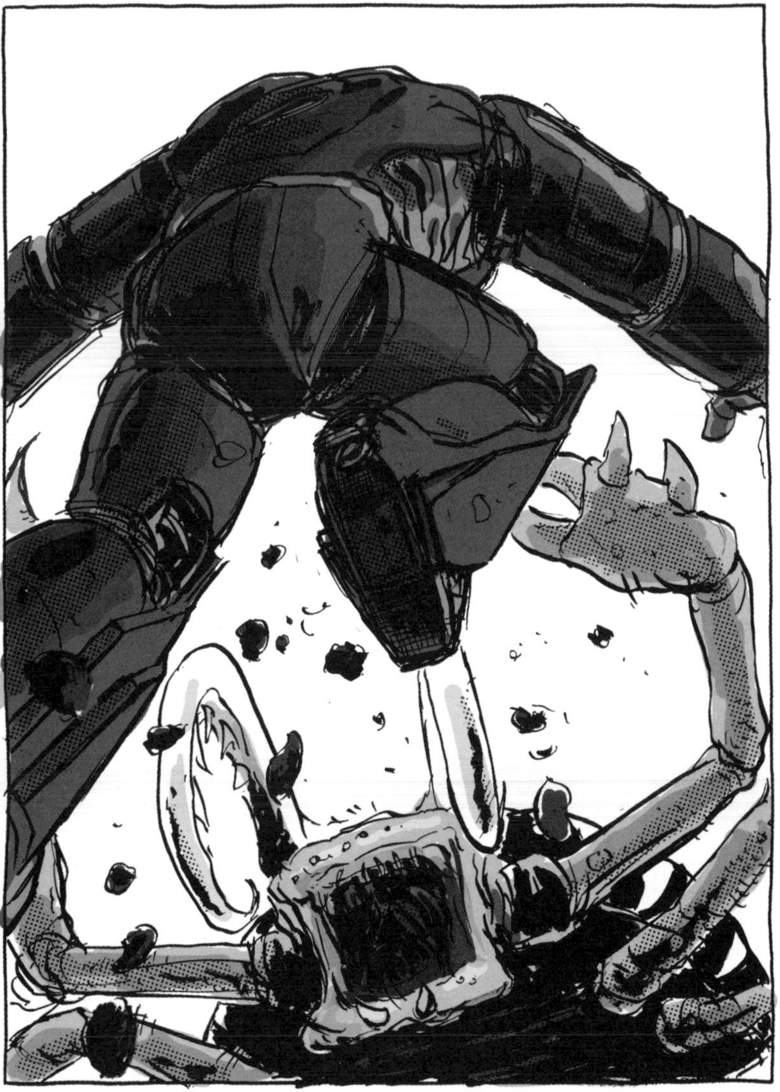

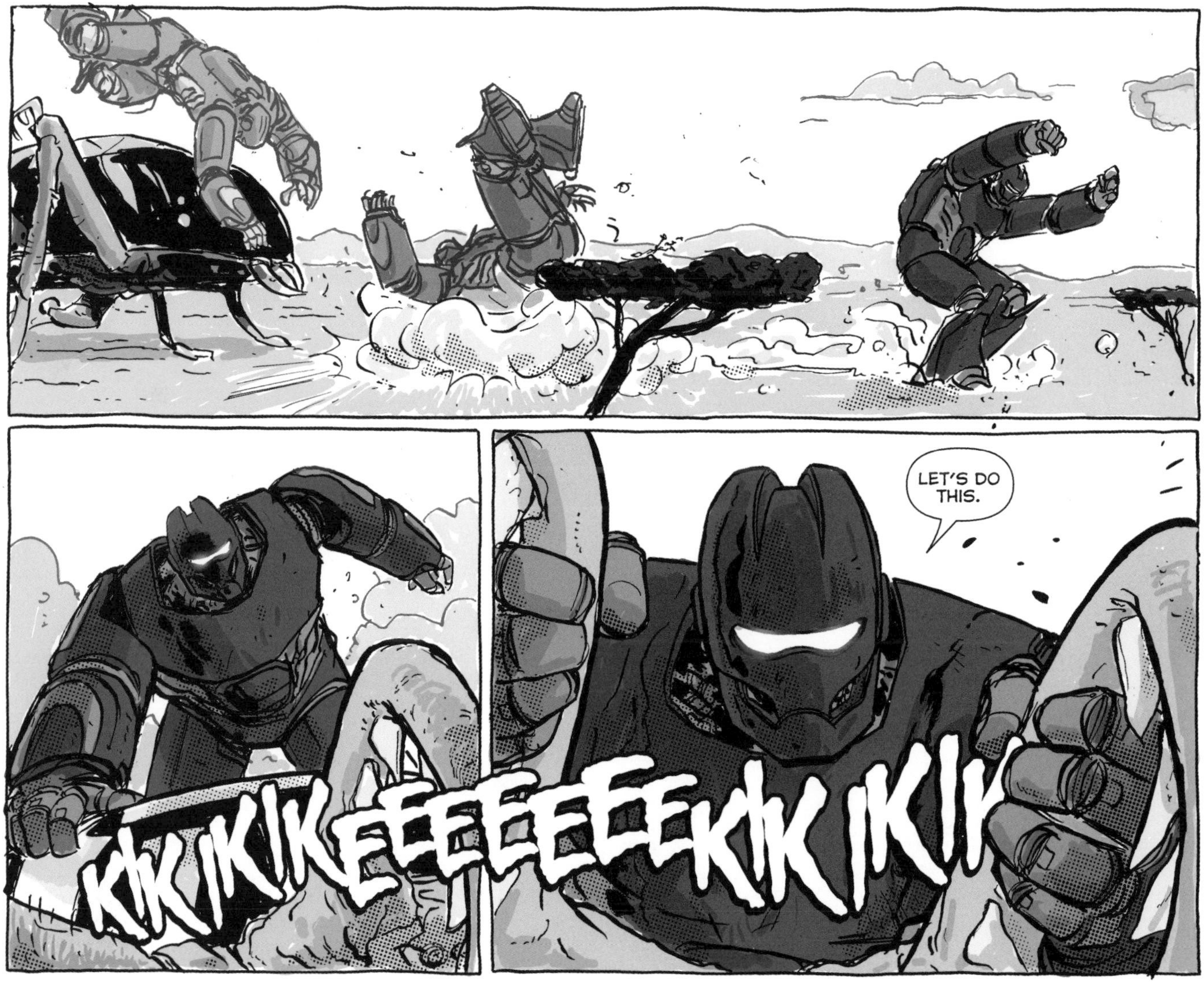
LET'S DO THIS.
KIKIKIKEEEEEEEEKIKIKIK

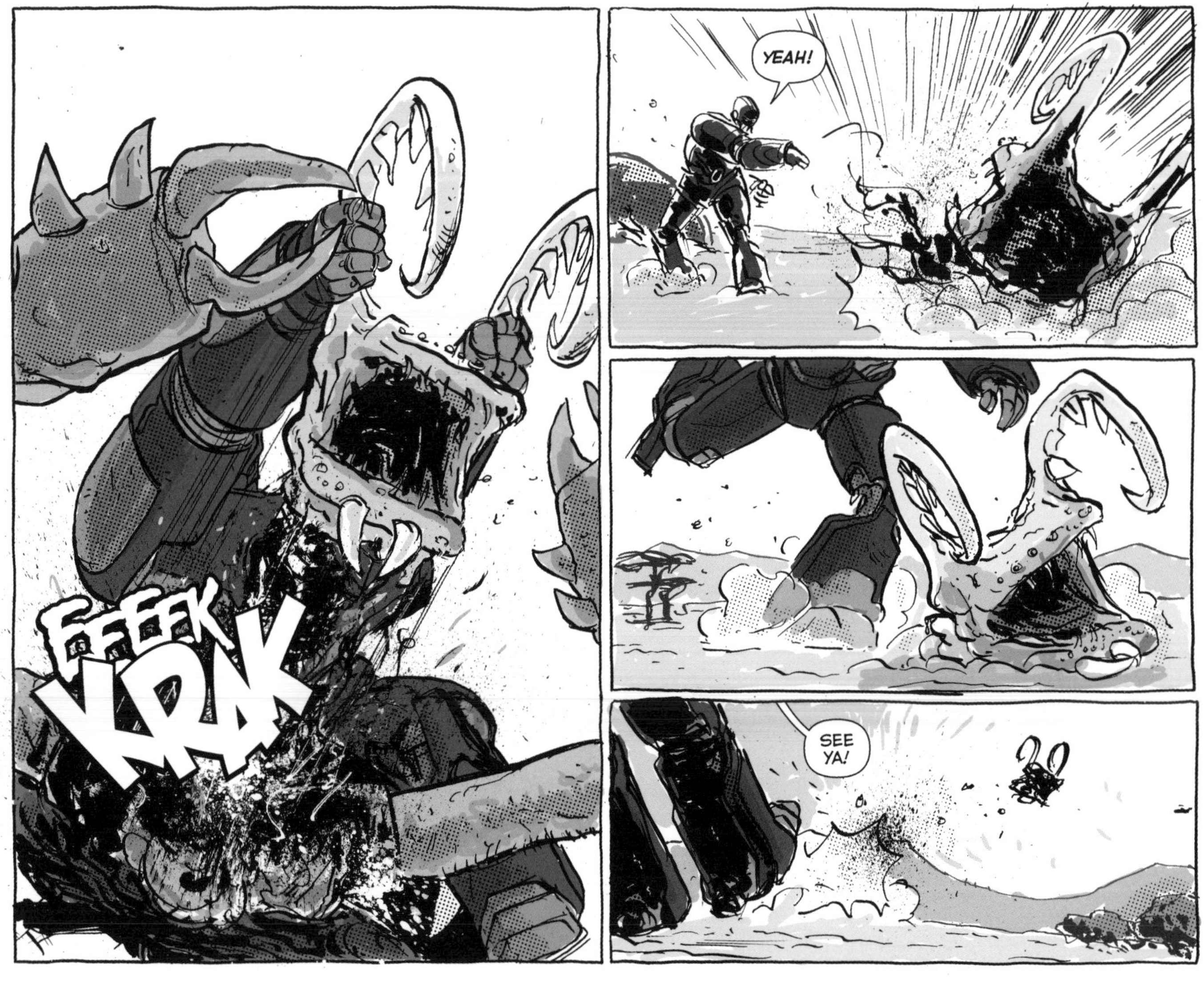
EEEEK
KRAK
YEAH!
SEE YA!

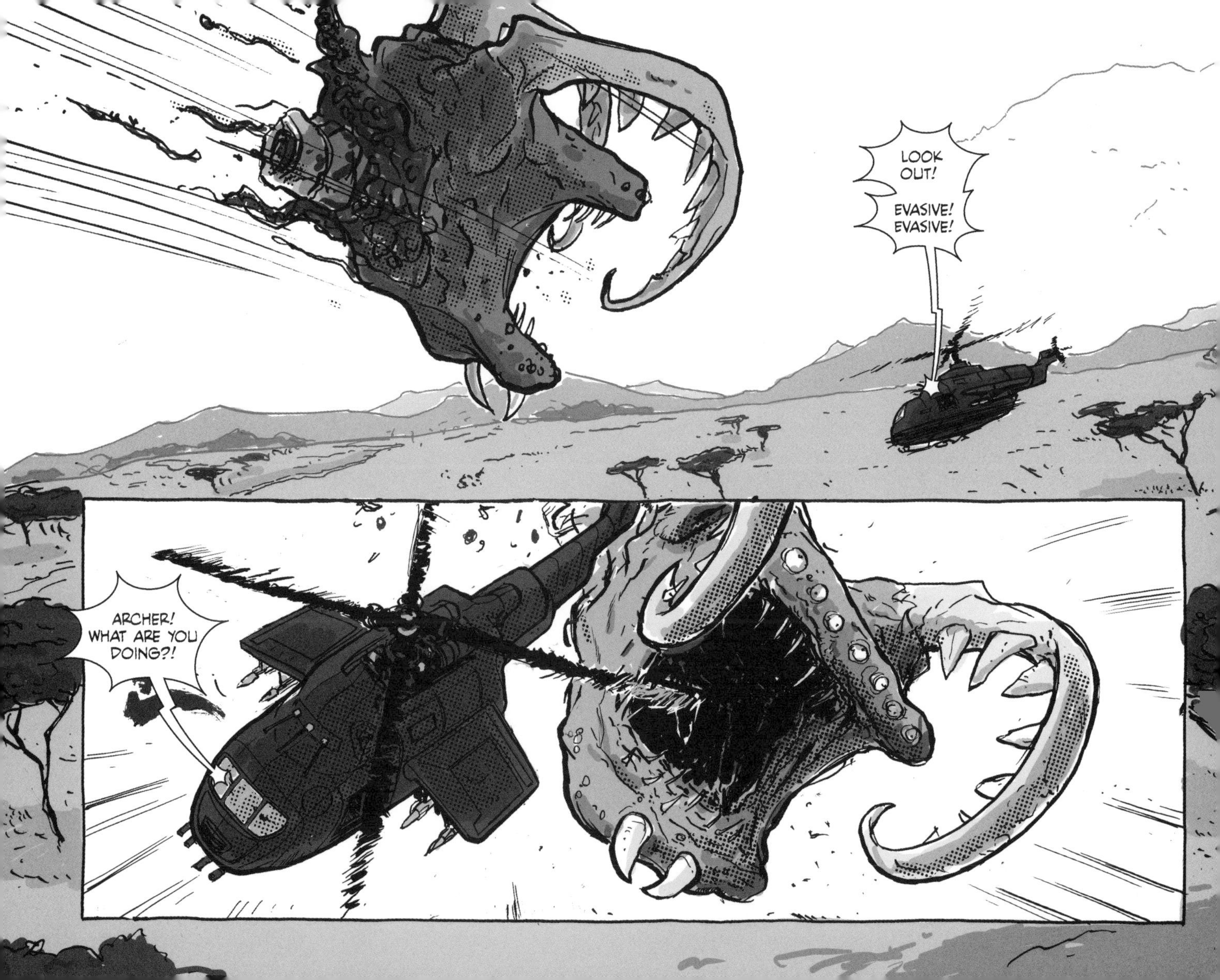
LOOK OUT!
EVASIVE! EVASIVE!
ARCHER! WHAT ARE YOU DOING?!

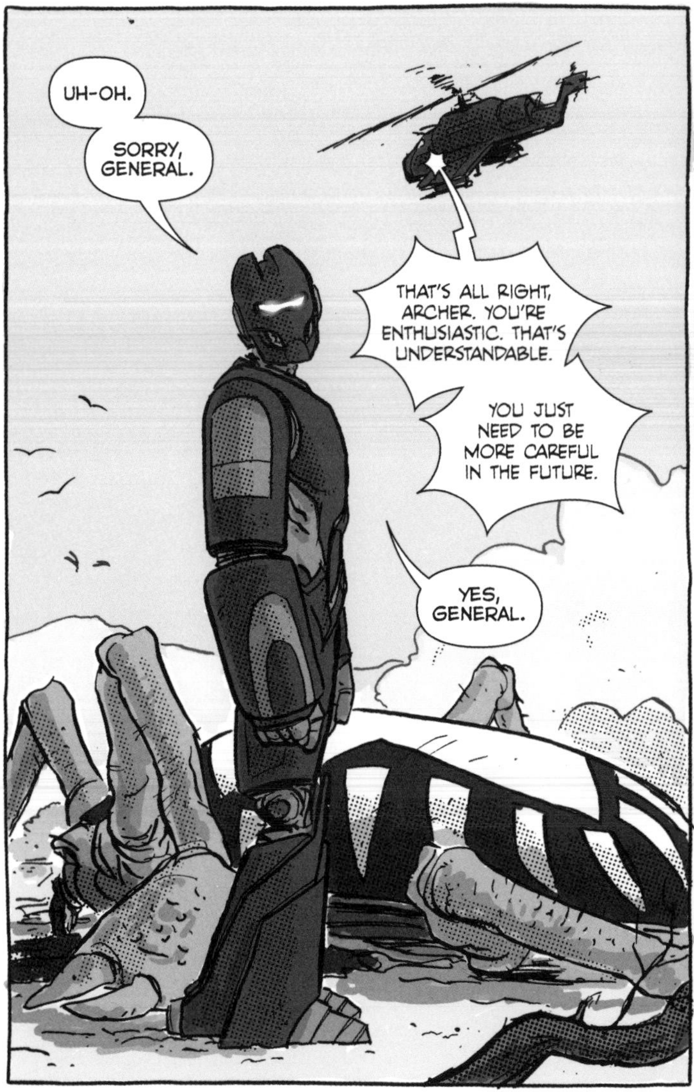
UH-OH.
SORRY, GENERAL.
THAT'S ALL RIGHT, ARCHER. YOU'RE ENTHUSIASTIC. THAT'S UNDERSTANDABLE.
YOU JUST NEED TO BE MORE CAREFUL IN THE FUTURE.
YES, GENERAL.
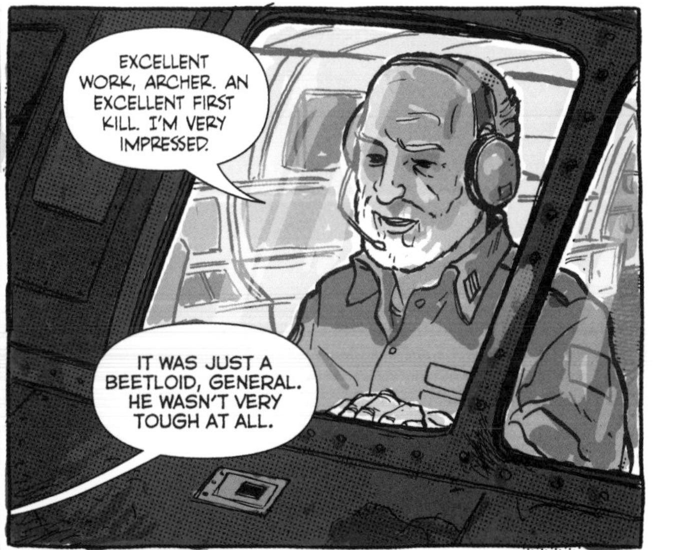
EXCELLENT WORK, ARCHER. AN EXCELLENT FIRST KILL. I'M VERY IMPRESSED.
IT WAS JUST A BEETLOID, GENERAL. HE WASN'T VERY TOUGH AT ALL.
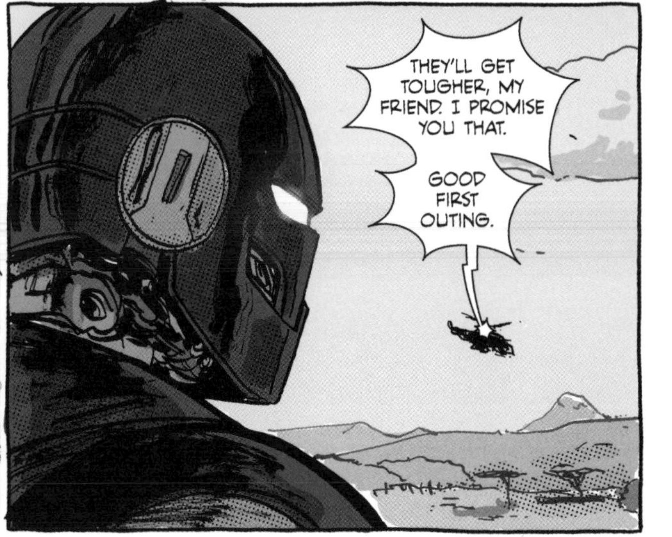
THEY'LL GET TOUGHER, MY FRIEND. I PROMISE YOU THAT.
GOOD FIRST OUTING.

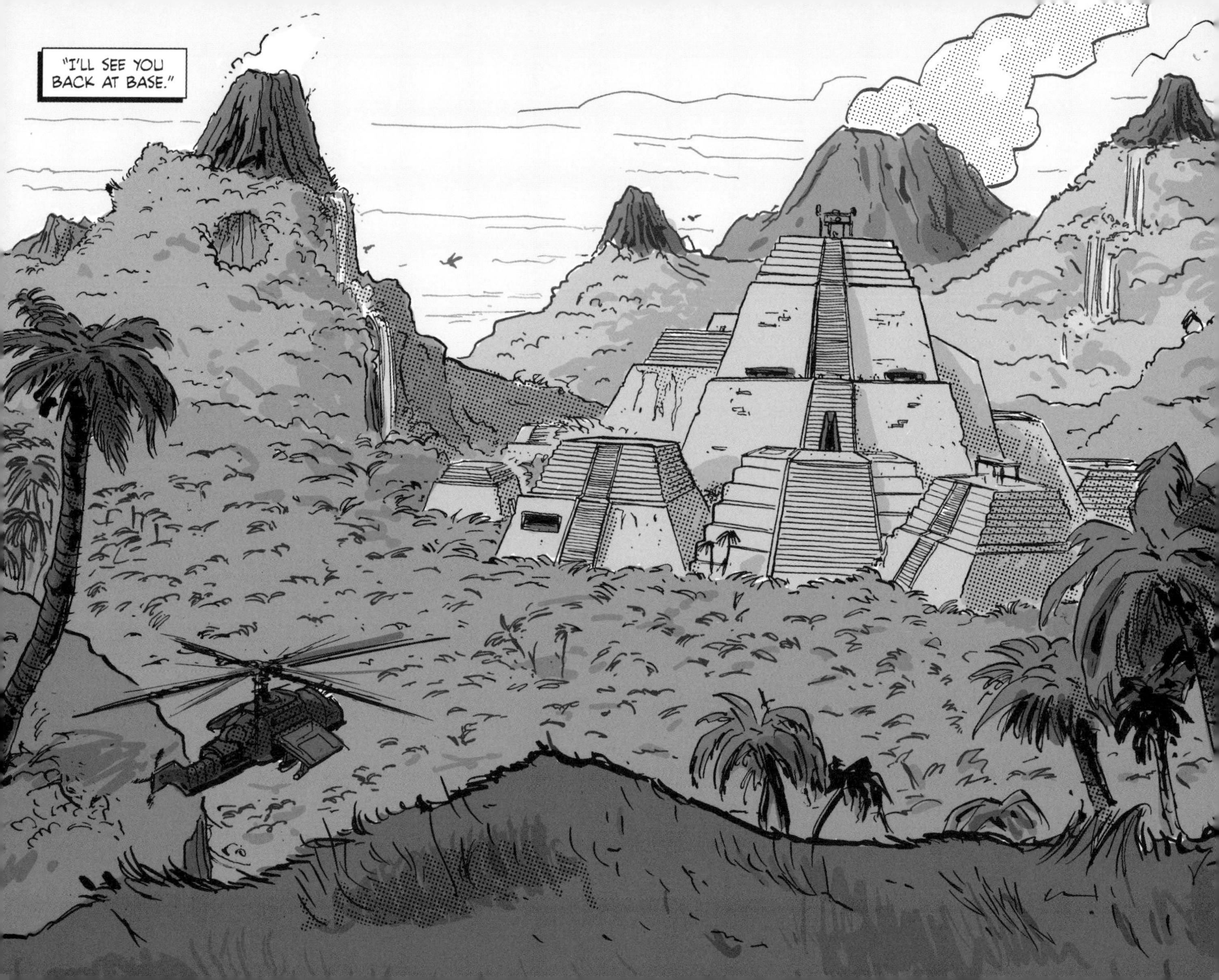
"I'LL SEE YOU BACK AT BASE."

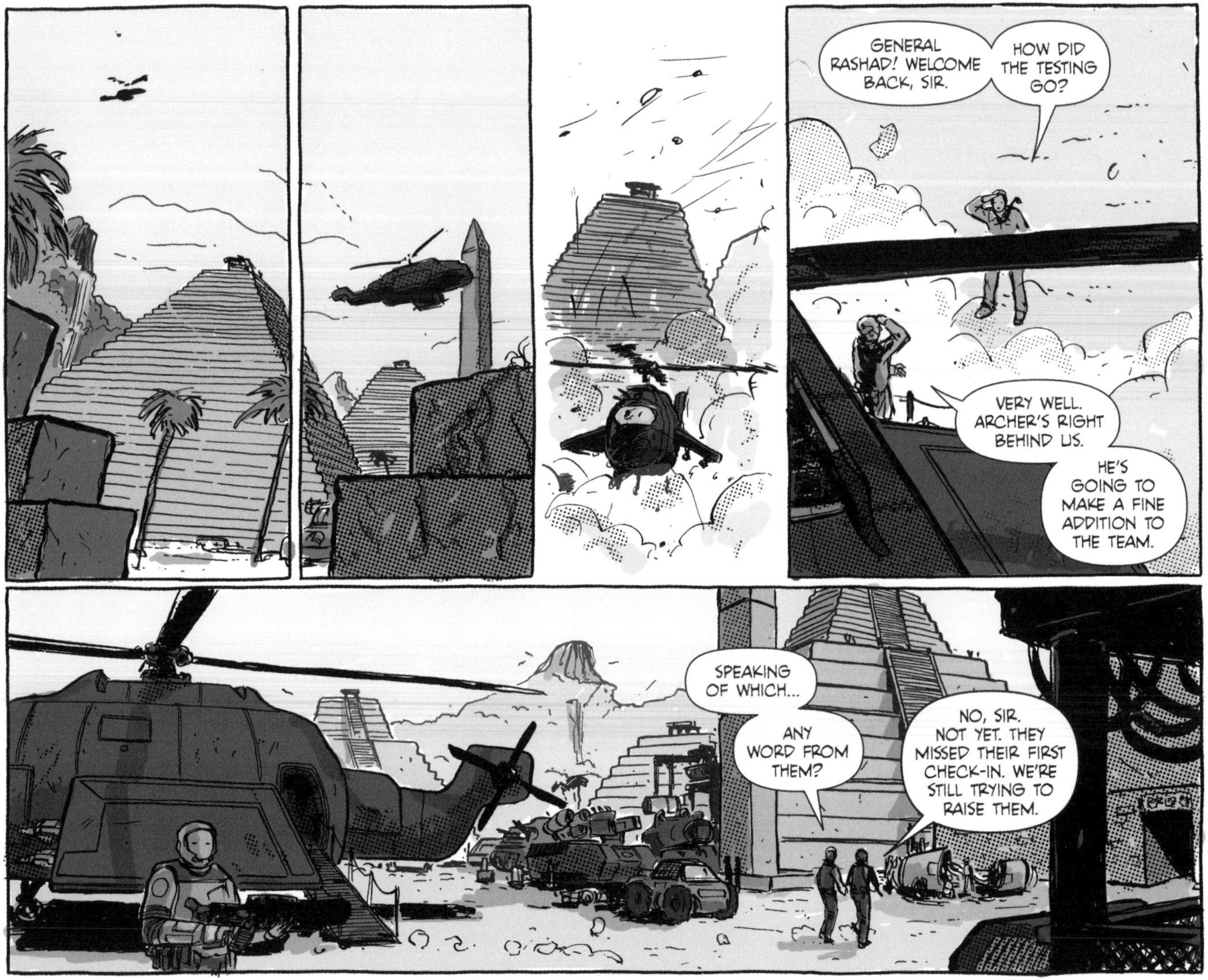
GENERAL RASHAD! WELCOME BACK, SIR.
HOW DID THE TESTING GO?
VERY WELL. ARCHER'S RIGHT BEHIND US.
HE'S GOING TO MAKE A FINE ADDITION TO THE TEAM.
SPEAKING OF WHICH...
ANY WORD FROM THEM?
NO, SIR. NOT YET. THEY MISSED THEIR FIRST CHECK-IN. WE'RE STILL TRYING TO RAISE THEM.

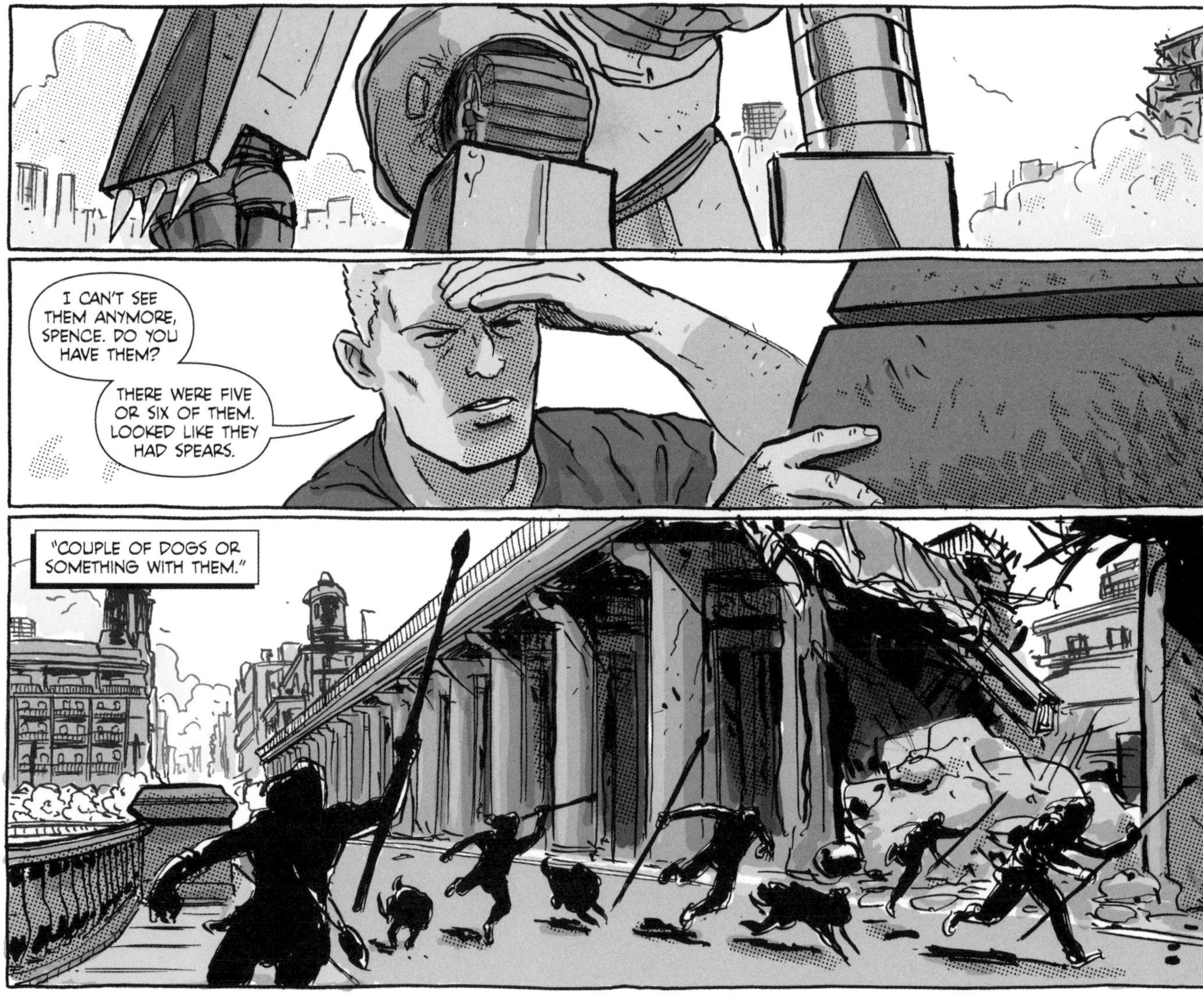
I CAN'T SEE THEM ANYMORE, SPENCE. DO YOU HAVE THEM?
THERE WERE FIVE OR SIX OF THEM. LOOKED LIKE THEY HAD SPEARS.
"COUPLE OF DOGS OR SOMETHING WITH THEM."

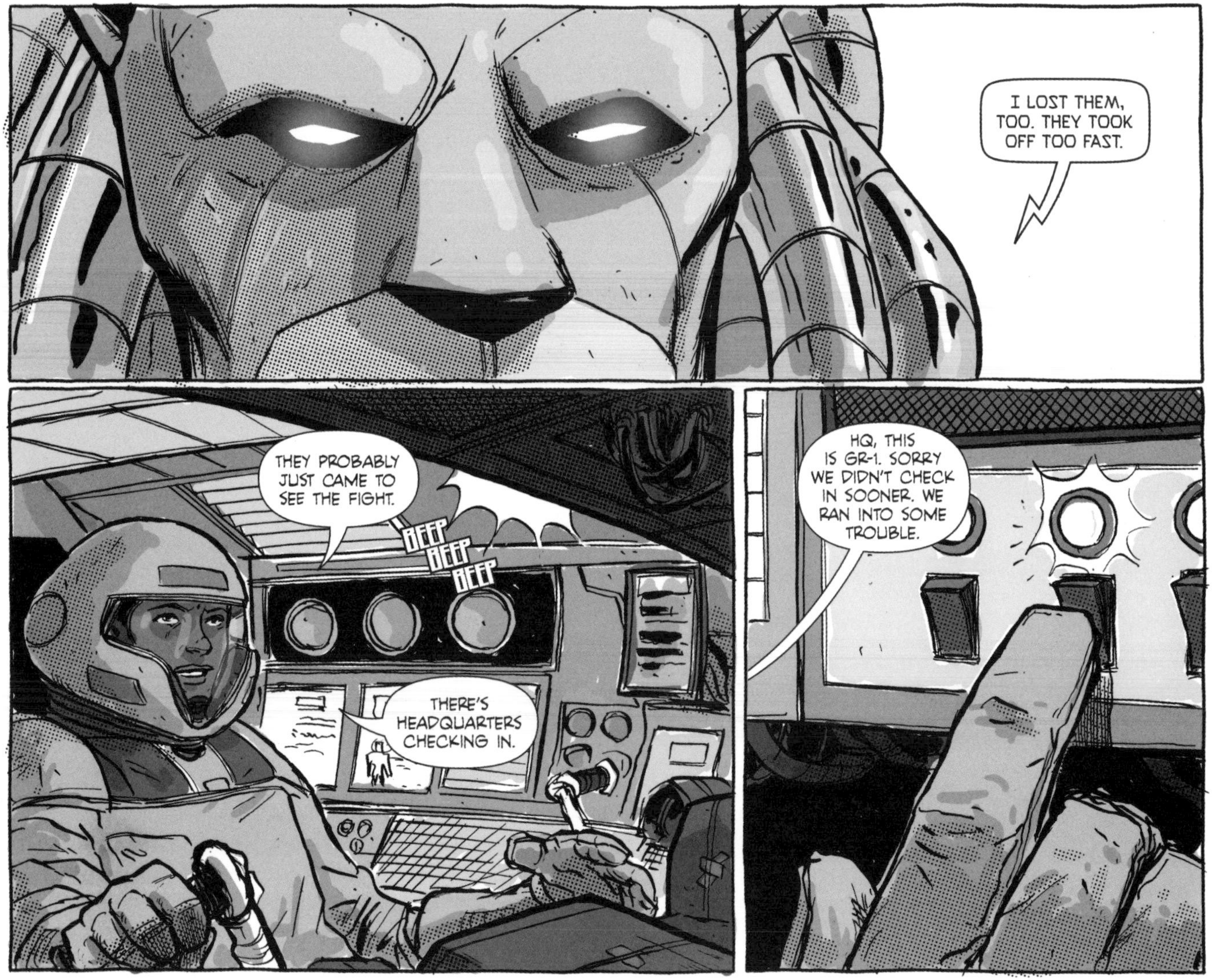
I LOST THEM, TOO. THEY TOOK OFF TOO FAST.
THEY PROBABLY JUST CAME TO SEE THE FIGHT.
BEEP BEEP BEEP
THERE'S HEADQUARTERS CHECKING IN.
HQ, THIS IS GR-1. SORRY WE DIDN'T CHECK IN SOONER. WE RAN INTO SOME TROUBLE.

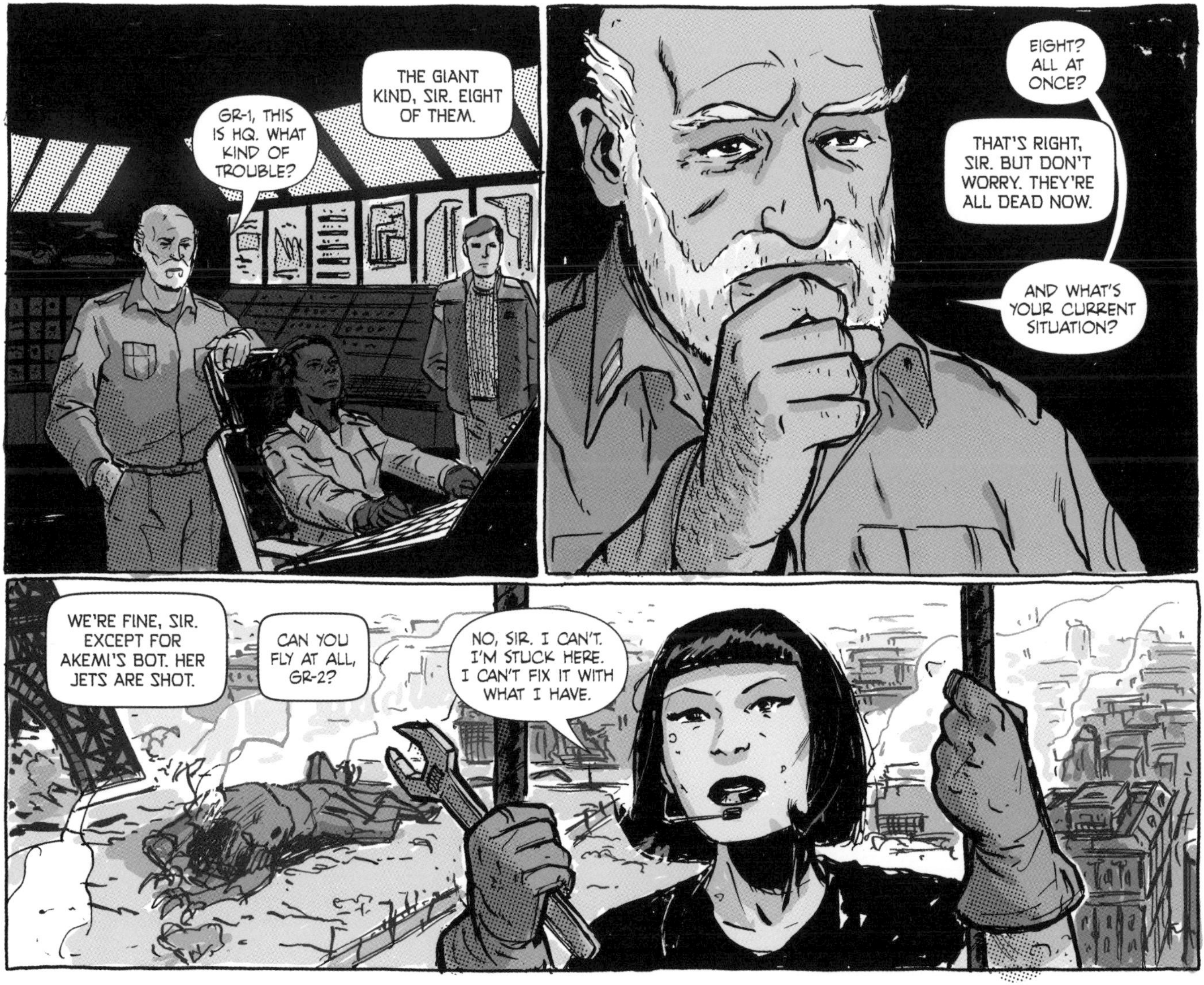
GR-1, THIS IS HQ. WHAT KIND OF TROUBLE?
THE GIANT KIND, SIR. EIGHT OF THEM.
EIGHT? ALL AT ONCE?
THAT'S RIGHT, SIR. BUT DON'T WORRY. THEY'RE ALL DEAD NOW.
AND WHAT'S YOUR CURRENT SITUATION?
WE'RE FINE, SIR. EXCEPT FOR AKEMI'S BOT. HER JETS ARE SHOT.
CAN YOU FLY AT ALL, GR-2?
NO, SIR. I CAN'T. I'M STUCK HERE. I CAN'T FIX IT WITH WHAT I HAVE.

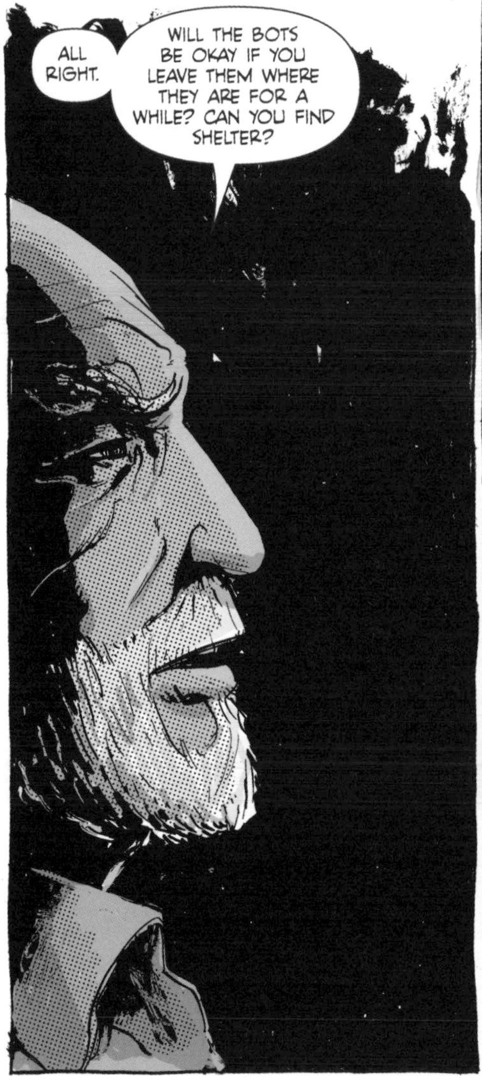
ALL RIGHT.
WILL THE BOTS BE OKAY IF YOU LEAVE THEM WHERE THEY ARE FOR A WHILE? CAN YOU FIND SHELTER?

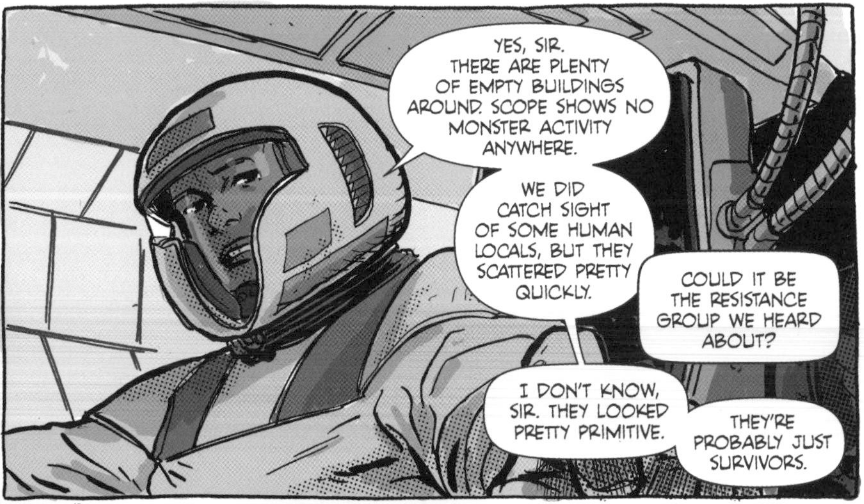
YES, SIR. THERE ARE PLENTY OF EMPTY BUILDINGS AROUND. SCOPE SHOWS NO MONSTER ACTIVITY ANYWHERE.
WE DID CATCH SIGHT OF SOME HUMAN LOCALS, BUT THEY SCATTERED PRETTY QUICKLY.
COULD IT BE THE RESISTANCE GROUP WE HEARD ABOUT?
I DON'T KNOW, SIR. THEY LOOKED PRETTY PRIMITIVE.
THEY'RE PROBABLY JUST SURVIVORS.

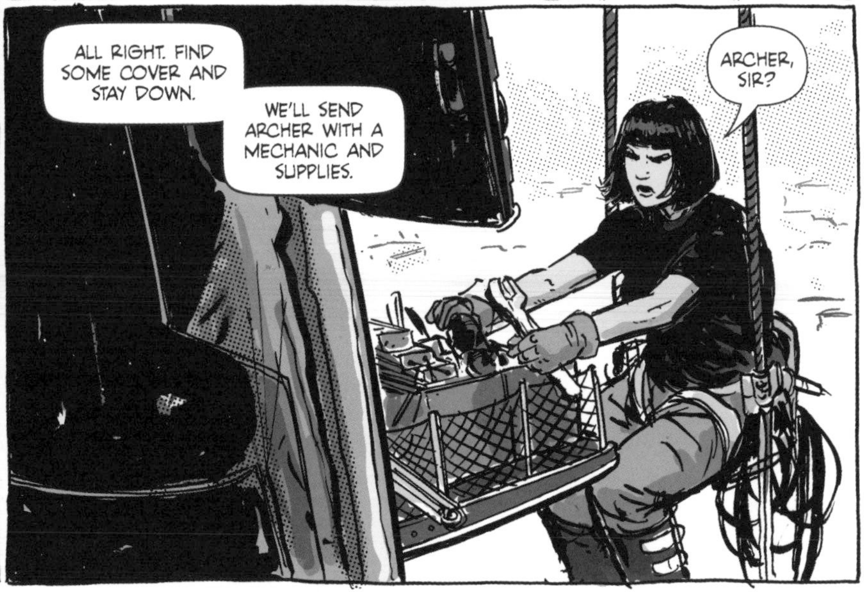
ALL RIGHT. FIND SOME COVER AND STAY DOWN.
WE'LL SEND ARCHER WITH A MECHANIC AND SUPPLIES.
ARCHER, SIR?

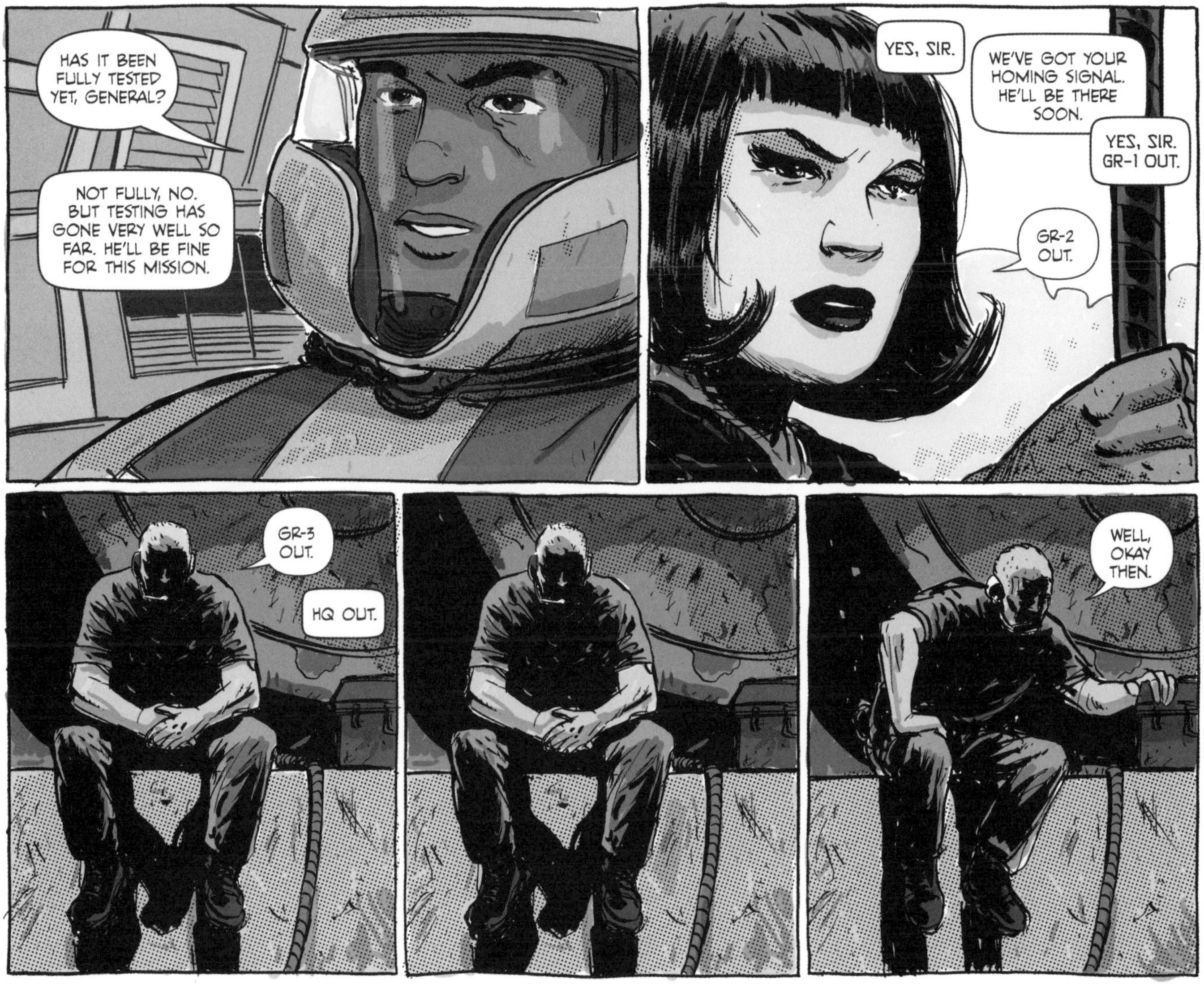
HAS IT BEEN FULLY TESTED YET, GENERAL?
NOT FULLY, NO. BUT TESTING HAS GONE VERY WELL SO FAR. HE'LL BE FINE FOR THIS MISSION.
YES, SIR.
WE'VE GOT YOUR HOMING SIGNAL. HE'LL BE THERE SOON.
YES, SIR. GR-1 OUT.
GR-2 OUT.
GR-3 OUT.
HQ OUT.
WELL, OKAY THEN.

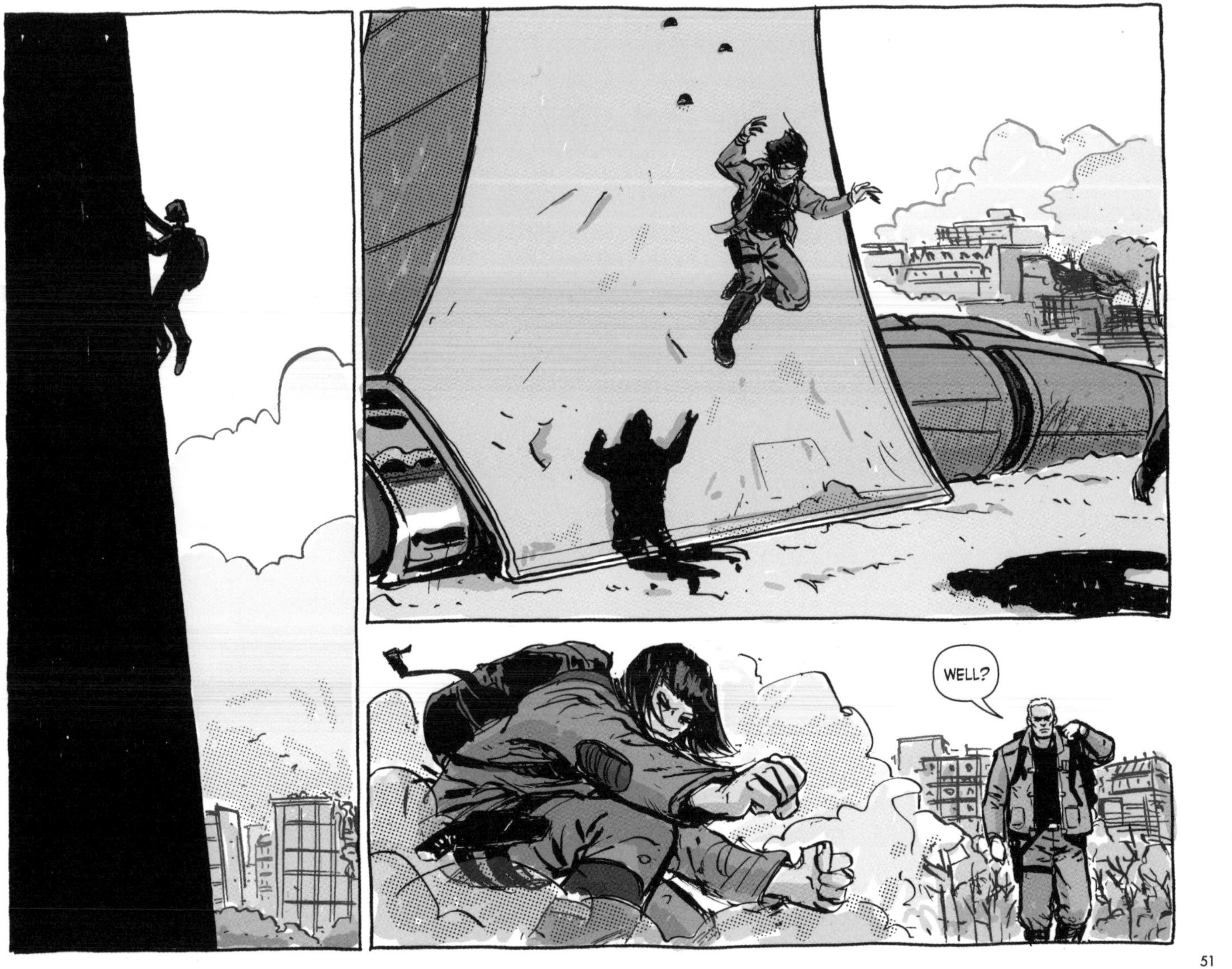
WELL?

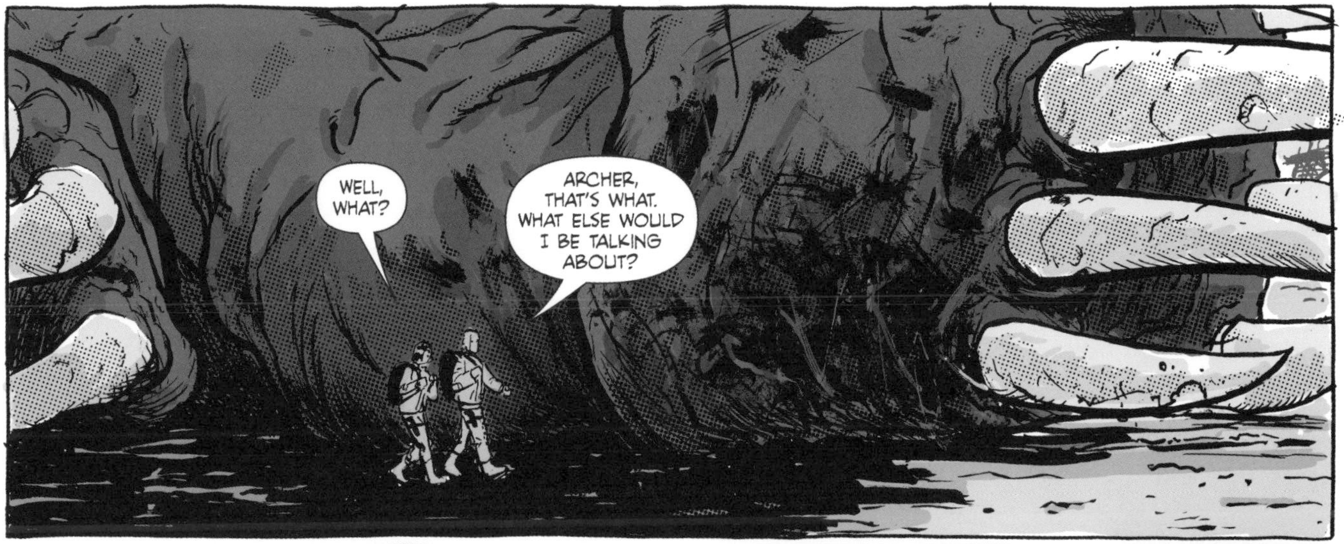
WELL, WHAT?
ARCHER, THAT'S WHAT. WHAT ELSE WOULD I BE TALKING ABOUT?

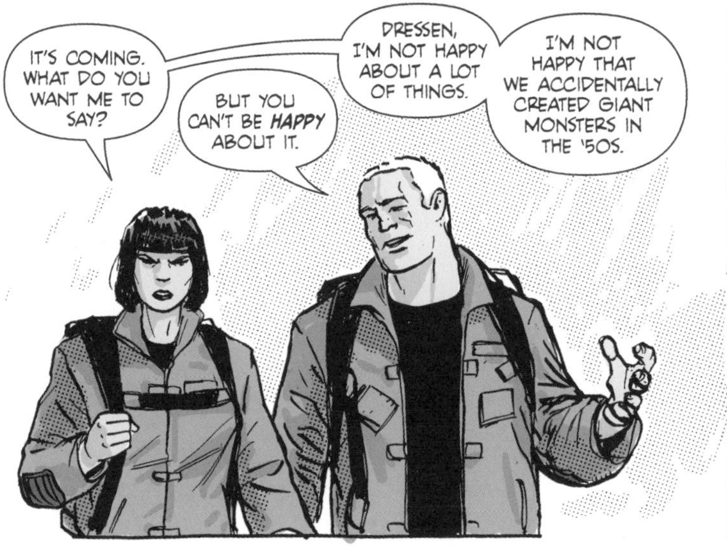
IT'S COMING. WHAT DO YOU WANT ME TO SAY?
BUT YOU CAN'T BE ***HAPPY*** ABOUT IT.
DRESSEN, I'M NOT HAPPY ABOUT A LOT OF THINGS.
I'M NOT HAPPY THAT WE ACCIDENTALLY CREATED GIANT MONSTERS IN THE '50S.

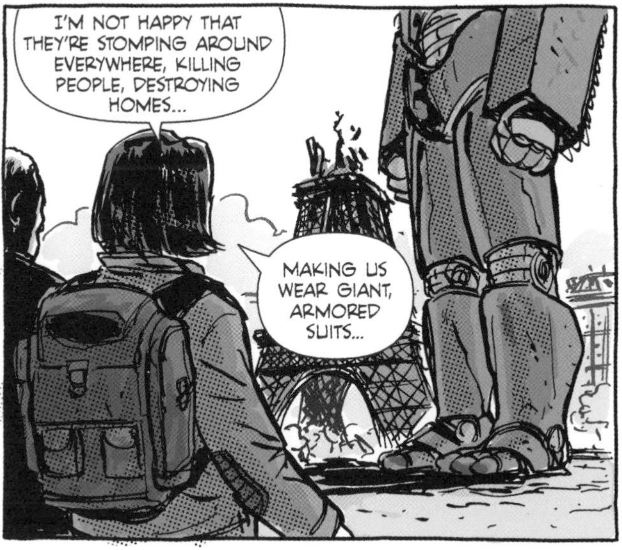
I'M NOT HAPPY THAT THEY'RE STOMPING AROUND EVERYWHERE, KILLING PEOPLE, DESTROYING HOMES...
MAKING US WEAR GIANT, ARMORED SUITS...

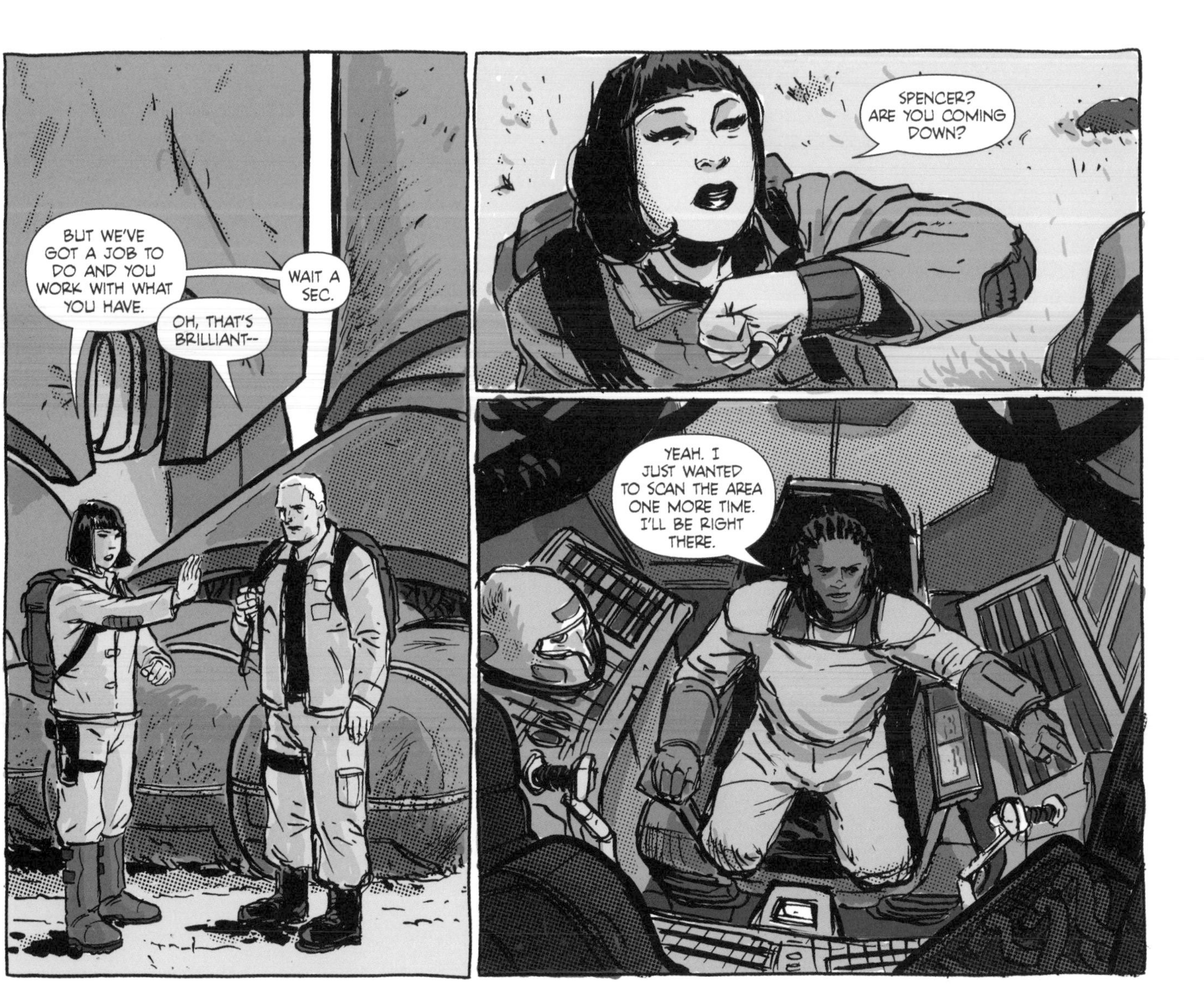
BUT WE'VE GOT A JOB TO DO AND YOU WORK WITH WHAT YOU HAVE.
WAIT A SEC.
OH, THAT'S BRILLIANT--
SPENCER? ARE YOU COMING DOWN?
YEAH. I JUST WANTED TO SCAN THE AREA ONE MORE TIME. I'LL BE RIGHT THERE.

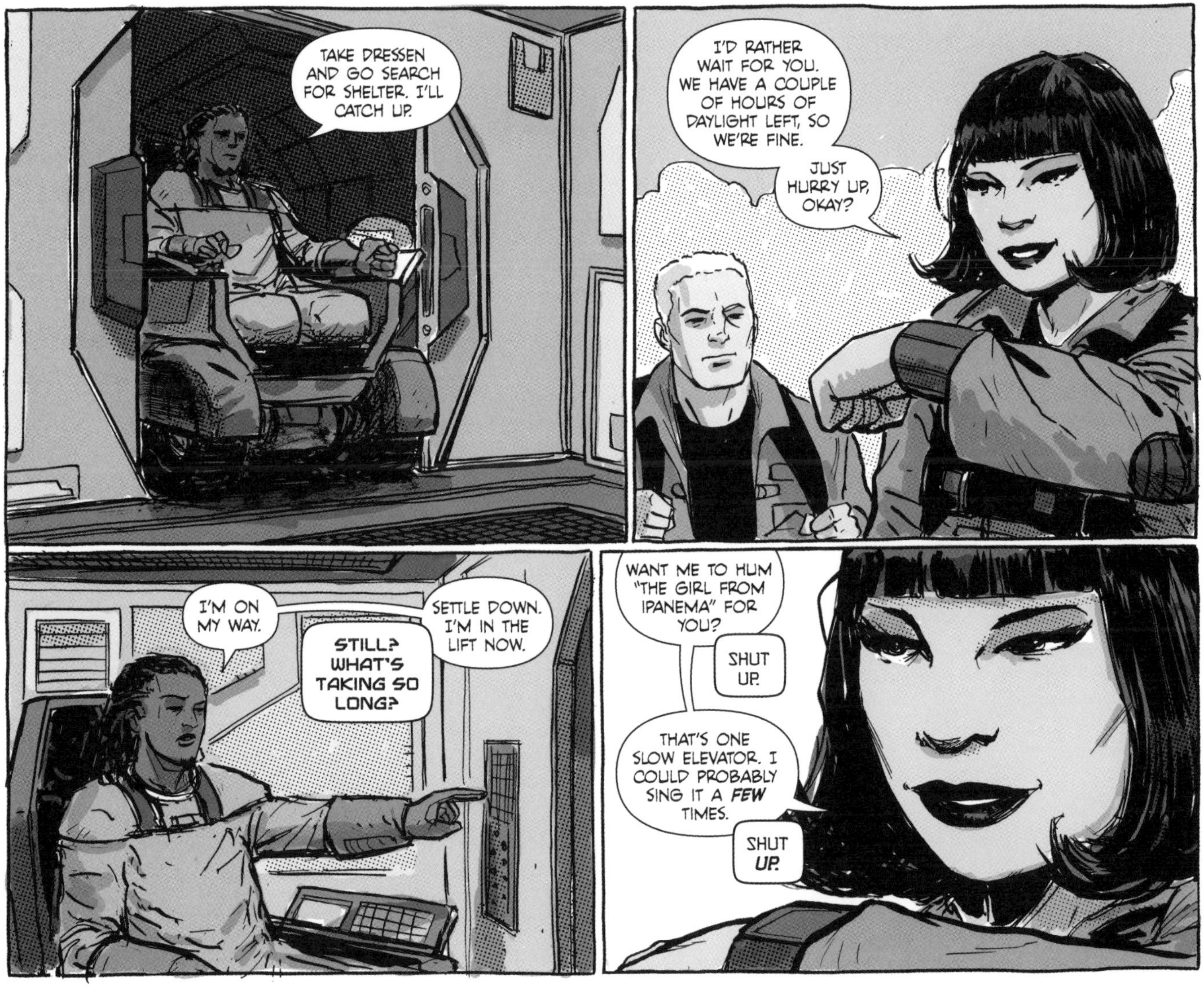
TAKE DRESSEN AND GO SEARCH FOR SHELTER. I'LL CATCH UP.
I'D RATHER WAIT FOR YOU. WE HAVE A COUPLE OF HOURS OF DAYLIGHT LEFT, SO WE'RE FINE.
JUST HURRY UP, OKAY?
I'M ON MY WAY.
SETTLE DOWN. I'M IN THE LIFT NOW.
STILL? WHAT'S TAKING SO LONG?
WANT ME TO HUM "THE GIRL FROM IPANEMA" FOR YOU?
SHUT UP.
THAT'S ONE SLOW ELEVATOR. I COULD PROBABLY SING IT A *FEW* TIMES.
SHUT *UP.*

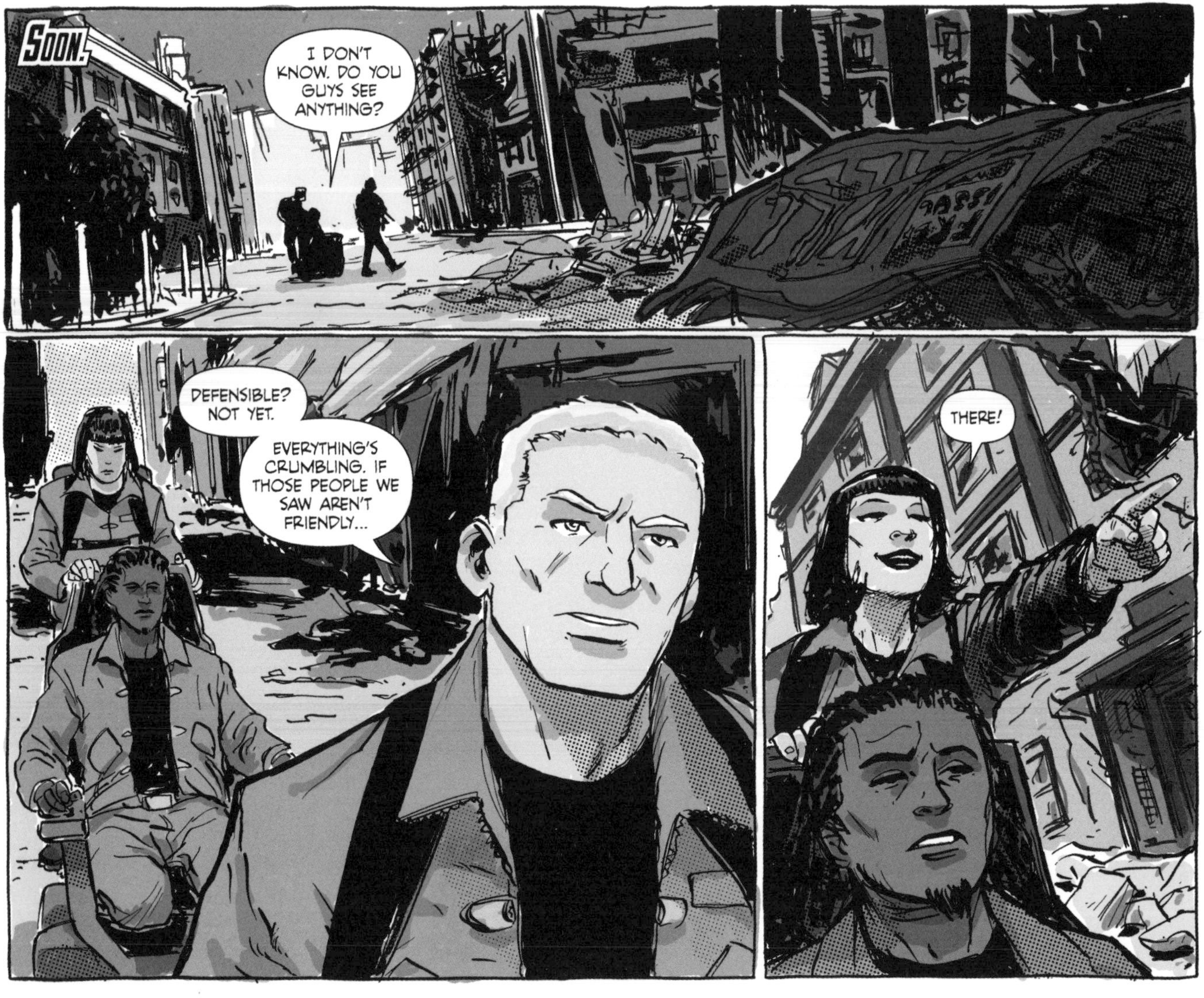
SOON.
I DON'T KNOW. DO YOU GUYS SEE ANYTHING?
DEFENSIBLE? NOT YET.
EVERYTHING'S CRUMBLING. IF THOSE PEOPLE WE SAW AREN'T FRIENDLY...
THERE!

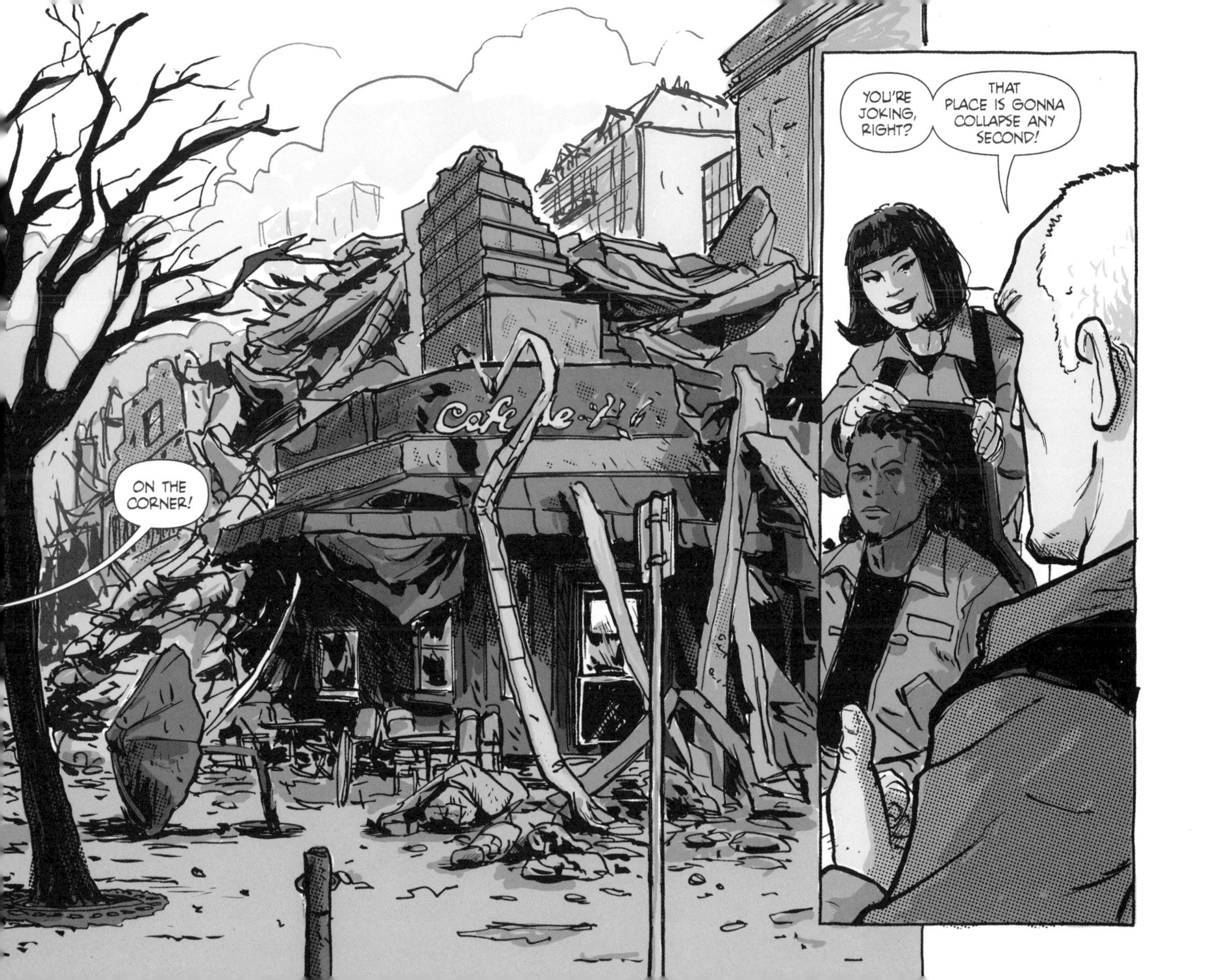
ON THE CORNER!
Cafe de ...
YOU'RE JOKING, RIGHT?
THAT PLACE IS GONNA COLLAPSE ANY SECOND!

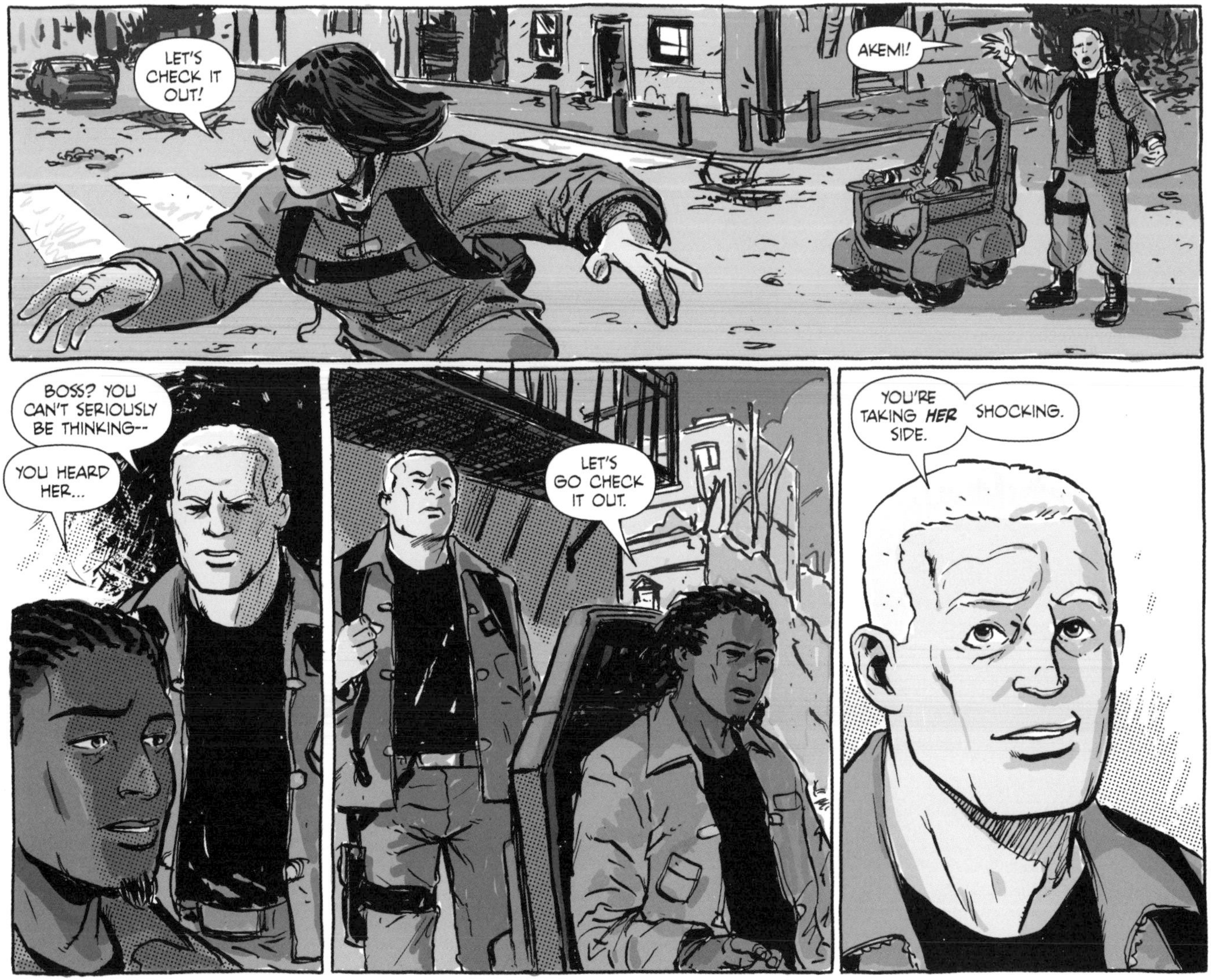
LET'S CHECK IT OUT!
AKEMI!
BOSS? YOU CAN'T SERIOUSLY BE THINKING--
YOU HEARD HER...
LET'S GO CHECK IT OUT.
YOU'RE TAKING **HER** SIDE.
SHOCKING.

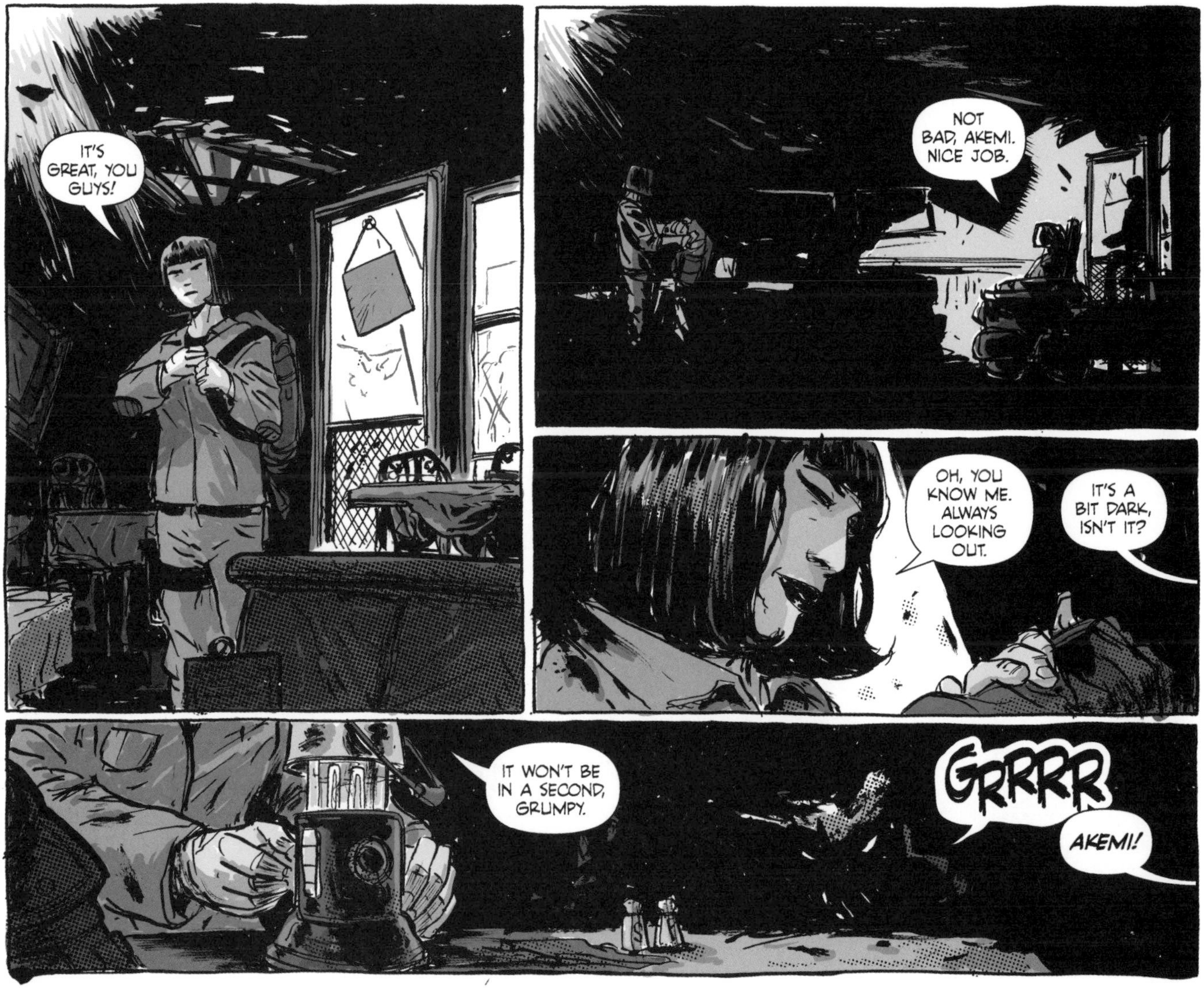
IT'S GREAT, YOU GUYS!
NOT BAD, AKEMI. NICE JOB.
OH, YOU KNOW ME. ALWAYS LOOKING OUT.
IT'S A BIT DARK, ISN'T IT?
IT WON'T BE IN A SECOND, GRUMPY.
GRRRR
AKEMI!

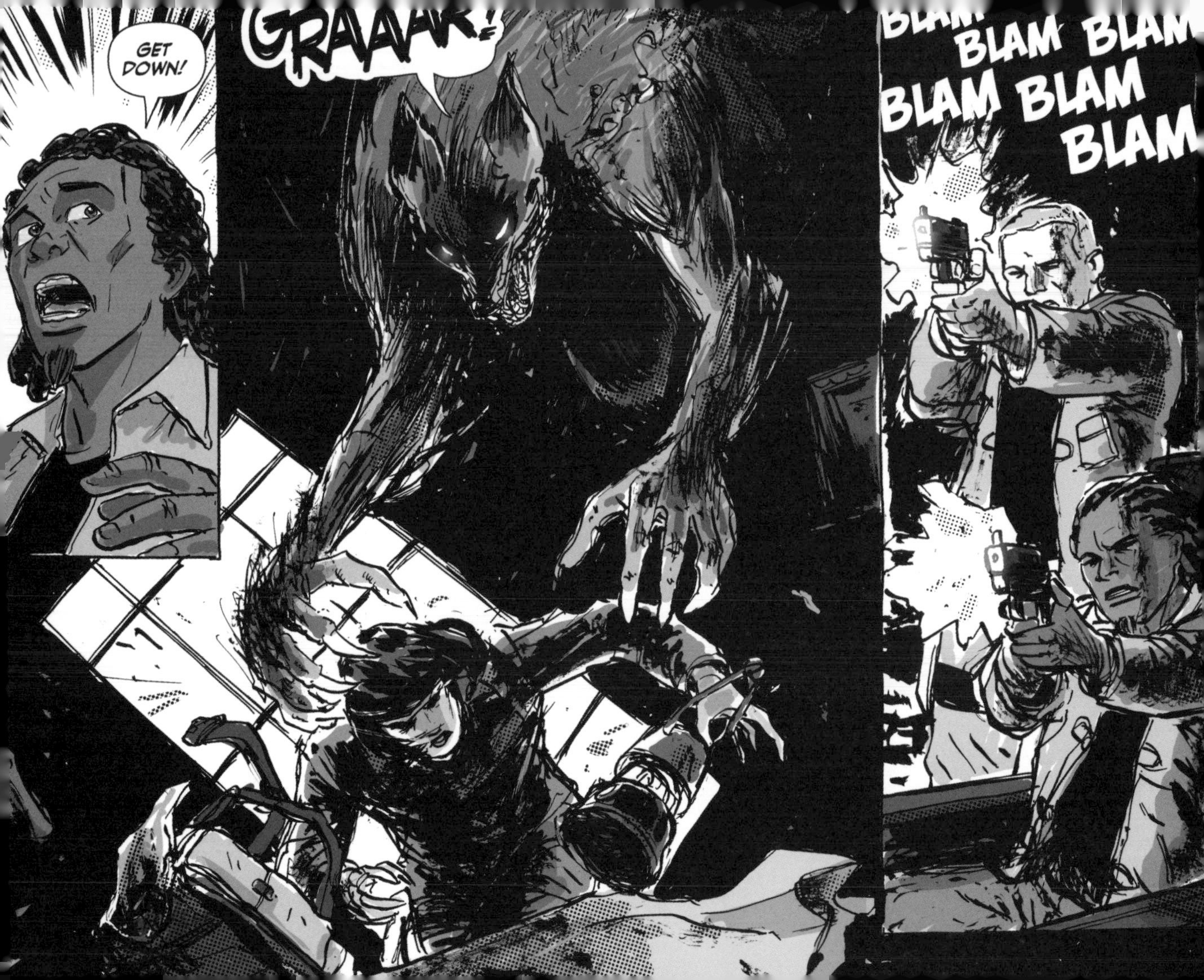
GET DOWN!
GRAAAK!
BLAM BLAM BLAM
BLAM BLAM
BLAM

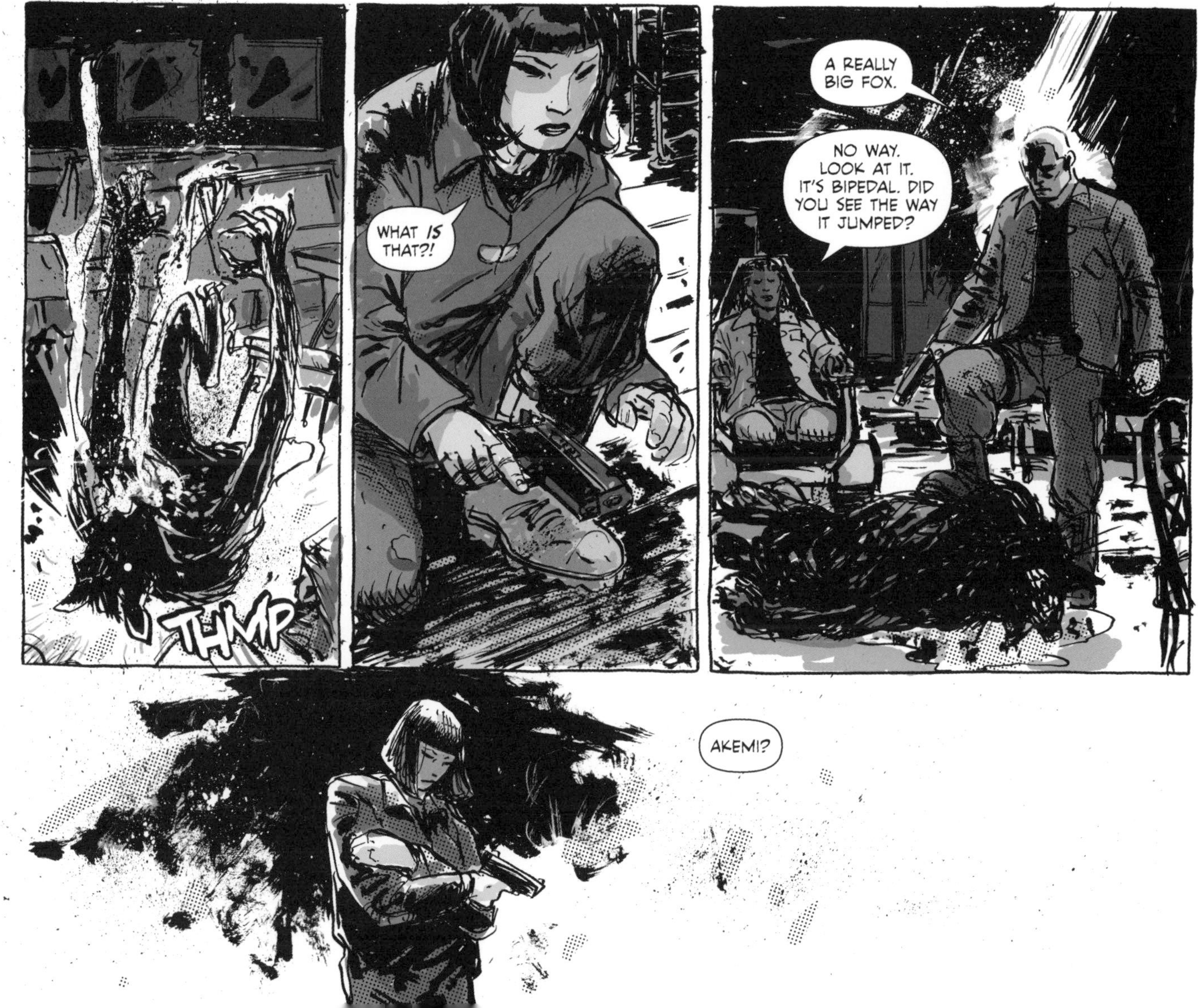
THMP
WHAT IS THAT?!
A REALLY BIG FOX.
NO WAY. LOOK AT IT. IT'S BIPEDAL. DID YOU SEE THE WAY IT JUMPED?
AKEMI?

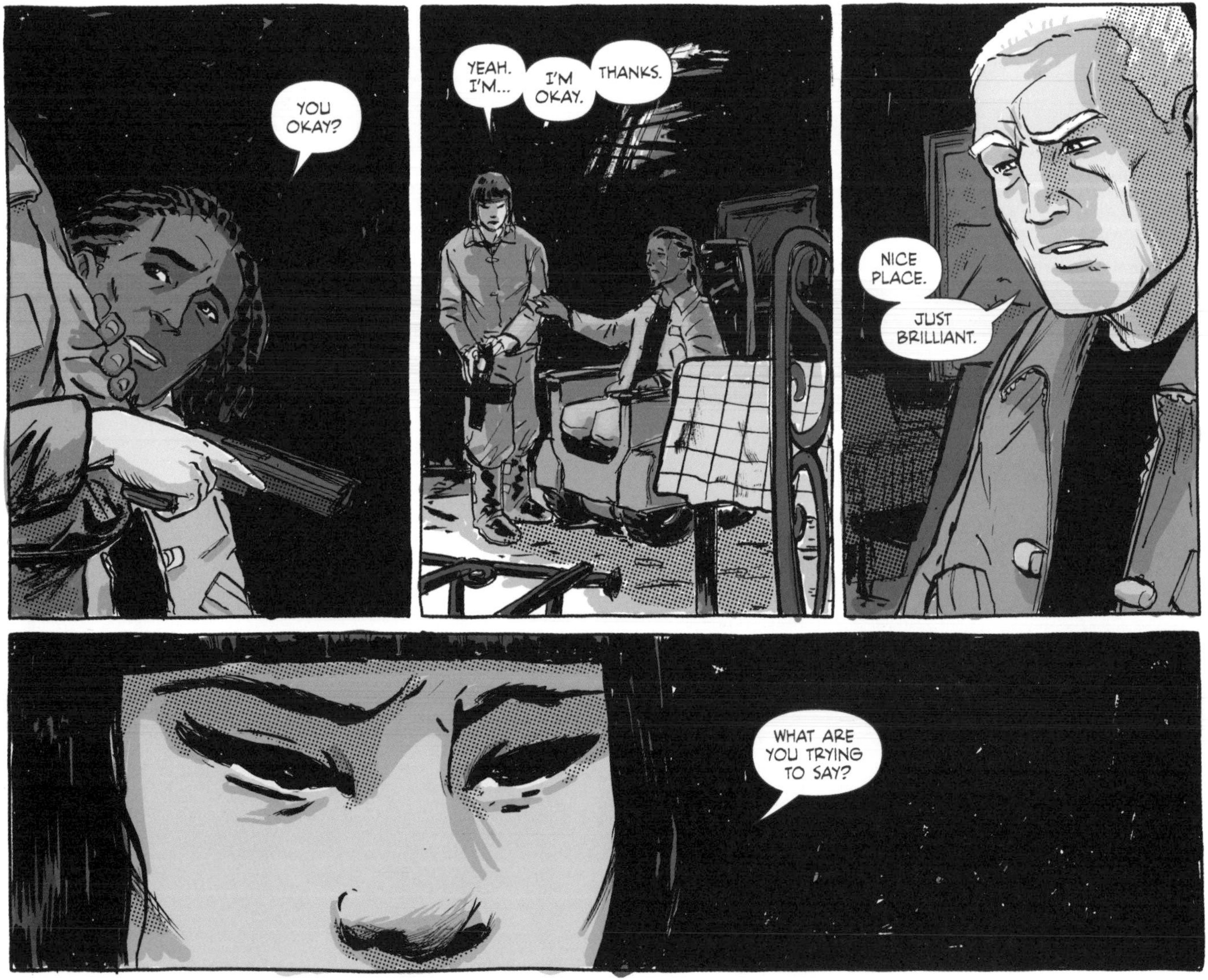
YOU OKAY?
YEAH. I'M...
I'M OKAY.
THANKS.
NICE PLACE.
JUST BRILLIANT.
WHAT ARE YOU TRYING TO SAY?

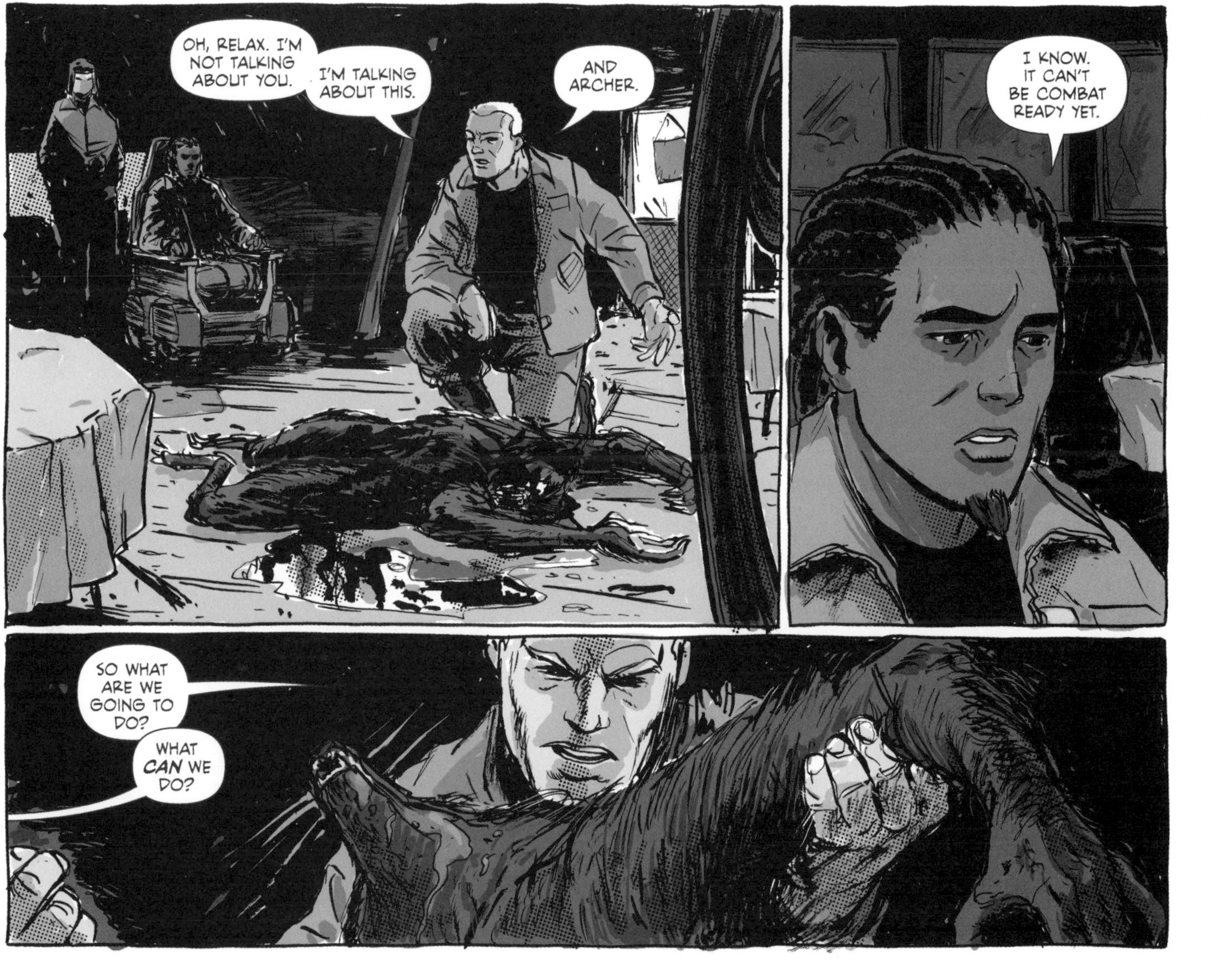
OH, RELAX. I'M NOT TALKING ABOUT YOU.
I'M TALKING ABOUT THIS.
AND ARCHER.
I KNOW. IT CAN'T BE COMBAT READY YET.
SO WHAT ARE WE GOING TO DO?
WHAT *CAN* WE DO?

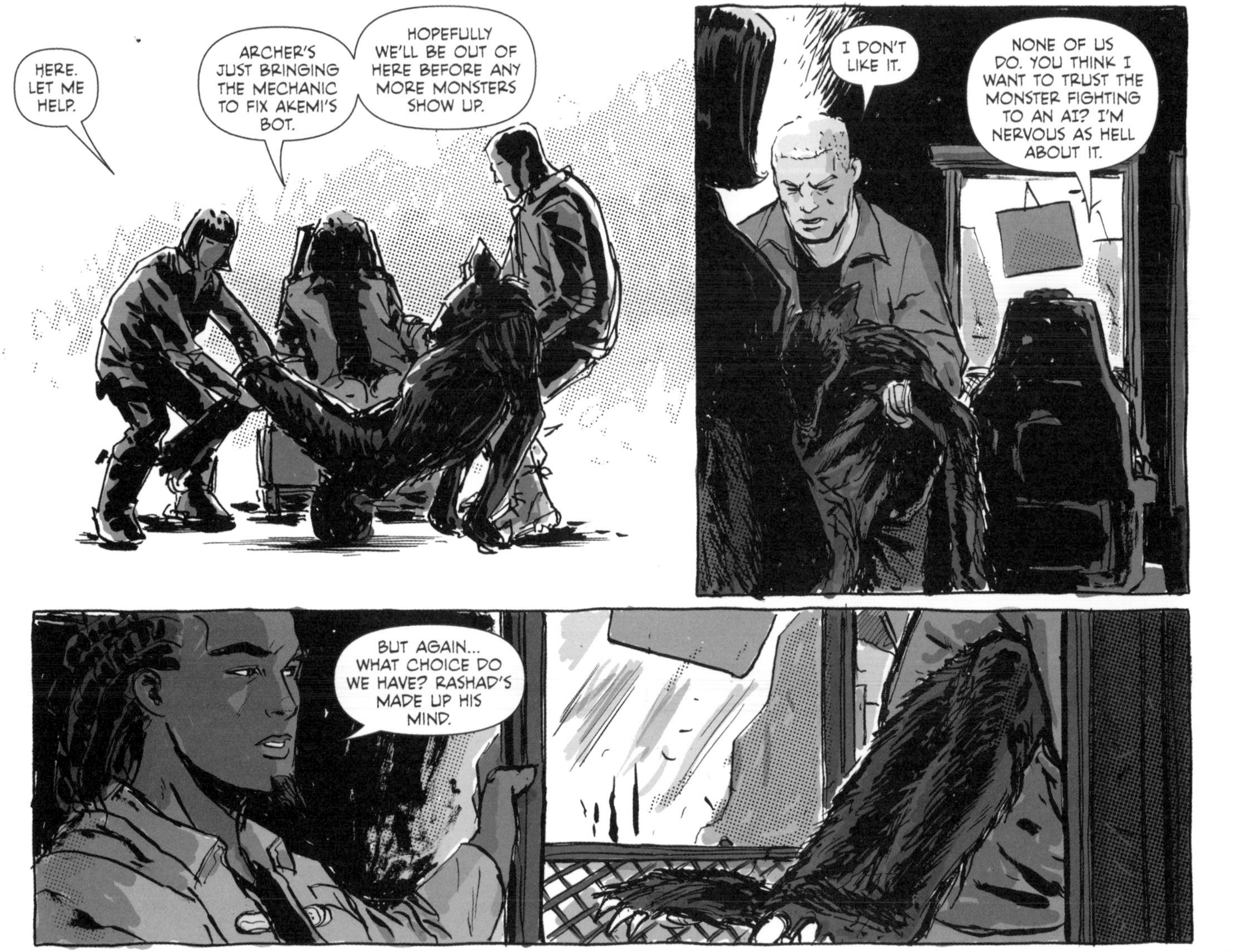
HERE. LET ME HELP.
ARCHER'S JUST BRINGING THE MECHANIC TO FIX AKEMI'S BOT.
HOPEFULLY WE'LL BE OUT OF HERE BEFORE ANY MORE MONSTERS SHOW UP.
I DON'T LIKE IT.
NONE OF US DO. YOU THINK I WANT TO TRUST THE MONSTER FIGHTING TO AN AI? I'M NERVOUS AS HELL ABOUT IT.
BUT AGAIN... WHAT CHOICE DO WE HAVE? RASHAD'S MADE UP HIS MIND.

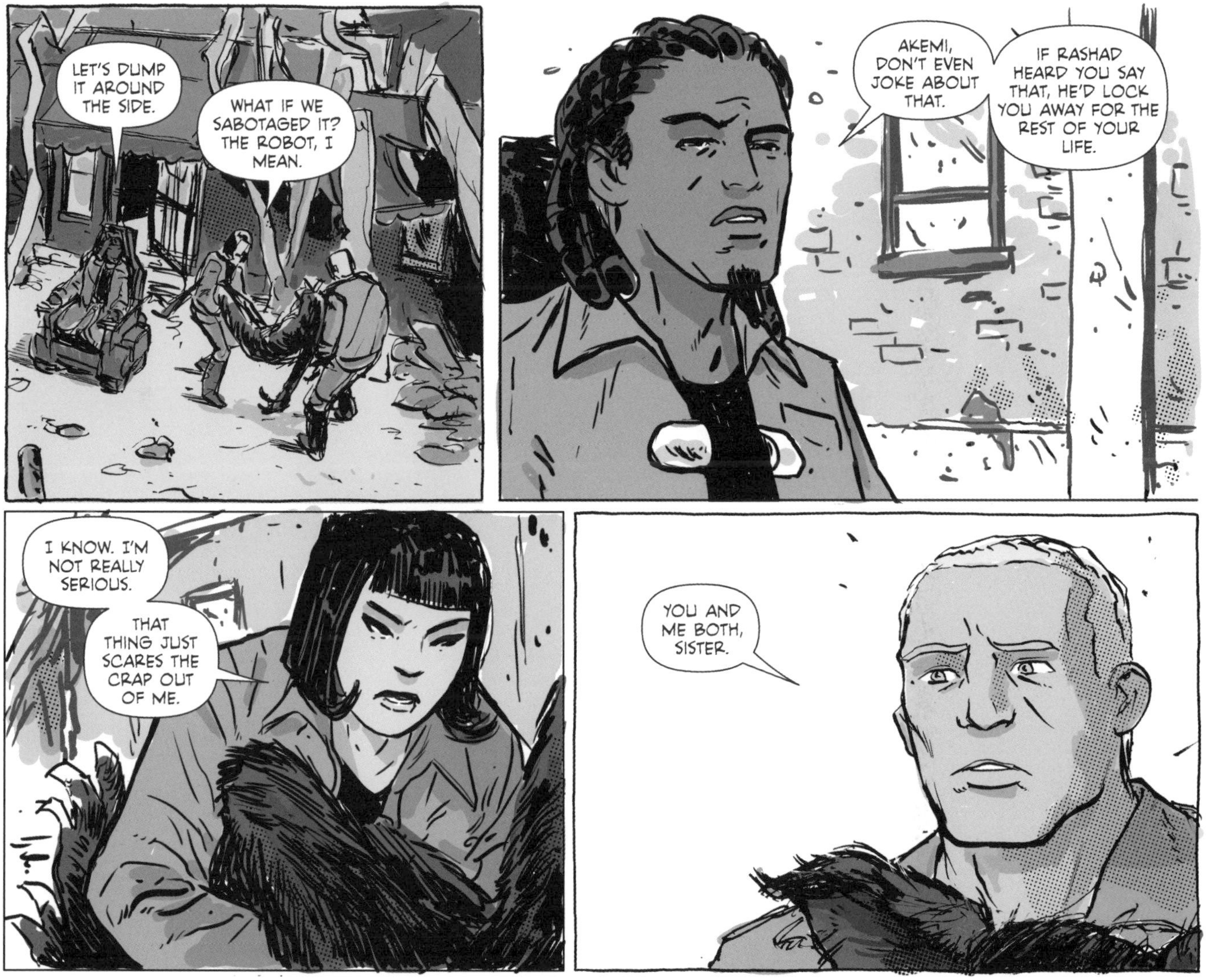
LET'S DUMP IT AROUND THE SIDE.
WHAT IF WE SABOTAGED IT? THE ROBOT, I MEAN.
AKEMI, DON'T EVEN JOKE ABOUT THAT.
IF RASHAD HEARD YOU SAY THAT, HE'D LOCK YOU AWAY FOR THE REST OF YOUR LIFE.
I KNOW. I'M NOT REALLY SERIOUS.
THAT THING JUST SCARES THE CRAP OUT OF ME.
YOU AND ME BOTH, SISTER.

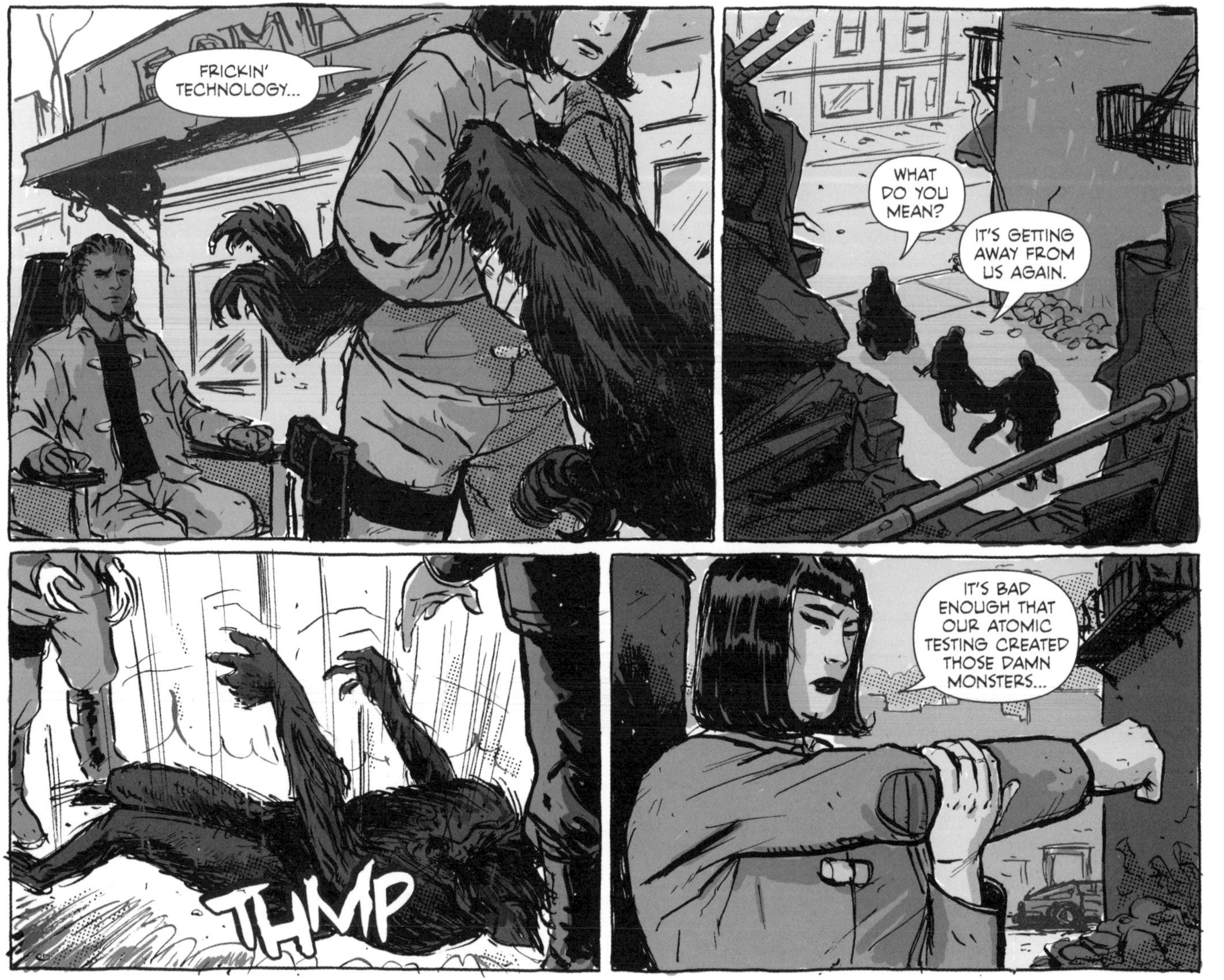
FRICKIN' TECHNOLOGY...
WHAT DO YOU MEAN?
IT'S GETTING AWAY FROM US AGAIN.
THMP
IT'S BAD ENOUGH THAT OUR ATOMIC TESTING CREATED THOSE DAMN MONSTERS...

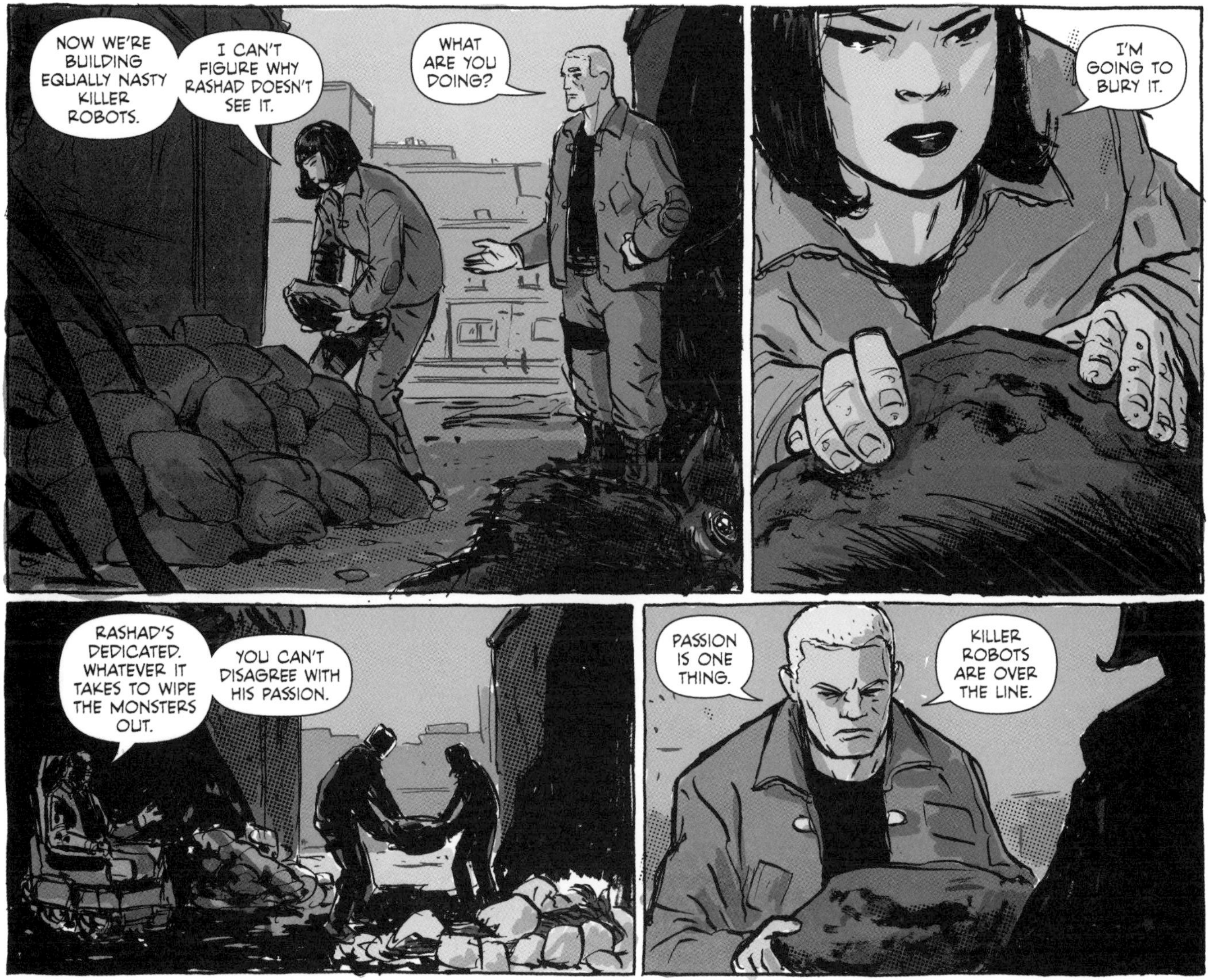
NOW WE'RE BUILDING EQUALLY NASTY KILLER ROBOTS.
I CAN'T FIGURE WHY RASHAD DOESN'T SEE IT.
WHAT ARE YOU DOING?
I'M GOING TO BURY IT.
RASHAD'S DEDICATED. WHATEVER IT TAKES TO WIPE THE MONSTERS OUT.
YOU CAN'T DISAGREE WITH HIS PASSION.
PASSION IS ONE THING.
KILLER ROBOTS ARE OVER THE LINE.

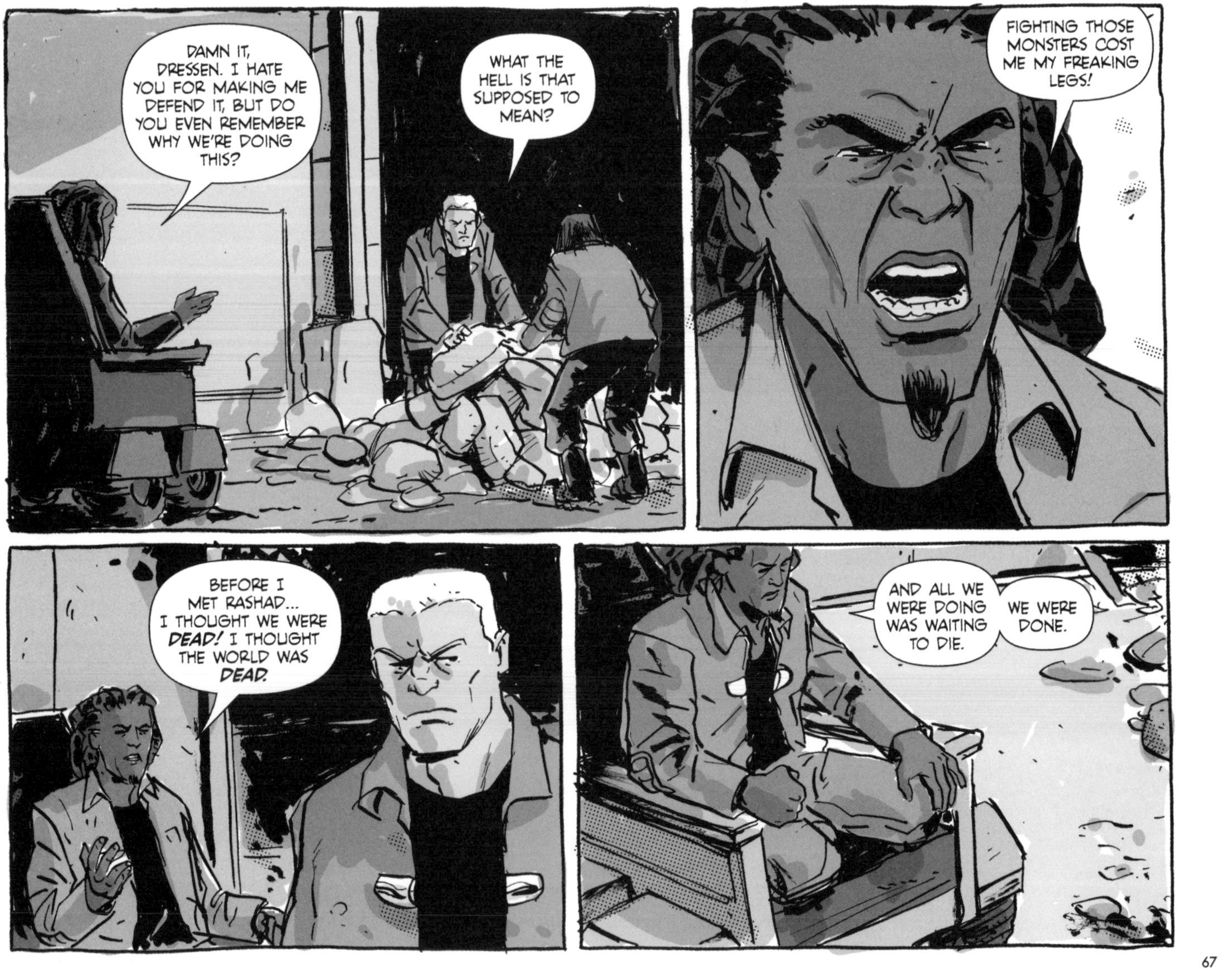
DAMN IT, DRESSEN. I HATE YOU FOR MAKING ME DEFEND IT, BUT DO YOU EVEN REMEMBER WHY WE'RE DOING THIS?
WHAT THE HELL IS THAT SUPPOSED TO MEAN?
FIGHTING THOSE MONSTERS COST ME MY FREAKING LEGS!
BEFORE I MET RASHAD... I THOUGHT WE WERE ***DEAD!*** I THOUGHT THE WORLD WAS ***DEAD.***
AND ALL WE WERE DOING WAS WAITING TO DIE.
WE WERE DONE.

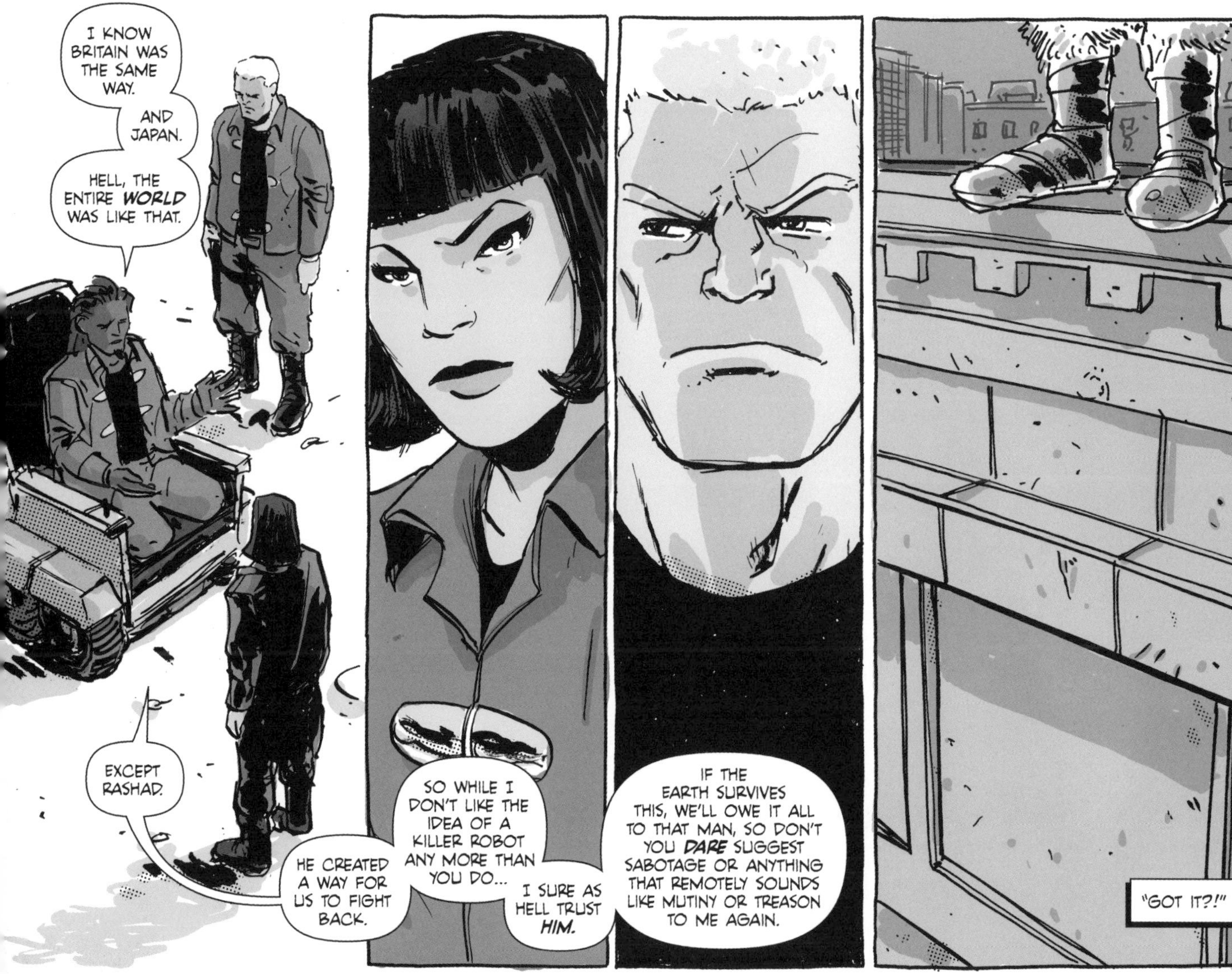
I KNOW BRITAIN WAS THE SAME WAY.
AND JAPAN.
HELL, THE ENTIRE *WORLD* WAS LIKE THAT.
EXCEPT RASHAD.
HE CREATED A WAY FOR US TO FIGHT BACK.
SO WHILE I DON'T LIKE THE IDEA OF A KILLER ROBOT ANY MORE THAN YOU DO...
I SURE AS HELL TRUST *HIM.*
IF THE EARTH SURVIVES THIS, WE'LL OWE IT ALL TO THAT MAN, SO DON'T YOU *DARE* SUGGEST SABOTAGE OR ANYTHING THAT REMOTELY SOUNDS LIKE MUTINY OR TREASON TO ME AGAIN.
"GOT IT?!"

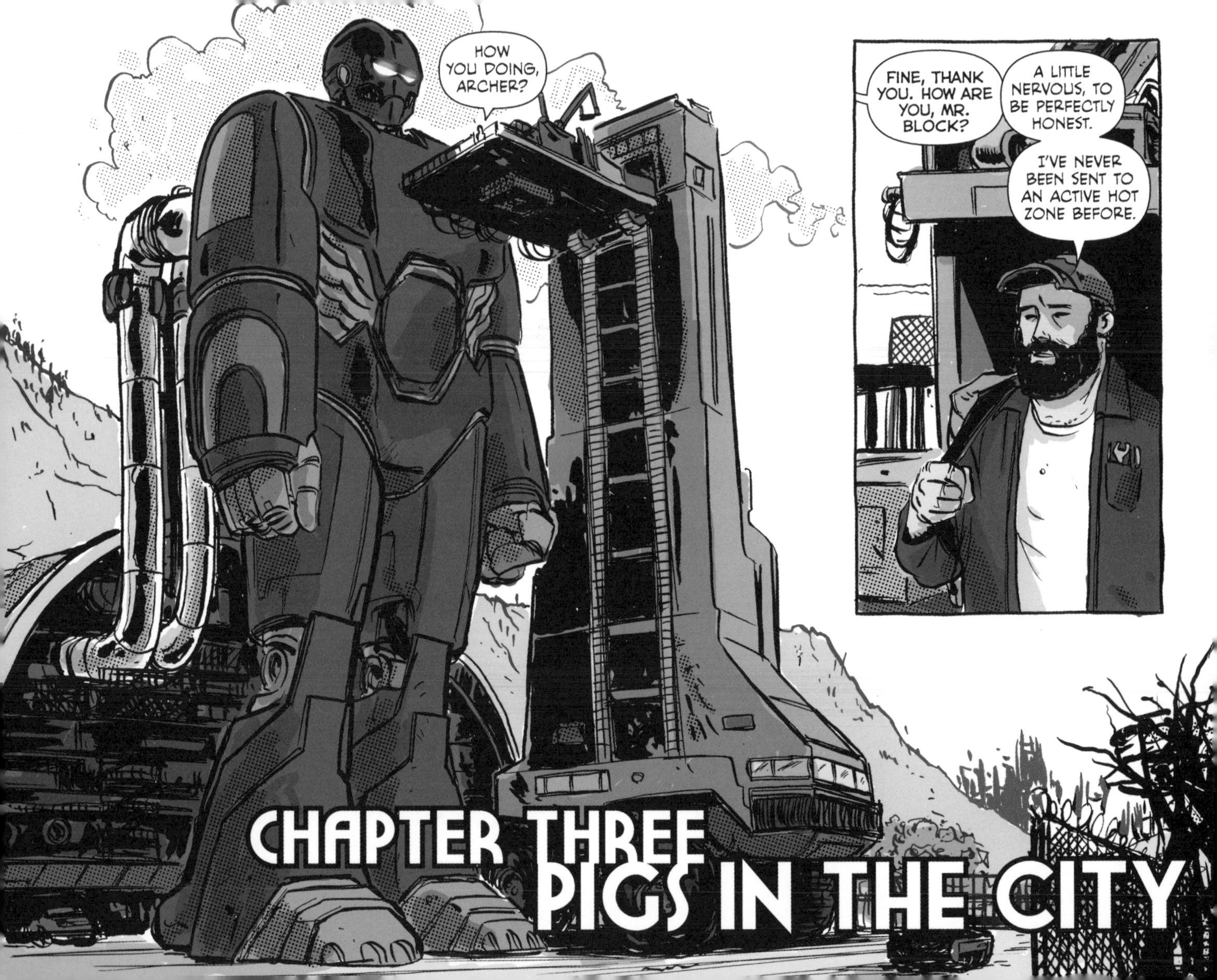
HOW YOU DOING, ARCHER?
CHAPTER THREE
PIGS IN THE CITY
FINE, THANK YOU. HOW ARE YOU, MR. BLOCK?
A LITTLE NERVOUS, TO BE PERFECTLY HONEST.
I'VE NEVER BEEN SENT TO AN ACTIVE HOT ZONE BEFORE.

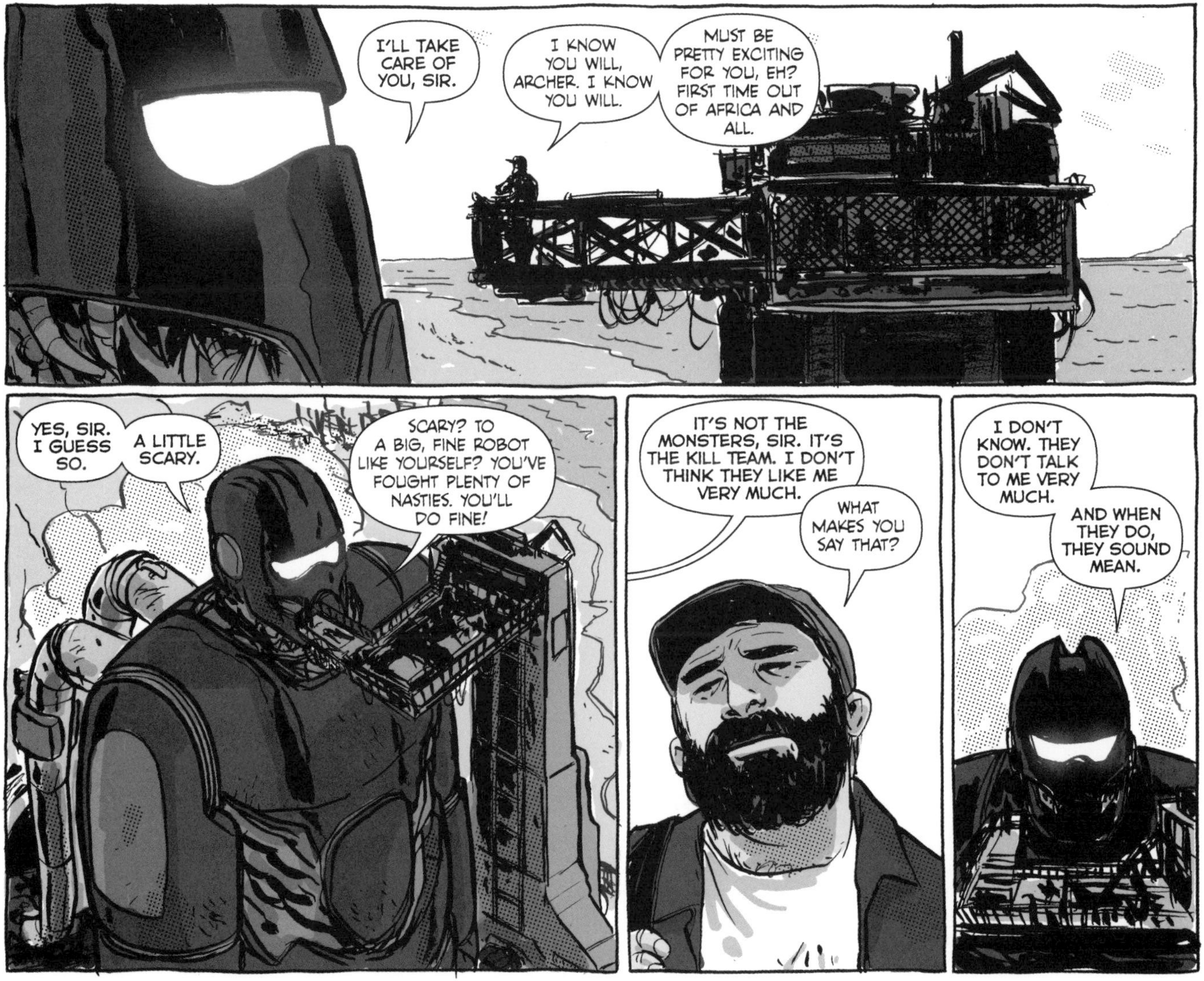
I'LL TAKE CARE OF YOU, SIR.
I KNOW YOU WILL, ARCHER. I KNOW YOU WILL.
MUST BE PRETTY EXCITING FOR YOU, EH? FIRST TIME OUT OF AFRICA AND ALL.
YES, SIR. I GUESS SO.
A LITTLE SCARY.
SCARY? TO A BIG, FINE ROBOT LIKE YOURSELF? YOU'VE FOUGHT PLENTY OF NASTIES. YOU'LL DO FINE!
IT'S NOT THE MONSTERS, SIR. IT'S THE KILL TEAM. I DON'T THINK THEY LIKE ME VERY MUCH.
WHAT MAKES YOU SAY THAT?
I DON'T KNOW. THEY DON'T TALK TO ME VERY MUCH.
AND WHEN THEY DO, THEY SOUND MEAN.

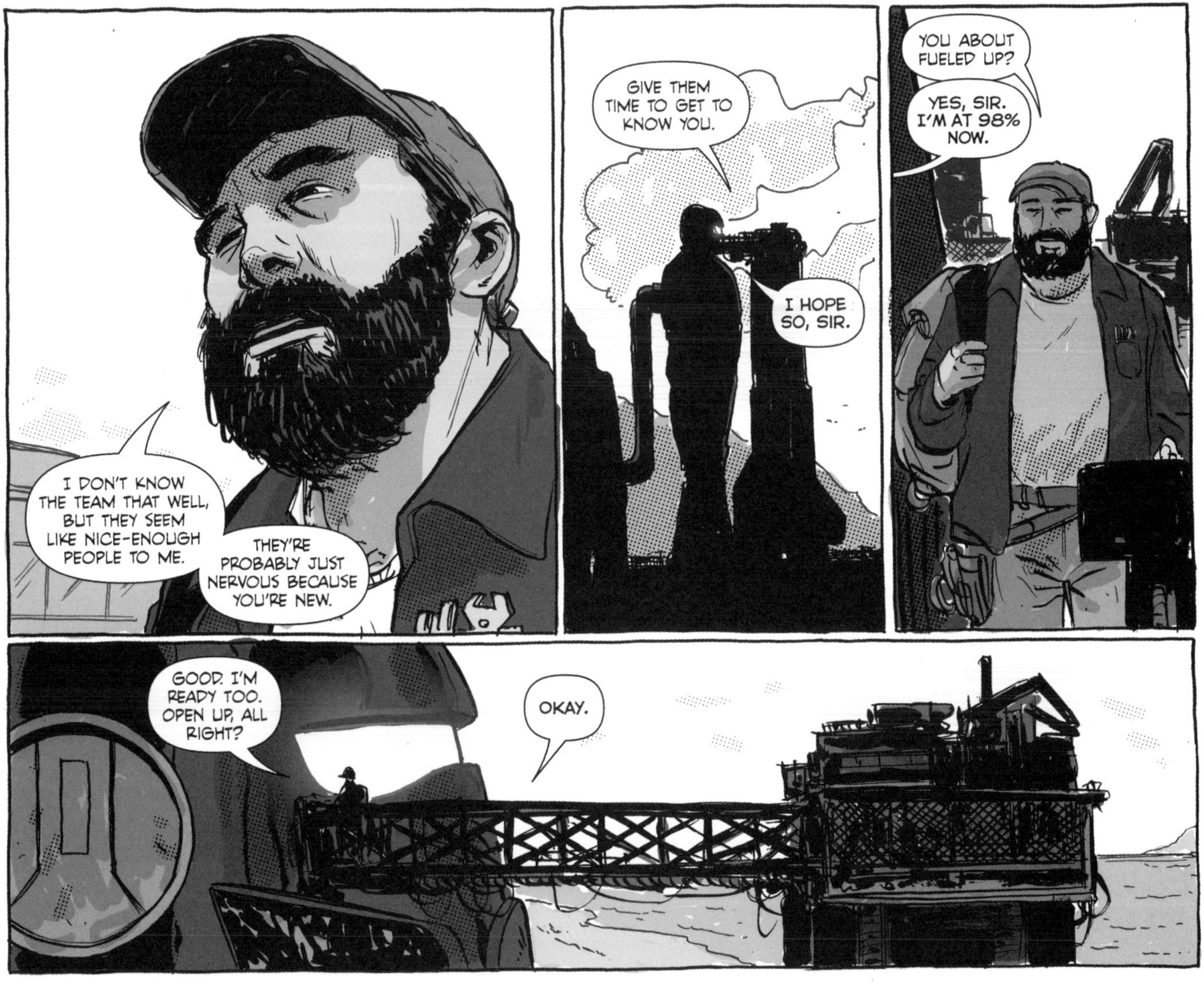
I DON'T KNOW THE TEAM THAT WELL, BUT THEY SEEM LIKE NICE-ENOUGH PEOPLE TO ME.
THEY'RE PROBABLY JUST NERVOUS BECAUSE YOU'RE NEW.
GIVE THEM TIME TO GET TO KNOW YOU.
I HOPE SO, SIR.
YOU ABOUT FUELED UP?
YES, SIR. I'M AT 98% NOW.
GOOD. I'M READY TOO. OPEN UP, ALL RIGHT?
OKAY.

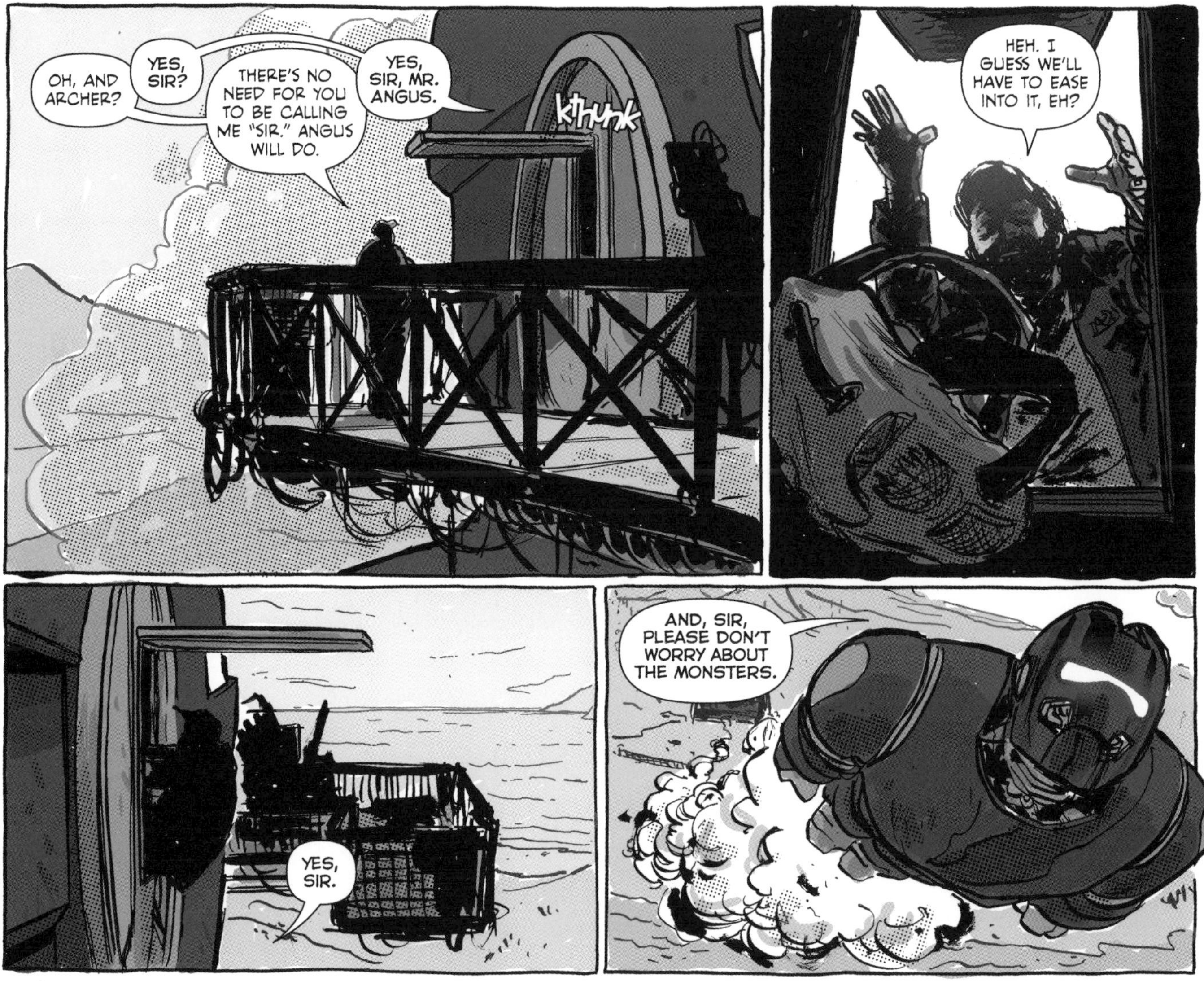
OH, AND ARCHER?
YES, SIR?
THERE'S NO NEED FOR YOU TO BE CALLING ME "SIR." ANGUS WILL DO.
YES, SIR, MR. ANGUS.
KTHUNK
HEH. I GUESS WE'LL HAVE TO EASE INTO IT, EH?
YES, SIR.
AND, SIR, PLEASE DON'T WORRY ABOUT THE MONSTERS.

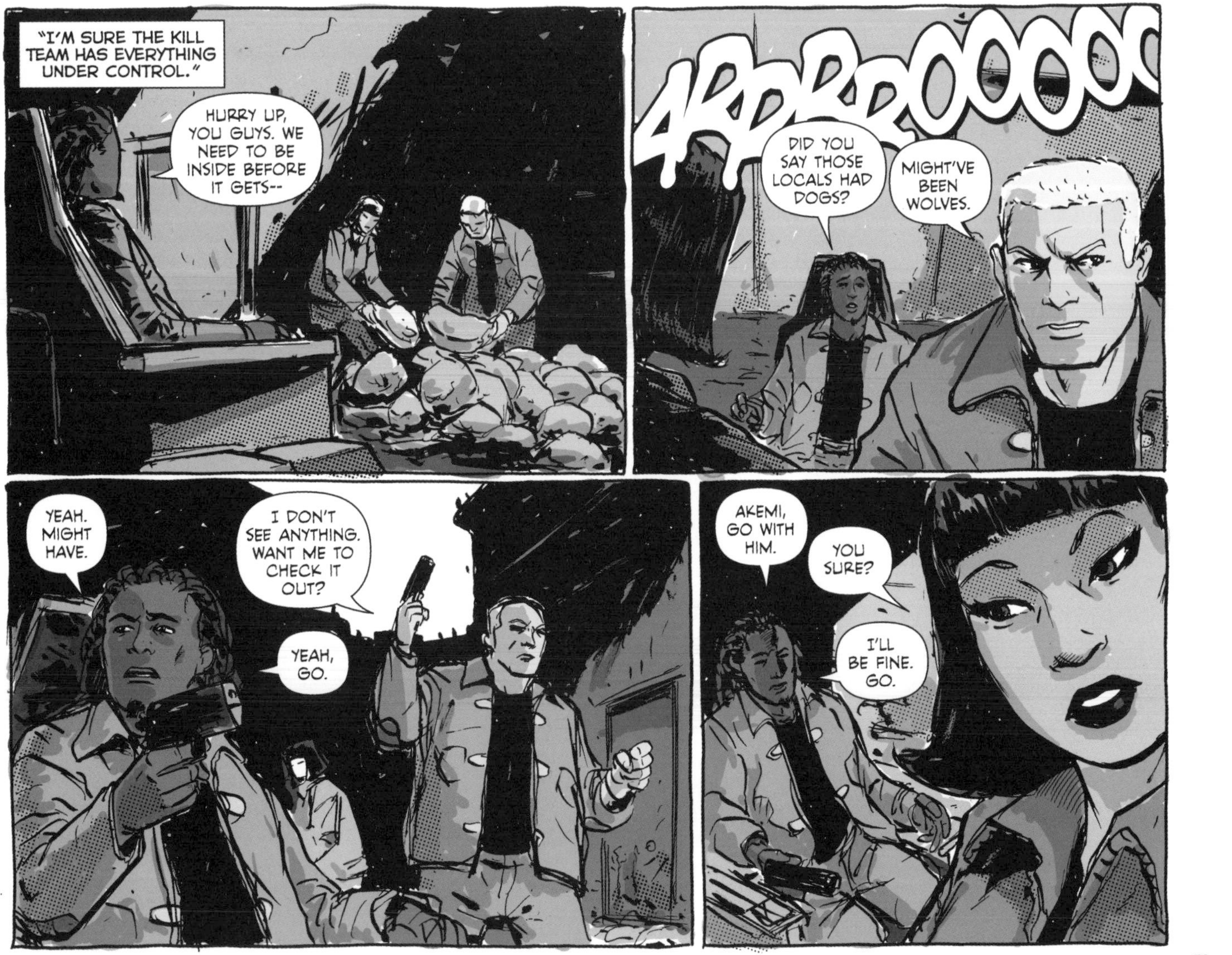
"I'M SURE THE KILL TEAM HAS EVERYTHING UNDER CONTROL."
HURRY UP, YOU GUYS. WE NEED TO BE INSIDE BEFORE IT GETS--
ARRROOOOOO
DID YOU SAY THOSE LOCALS HAD DOGS?
MIGHT'VE BEEN WOLVES.
YEAH. MIGHT HAVE.
I DON'T SEE ANYTHING. WANT ME TO CHECK IT OUT?
YEAH, GO.
AKEMI, GO WITH HIM.
YOU SURE?
I'LL BE FINE. GO.

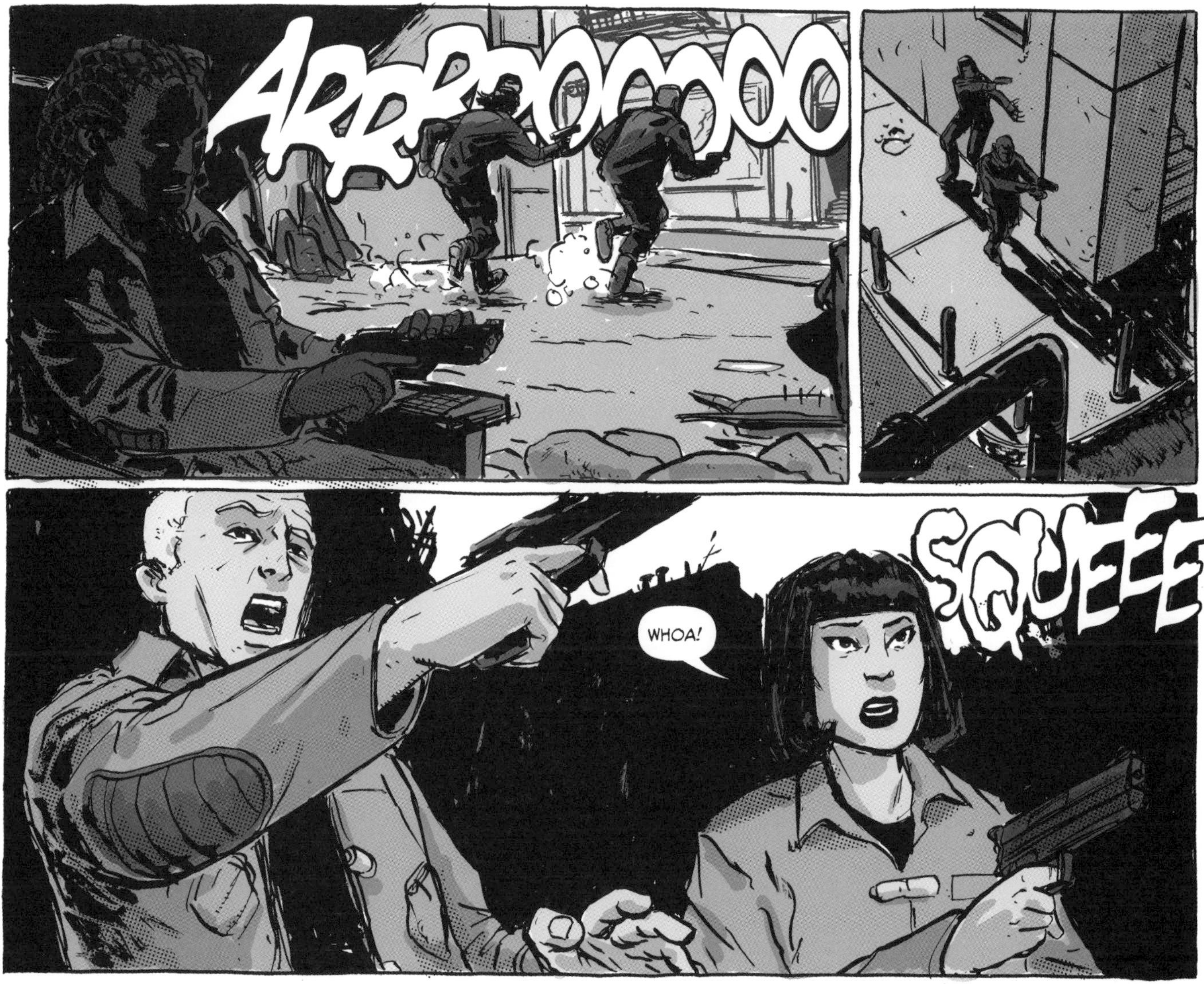
ARRRROOOOOO
SQUEEE
WHOA!

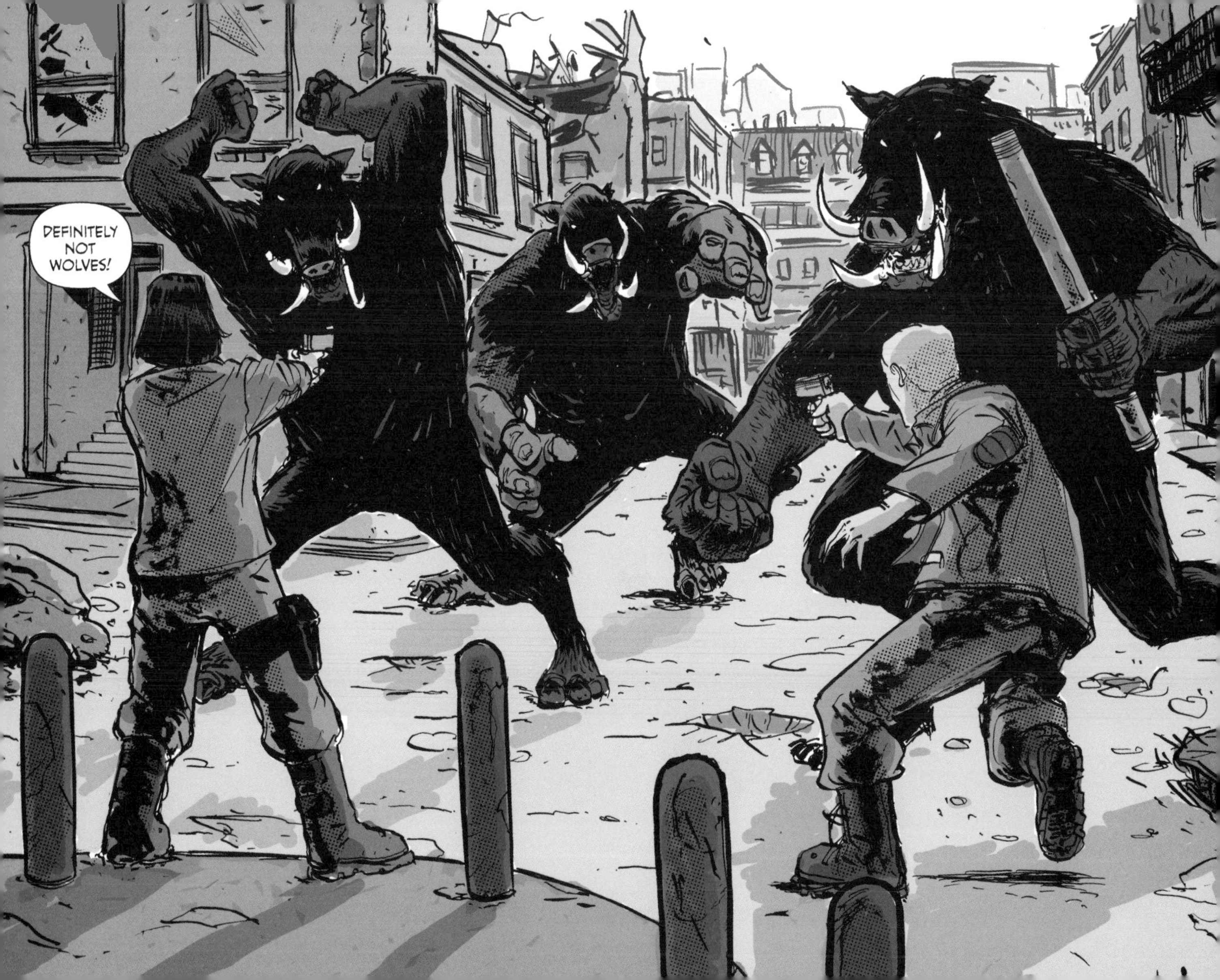
DEFINITELY NOT WOLVES!

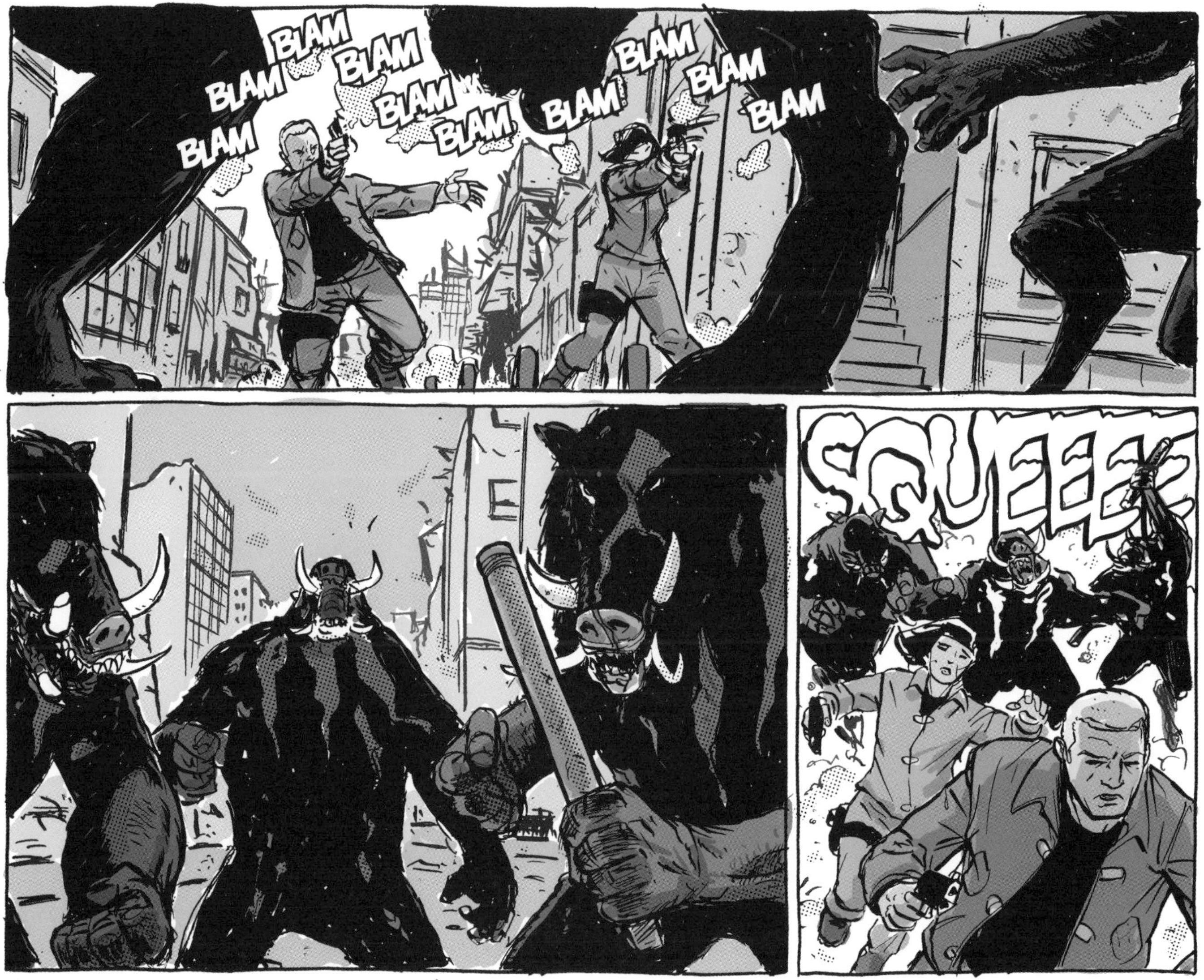
BLAM
BLAM
BLAM
BLAM
BLAM
BLAM
BLAM
BLAM
BLAM
BLAM
BLAM
SQUEEEE

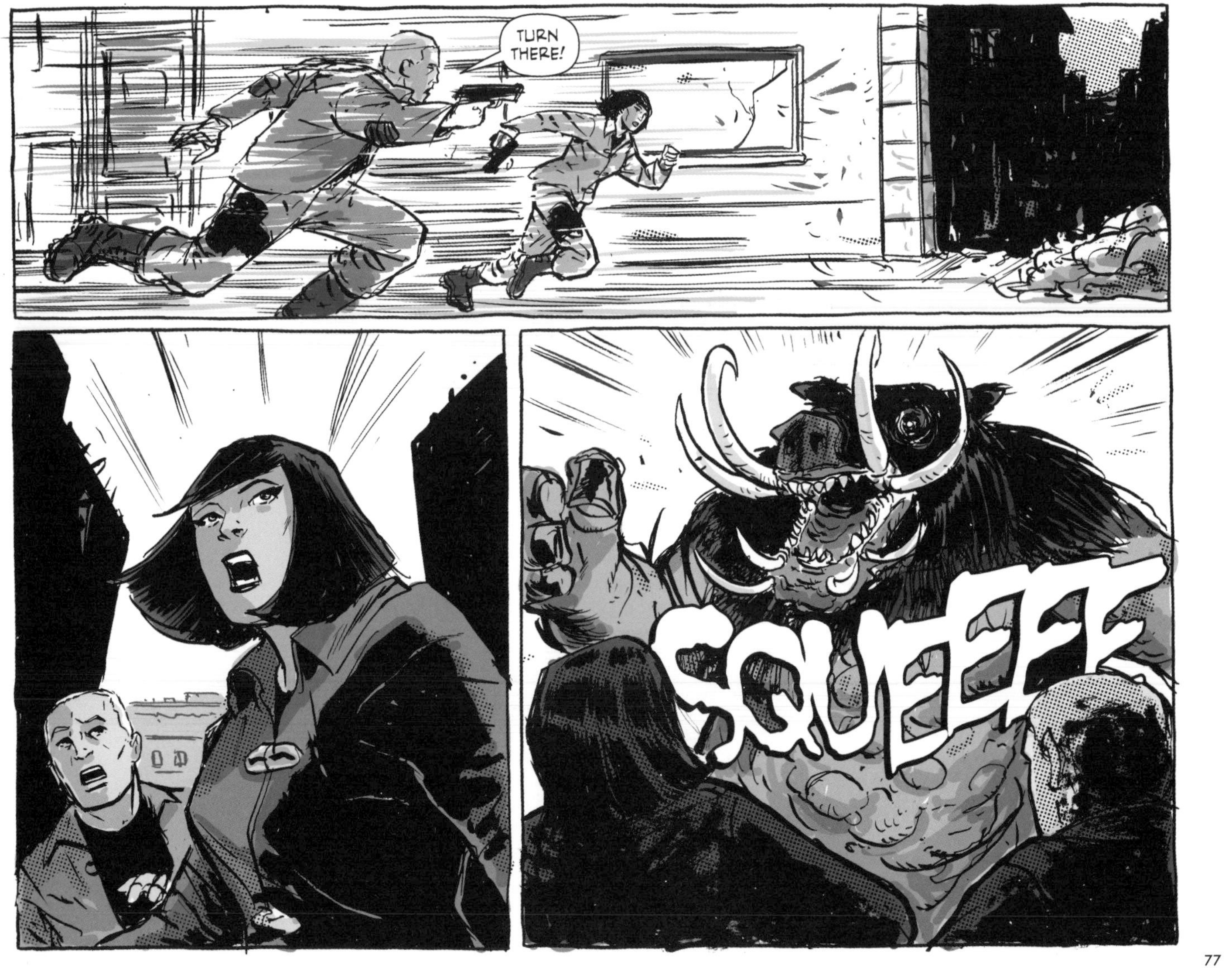
TURN THERE!
SQUEEFF

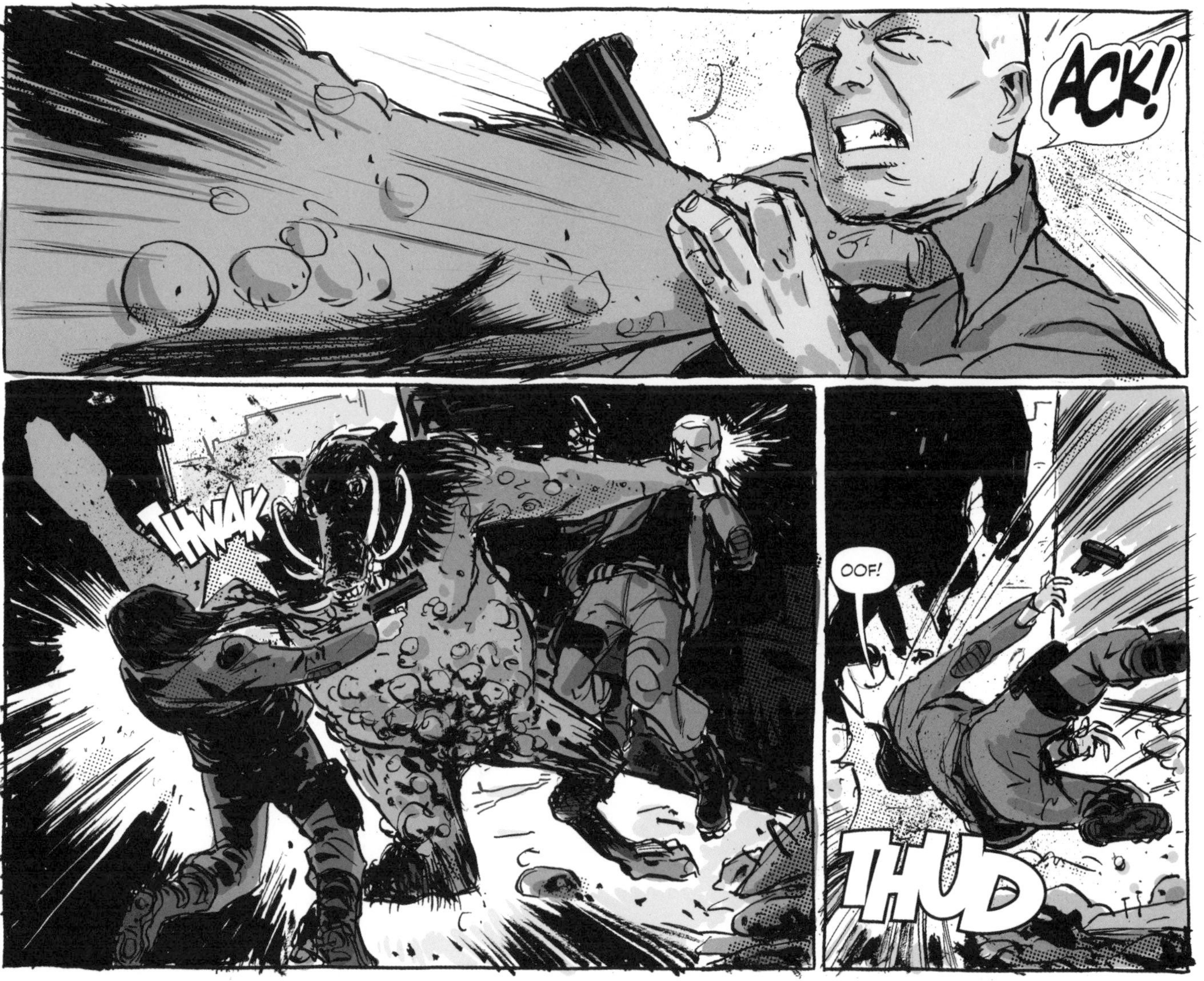
ACK!
THWAK
OOF!
THUD

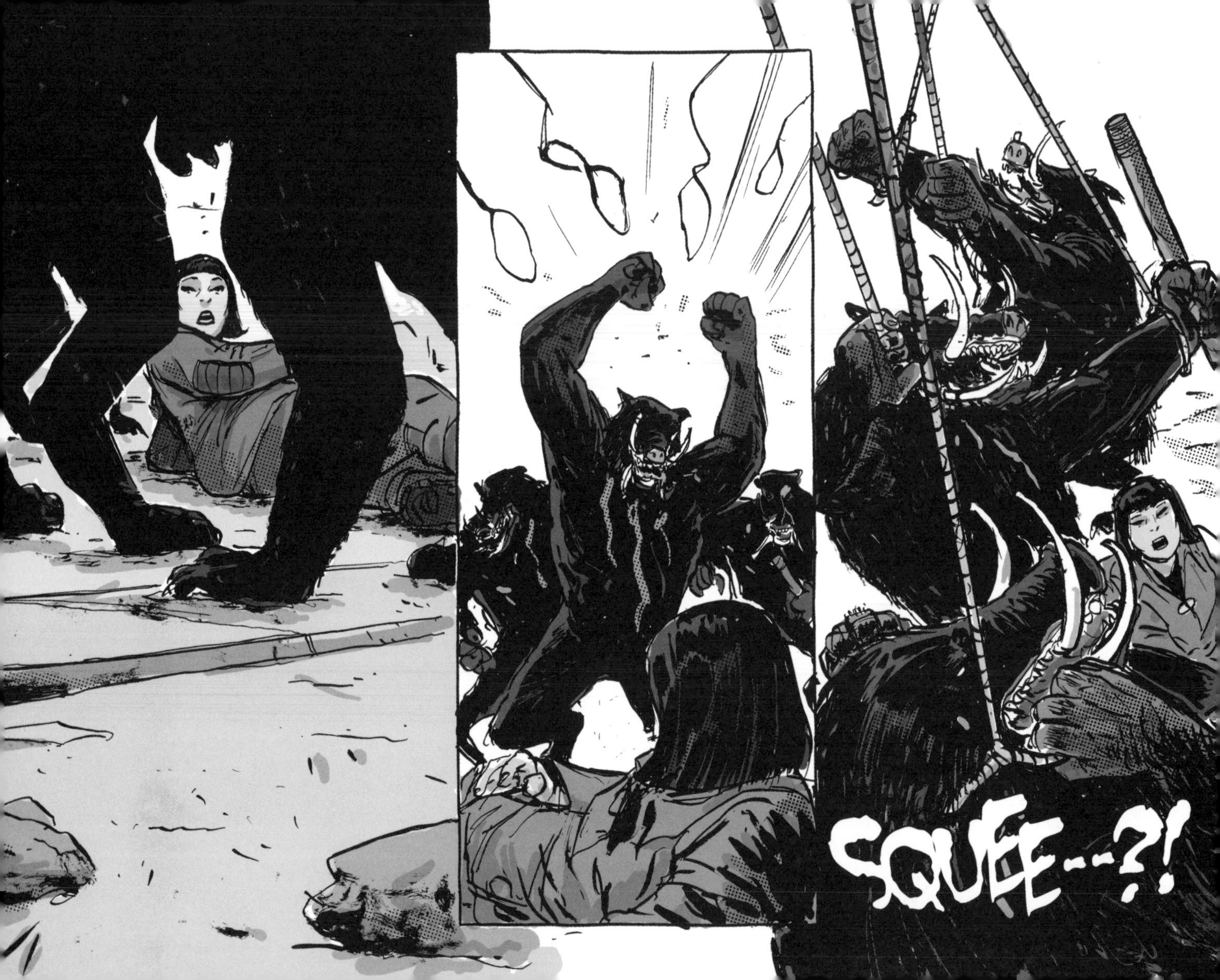
SQUEE--?!

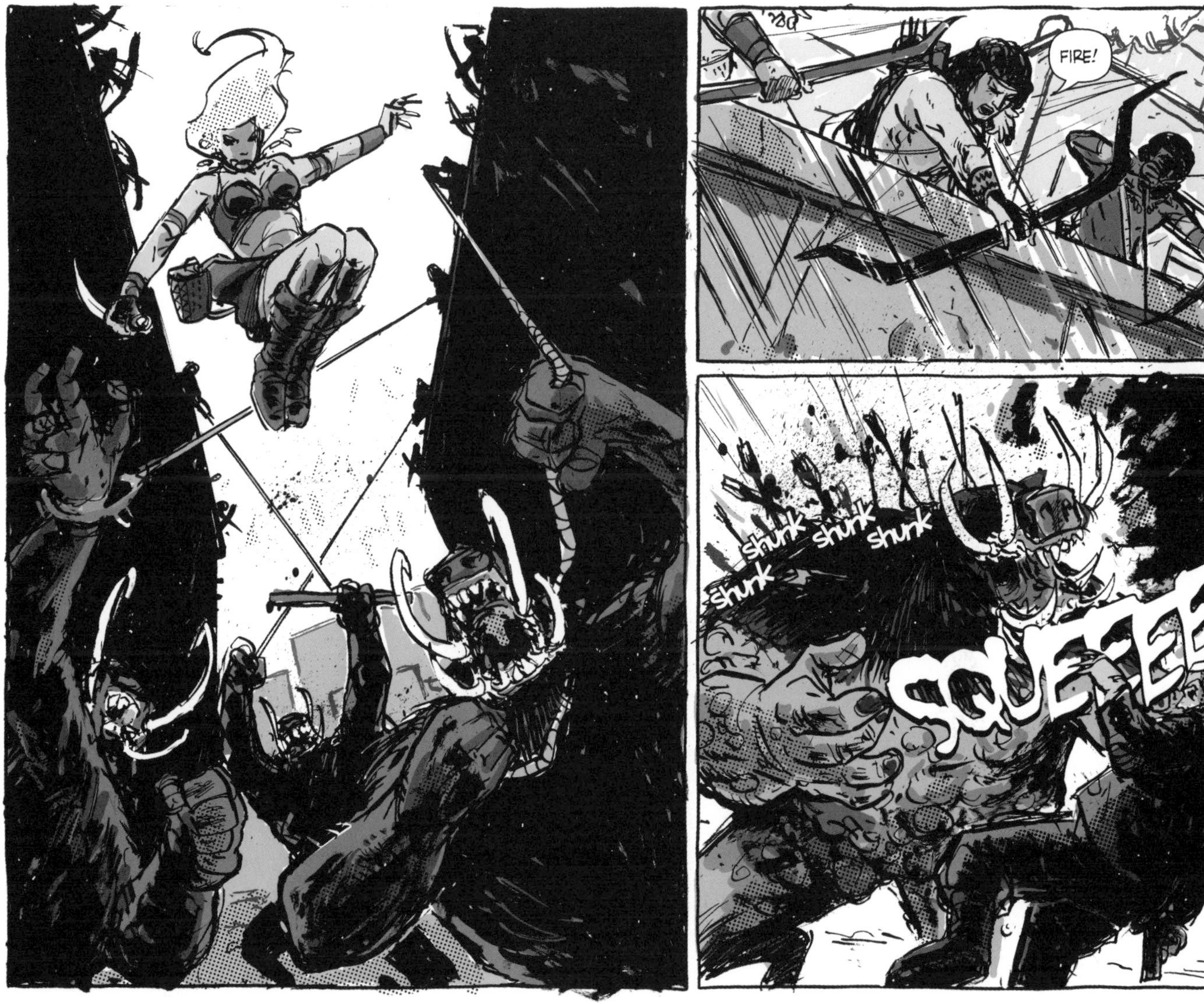
FIRE!
shunk shunk shunk shunk
SQUEEEE

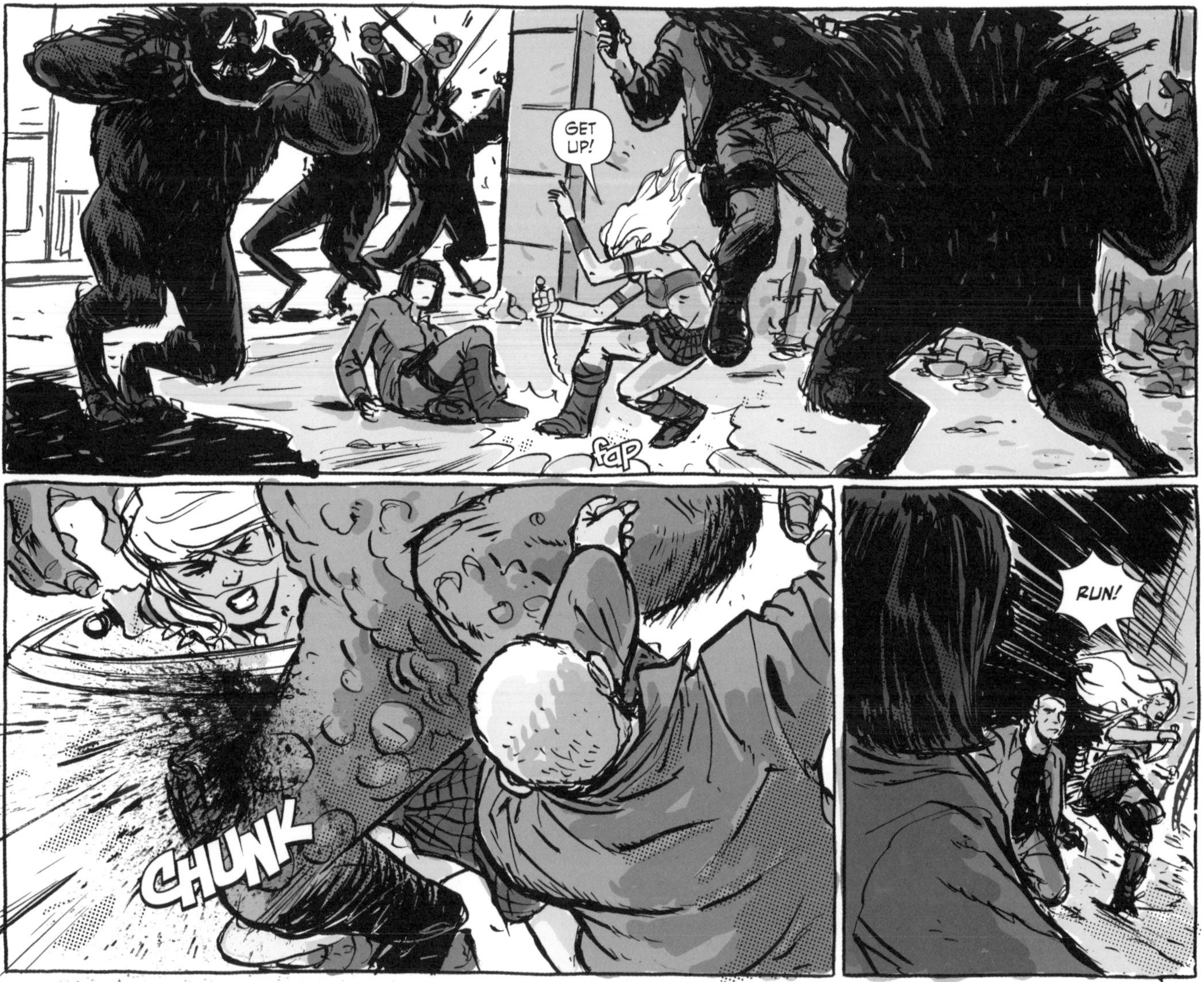
GET UP!
fap
CHUNK
RUN!

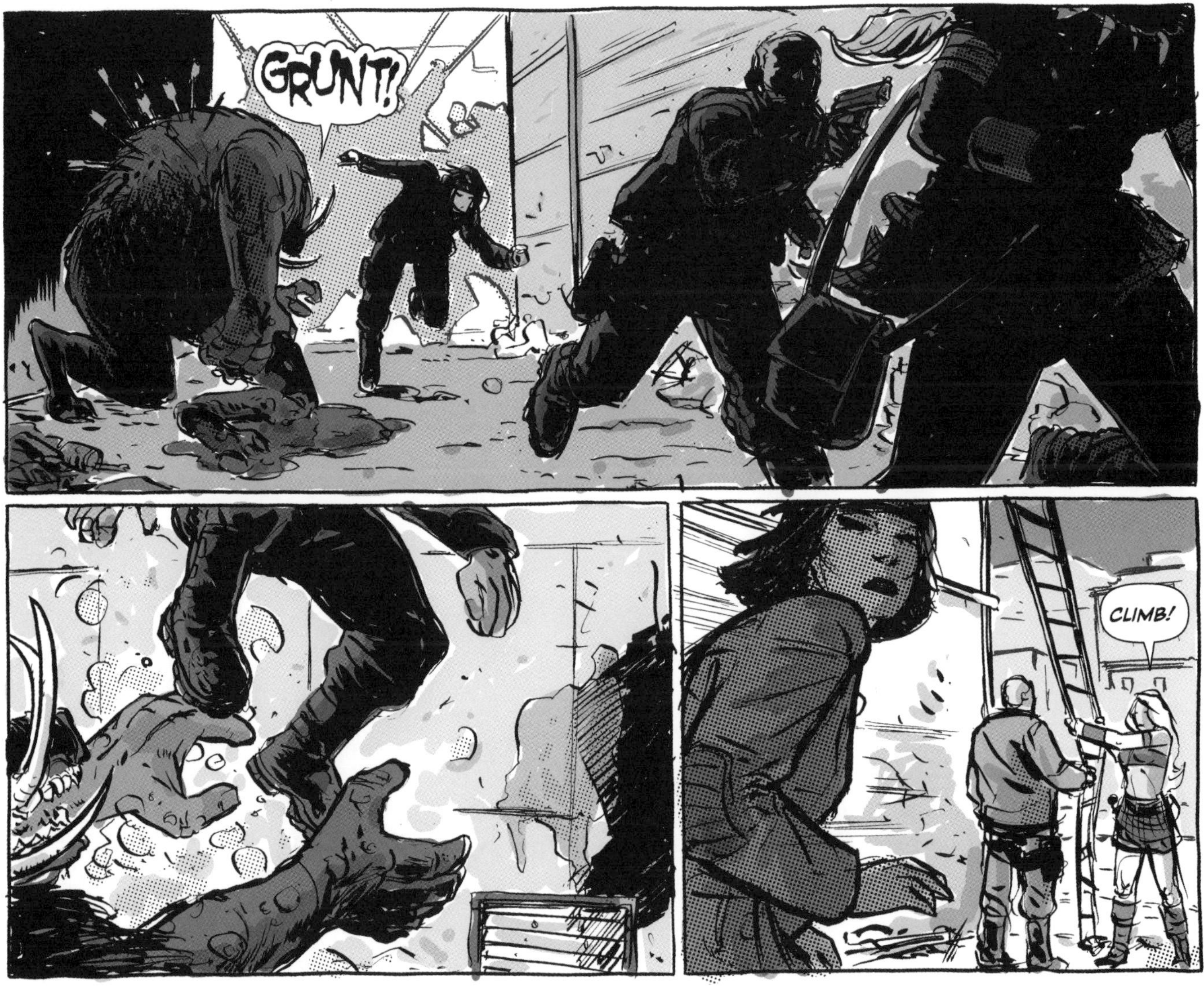
GRUNT!
CLIMB!

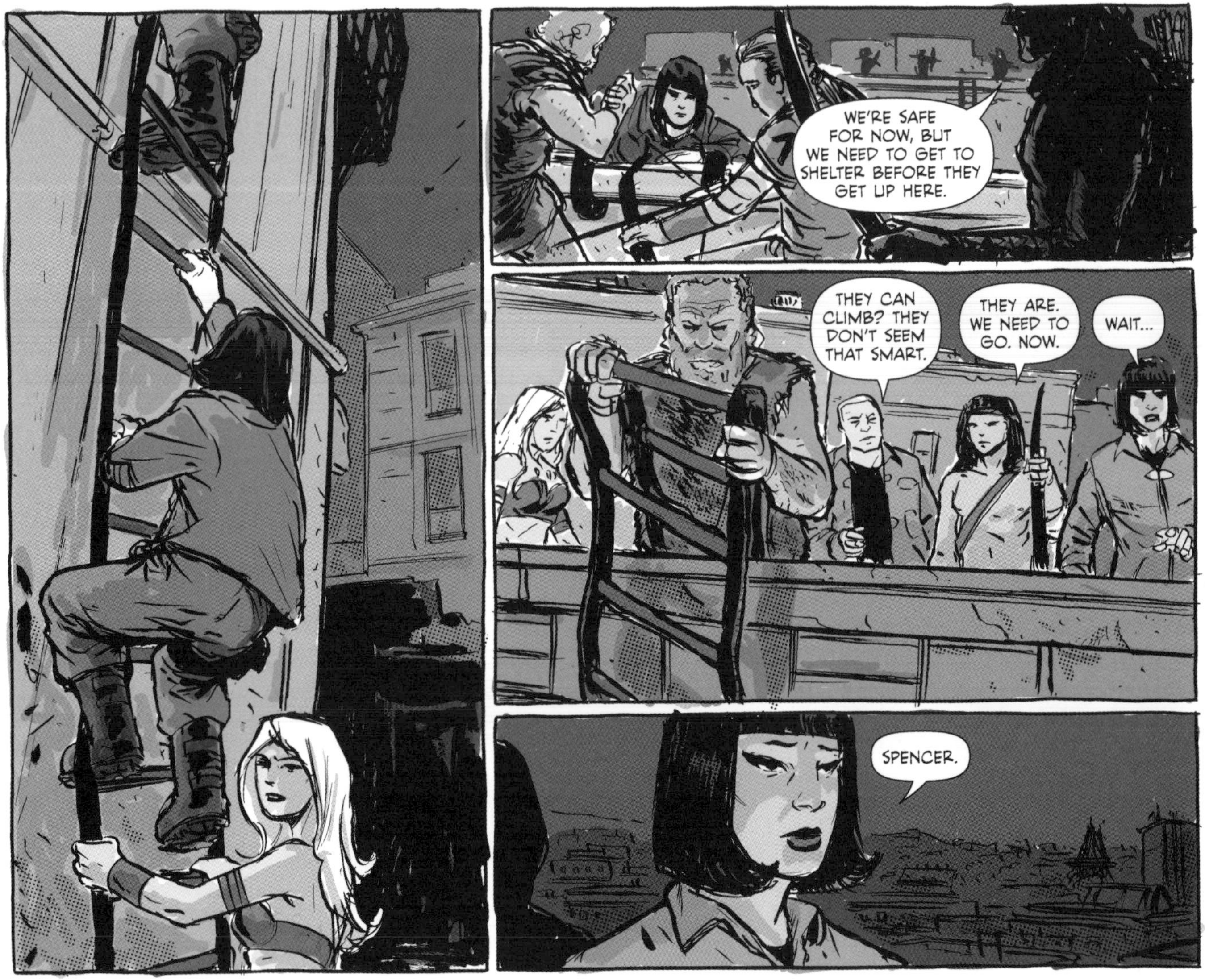
WE'RE SAFE FOR NOW, BUT WE NEED TO GET TO SHELTER BEFORE THEY GET UP HERE.
THEY CAN CLIMB? THEY DON'T SEEM THAT SMART.
THEY ARE. WE NEED TO GO. NOW.
WAIT...
SPENCER.

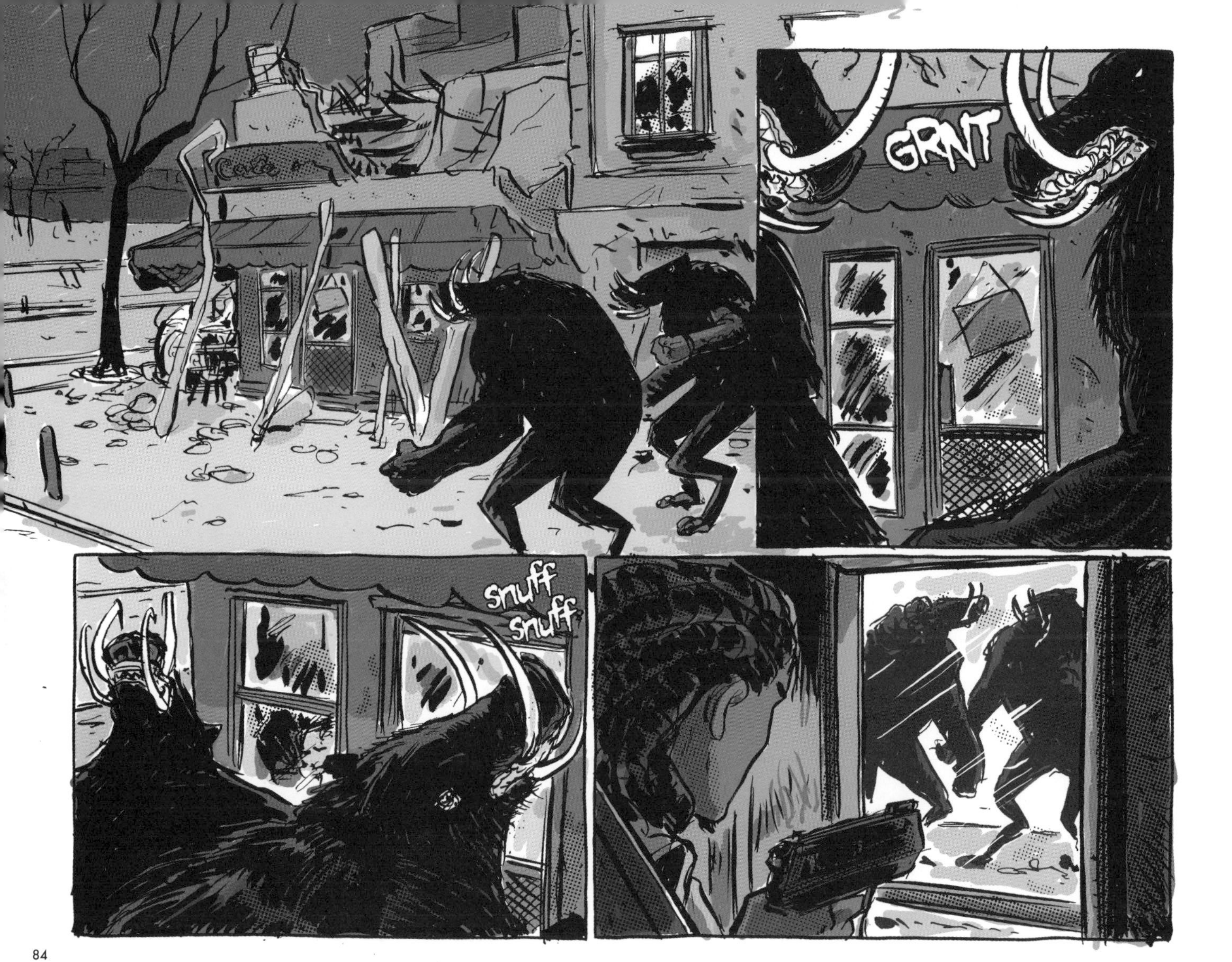
Cafe
GRNT
snuff
snuff

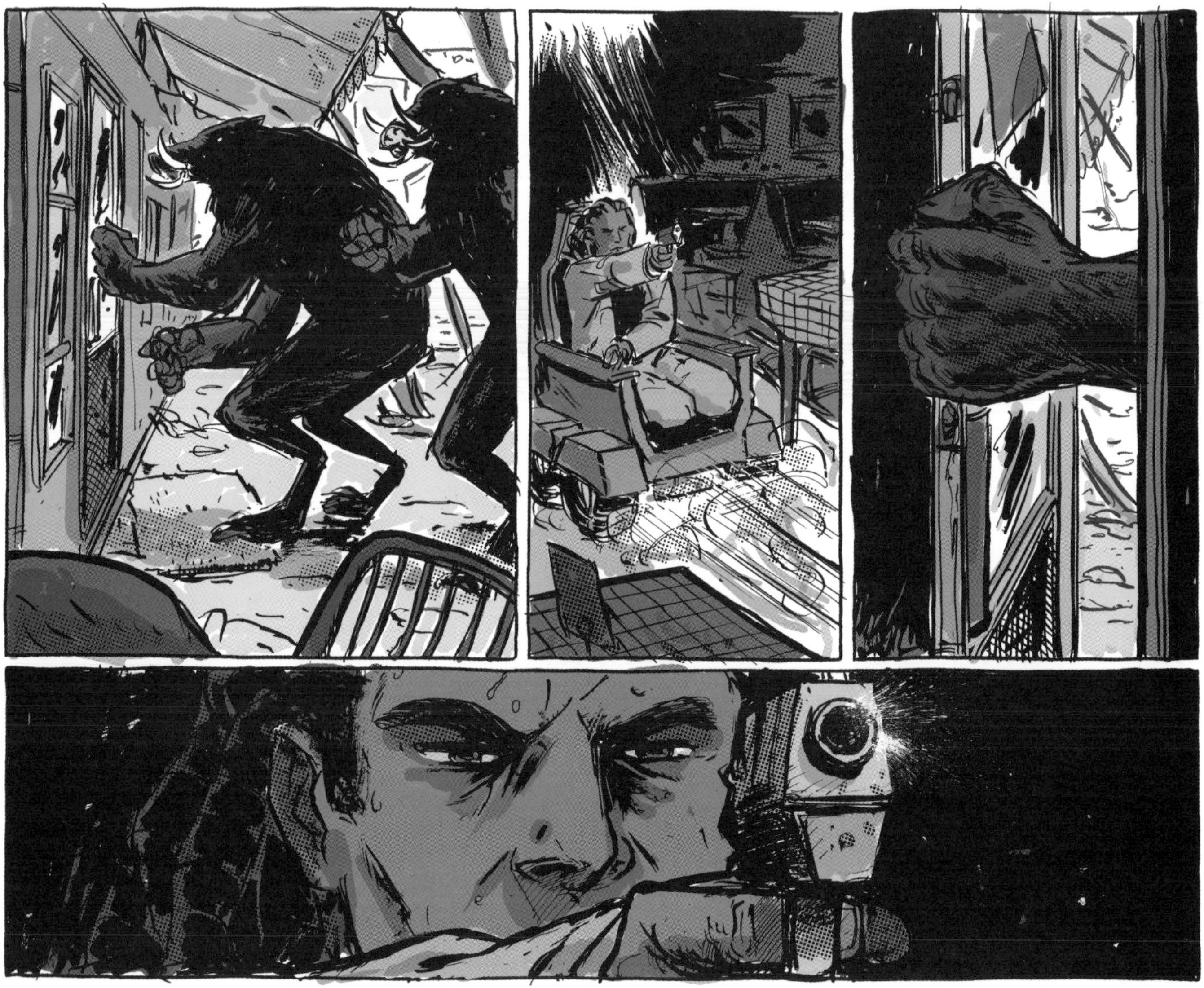

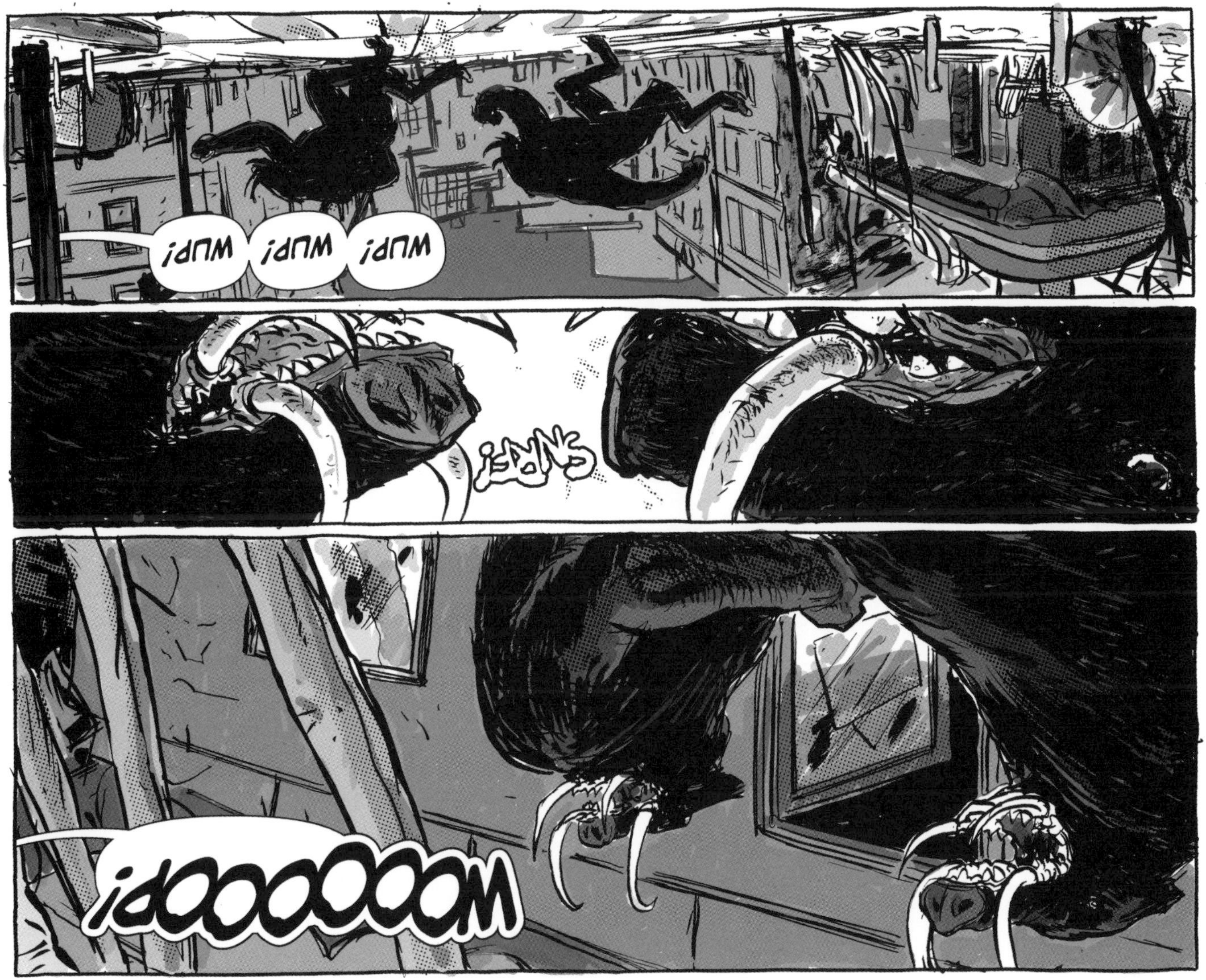
WUP!
WUP!
WUP!
SNAP!
WOOOOOOP!

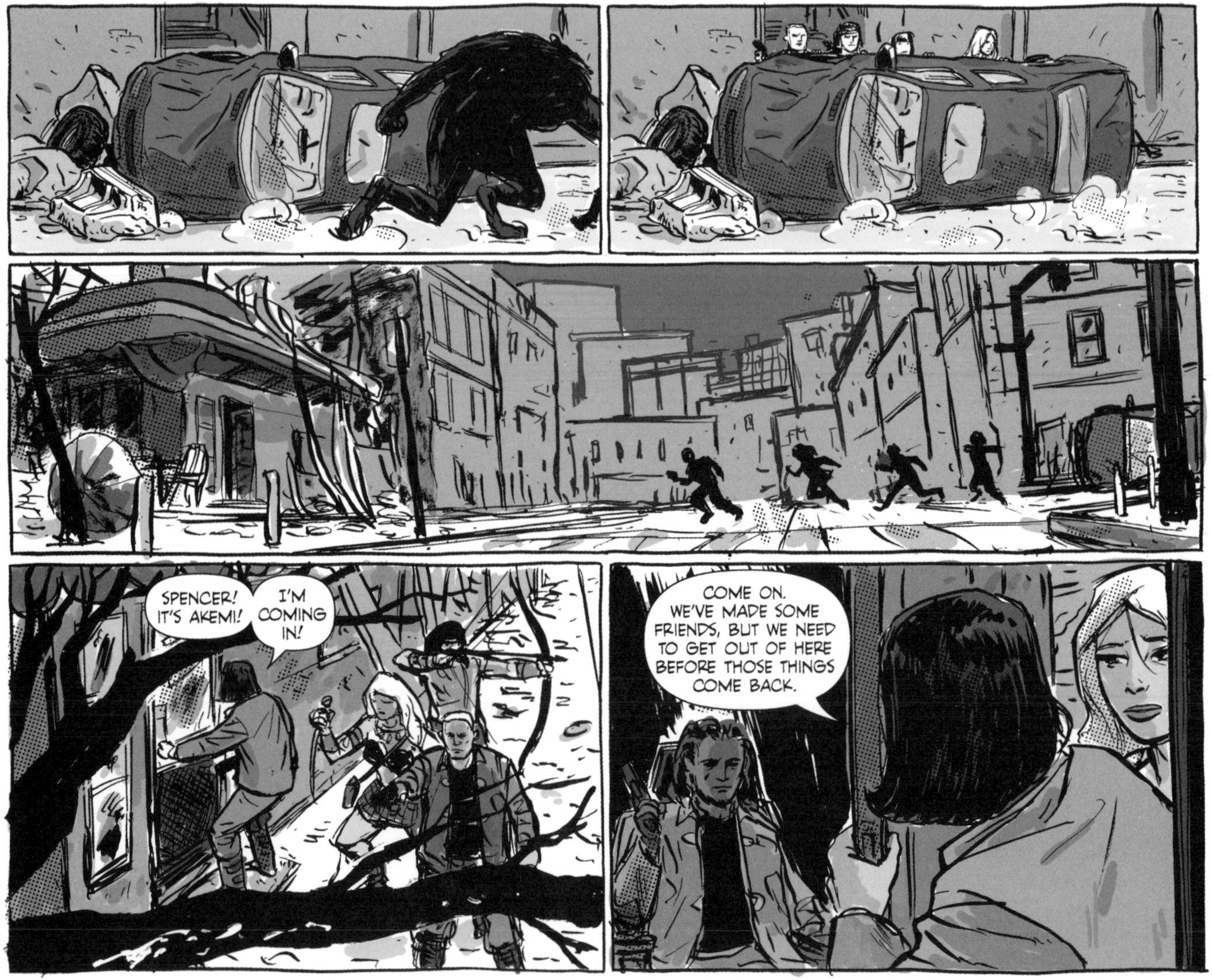
SPENCER! IT'S AKEMI!
I'M COMING IN!
COME ON. WE'VE MADE SOME FRIENDS, BUT WE NEED TO GET OUT OF HERE BEFORE THOSE THINGS COME BACK.

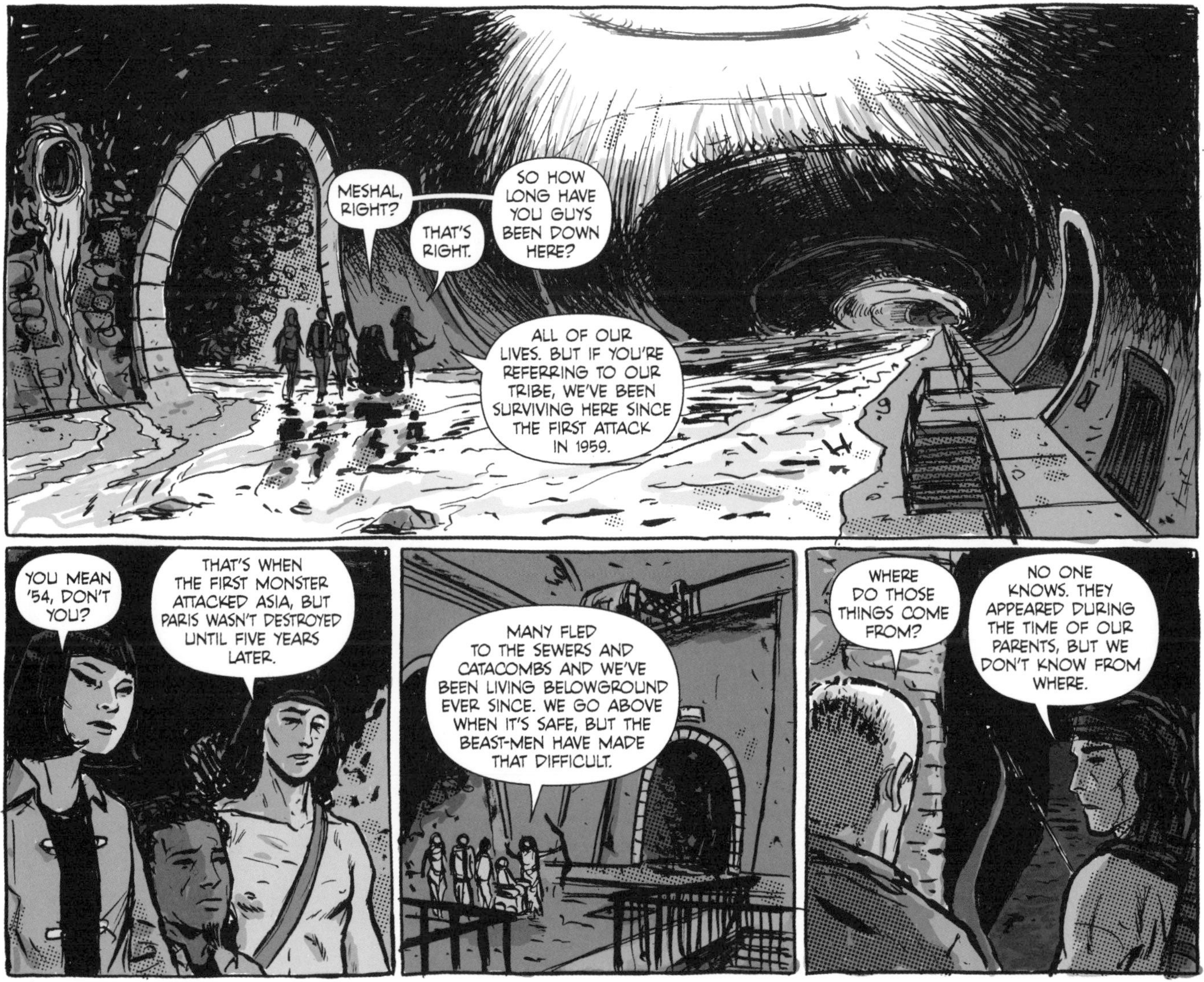
MESHAL, RIGHT?
SO HOW LONG HAVE YOU GUYS BEEN DOWN HERE?
THAT'S RIGHT.
ALL OF OUR LIVES. BUT IF YOU'RE REFERRING TO OUR TRIBE, WE'VE BEEN SURVIVING HERE SINCE THE FIRST ATTACK IN 1959.
YOU MEAN '54, DON'T YOU?
THAT'S WHEN THE FIRST MONSTER ATTACKED ASIA, BUT PARIS WASN'T DESTROYED UNTIL FIVE YEARS LATER.
MANY FLED TO THE SEWERS AND CATACOMBS AND WE'VE BEEN LIVING BELOWGROUND EVER SINCE. WE GO ABOVE WHEN IT'S SAFE, BUT THE BEAST-MEN HAVE MADE THAT DIFFICULT.
WHERE DO THOSE THINGS COME FROM?
NO ONE KNOWS. THEY APPEARED DURING THE TIME OF OUR PARENTS, BUT WE DON'T KNOW FROM WHERE.

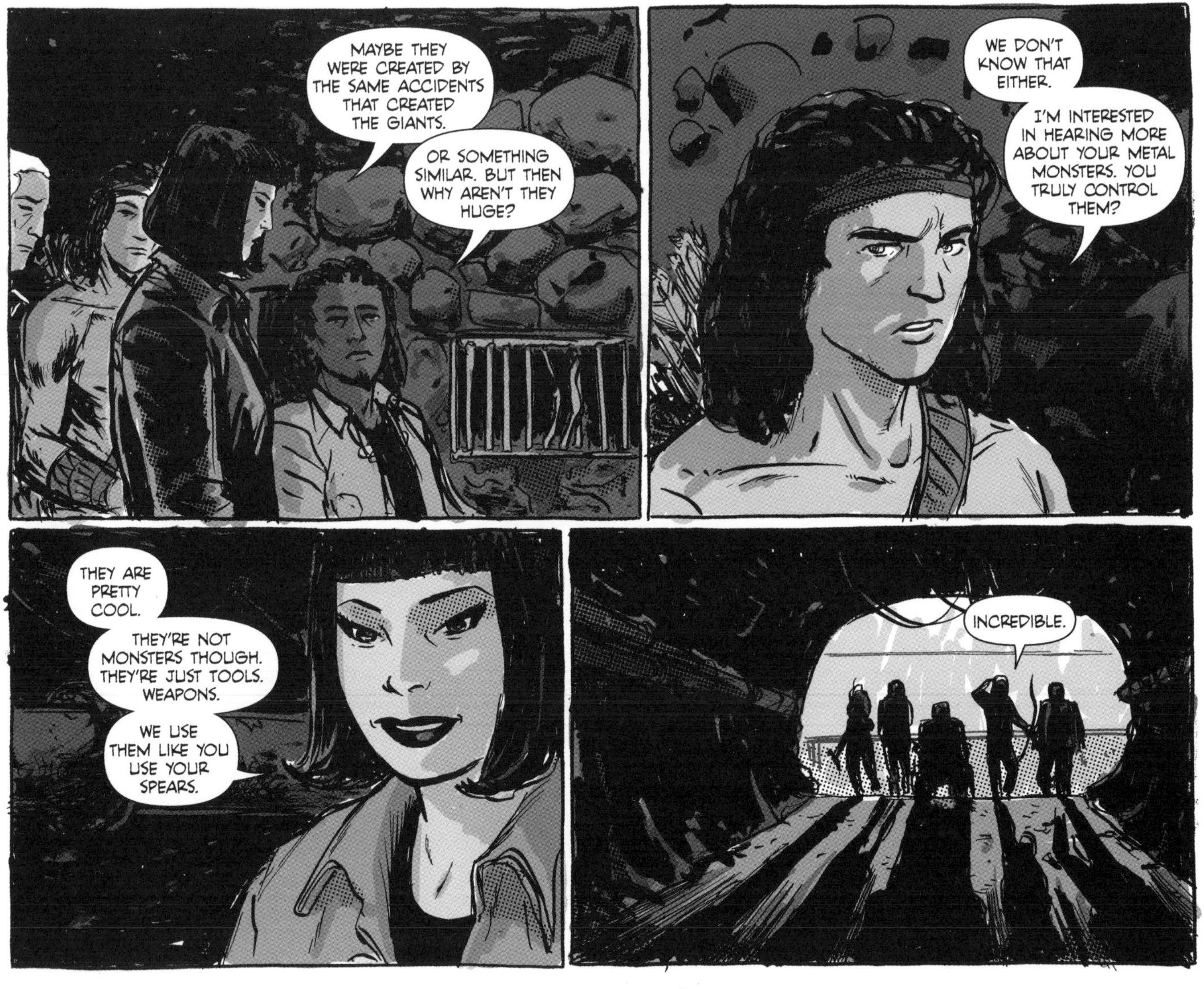
MAYBE THEY WERE CREATED BY THE SAME ACCIDENTS THAT CREATED THE GIANTS.
OR SOMETHING SIMILAR. BUT THEN WHY AREN'T THEY HUGE?
WE DON'T KNOW THAT EITHER.
I'M INTERESTED IN HEARING MORE ABOUT YOUR METAL MONSTERS. YOU TRULY CONTROL THEM?
THEY ARE PRETTY COOL.
THEY'RE NOT MONSTERS THOUGH. THEY'RE JUST TOOLS. WEAPONS.
WE USE THEM LIKE YOU USE YOUR SPEARS.
INCREDIBLE.

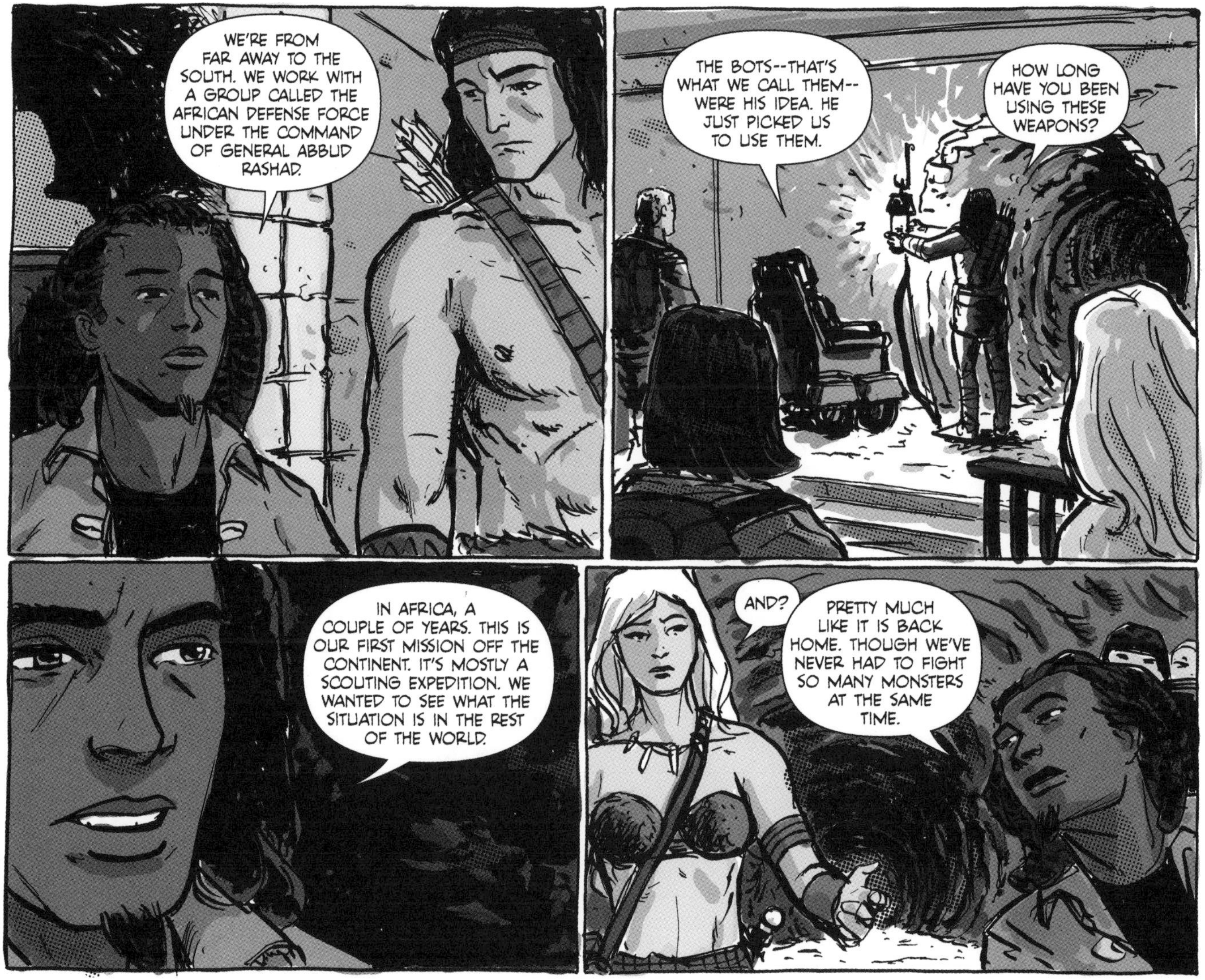
WE'RE FROM FAR AWAY TO THE SOUTH. WE WORK WITH A GROUP CALLED THE AFRICAN DEFENSE FORCE UNDER THE COMMAND OF GENERAL ABBUD RASHAD.
THE BOTS--THAT'S WHAT WE CALL THEM--WERE HIS IDEA. HE JUST PICKED US TO USE THEM.
HOW LONG HAVE YOU BEEN USING THESE WEAPONS?
IN AFRICA, A COUPLE OF YEARS. THIS IS OUR FIRST MISSION OFF THE CONTINENT. IT'S MOSTLY A SCOUTING EXPEDITION. WE WANTED TO SEE WHAT THE SITUATION IS IN THE REST OF THE WORLD.
AND?
PRETTY MUCH LIKE IT IS BACK HOME. THOUGH WE'VE NEVER HAD TO FIGHT SO MANY MONSTERS AT THE SAME TIME.

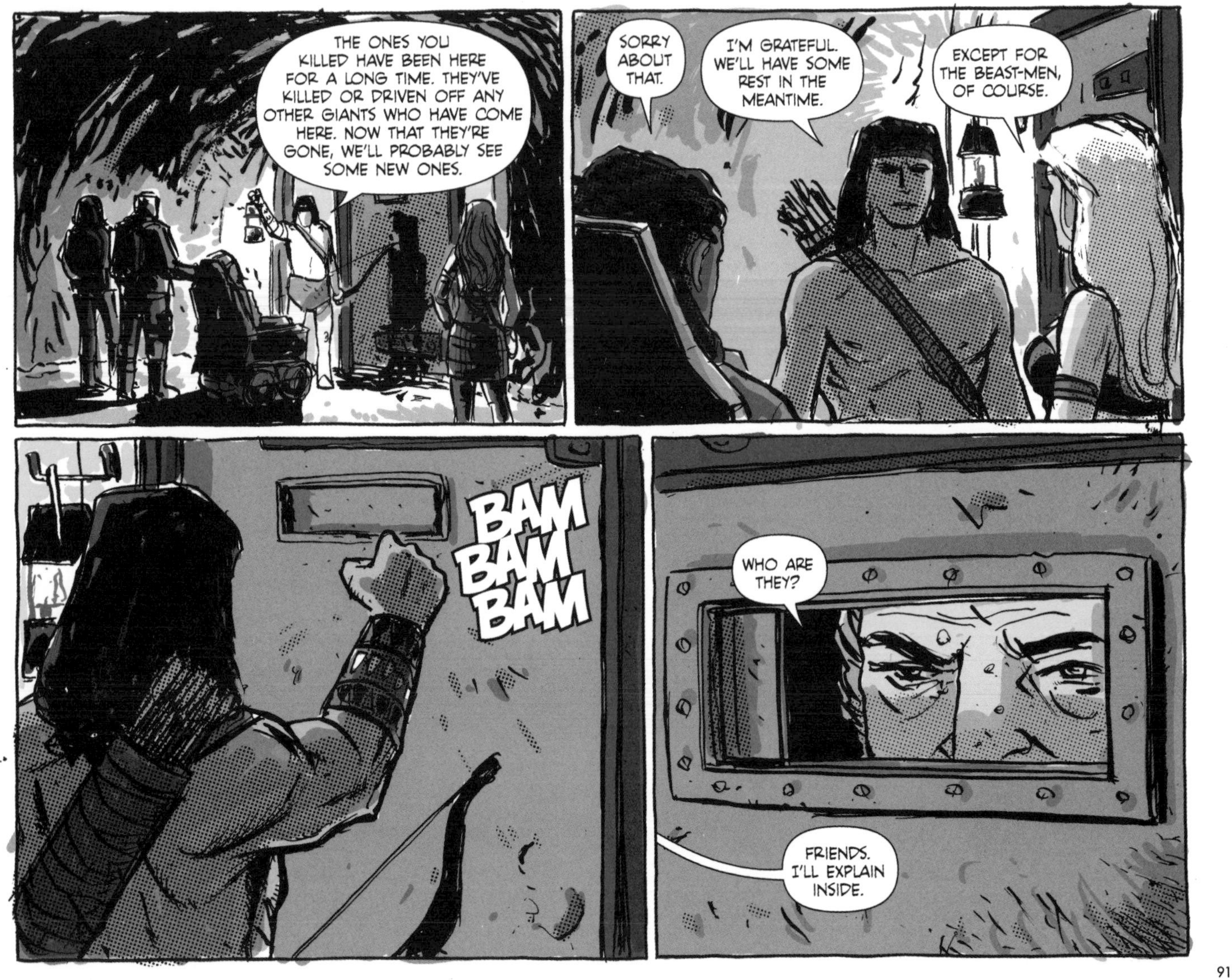
THE ONES YOU KILLED HAVE BEEN HERE FOR A LONG TIME. THEY'VE KILLED OR DRIVEN OFF ANY OTHER GIANTS WHO HAVE COME HERE. NOW THAT THEY'RE GONE, WE'LL PROBABLY SEE SOME NEW ONES.
SORRY ABOUT THAT.
I'M GRATEFUL. WE'LL HAVE SOME REST IN THE MEANTIME.
EXCEPT FOR THE BEAST-MEN, OF COURSE.
BAM BAM BAM
WHO ARE THEY?
FRIENDS. I'LL EXPLAIN INSIDE.

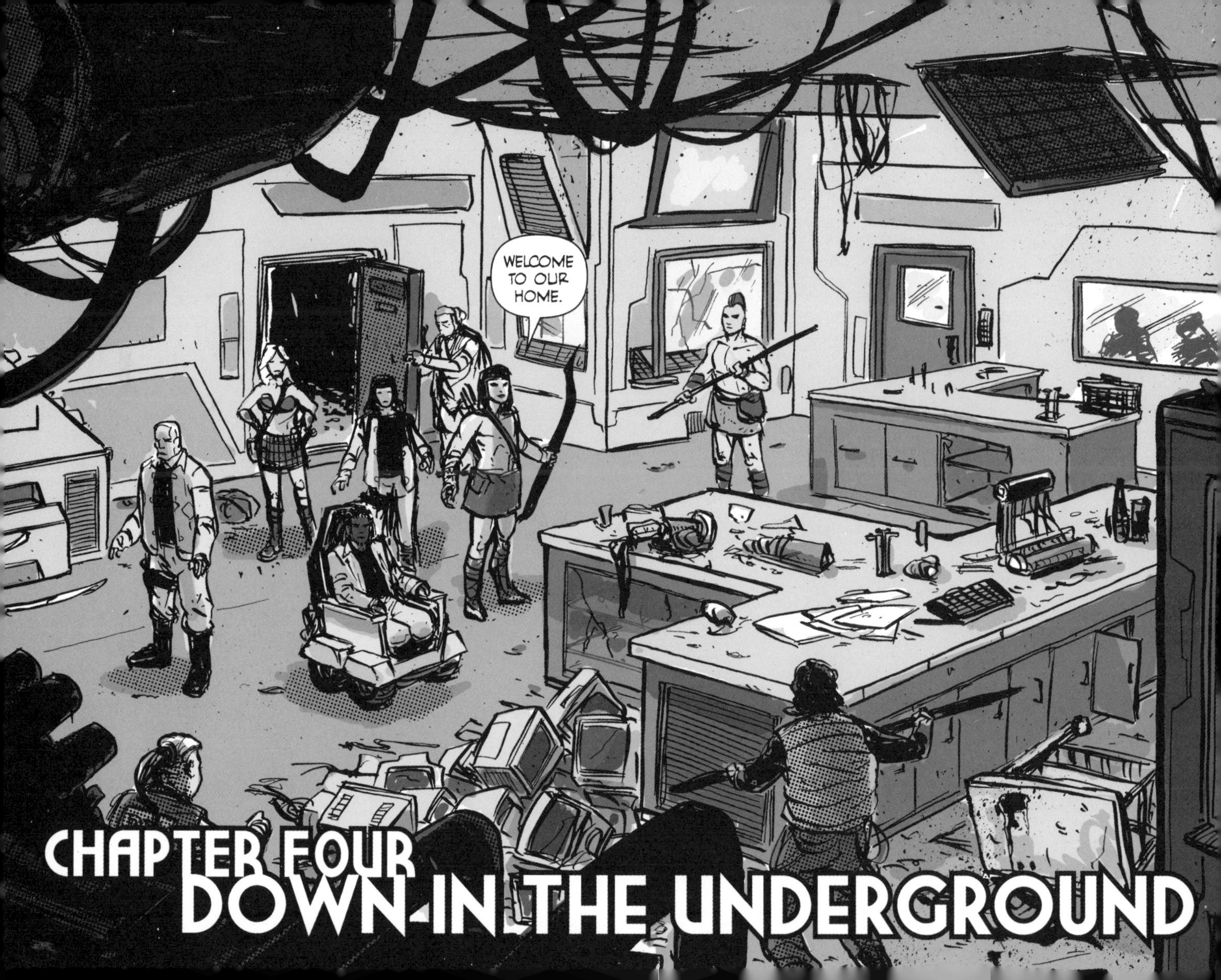
WELCOME TO OUR HOME.
CHAPTER FOUR
DOWN IN THE UNDERGROUND

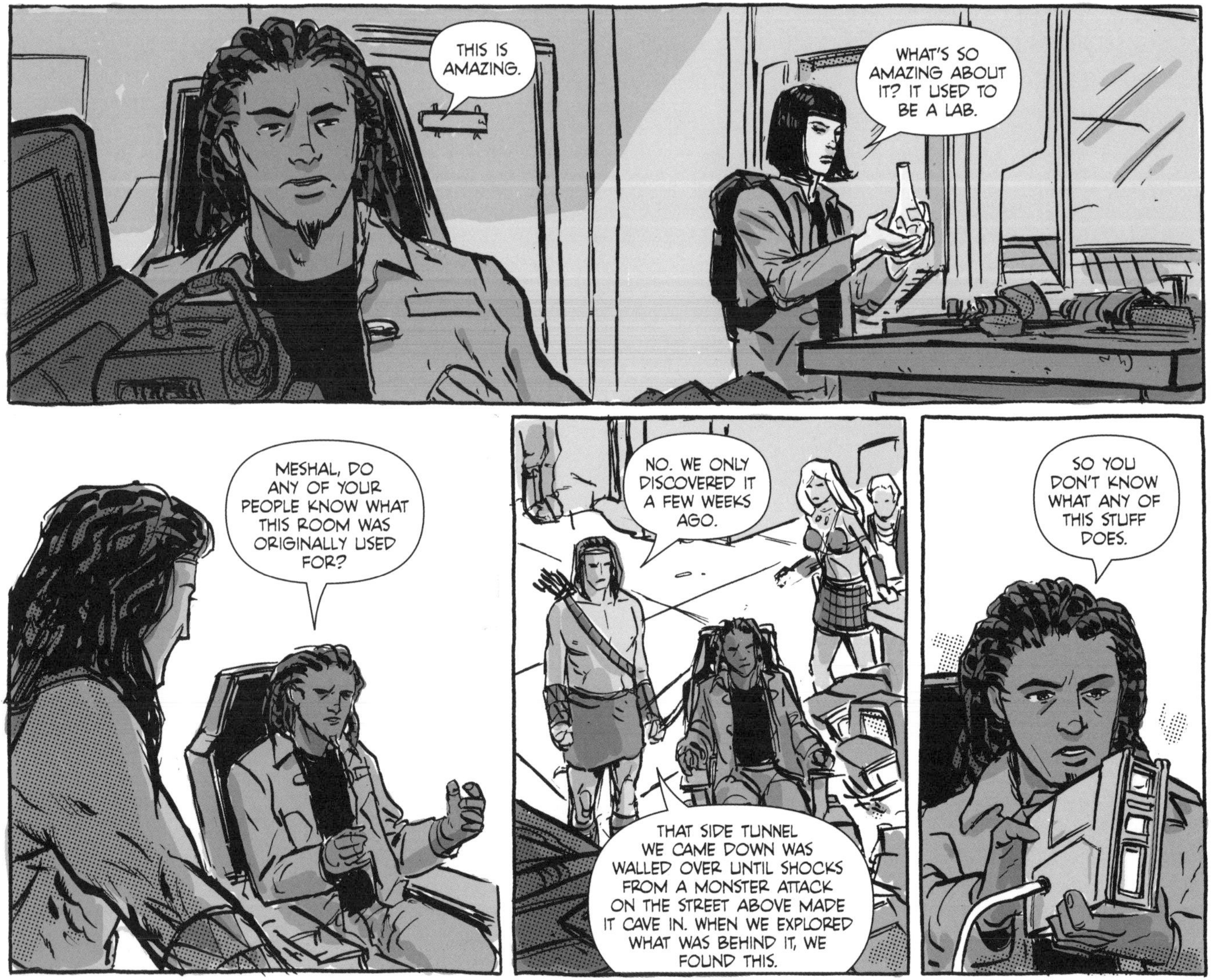
THIS IS AMAZING.
WHAT'S SO AMAZING ABOUT IT? IT USED TO BE A LAB.
MESHAL, DO ANY OF YOUR PEOPLE KNOW WHAT THIS ROOM WAS ORIGINALLY USED FOR?
NO. WE ONLY DISCOVERED IT A FEW WEEKS AGO.
THAT SIDE TUNNEL WE CAME DOWN WAS WALLED OVER UNTIL SHOCKS FROM A MONSTER ATTACK ON THE STREET ABOVE MADE IT CAVE IN. WHEN WE EXPLORED WHAT WAS BEHIND IT, WE FOUND THIS.
SO YOU DON'T KNOW WHAT ANY OF THIS STUFF DOES.

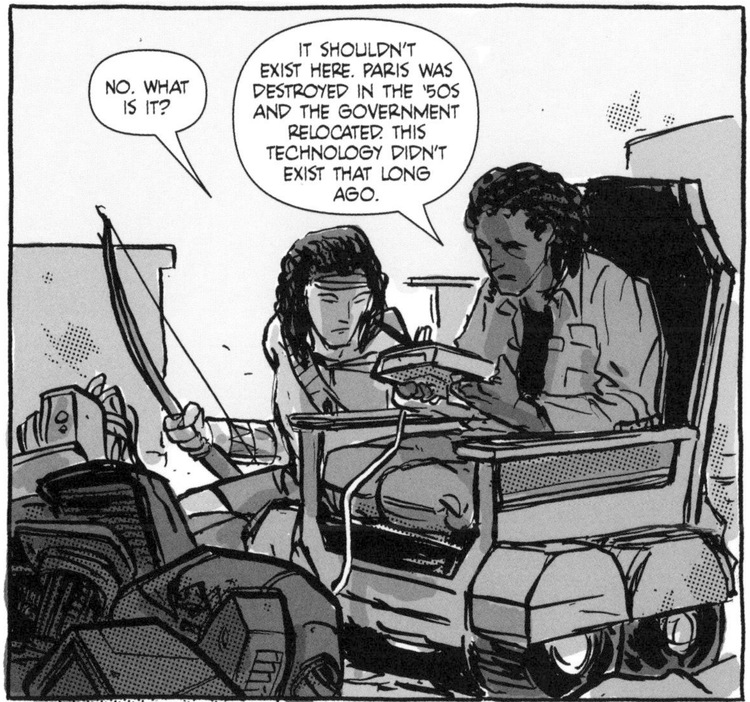
NO. WHAT IS IT?
IT SHOULDN'T EXIST HERE. PARIS WAS DESTROYED IN THE '50S AND THE GOVERNMENT RELOCATED. THIS TECHNOLOGY DIDN'T EXIST THAT LONG AGO.
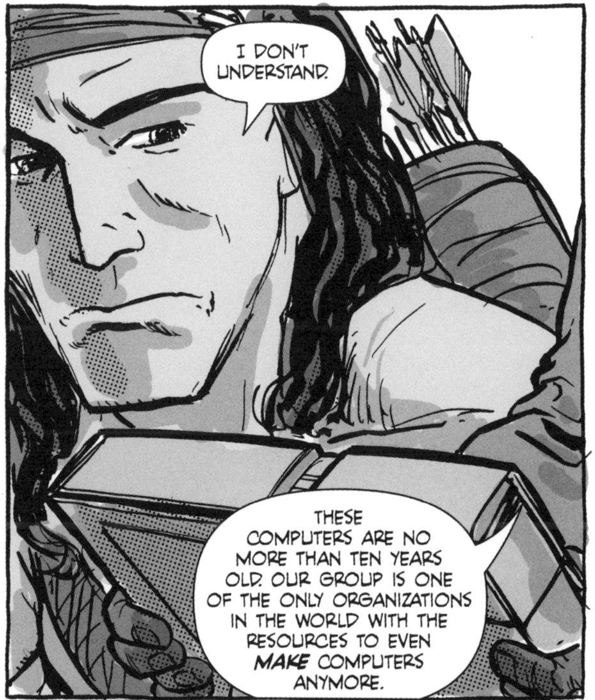
I DON'T UNDERSTAND.
THESE COMPUTERS ARE NO MORE THAN TEN YEARS OLD. OUR GROUP IS ONE OF THE ONLY ORGANIZATIONS IN THE WORLD WITH THE RESOURCES TO EVEN ***MAKE*** COMPUTERS ANYMORE.
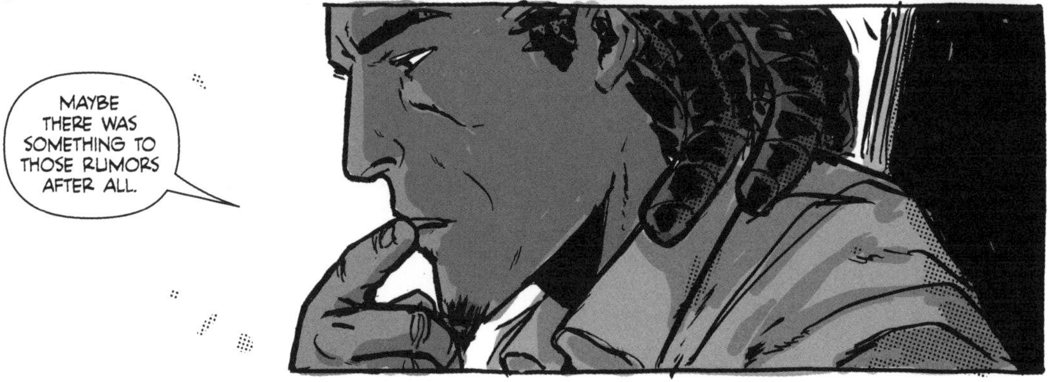
MAYBE THERE WAS SOMETHING TO THOSE RUMORS AFTER ALL.

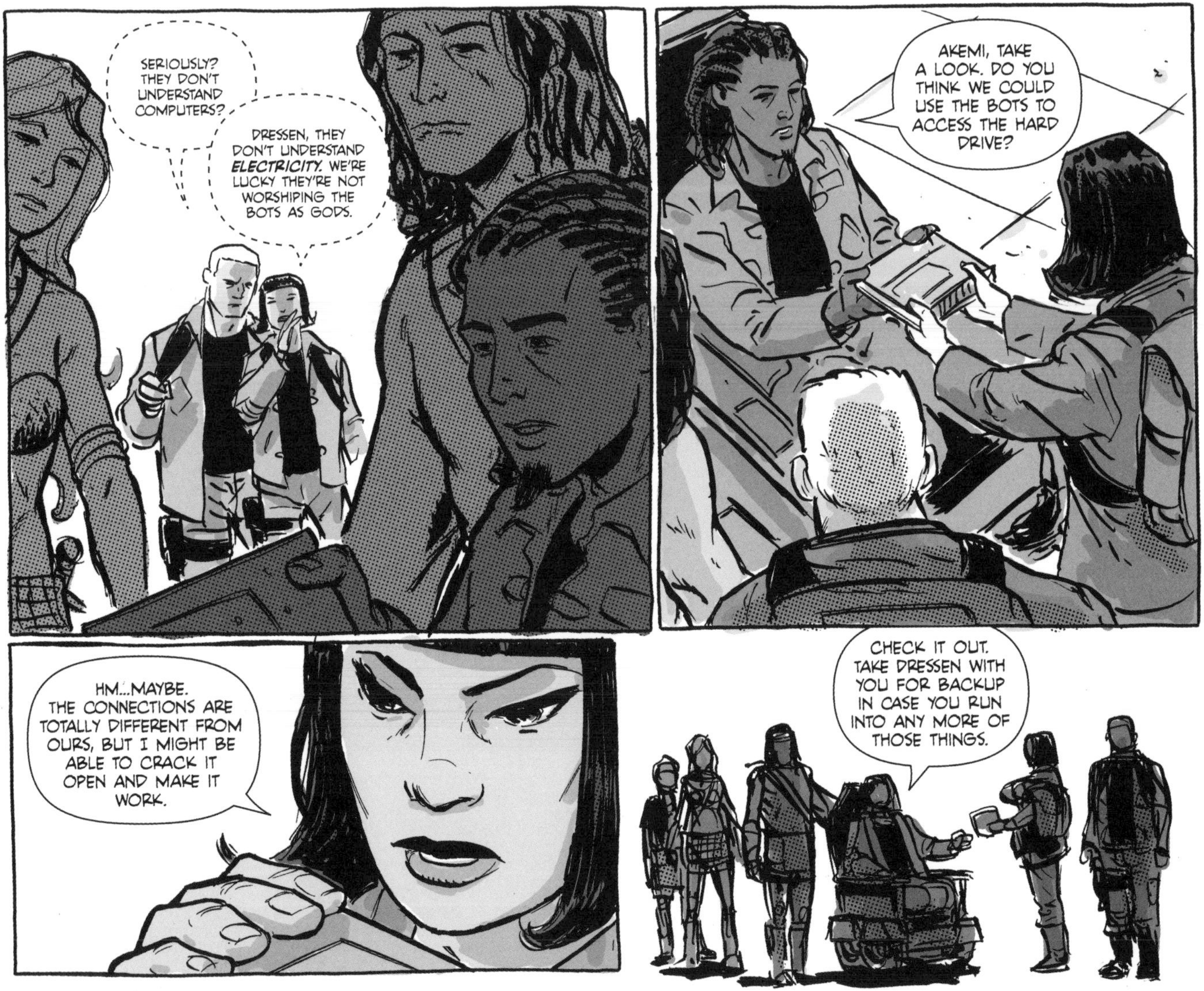
SERIOUSLY? THEY DON'T UNDERSTAND COMPUTERS?
DRESSEN, THEY DON'T UNDERSTAND ***ELECTRICITY.*** WE'RE LUCKY THEY'RE NOT WORSHIPING THE BOTS AS GODS.
AKEMI, TAKE A LOOK. DO YOU THINK WE COULD USE THE BOTS TO ACCESS THE HARD DRIVE?
HM...MAYBE. THE CONNECTIONS ARE TOTALLY DIFFERENT FROM OURS, BUT I MIGHT BE ABLE TO CRACK IT OPEN AND MAKE IT WORK.
CHECK IT OUT. TAKE DRESSEN WITH YOU FOR BACKUP IN CASE YOU RUN INTO ANY MORE OF THOSE THINGS.

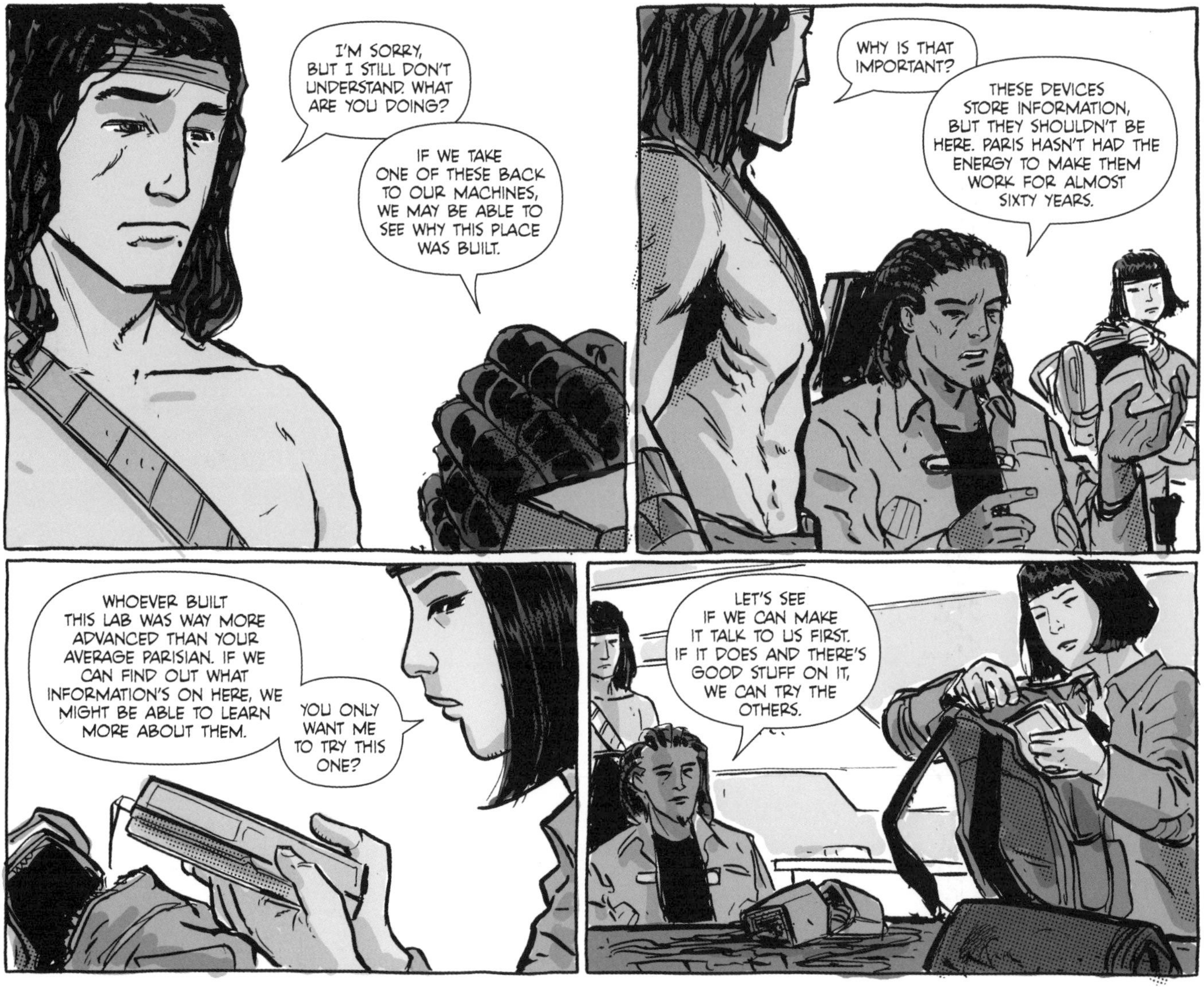
I'M SORRY, BUT I STILL DON'T UNDERSTAND. WHAT ARE YOU DOING?
IF WE TAKE ONE OF THESE BACK TO OUR MACHINES, WE MAY BE ABLE TO SEE WHY THIS PLACE WAS BUILT.
WHY IS THAT IMPORTANT?
THESE DEVICES STORE INFORMATION, BUT THEY SHOULDN'T BE HERE. PARIS HASN'T HAD THE ENERGY TO MAKE THEM WORK FOR ALMOST SIXTY YEARS.
WHOEVER BUILT THIS LAB WAS WAY MORE ADVANCED THAN YOUR AVERAGE PARISIAN. IF WE CAN FIND OUT WHAT INFORMATION'S ON HERE, WE MIGHT BE ABLE TO LEARN MORE ABOUT THEM.
YOU ONLY WANT ME TO TRY THIS ONE?
LET'S SEE IF WE CAN MAKE IT TALK TO US FIRST. IF IT DOES AND THERE'S GOOD STUFF ON IT, WE CAN TRY THE OTHERS.

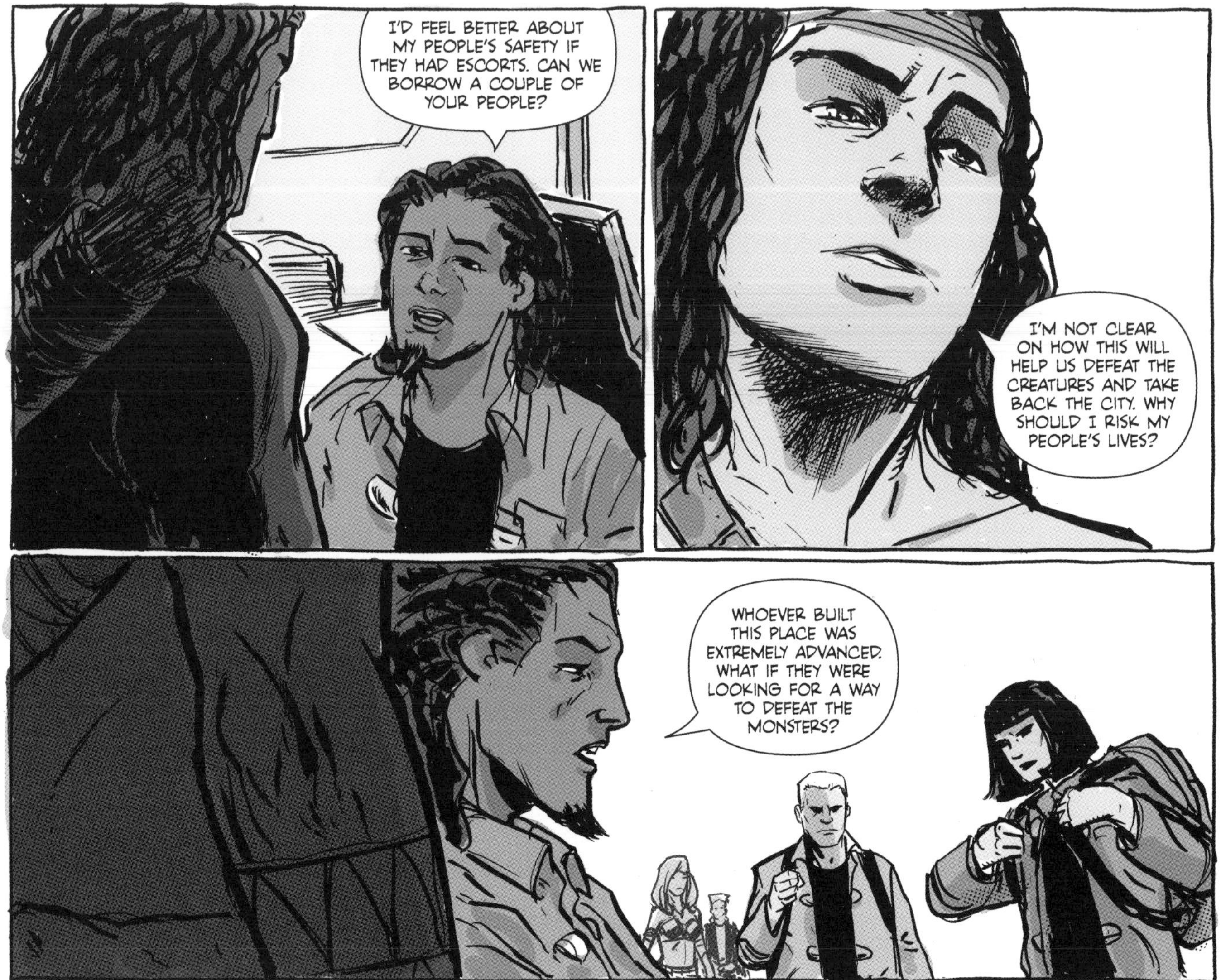
I'D FEEL BETTER ABOUT MY PEOPLE'S SAFETY IF THEY HAD ESCORTS. CAN WE BORROW A COUPLE OF YOUR PEOPLE?
I'M NOT CLEAR ON HOW THIS WILL HELP US DEFEAT THE CREATURES AND TAKE BACK THE CITY. WHY SHOULD I RISK MY PEOPLE'S LIVES?
WHOEVER BUILT THIS PLACE WAS EXTREMELY ADVANCED. WHAT IF THEY WERE LOOKING FOR A WAY TO DEFEAT THE MONSTERS?

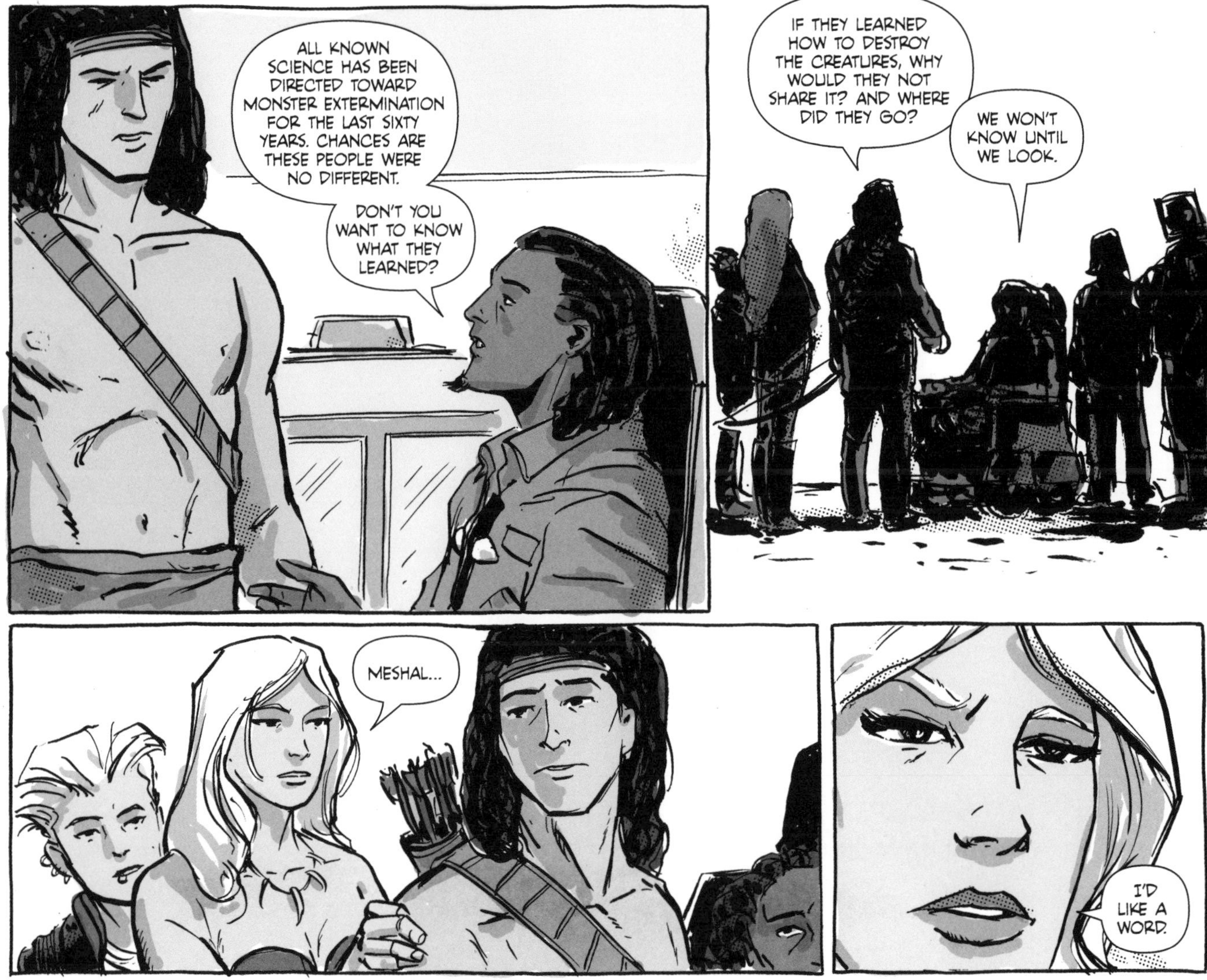
ALL KNOWN SCIENCE HAS BEEN DIRECTED TOWARD MONSTER EXTERMINATION FOR THE LAST SIXTY YEARS. CHANCES ARE THESE PEOPLE WERE NO DIFFERENT.
DON'T YOU WANT TO KNOW WHAT THEY LEARNED?
IF THEY LEARNED HOW TO DESTROY THE CREATURES, WHY WOULD THEY NOT SHARE IT? AND WHERE DID THEY GO?
WE WON'T KNOW UNTIL WE LOOK.
MESHAL...
I'D LIKE A WORD.

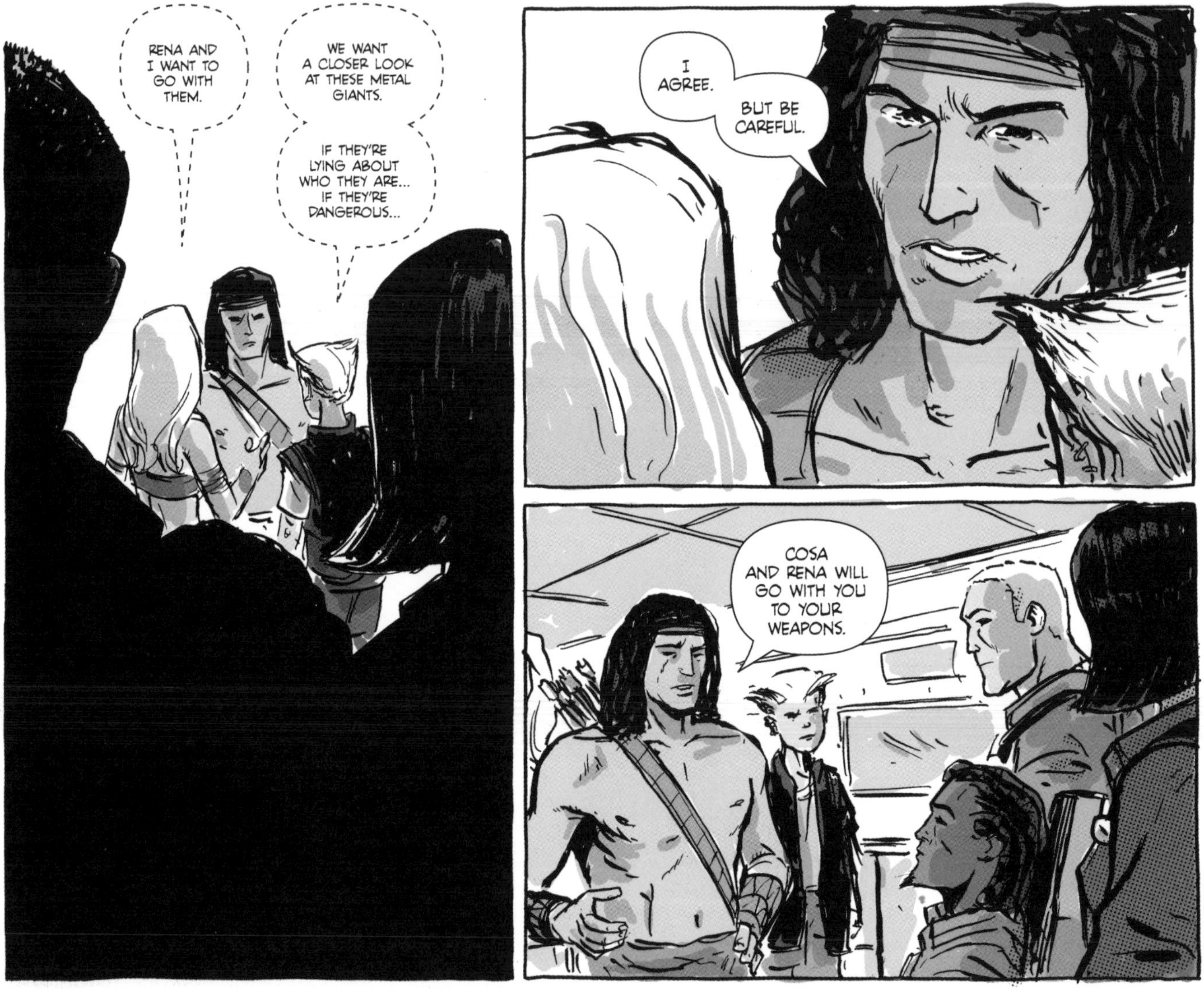
RENA AND I WANT TO GO WITH THEM.
WE WANT A CLOSER LOOK AT THESE METAL GIANTS.
IF THEY'RE LYING ABOUT WHO THEY ARE... IF THEY'RE DANGEROUS...
I AGREE.
BUT BE CAREFUL.
COSA AND RENA WILL GO WITH YOU TO YOUR WEAPONS.

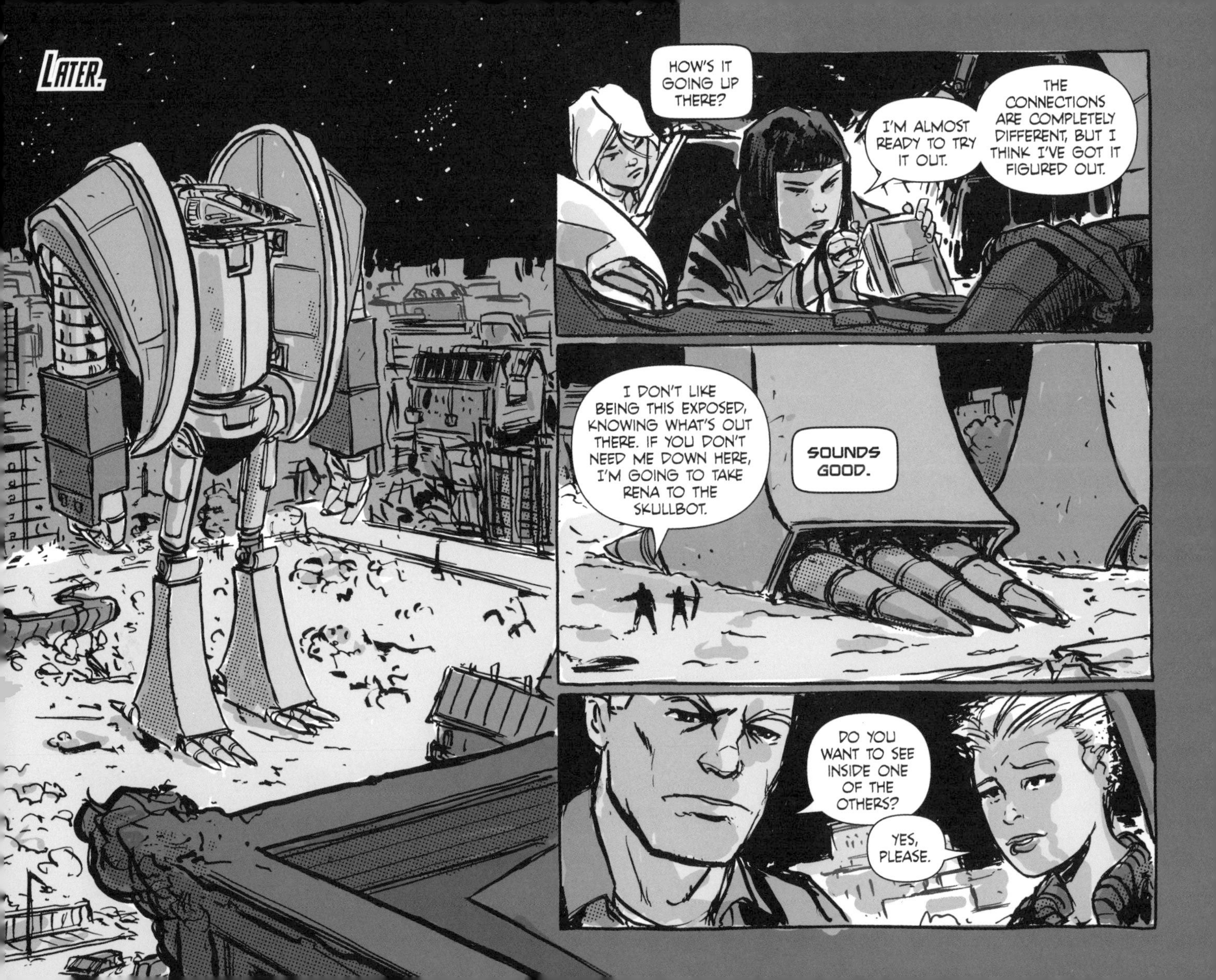
LATER.
HOW'S IT GOING UP THERE?
I'M ALMOST READY TO TRY IT OUT.
THE CONNECTIONS ARE COMPLETELY DIFFERENT, BUT I THINK I'VE GOT IT FIGURED OUT.
I DON'T LIKE BEING THIS EXPOSED, KNOWING WHAT'S OUT THERE. IF YOU DON'T NEED ME DOWN HERE, I'M GOING TO TAKE RENA TO THE SKULLBOT.
SOUNDS GOOD.
DO YOU WANT TO SEE INSIDE ONE OF THE OTHERS?
YES, PLEASE.

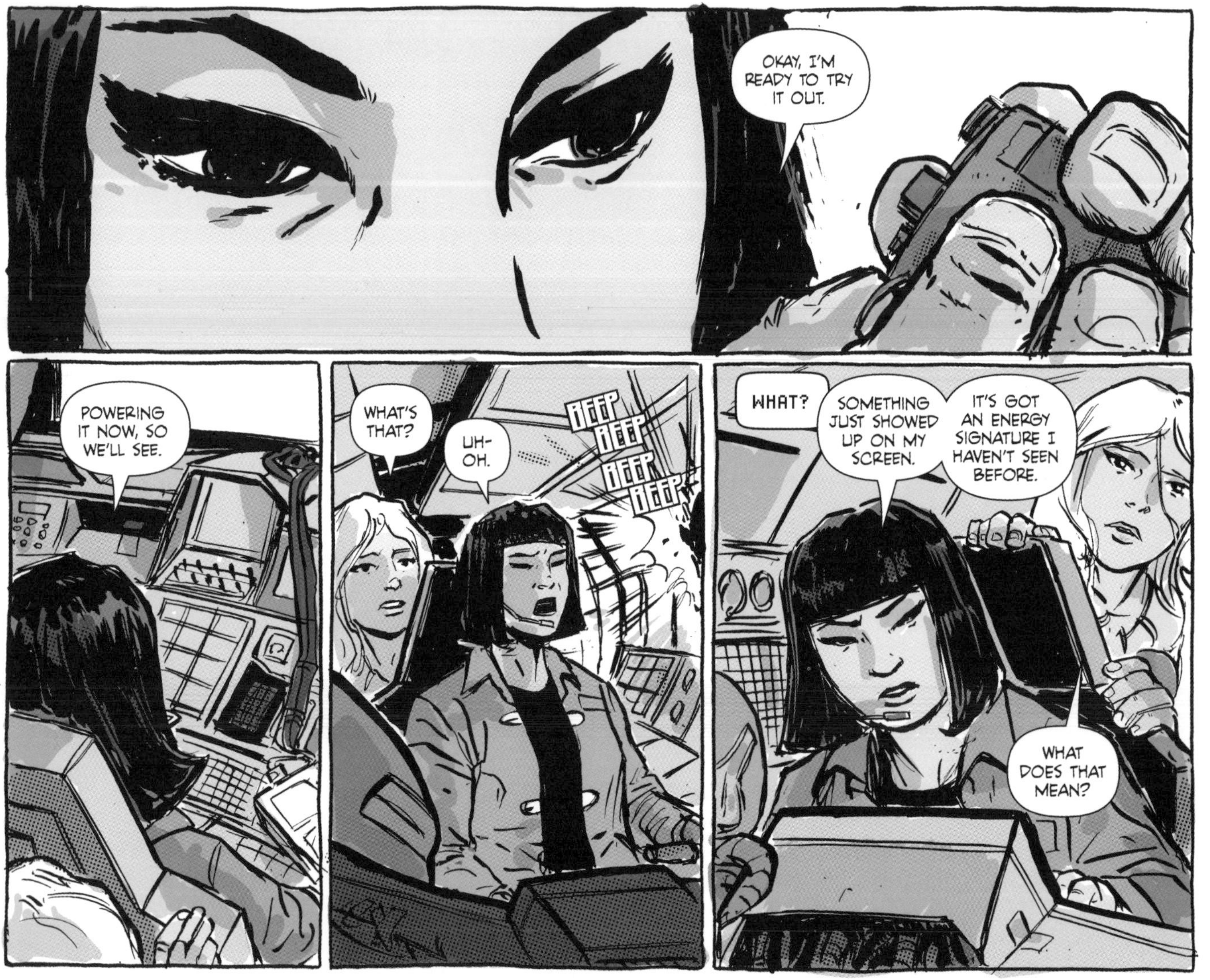
OKAY, I'M READY TO TRY IT OUT.
POWERING IT NOW, SO WE'LL SEE.
WHAT'S THAT?
UH-OH.
BEEP BEEP BEEP BEEP
WHAT?
SOMETHING JUST SHOWED UP ON MY SCREEN.
IT'S GOT AN ENERGY SIGNATURE I HAVEN'T SEEN BEFORE.
WHAT DOES THAT MEAN?

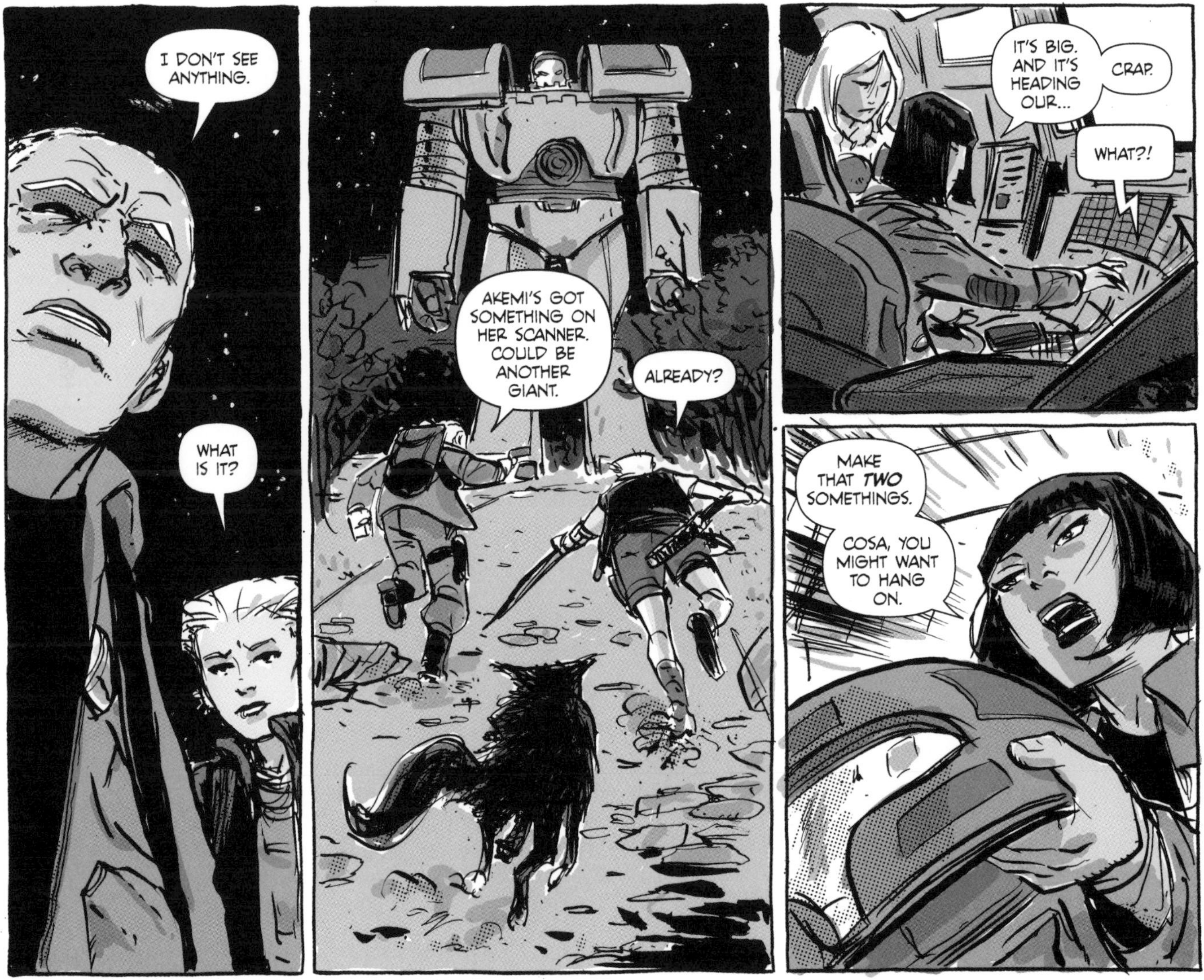
I DON'T SEE ANYTHING.
WHAT IS IT?
AKEMI'S GOT SOMETHING ON HER SCANNER. COULD BE ANOTHER GIANT.
ALREADY?
IT'S BIG. AND IT'S HEADING OUR...
CRAP.
WHAT?!
MAKE THAT *TWO* SOMETHINGS.
COSA, YOU MIGHT WANT TO HANG ON.

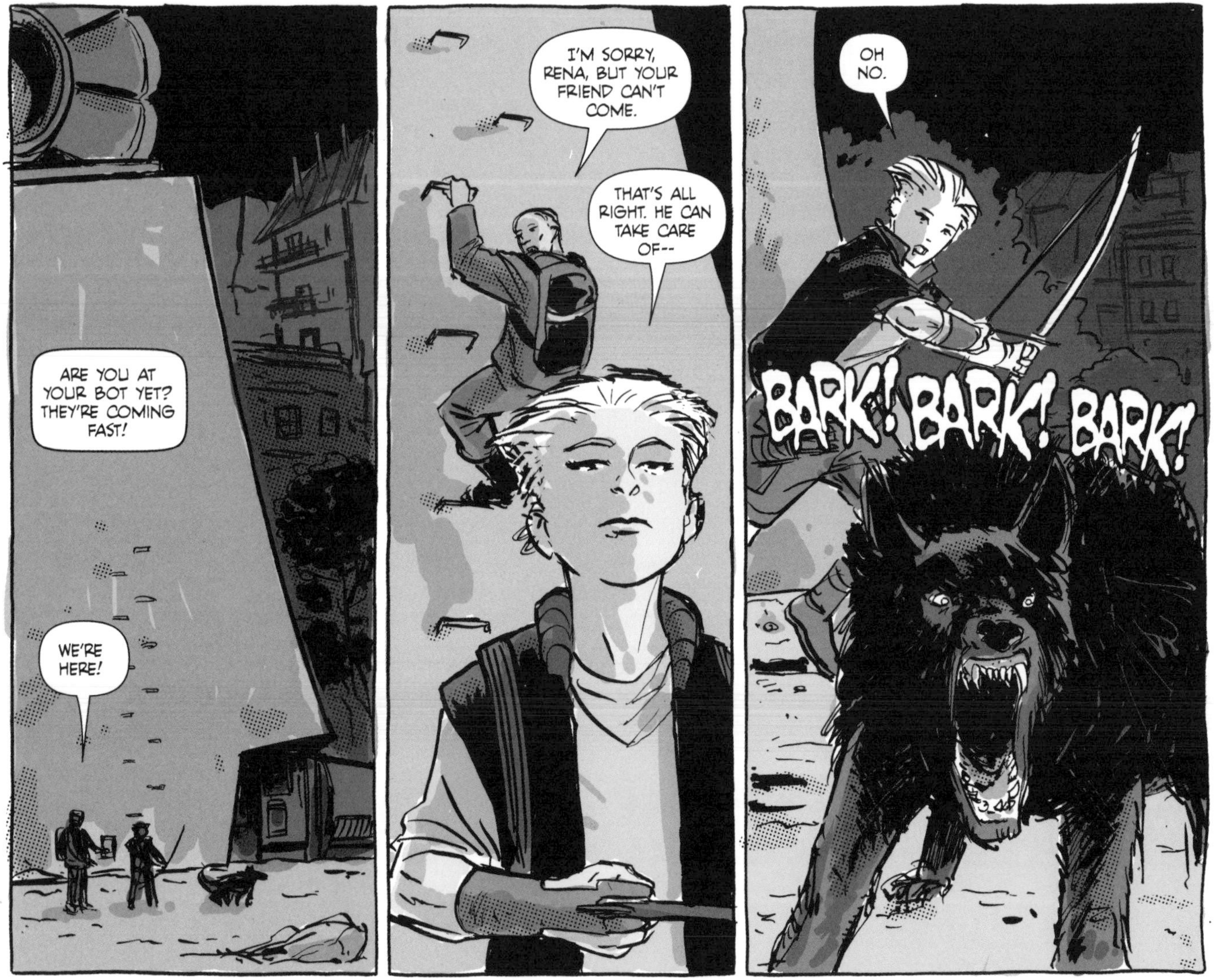
ARE YOU AT YOUR BOT YET? THEY'RE COMING FAST!
WE'RE HERE!
I'M SORRY, RENA, BUT YOUR FRIEND CAN'T COME.
THAT'S ALL RIGHT. HE CAN TAKE CARE OF--
OH NO.
BARK! BARK! BARK!

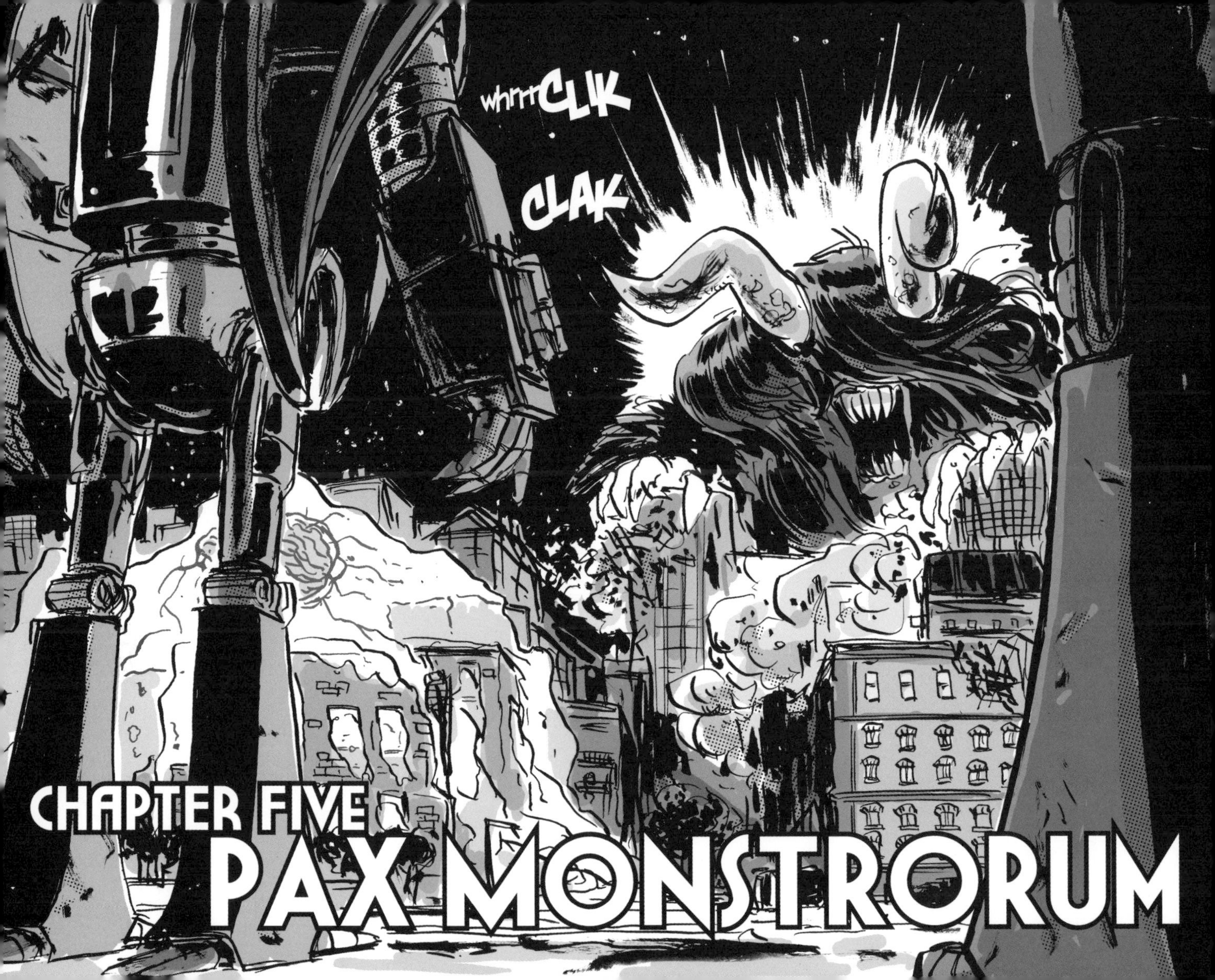
whrrrCLIK
CLAK
CHAPTER FIVE
PAX MONSTRORUM

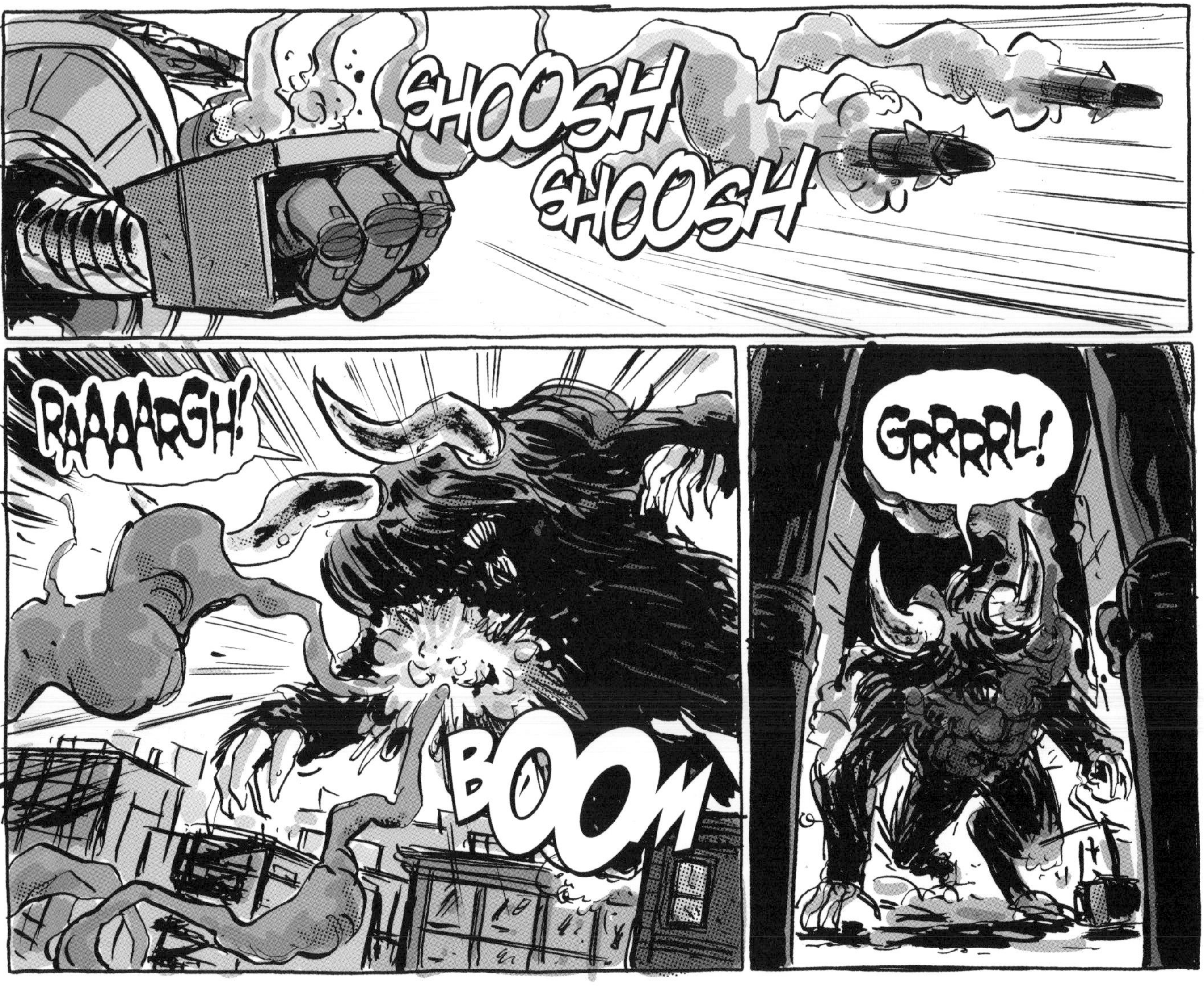
SHOOSH
SHOOSH
RAAAARGH!
BOOM
GRRRRL!

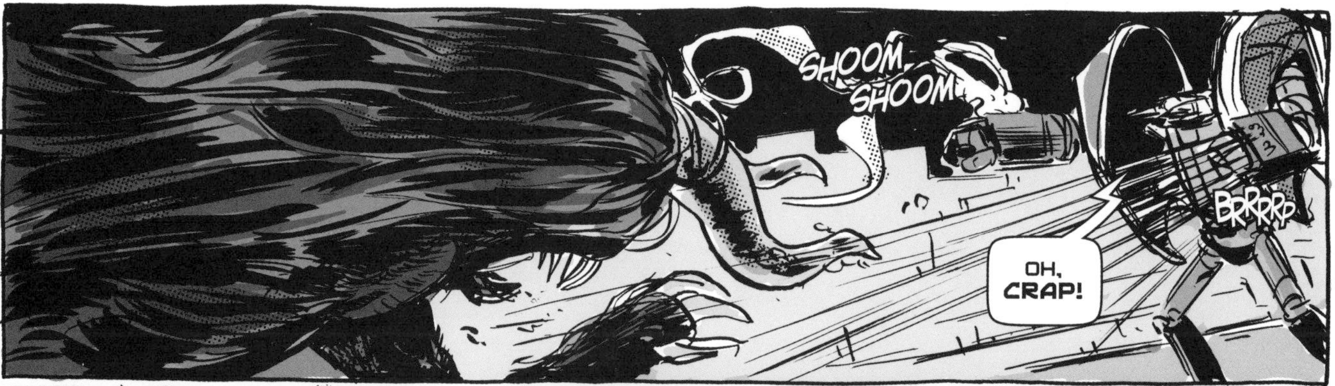
SHOOM
SHOOM
BRRRRP
OH, CRAP!

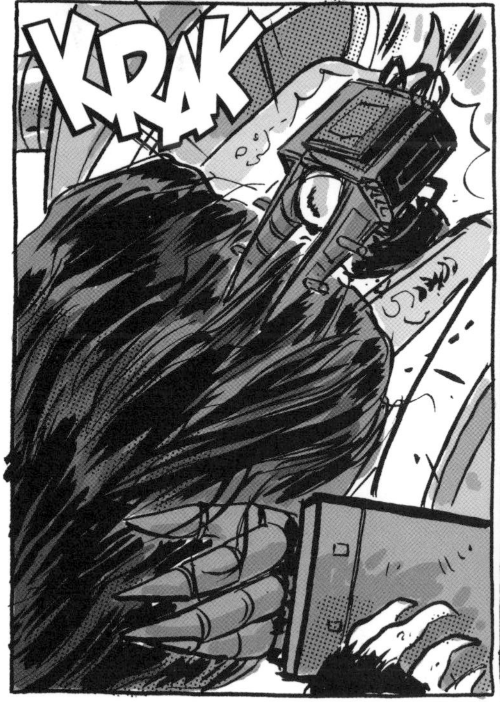
KRAK

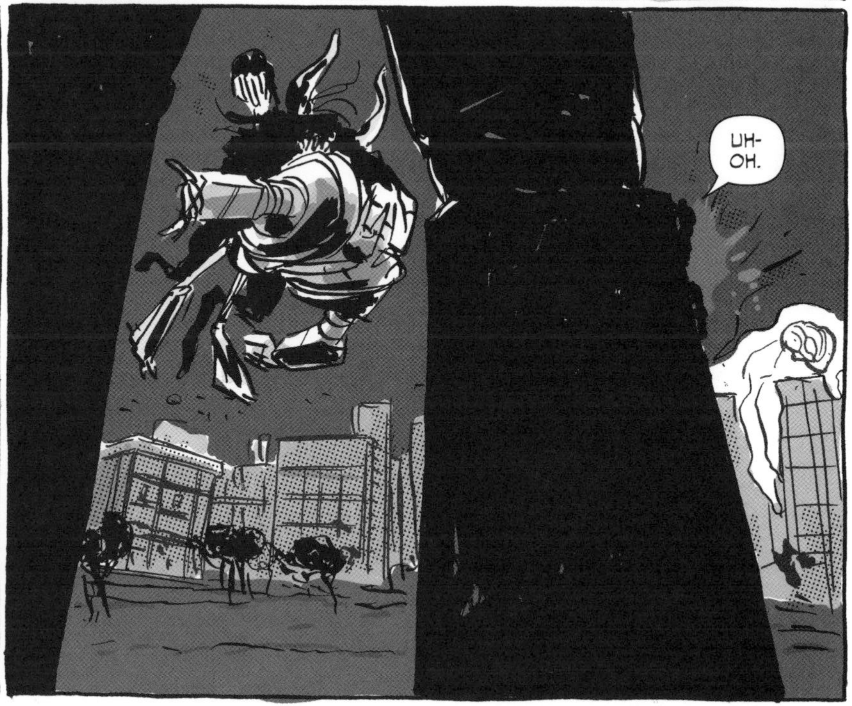
UH-OH.

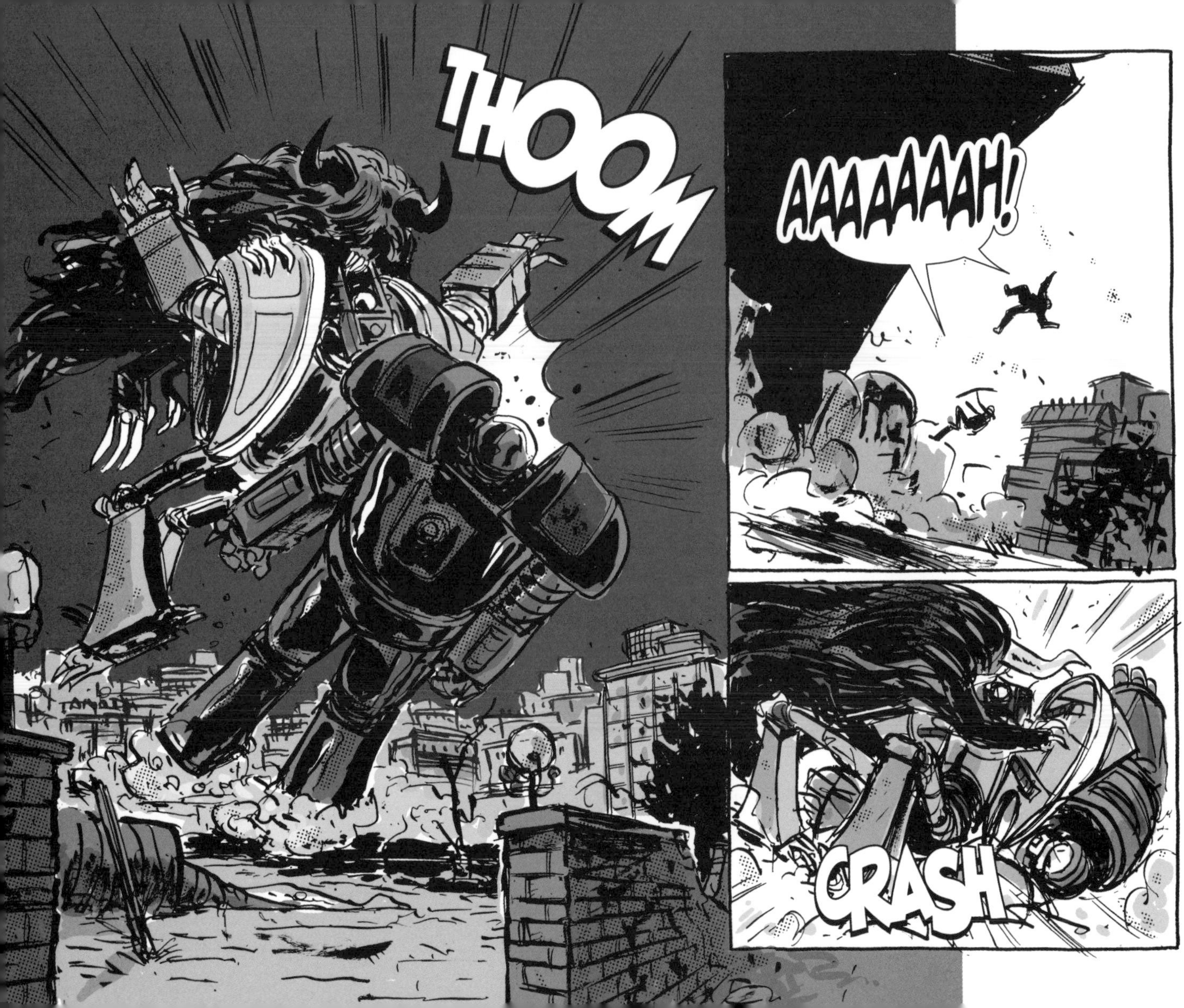
THOOM
AAAAAAAH!
CRASH

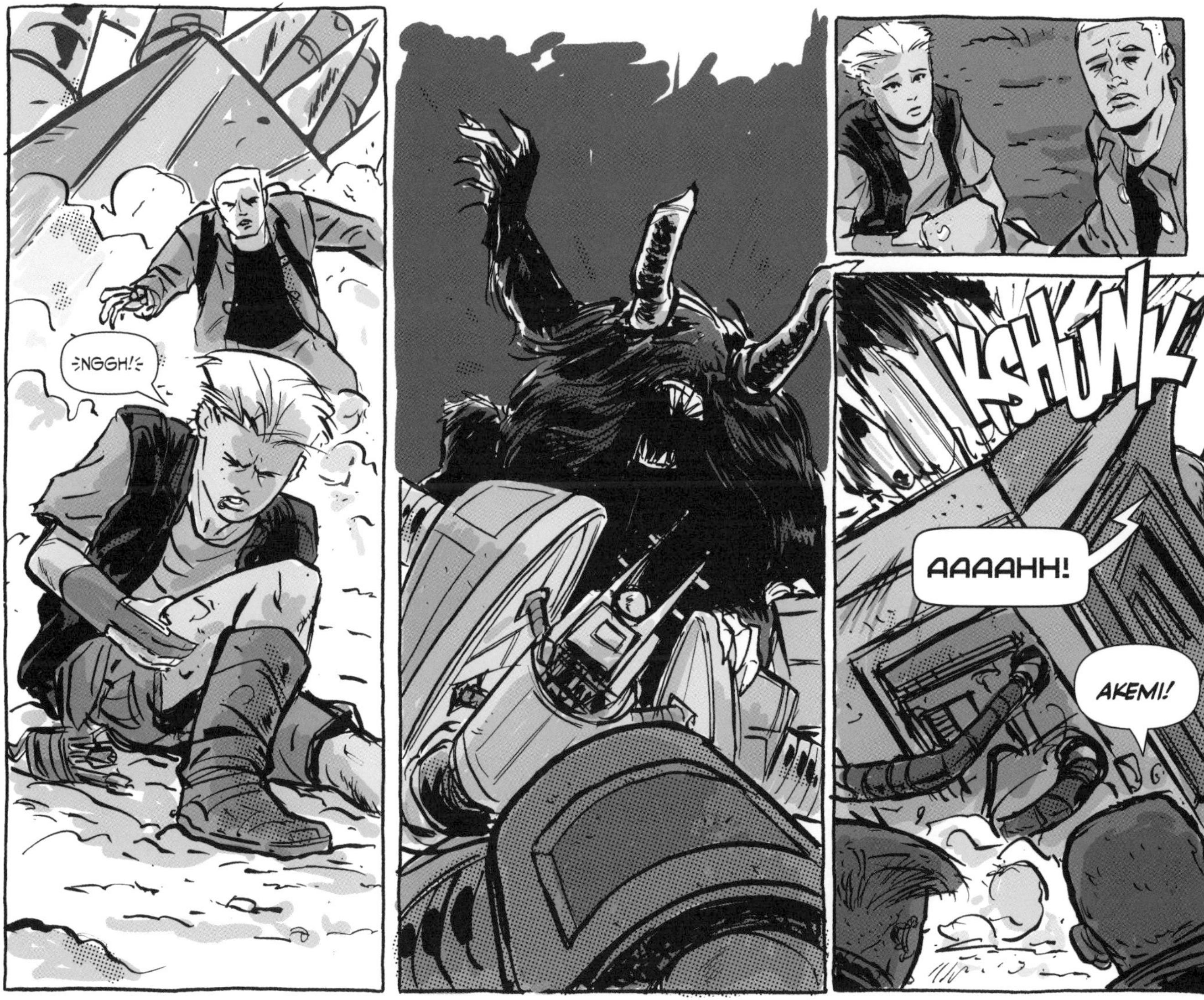
NGGH!
KSHUNK
AAAAHH!
AKEMI!

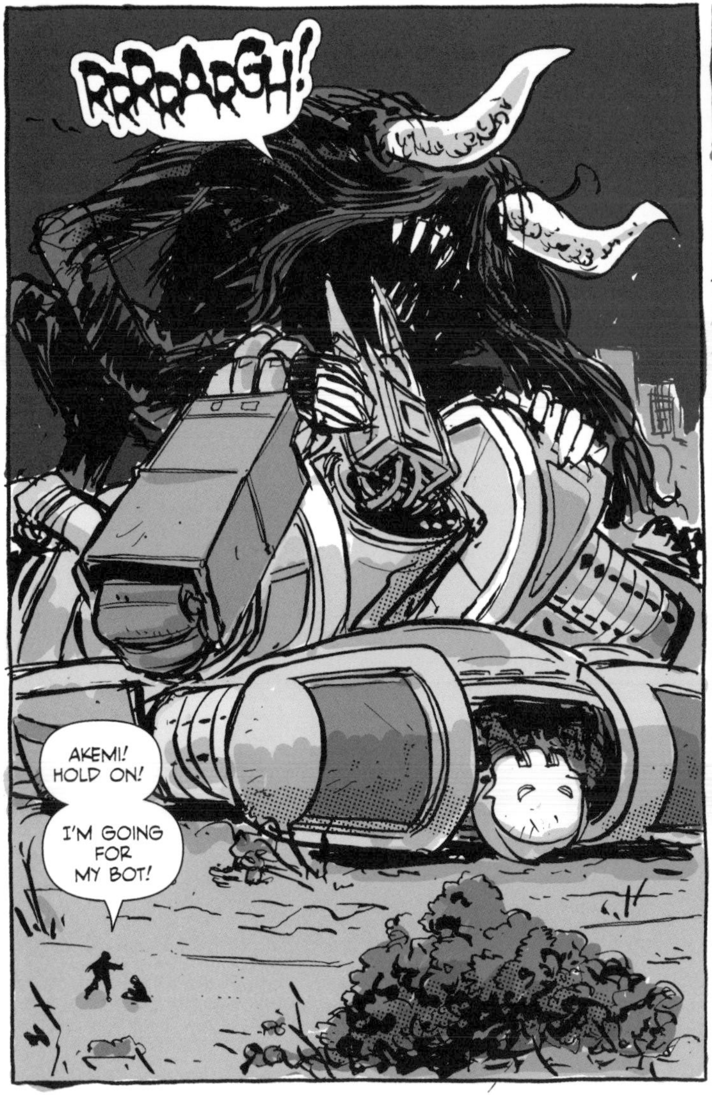
RRRRARGH!
AKEMI! HOLD ON!
I'M GOING FOR MY BOT!

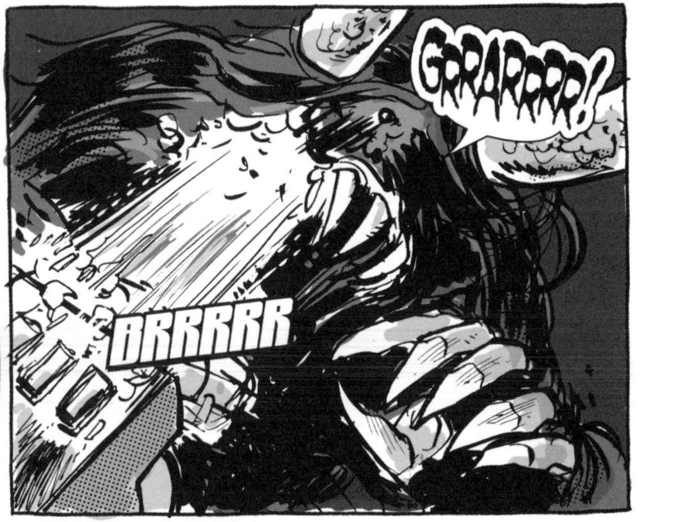
GRRARRRR!
BRRRRR

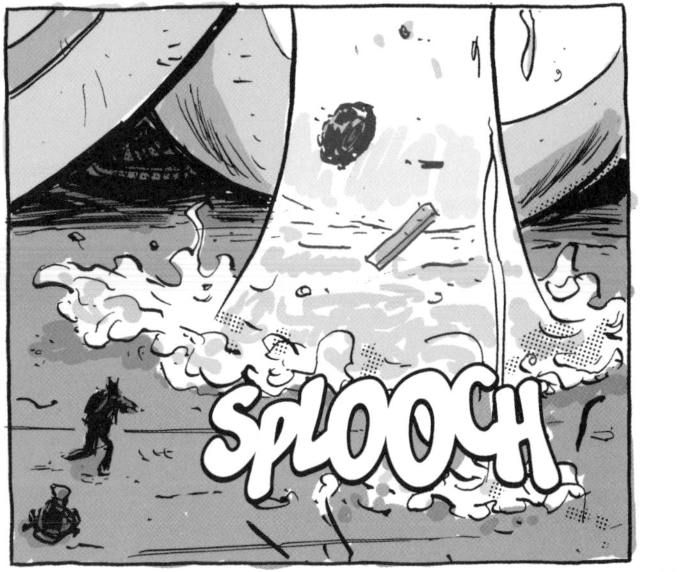
SPLOOCH

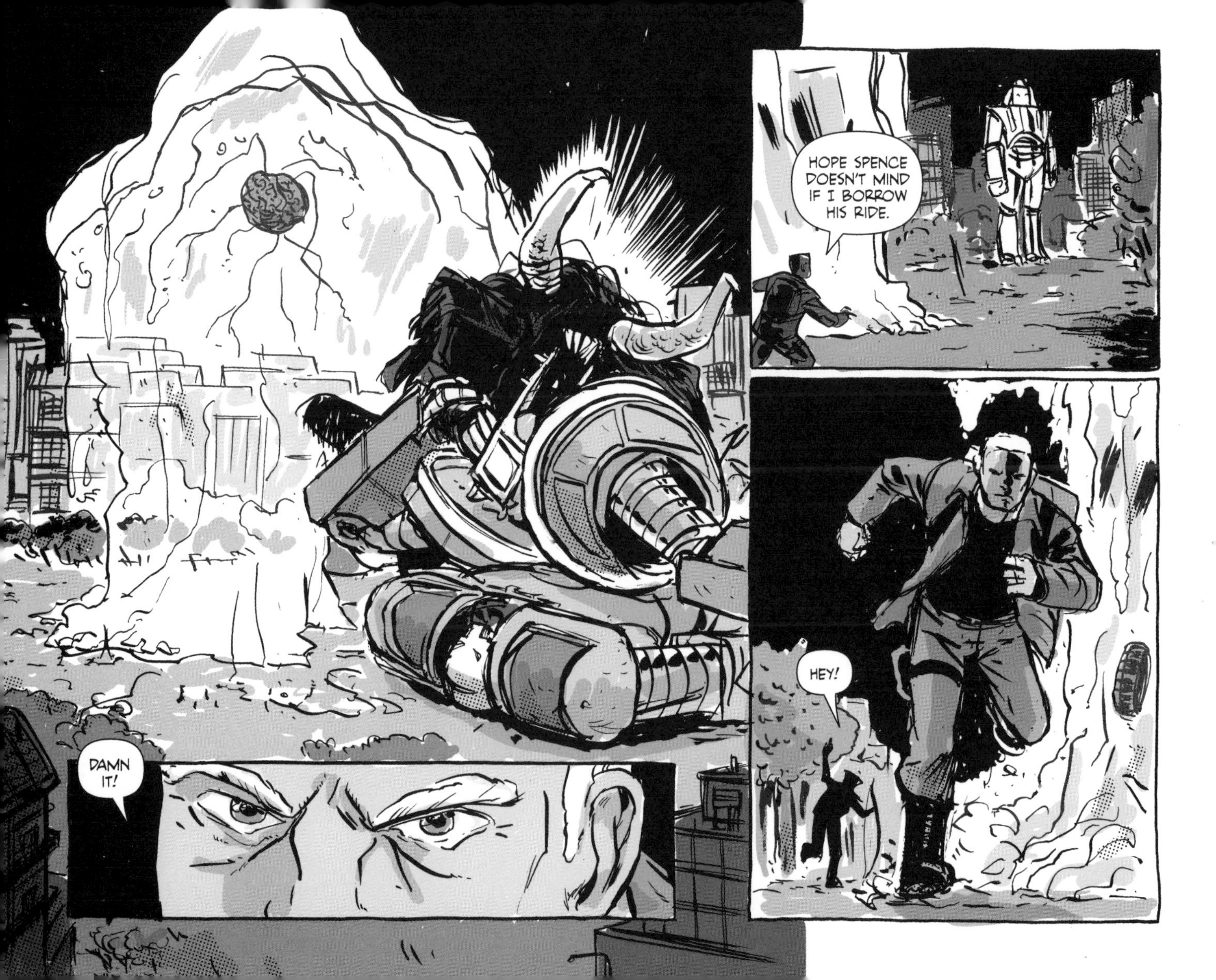
DAMN IT!
HOPE SPENCE DOESN'T MIND IF I BORROW HIS RIDE.
HEY!

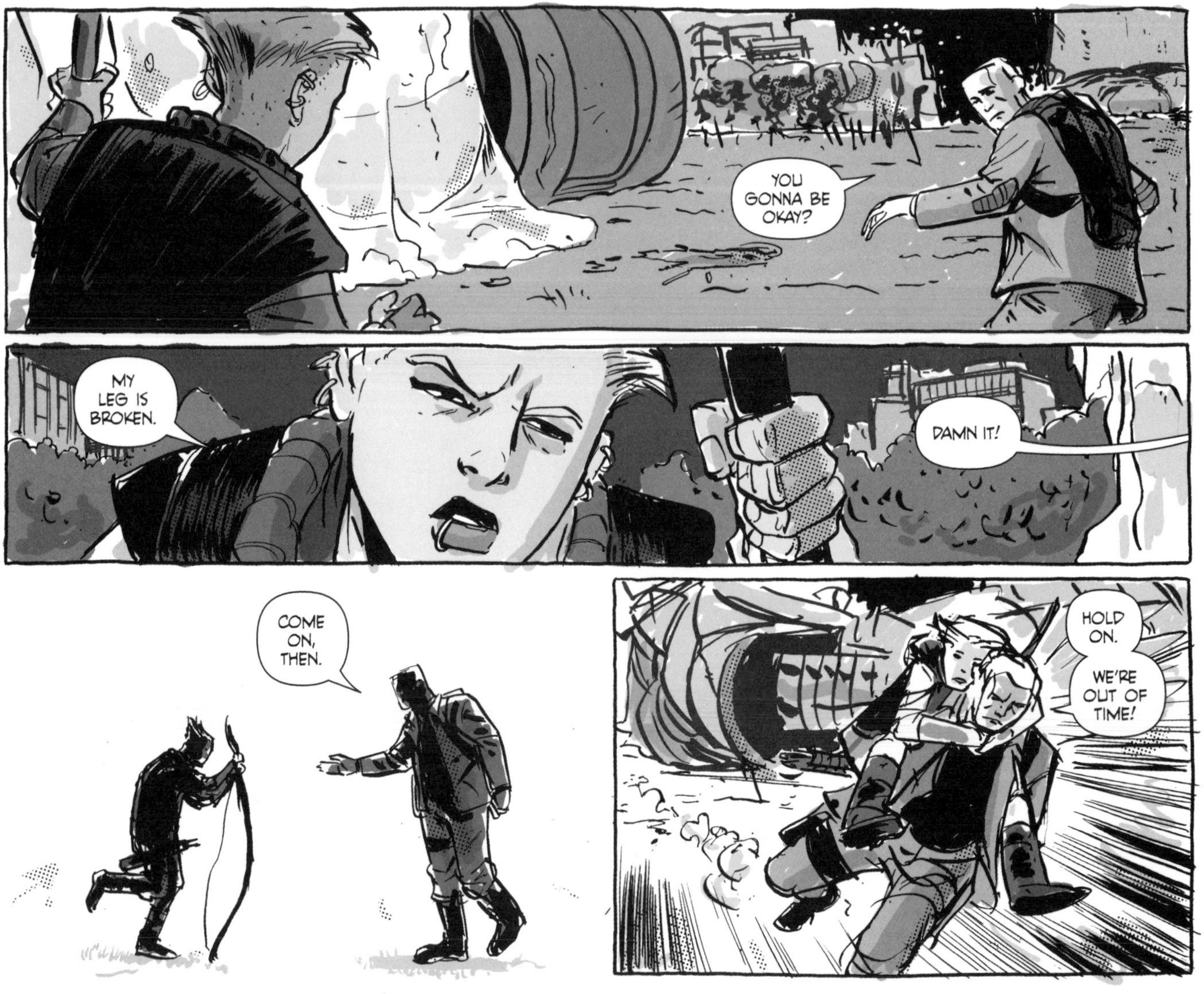
YOU GONNA BE OKAY?
MY LEG IS BROKEN.
DAMN IT!
COME ON, THEN.
HOLD ON.
WE'RE OUT OF TIME!

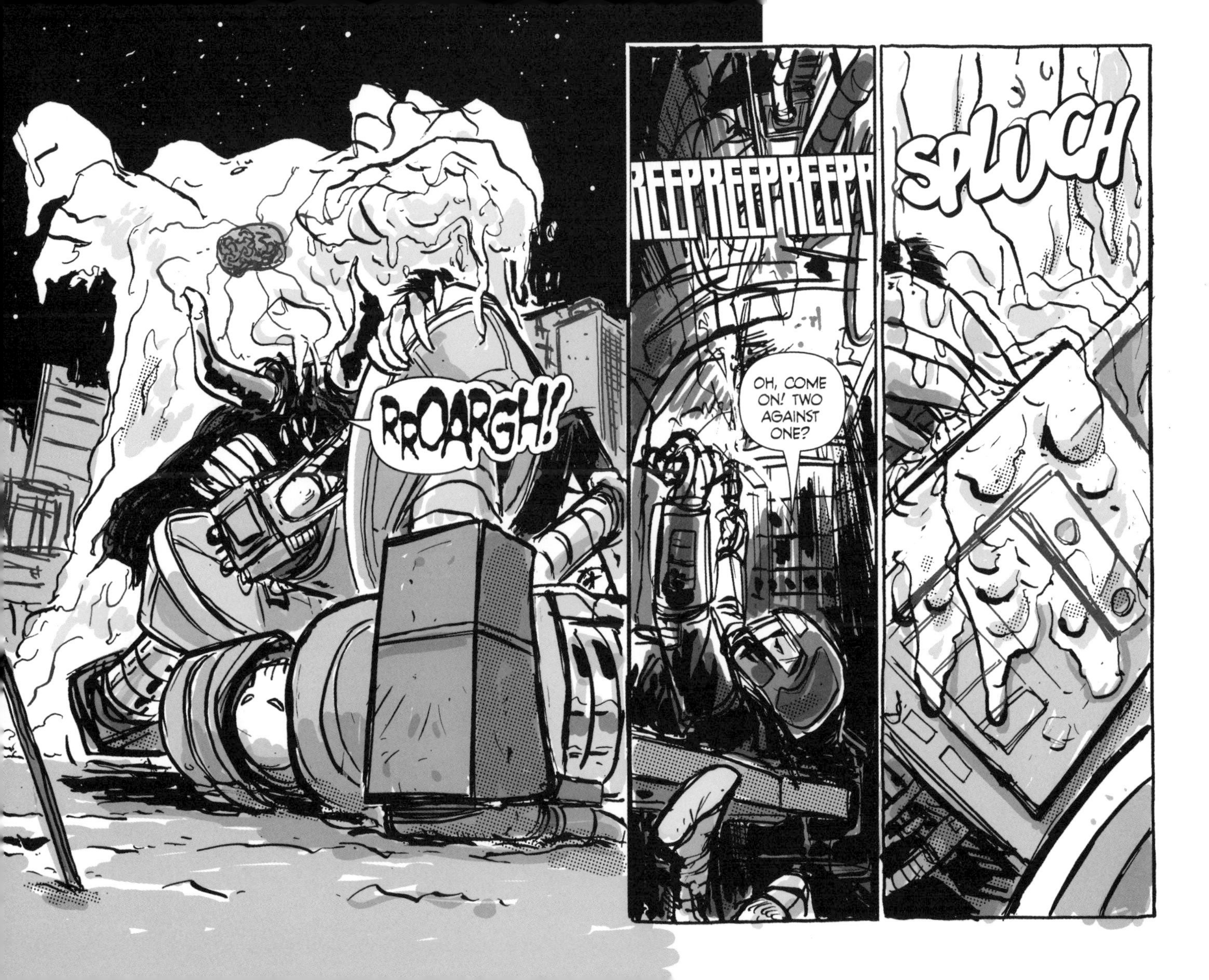
RRROARGH!
REEPREEPREEPR
OH, COME ON! TWO AGAINST ONE?
SPLUCH

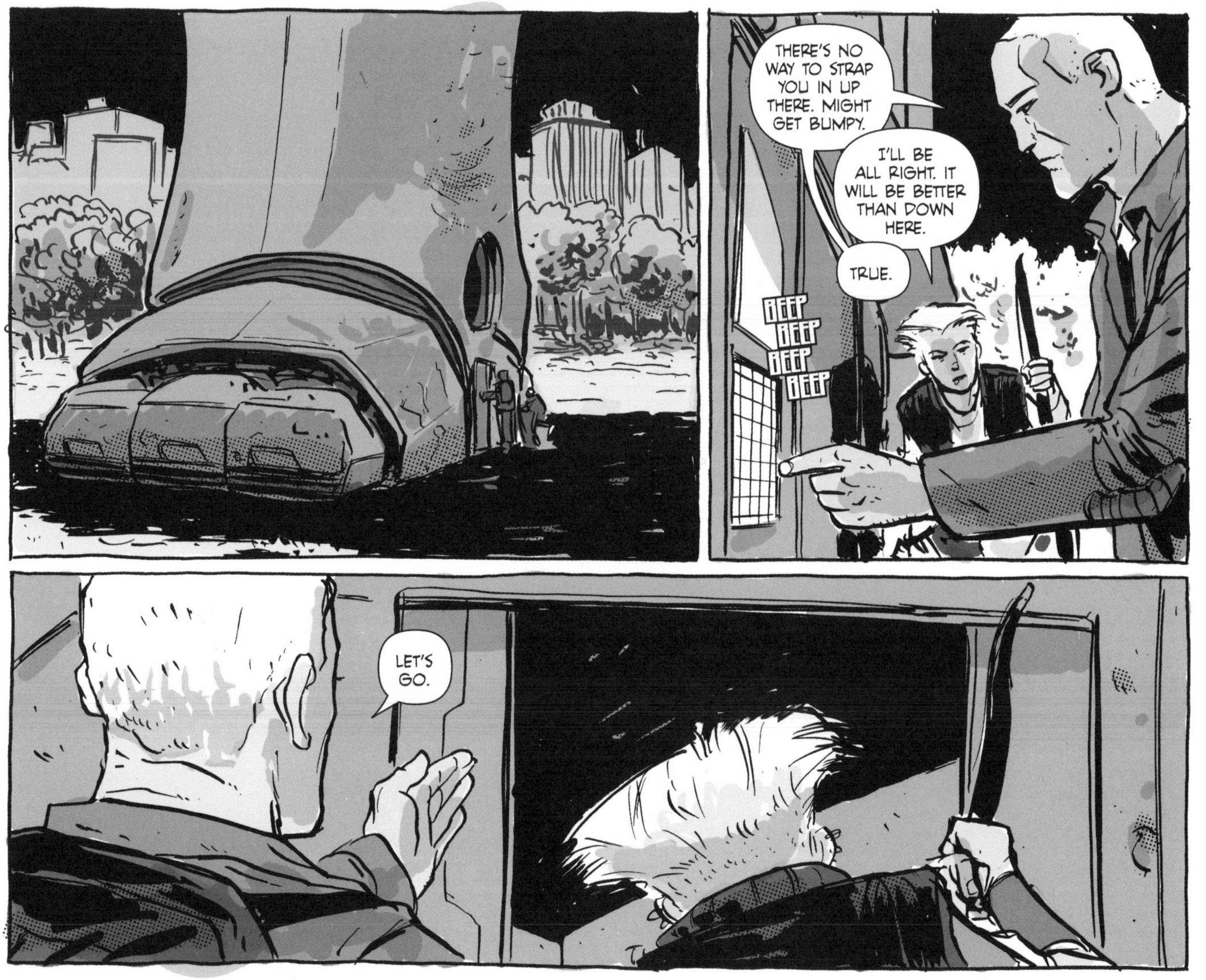
THERE'S NO WAY TO STRAP YOU IN UP THERE. MIGHT GET BUMPY.
I'LL BE ALL RIGHT. IT WILL BE BETTER THAN DOWN HERE.
TRUE.
BEEP BEEP BEEP BEEP
LET'S GO.

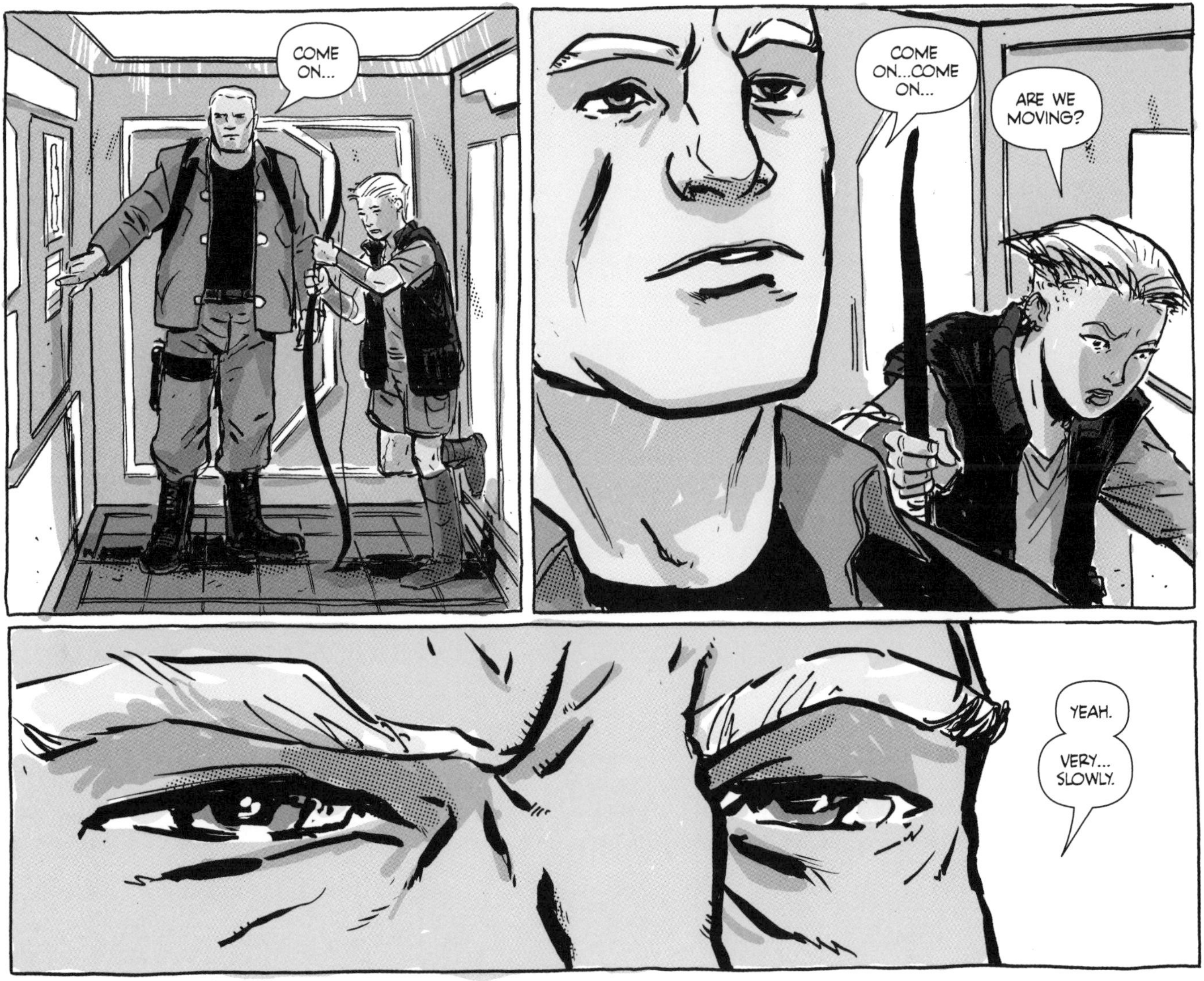
COME ON...
COME ON...COME ON...
ARE WE MOVING?
YEAH.
VERY... SLOWLY.

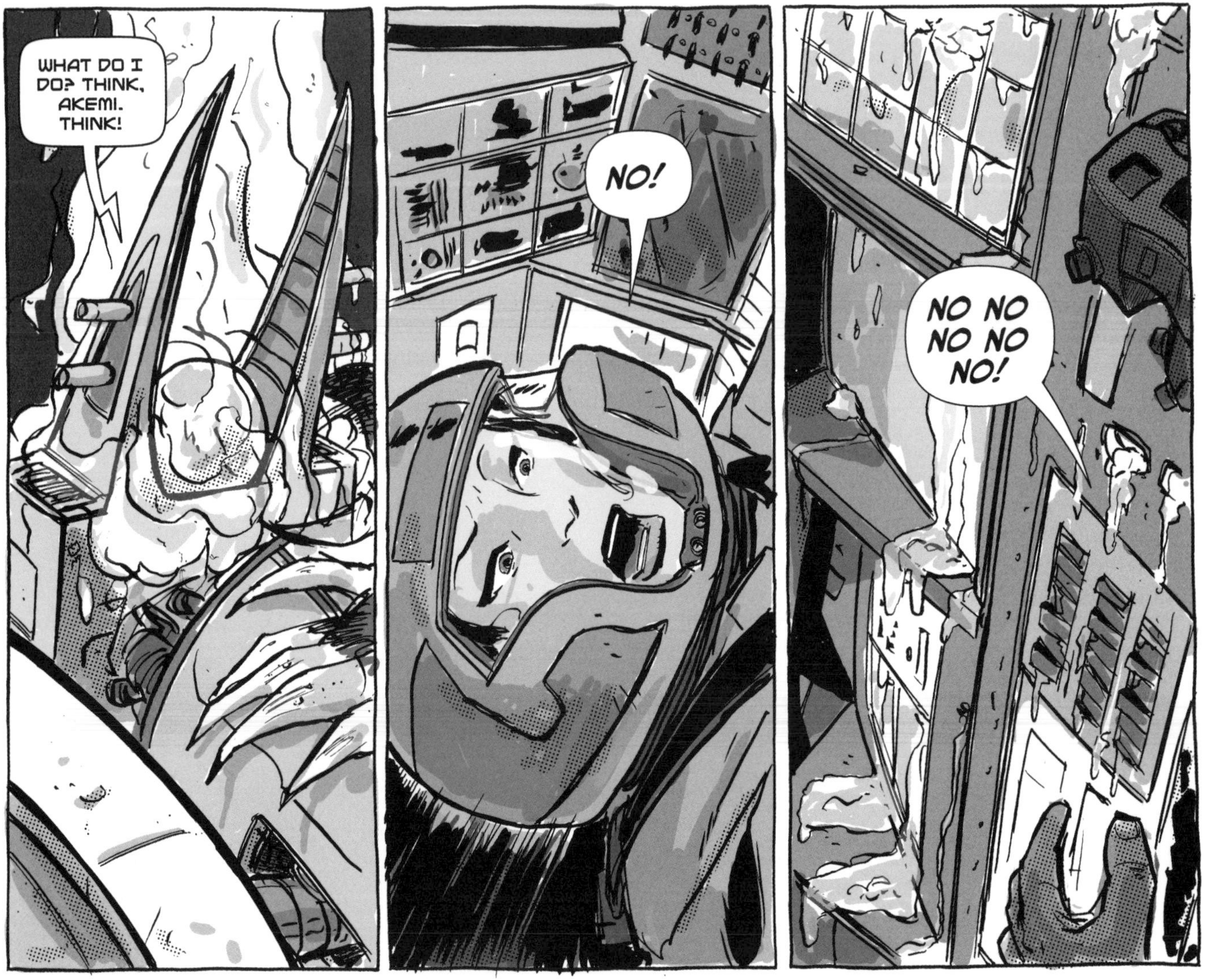
WHAT DO I DO? THINK, AKEMI. THINK!
NO!
NO NO NO NO NO!

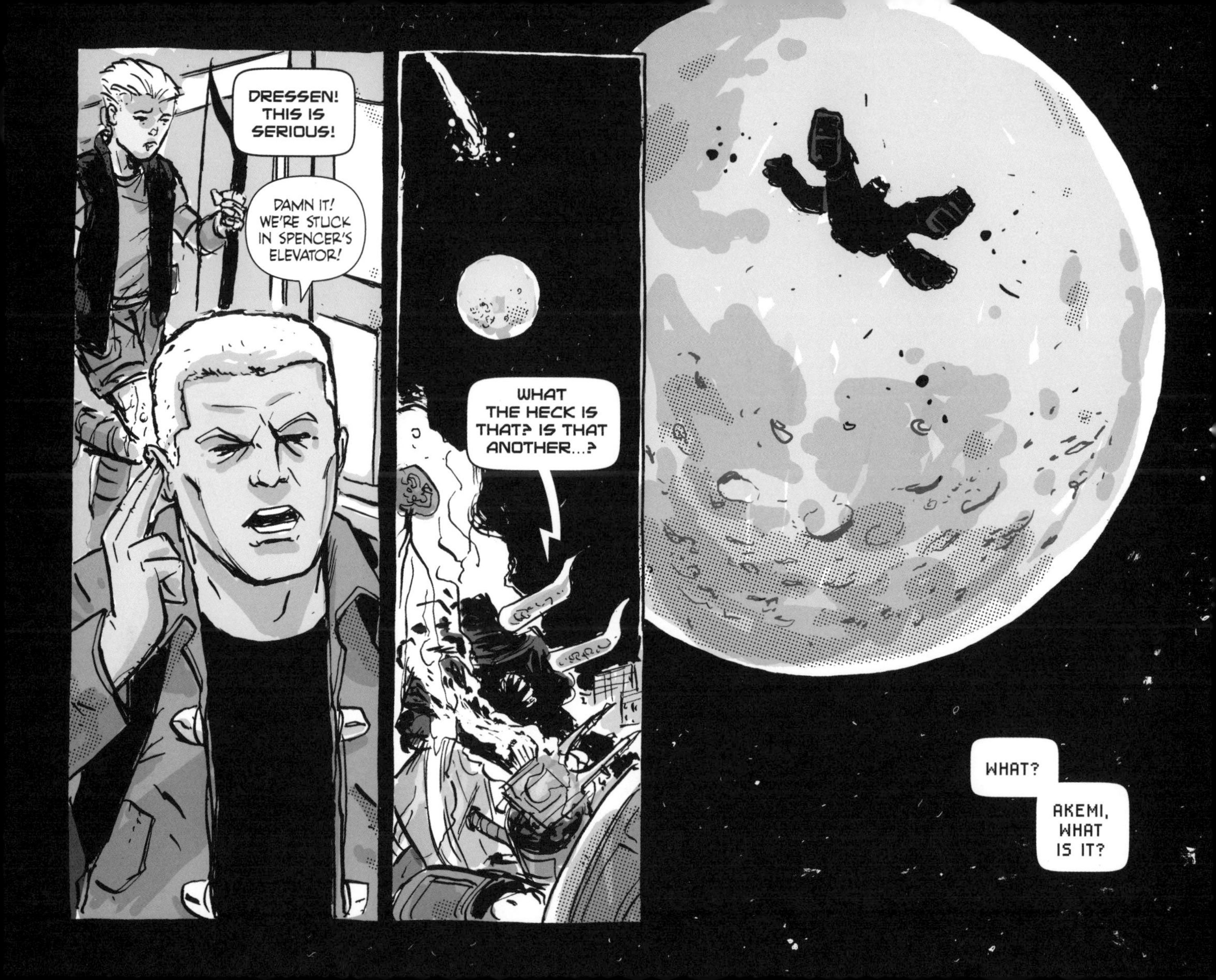
DRESSEN! THIS IS SERIOUS!
DAMN IT! WE'RE STUCK IN SPENCER'S ELEVATOR!
WHAT THE HECK IS THAT? IS THAT ANOTHER...?
WHAT?
AKEMI, WHAT IS IT?

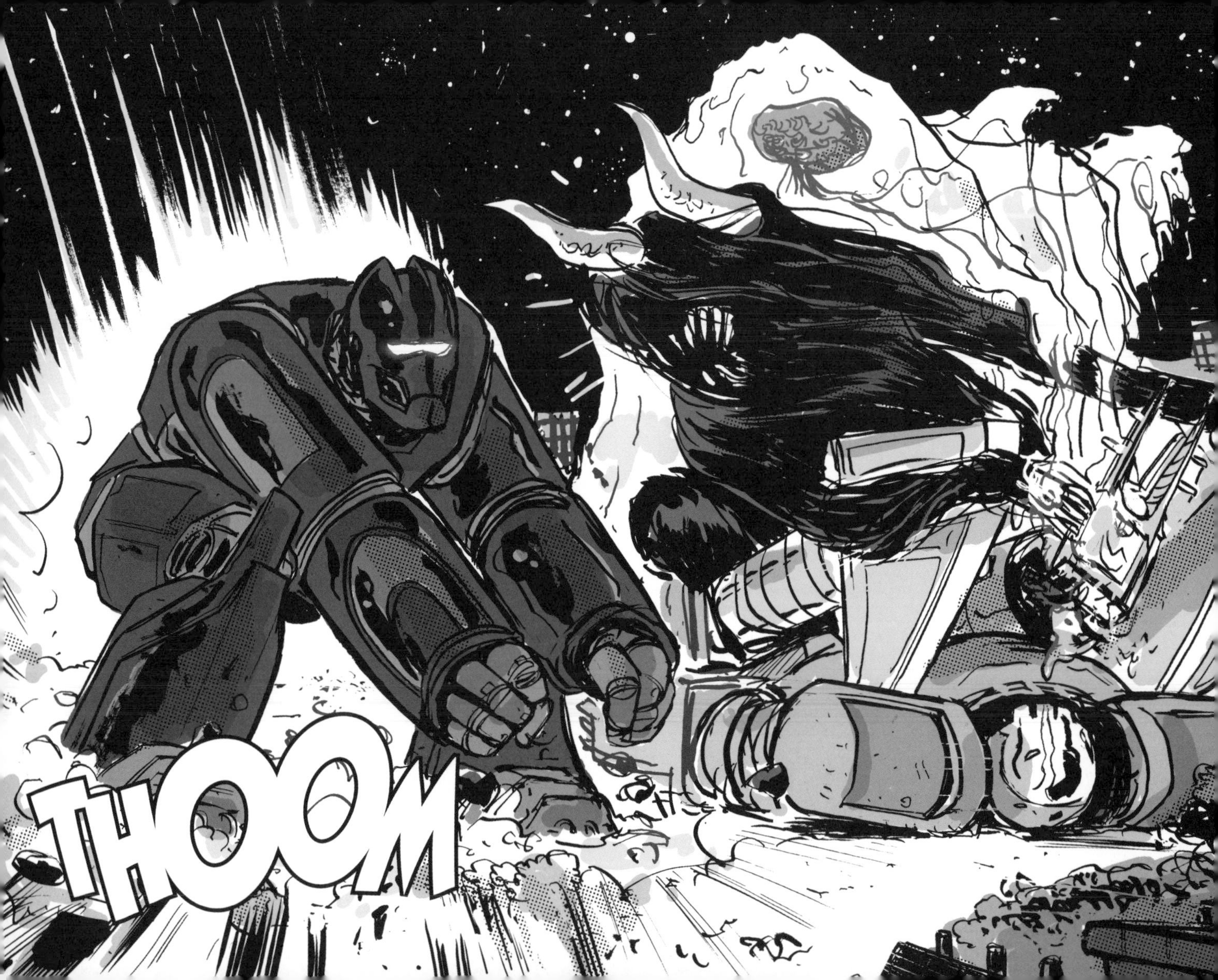
THOOM

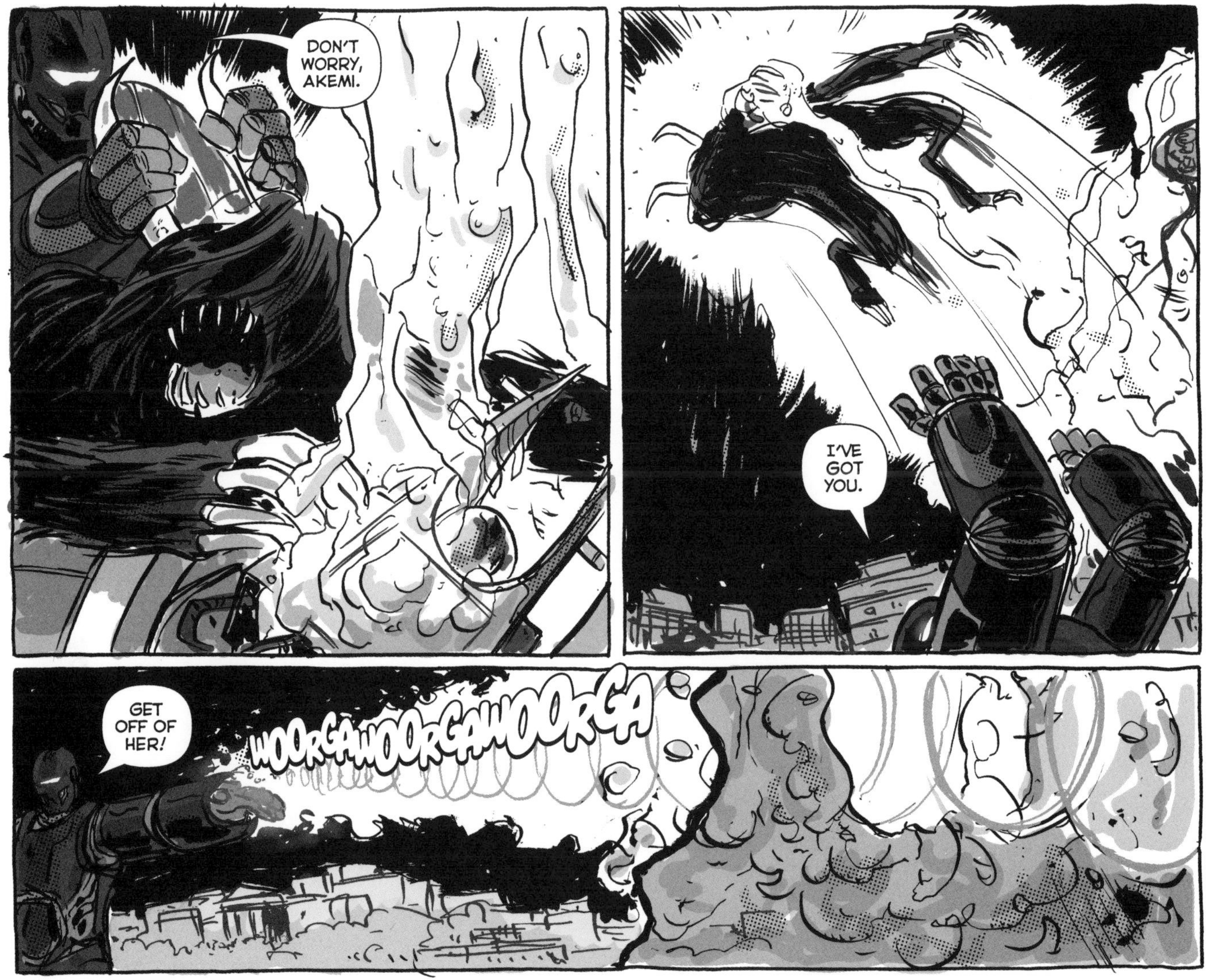
DON'T WORRY, AKEMI.
I'VE GOT YOU.
GET OFF OF HER!
WOORGAWOORGAWOORGA

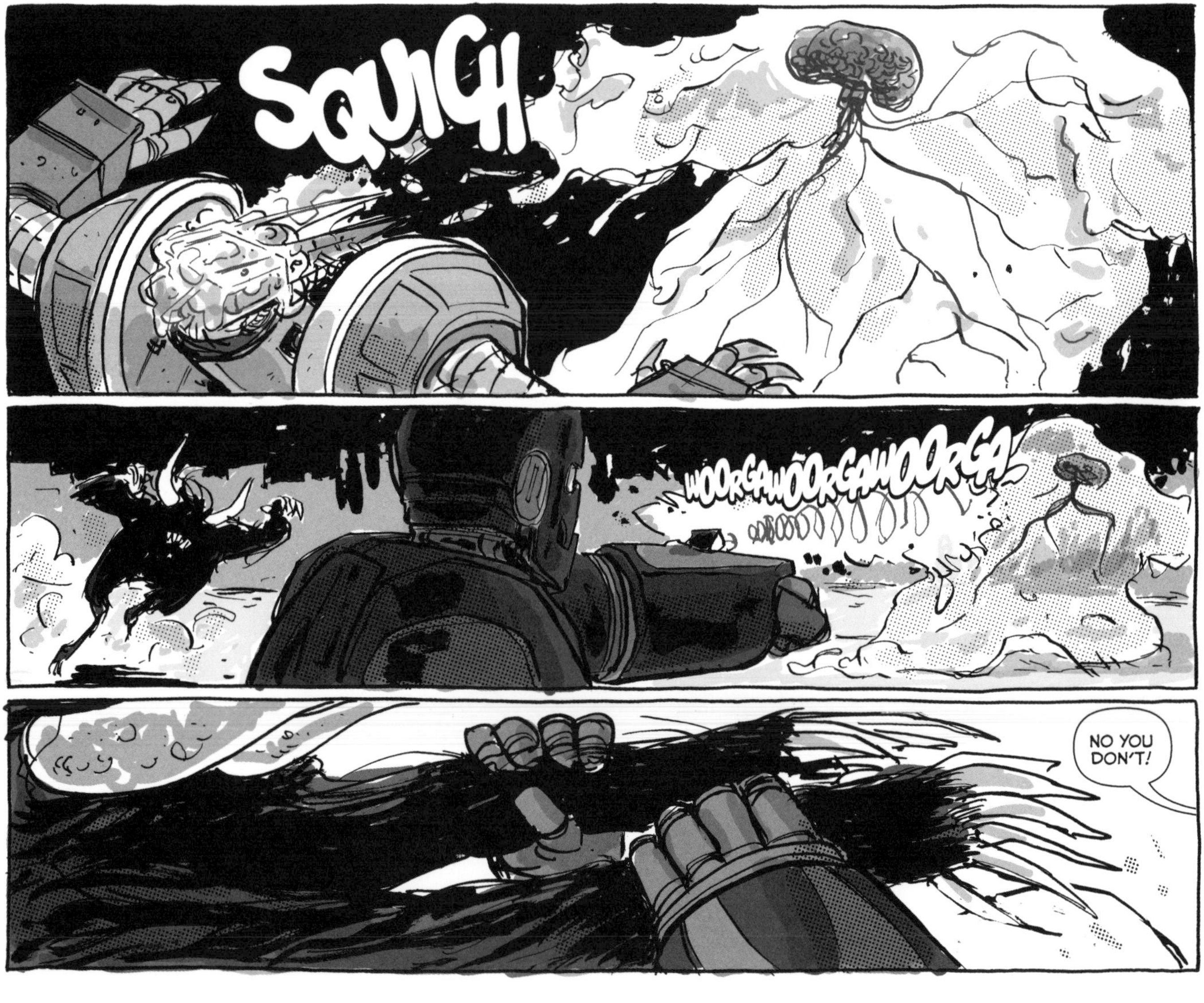
SQUICH
WOORGAWOORGAWOORGA
NO YOU DON'T!

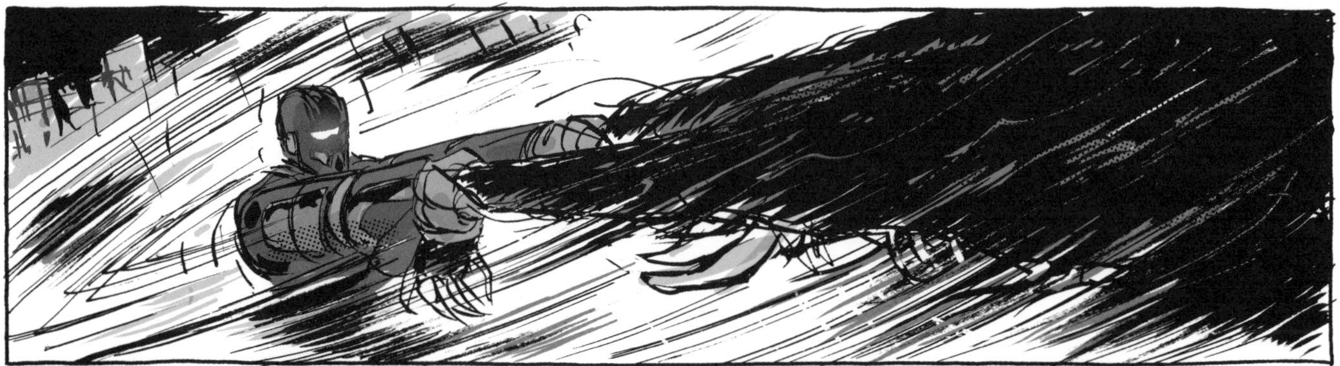

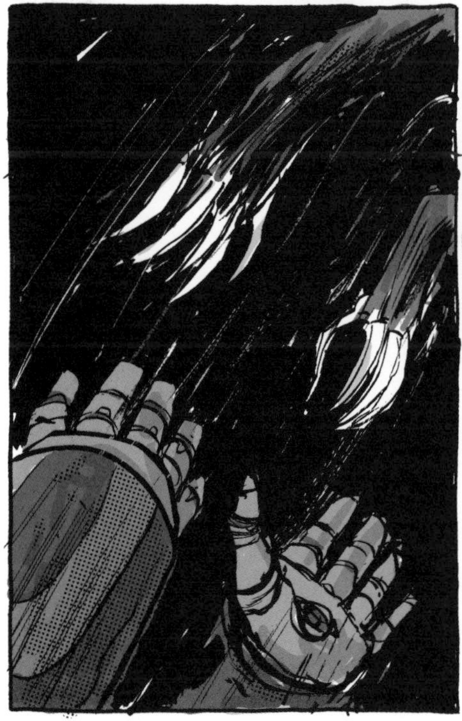

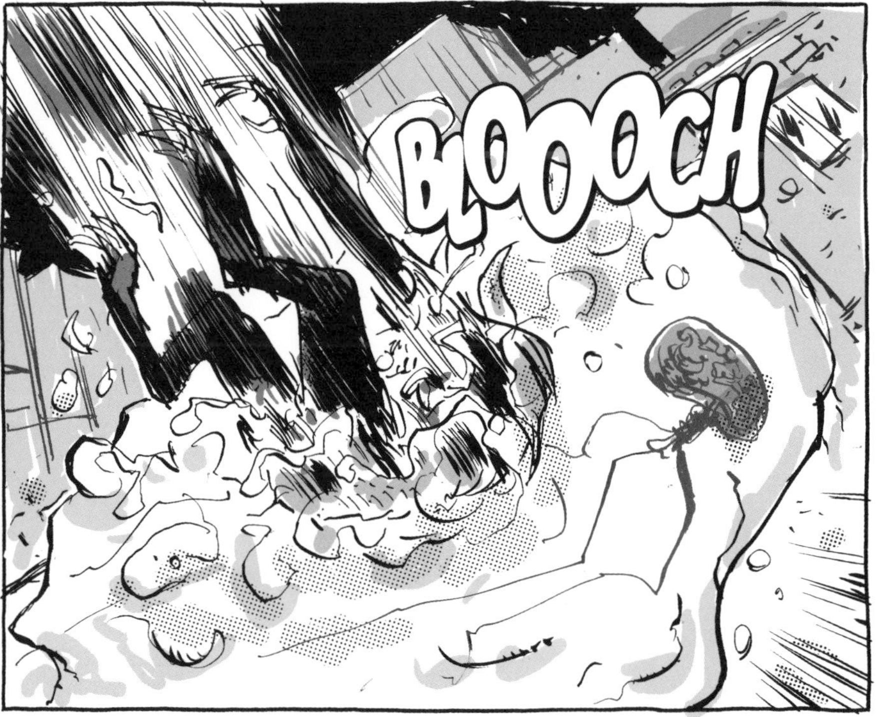
BLOOOCH

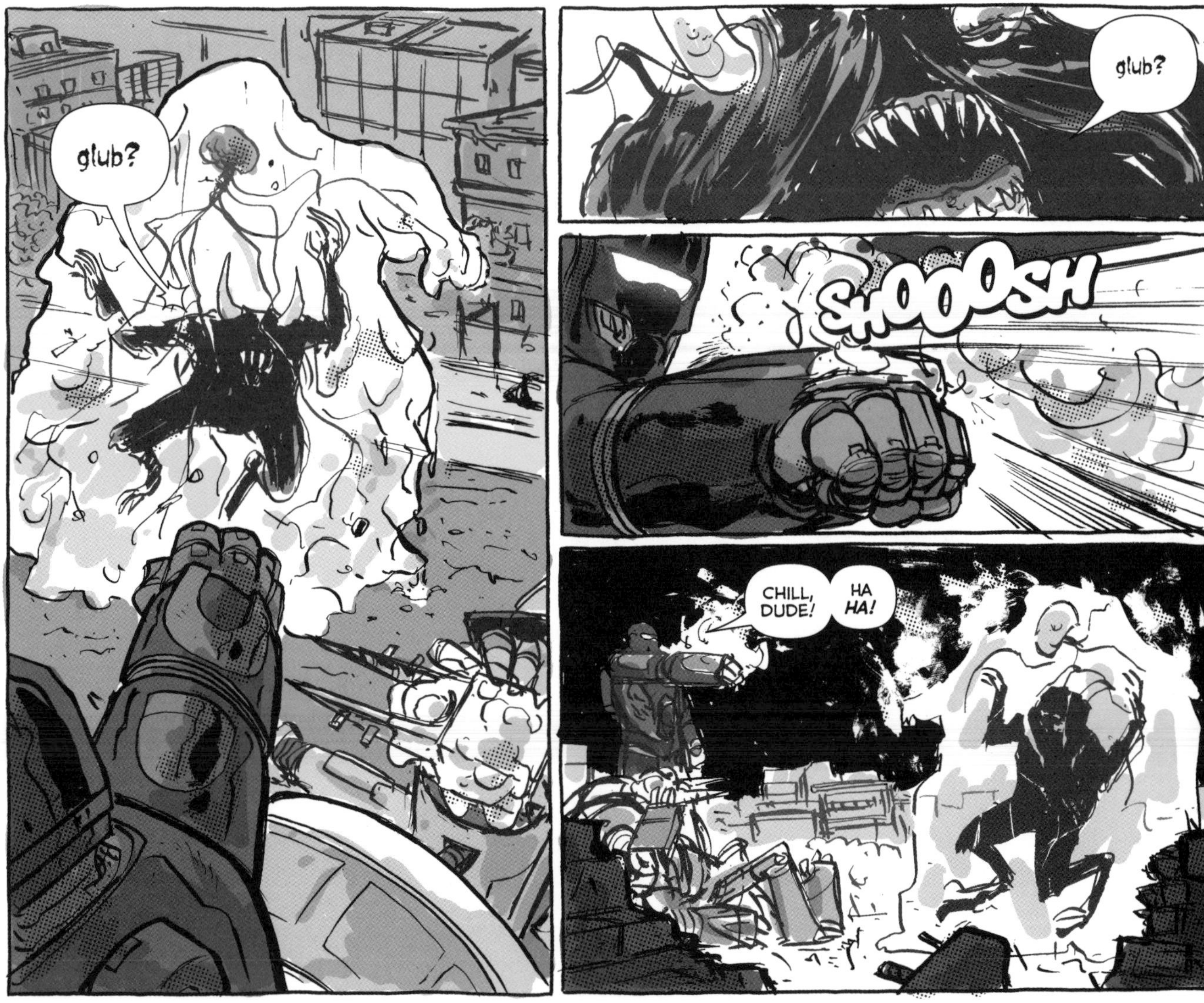
glub?
glub?
SHOOOOSH
CHILL, DUDE!
HA *HA!*

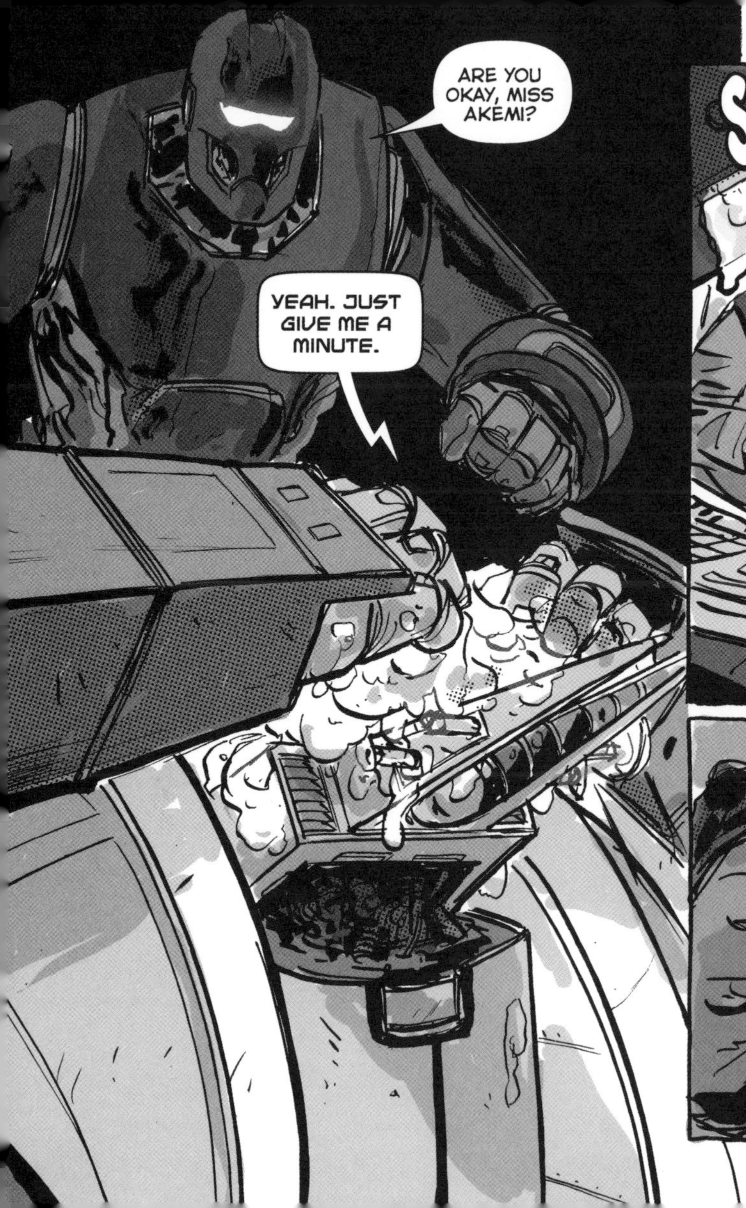
ARE YOU OKAY, MISS AKEMI?
YEAH. JUST GIVE ME A MINUTE.

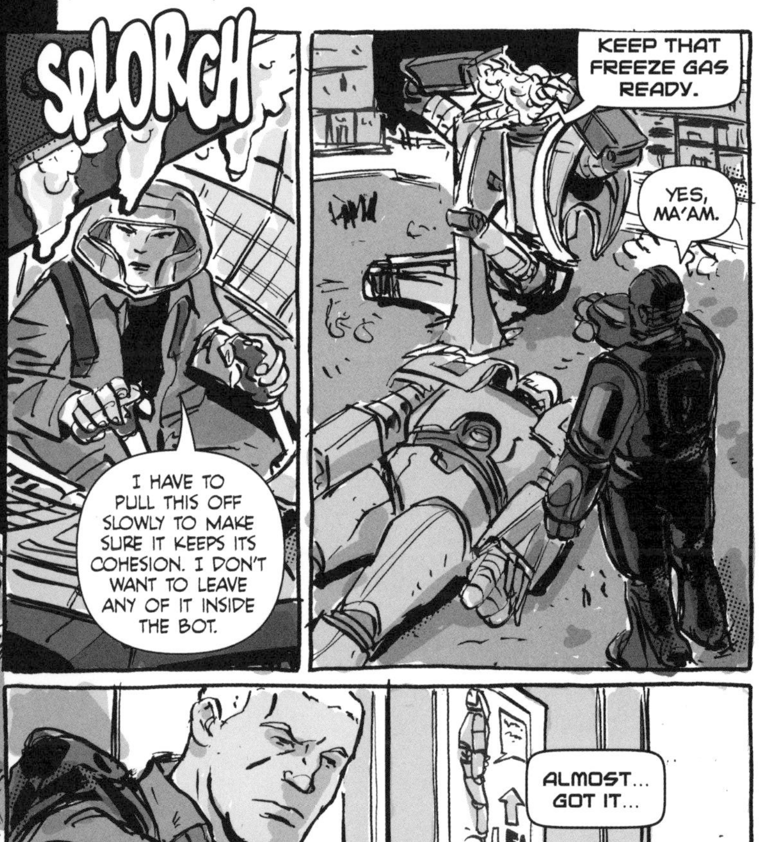
SPLORCH
I HAVE TO PULL THIS OFF SLOWLY TO MAKE SURE IT KEEPS ITS COHESION. I DON'T WANT TO LEAVE ANY OF IT INSIDE THE BOT.
KEEP THAT FREEZE GAS READY.
YES, MA'AM.
ALMOST... GOT IT...

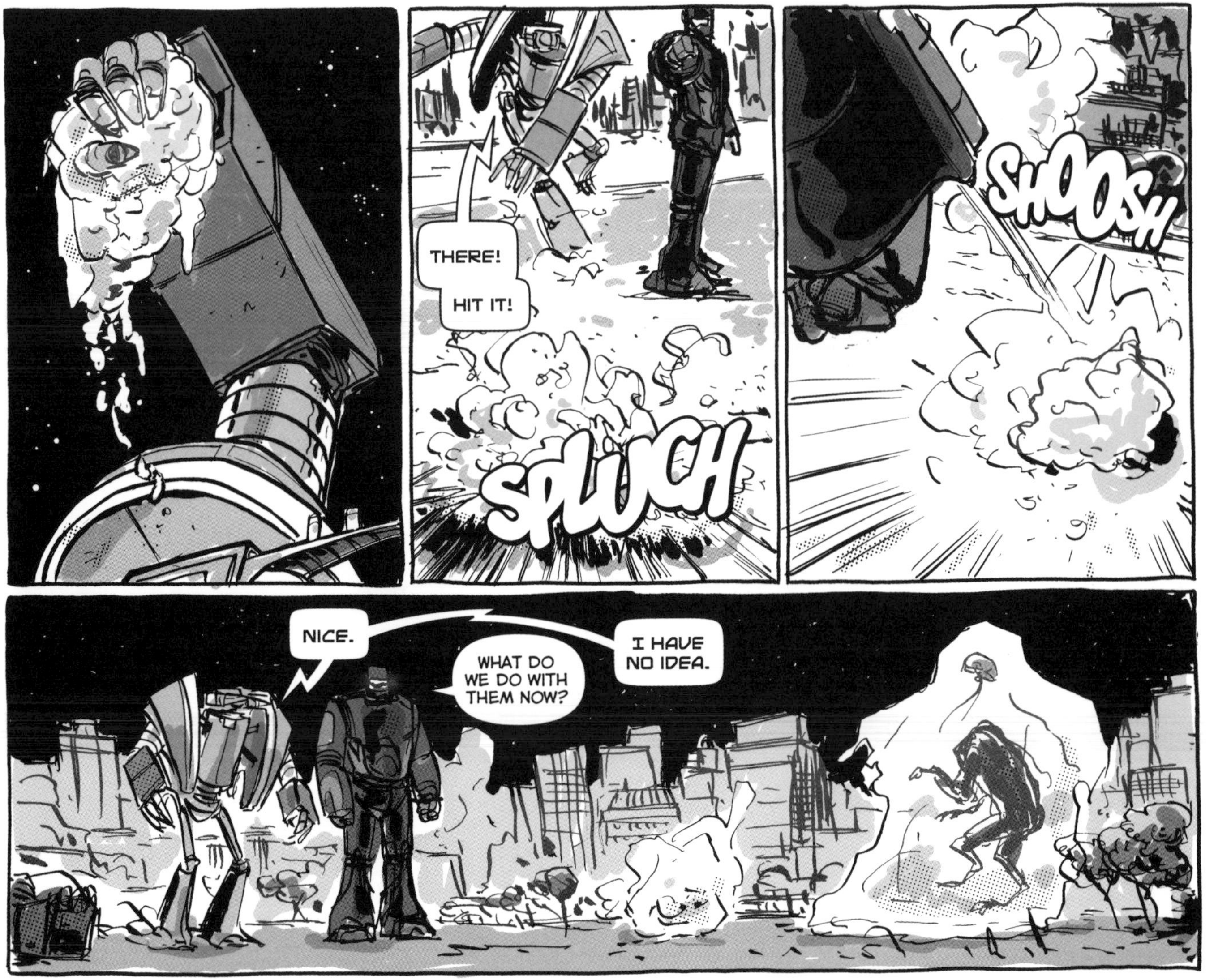
THERE!
HIT IT!
SPLUCH
SHOOSH
NICE.
WHAT DO WE DO WITH THEM NOW?
I HAVE NO IDEA.

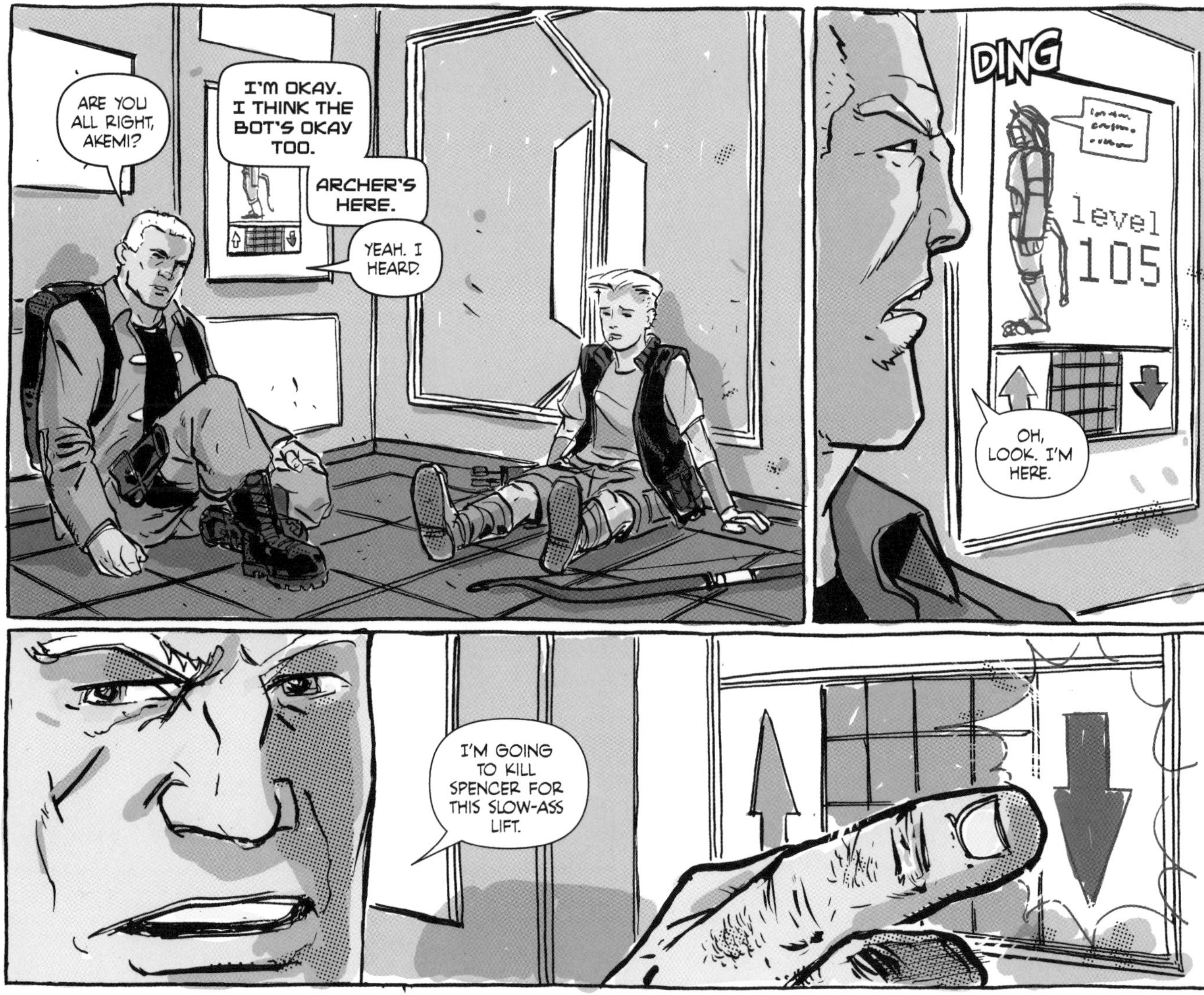
ARE YOU ALL RIGHT, AKEMI?
I'M OKAY. I THINK THE BOT'S OKAY TOO.
ARCHER'S HERE.
YEAH. I HEARD.
DING
level
105
OH, LOOK. I'M HERE.
I'M GOING TO KILL SPENCER FOR THIS SLOW-ASS LIFT.

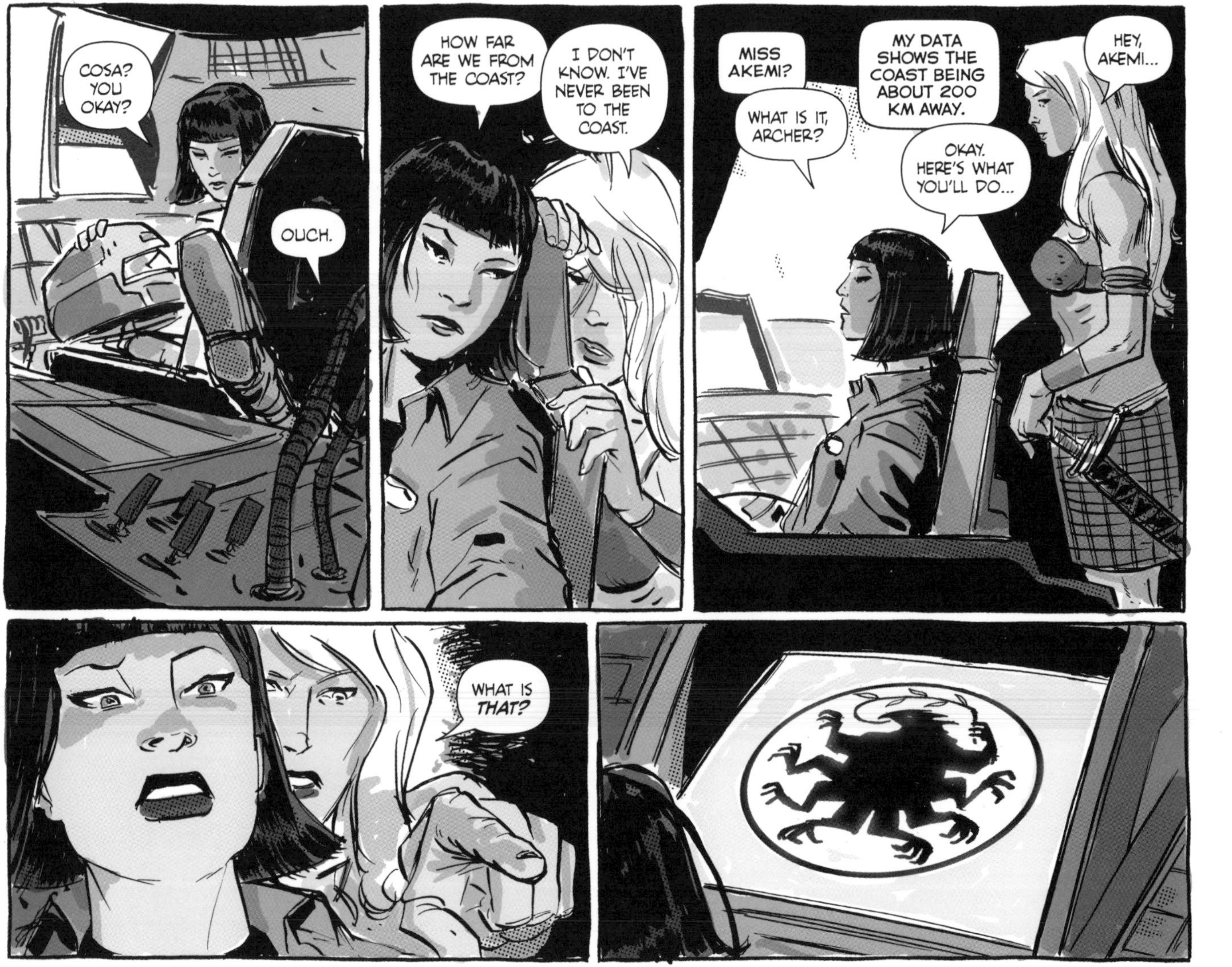
COSA? YOU OKAY?
OUCH.
HOW FAR ARE WE FROM THE COAST?
I DON'T KNOW. I'VE NEVER BEEN TO THE COAST.
MISS AKEMI?
WHAT IS IT, ARCHER?
MY DATA SHOWS THE COAST BEING ABOUT 200 KM AWAY.
OKAY. HERE'S WHAT YOU'LL DO...
HEY, AKEMI...
WHAT IS *THAT?*

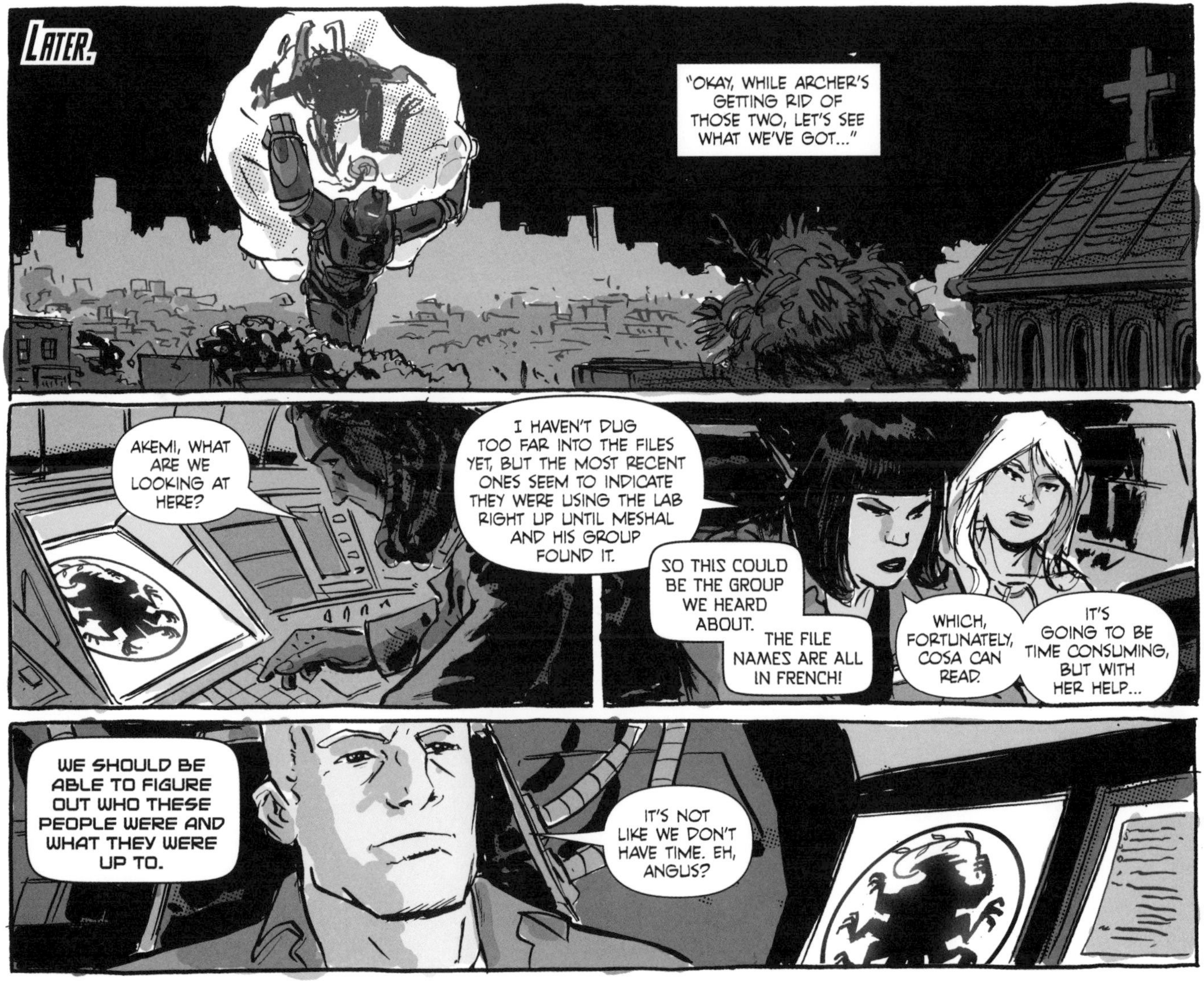
LATER.
"OKAY, WHILE ARCHER'S GETTING RID OF THOSE TWO, LET'S SEE WHAT WE'VE GOT..."
AKEMI, WHAT ARE WE LOOKING AT HERE?
I HAVEN'T DUG TOO FAR INTO THE FILES YET, BUT THE MOST RECENT ONES SEEM TO INDICATE THEY WERE USING THE LAB RIGHT UP UNTIL MESHAL AND HIS GROUP FOUND IT.
SO THIS COULD BE THE GROUP WE HEARD ABOUT.
THE FILE NAMES ARE ALL IN FRENCH!
WHICH, FORTUNATELY, COSA CAN READ.
IT'S GOING TO BE TIME CONSUMING, BUT WITH HER HELP...
WE SHOULD BE ABLE TO FIGURE OUT WHO THESE PEOPLE WERE AND WHAT THEY WERE UP TO.
IT'S NOT LIKE WE DON'T HAVE TIME. EH, ANGUS?

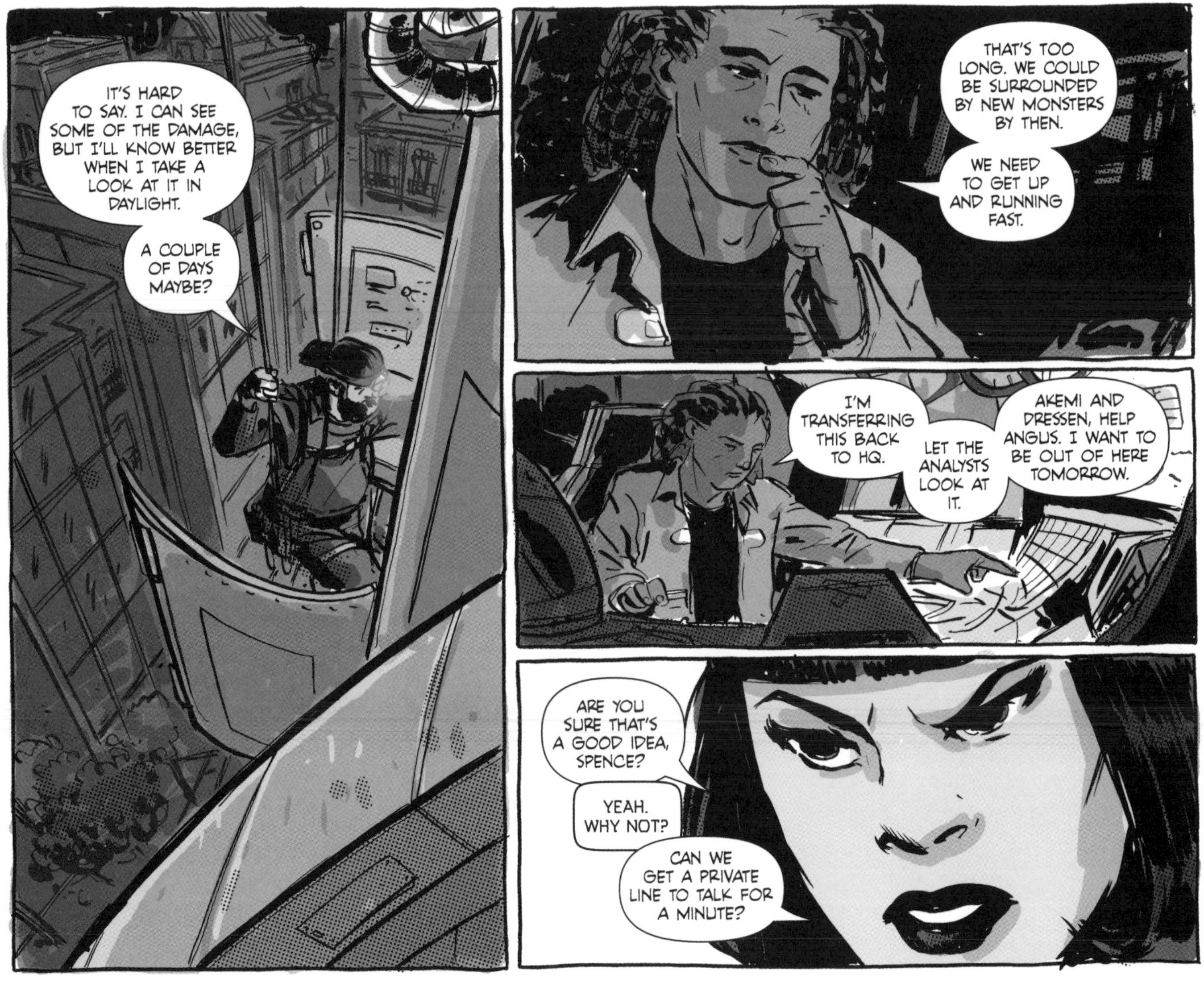
IT'S HARD TO SAY. I CAN SEE SOME OF THE DAMAGE, BUT I'LL KNOW BETTER WHEN I TAKE A LOOK AT IT IN DAYLIGHT.
A COUPLE OF DAYS MAYBE?
THAT'S TOO LONG. WE COULD BE SURROUNDED BY NEW MONSTERS BY THEN.
WE NEED TO GET UP AND RUNNING FAST.
I'M TRANSFERRING THIS BACK TO HQ.
LET THE ANALYSTS LOOK AT IT.
AKEMI AND DRESSEN, HELP ANGUS. I WANT TO BE OUT OF HERE TOMORROW.
ARE YOU SURE THAT'S A GOOD IDEA, SPENCE?
YEAH. WHY NOT?
CAN WE GET A PRIVATE LINE TO TALK FOR A MINUTE?

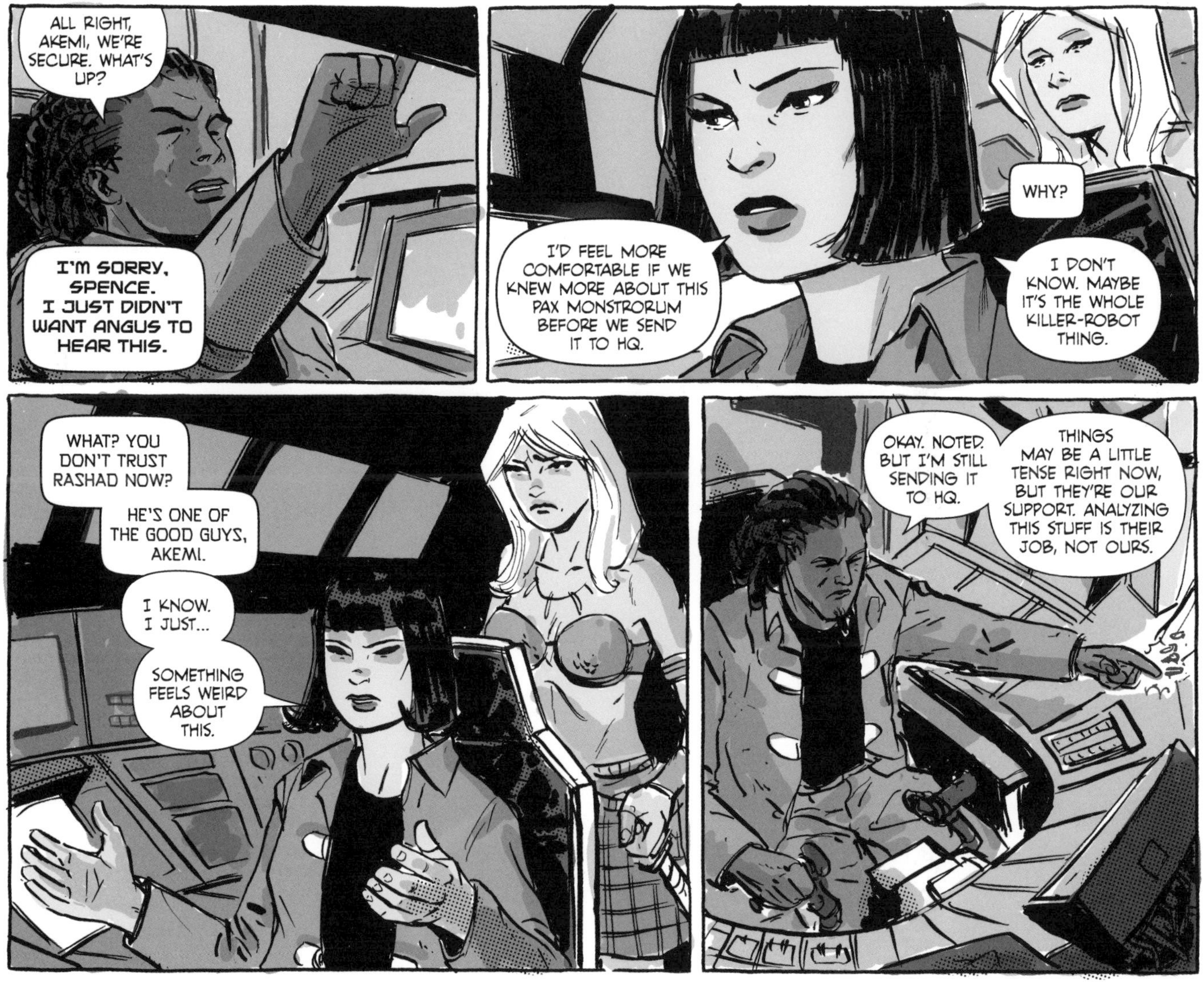
ALL RIGHT, AKEMI, WE'RE SECURE. WHAT'S UP?
I'M SORRY, SPENCE. I JUST DIDN'T WANT ANGUS TO HEAR THIS.
I'D FEEL MORE COMFORTABLE IF WE KNEW MORE ABOUT THIS PAX MONSTRORUM BEFORE WE SEND IT TO HQ.
WHY?
I DON'T KNOW. MAYBE IT'S THE WHOLE KILLER-ROBOT THING.
WHAT? YOU DON'T TRUST RASHAD NOW?
HE'S ONE OF THE GOOD GUYS, AKEMI.
I KNOW. I JUST...
SOMETHING FEELS WEIRD ABOUT THIS.
OKAY. NOTED. BUT I'M STILL SENDING IT TO HQ.
THINGS MAY BE A LITTLE TENSE RIGHT NOW, BUT THEY'RE OUR SUPPORT. ANALYZING THIS STUFF IS THEIR JOB, NOT OURS.

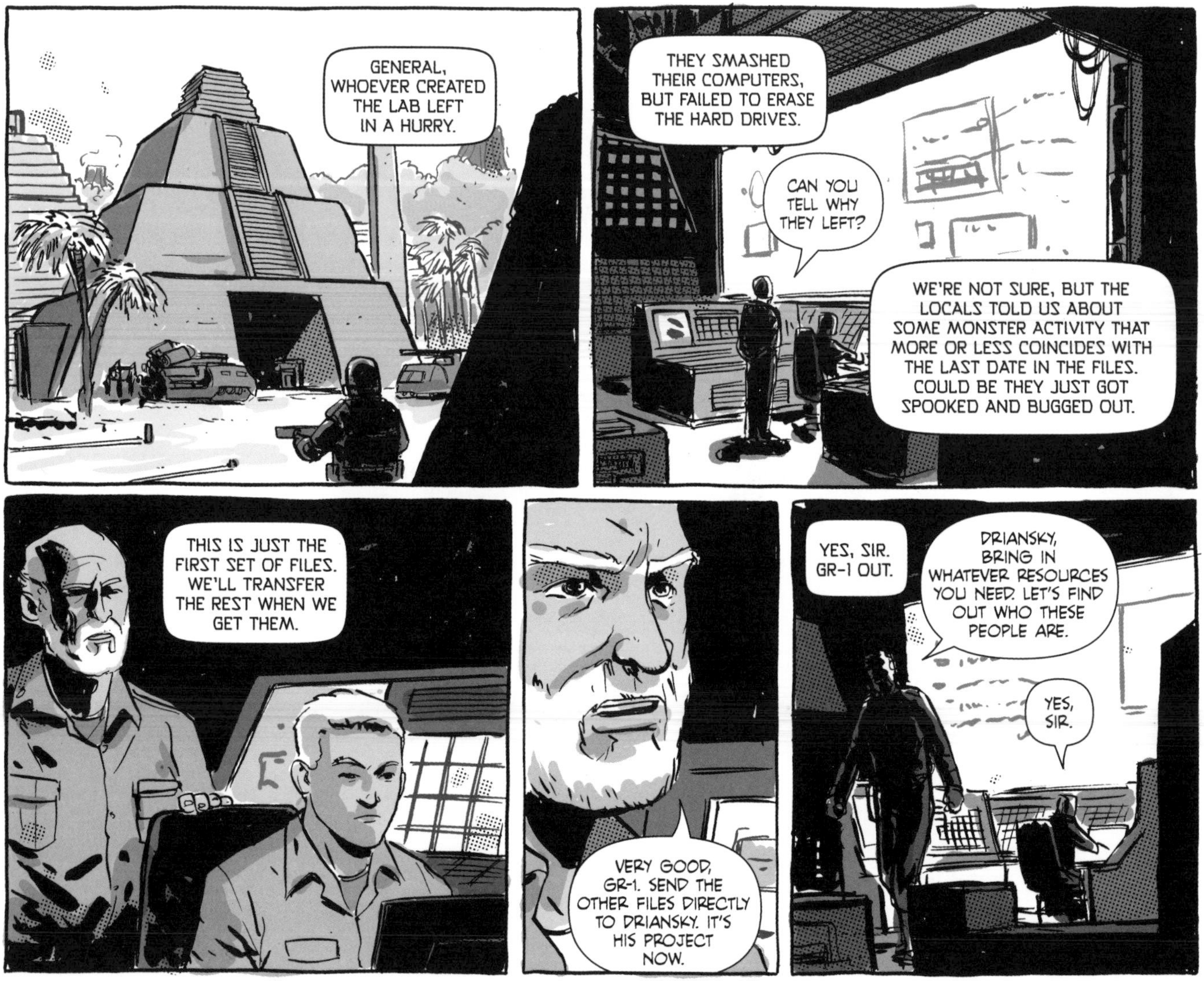
GENERAL, WHOEVER CREATED THE LAB LEFT IN A HURRY.
THEY SMASHED THEIR COMPUTERS, BUT FAILED TO ERASE THE HARD DRIVES.
CAN YOU TELL WHY THEY LEFT?
WE'RE NOT SURE, BUT THE LOCALS TOLD US ABOUT SOME MONSTER ACTIVITY THAT MORE OR LESS COINCIDES WITH THE LAST DATE IN THE FILES. COULD BE THEY JUST GOT SPOOKED AND BUGGED OUT.
THIS IS JUST THE FIRST SET OF FILES. WE'LL TRANSFER THE REST WHEN WE GET THEM.
VERY GOOD, GR-1. SEND THE OTHER FILES DIRECTLY TO DRIANSKY. IT'S HIS PROJECT NOW.
YES, SIR. GR-1 OUT.
DRIANSKY, BRING IN WHATEVER RESOURCES YOU NEED. LET'S FIND OUT WHO THESE PEOPLE ARE.
YES, SIR.

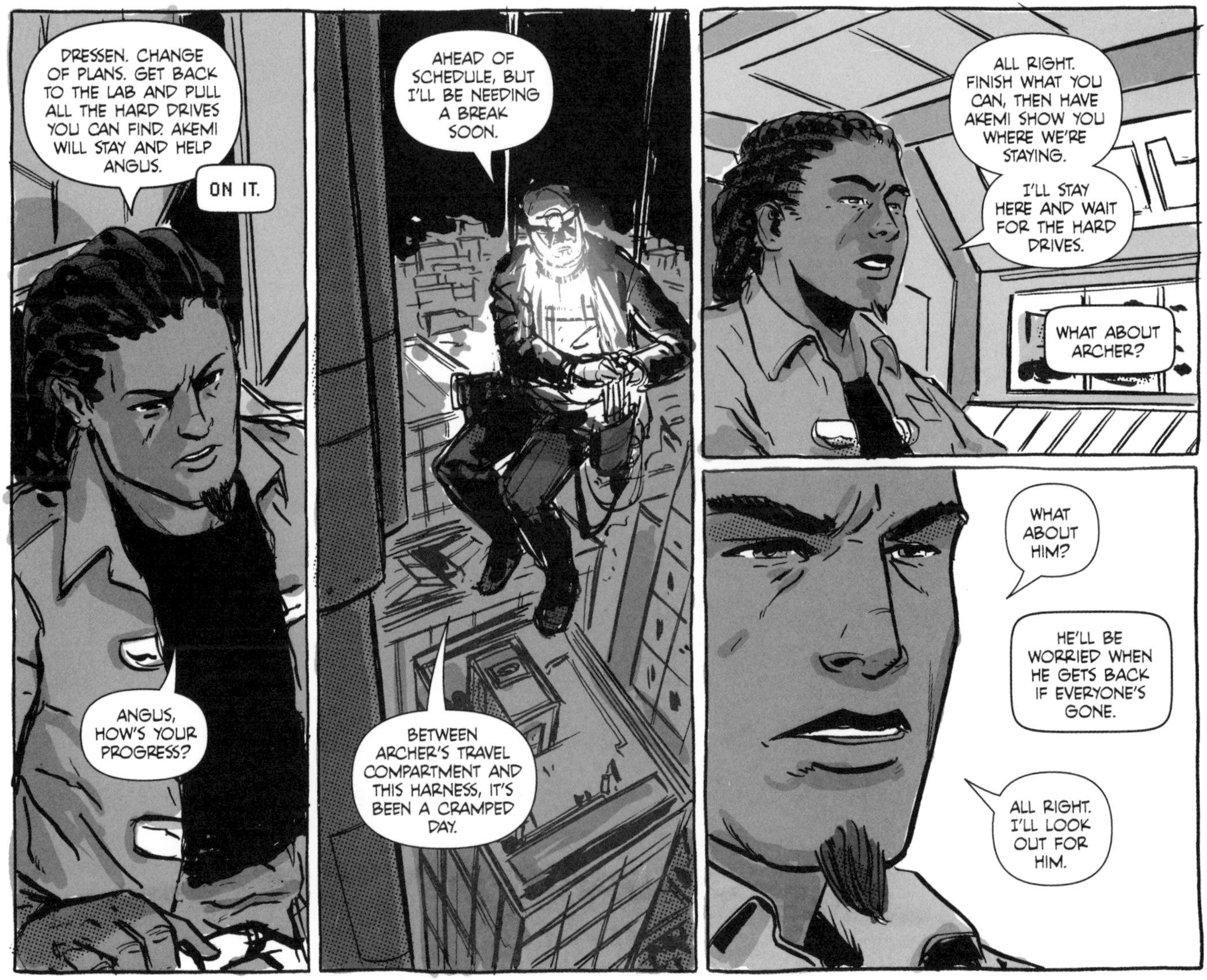
DRESSEN. CHANGE OF PLANS. GET BACK TO THE LAB AND PULL ALL THE HARD DRIVES YOU CAN FIND. AKEMI WILL STAY AND HELP ANGUS.
ON IT.
ANGUS, HOW'S YOUR PROGRESS?
AHEAD OF SCHEDULE, BUT I'LL BE NEEDING A BREAK SOON.
BETWEEN ARCHER'S TRAVEL COMPARTMENT AND THIS HARNESS, IT'S BEEN A CRAMPED DAY.
ALL RIGHT. FINISH WHAT YOU CAN, THEN HAVE AKEMI SHOW YOU WHERE WE'RE STAYING.
I'LL STAY HERE AND WAIT FOR THE HARD DRIVES.
WHAT ABOUT ARCHER?
WHAT ABOUT HIM?
HE'LL BE WORRIED WHEN HE GETS BACK IF EVERYONE'S GONE.
ALL RIGHT. I'LL LOOK OUT FOR HIM.

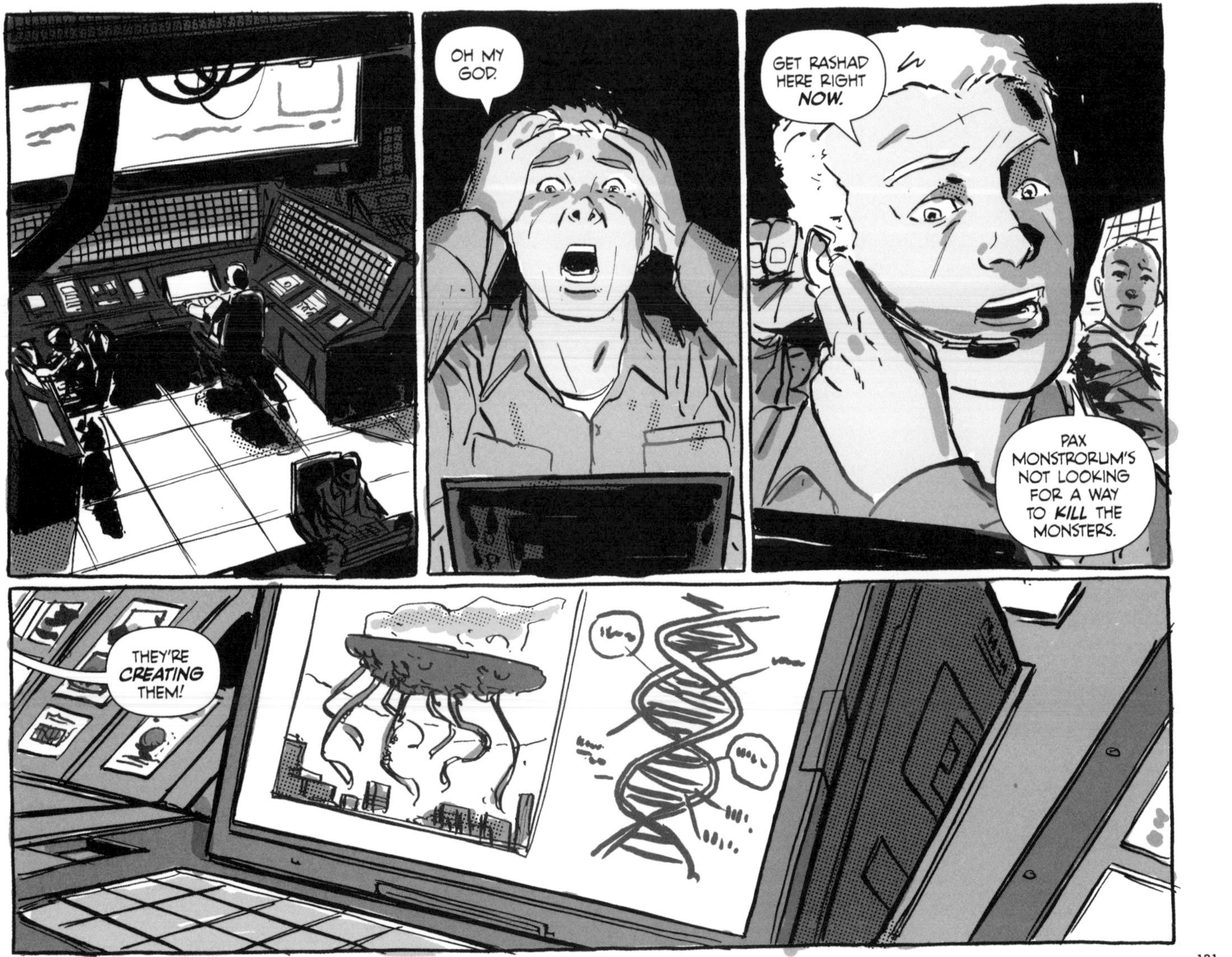
OH MY GOD.
GET RASHAD HERE RIGHT ***NOW.***
PAX MONSTRORUM'S NOT LOOKING FOR A WAY TO ***KILL*** THE MONSTERS.
THEY'RE ***CREATING*** THEM!

CHAPTER SIX INTO THE TREES

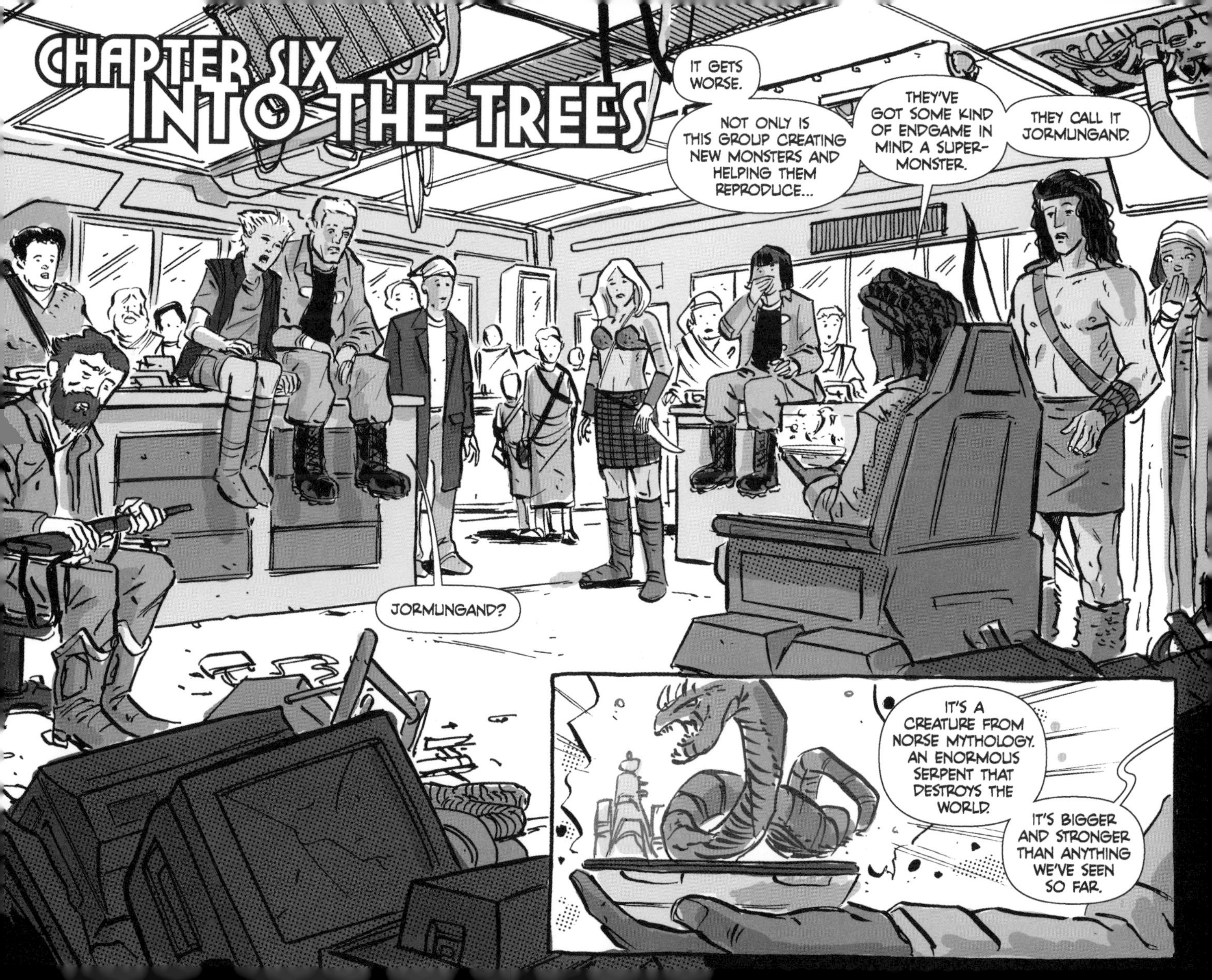
IT GETS WORSE.
NOT ONLY IS THIS GROUP CREATING NEW MONSTERS AND HELPING THEM REPRODUCE...
THEY'VE GOT SOME KIND OF ENDGAME IN MIND. A SUPER-MONSTER.
THEY CALL IT JORMUNGAND.
JORMUNGAND?
IT'S A CREATURE FROM NORSE MYTHOLOGY. AN ENORMOUS SERPENT THAT DESTROYS THE WORLD.
IT'S BIGGER AND STRONGER THAN ANYTHING WE'VE SEEN SO FAR.

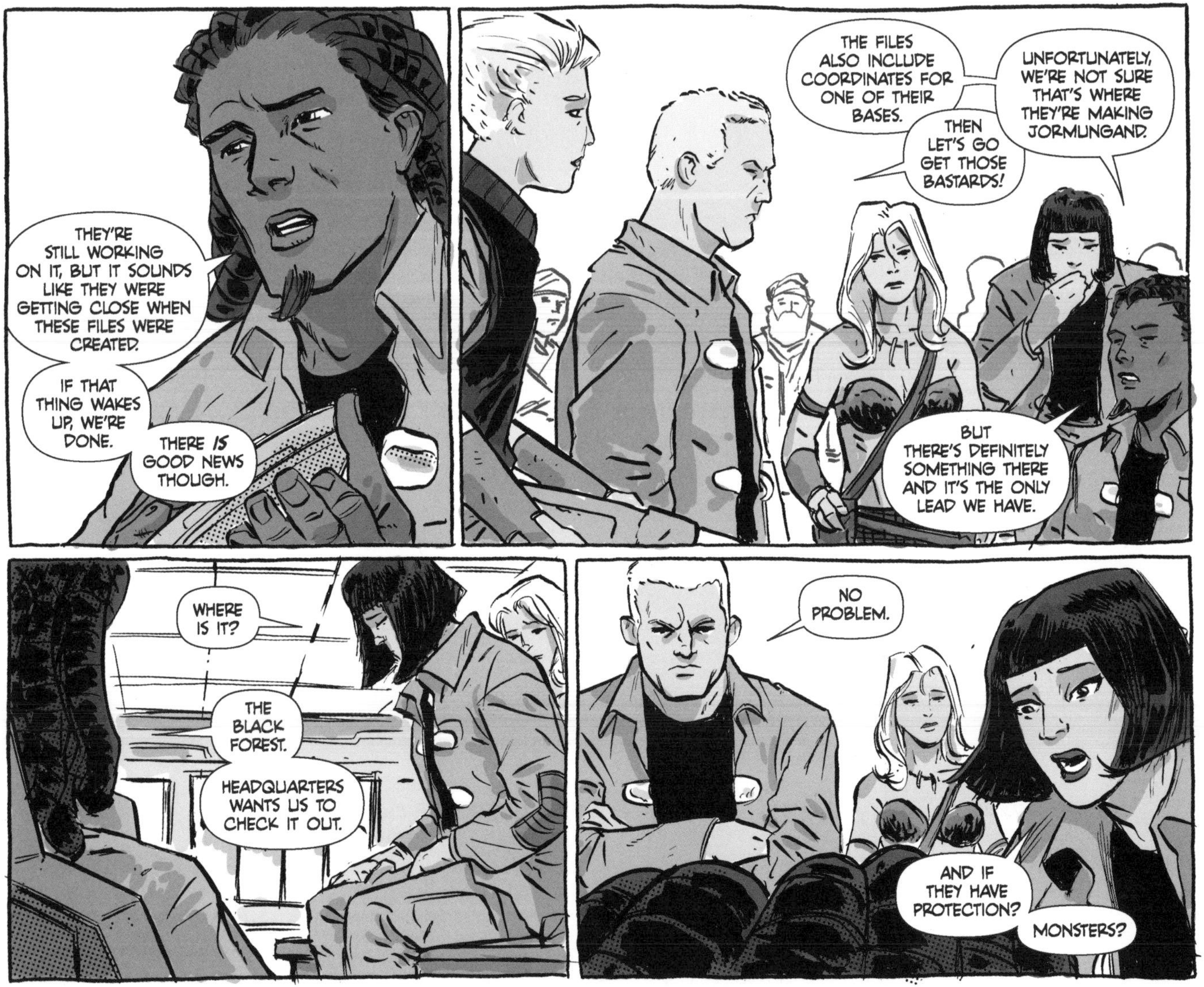
THEY'RE STILL WORKING ON IT, BUT IT SOUNDS LIKE THEY WERE GETTING CLOSE WHEN THESE FILES WERE CREATED.
IF THAT THING WAKES UP, WE'RE DONE.
THERE *IS* GOOD NEWS THOUGH.
THE FILES ALSO INCLUDE COORDINATES FOR ONE OF THEIR BASES.
UNFORTUNATELY, WE'RE NOT SURE THAT'S WHERE THEY'RE MAKING JORMUNGAND.
THEN LET'S GO GET THOSE BASTARDS!
BUT THERE'S DEFINITELY SOMETHING THERE AND IT'S THE ONLY LEAD WE HAVE.
WHERE IS IT?
THE BLACK FOREST.
HEADQUARTERS WANTS US TO CHECK IT OUT.
NO PROBLEM.
AND IF THEY HAVE PROTECTION?
MONSTERS?

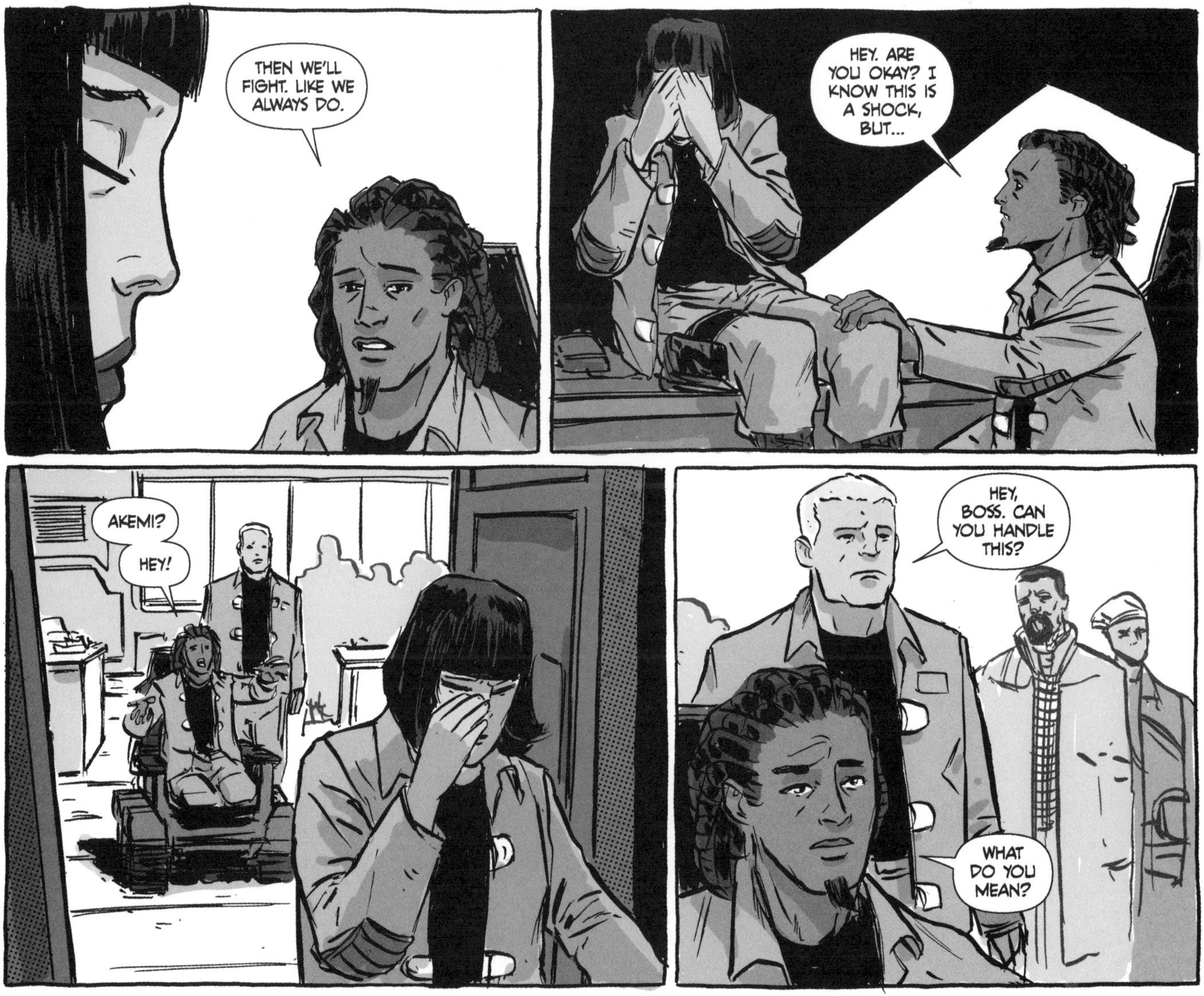
THEN WE'LL FIGHT. LIKE WE ALWAYS DO.
HEY. ARE YOU OKAY? I KNOW THIS IS A SHOCK, BUT...
AKEMI?
HEY!
HEY, BOSS. CAN YOU HANDLE THIS?
WHAT DO YOU MEAN?

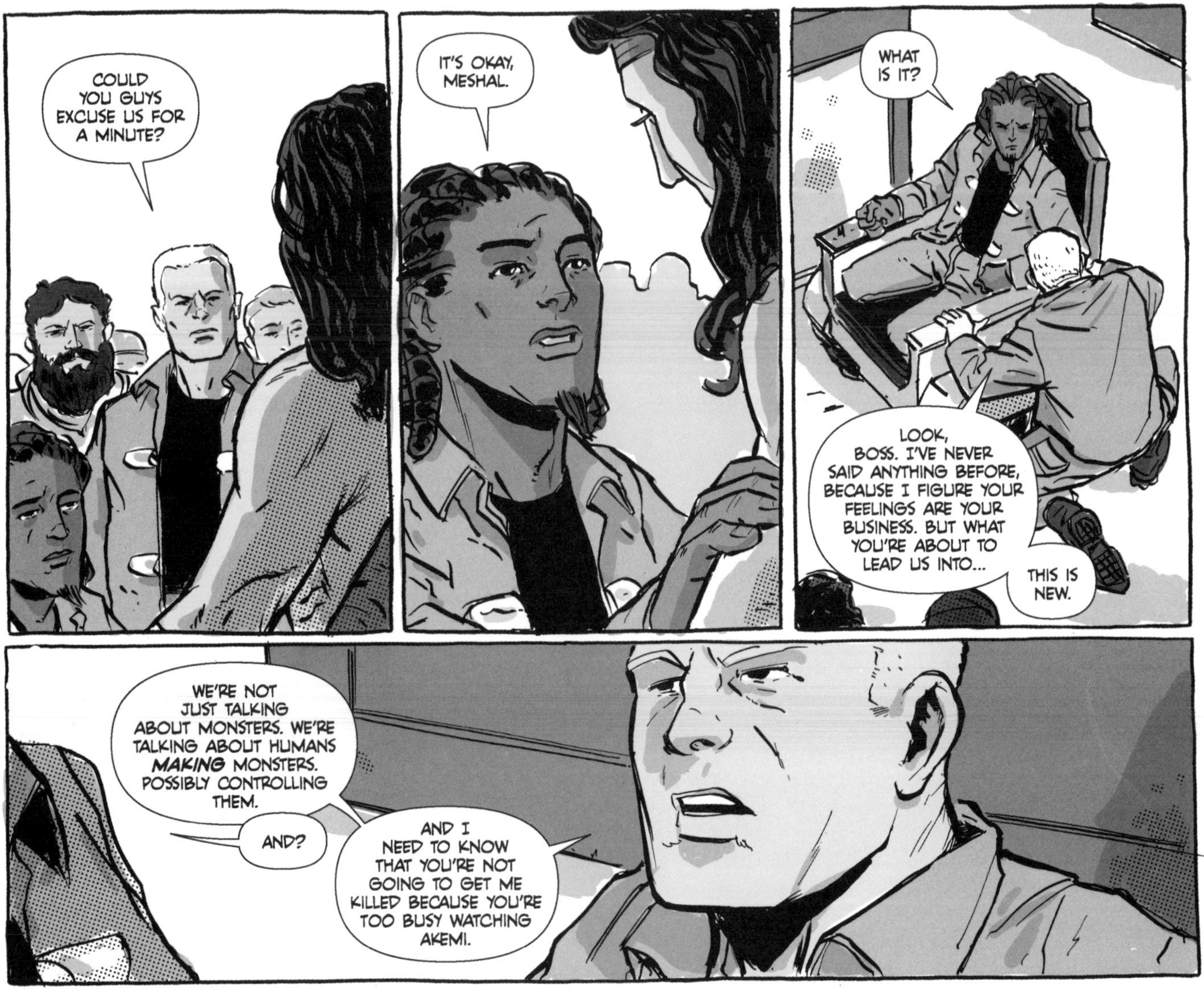
COULD YOU GUYS EXCUSE US FOR A MINUTE?
IT'S OKAY, MESHAL.
WHAT IS IT?
LOOK, BOSS. I'VE NEVER SAID ANYTHING BEFORE, BECAUSE I FIGURE YOUR FEELINGS ARE YOUR BUSINESS. BUT WHAT YOU'RE ABOUT TO LEAD US INTO...
THIS IS NEW.
WE'RE NOT JUST TALKING ABOUT MONSTERS. WE'RE TALKING ABOUT HUMANS **MAKING** MONSTERS. POSSIBLY CONTROLLING THEM.
AND?
AND I NEED TO KNOW THAT YOU'RE NOT GOING TO GET ME KILLED BECAUSE YOU'RE TOO BUSY WATCHING AKEMI.

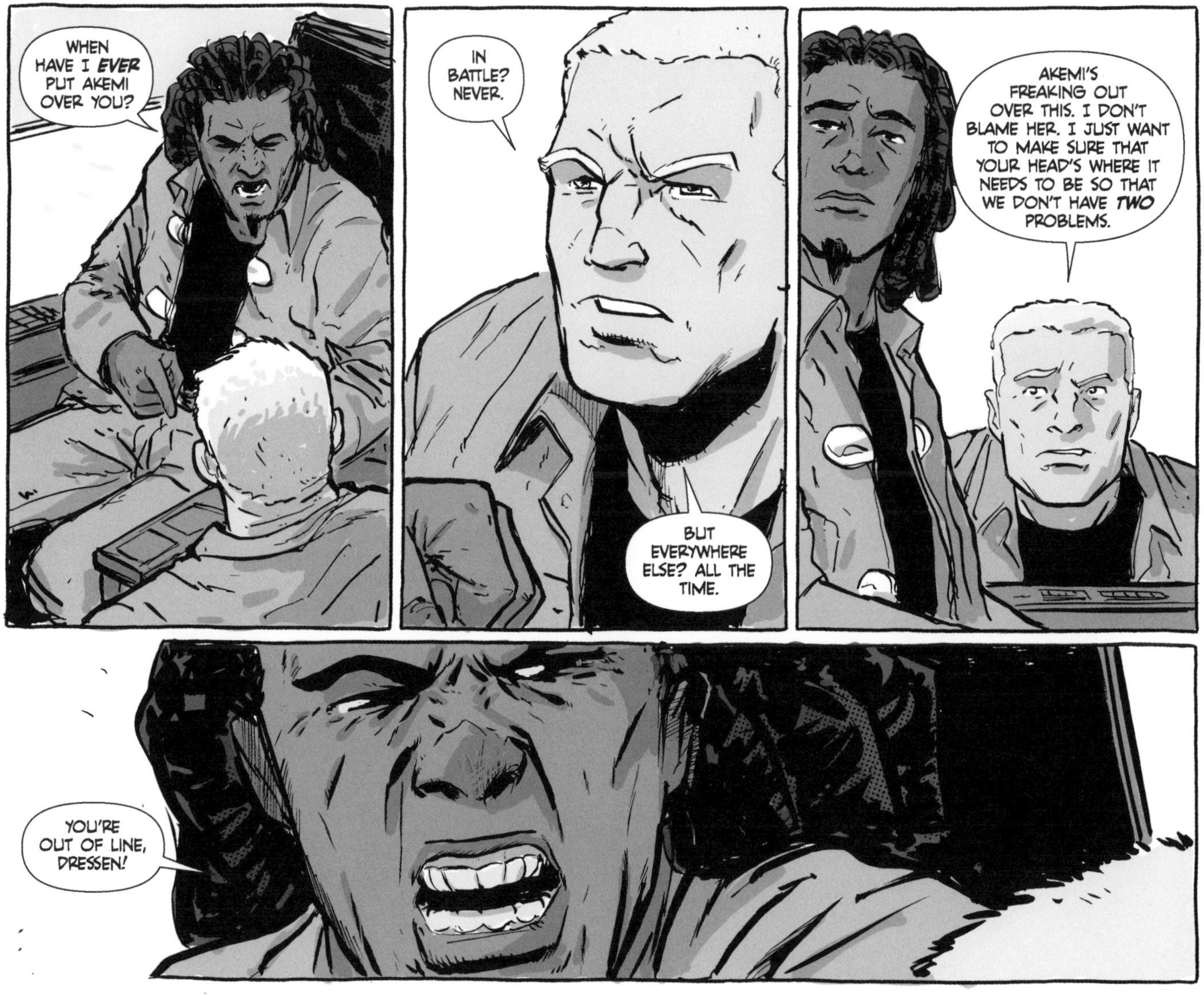
WHEN HAVE I **EVER** PUT AKEMI OVER YOU?
IN BATTLE? NEVER.
BUT EVERYWHERE ELSE? ALL THE TIME.
AKEMI'S FREAKING OUT OVER THIS. I DON'T BLAME HER. I JUST WANT TO MAKE SURE THAT YOUR HEAD'S WHERE IT NEEDS TO BE SO THAT WE DON'T HAVE **TWO** PROBLEMS.
YOU'RE OUT OF LINE, DRESSEN!

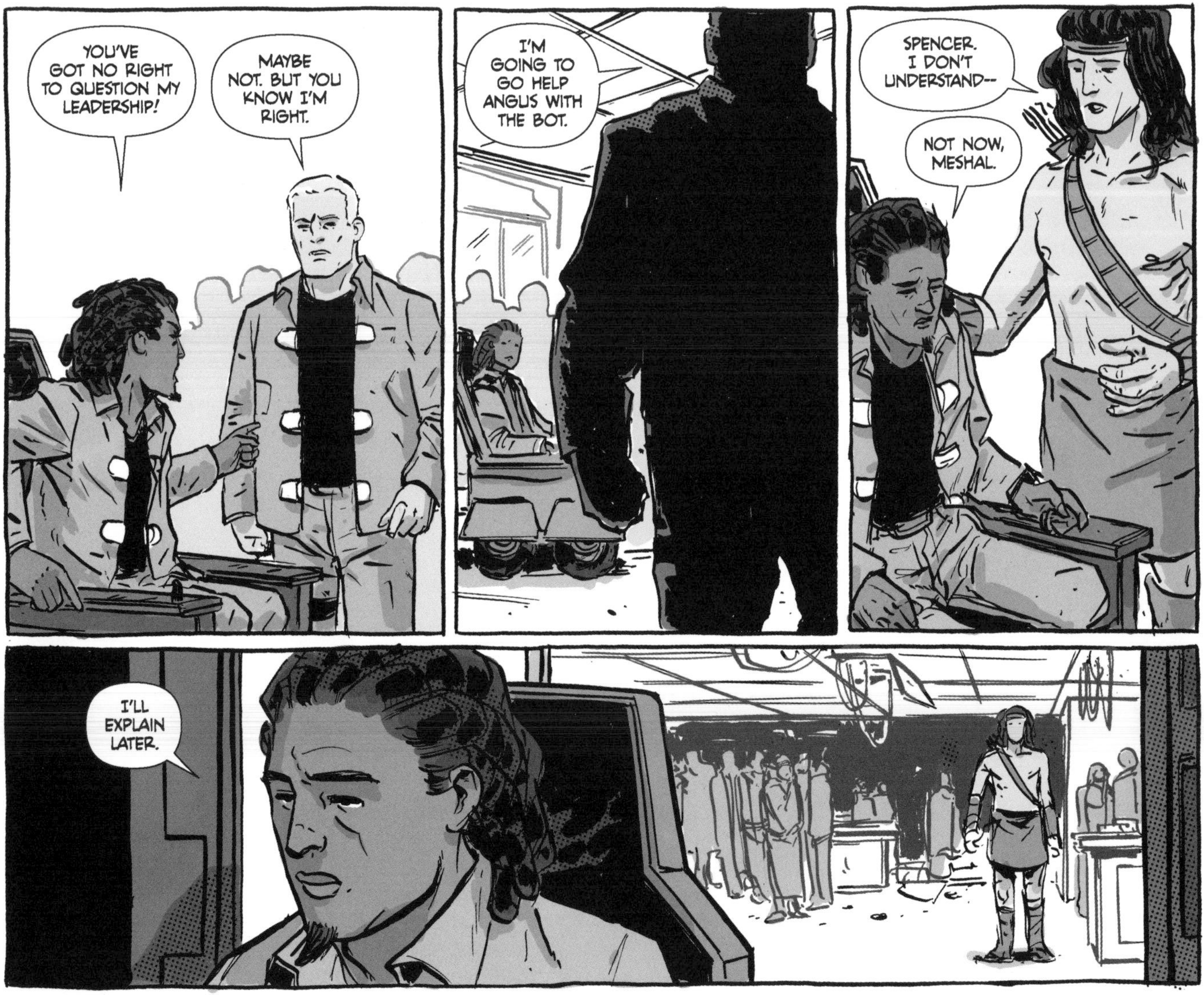
YOU'VE GOT NO RIGHT TO QUESTION MY LEADERSHIP!
MAYBE NOT. BUT YOU KNOW I'M RIGHT.
I'M GOING TO GO HELP ANGUS WITH THE BOT.
SPENCER. I DON'T UNDERSTAND--
NOT NOW, MESHAL.
I'LL EXPLAIN LATER.

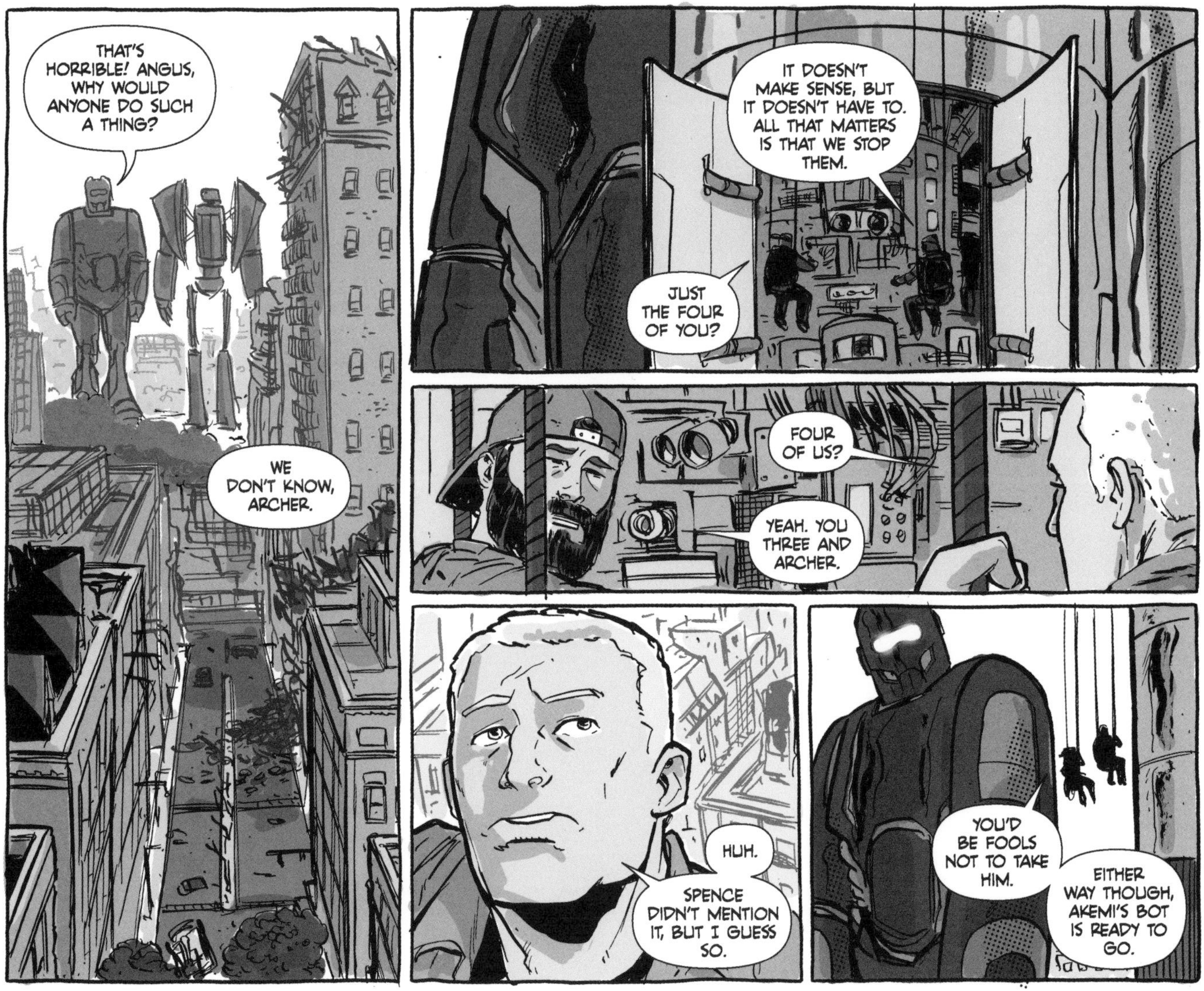
THAT'S HORRIBLE! ANGUS, WHY WOULD ANYONE DO SUCH A THING?
WE DON'T KNOW, ARCHER.
IT DOESN'T MAKE SENSE, BUT IT DOESN'T HAVE TO. ALL THAT MATTERS IS THAT WE STOP THEM.
JUST THE FOUR OF YOU?
FOUR OF US?
YEAH. YOU THREE AND ARCHER.
HUH.
SPENCE DIDN'T MENTION IT, BUT I GUESS SO.
YOU'D BE FOOLS NOT TO TAKE HIM.
EITHER WAY THOUGH, AKEMI'S BOT IS READY TO GO.

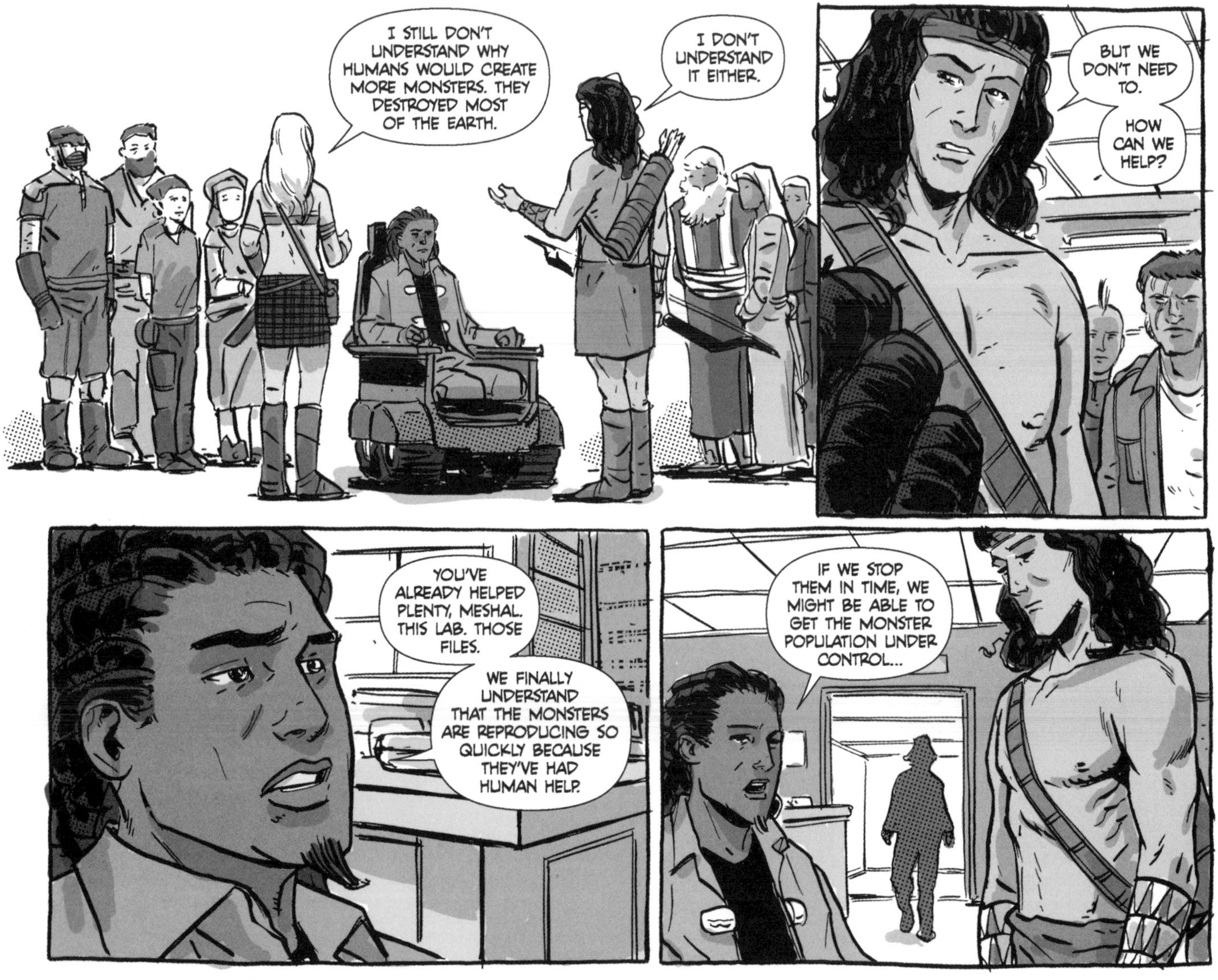
I STILL DON'T UNDERSTAND WHY HUMANS WOULD CREATE MORE MONSTERS. THEY DESTROYED MOST OF THE EARTH.
I DON'T UNDERSTAND IT EITHER.
BUT WE DON'T NEED TO.
HOW CAN WE HELP?
YOU'VE ALREADY HELPED PLENTY, MESHAL. THIS LAB. THOSE FILES.
WE FINALLY UNDERSTAND THAT THE MONSTERS ARE REPRODUCING SO QUICKLY BECAUSE THEY'VE HAD HUMAN HELP.
IF WE STOP THEM IN TIME, WE MIGHT BE ABLE TO GET THE MONSTER POPULATION UNDER CONTROL...

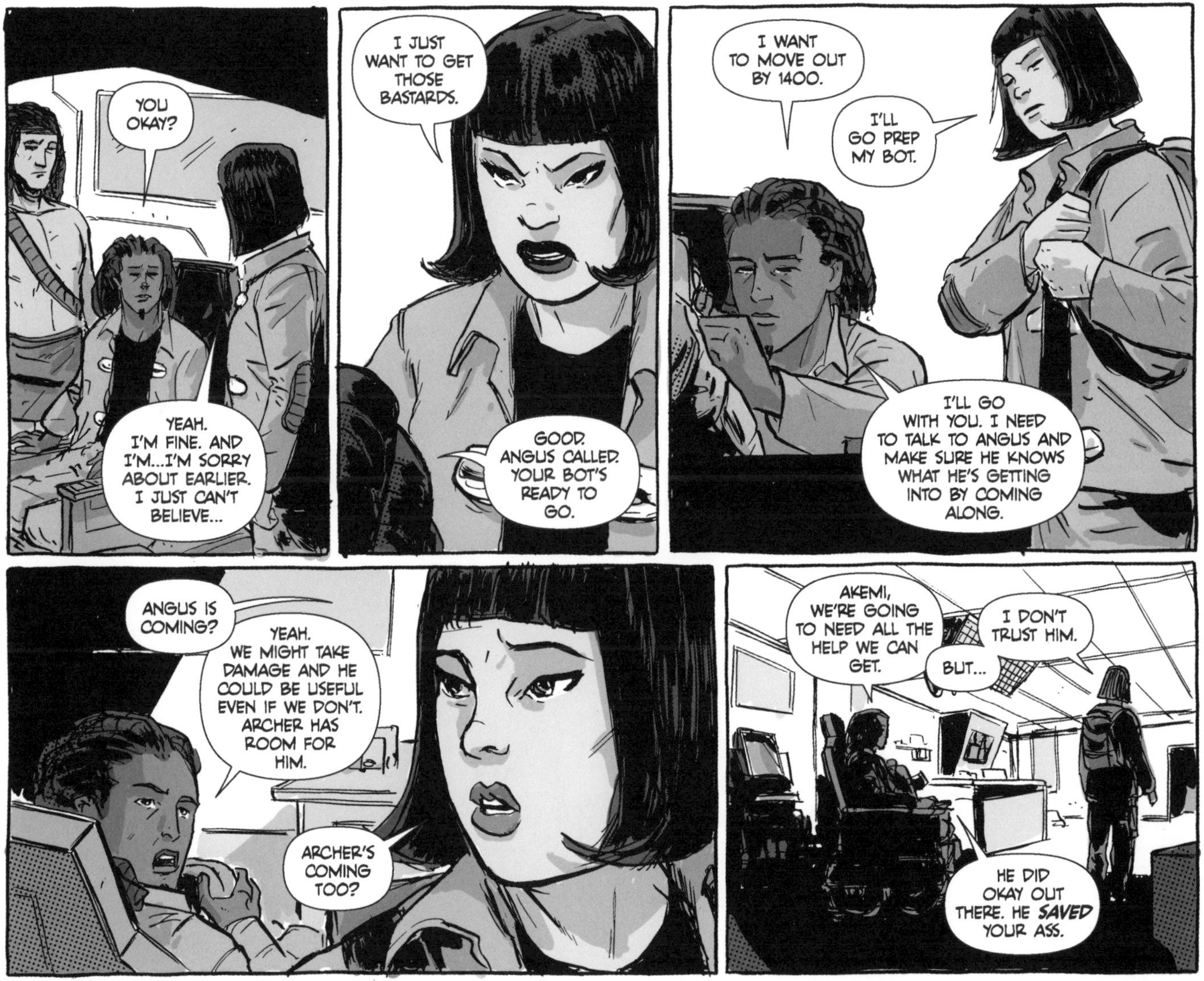

YOU OKAY?
YEAH. I'M FINE. AND I'M...I'M SORRY ABOUT EARLIER. I JUST CAN'T BELIEVE...
I JUST WANT TO GET THOSE BASTARDS.
GOOD. ANGUS CALLED. YOUR BOT'S READY TO GO.
I WANT TO MOVE OUT BY 1400.
I'LL GO PREP MY BOT.
I'LL GO WITH YOU. I NEED TO TALK TO ANGUS AND MAKE SURE HE KNOWS WHAT HE'S GETTING INTO BY COMING ALONG.
ANGUS IS COMING?
YEAH. WE MIGHT TAKE DAMAGE AND HE COULD BE USEFUL EVEN IF WE DON'T. ARCHER HAS ROOM FOR HIM.
ARCHER'S COMING TOO?
AKEMI, WE'RE GOING TO NEED ALL THE HELP WE CAN GET.
I DON'T TRUST HIM.
BUT...
HE DID OKAY OUT THERE. HE *SAVED* YOUR ASS.

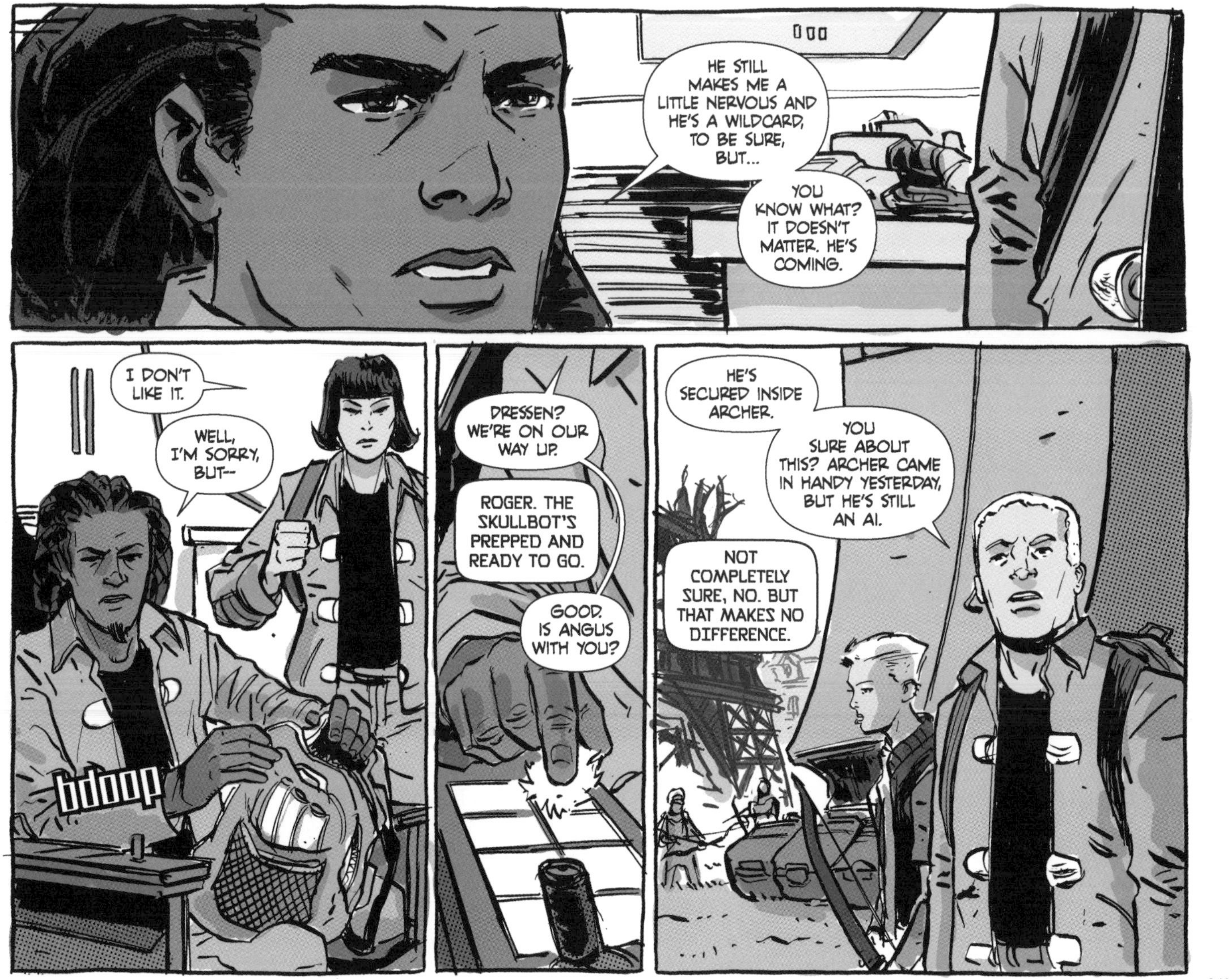
HE STILL MAKES ME A LITTLE NERVOUS AND HE'S A WILDCARD, TO BE SURE, BUT...
YOU KNOW WHAT? IT DOESN'T MATTER. HE'S COMING.
I DON'T LIKE IT.
WELL, I'M SORRY, BUT--
bdoop
DRESSEN? WE'RE ON OUR WAY UP.
ROGER. THE SKULLBOT'S PREPPED AND READY TO GO.
GOOD. IS ANGUS WITH YOU?
HE'S SECURED INSIDE ARCHER.
YOU SURE ABOUT THIS? ARCHER CAME IN HANDY YESTERDAY, BUT HE'S STILL AN AI.
NOT COMPLETELY SURE, NO. BUT THAT MAKES NO DIFFERENCE.

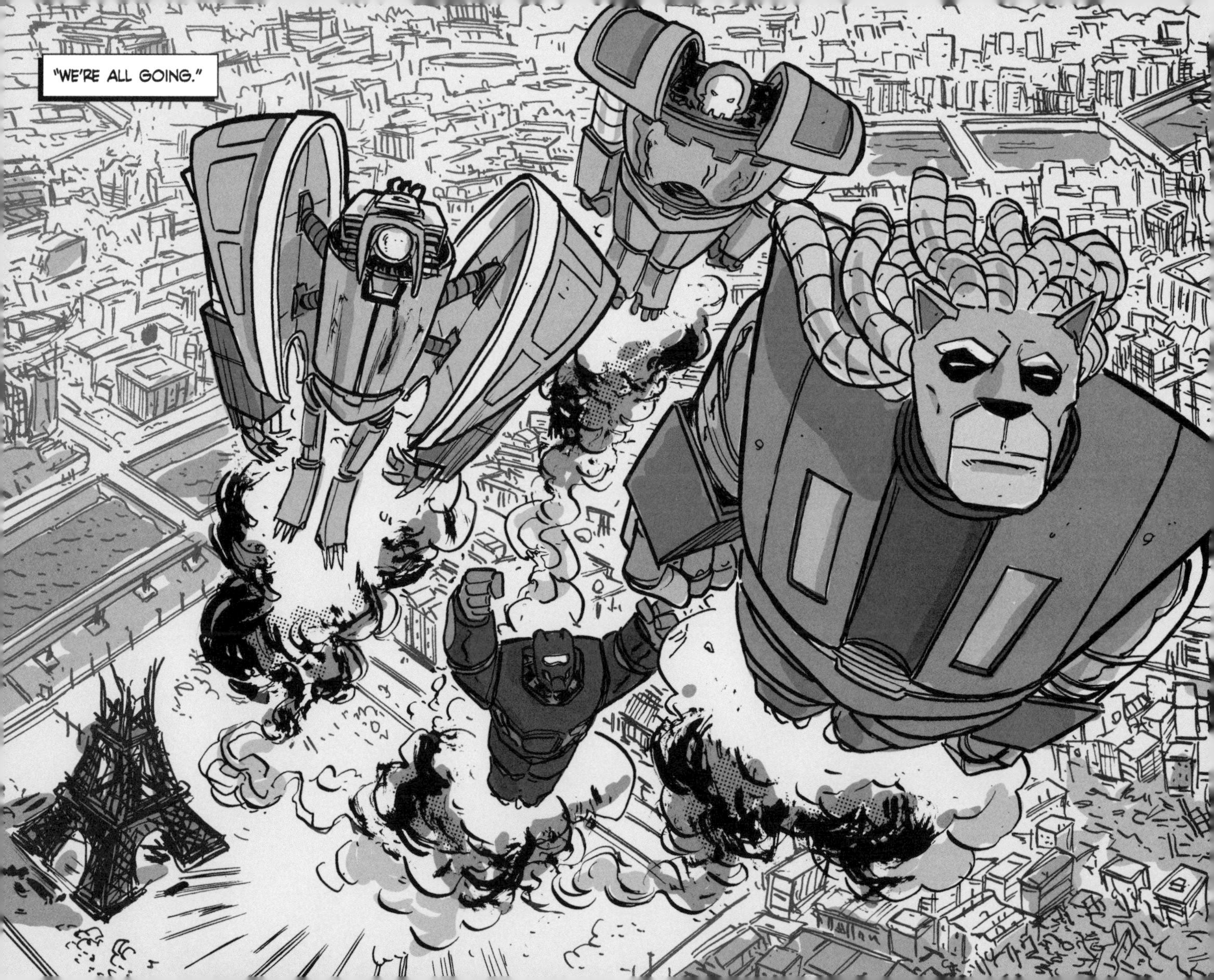
"WE'RE ALL GOING."

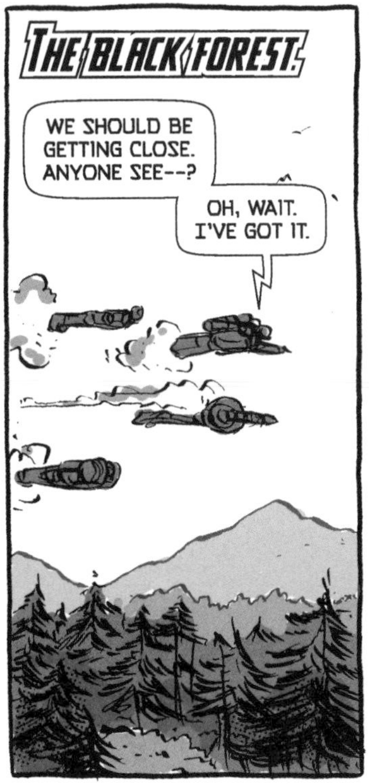
THE BLACK FOREST.
WE SHOULD BE GETTING CLOSE. ANYONE SEE--?
OH, WAIT. I'VE GOT IT.

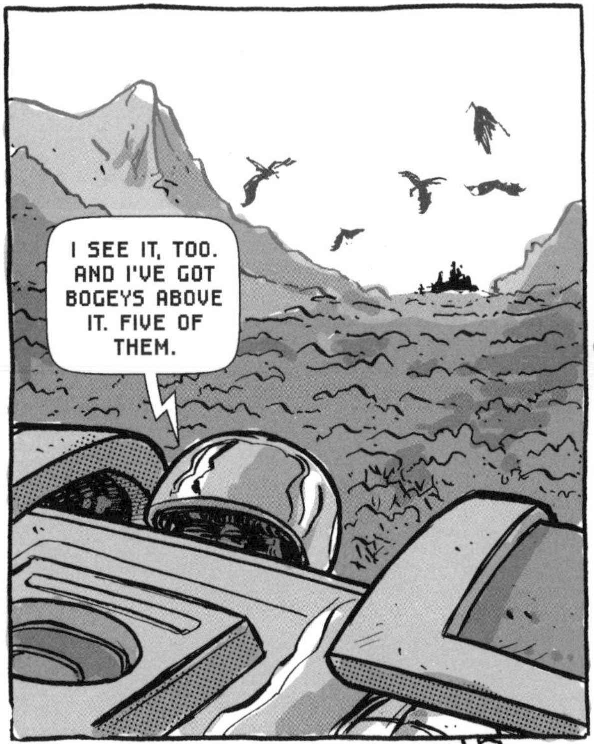
I SEE IT, TOO. AND I'VE GOT BOGEYS ABOVE IT. FIVE OF THEM.

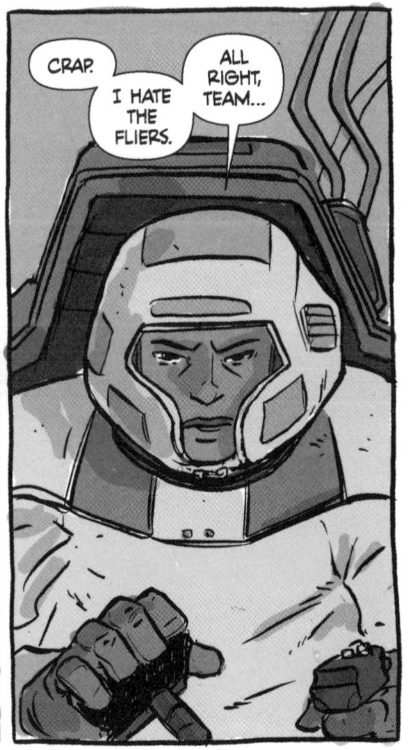
CRAP.
I HATE THE FLIERS.
ALL RIGHT, TEAM...

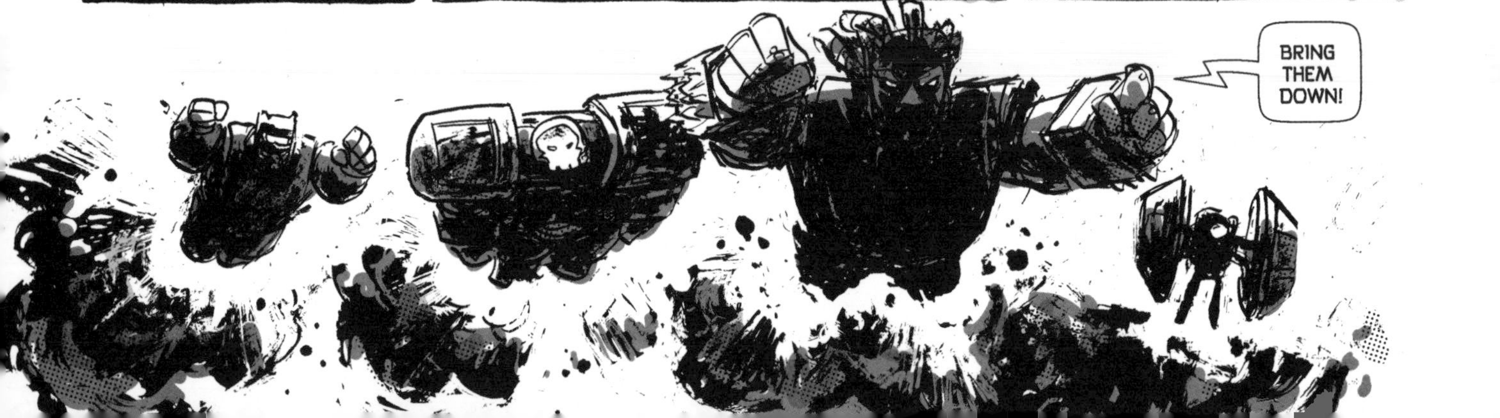
BRING THEM DOWN!

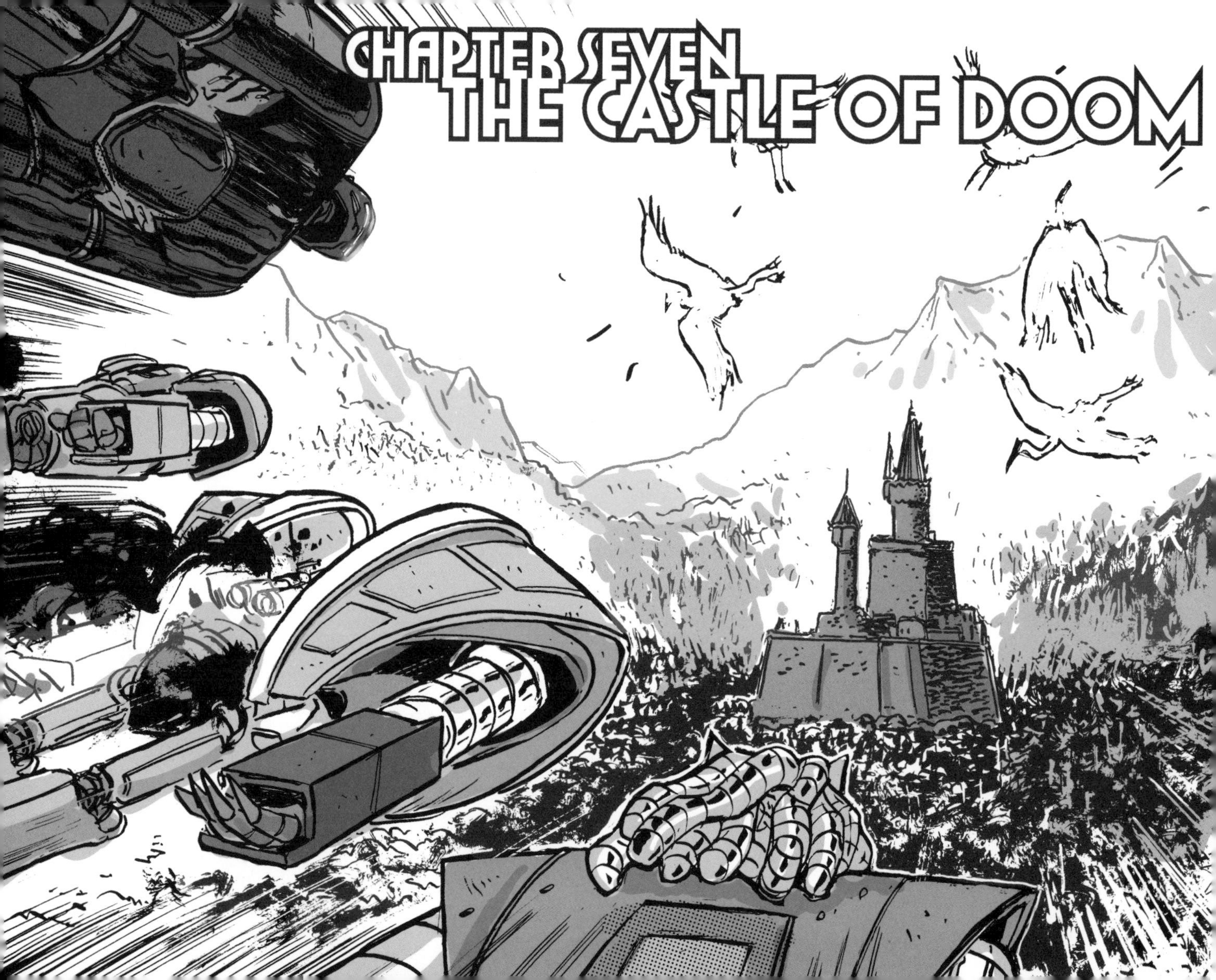
CHAPTER SEVEN
THE CASTLE OF DOOM

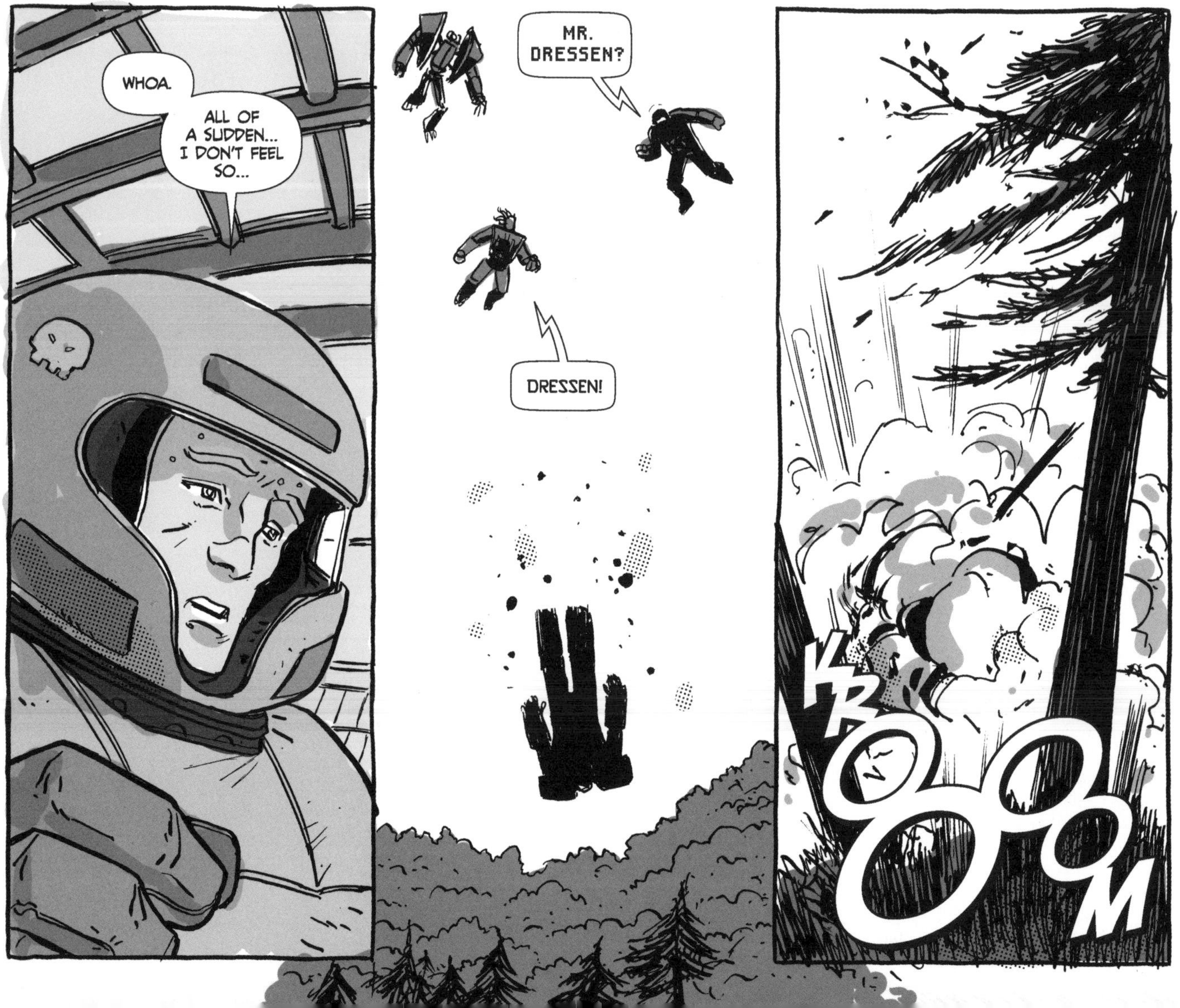
WHOA.
ALL OF A SUDDEN... I DON'T FEEL SO...
MR. DRESSEN?
DRESSEN!
KRBOOOOM

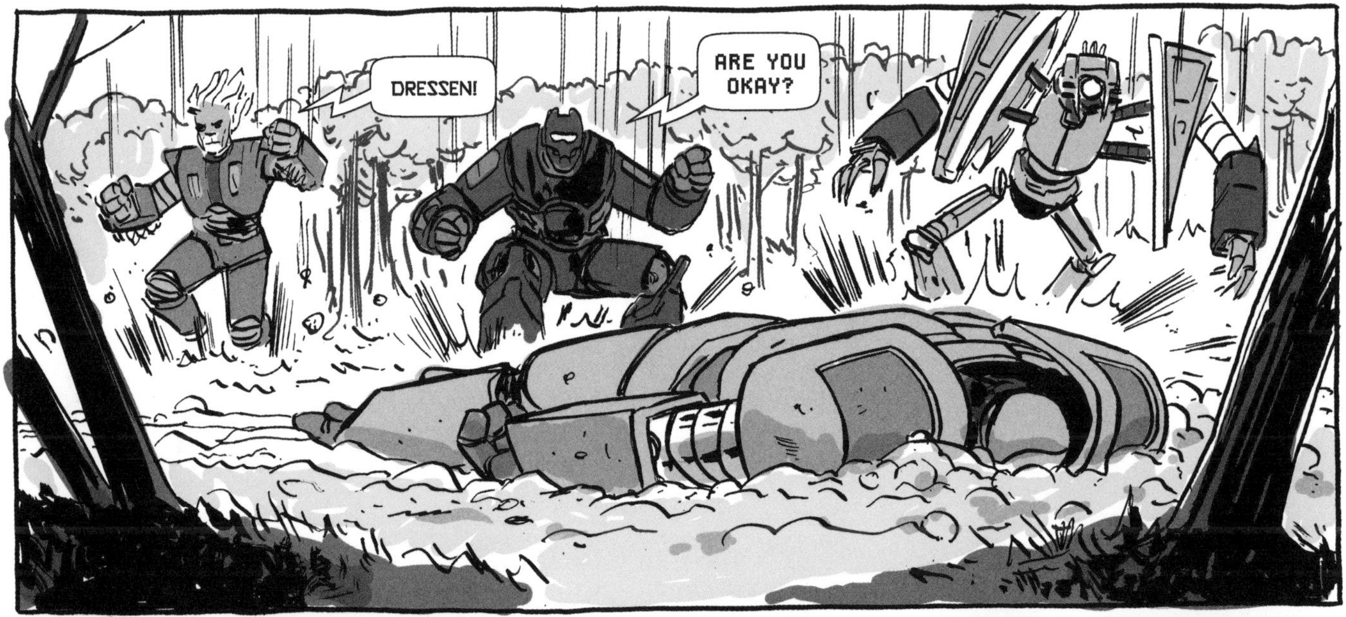
DRESSEN!
ARE YOU OKAY?

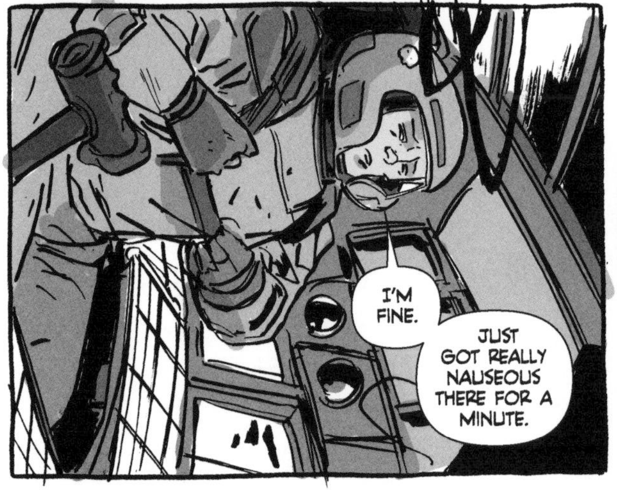
I'M FINE.
JUST GOT REALLY NAUSEOUS THERE FOR A MINUTE.

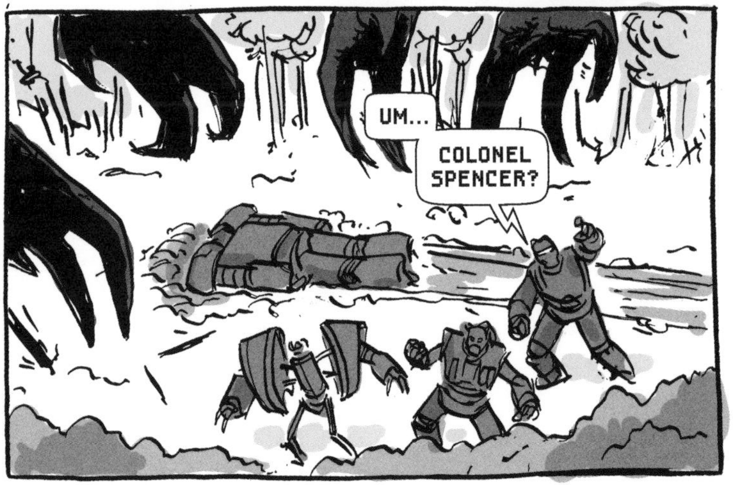
UM...
COLONEL SPENCER?

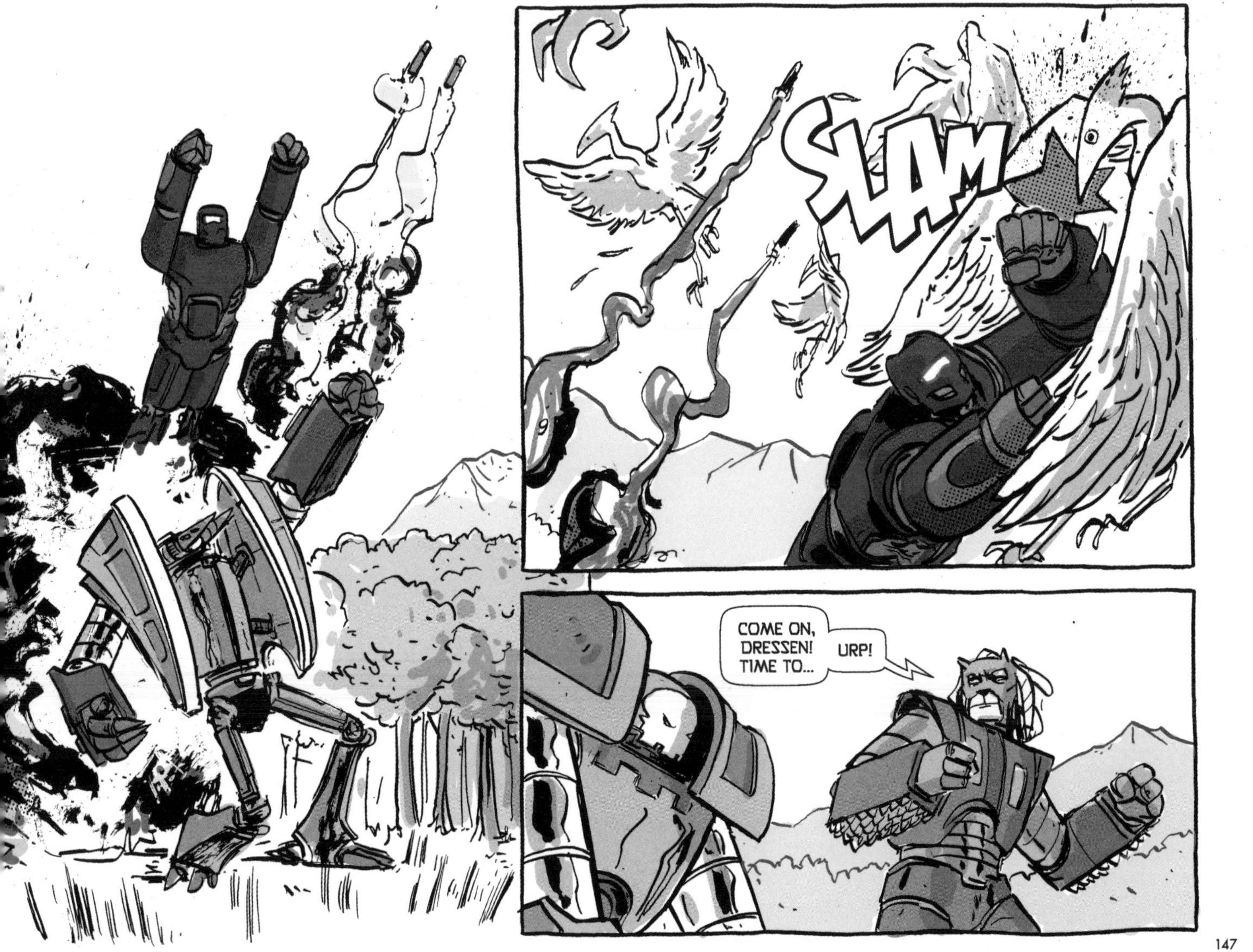
SLAM
COME ON, DRESSEN! TIME TO...
URP!

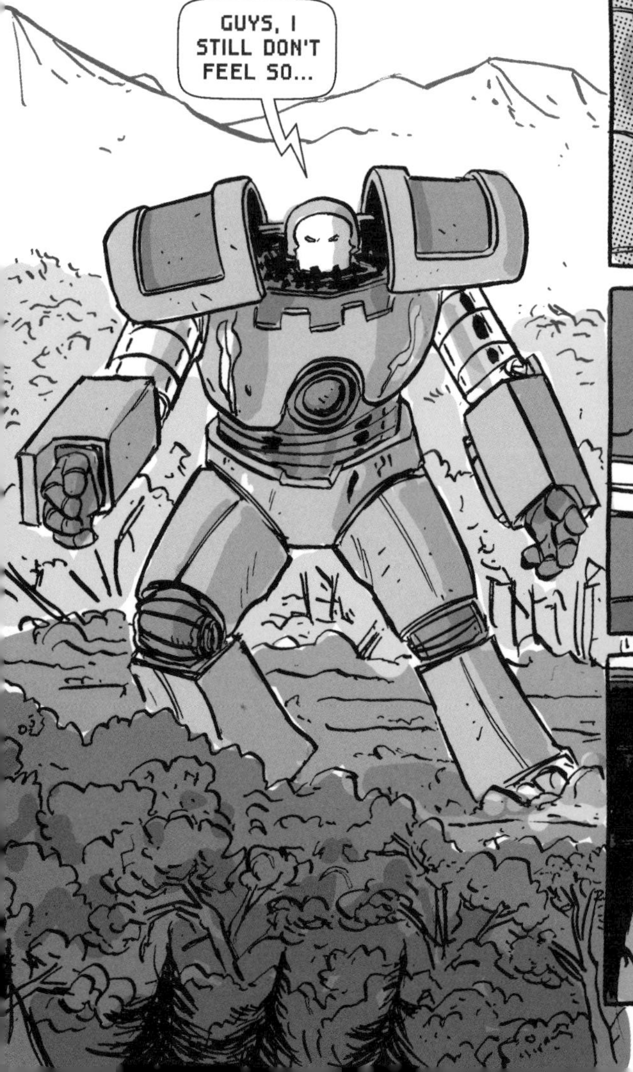
GUYS, I STILL DON'T FEEL SO...
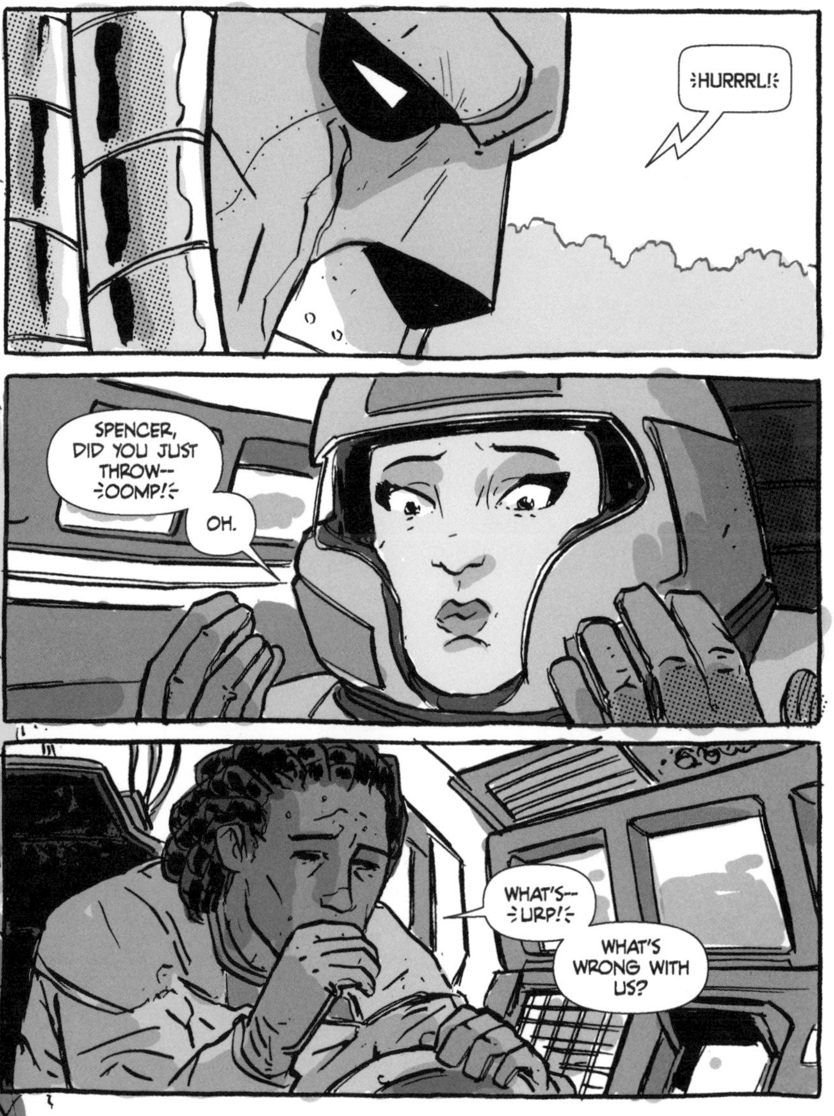
⁝HURRRL!⁝
SPENCER, DID YOU JUST THROW-- ⁝OOMP!⁝
OH.
WHAT'S-- ⁝URP!⁝
WHAT'S WRONG WITH US?

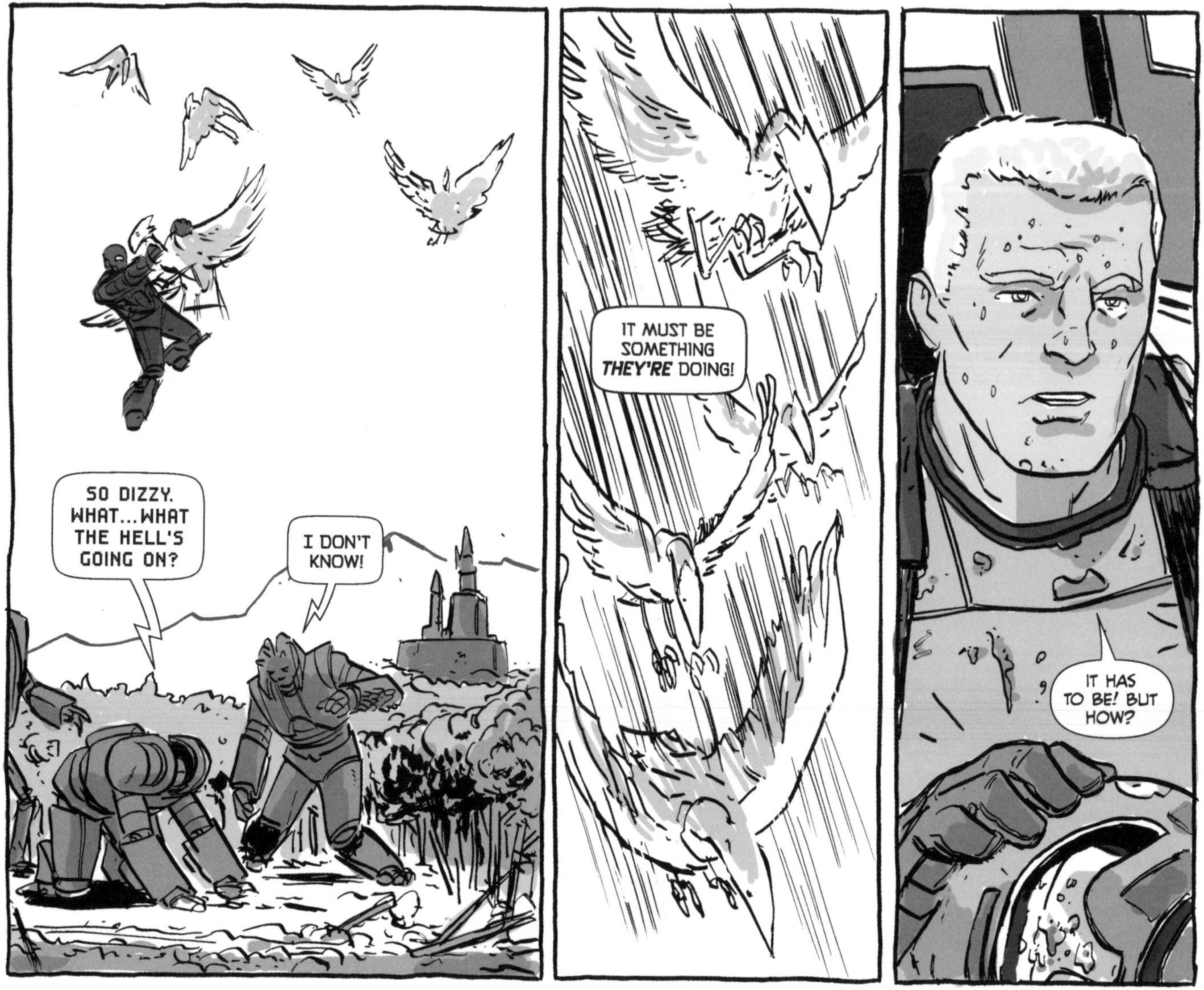
SO DIZZY. WHAT...WHAT THE HELL'S GOING ON?
I DON'T KNOW!
IT MUST BE SOMETHING ***THEY'RE*** DOING!
IT HAS TO BE! BUT HOW?

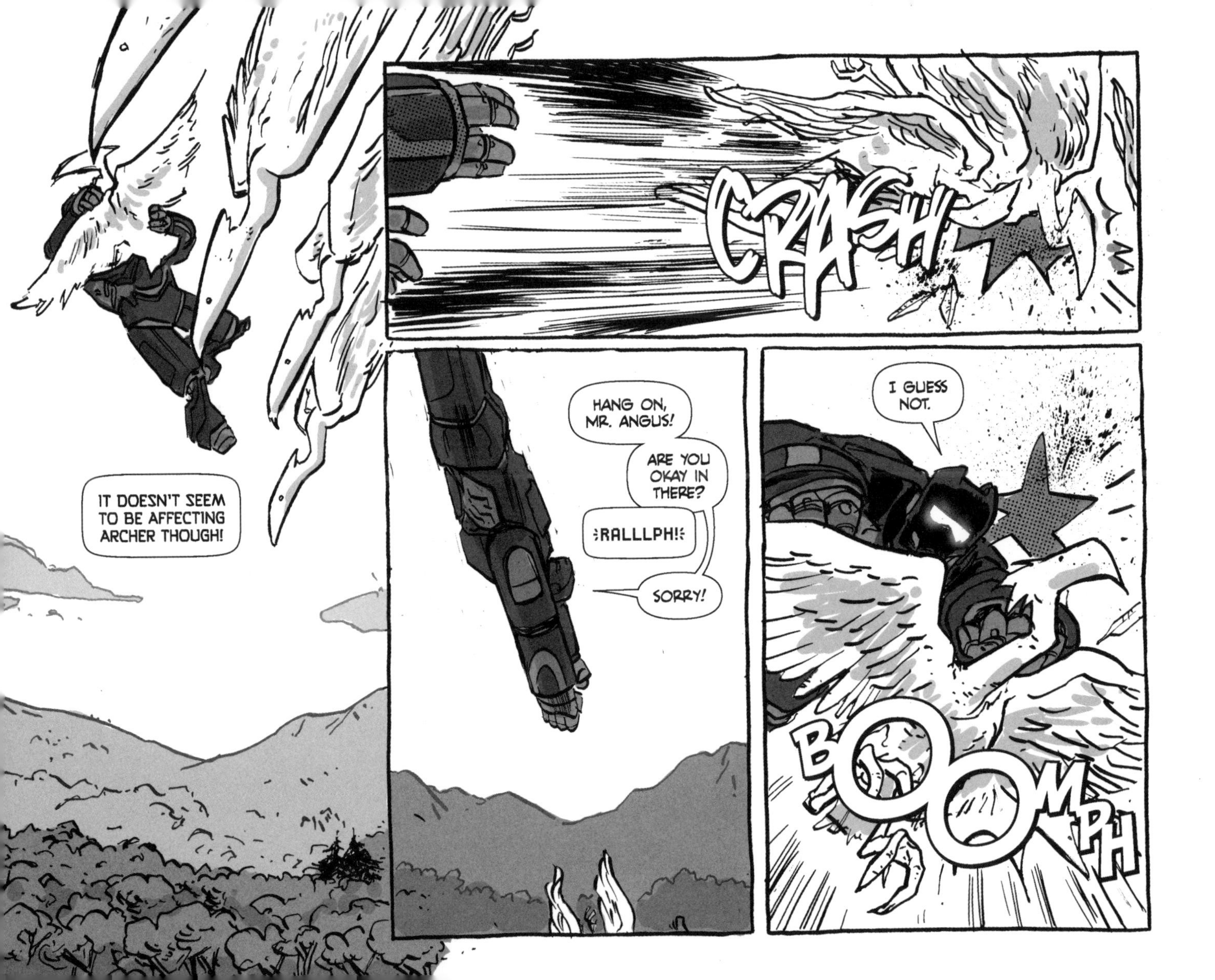
IT DOESN'T SEEM TO BE AFFECTING ARCHER THOUGH!
CRASH
HANG ON, MR. ANGUS!
ARE YOU OKAY IN THERE?
RALLLPH!
SORRY!
I GUESS NOT.
BOOOMPH

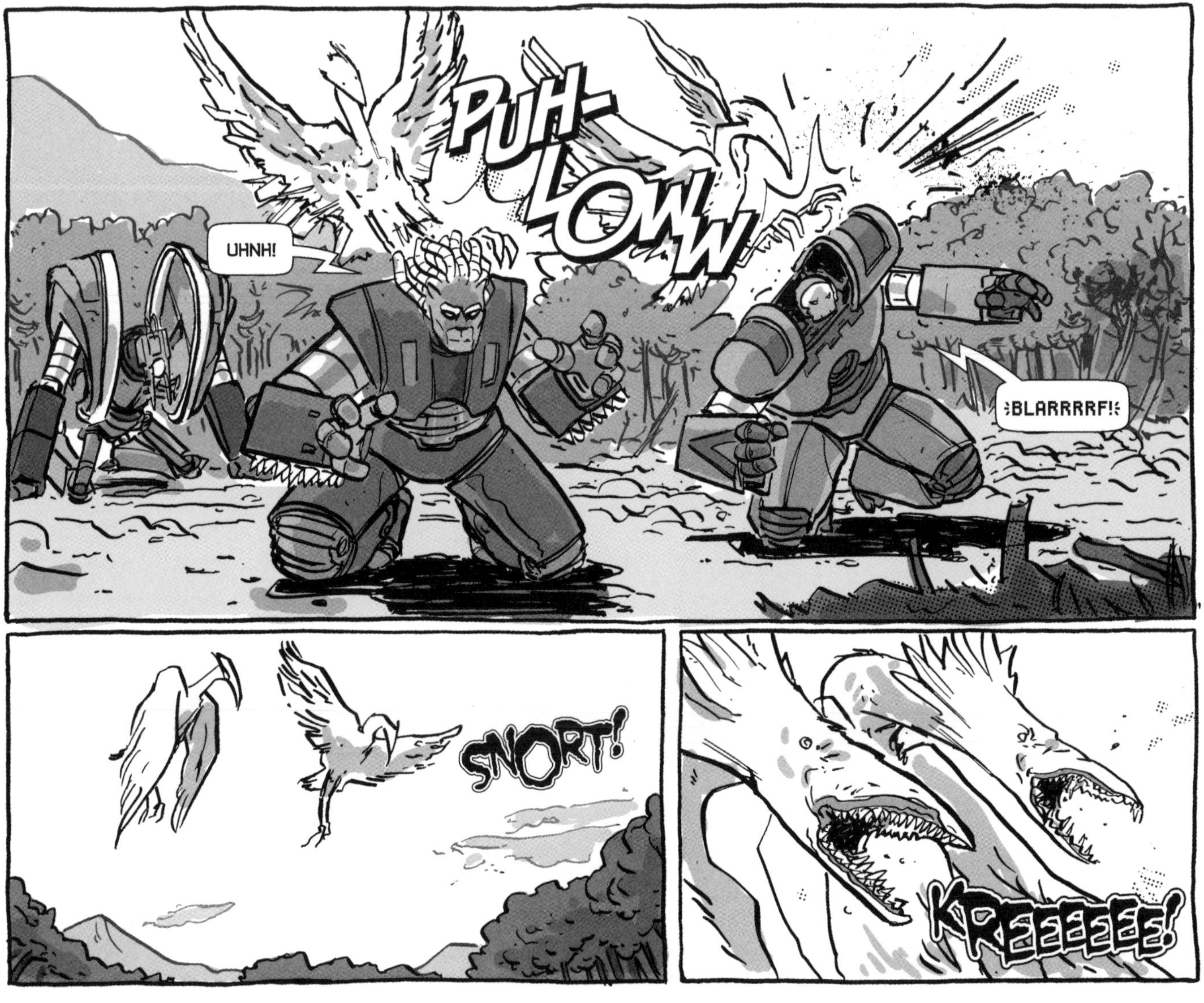
PUH-LOWW
UHNH!
BLARRRRF!
SNORT!
KREEEEEE!

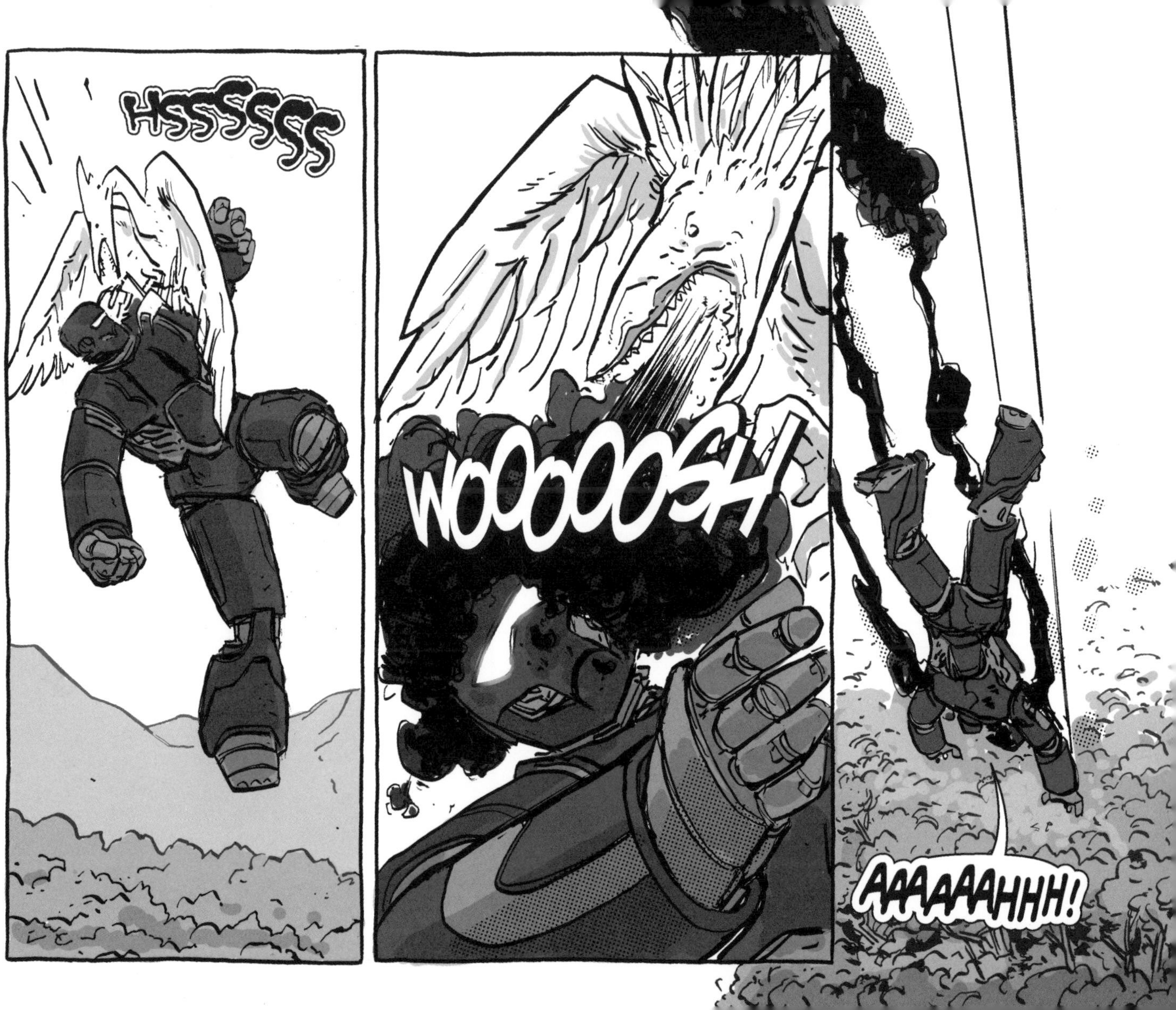
HSSSSSS
WOOOOOSH
AAAAAAHHH!

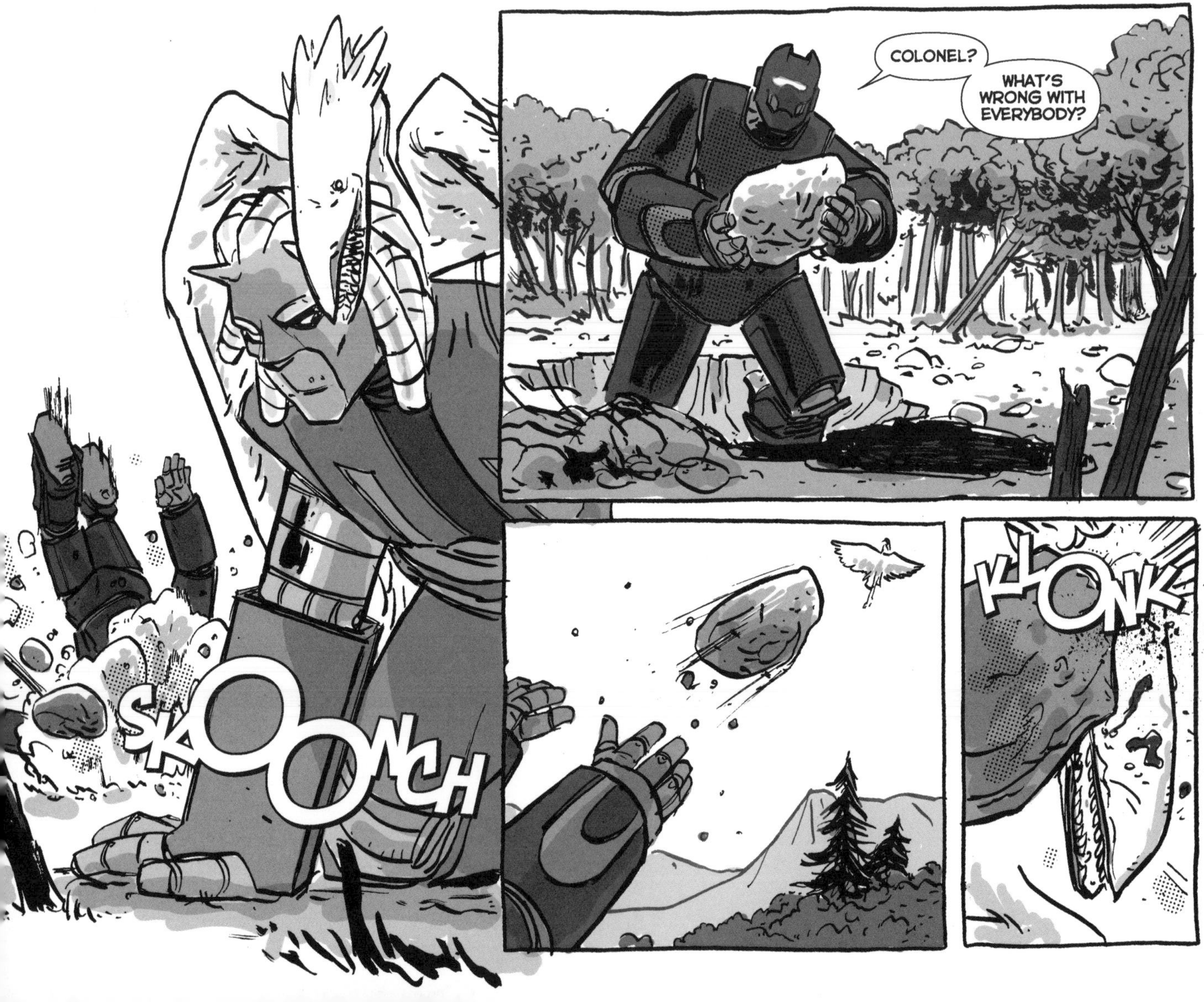

SKOONCH
COLONEL?
WHAT'S WRONG WITH EVERYBODY?
KLONK

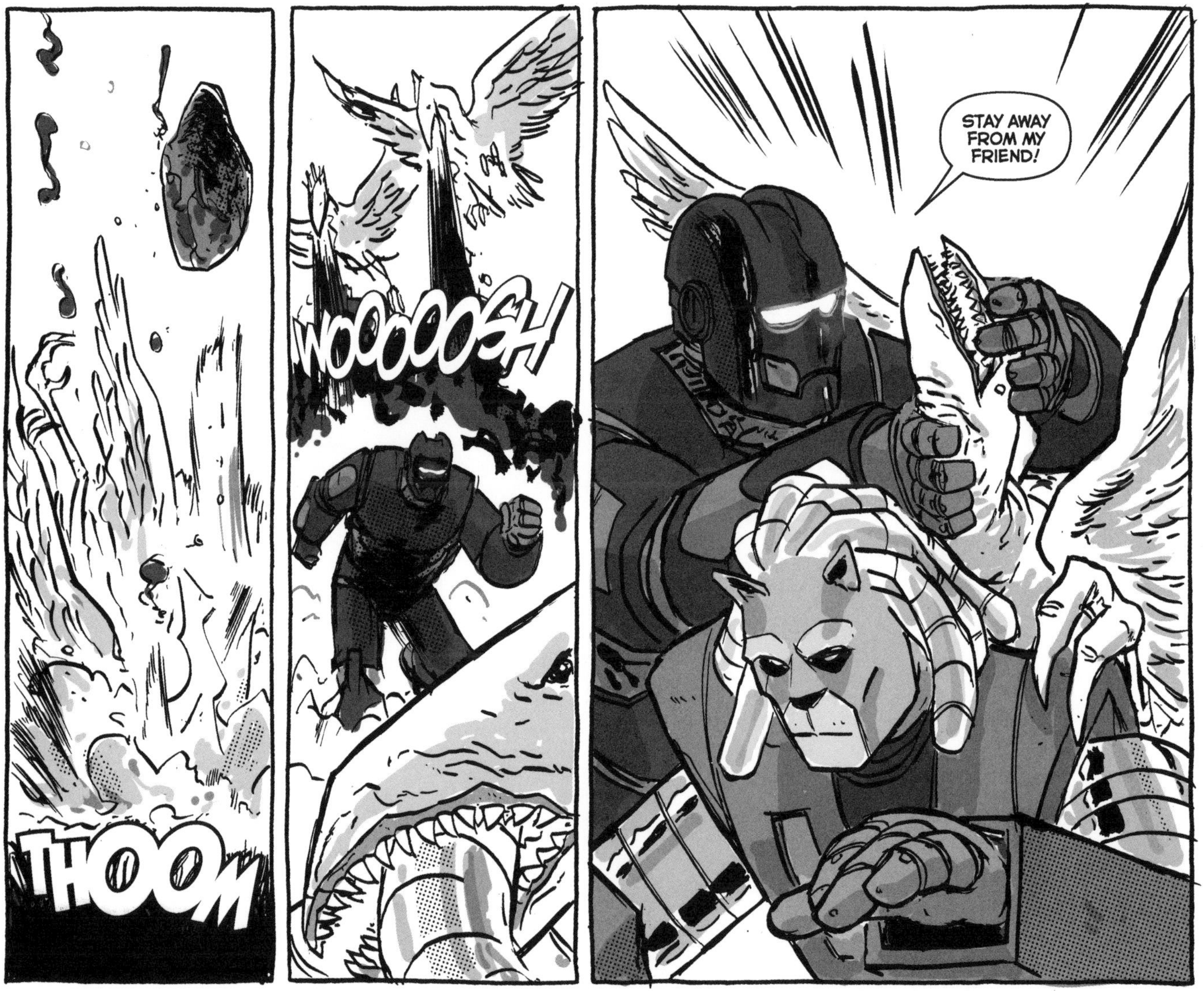
THOOM
WOOOOOSH
STAY AWAY FROM MY FRIEND!

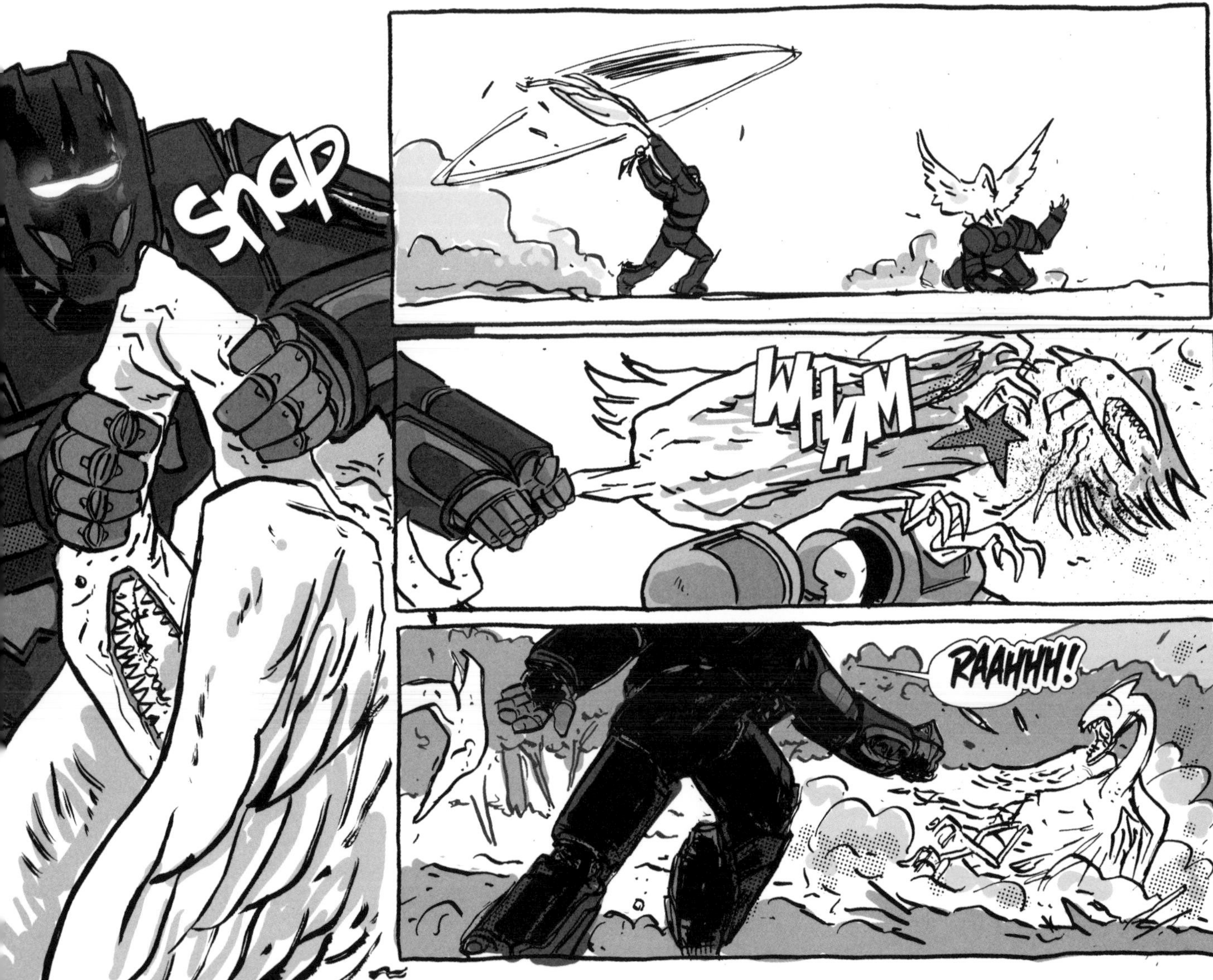
SNAP
WHAM
RAAHHH!

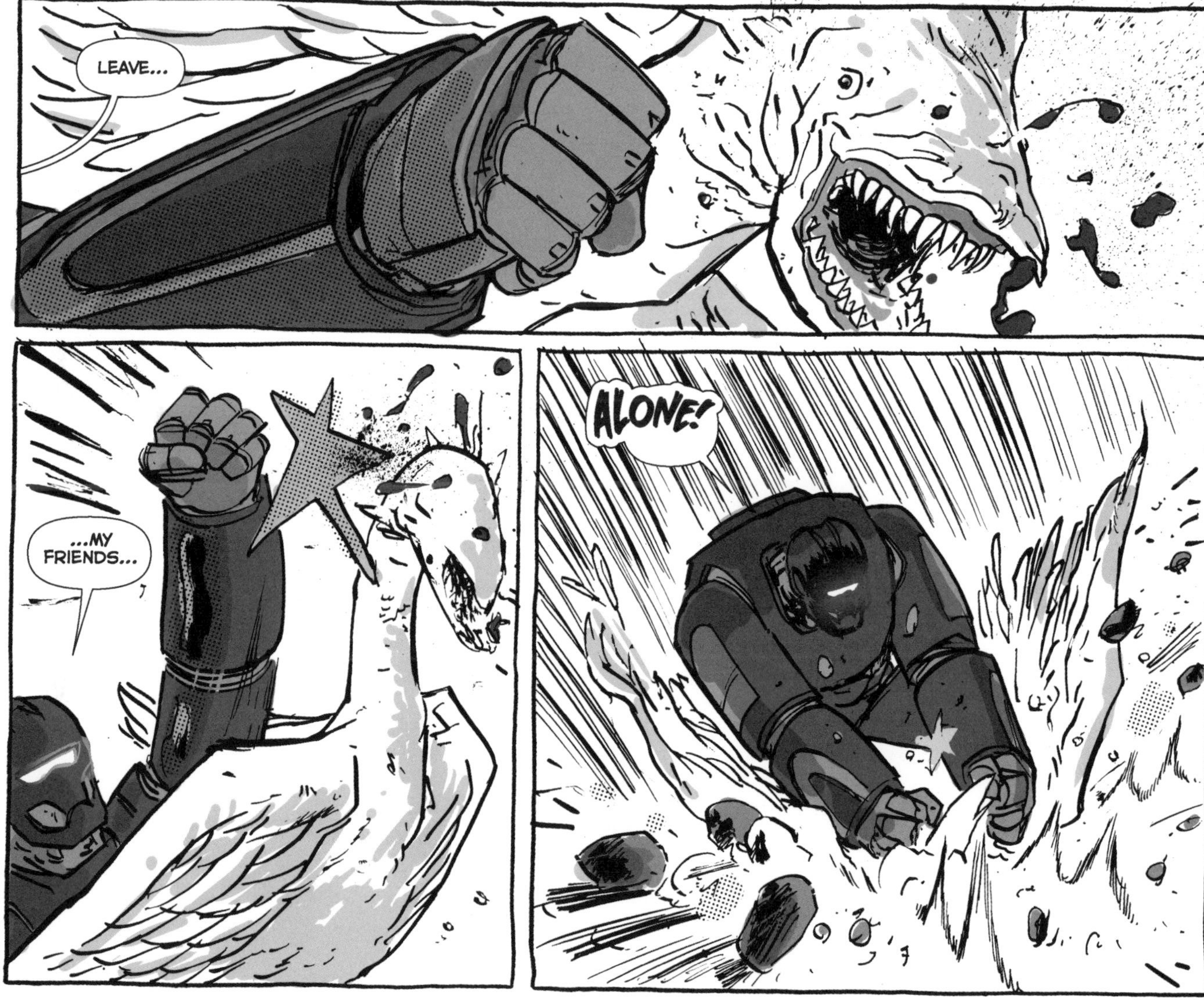
LEAVE...
...MY FRIENDS...
ALONE!

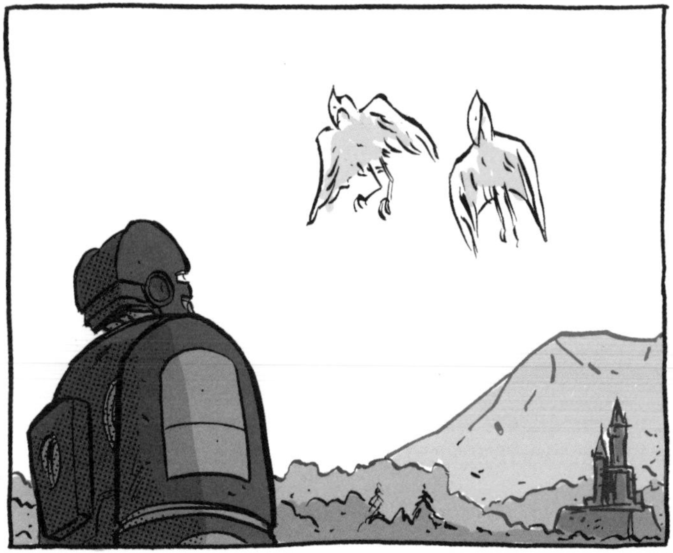
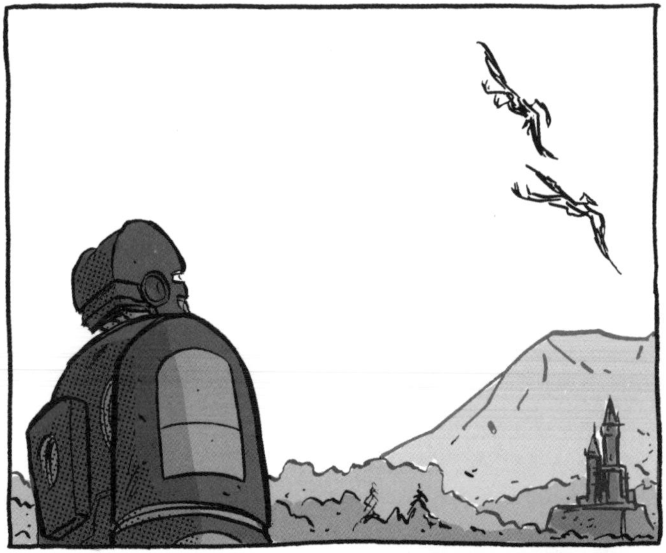
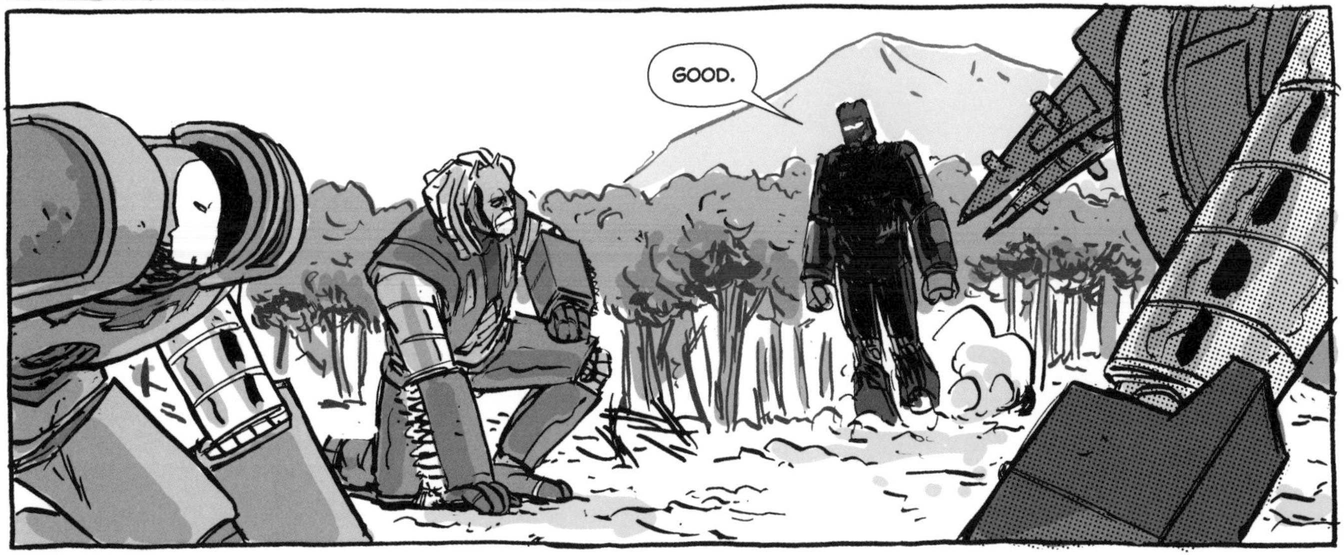
GOOD.

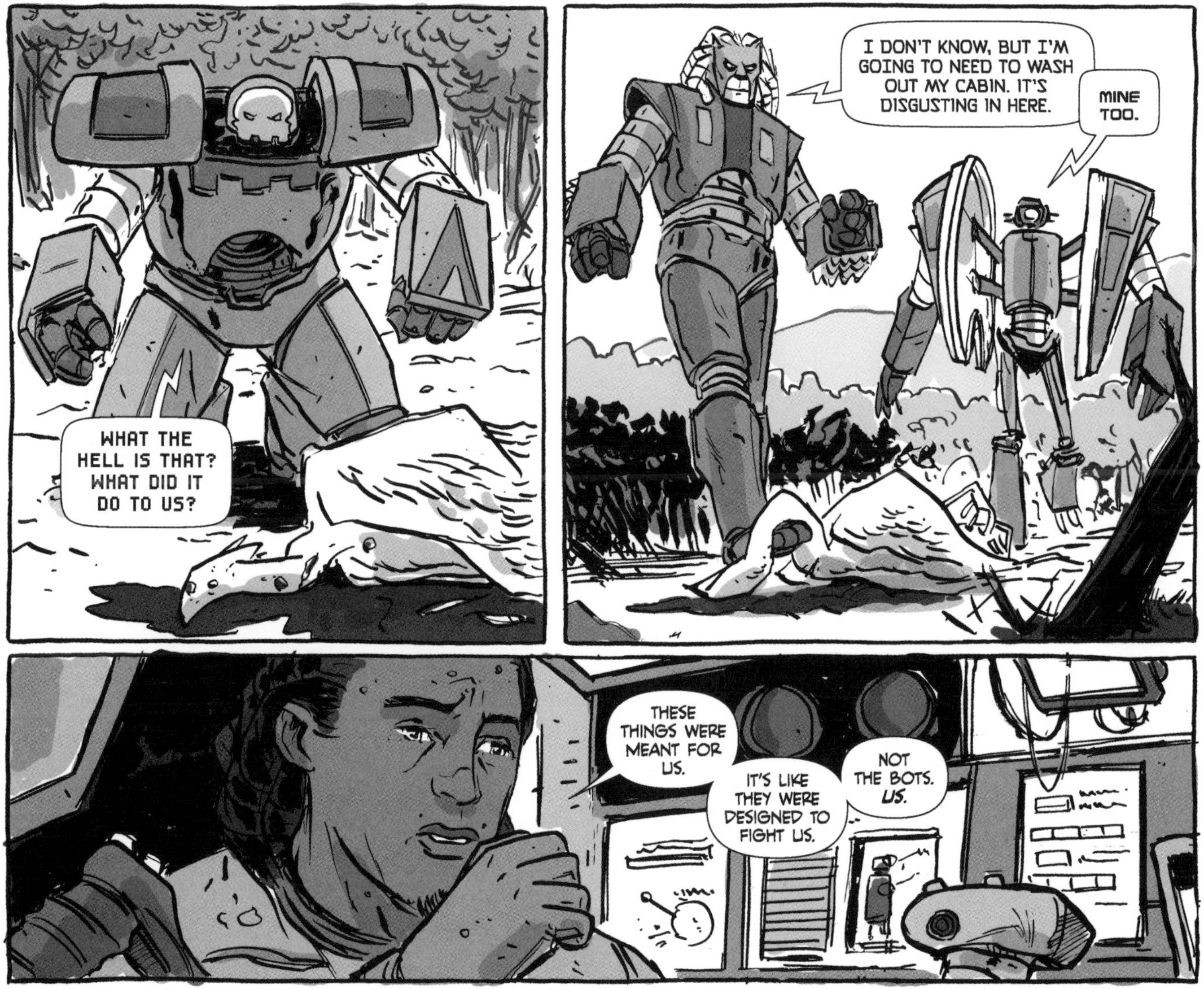
WHAT THE HELL IS THAT? WHAT DID IT DO TO US?
I DON'T KNOW, BUT I'M GOING TO NEED TO WASH OUT MY CABIN. IT'S DISGUSTING IN HERE.
MINE TOO.
THESE THINGS WERE MEANT FOR US.
IT'S LIKE THEY WERE DESIGNED TO FIGHT US.
NOT THE BOTS. *US.*

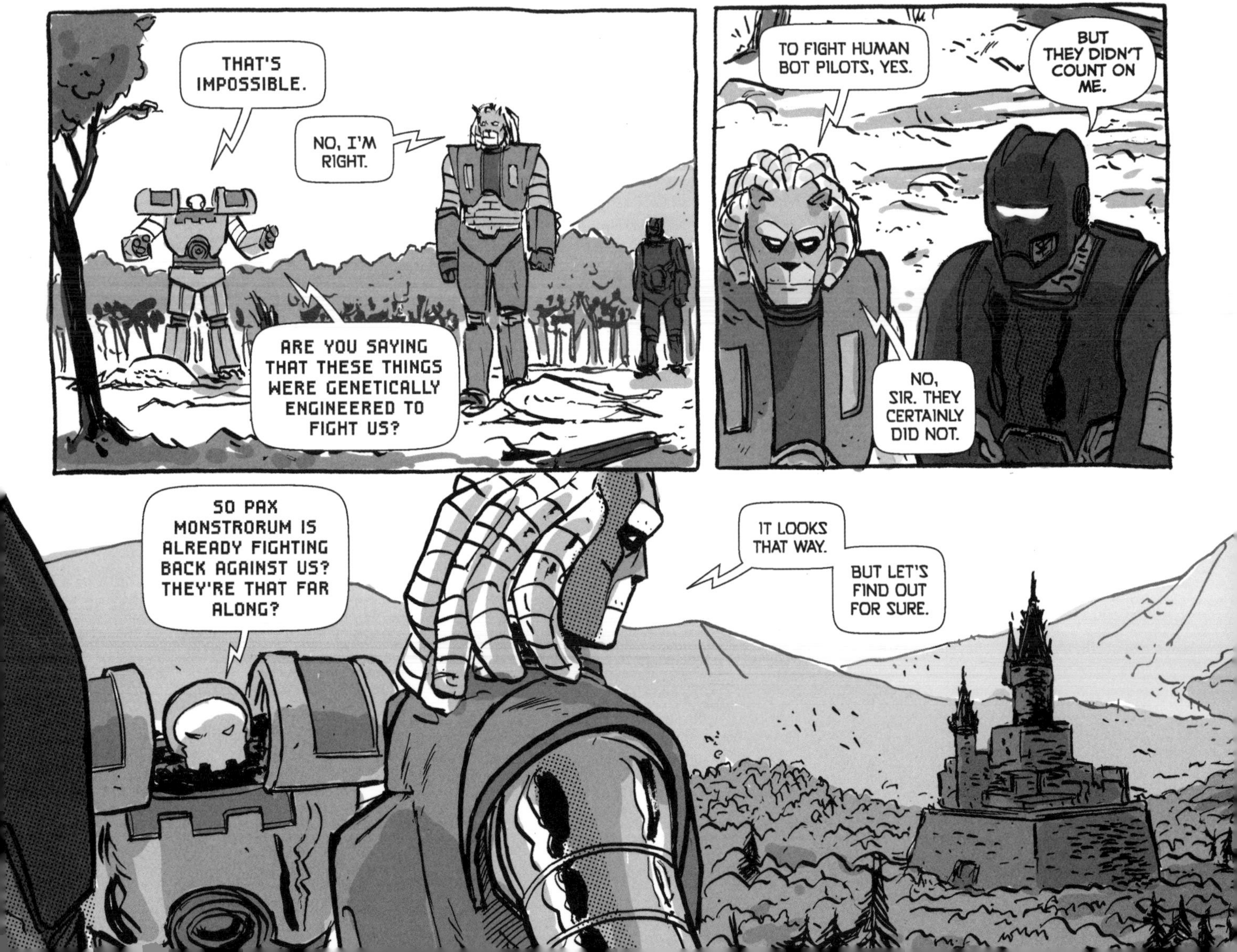
THAT'S IMPOSSIBLE.
NO, I'M RIGHT.
ARE YOU SAYING THAT THESE THINGS WERE GENETICALLY ENGINEERED TO FIGHT US?
TO FIGHT HUMAN BOT PILOTS, YES.
BUT THEY DIDN'T COUNT ON ME.
NO, SIR. THEY CERTAINLY DID NOT.
SO PAX MONSTRORUM IS ALREADY FIGHTING BACK AGAINST US? THEY'RE THAT FAR ALONG?
IT LOOKS THAT WAY.
BUT LET'S FIND OUT FOR SURE.

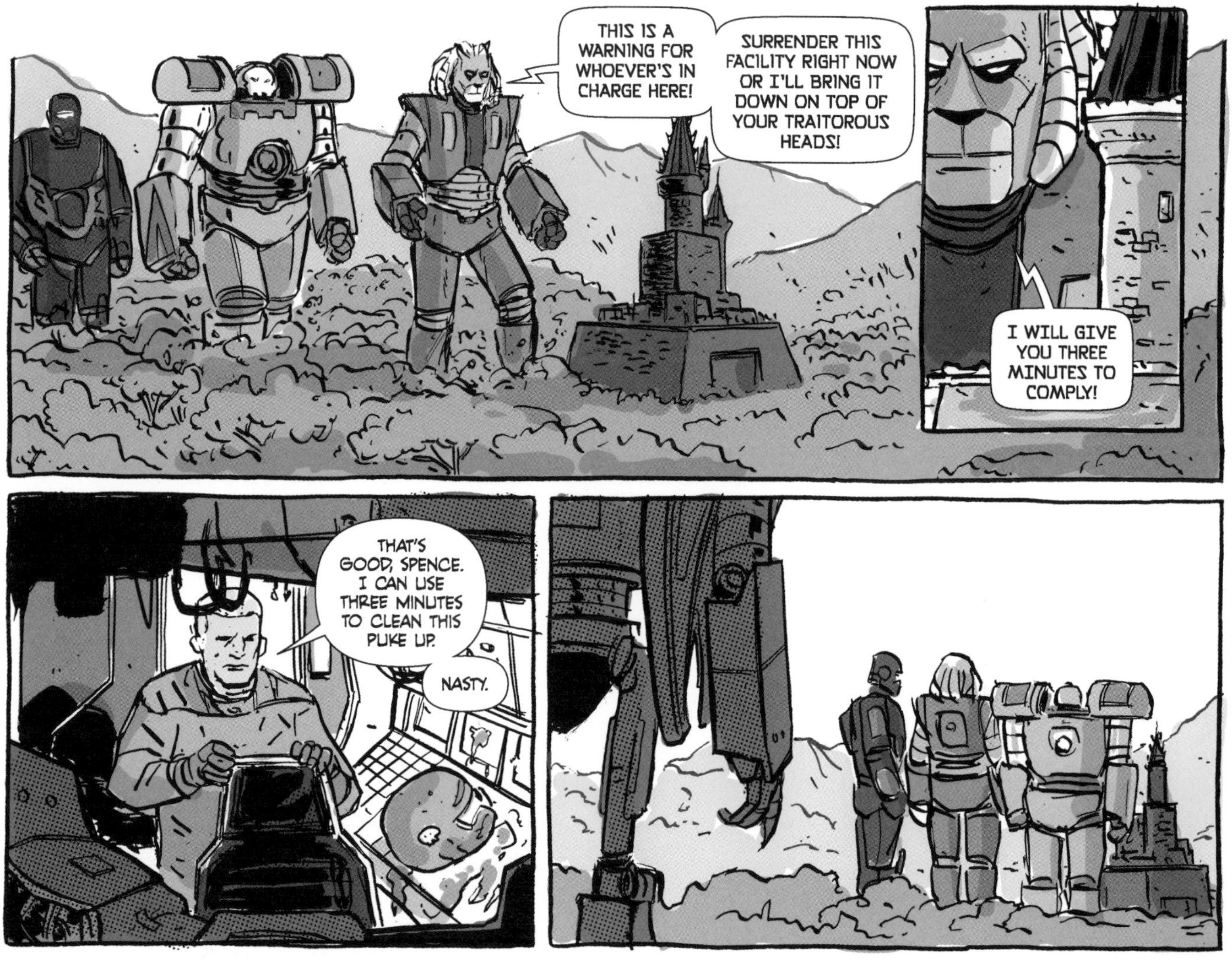
THIS IS A WARNING FOR WHOEVER'S IN CHARGE HERE!
SURRENDER THIS FACILITY RIGHT NOW OR I'LL BRING IT DOWN ON TOP OF YOUR TRAITOROUS HEADS!
I WILL GIVE YOU THREE MINUTES TO COMPLY!
THAT'S GOOD, SPENCE. I CAN USE THREE MINUTES TO CLEAN THIS PUKE UP.
NASTY.

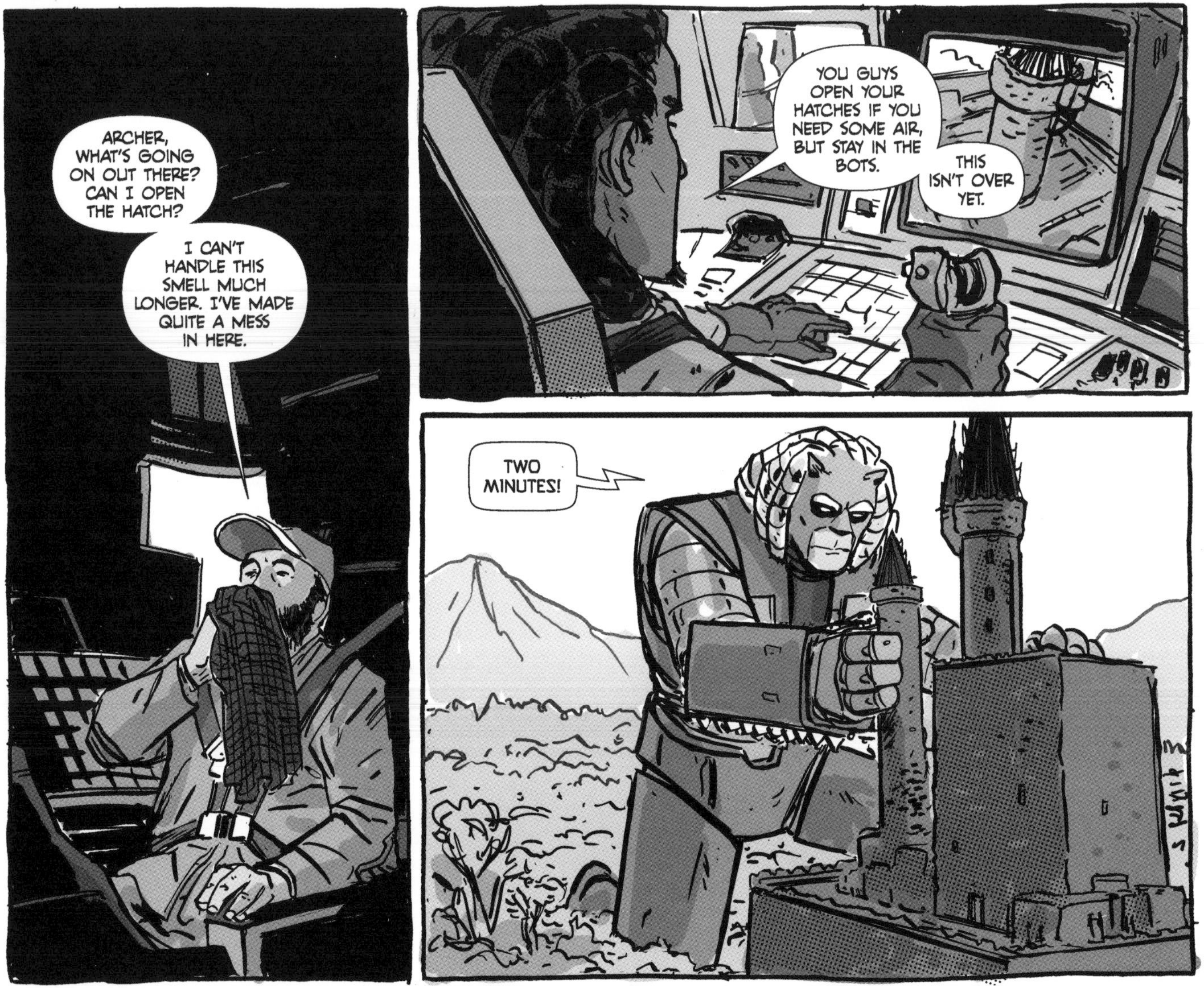
ARCHER, WHAT'S GOING ON OUT THERE? CAN I OPEN THE HATCH?
I CAN'T HANDLE THIS SMELL MUCH LONGER. I'VE MADE QUITE A MESS IN HERE.
YOU GUYS OPEN YOUR HATCHES IF YOU NEED SOME AIR, BUT STAY IN THE BOTS.
THIS ISN'T OVER YET.
TWO MINUTES!

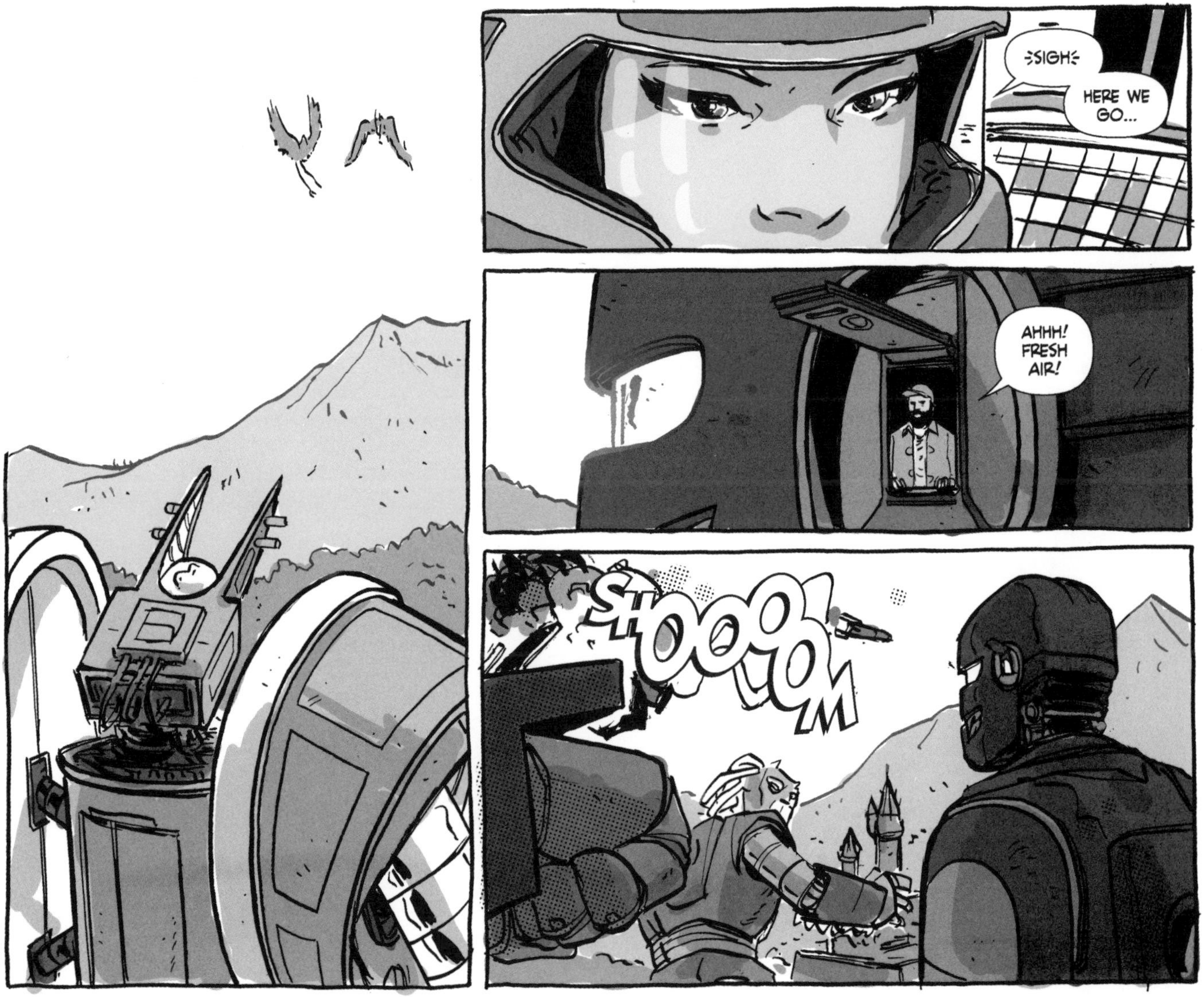
⁼SIGH⁼
HERE WE GO...
AHHH! FRESH AIR!
SHOOOOOOM

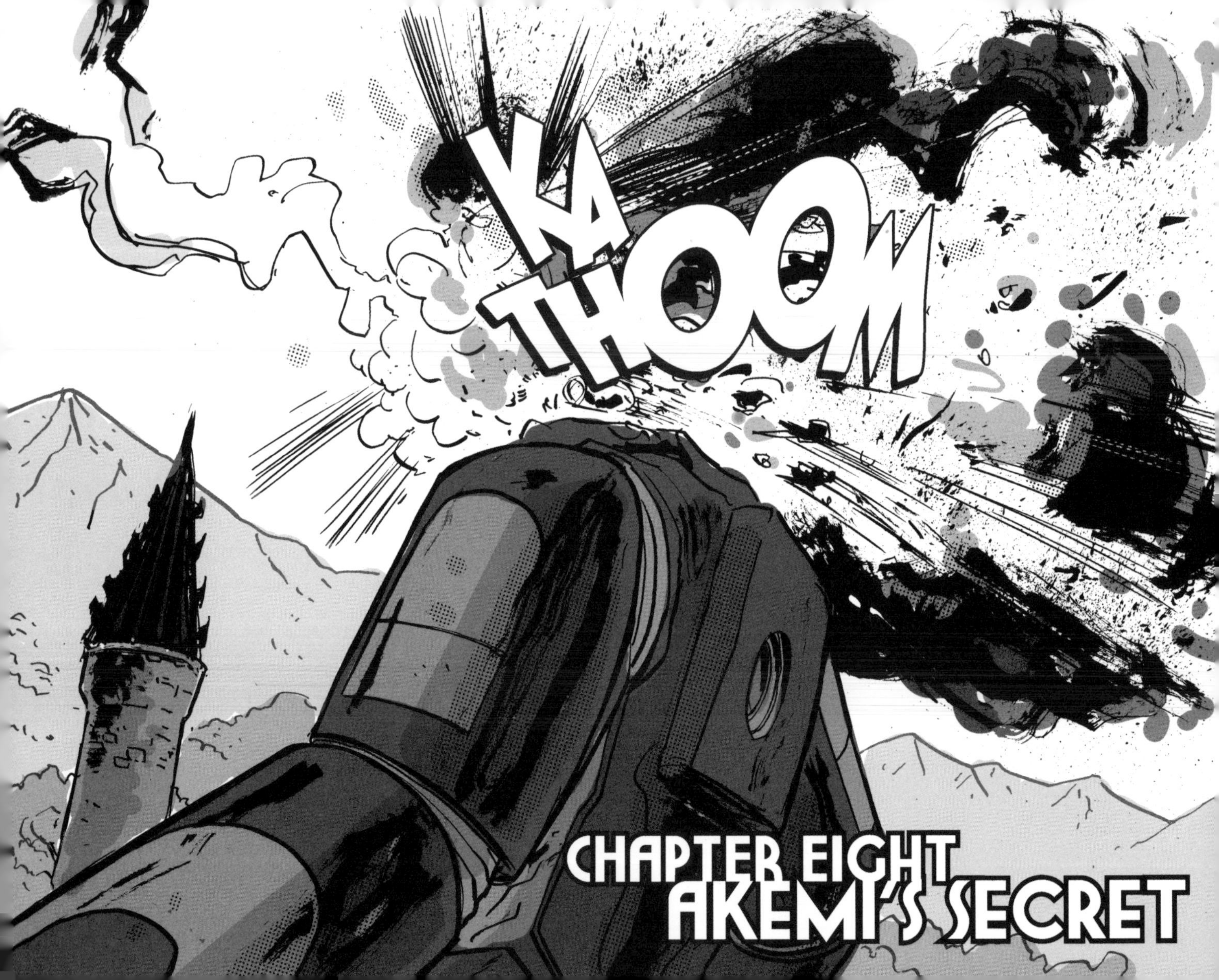
KA
THOOM
CHAPTER EIGHT
AKEMI'S SECRET

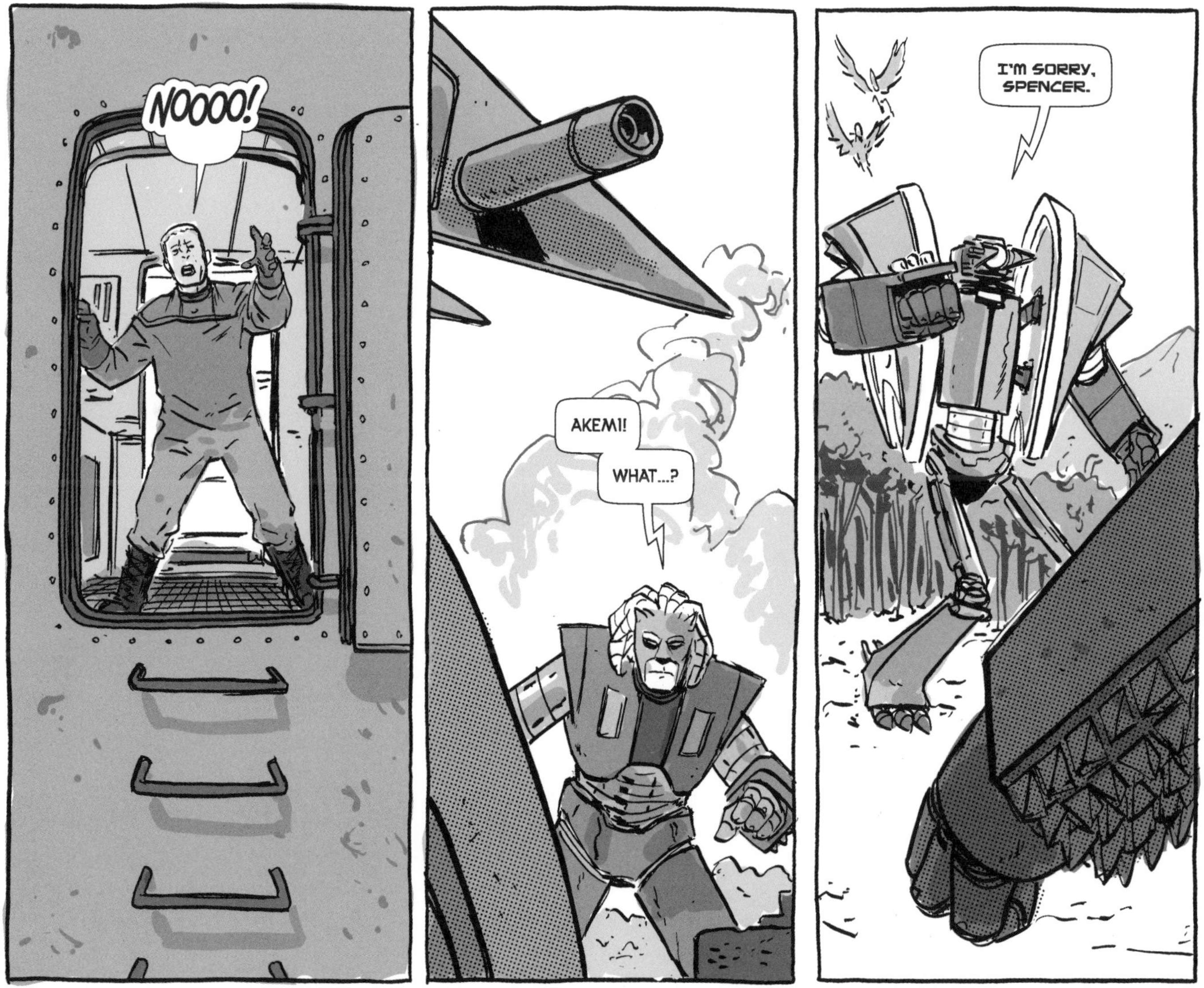
NOOOO!
AKEMI!
WHAT...?
I'M SORRY, SPENCER.

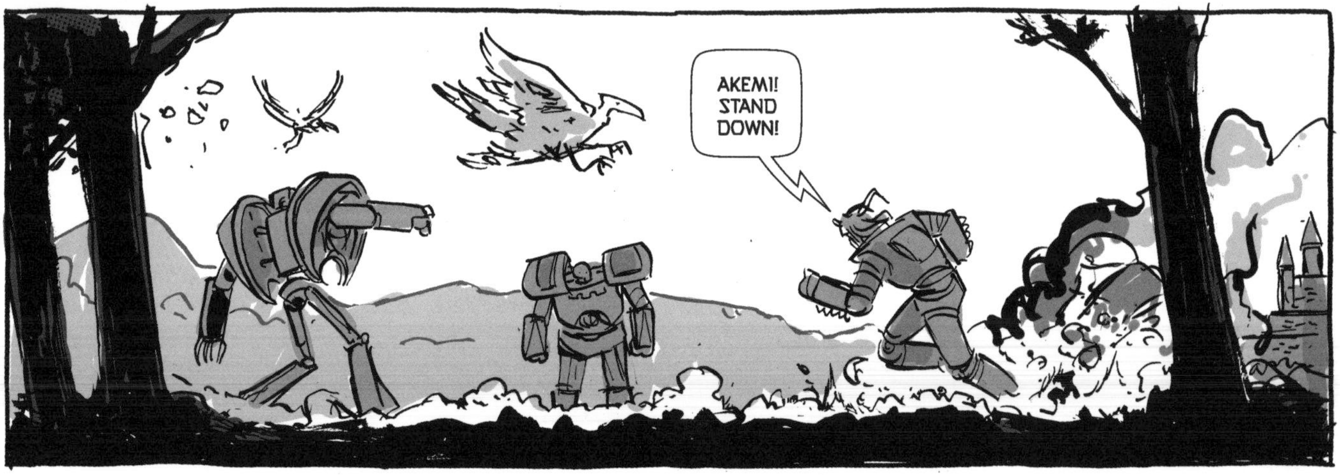
AKEMI! STAND DOWN!

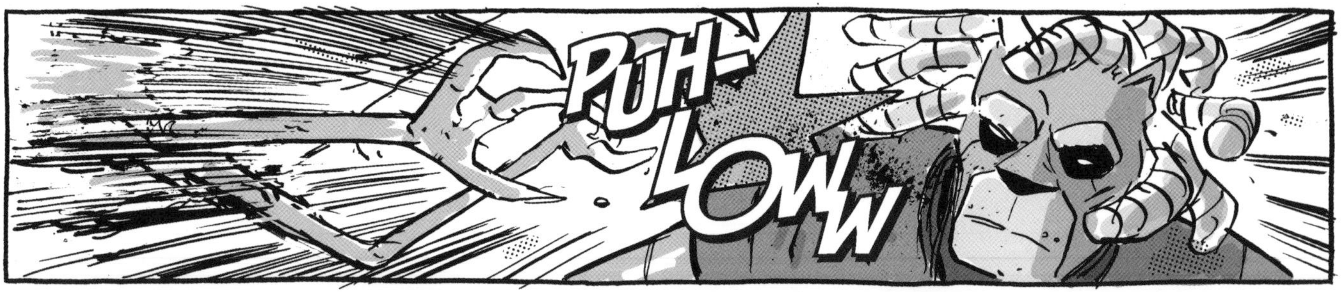
PUH-LOWW

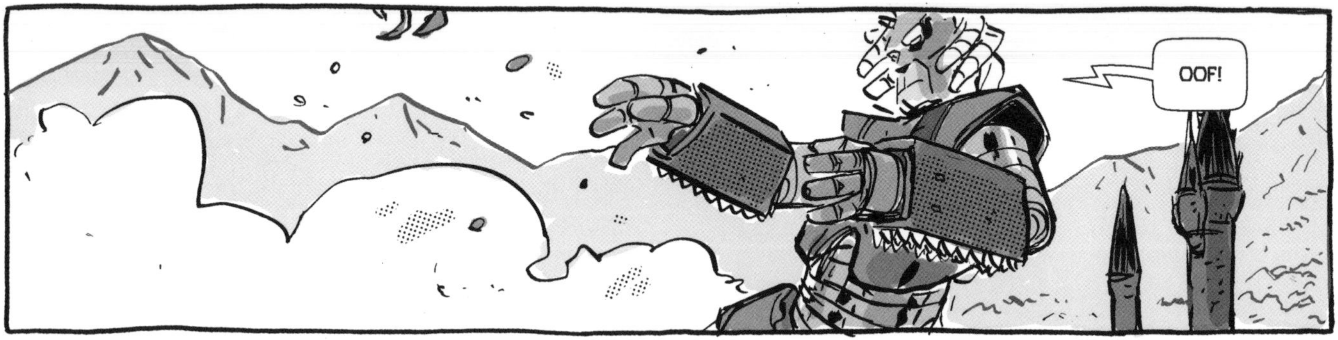
OOF!

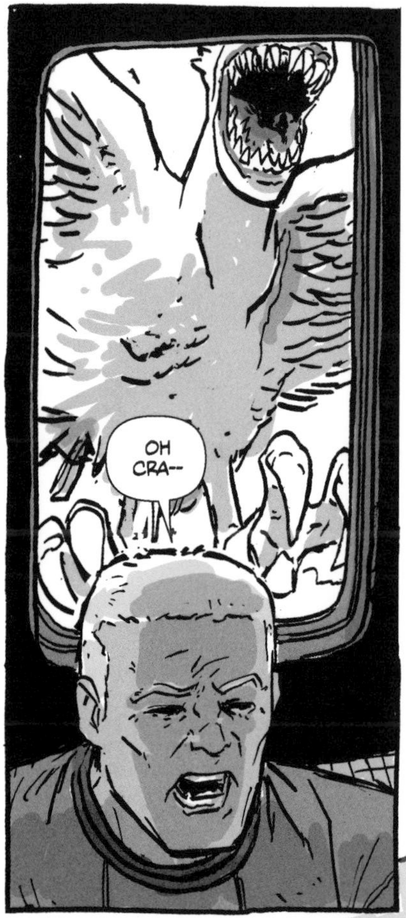
OH CRA--
SLAMMO

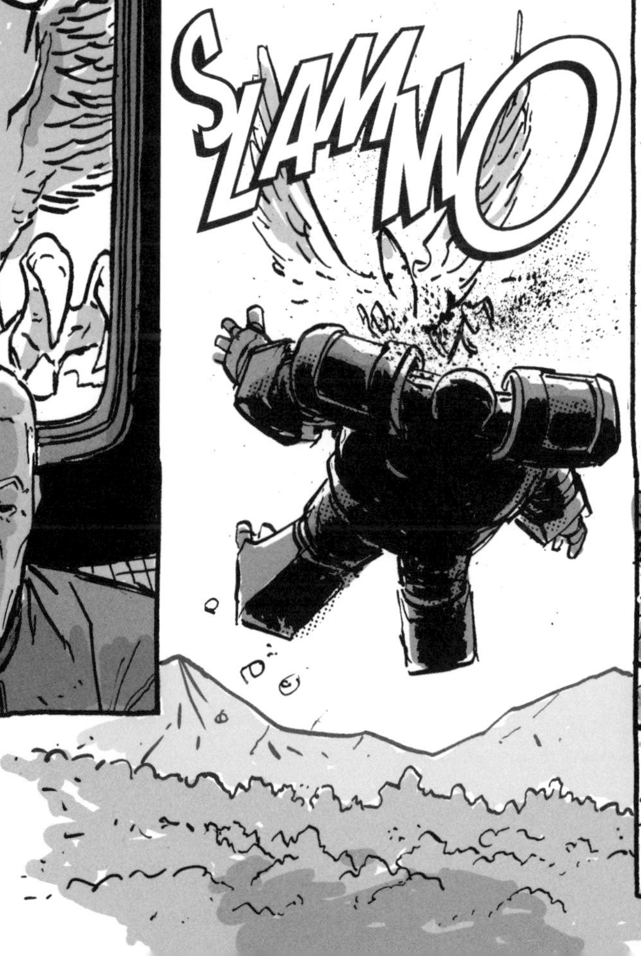

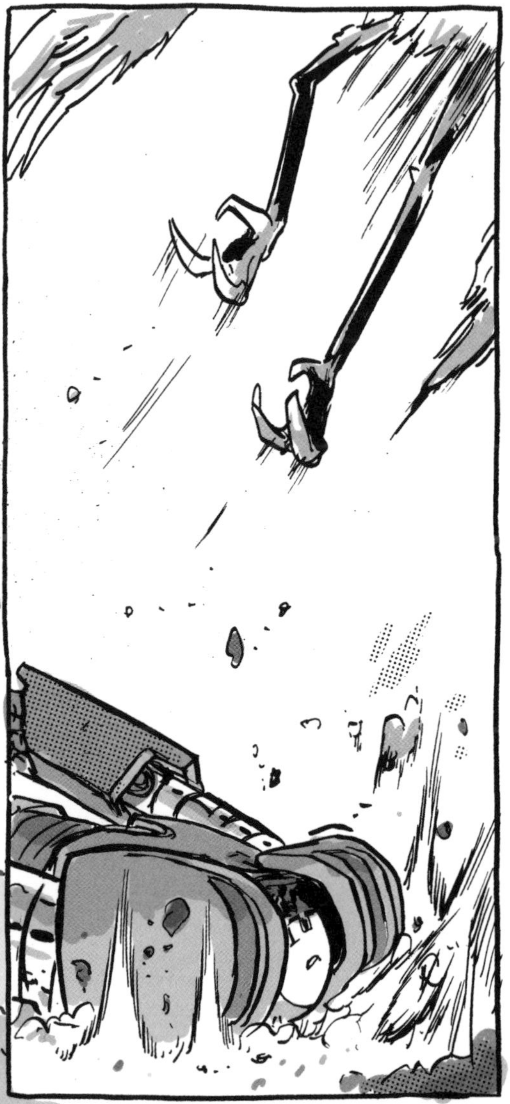

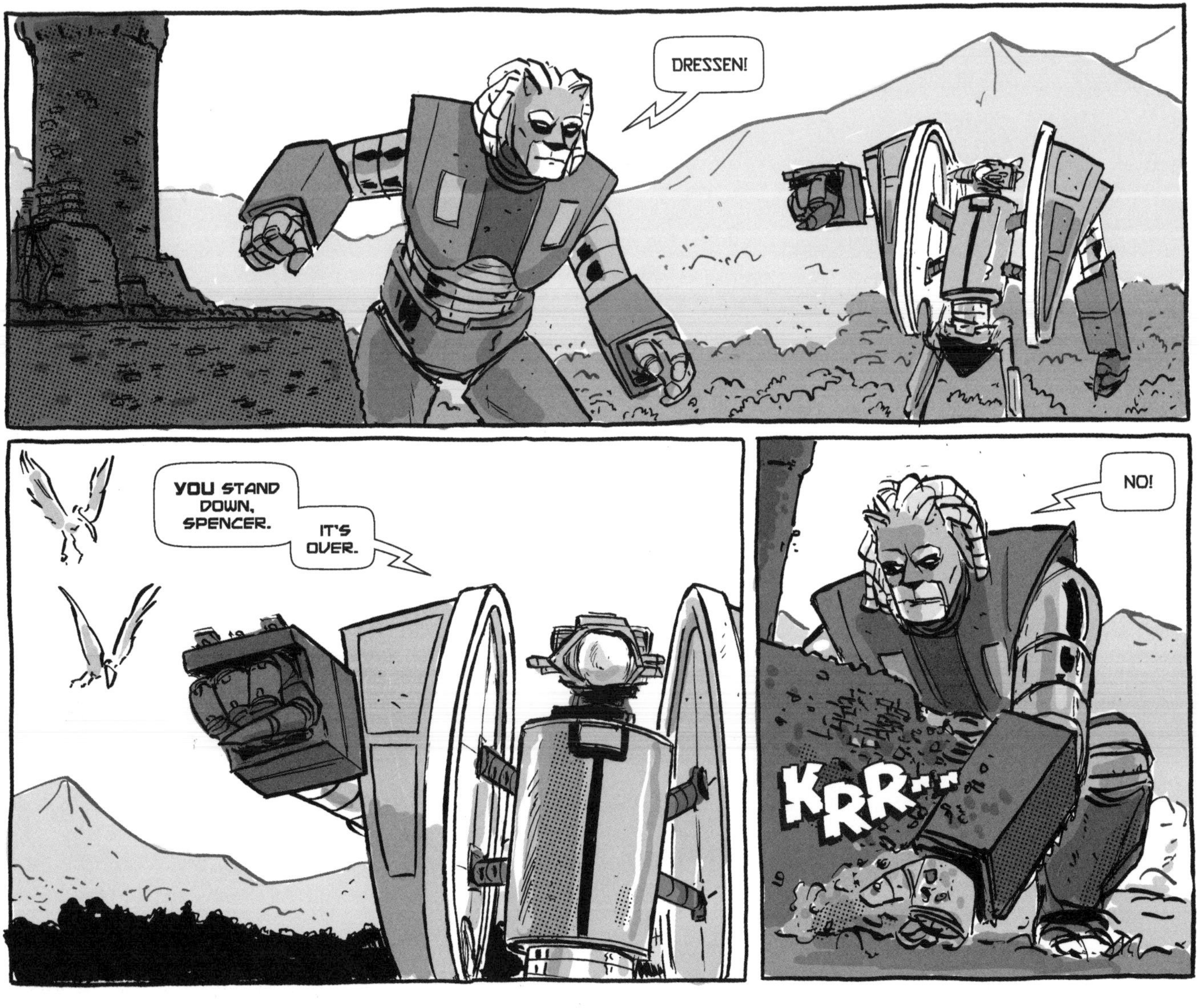
DRESSEN!
YOU STAND DOWN, SPENCER.
IT'S OVER.
NO!
KRR...

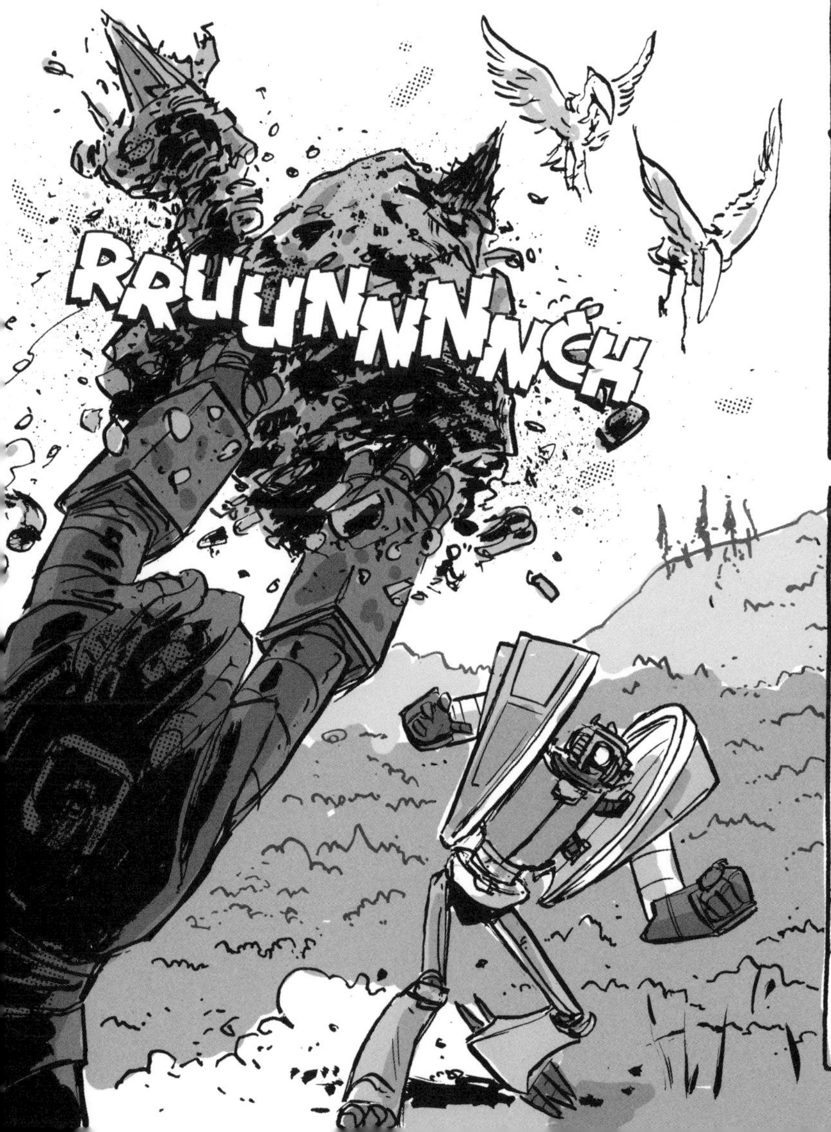
RRUUNNNNNCH
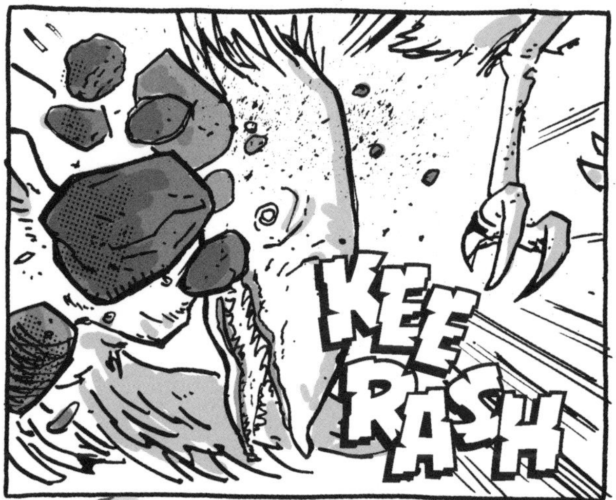
KEE RASH
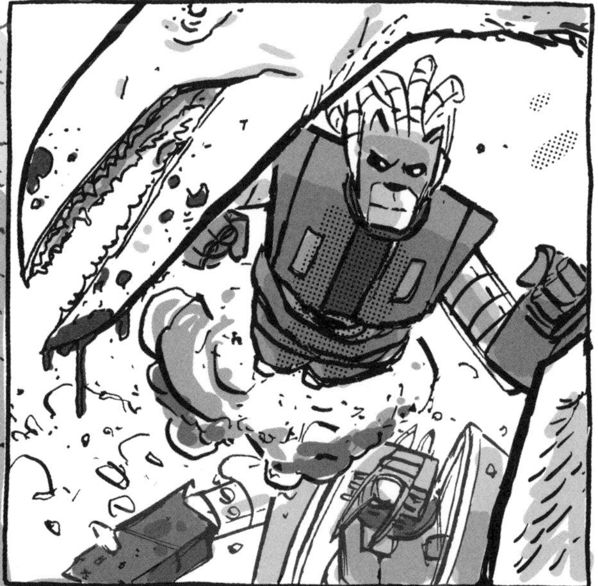

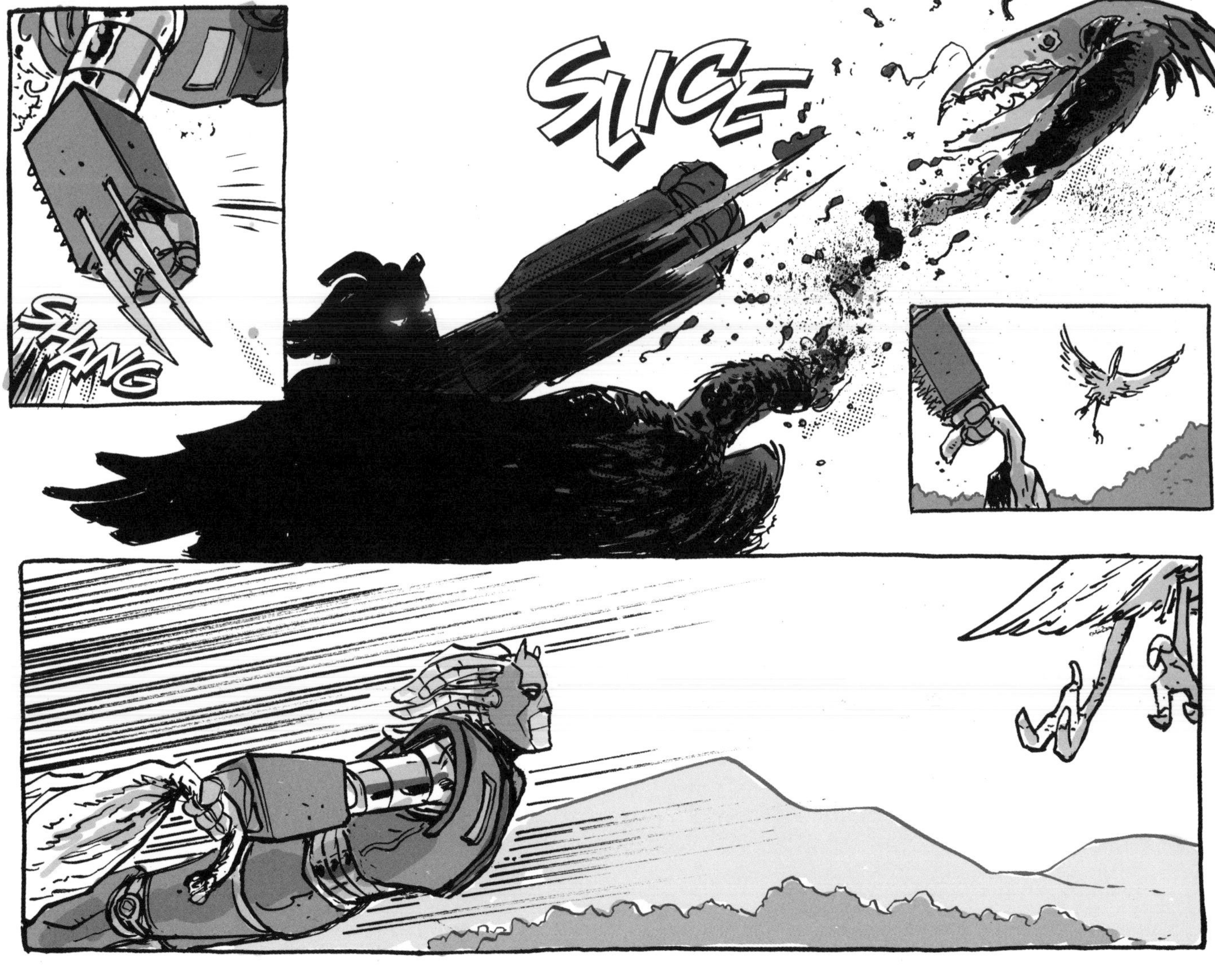
SHANG
SLICE

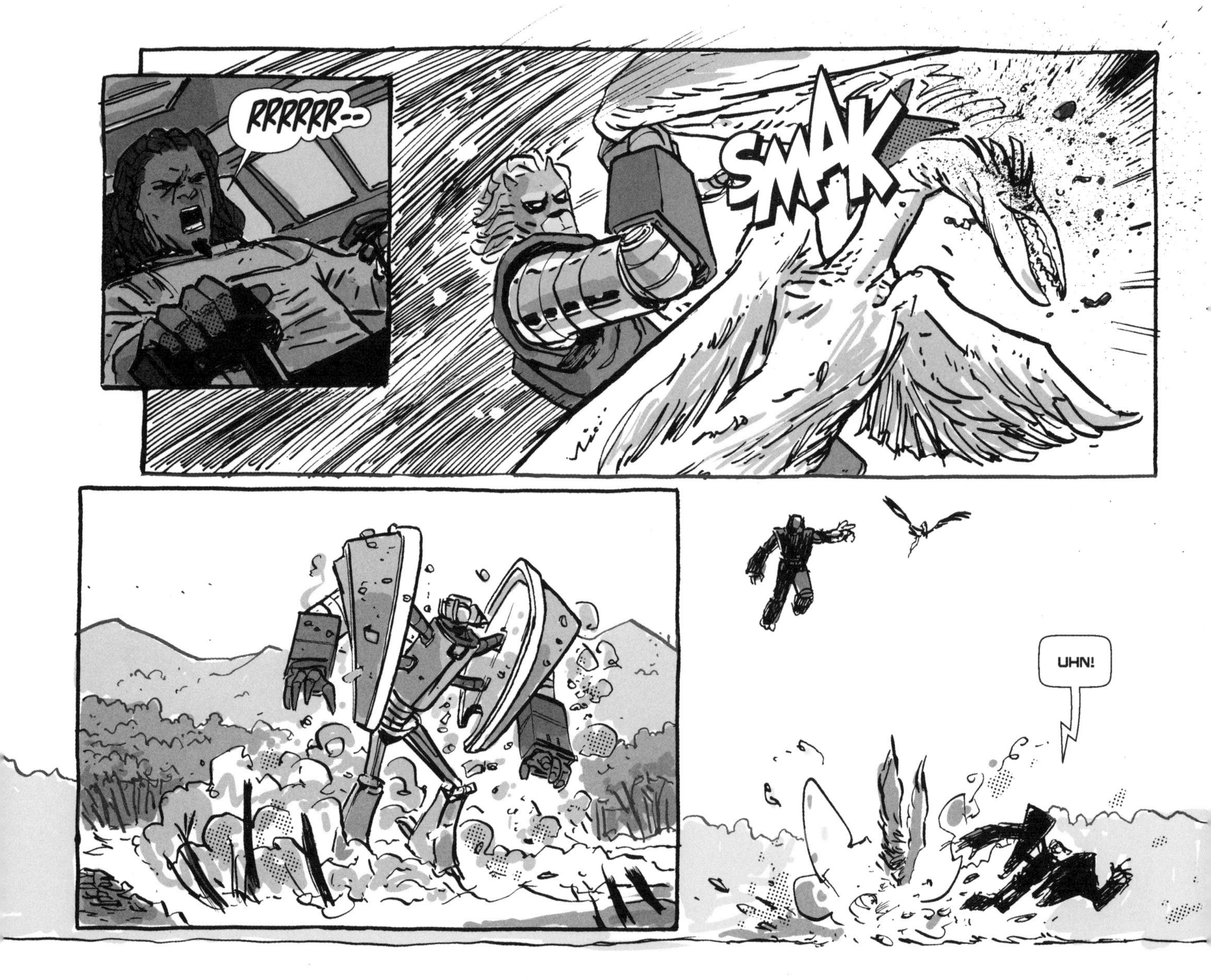
RRRRRR--
SMAK
UHN!

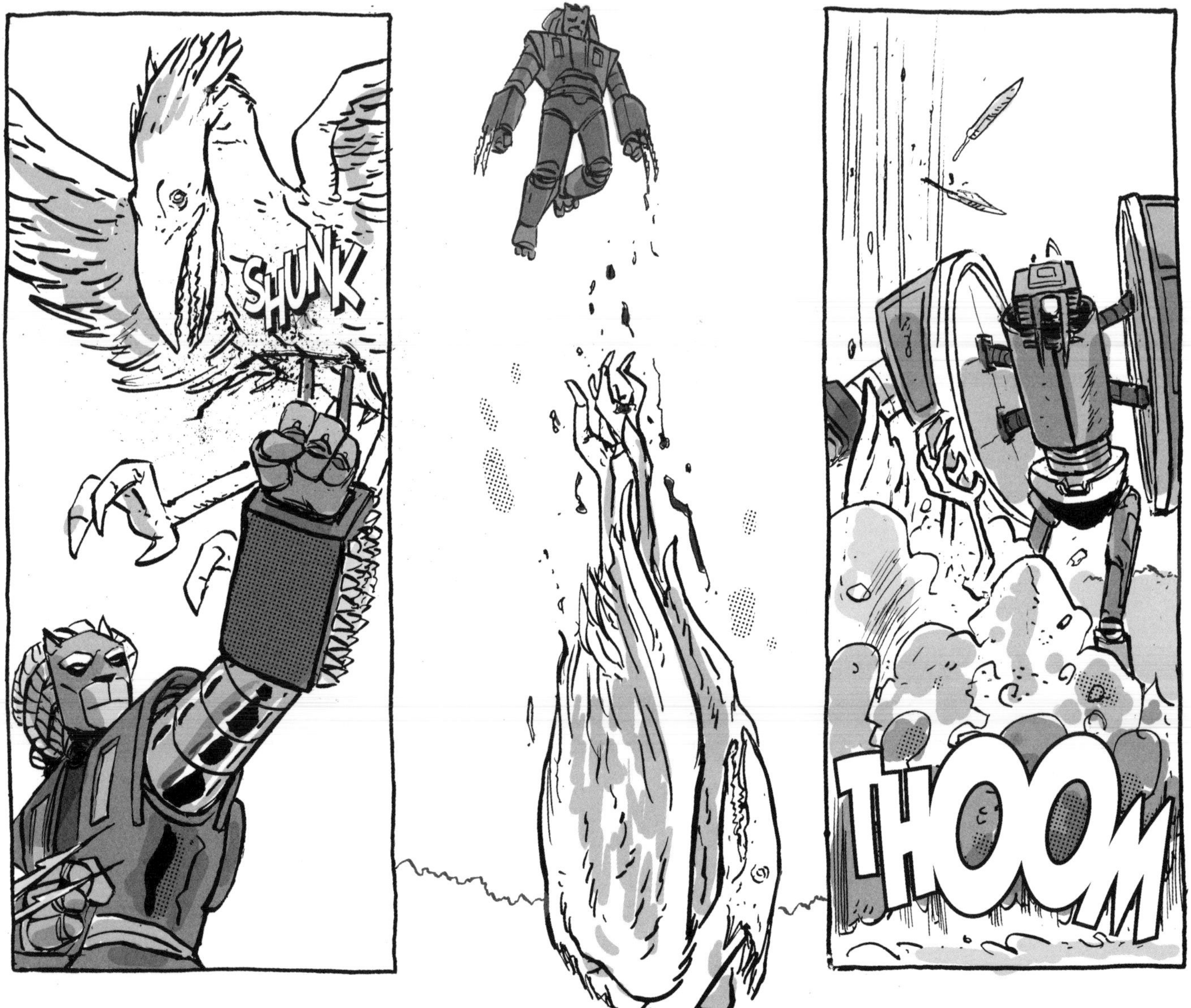
SHUNK
THOOM

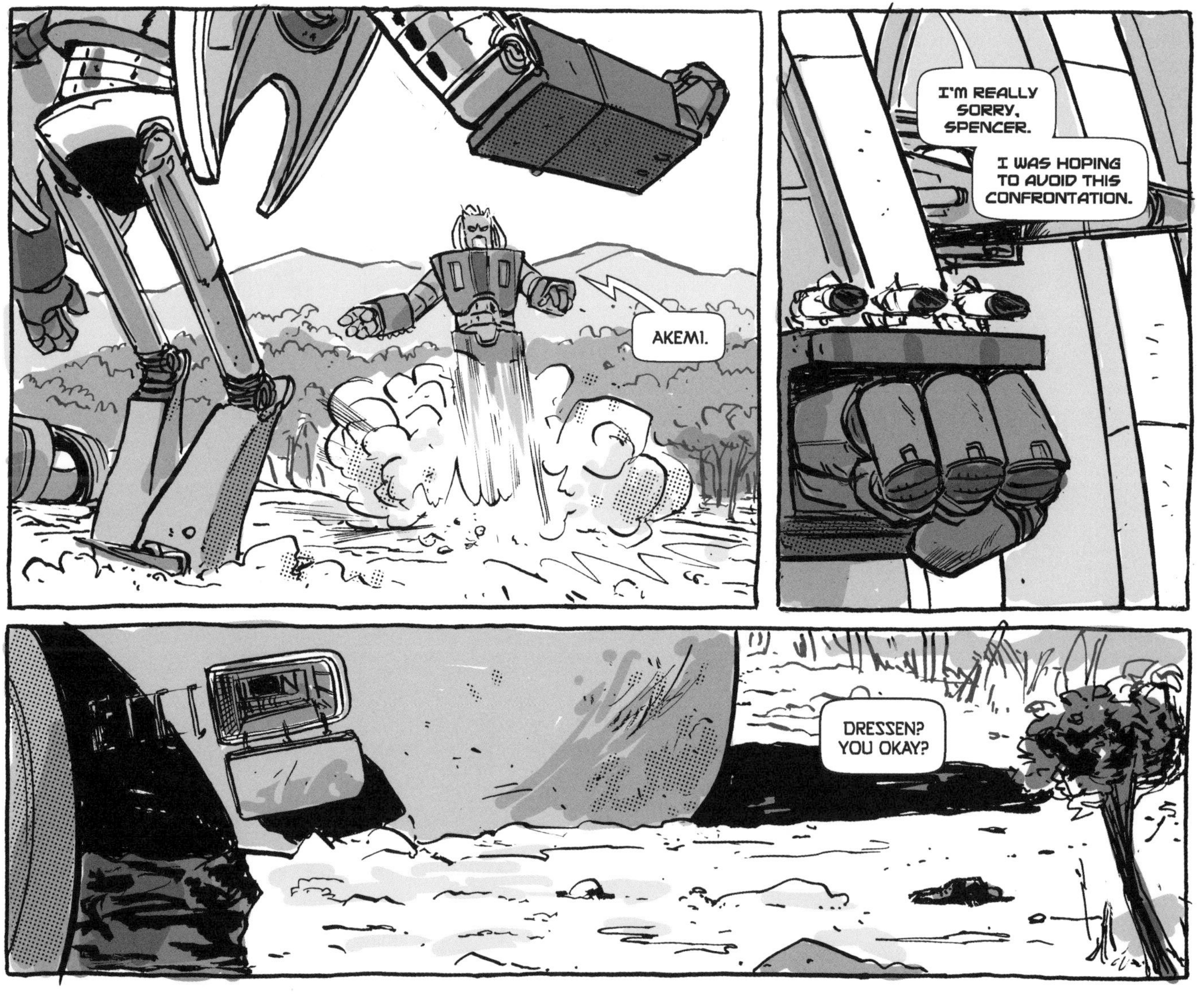
AKEMI.
I'M REALLY SORRY, SPENCER.
I WAS HOPING TO AVOID THIS CONFRONTATION.
DRESSEN? YOU OKAY?

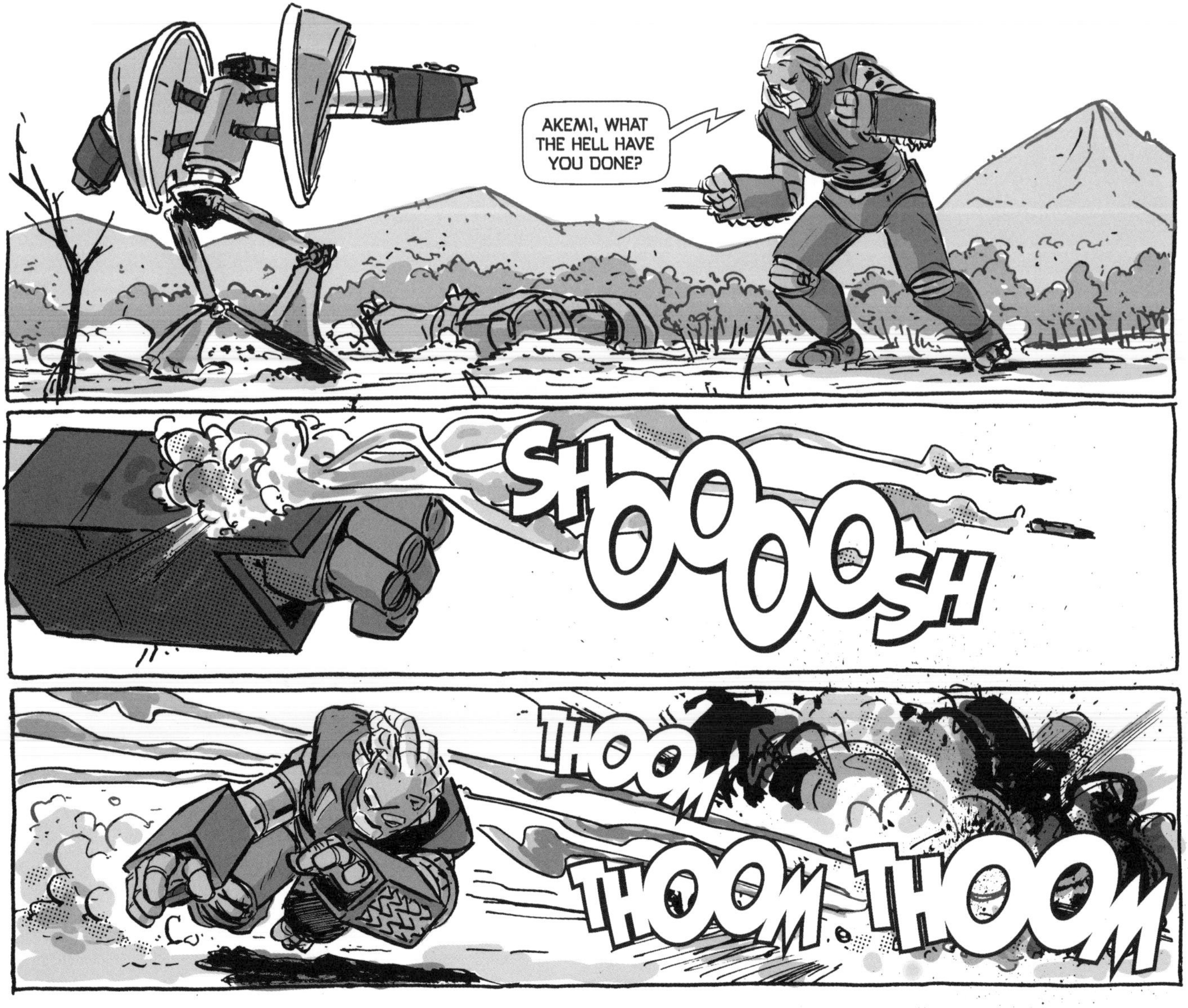
AKEMI, WHAT THE HELL HAVE YOU DONE?
SHOOOOOSH
THOOM
THOOM
THOOM

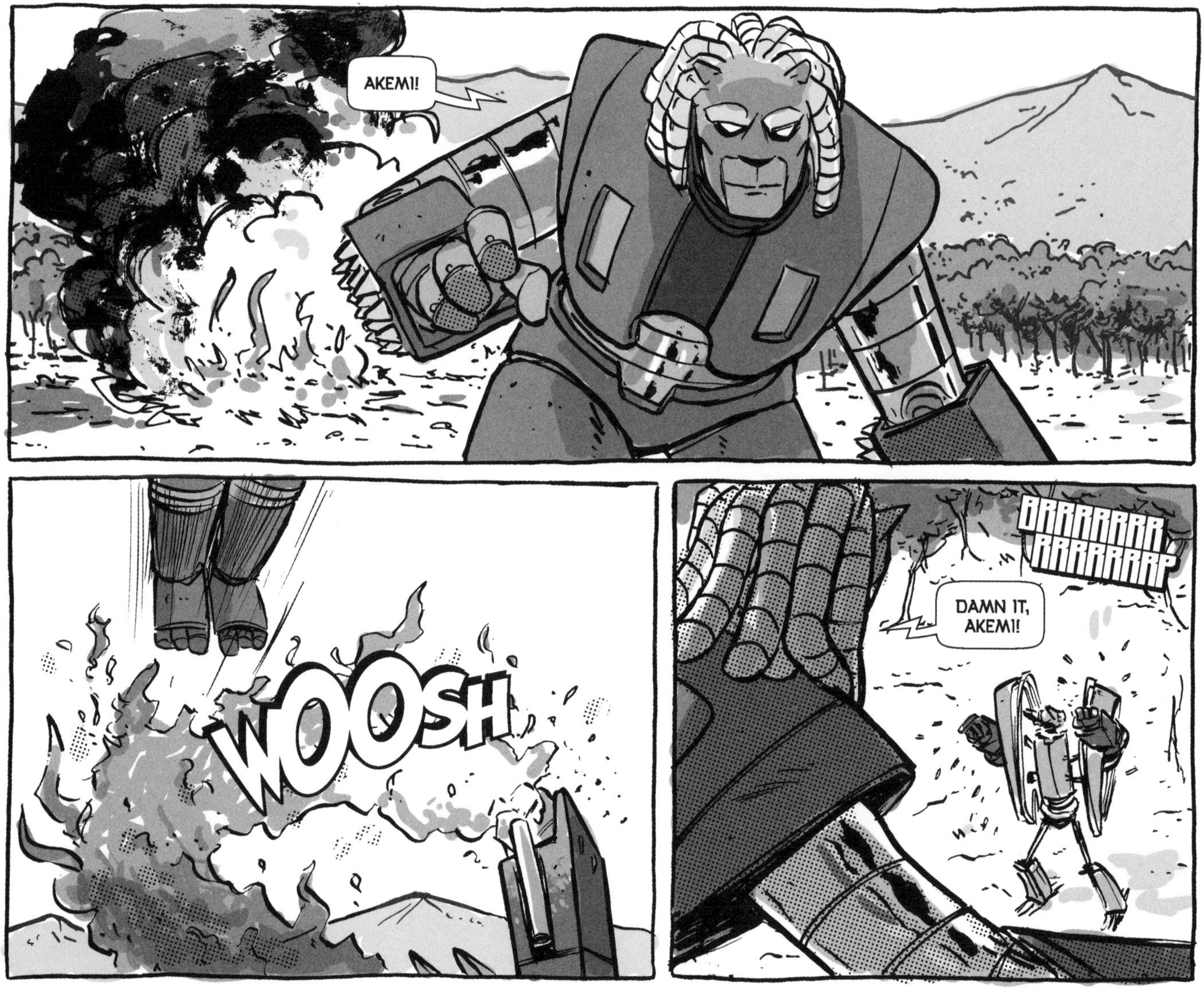
AKEMI!
WOOSH
BRRRRRRR RRRRRRRP
DAMN IT, AKEMI!

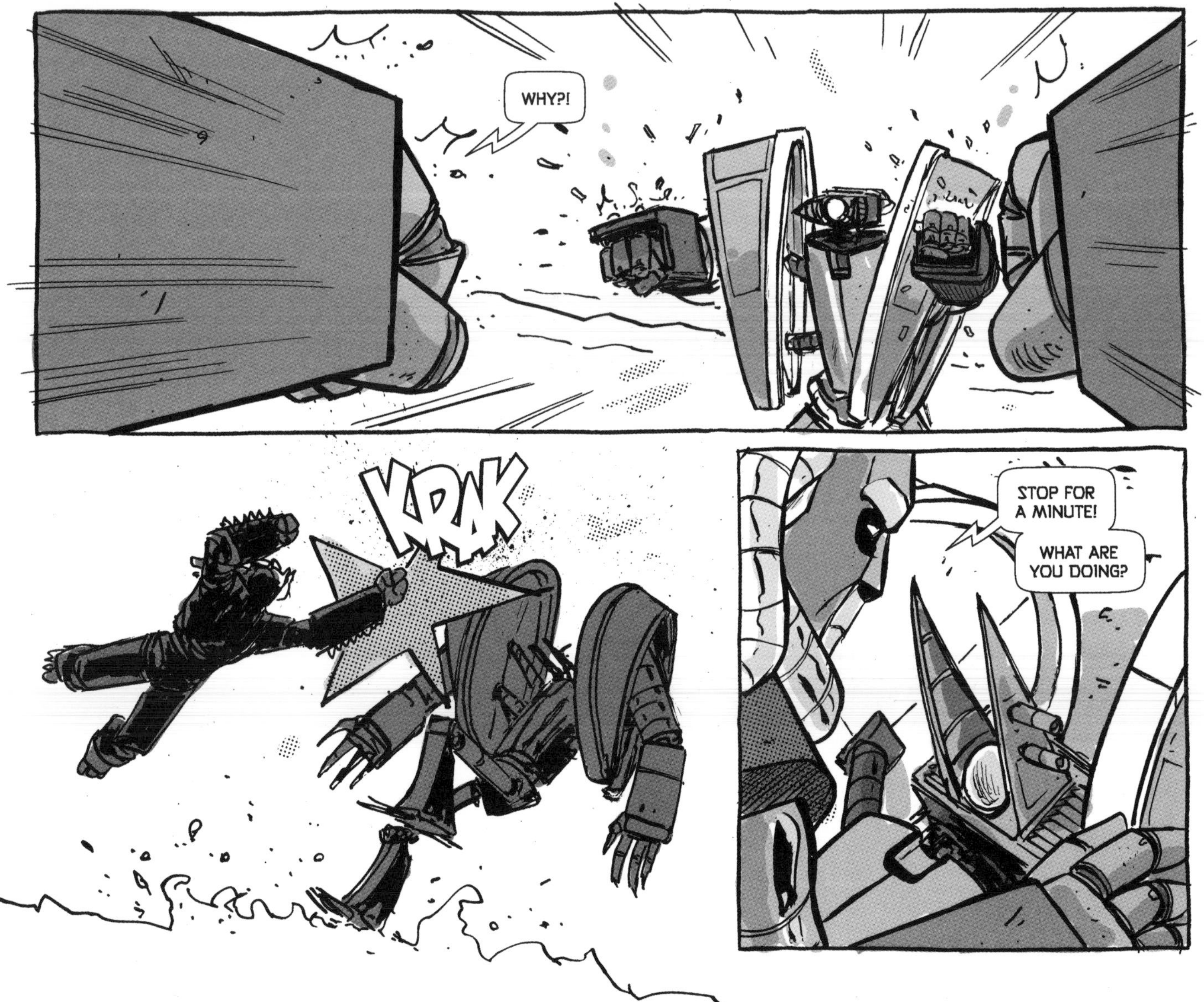
WHY?!
KRAK
STOP FOR A MINUTE!
WHAT ARE YOU DOING?

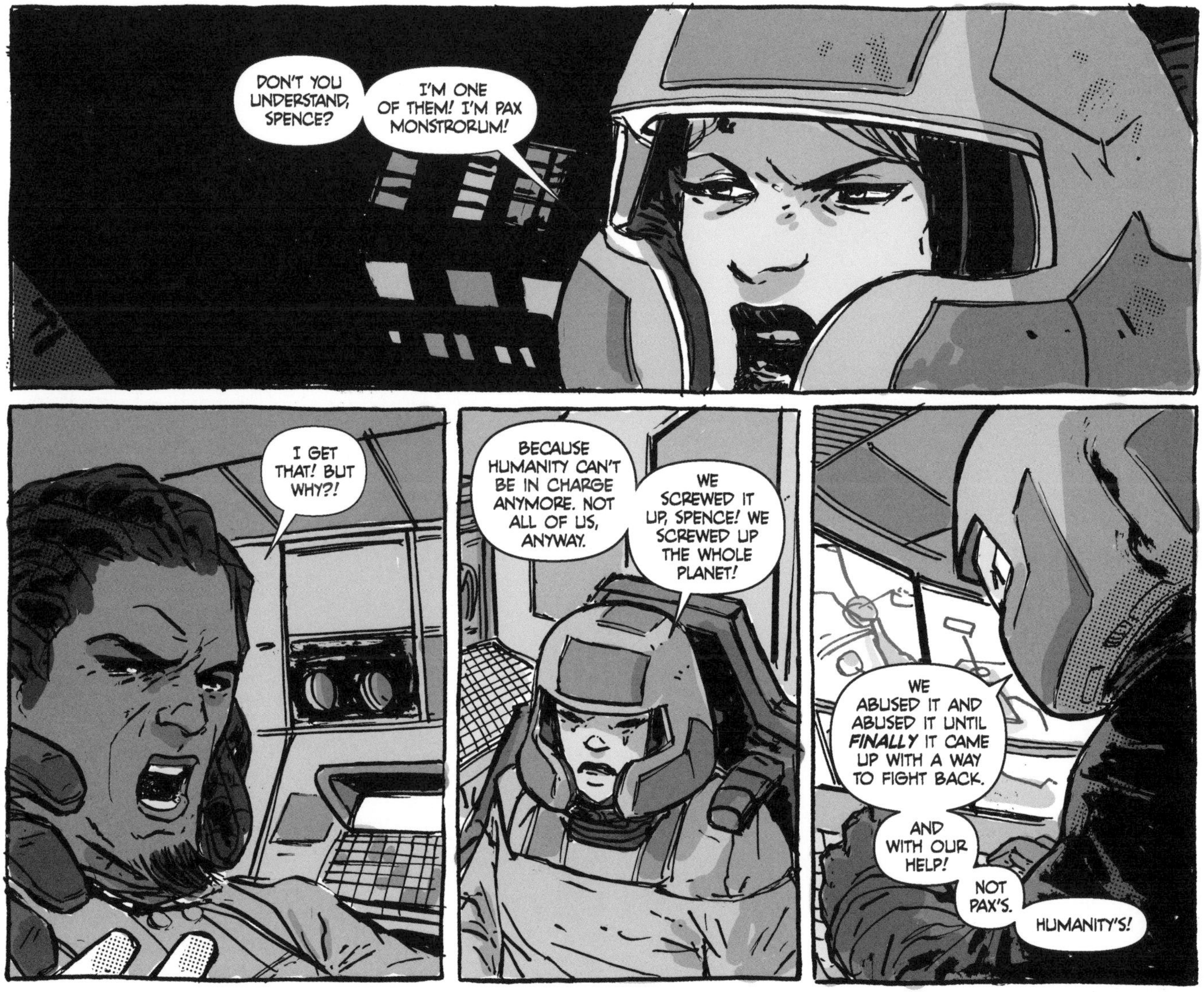
DON'T YOU UNDERSTAND, SPENCE?
I'M ONE OF THEM! I'M PAX MONSTRORUM!
I GET THAT! BUT WHY?!
BECAUSE HUMANITY CAN'T BE IN CHARGE ANYMORE. NOT ALL OF US, ANYWAY.
WE SCREWED IT UP, SPENCE! WE SCREWED UP THE WHOLE PLANET!
WE ABUSED IT AND ABUSED IT UNTIL *FINALLY* IT CAME UP WITH A WAY TO FIGHT BACK.
AND WITH OUR HELP!
NOT PAX'S.
HUMANITY'S!

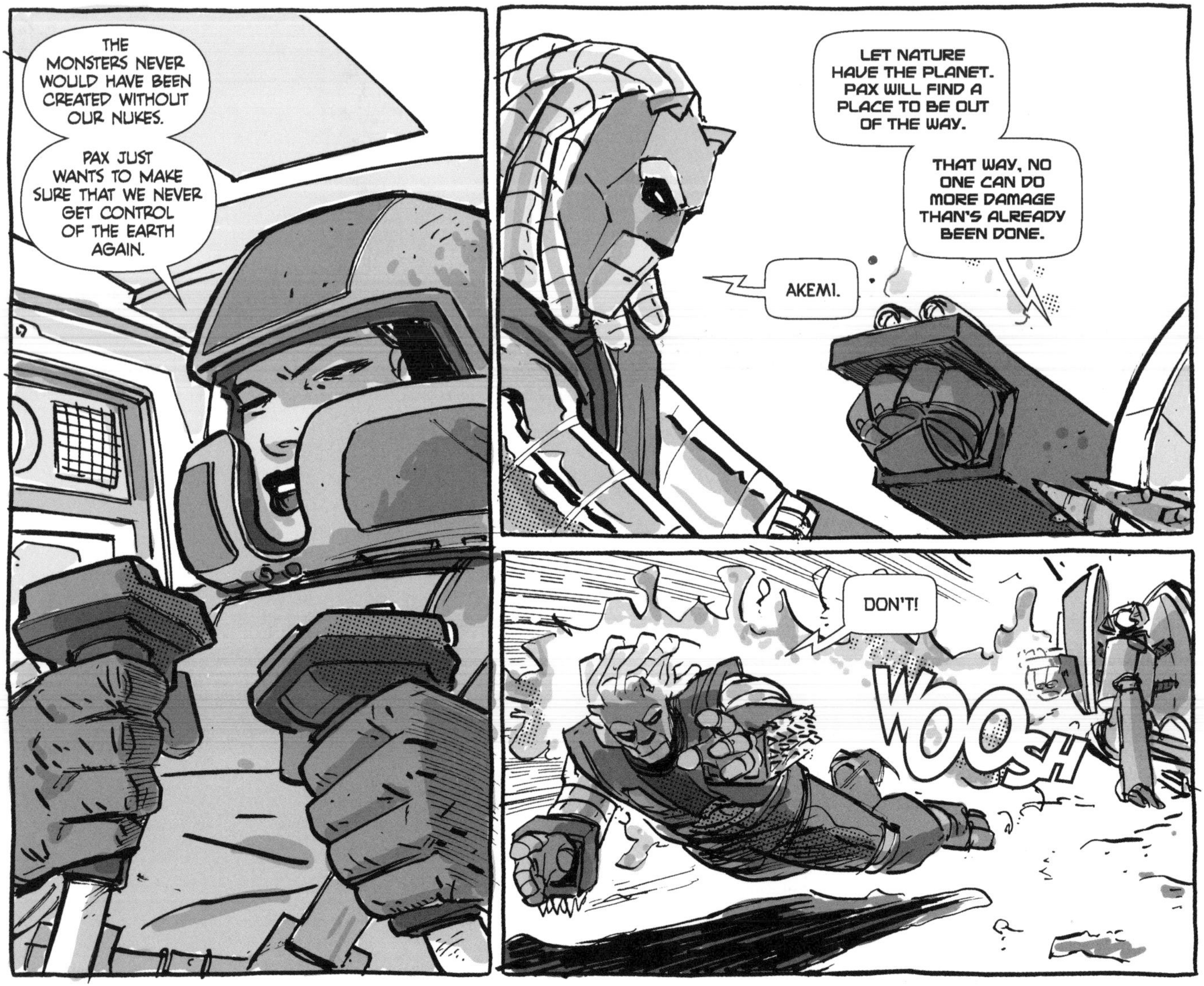
THE MONSTERS NEVER WOULD HAVE BEEN CREATED WITHOUT OUR NUKES.
PAX JUST WANTS TO MAKE SURE THAT WE NEVER GET CONTROL OF THE EARTH AGAIN.
LET NATURE HAVE THE PLANET. PAX WILL FIND A PLACE TO BE OUT OF THE WAY.
THAT WAY, NO ONE CAN DO MORE DAMAGE THAN'S ALREADY BEEN DONE.
AKEMI.
DON'T!
WOOSH

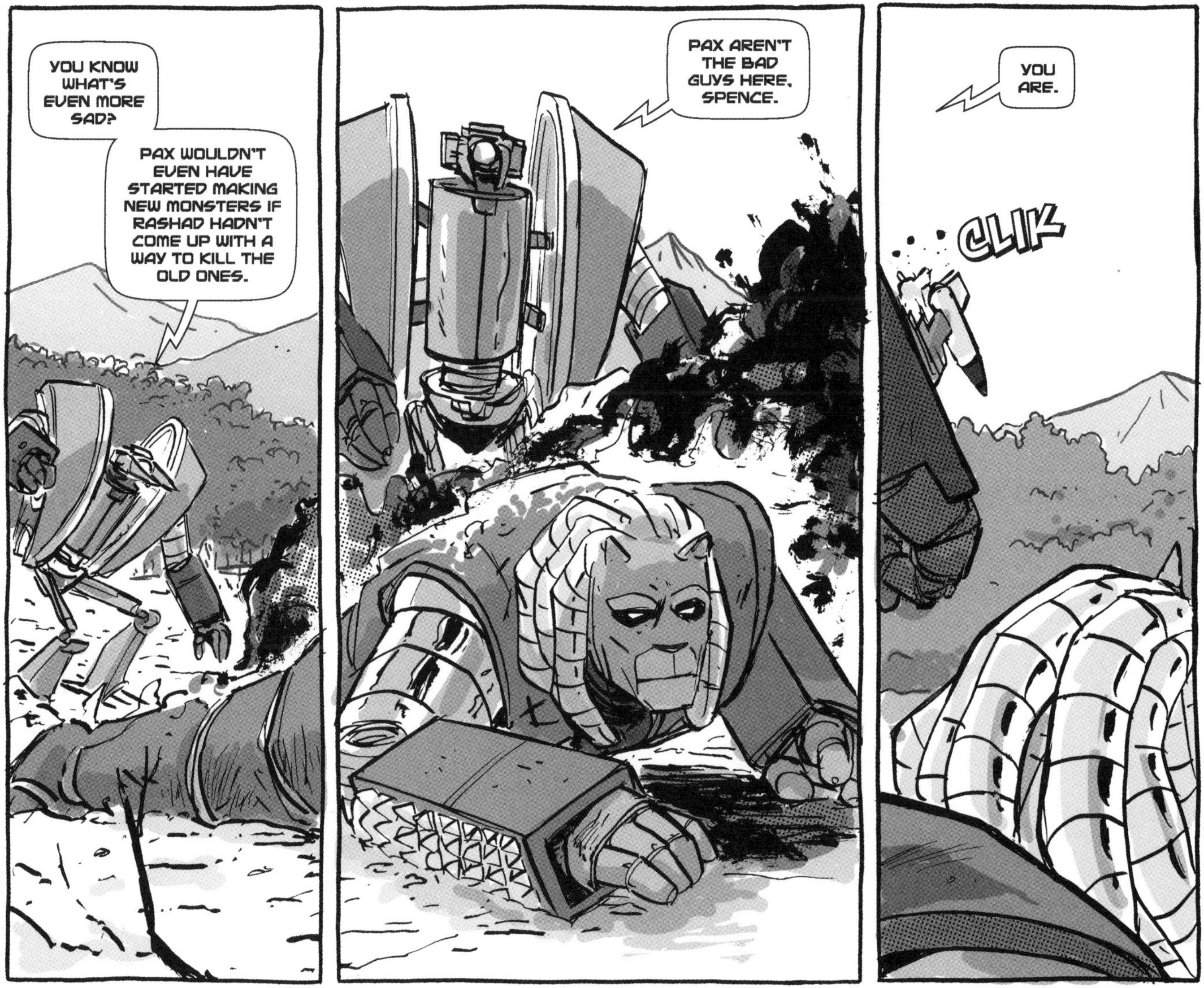
YOU KNOW WHAT'S EVEN MORE SAD?
PAX WOULDN'T EVEN HAVE STARTED MAKING NEW MONSTERS IF RASHAD HADN'T COME UP WITH A WAY TO KILL THE OLD ONES.
PAX AREN'T THE BAD GUYS HERE, SPENCE.
YOU ARE.
CLIK

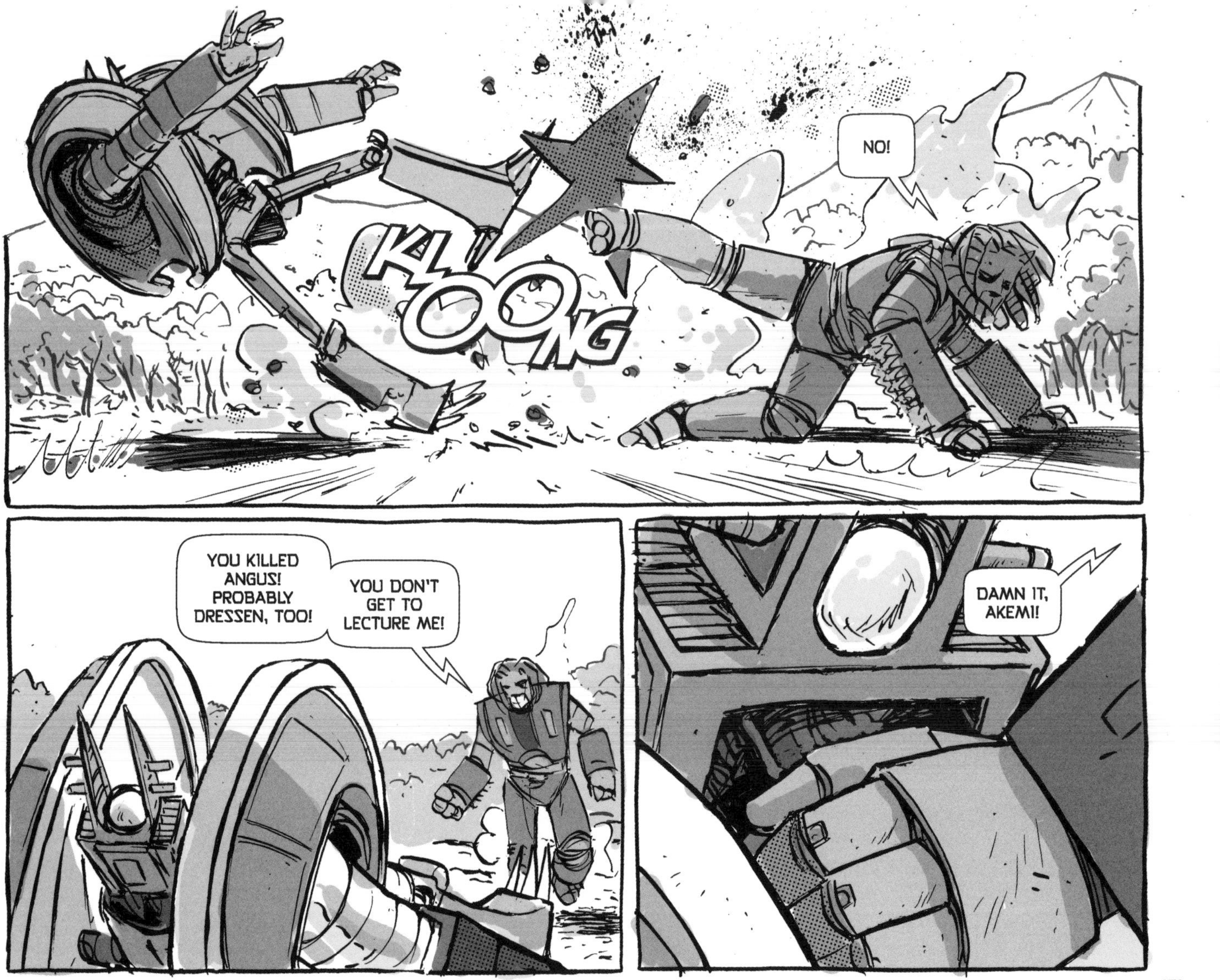
KLOOONG
NO!
YOU KILLED ANGUS! PROBABLY DRESSEN, TOO!
YOU DON'T GET TO LECTURE ME!
DAMN IT, AKEMI!

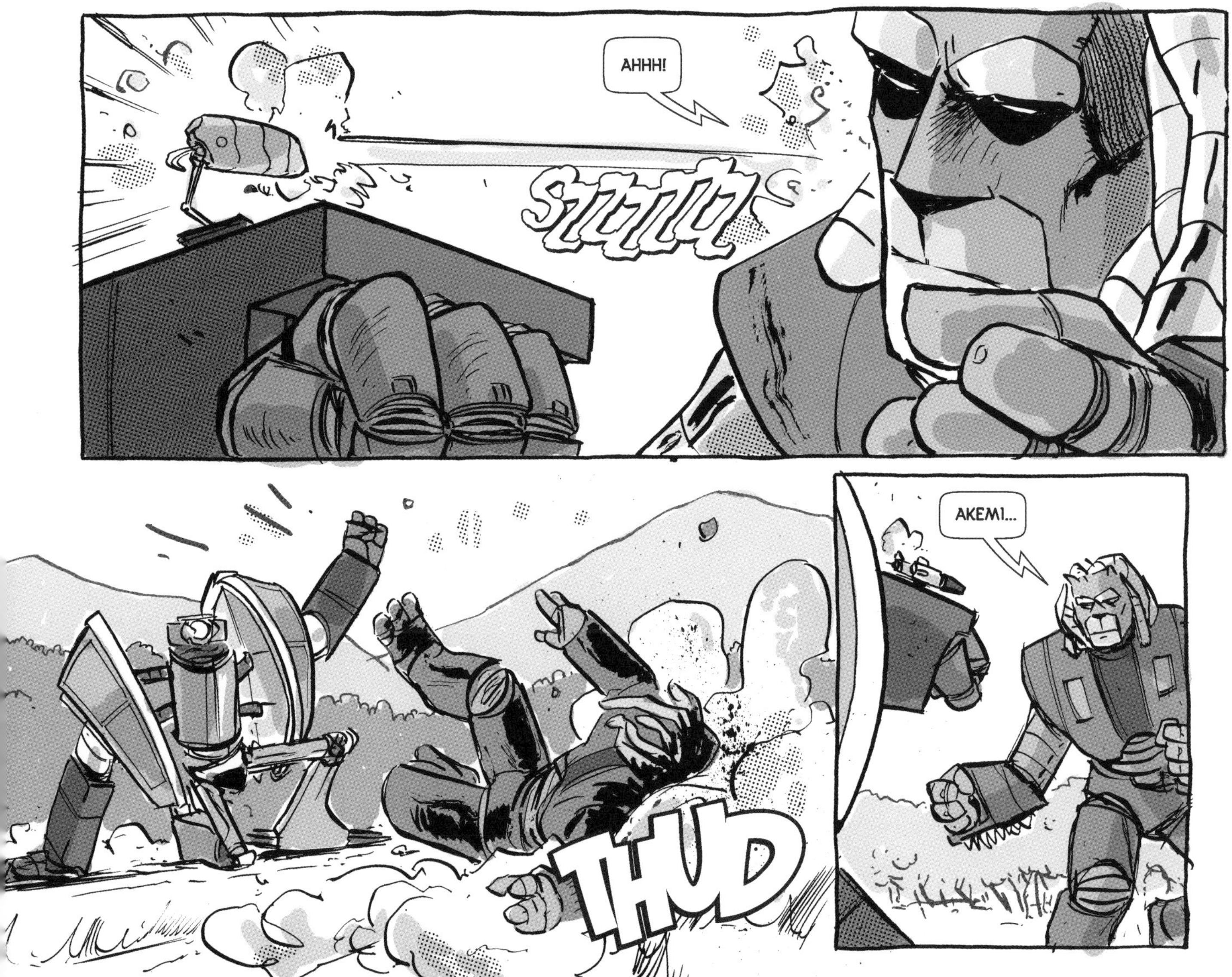
SZZZTT
AHHH!
THUD
AKEMI...

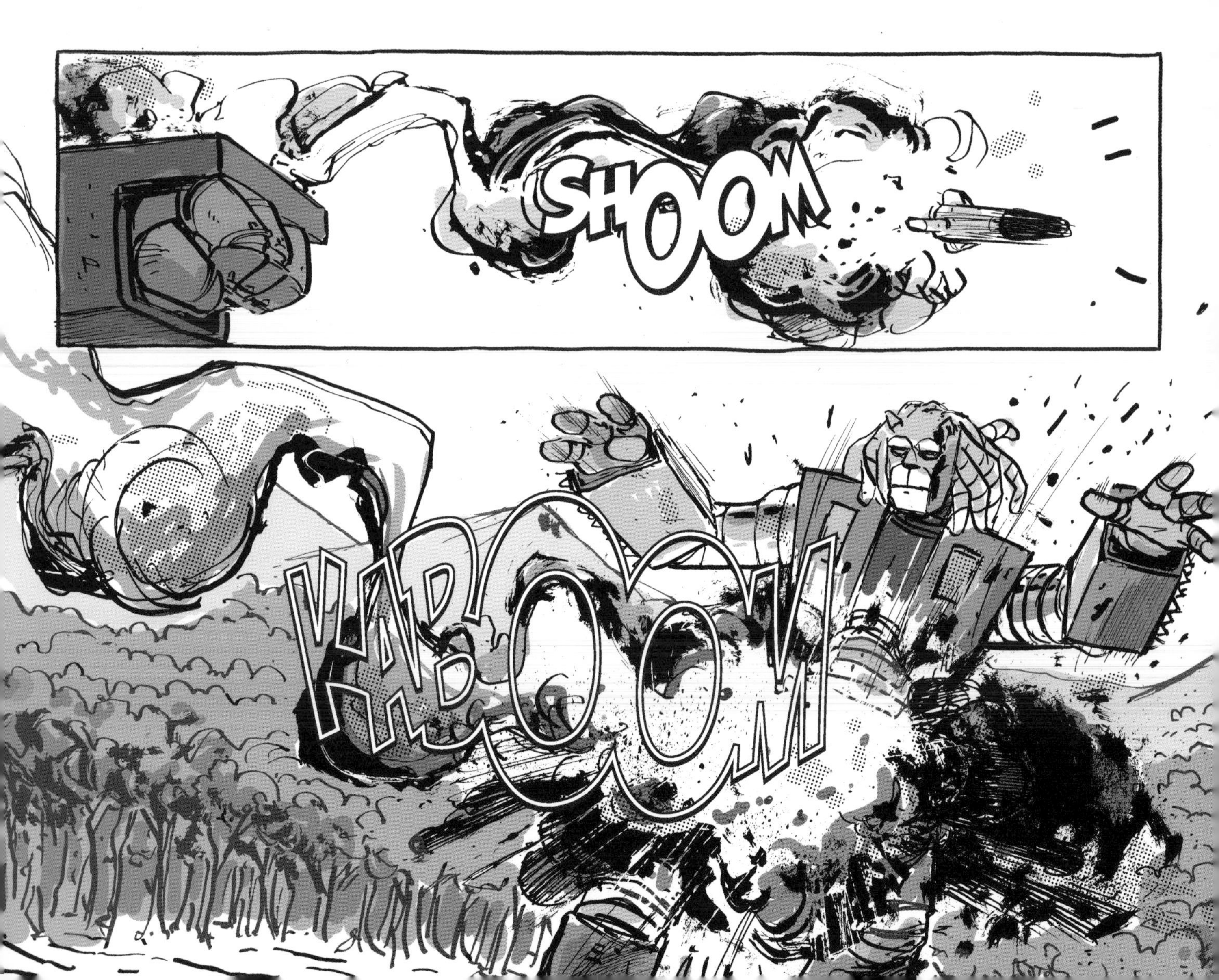
SHOOM
KABOOM

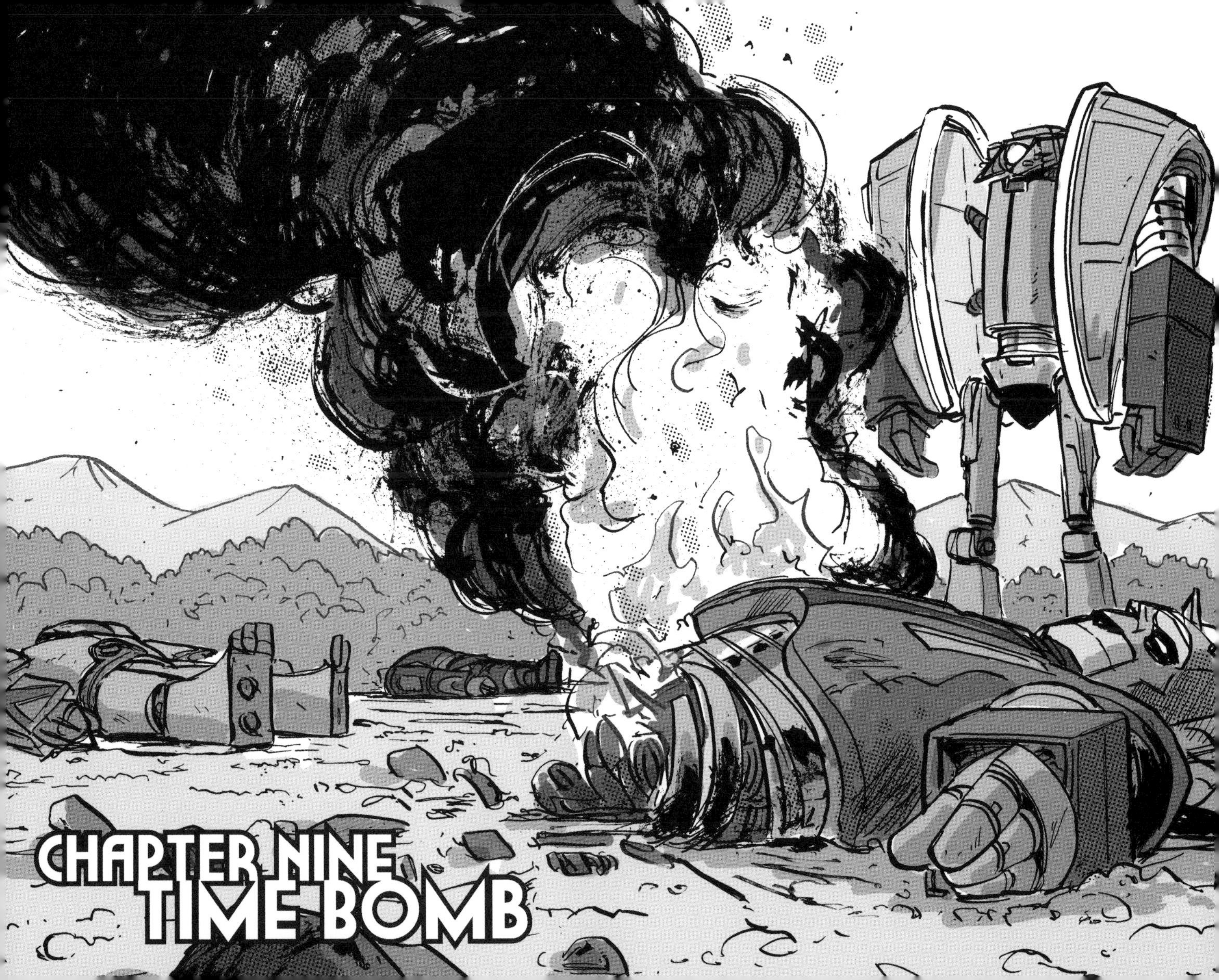
CHAPTER NINE
TIME BOMB

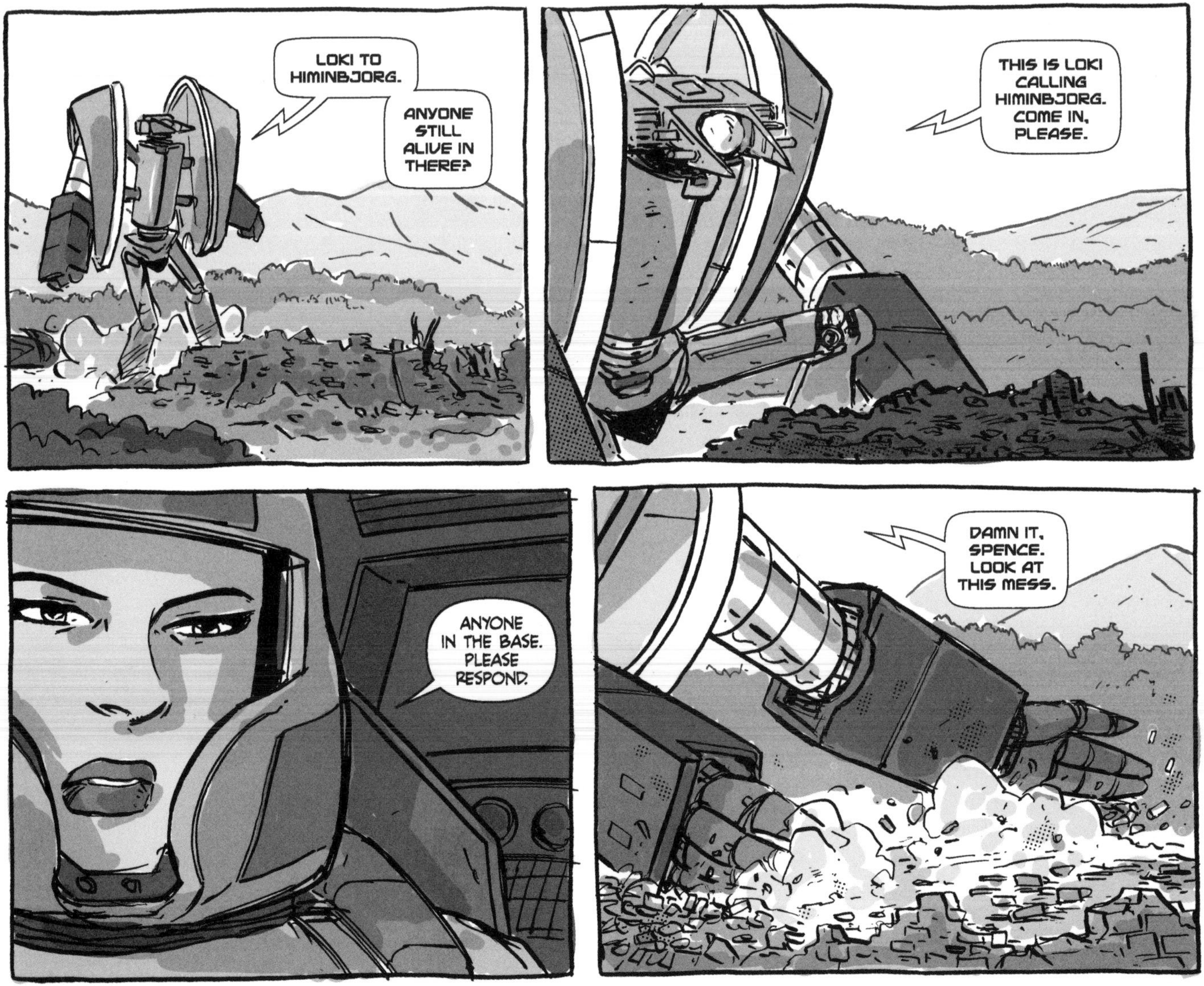
LOKI TO HIMINBJORG.
ANYONE STILL ALIVE IN THERE?
THIS IS LOKI CALLING HIMINBJORG. COME IN, PLEASE.
ANYONE IN THE BASE. PLEASE RESPOND.
DAMN IT, SPENCE. LOOK AT THIS MESS.

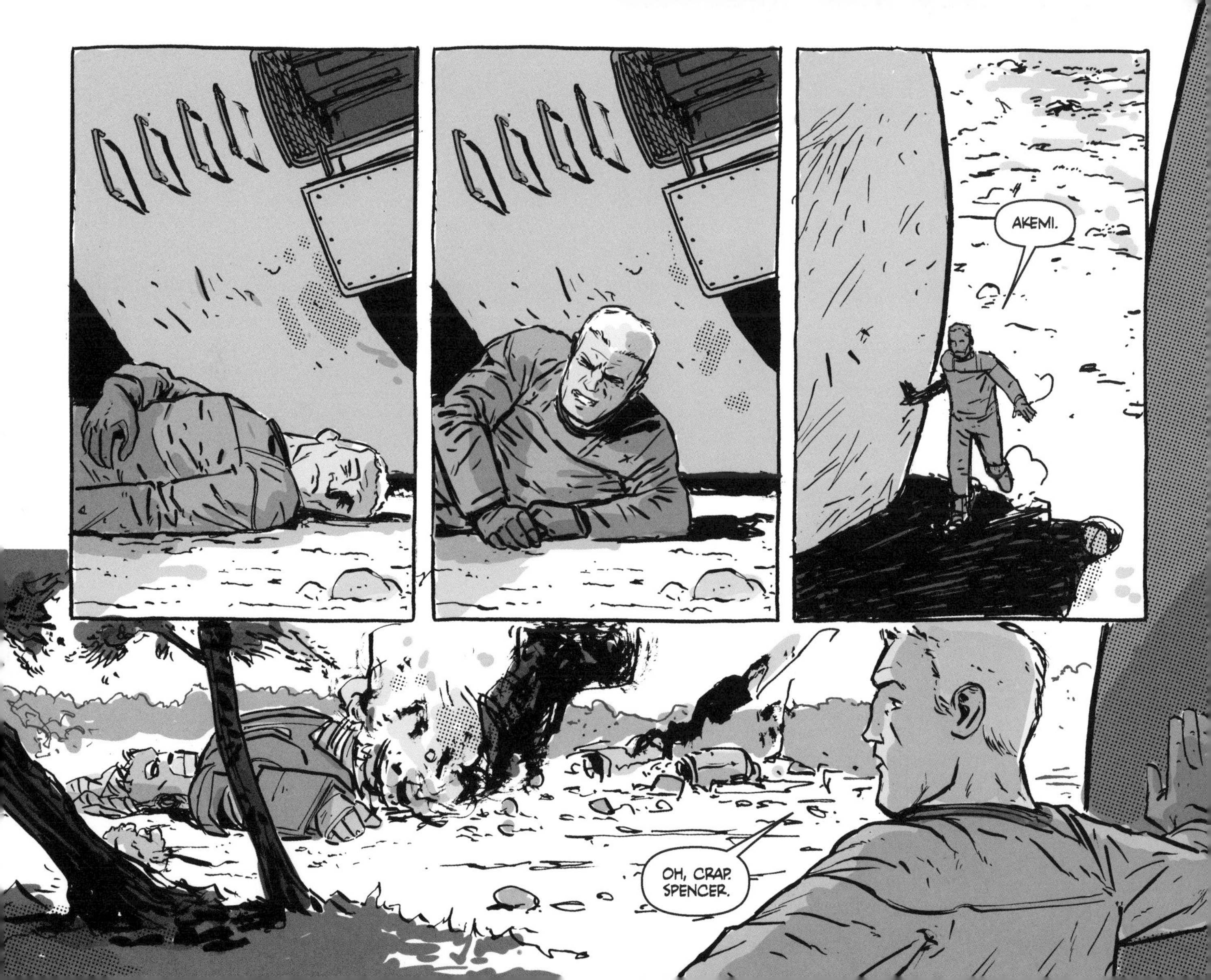
AKEMI.
OH, CRAP. SPENCER.

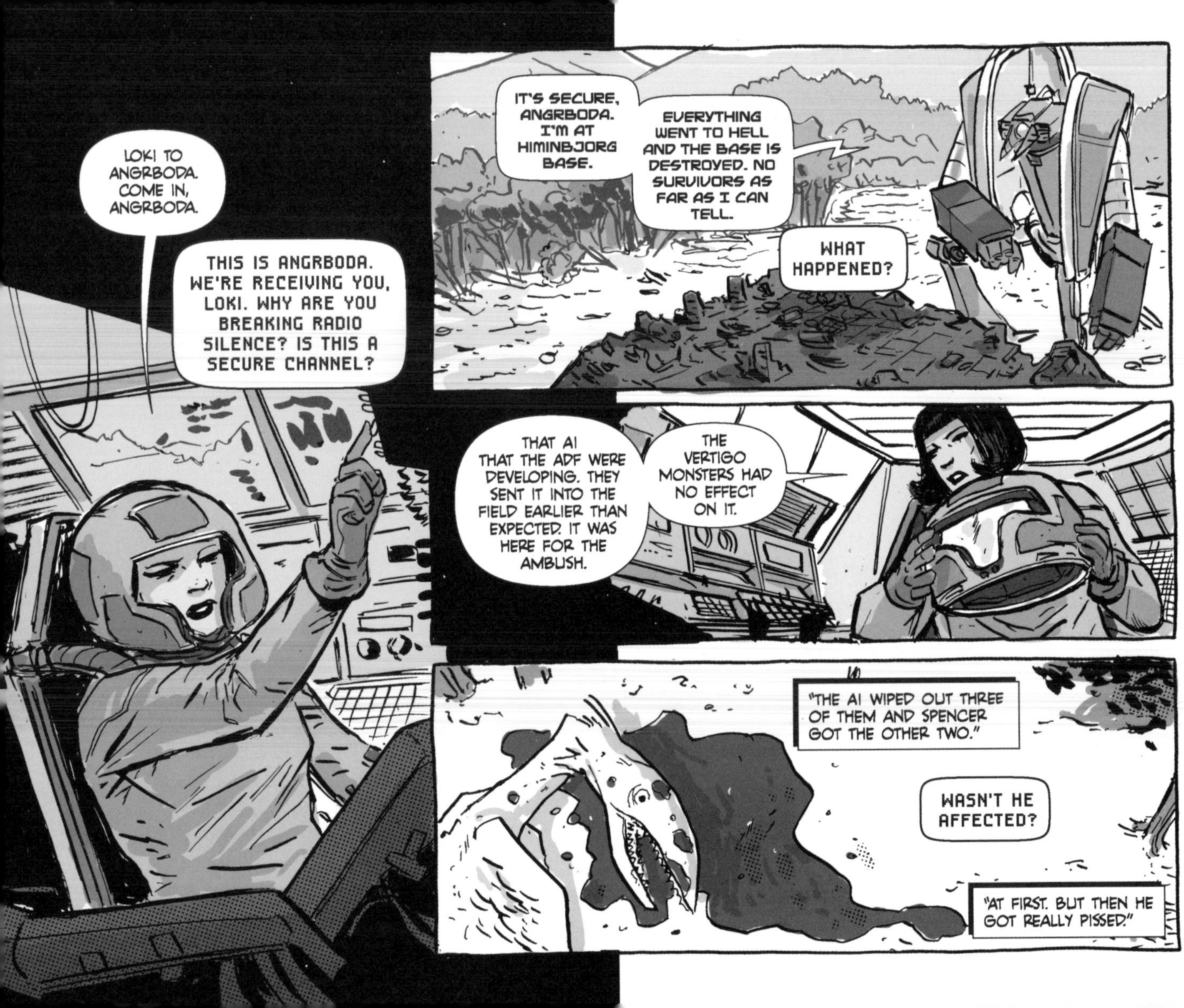
LOKI TO ANGRBODA. COME IN, ANGRBODA.
THIS IS ANGRBODA. WE'RE RECEIVING YOU, LOKI. WHY ARE YOU BREAKING RADIO SILENCE? IS THIS A SECURE CHANNEL?
IT'S SECURE, ANGRBODA. I'M AT HIMINBJORG BASE.
EVERYTHING WENT TO HELL AND THE BASE IS DESTROYED. NO SURVIVORS AS FAR AS I CAN TELL.
WHAT HAPPENED?
THAT AI THAT THE ADF WERE DEVELOPING. THEY SENT IT INTO THE FIELD EARLIER THAN EXPECTED. IT WAS HERE FOR THE AMBUSH.
THE VERTIGO MONSTERS HAD NO EFFECT ON IT.
"THE AI WIPED OUT THREE OF THEM AND SPENCER GOT THE OTHER TWO."
WASN'T HE AFFECTED?
"AT FIRST. BUT THEN HE GOT REALLY PISSED."

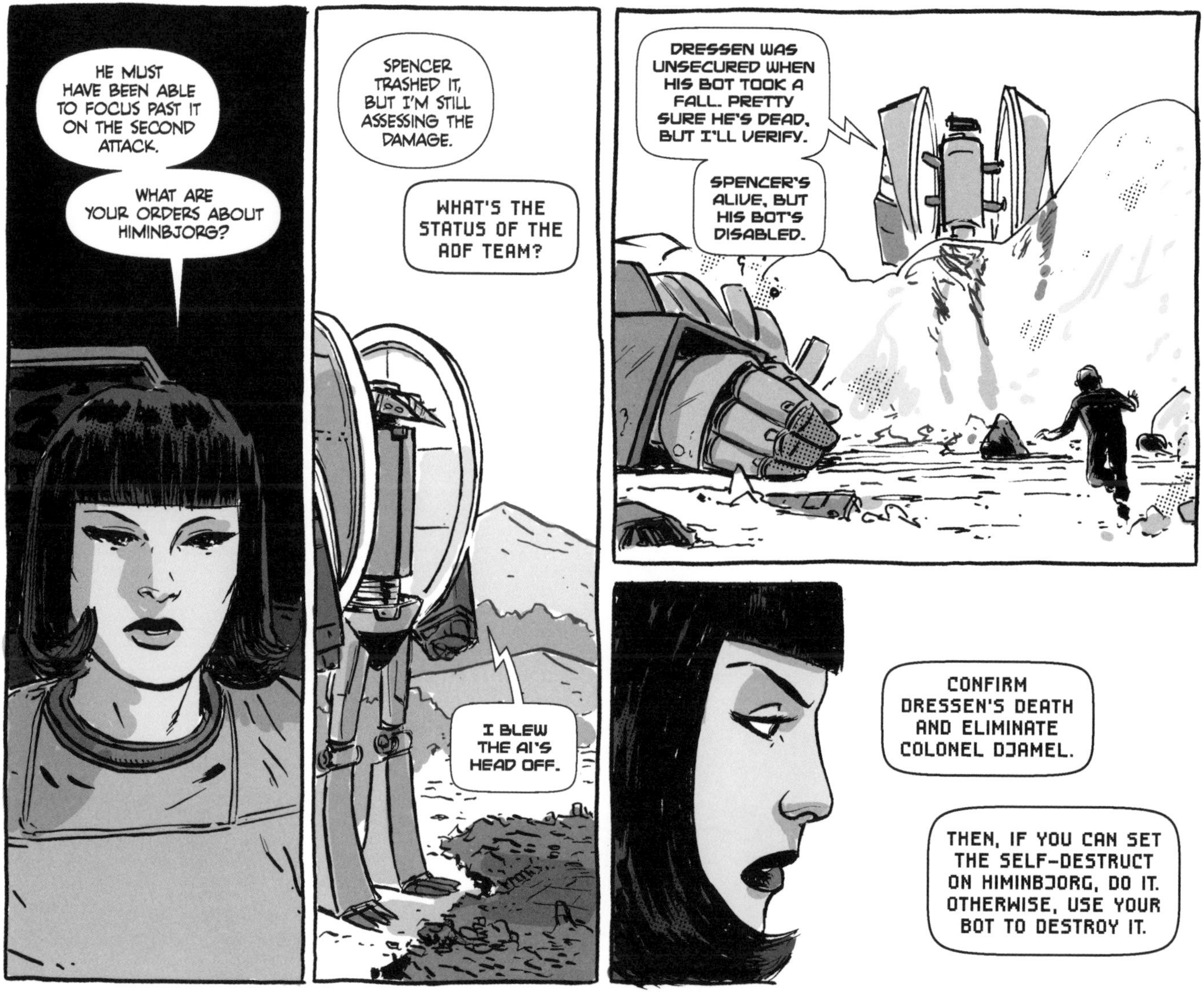
HE MUST HAVE BEEN ABLE TO FOCUS PAST IT ON THE SECOND ATTACK.
WHAT ARE YOUR ORDERS ABOUT HIMINBJORG?
SPENCER TRASHED IT, BUT I'M STILL ASSESSING THE DAMAGE.
WHAT'S THE STATUS OF THE ADF TEAM?
I BLEW THE AI'S HEAD OFF.
DRESSEN WAS UNSECURED WHEN HIS BOT TOOK A FALL. PRETTY SURE HE'S DEAD, BUT I'LL VERIFY.
SPENCER'S ALIVE, BUT HIS BOT'S DISABLED.
CONFIRM DRESSEN'S DEATH AND ELIMINATE COLONEL DJAMEL.
THEN, IF YOU CAN SET THE SELF-DESTRUCT ON HIMINBJORG, DO IT. OTHERWISE, USE YOUR BOT TO DESTROY IT.

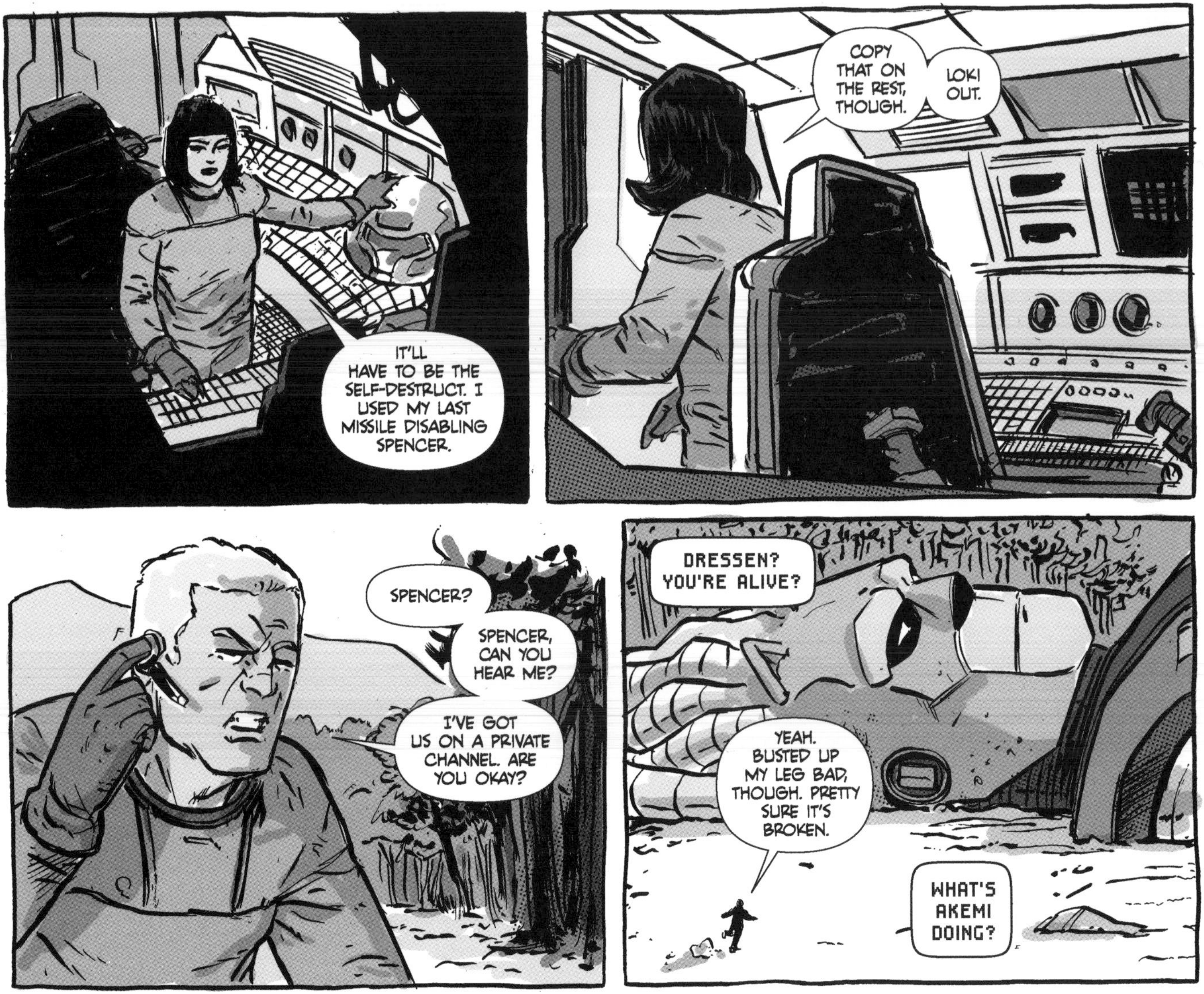
IT'LL HAVE TO BE THE SELF-DESTRUCT. I USED MY LAST MISSILE DISABLING SPENCER.
COPY THAT ON THE REST, THOUGH.
LOKI OUT.
SPENCER?
SPENCER, CAN YOU HEAR ME?
I'VE GOT US ON A PRIVATE CHANNEL. ARE YOU OKAY?
DRESSEN? YOU'RE ALIVE?
YEAH. BUSTED UP MY LEG BAD, THOUGH. PRETTY SURE IT'S BROKEN.
WHAT'S AKEMI DOING?

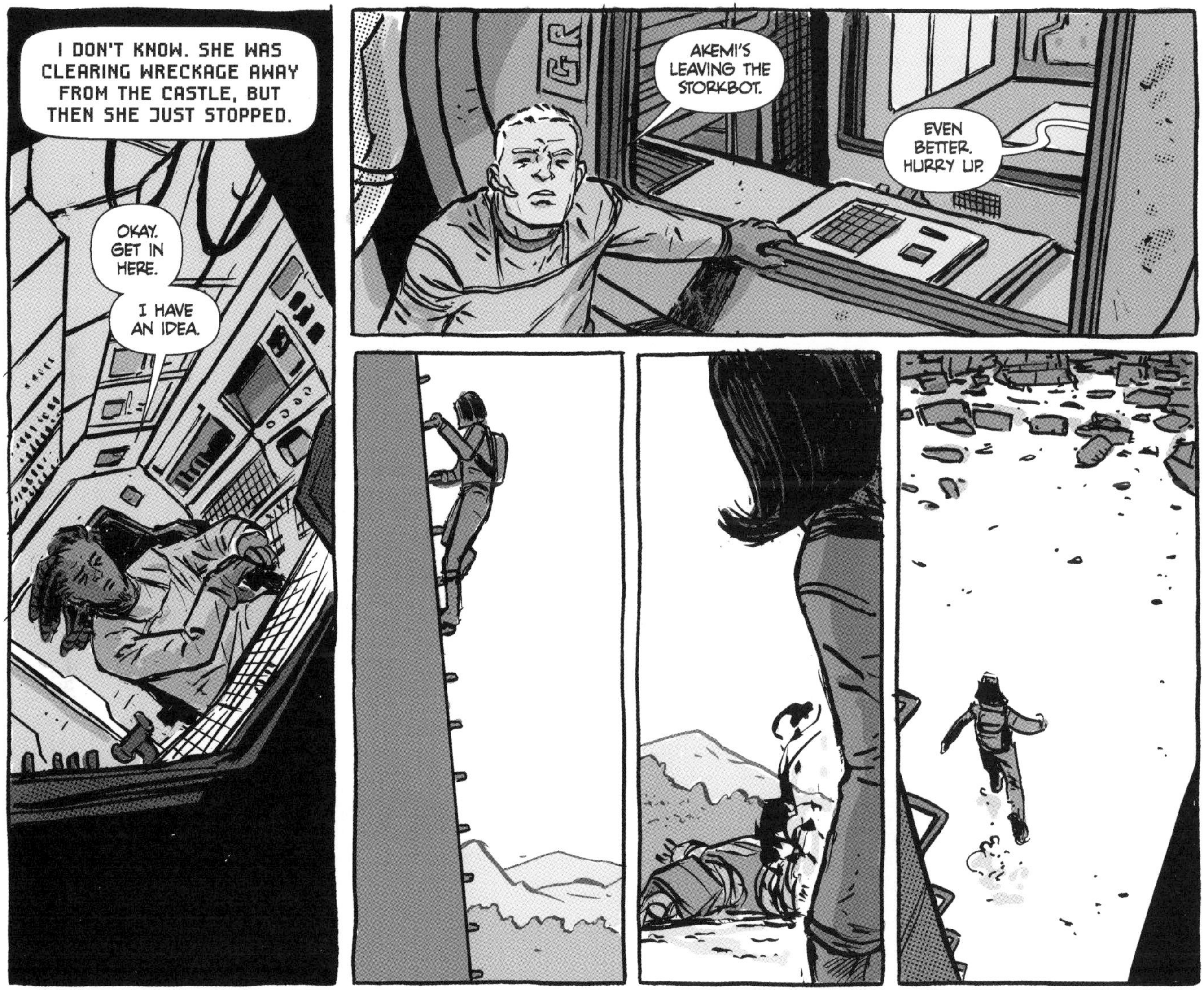
I DON'T KNOW. SHE WAS CLEARING WRECKAGE AWAY FROM THE CASTLE, BUT THEN SHE JUST STOPPED.
OKAY. GET IN HERE.
I HAVE AN IDEA.
AKEMI'S LEAVING THE STORKBOT.
EVEN BETTER. HURRY UP.

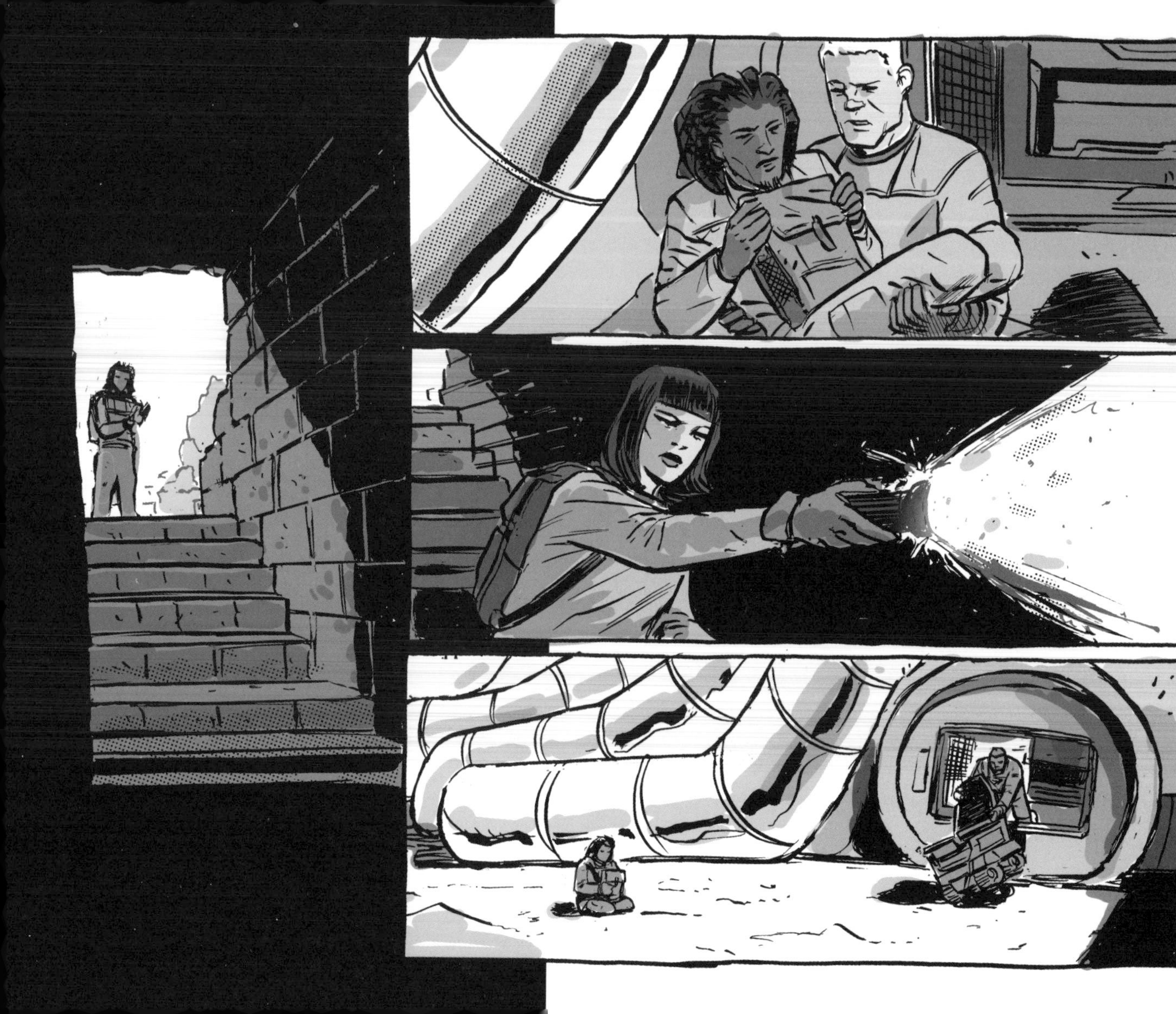

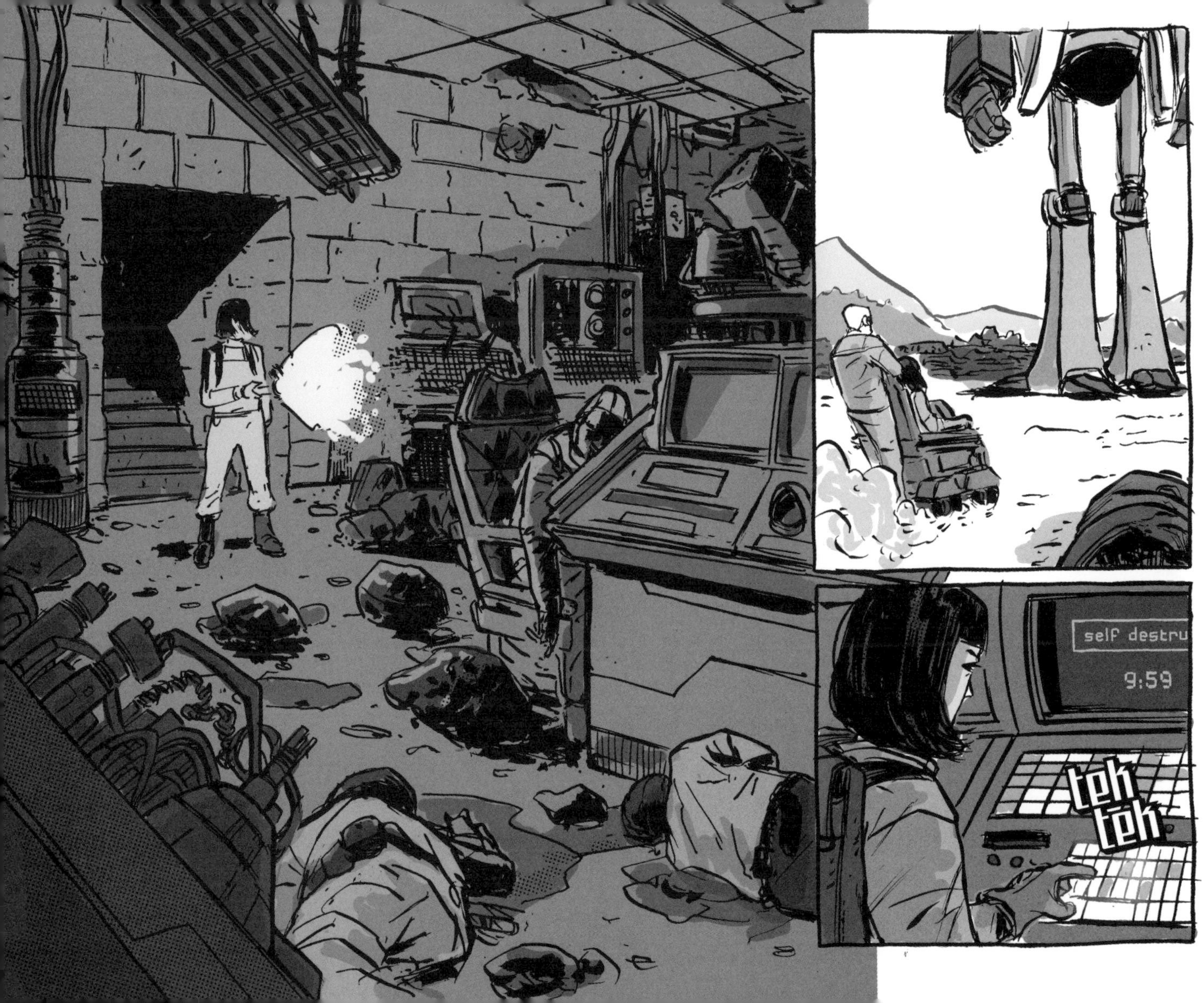
self destru
9:59
tek tek

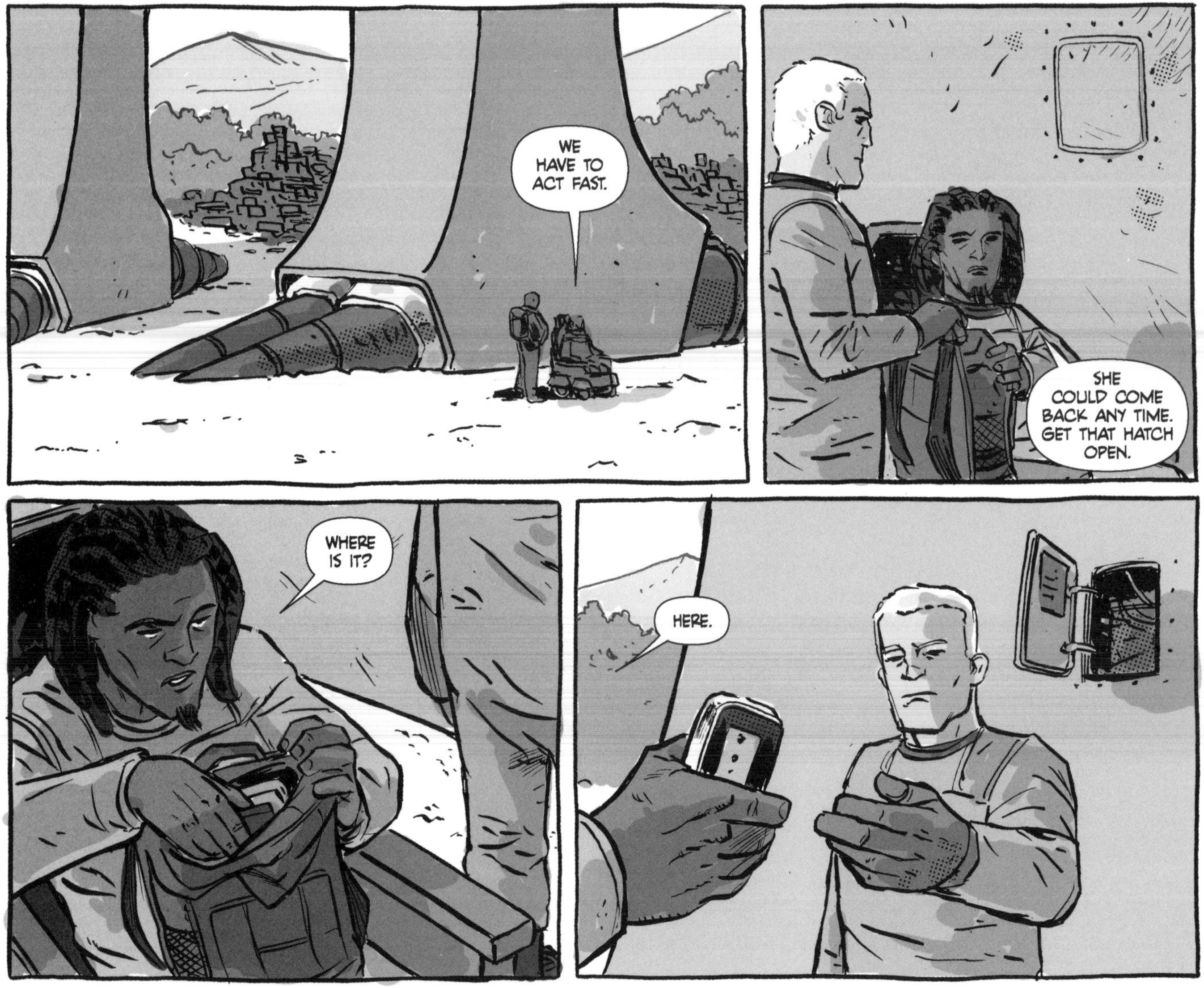
WE HAVE TO ACT FAST.
SHE COULD COME BACK ANY TIME. GET THAT HATCH OPEN.
WHERE IS IT?
HERE.

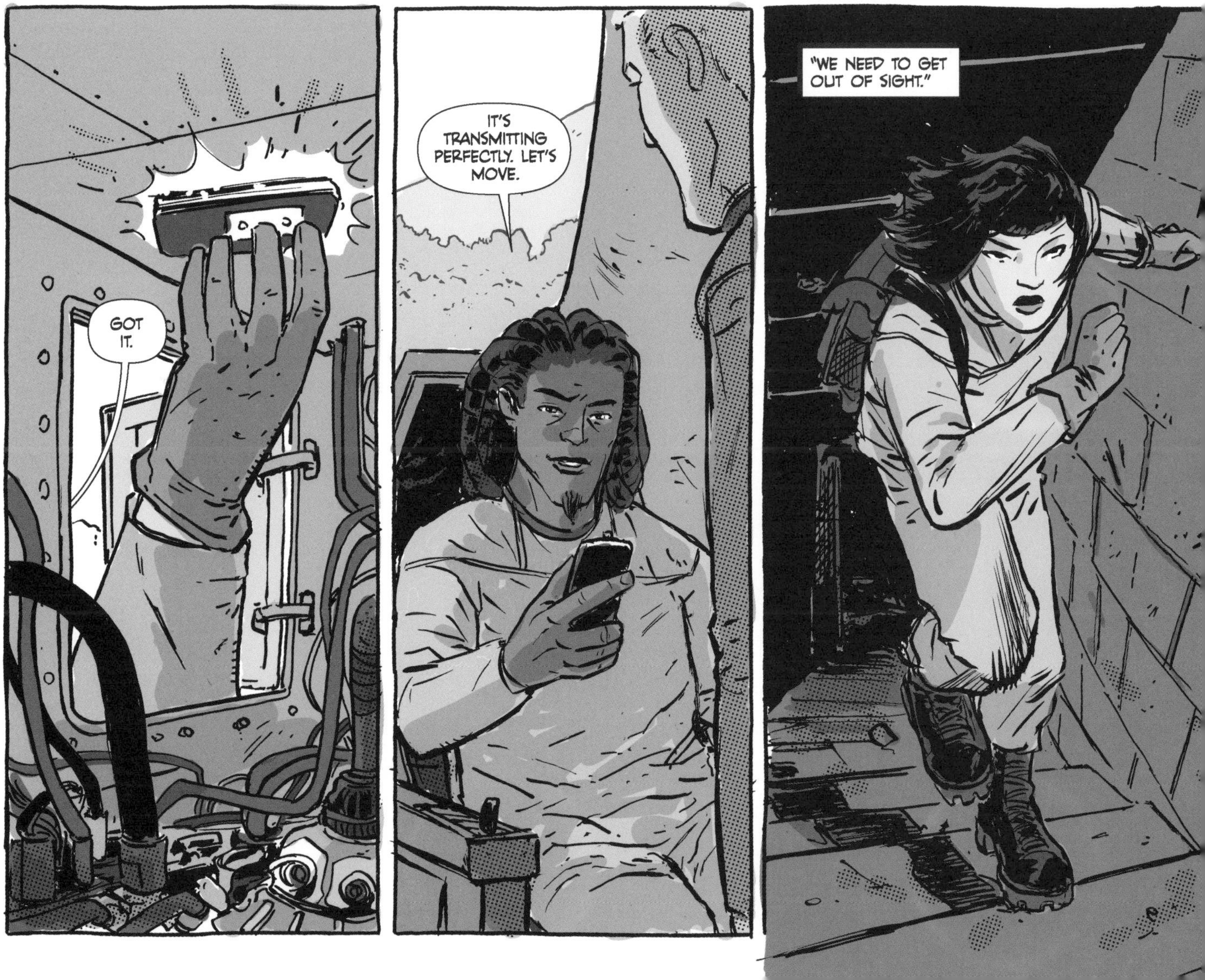
GOT IT.
IT'S TRANSMITTING PERFECTLY. LET'S MOVE.
"WE NEED TO GET OUT OF SIGHT."

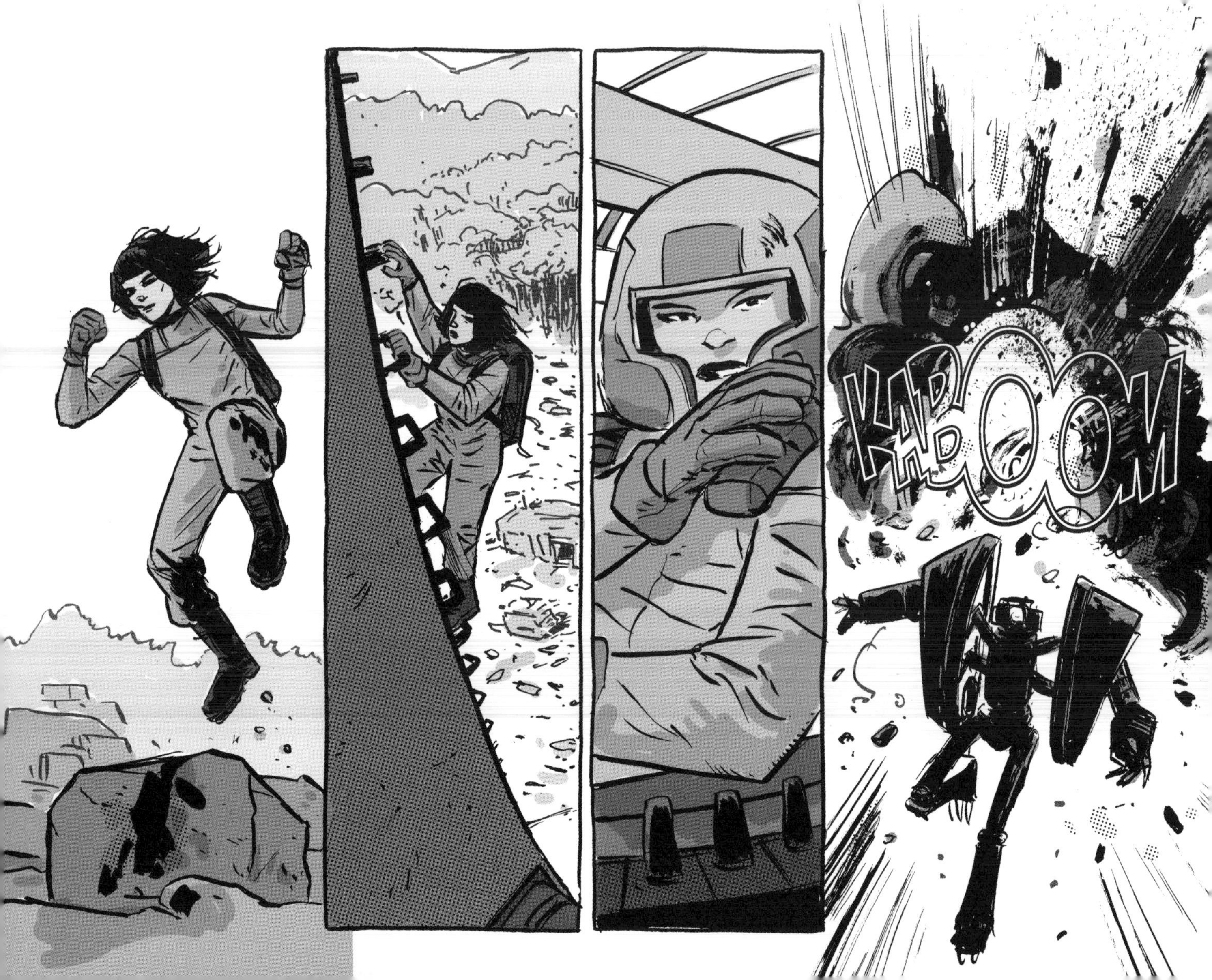
KABOOM

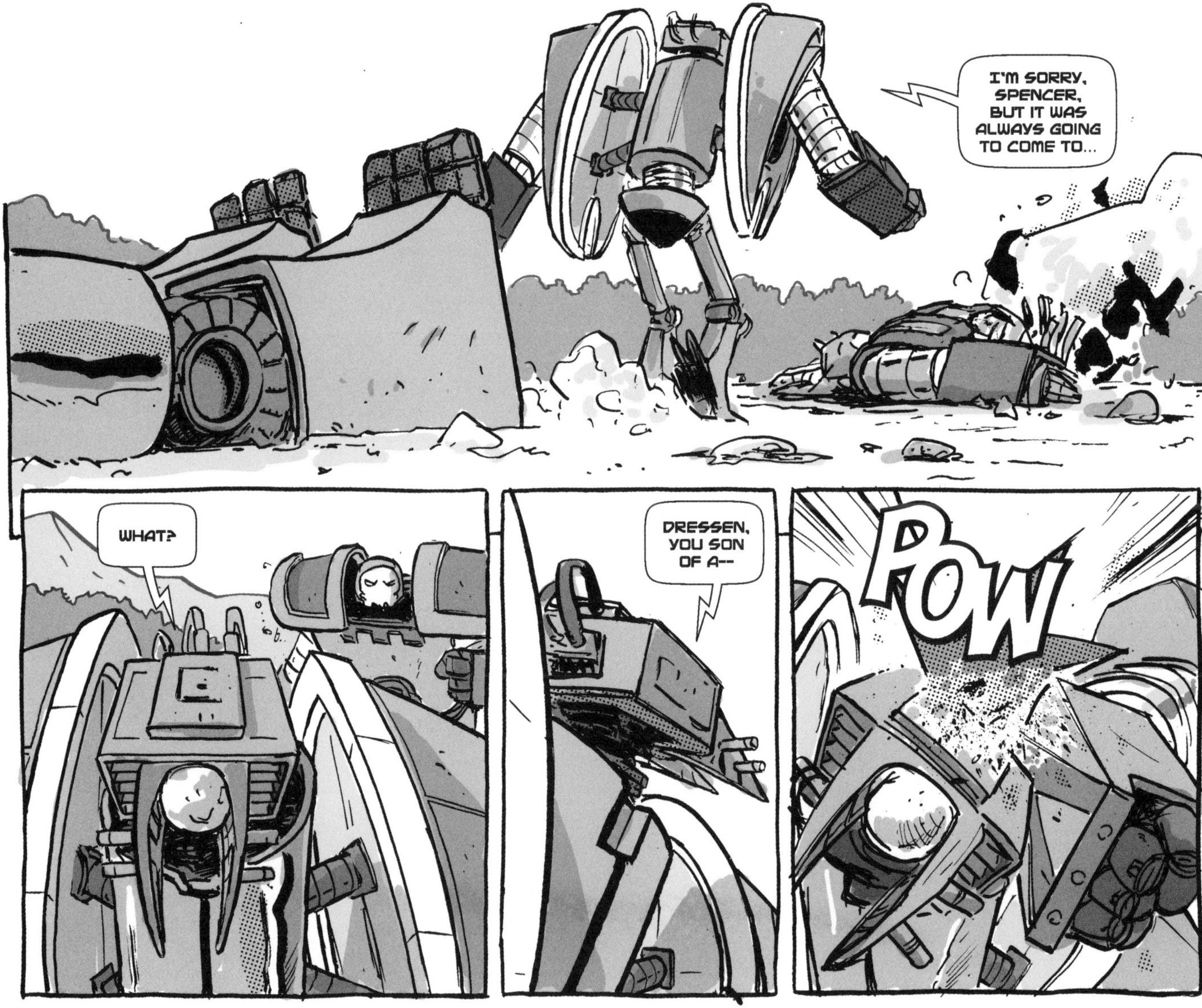
I'M SORRY, SPENCER, BUT IT WAS ALWAYS GOING TO COME TO...
WHAT?
DRESSEN, YOU SON OF A--
POW

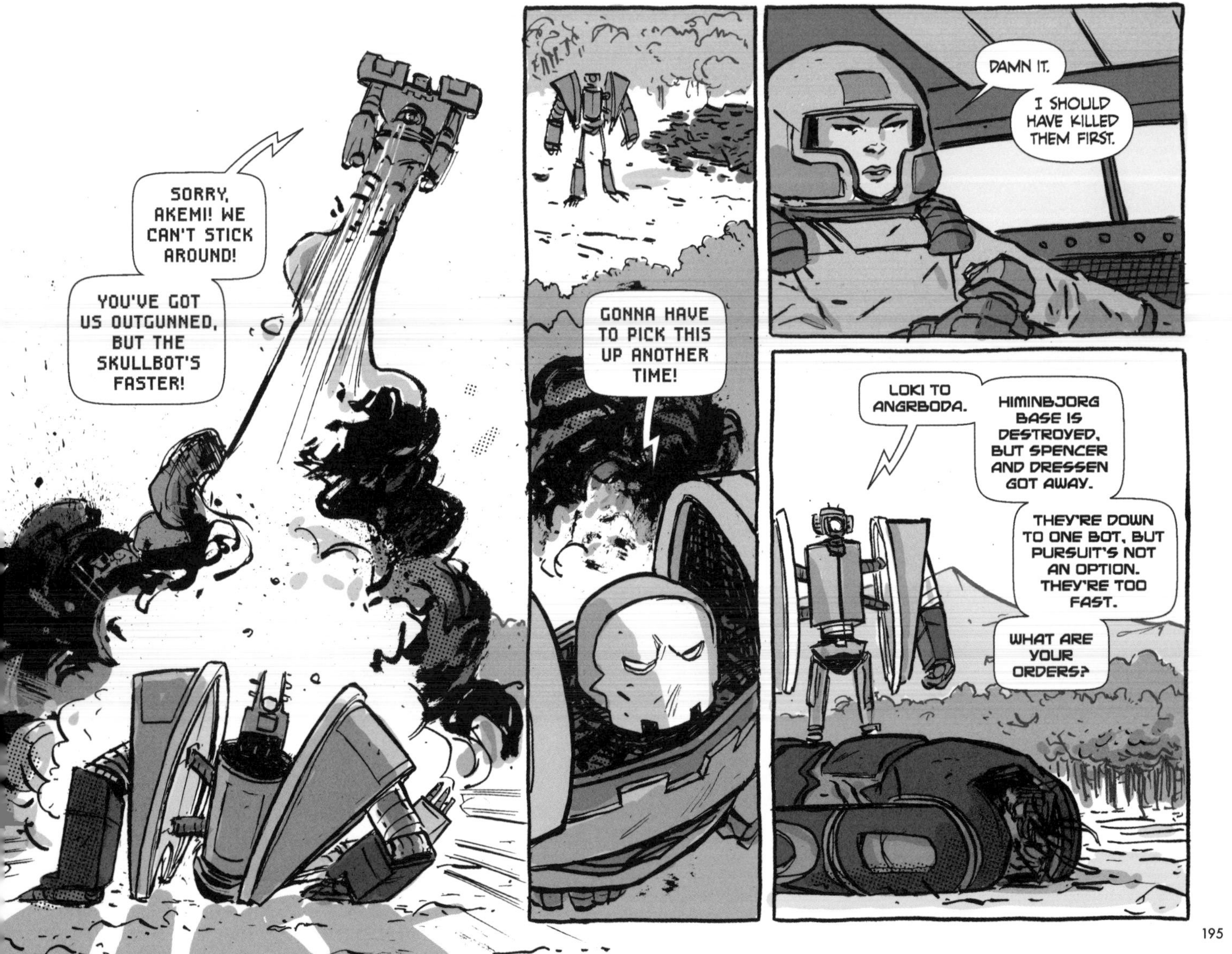
SORRY, AKEMI! WE CAN'T STICK AROUND!
YOU'VE GOT US OUTGUNNED, BUT THE SKULLBOT'S FASTER!
GONNA HAVE TO PICK THIS UP ANOTHER TIME!
DAMN IT.
I SHOULD HAVE KILLED THEM FIRST.
LOKI TO ANGRBODA.
HIMINBJORG BASE IS DESTROYED, BUT SPENCER AND DRESSEN GOT AWAY.
THEY'RE DOWN TO ONE BOT, BUT PURSUIT'S NOT AN OPTION. THEY'RE TOO FAST.
WHAT ARE YOUR ORDERS?

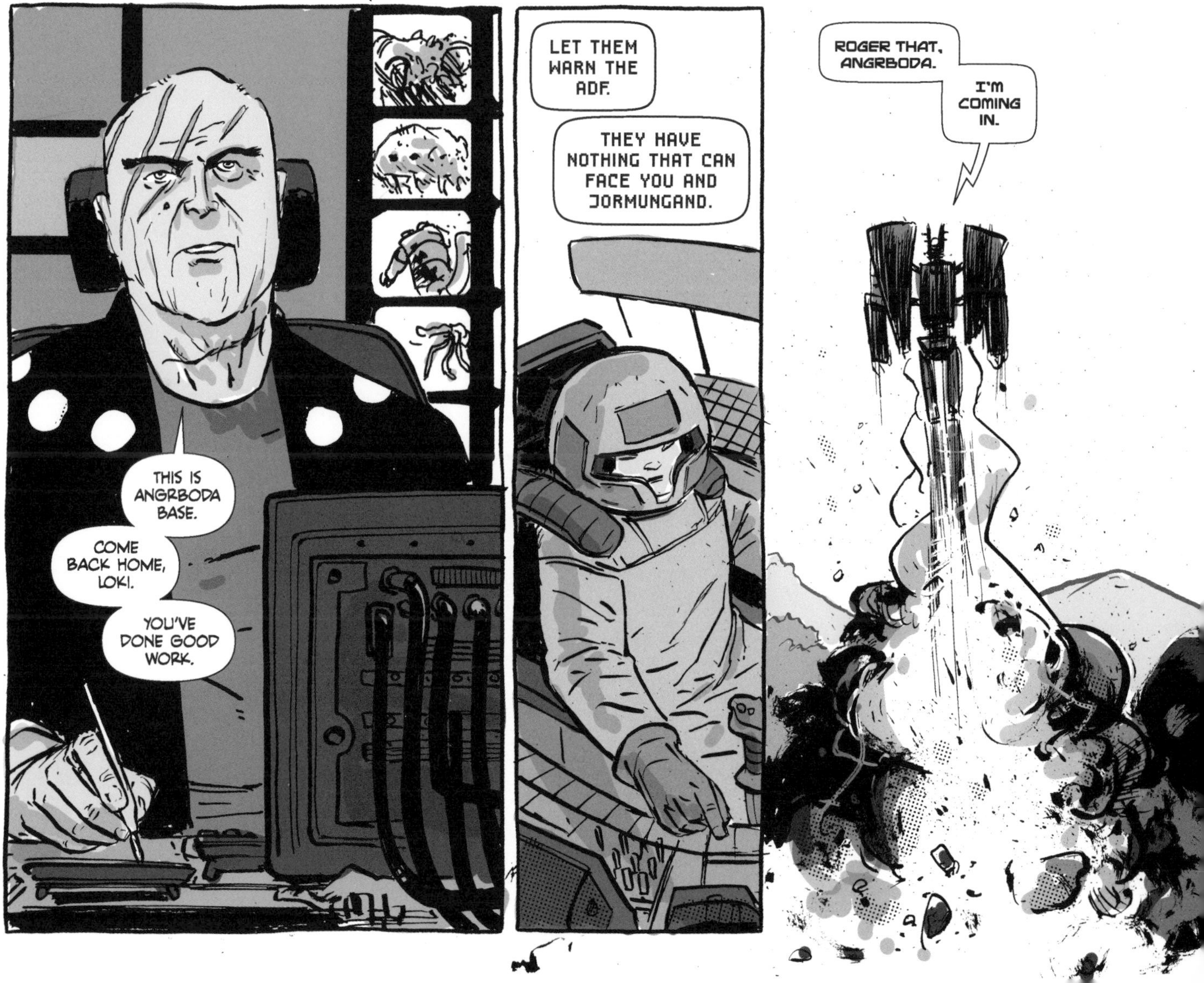
THIS IS ANGRBODA BASE.
COME BACK HOME, LOKI.
YOU'VE DONE GOOD WORK.
LET THEM WARN THE ADF.
THEY HAVE NOTHING THAT CAN FACE YOU AND JORMUNGAND.
ROGER THAT, ANGRBODA.
I'M COMING IN.

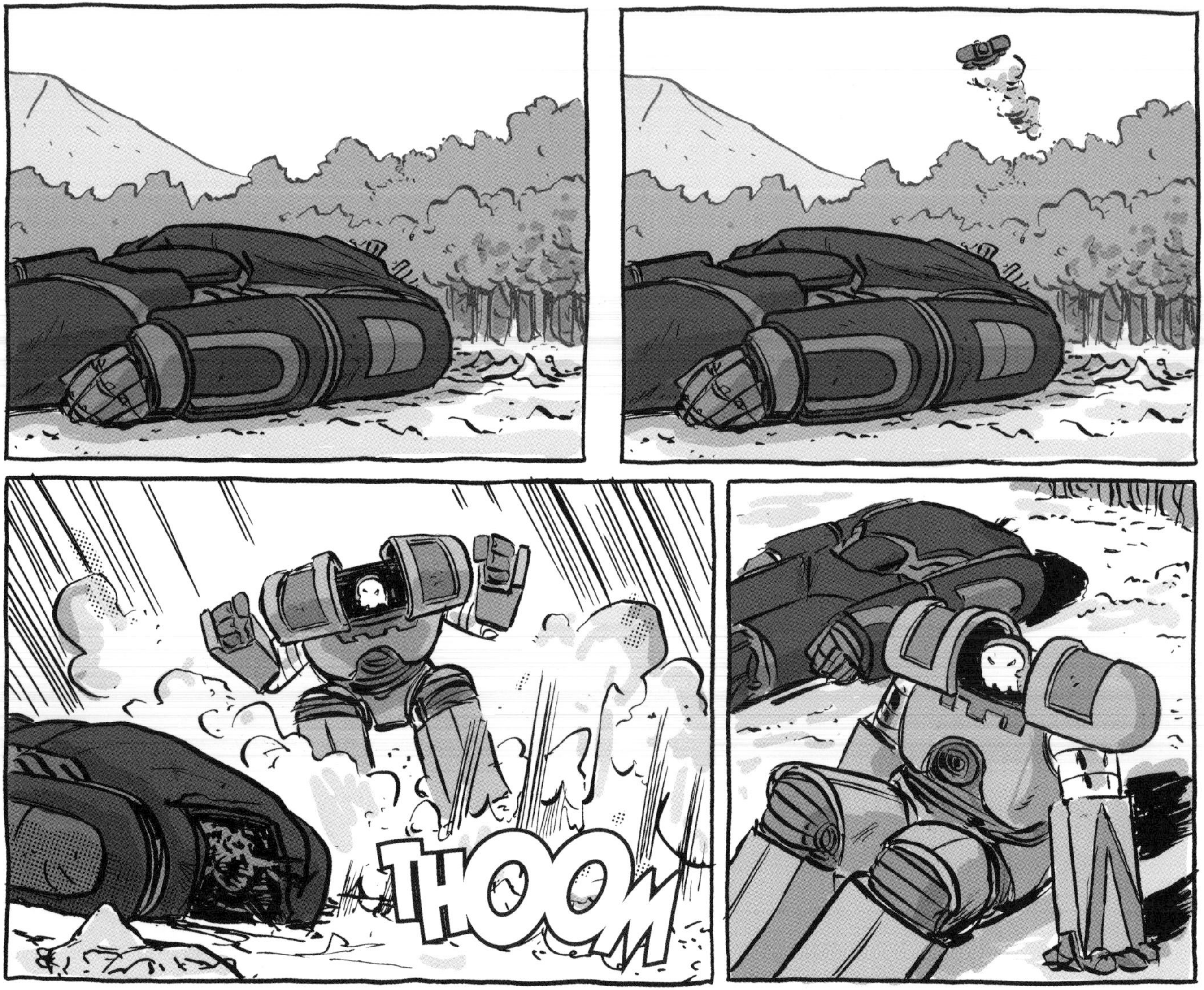
THOOM

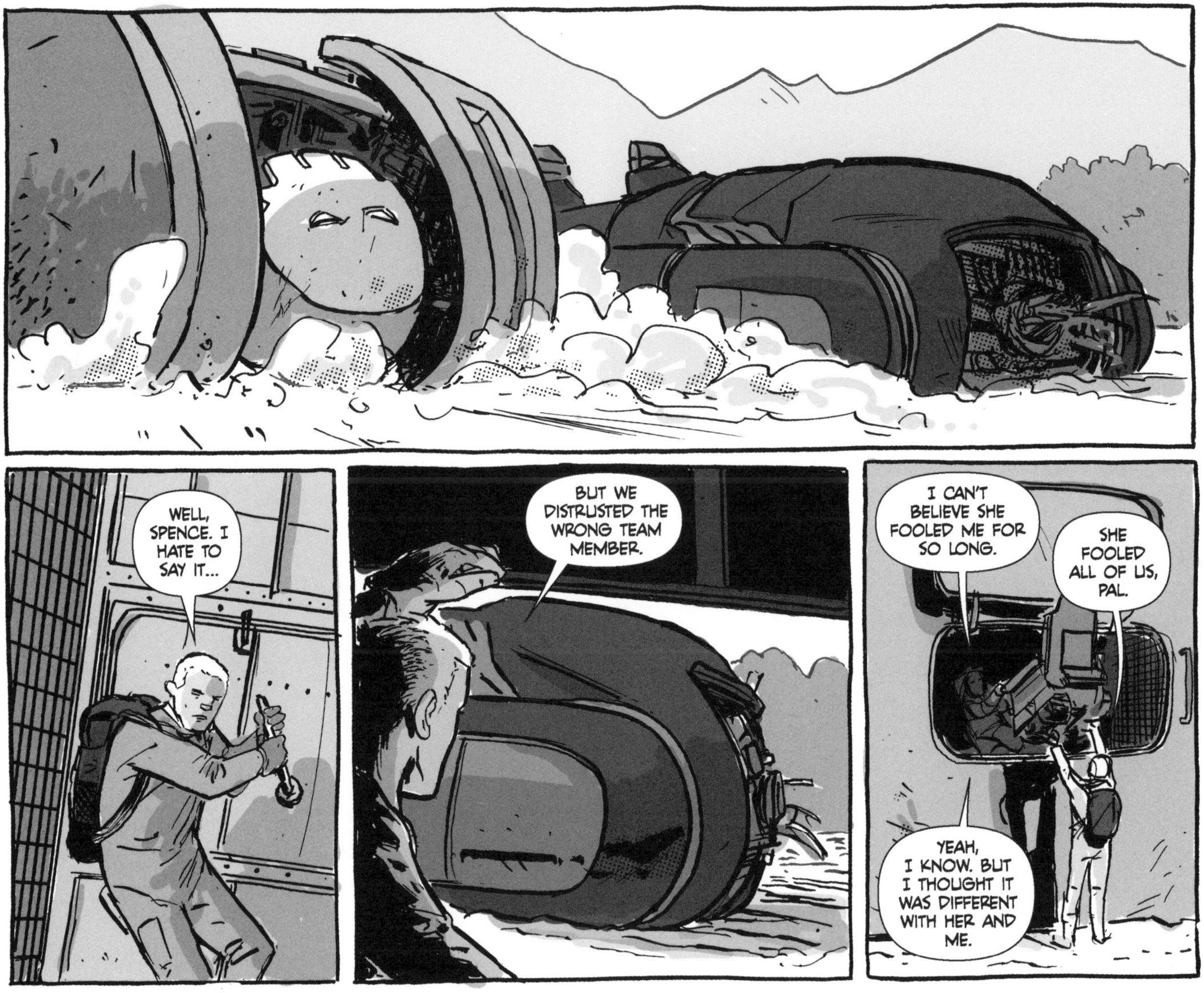
WELL, SPENCE. I HATE TO SAY IT...
BUT WE DISTRUSTED THE WRONG TEAM MEMBER.
I CAN'T BELIEVE SHE FOOLED ME FOR SO LONG.
SHE FOOLED ALL OF US, PAL.
YEAH, I KNOW. BUT I THOUGHT IT WAS DIFFERENT WITH HER AND ME.

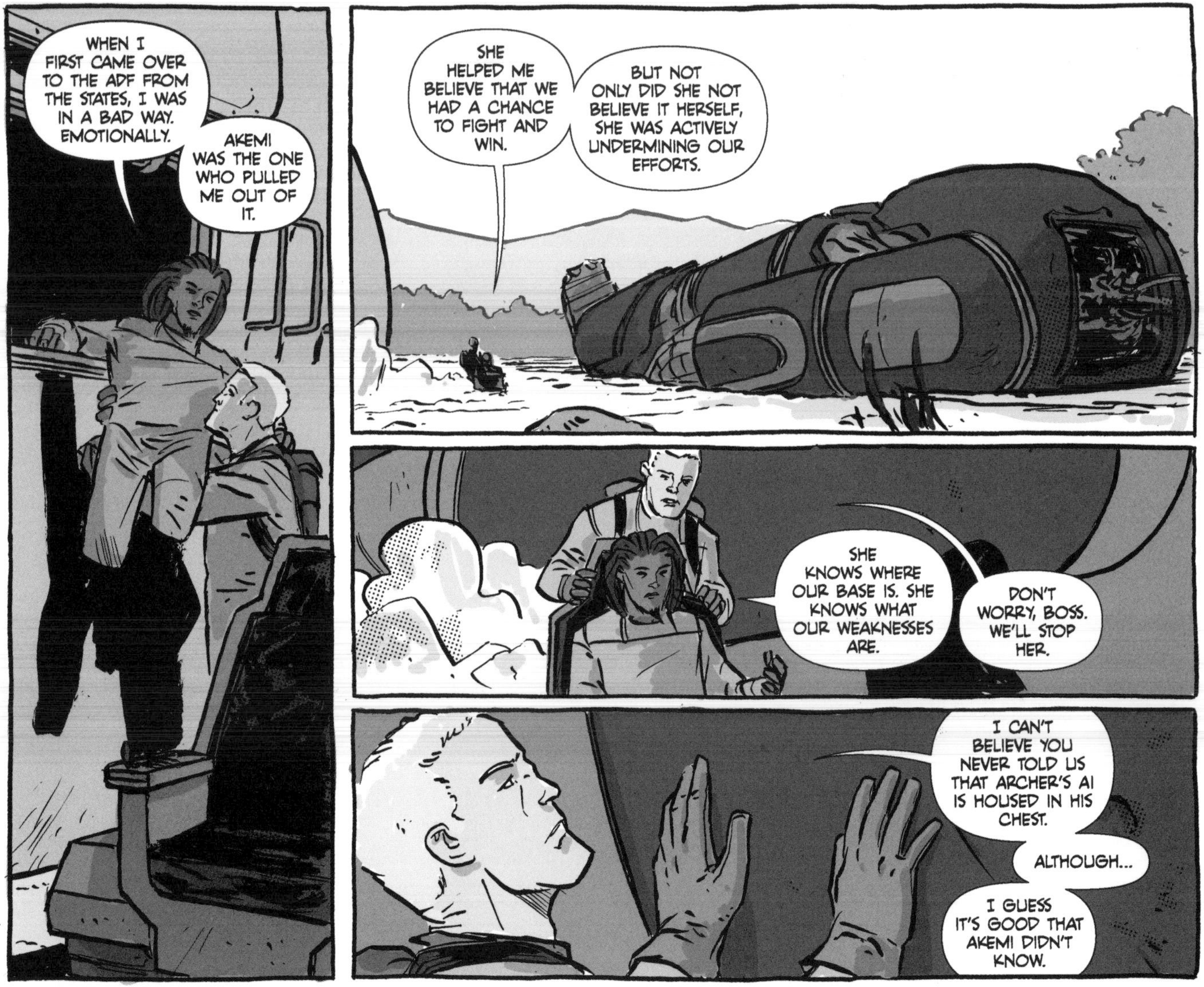
WHEN I FIRST CAME OVER TO THE ADF FROM THE STATES, I WAS IN A BAD WAY. EMOTIONALLY.
AKEMI WAS THE ONE WHO PULLED ME OUT OF IT.
SHE HELPED ME BELIEVE THAT WE HAD A CHANCE TO FIGHT AND WIN.
BUT NOT ONLY DID SHE NOT BELIEVE IT HERSELF, SHE WAS ACTIVELY UNDERMINING OUR EFFORTS.
SHE KNOWS WHERE OUR BASE IS. SHE KNOWS WHAT OUR WEAKNESSES ARE.
DON'T WORRY, BOSS. WE'LL STOP HER.
I CAN'T BELIEVE YOU NEVER TOLD US THAT ARCHER'S AI IS HOUSED IN HIS CHEST.
ALTHOUGH...
I GUESS IT'S GOOD THAT AKEMI DIDN'T KNOW.

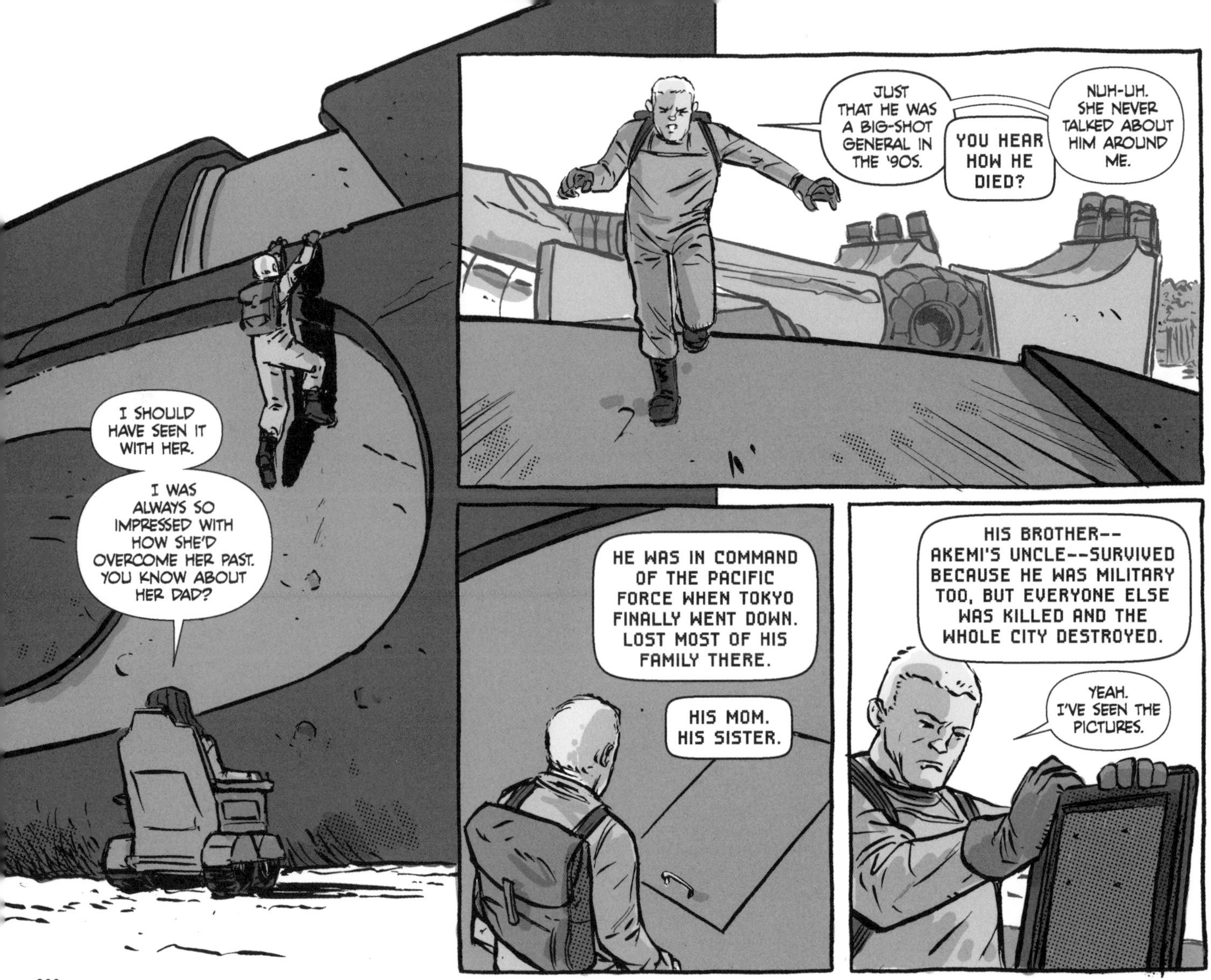
I SHOULD HAVE SEEN IT WITH HER.
I WAS ALWAYS SO IMPRESSED WITH HOW SHE'D OVERCOME HER PAST. YOU KNOW ABOUT HER DAD?
JUST THAT HE WAS A BIG-SHOT GENERAL IN THE '90S.
NUH-UH. SHE NEVER TALKED ABOUT HIM AROUND ME.
YOU HEAR HOW HE DIED?
HE WAS IN COMMAND OF THE PACIFIC FORCE WHEN TOKYO FINALLY WENT DOWN. LOST MOST OF HIS FAMILY THERE.
HIS MOM. HIS SISTER.
HIS BROTHER-- AKEMI'S UNCLE--SURVIVED BECAUSE HE WAS MILITARY TOO, BUT EVERYONE ELSE WAS KILLED AND THE WHOLE CITY DESTROYED.
YEAH. I'VE SEEN THE PICTURES.

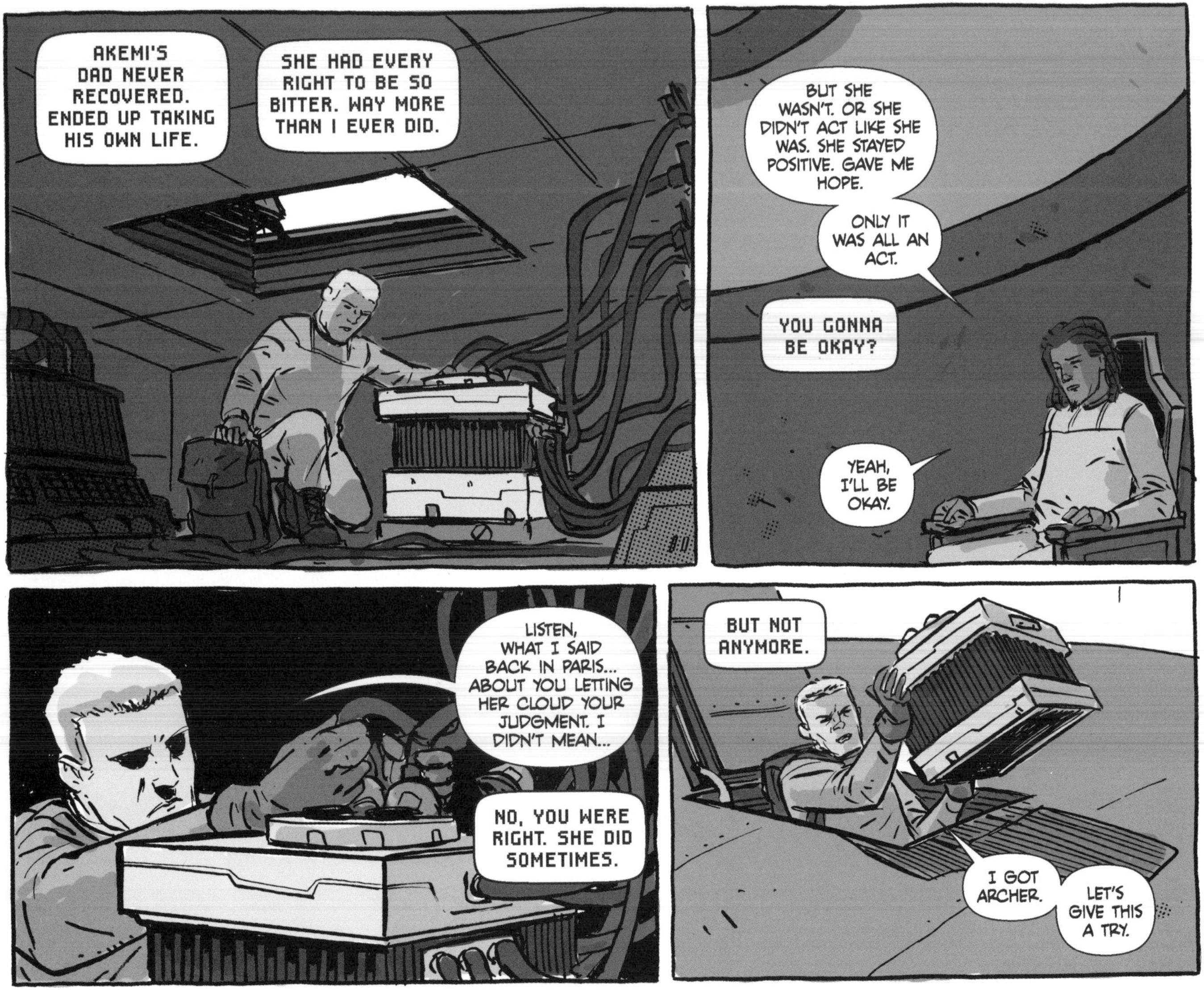
AKEMI'S DAD NEVER RECOVERED. ENDED UP TAKING HIS OWN LIFE.
SHE HAD EVERY RIGHT TO BE SO BITTER. WAY MORE THAN I EVER DID.
BUT SHE WASN'T. OR SHE DIDN'T ACT LIKE SHE WAS. SHE STAYED POSITIVE. GAVE ME HOPE.
ONLY IT WAS ALL AN ACT.
YOU GONNA BE OKAY?
YEAH, I'LL BE OKAY.
LISTEN, WHAT I SAID BACK IN PARIS... ABOUT YOU LETTING HER CLOUD YOUR JUDGMENT. I DIDN'T MEAN...
NO, YOU WERE RIGHT. SHE DID SOMETIMES.
BUT NOT ANYMORE.
I GOT ARCHER.
LET'S GIVE THIS A TRY.

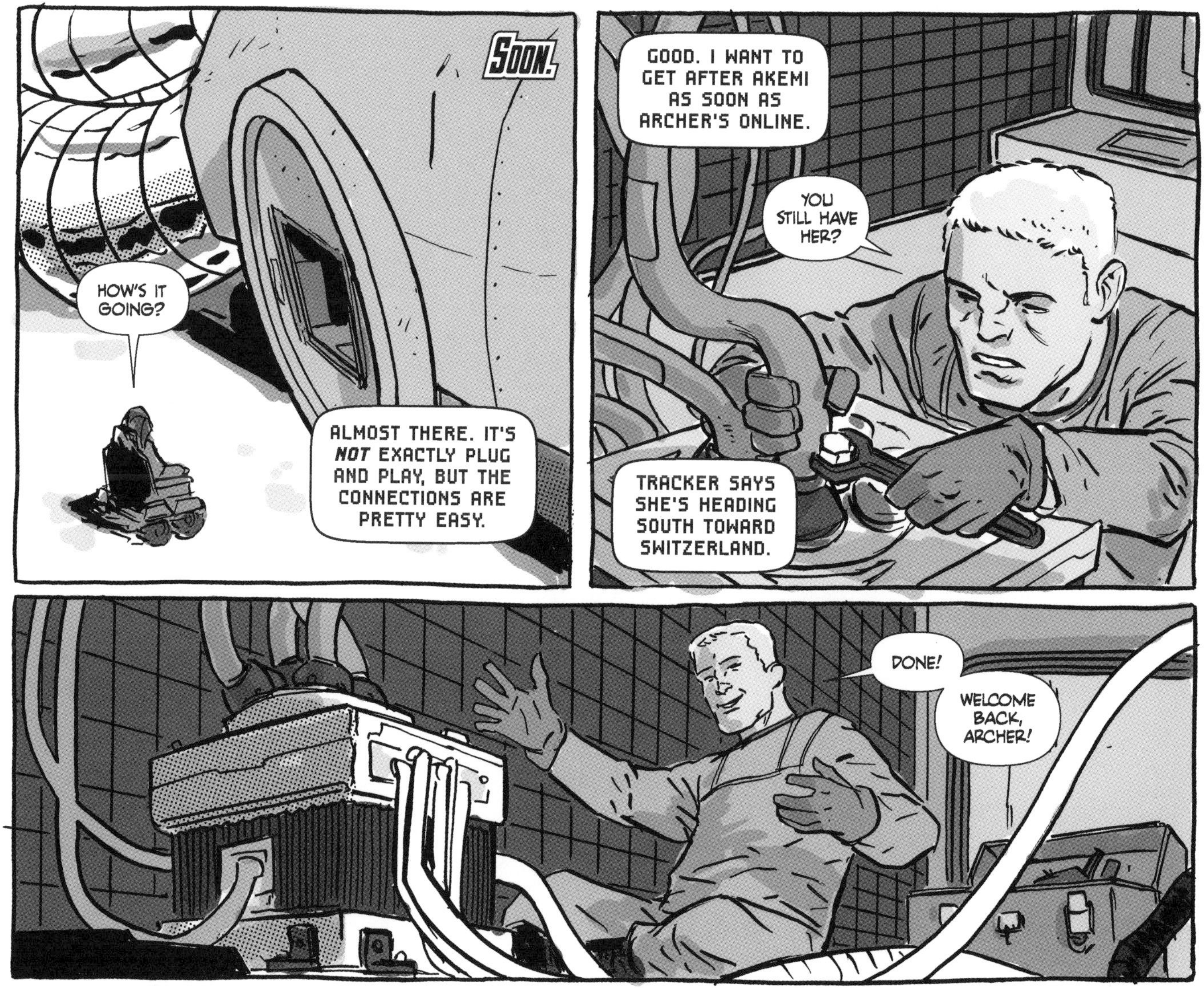
SOON.
HOW'S IT GOING?
ALMOST THERE. IT'S ***NOT*** EXACTLY PLUG AND PLAY, BUT THE CONNECTIONS ARE PRETTY EASY.
GOOD. I WANT TO GET AFTER AKEMI AS SOON AS ARCHER'S ONLINE.
YOU STILL HAVE HER?
TRACKER SAYS SHE'S HEADING SOUTH TOWARD SWITZERLAND.
DONE!
WELCOME BACK, ARCHER!

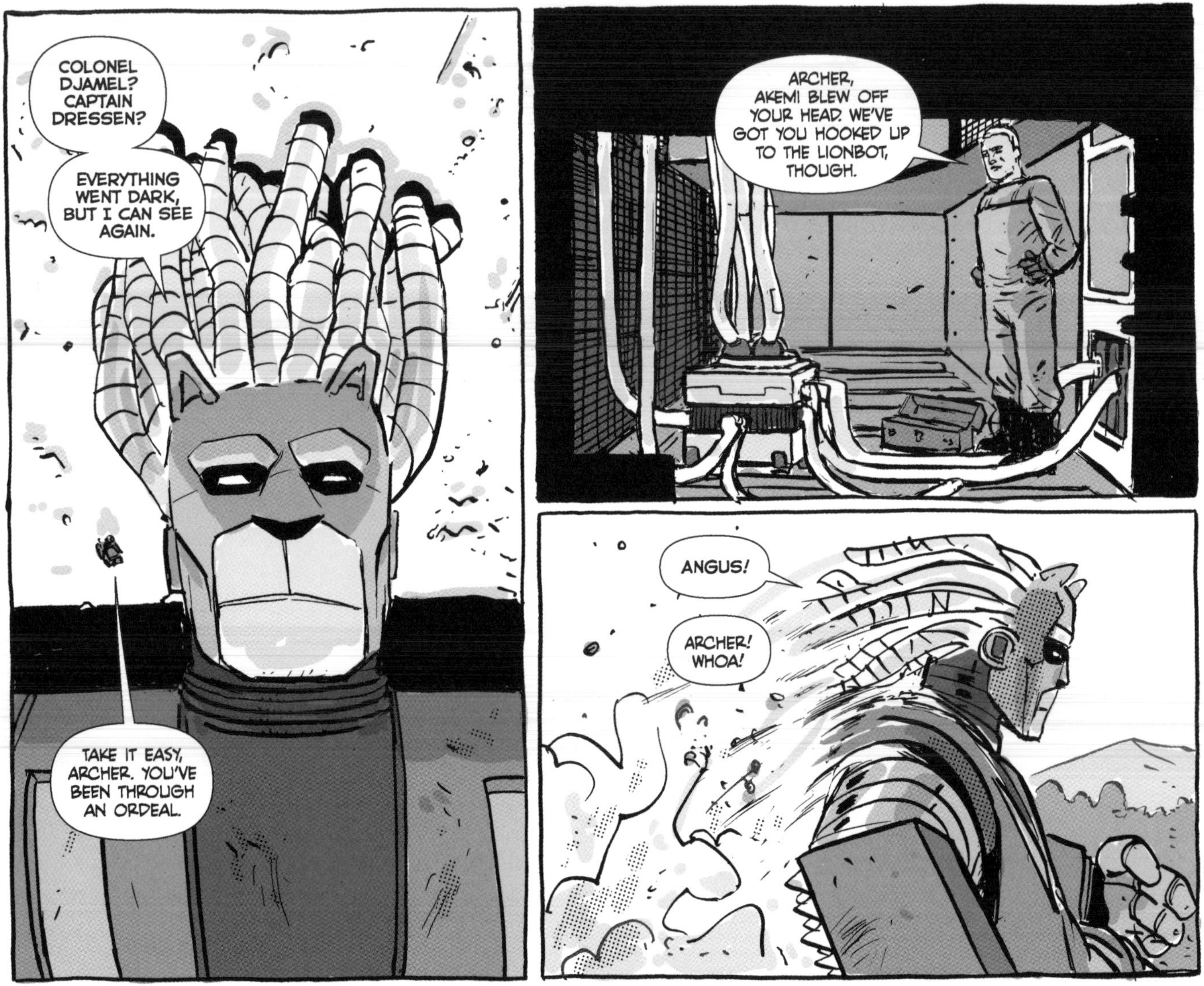
COLONEL DJAMEL? CAPTAIN DRESSEN?
EVERYTHING WENT DARK, BUT I CAN SEE AGAIN.
TAKE IT EASY, ARCHER. YOU'VE BEEN THROUGH AN ORDEAL.
ARCHER, AKEMI BLEW OFF YOUR HEAD. WE'VE GOT YOU HOOKED UP TO THE LIONBOT, THOUGH.
ANGUS!
ARCHER! WHOA!

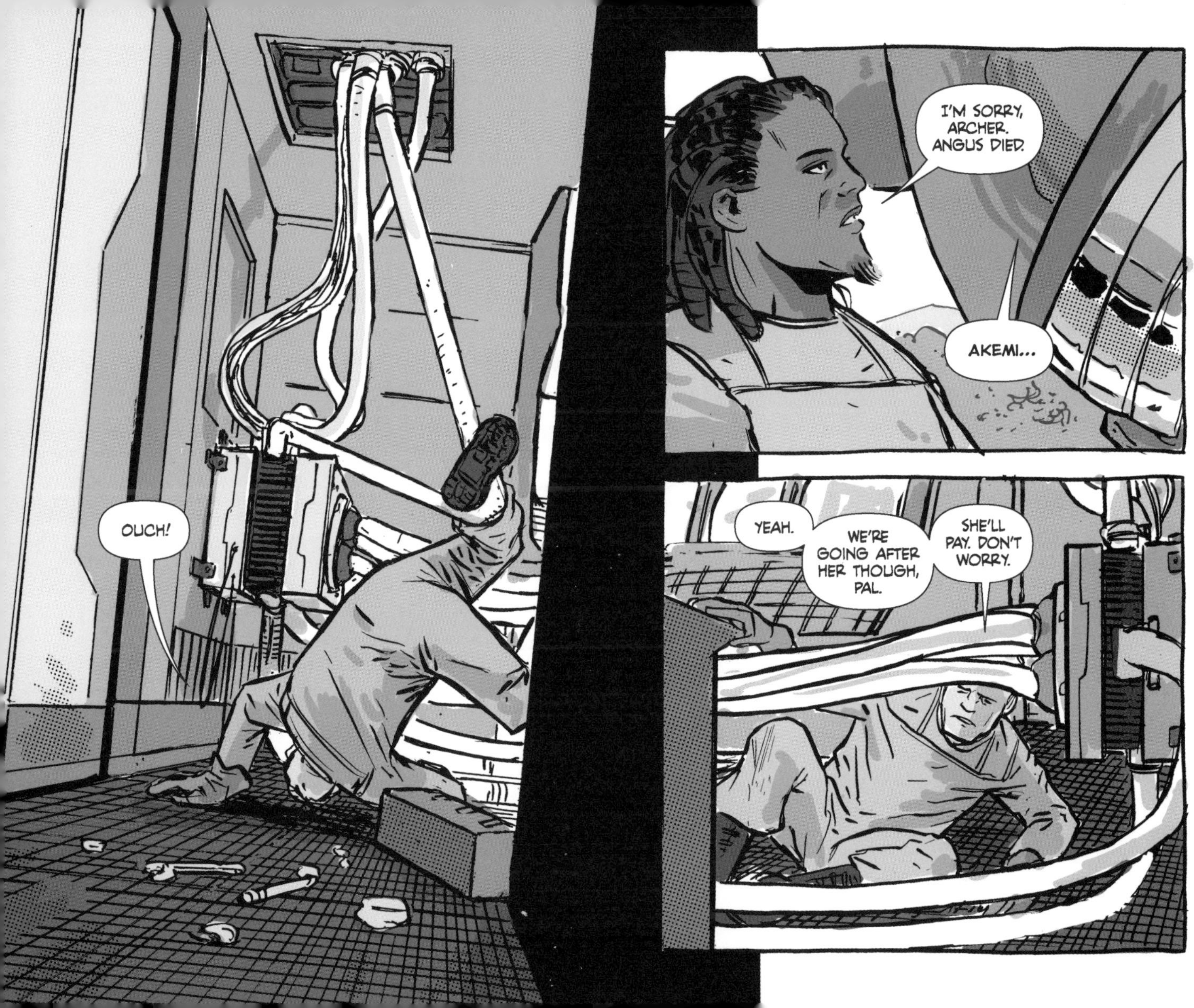
OUCH!
I'M SORRY, ARCHER. ANGUS DIED.
AKEMI...
YEAH.
WE'RE GOING AFTER HER THOUGH, PAL.
SHE'LL PAY. DON'T WORRY.

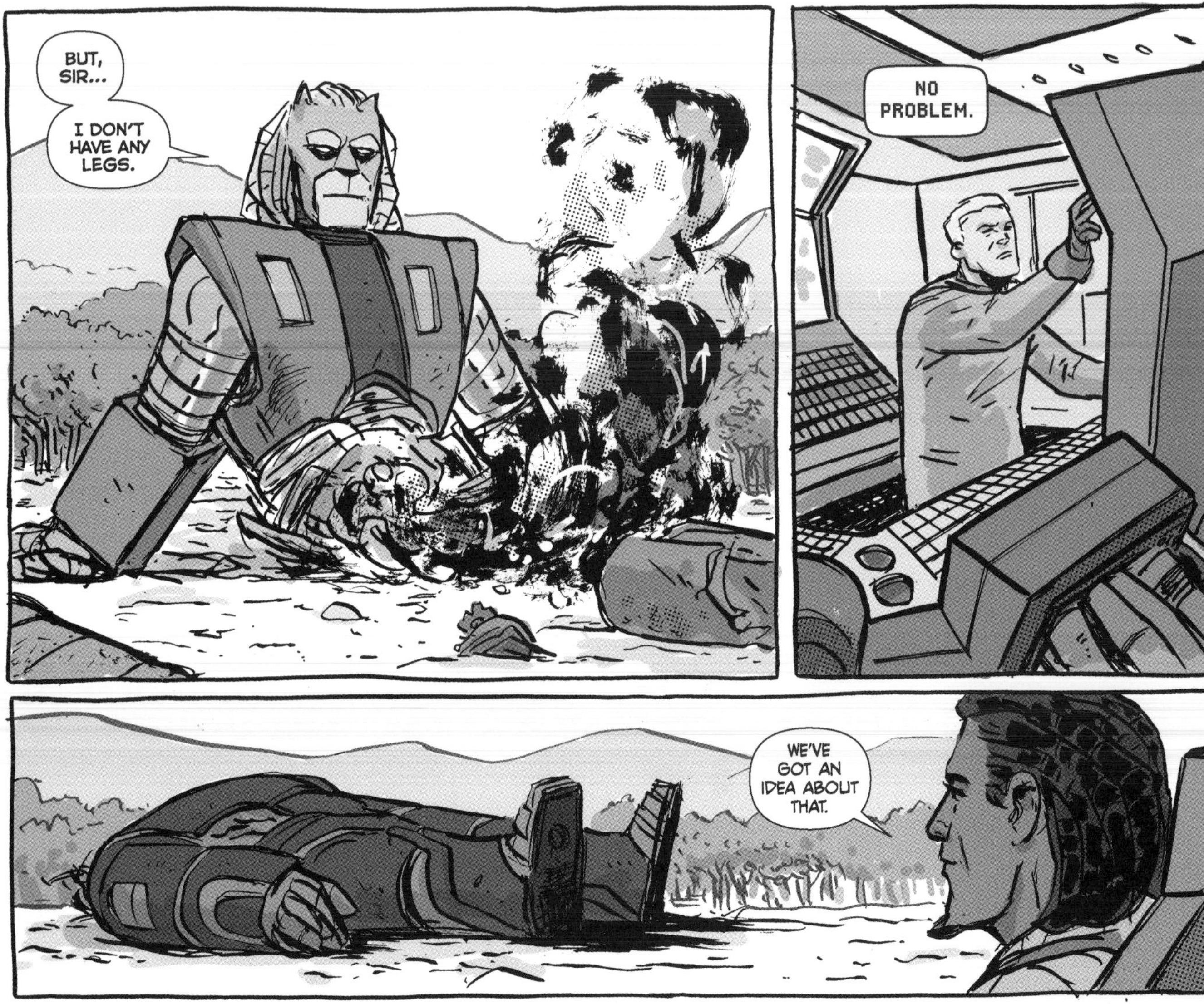
BUT, SIR...
I DON'T HAVE ANY LEGS.
NO PROBLEM.
WE'VE GOT AN IDEA ABOUT THAT.

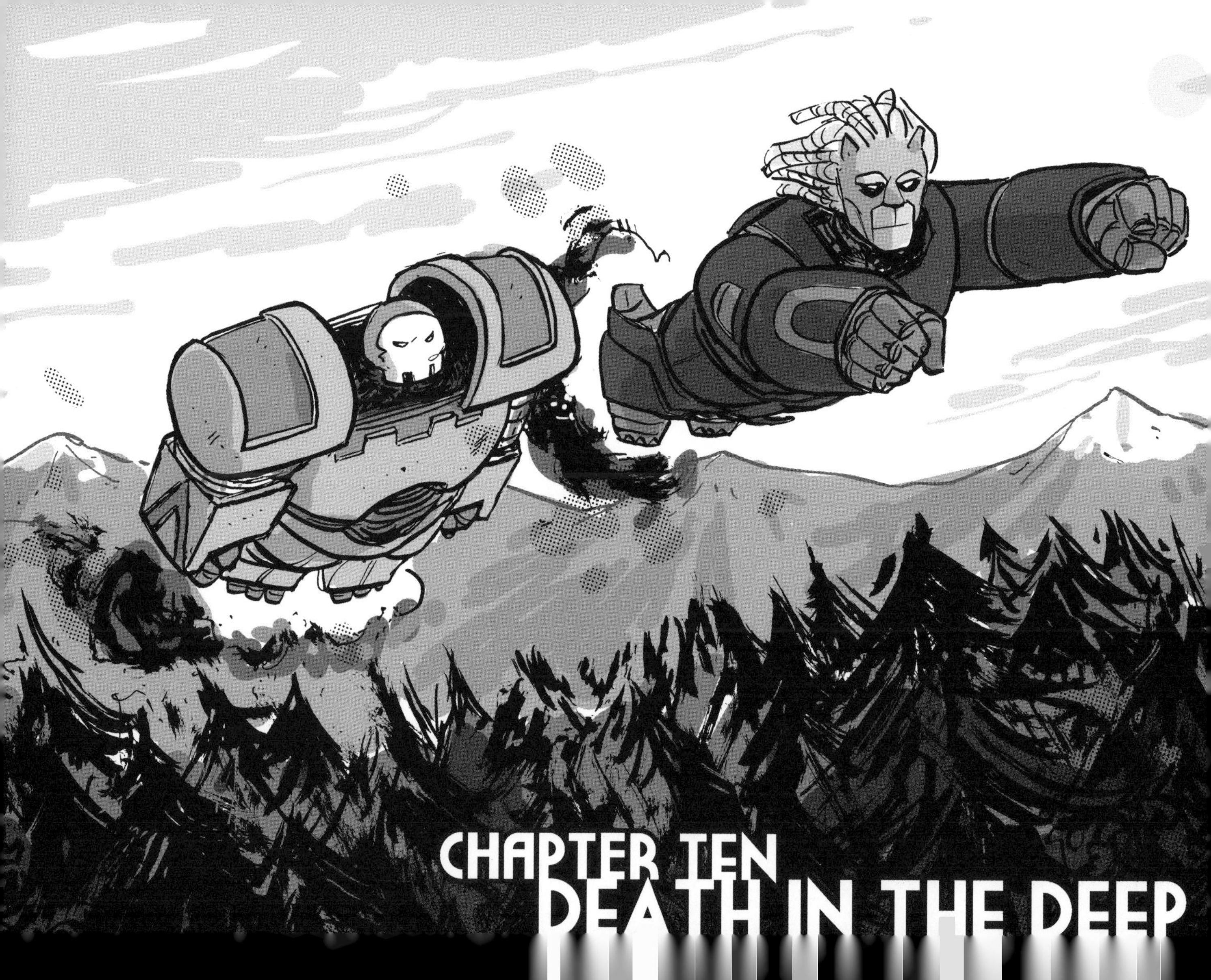
CHAPTER TEN
DEATH IN THE DEEP

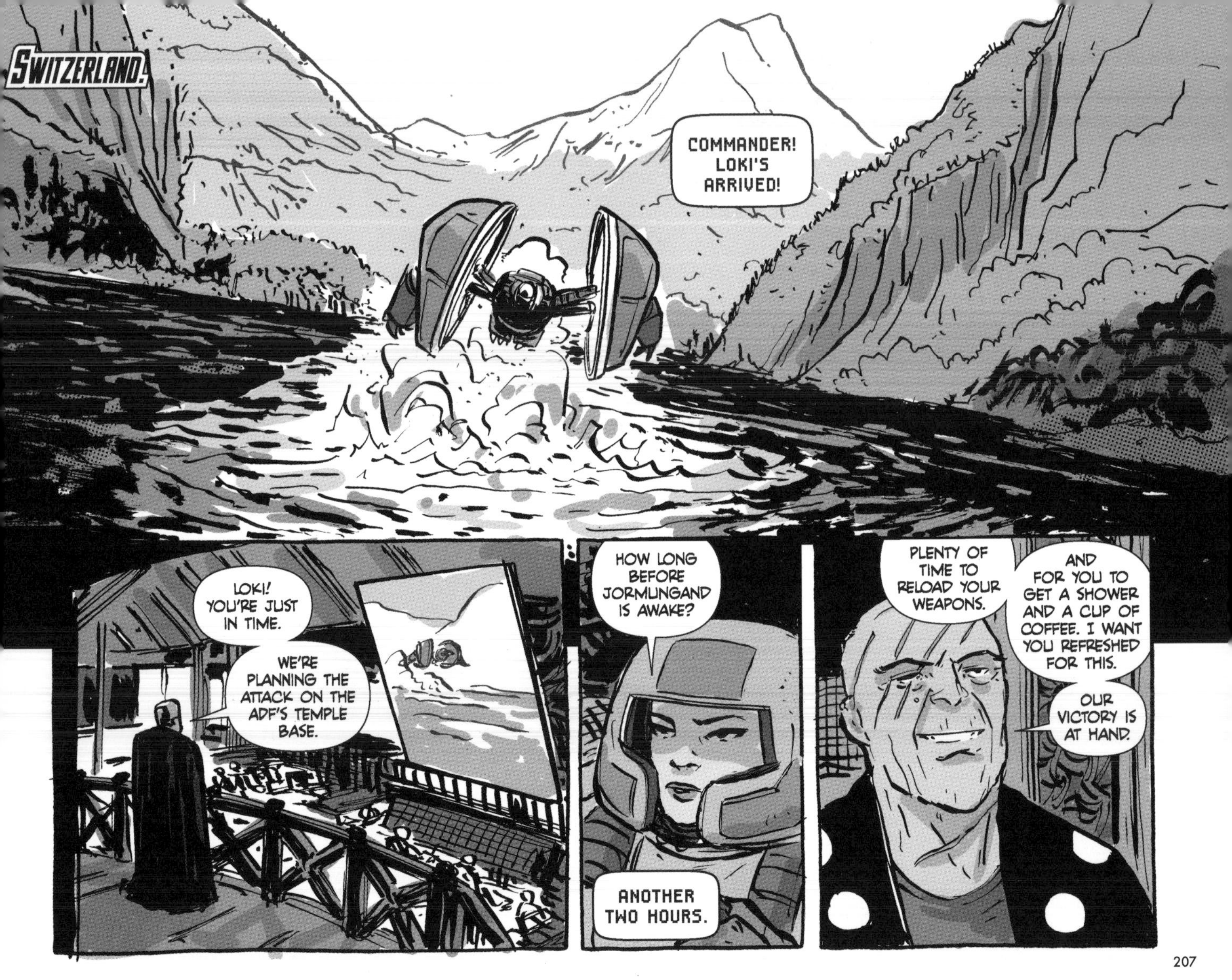
SWITZERLAND.
COMMANDER! LOKI'S ARRIVED!
LOKI! YOU'RE JUST IN TIME.
WE'RE PLANNING THE ATTACK ON THE ADF'S TEMPLE BASE.
HOW LONG BEFORE JORMUNGAND IS AWAKE?
ANOTHER TWO HOURS.
PLENTY OF TIME TO RELOAD YOUR WEAPONS.
AND FOR YOU TO GET A SHOWER AND A CUP OF COFFEE. I WANT YOU REFRESHED FOR THIS.
OUR VICTORY IS AT HAND.

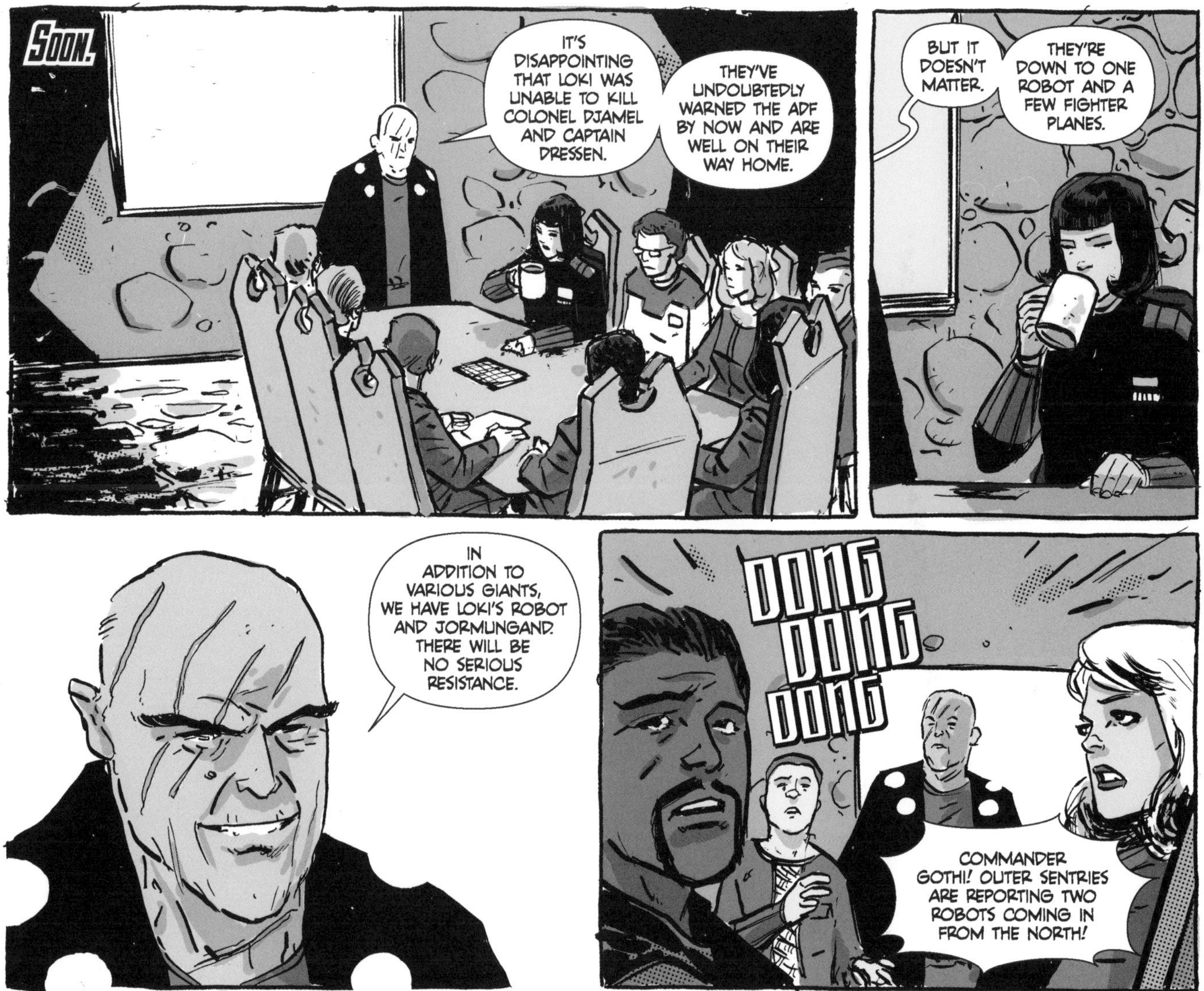
SOON.
IT'S DISAPPOINTING THAT LOKI WAS UNABLE TO KILL COLONEL DJAMEL AND CAPTAIN DRESSEN.
THEY'VE UNDOUBTEDLY WARNED THE ADF BY NOW AND ARE WELL ON THEIR WAY HOME.
BUT IT DOESN'T MATTER.
THEY'RE DOWN TO ONE ROBOT AND A FEW FIGHTER PLANES.
IN ADDITION TO VARIOUS GIANTS, WE HAVE LOKI'S ROBOT AND JORMUNGAND. THERE WILL BE NO SERIOUS RESISTANCE.
DONG DONG DONG
COMMANDER GOTHI! OUTER SENTRIES ARE REPORTING TWO ROBOTS COMING IN FROM THE NORTH!

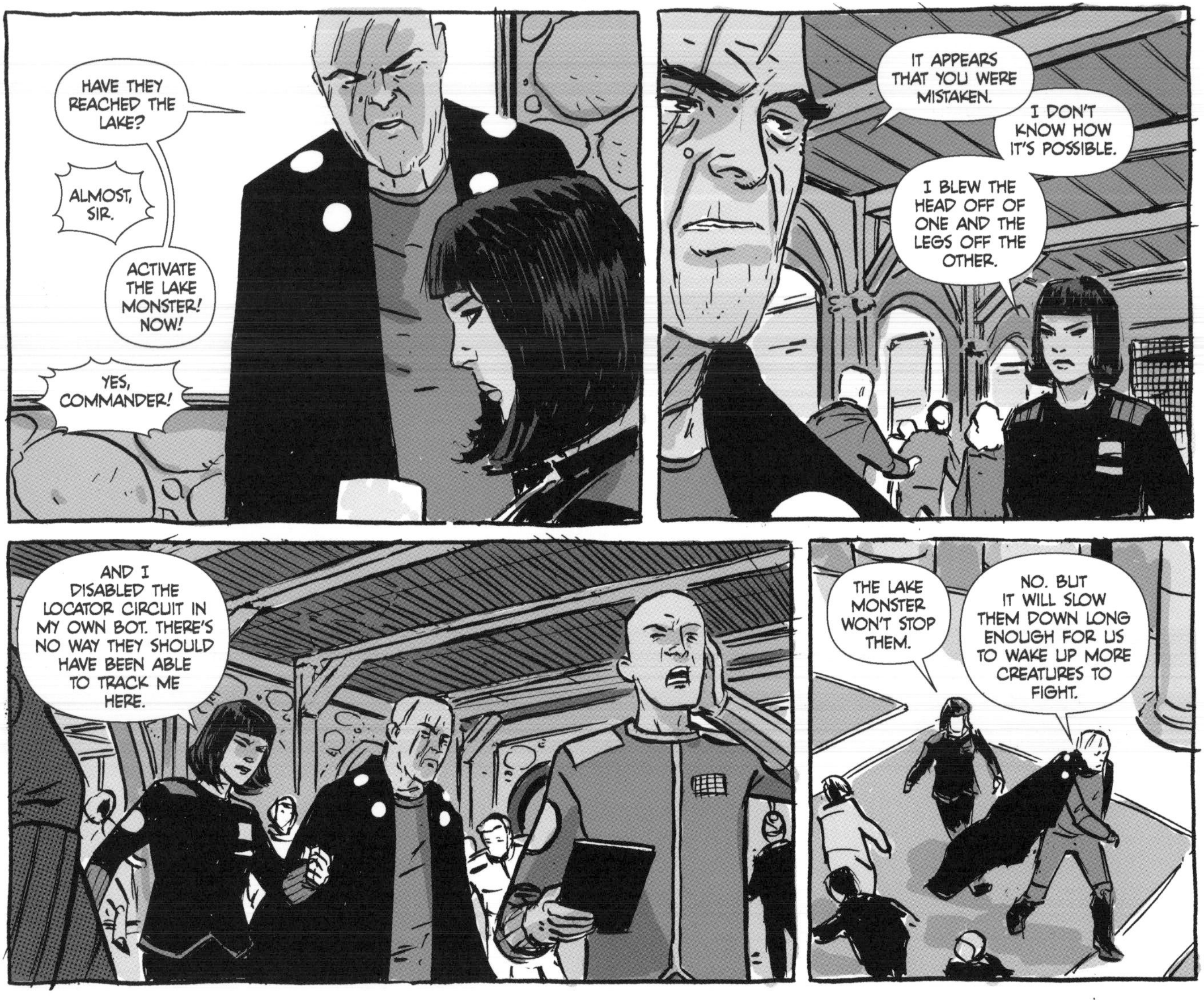
HAVE THEY REACHED THE LAKE?
ALMOST, SIR.
ACTIVATE THE LAKE MONSTER! NOW!
YES, COMMANDER!
IT APPEARS THAT YOU WERE MISTAKEN.
I DON'T KNOW HOW IT'S POSSIBLE.
I BLEW THE HEAD OFF OF ONE AND THE LEGS OFF THE OTHER.
AND I DISABLED THE LOCATOR CIRCUIT IN MY OWN BOT. THERE'S NO WAY THEY SHOULD HAVE BEEN ABLE TO TRACK ME HERE.
THE LAKE MONSTER WON'T STOP THEM.
NO. BUT IT WILL SLOW THEM DOWN LONG ENOUGH FOR US TO WAKE UP MORE CREATURES TO FIGHT.

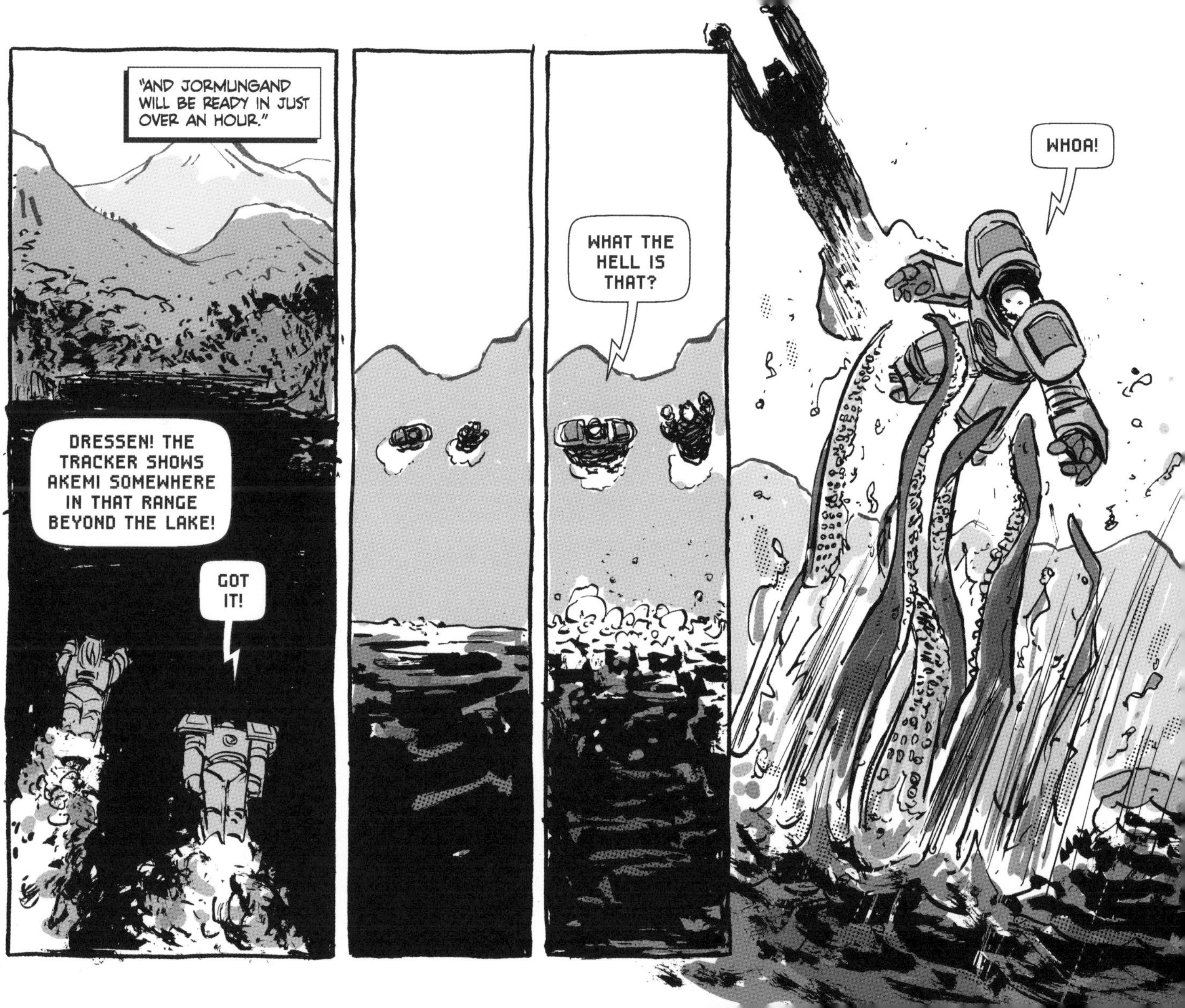
"AND JORMUNGAND WILL BE READY IN JUST OVER AN HOUR."
DRESSEN! THE TRACKER SHOWS AKEMI SOMEWHERE IN THAT RANGE BEYOND THE LAKE!
GOT IT!
WHAT THE HELL IS THAT?
WHOA!

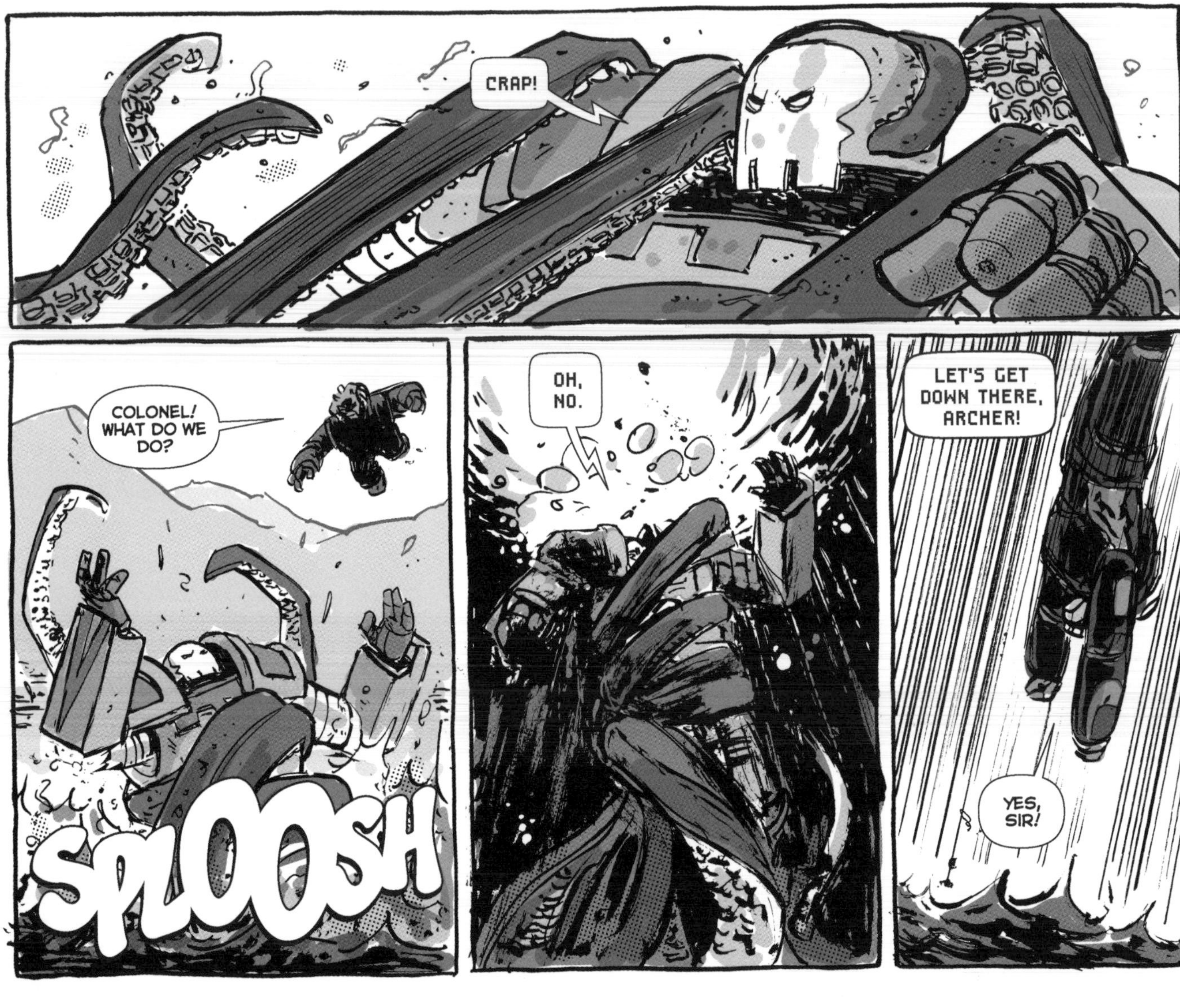
CRAP!
COLONEL! WHAT DO WE DO?
SPLOOSH
OH, NO.
LET'S GET DOWN THERE, ARCHER!
YES, SIR!

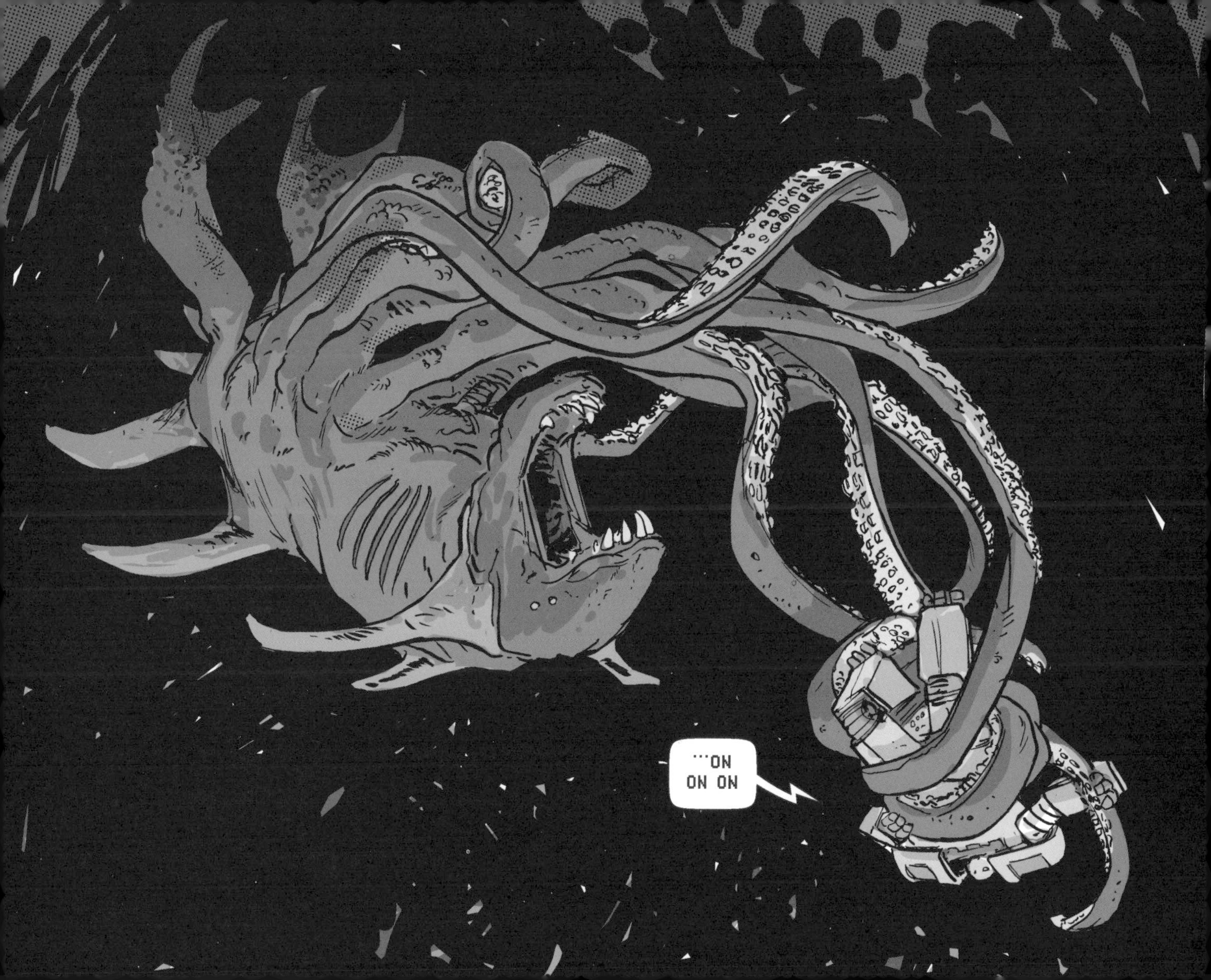
...ON
ON ON

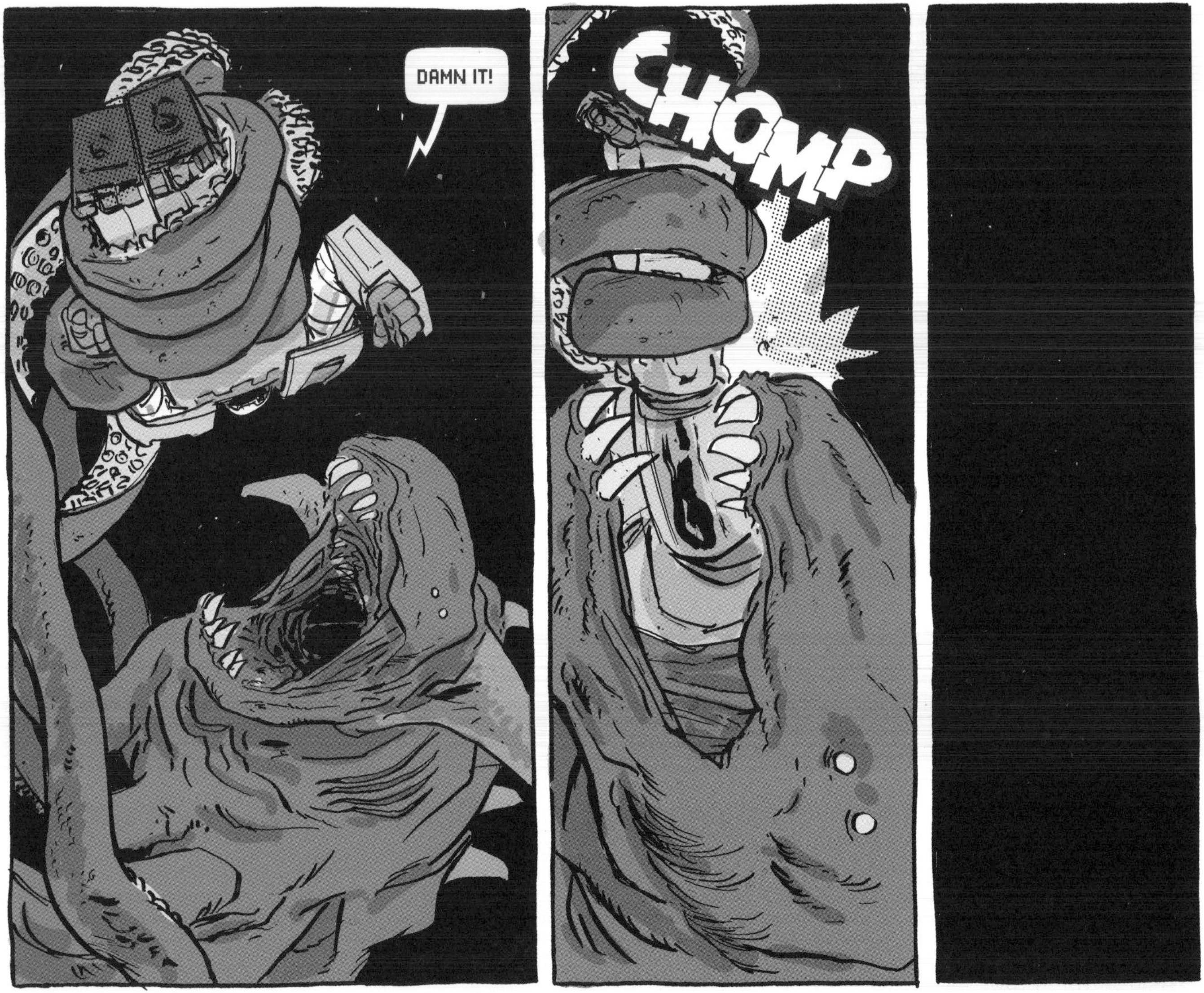
DAMN IT!
CHOMP

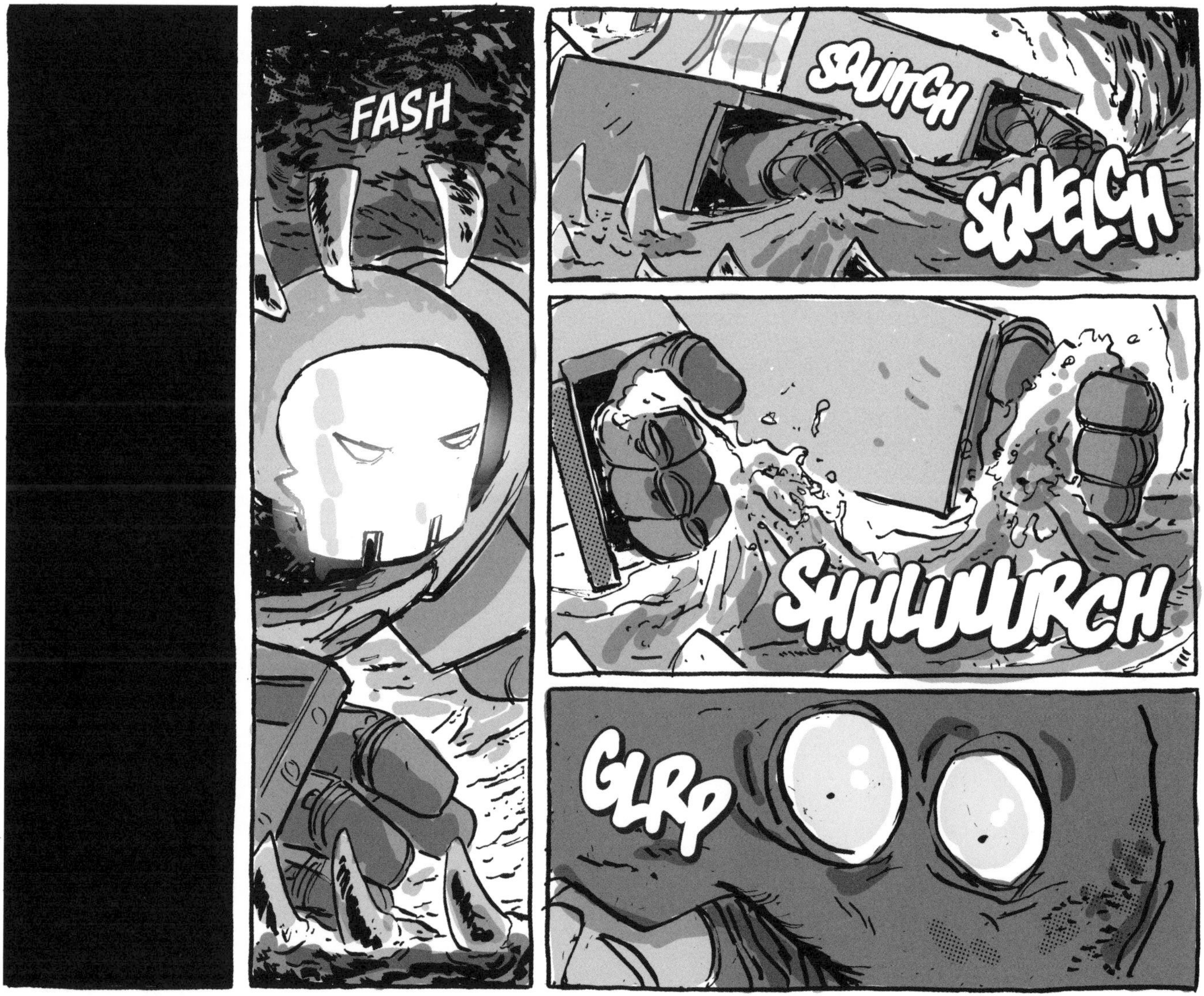
FASH
SQUITCH
SQUELCH
SHHLUUURCH
GLRP

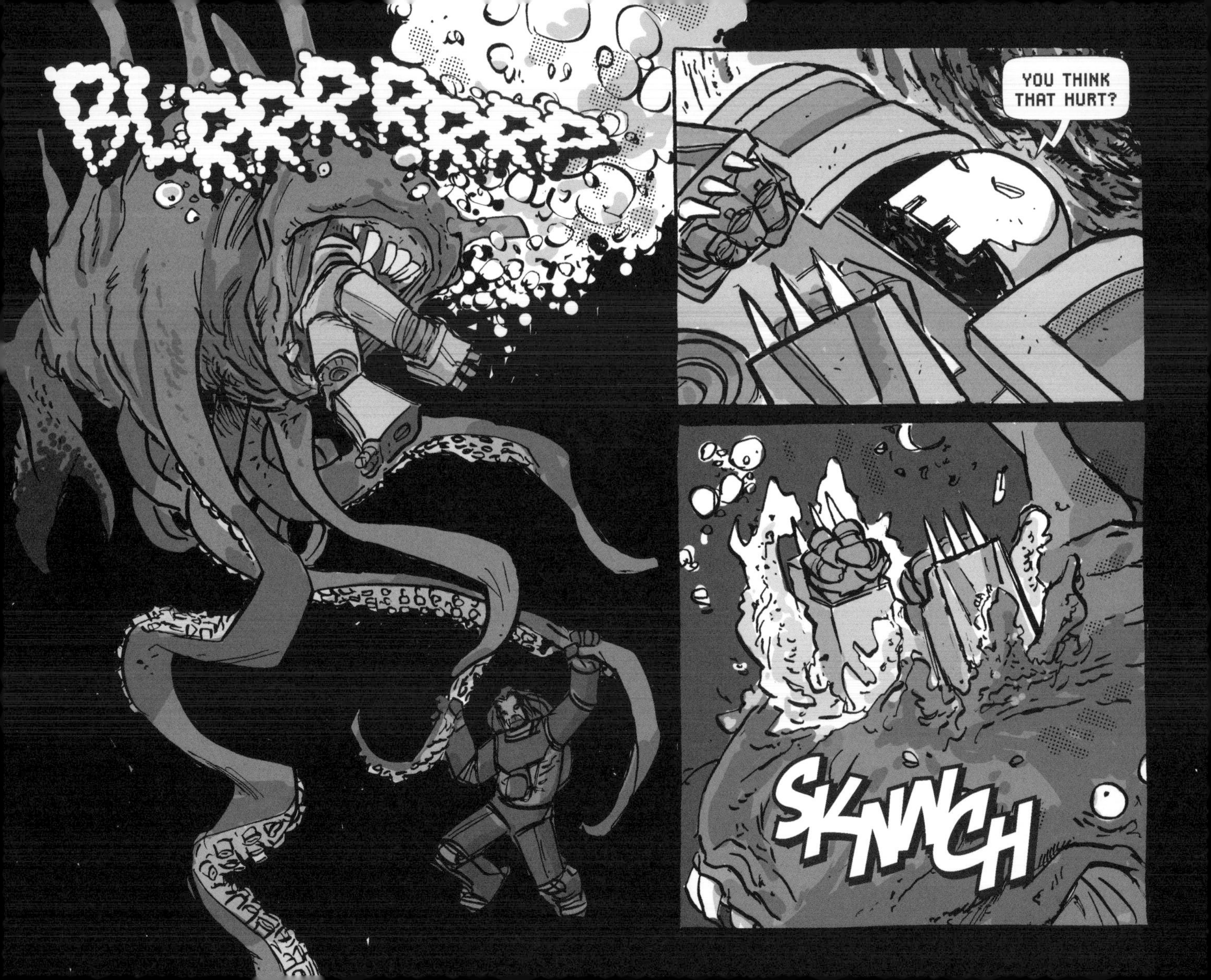
BLÜRRRRRP
YOU THINK THAT HURT?
SKNNCH

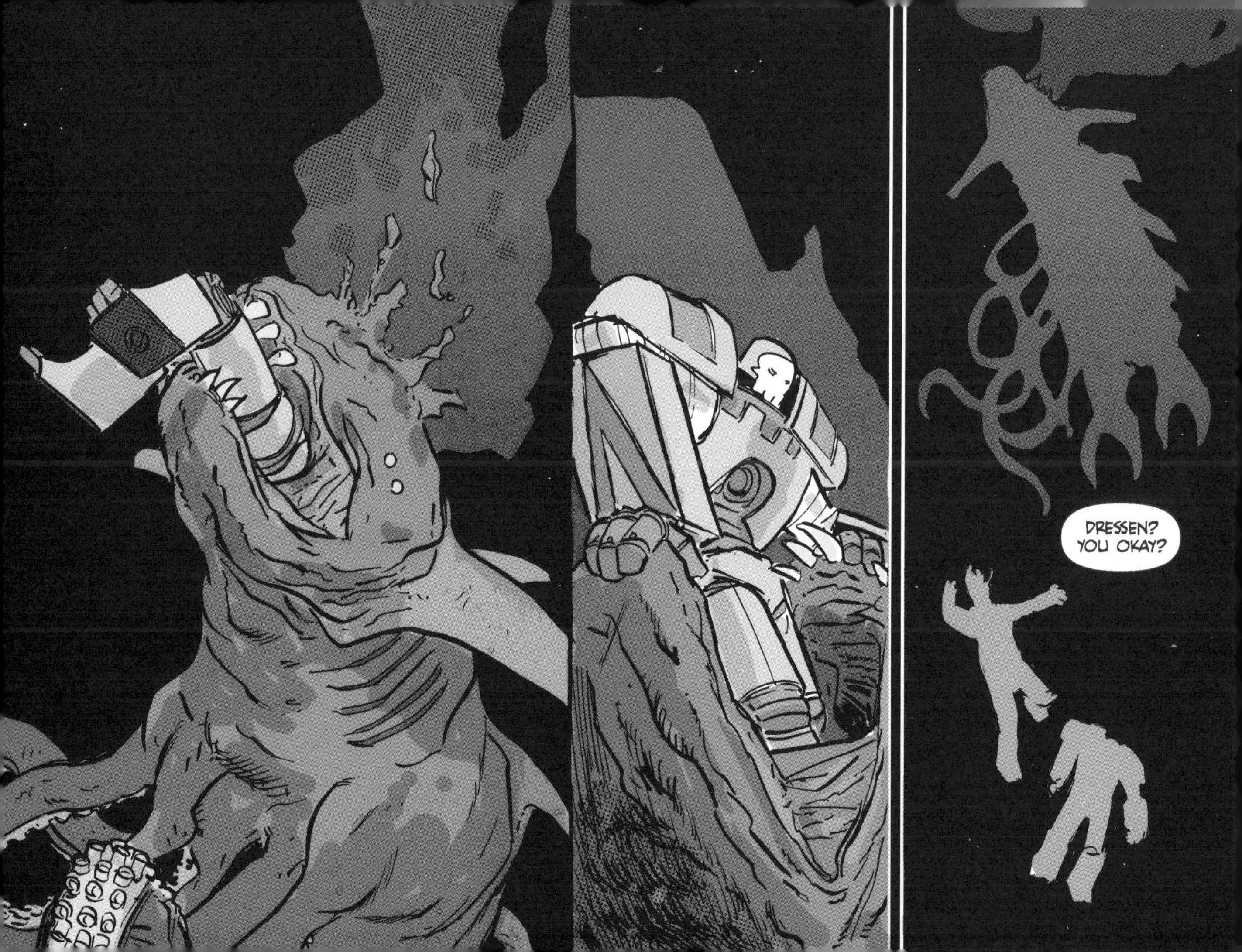
DRESSEN? YOU OKAY?

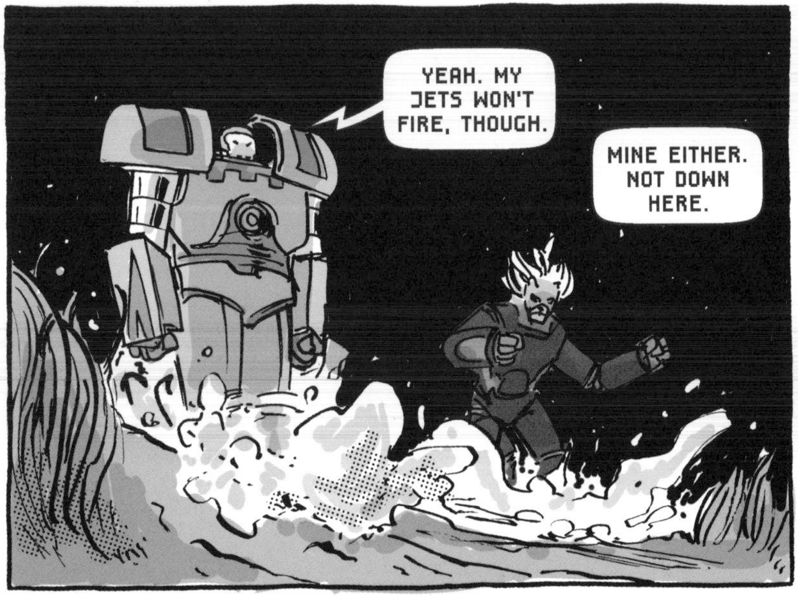
YEAH. MY JETS WON'T FIRE, THOUGH.
MINE EITHER. NOT DOWN HERE.

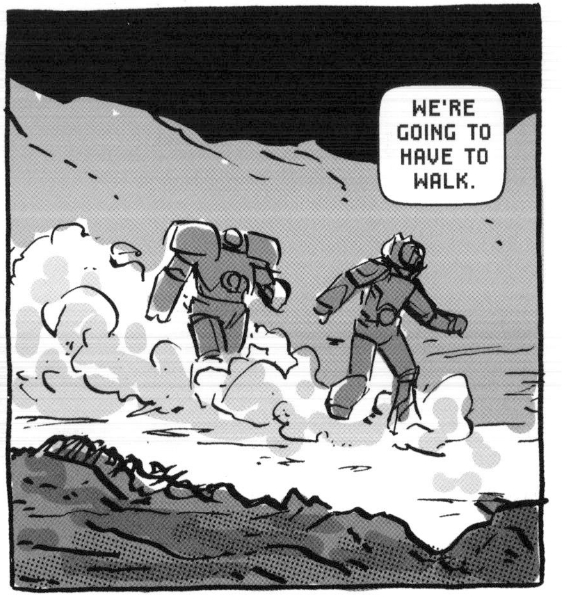
WE'RE GOING TO HAVE TO WALK.

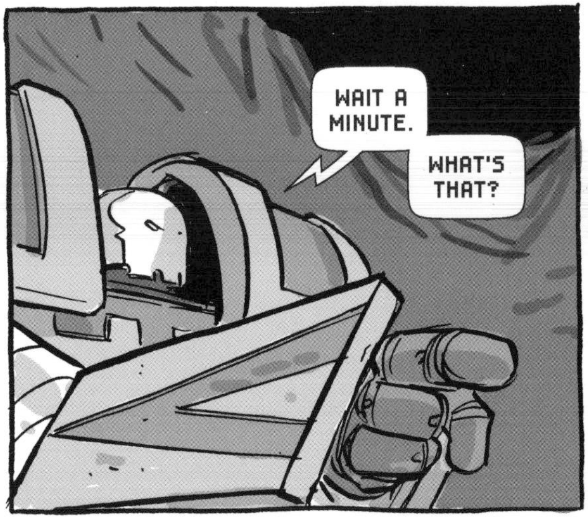
WAIT A MINUTE.
WHAT'S THAT?

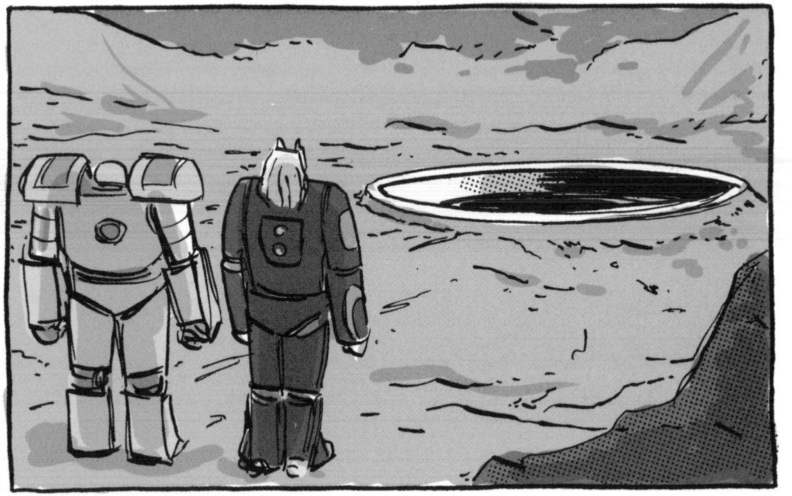

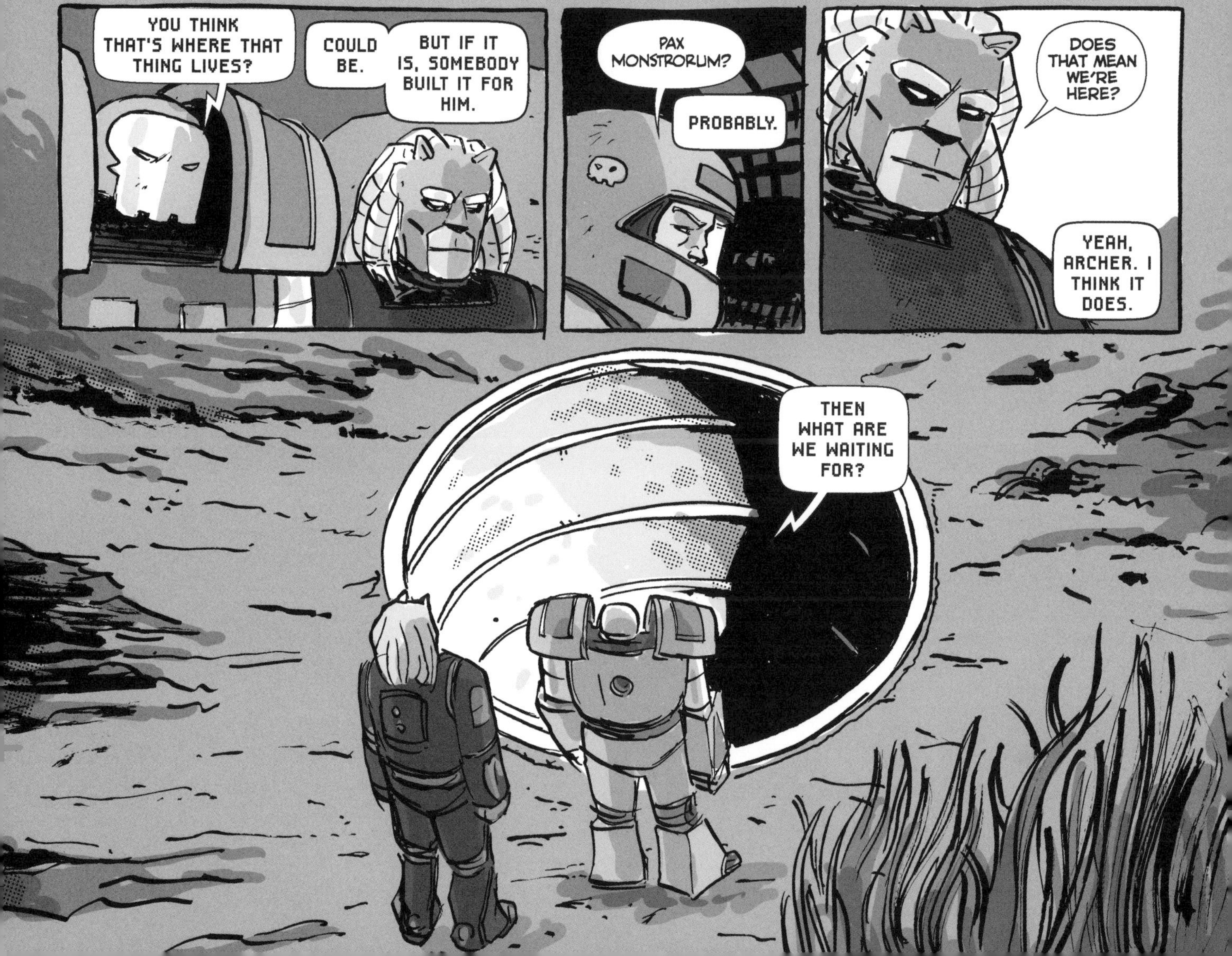
YOU THINK THAT'S WHERE THAT THING LIVES?
COULD BE.
BUT IF IT IS, SOMEBODY BUILT IT FOR HIM.
PAX MONSTRORUM?
PROBABLY.
DOES THAT MEAN WE'RE HERE?
YEAH, ARCHER. I THINK IT DOES.
THEN WHAT ARE WE WAITING FOR?

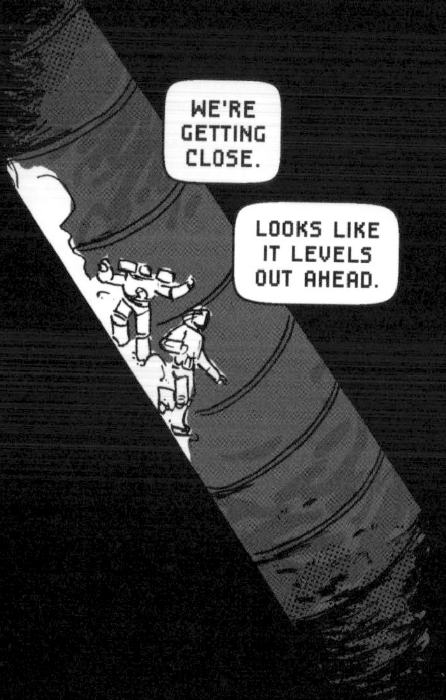
WE'RE GETTING CLOSE.
LOOKS LIKE IT LEVELS OUT AHEAD.

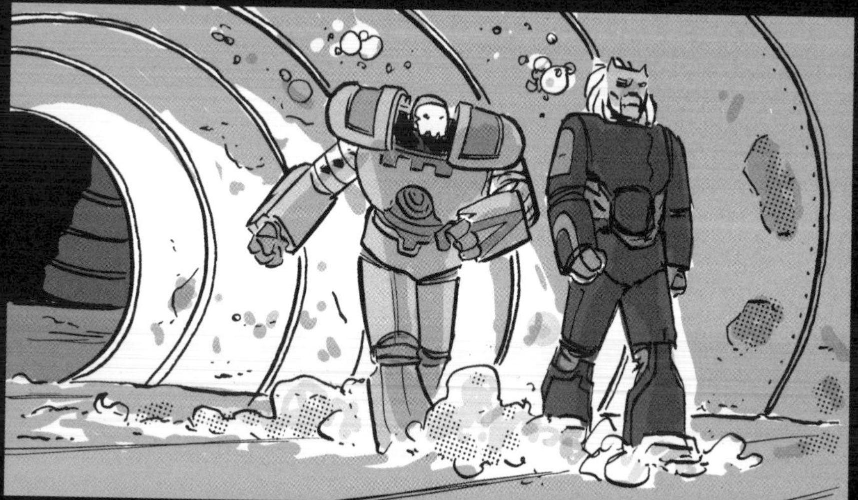

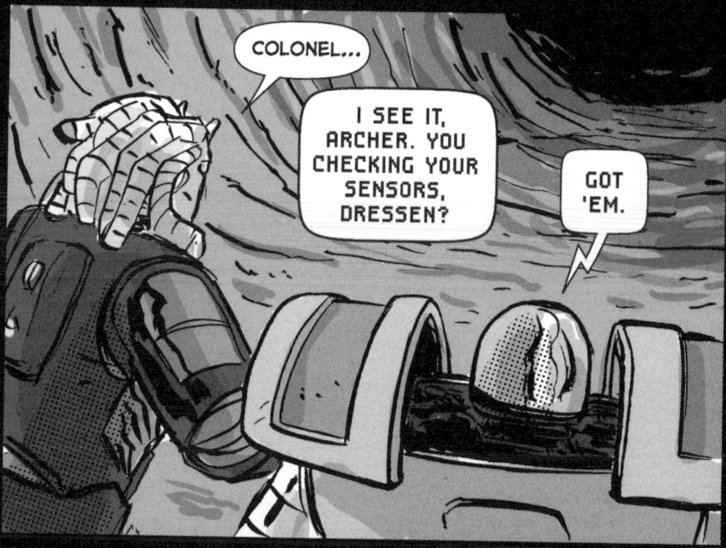
COLONEL...
I SEE IT, ARCHER. YOU CHECKING YOUR SENSORS, DRESSEN?
GOT 'EM.

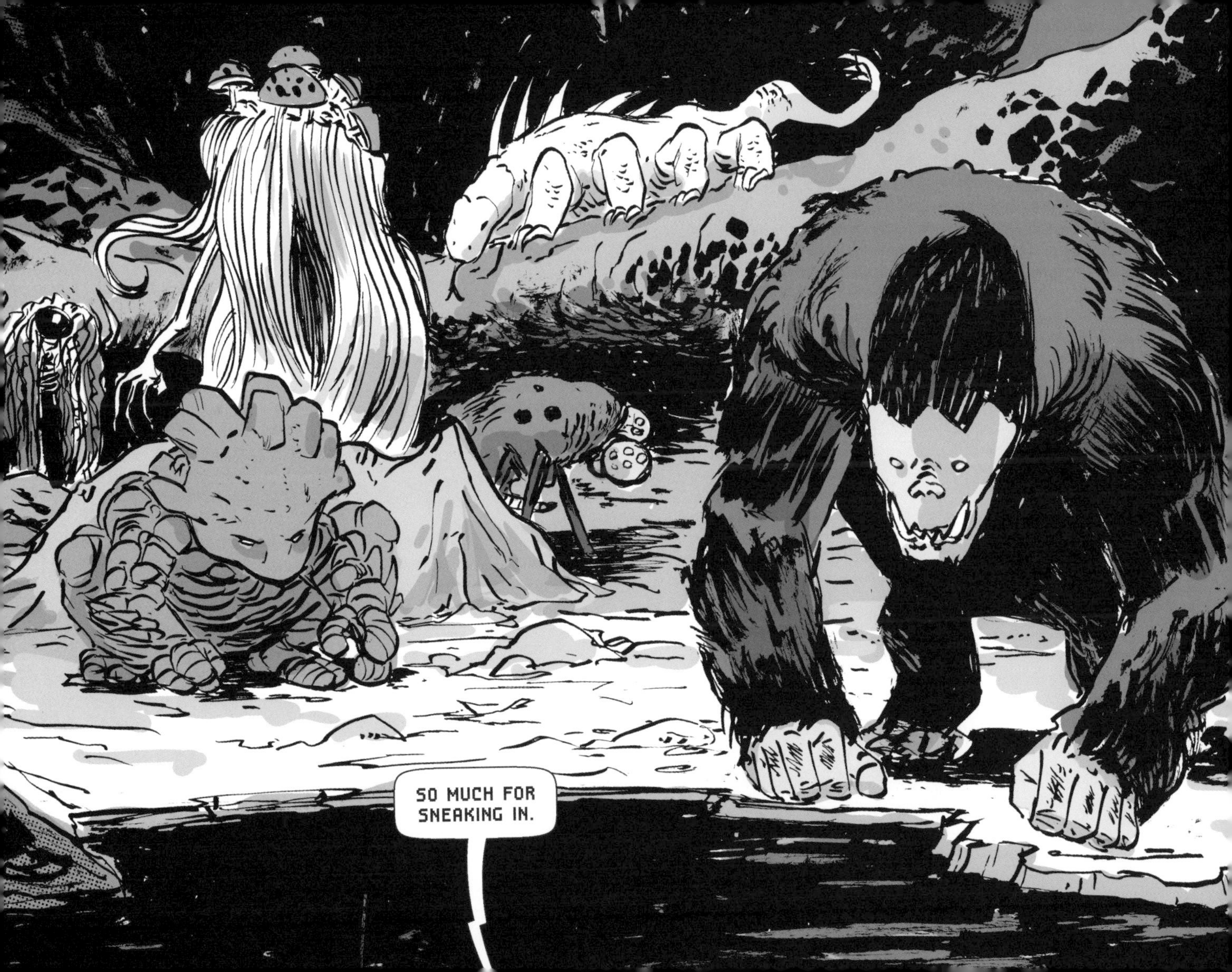
SO MUCH FOR SNEAKING IN.

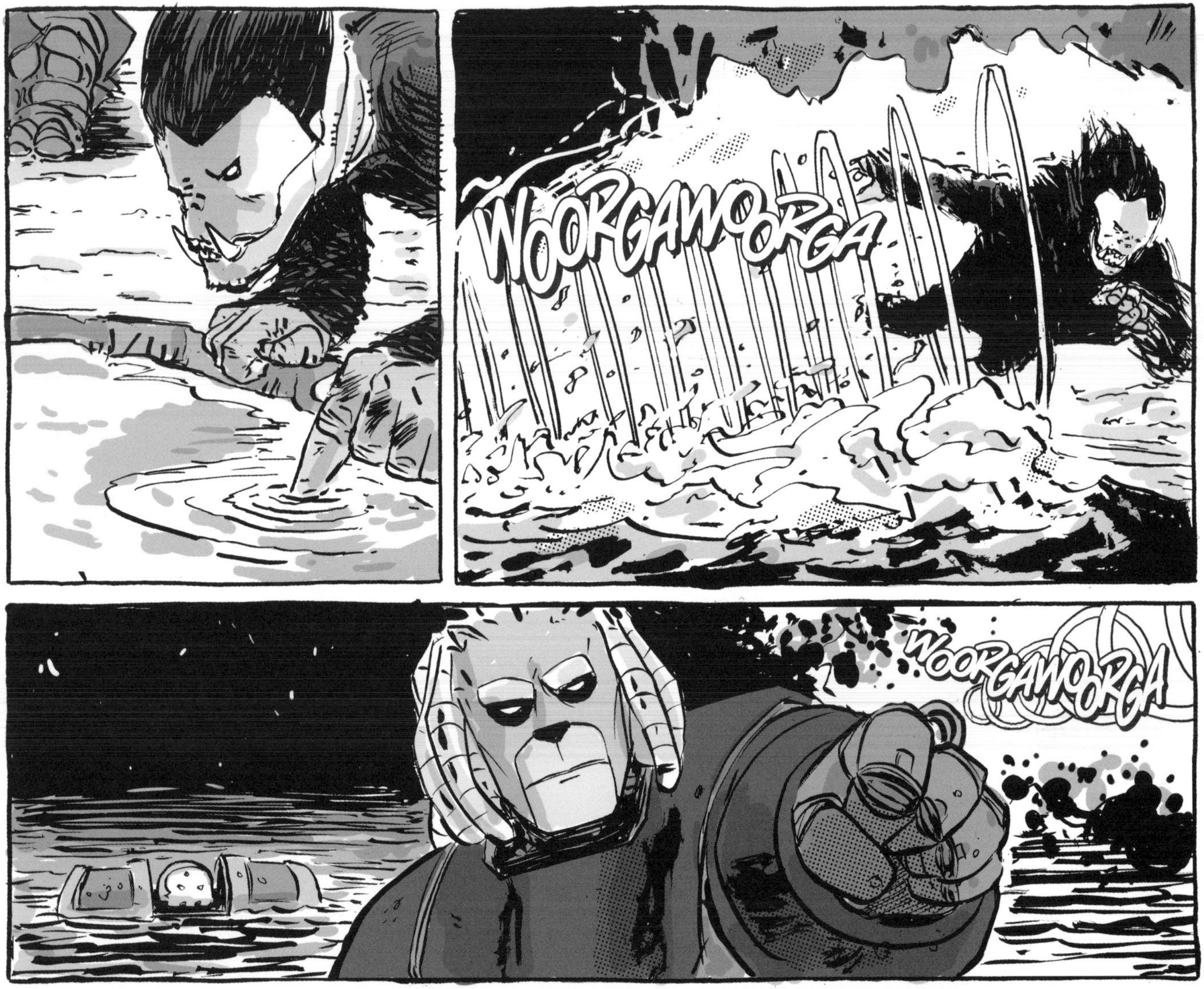
WOORGAWOORGA
WOORGAWOORGA

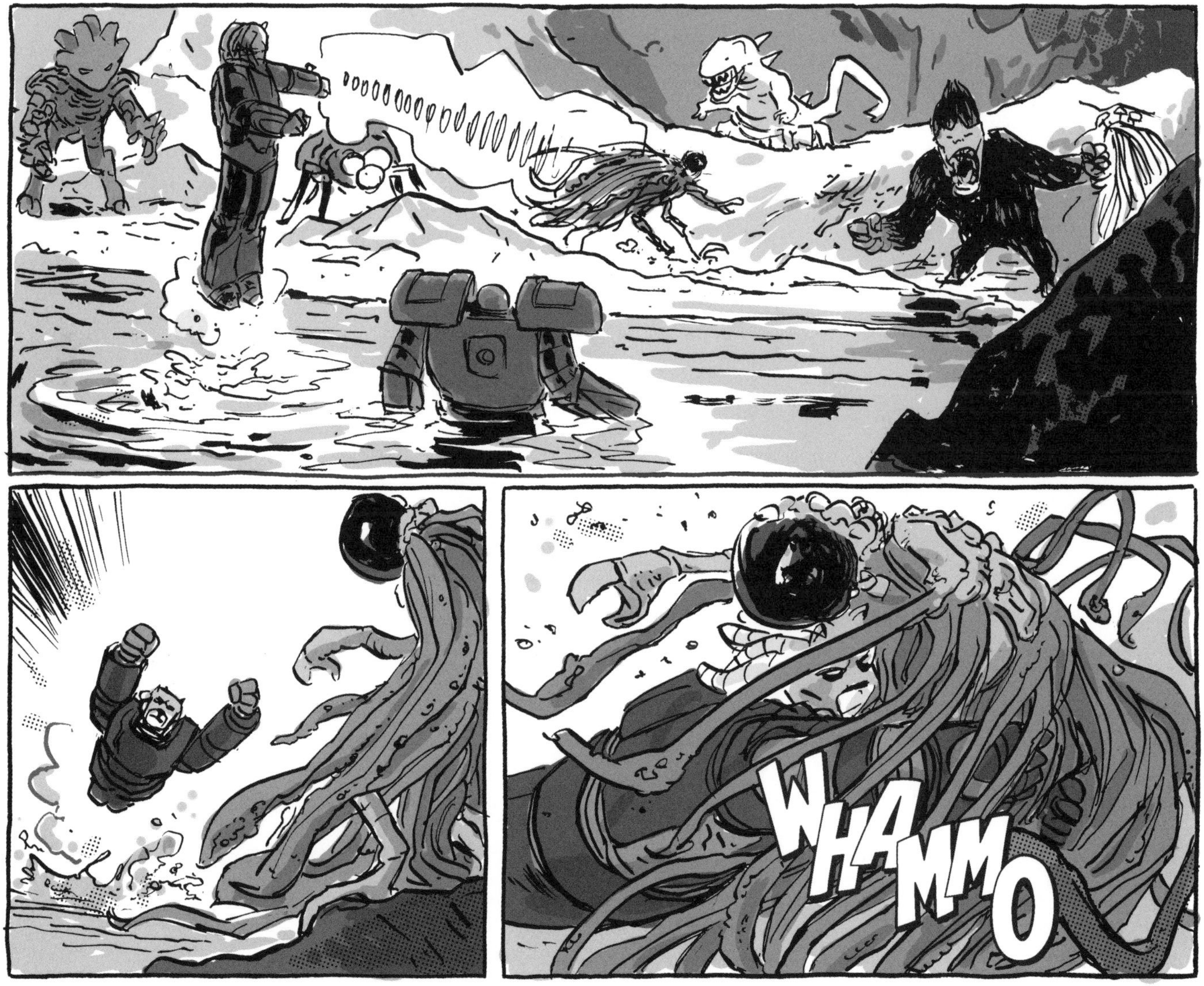
WHAMMO

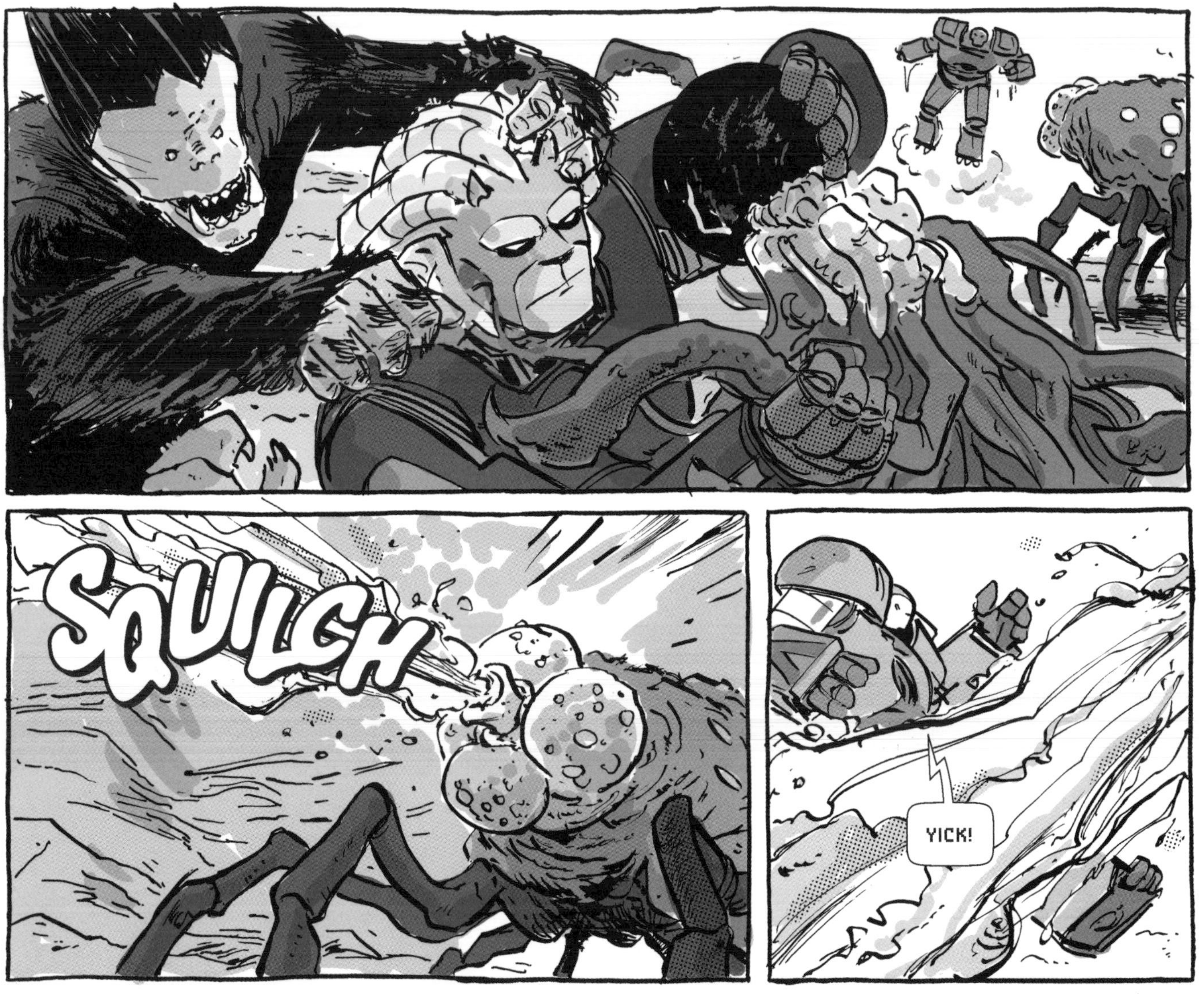
SQUILCH
YICK!

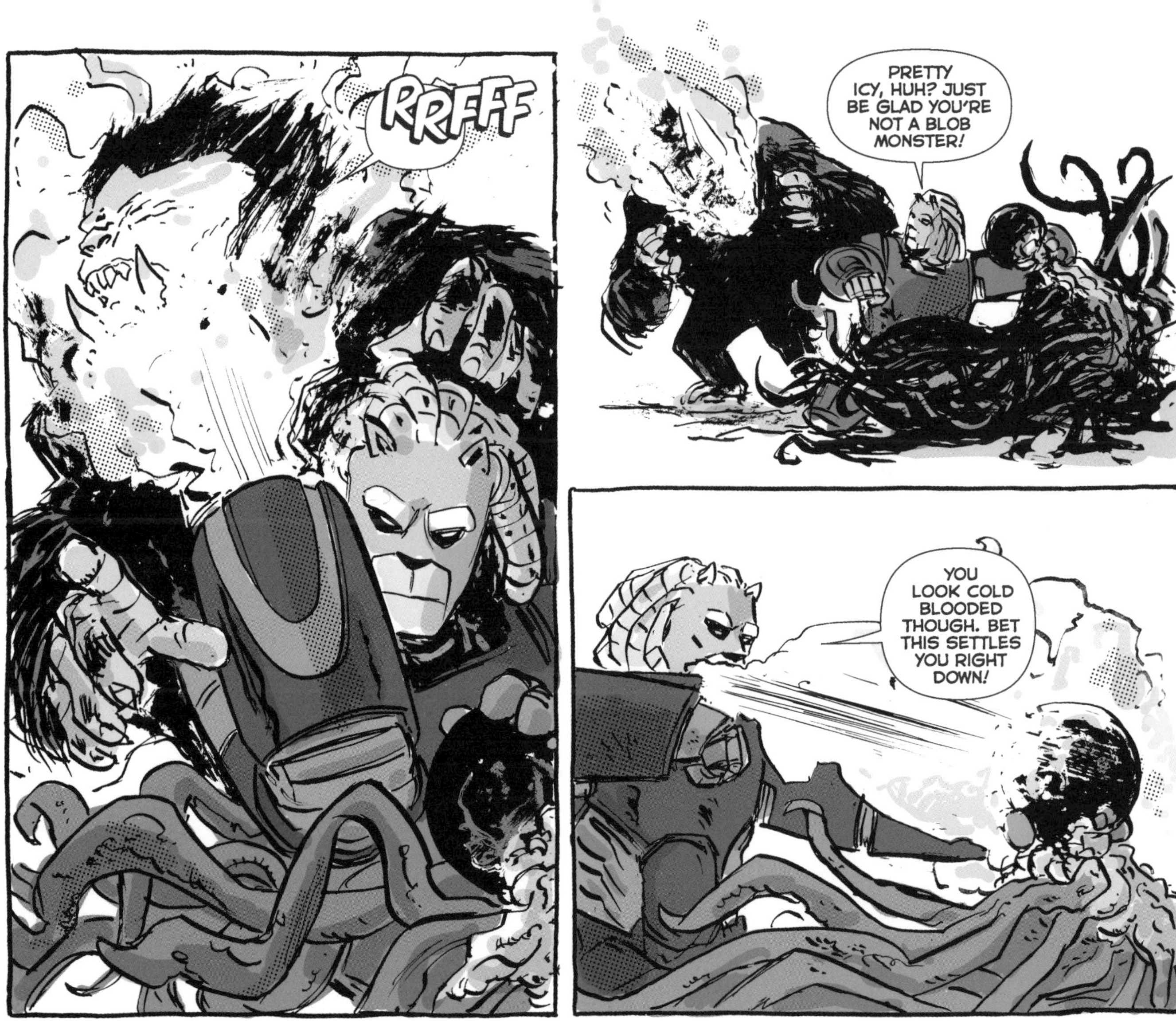
RRFFF
PRETTY ICY, HUH? JUST BE GLAD YOU'RE NOT A BLOB MONSTER!
YOU LOOK COLD BLOODED THOUGH. BET THIS SETTLES YOU RIGHT DOWN!

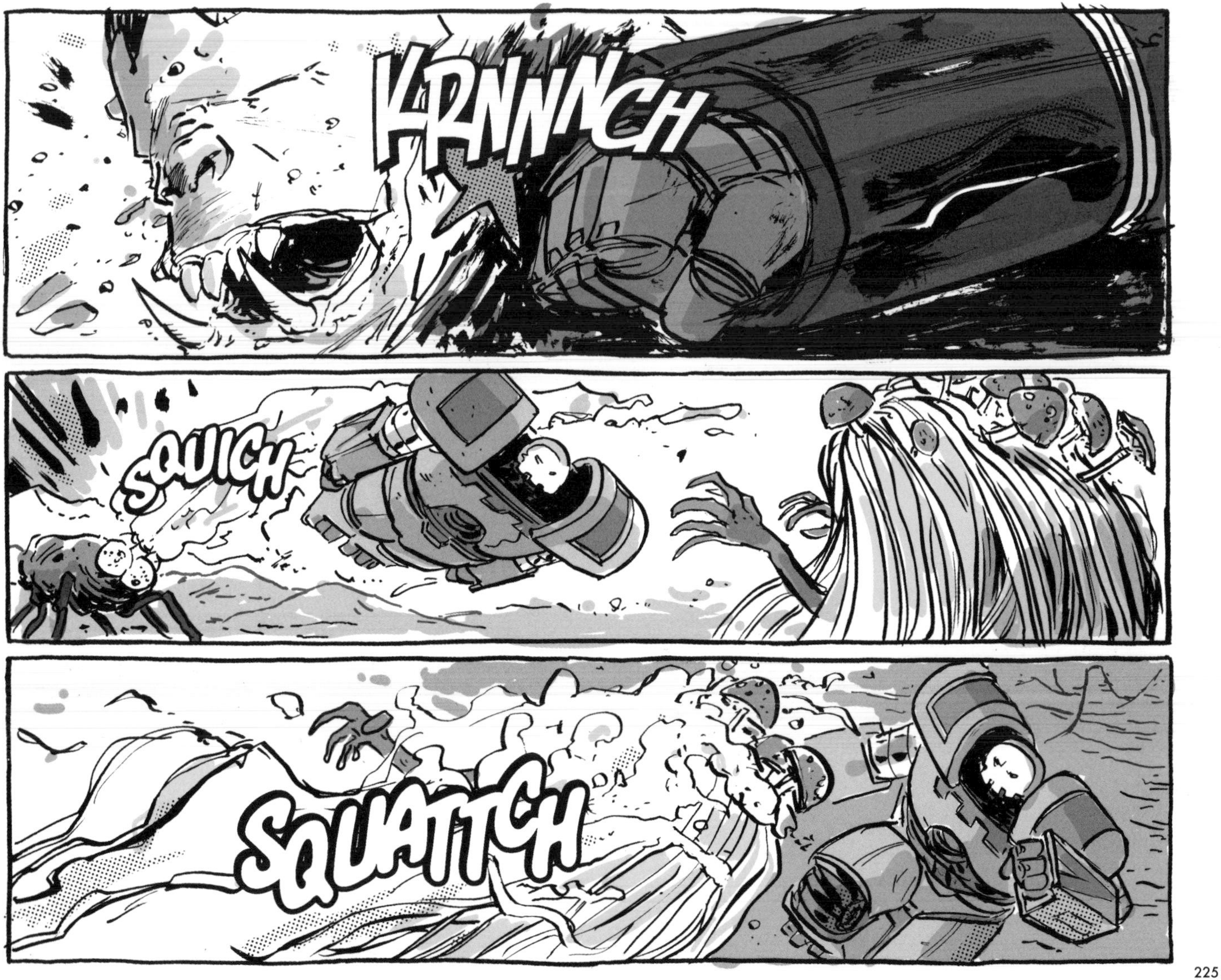
KRNNNCH
SQUICH
SQUATTCH

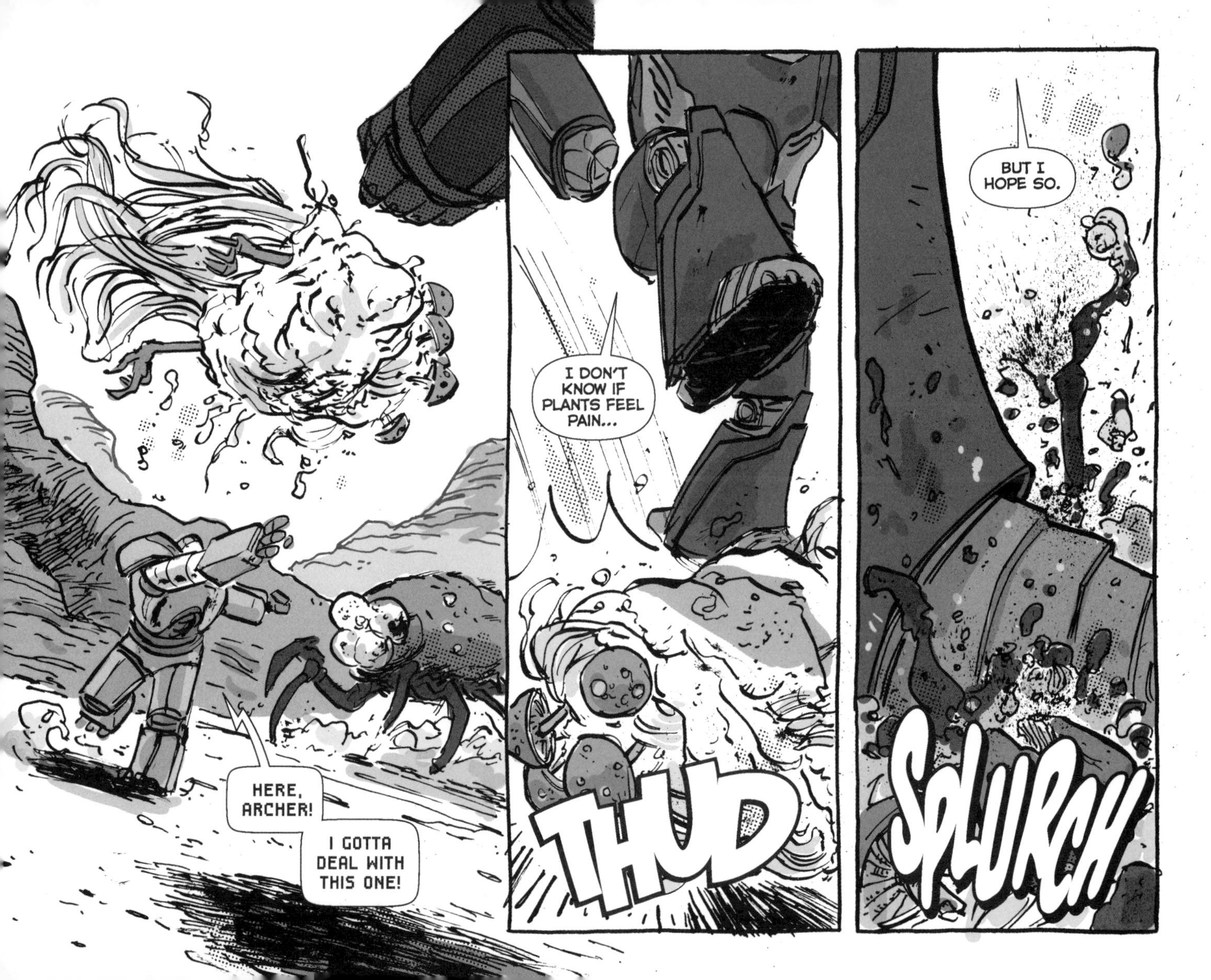
HERE, ARCHER!
I GOTTA DEAL WITH THIS ONE!
I DON'T KNOW IF PLANTS FEEL PAIN...
THUD
BUT I HOPE SO.
SPLURCH

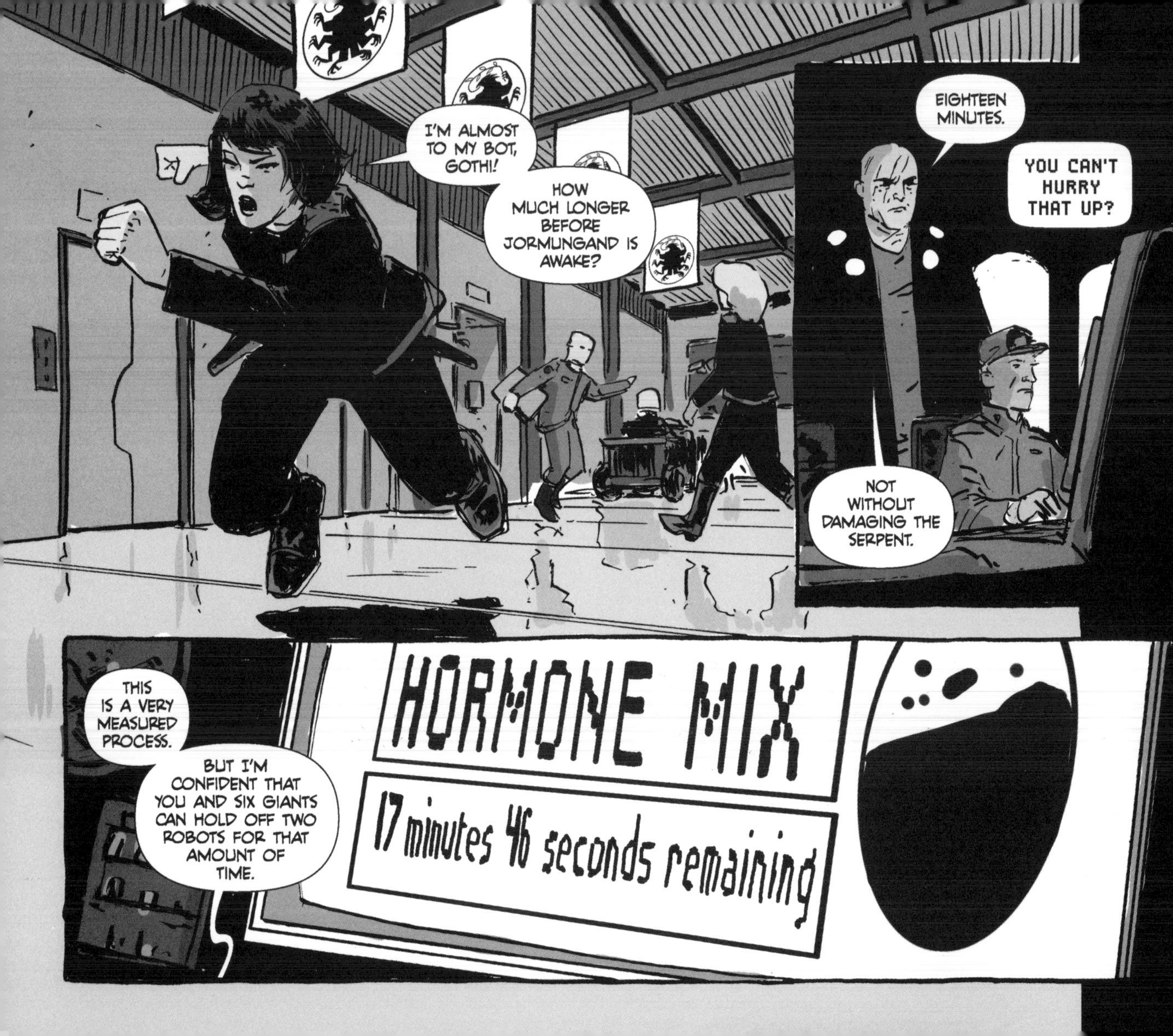
I'M ALMOST TO MY BOT, GOTHI!
HOW MUCH LONGER BEFORE JORMUNGAND IS AWAKE?
EIGHTEEN MINUTES.
YOU CAN'T HURRY THAT UP?
NOT WITHOUT DAMAGING THE SERPENT.
THIS IS A VERY MEASURED PROCESS.
BUT I'M CONFIDENT THAT YOU AND SIX GIANTS CAN HOLD OFF TWO ROBOTS FOR THAT AMOUNT OF TIME.
HORMONE MIX
17 minutes 46 seconds remaining

CHAPTER ELEVEN
REVENGE OF THE ROBOTS

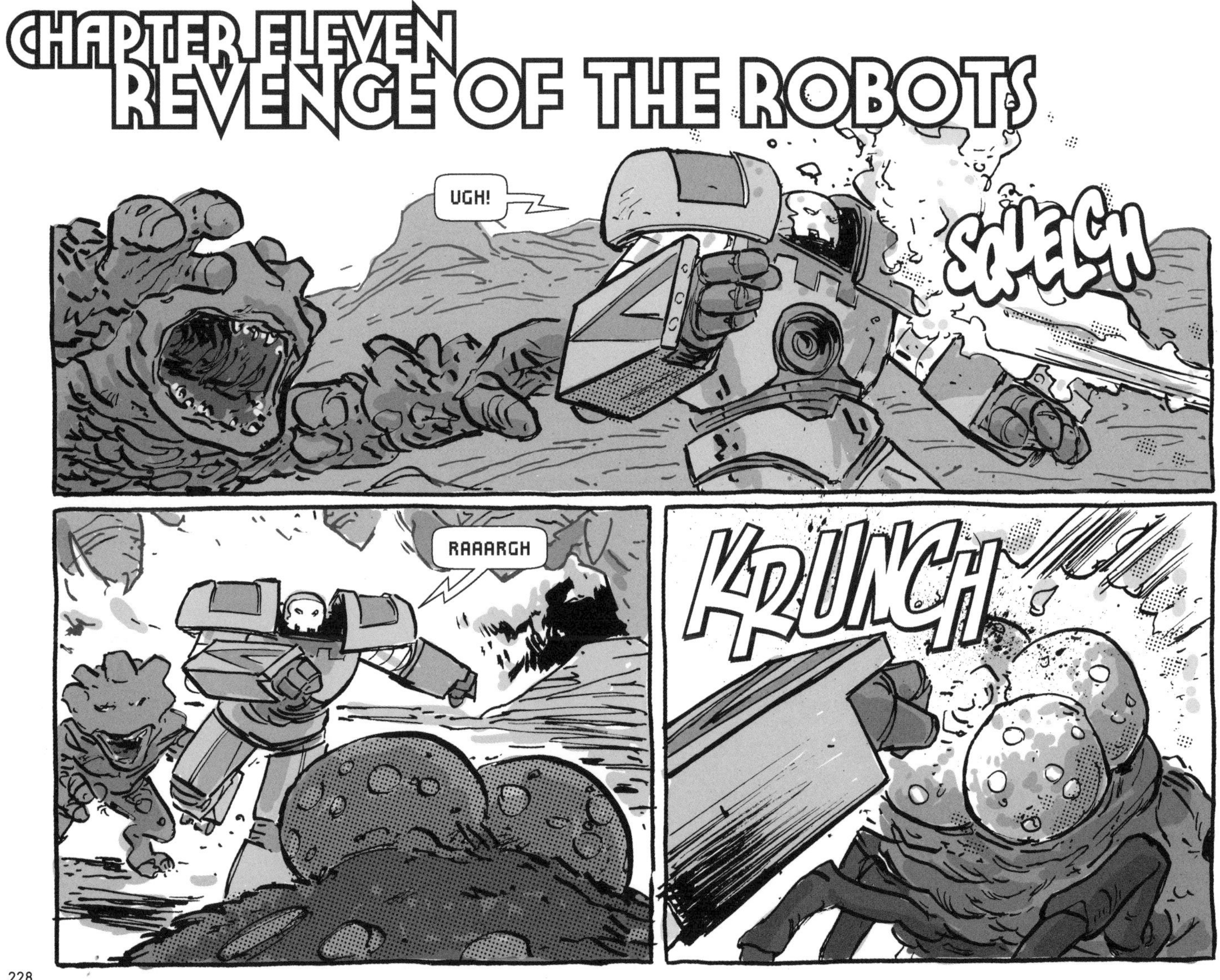
UGH!
SQUELCH
RAAARGH
KRUNCH

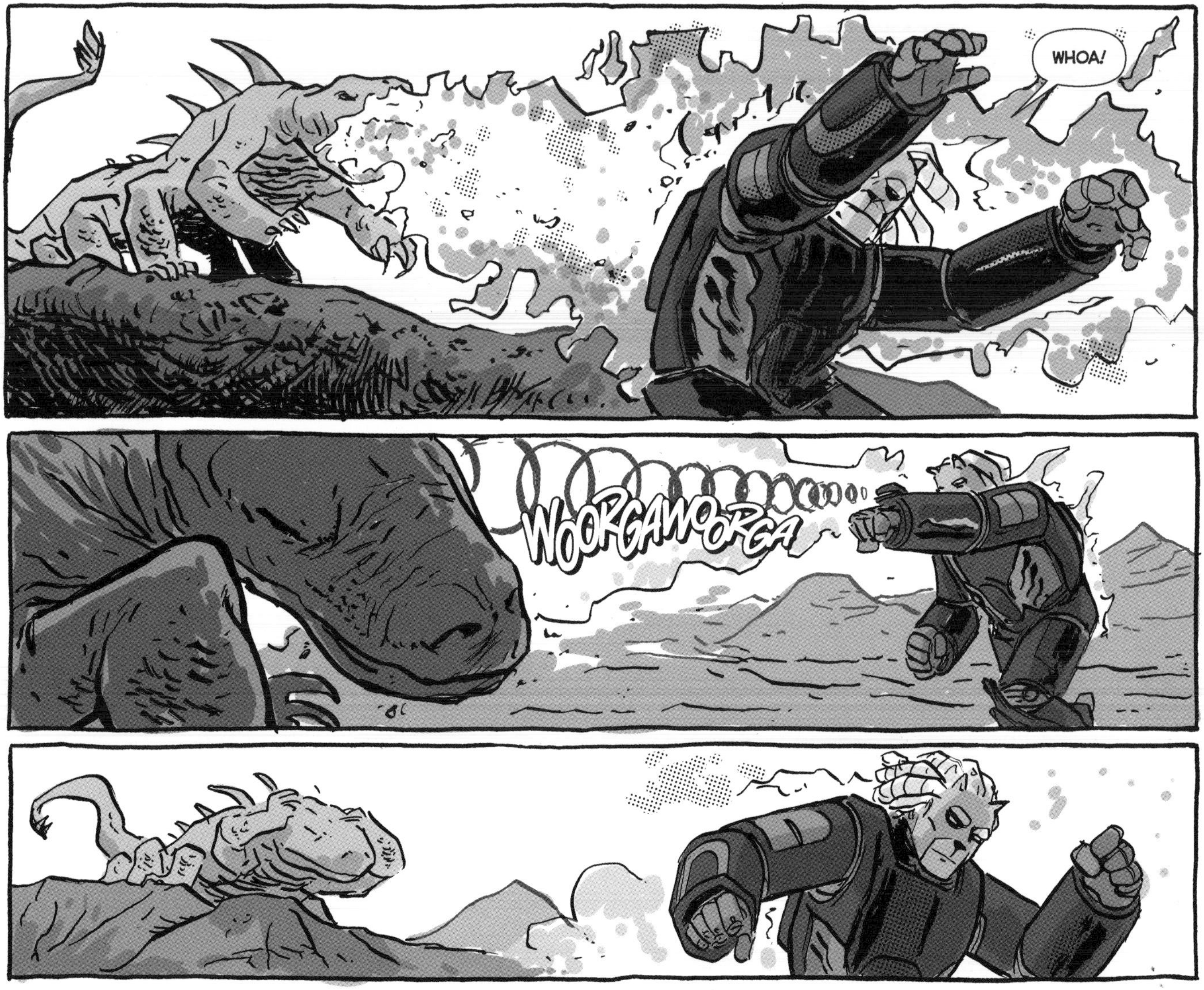
WHOA!
WOORGAWOORGA

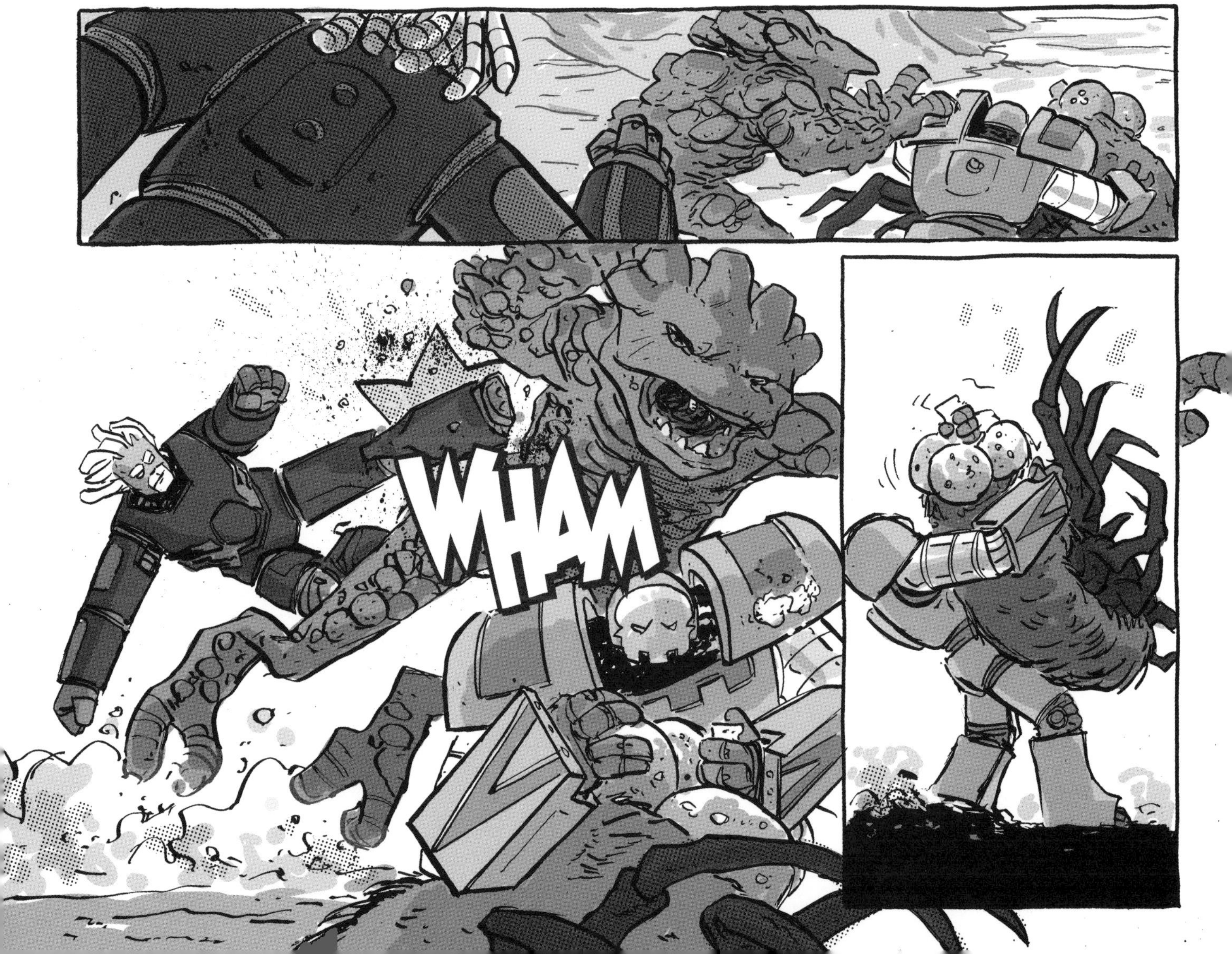
WHAM

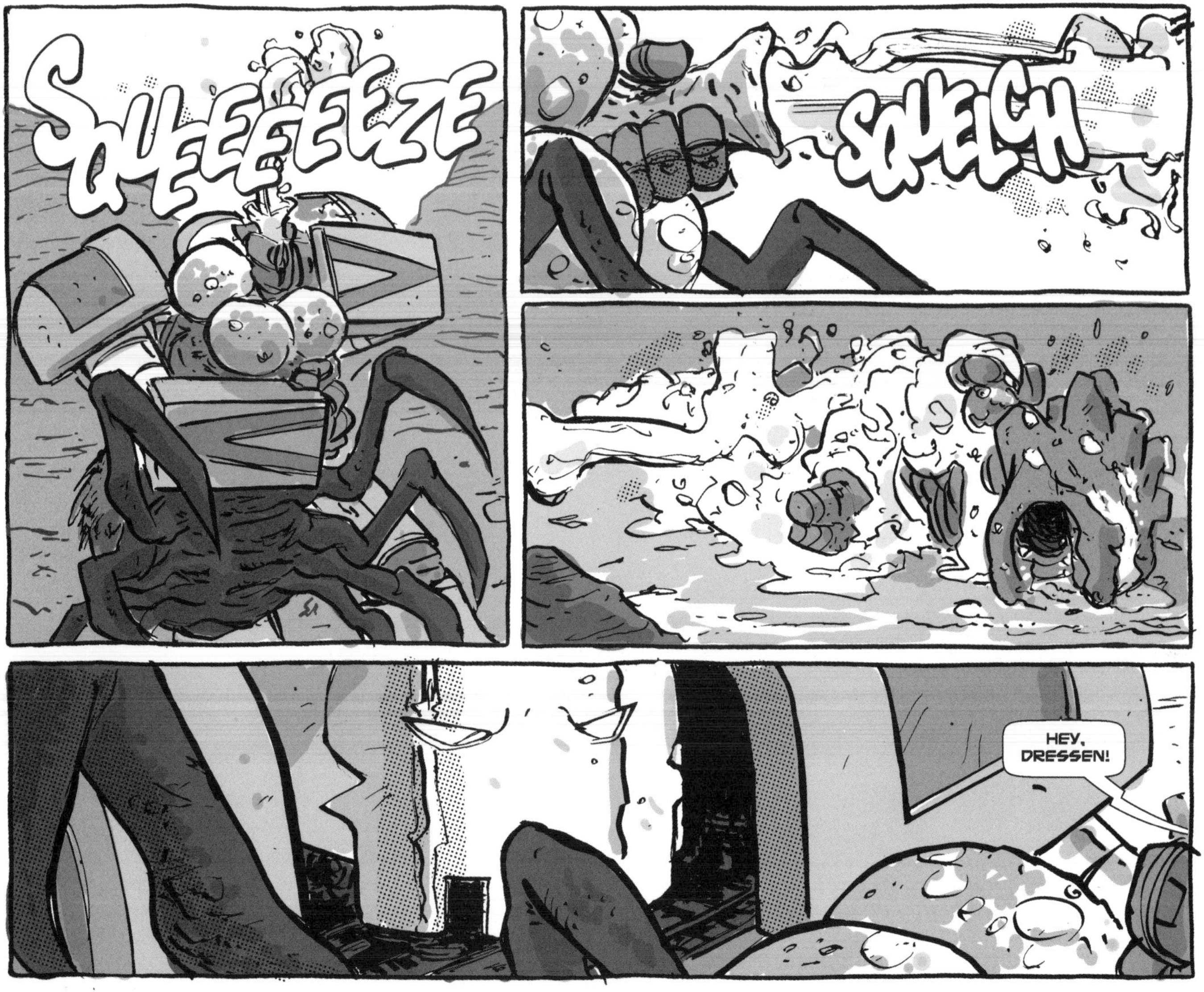
SQUEEEEEZE
SQUELCH
HEY, DRESSEN!

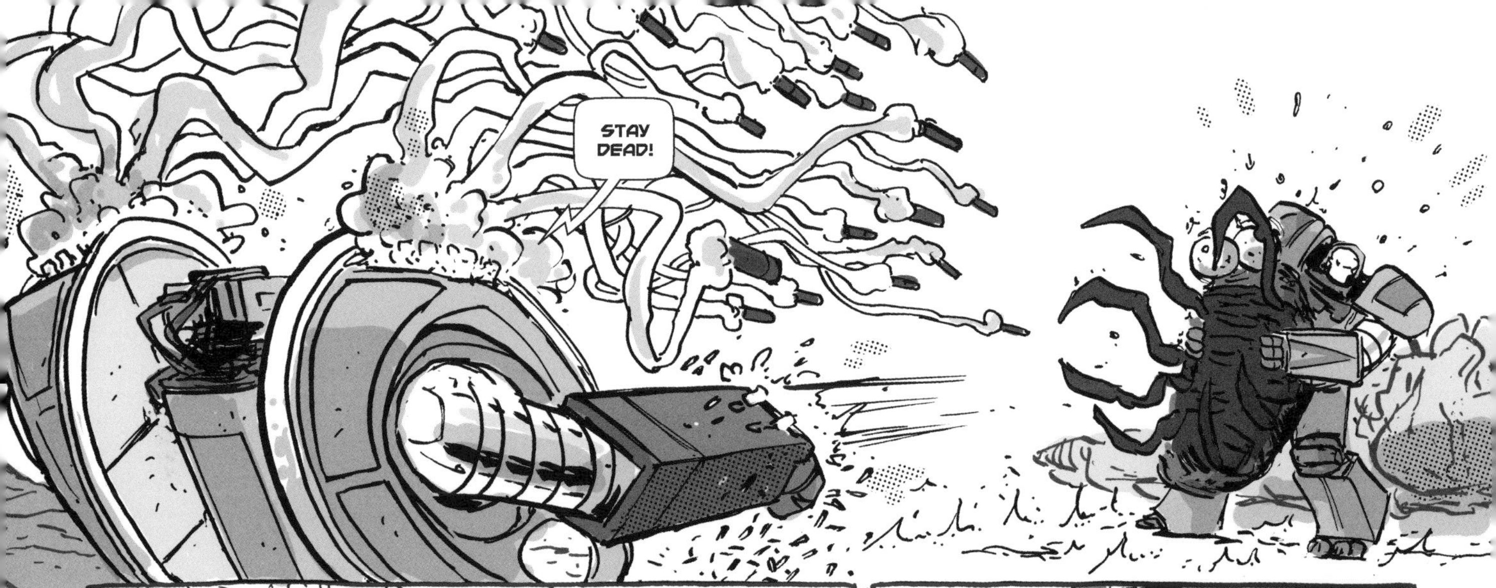
STAY DEAD!

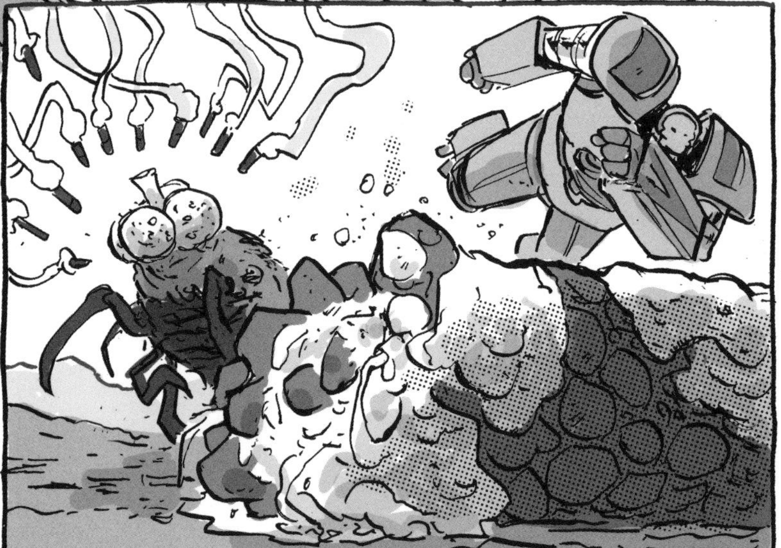

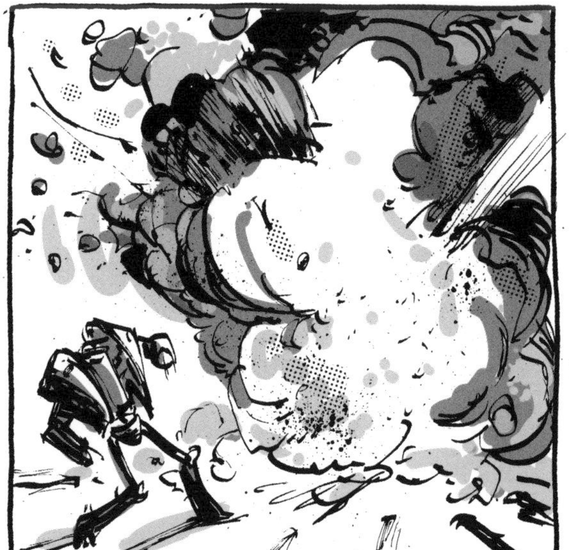

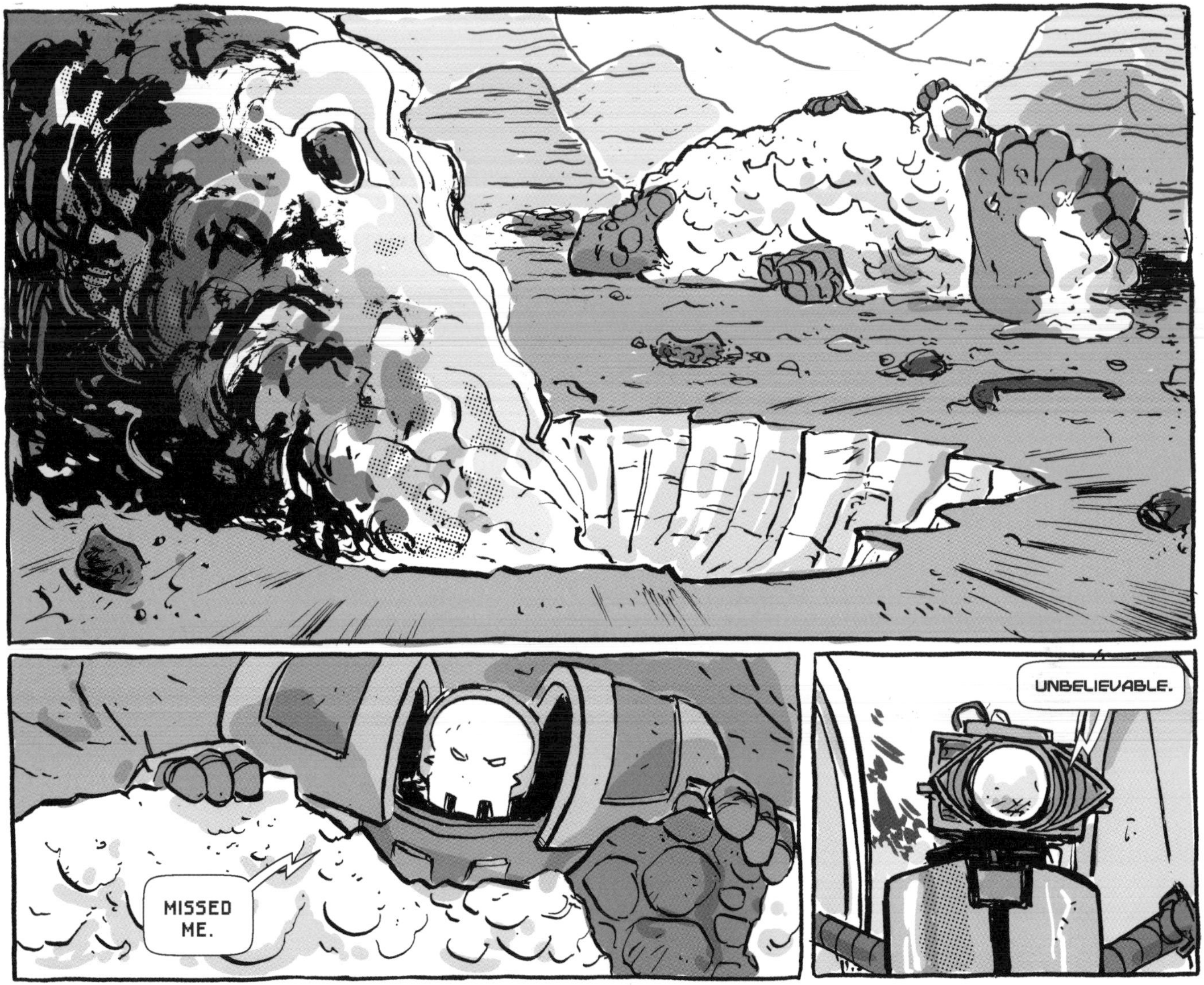
MISSED ME.
UNBELIEVABLE.

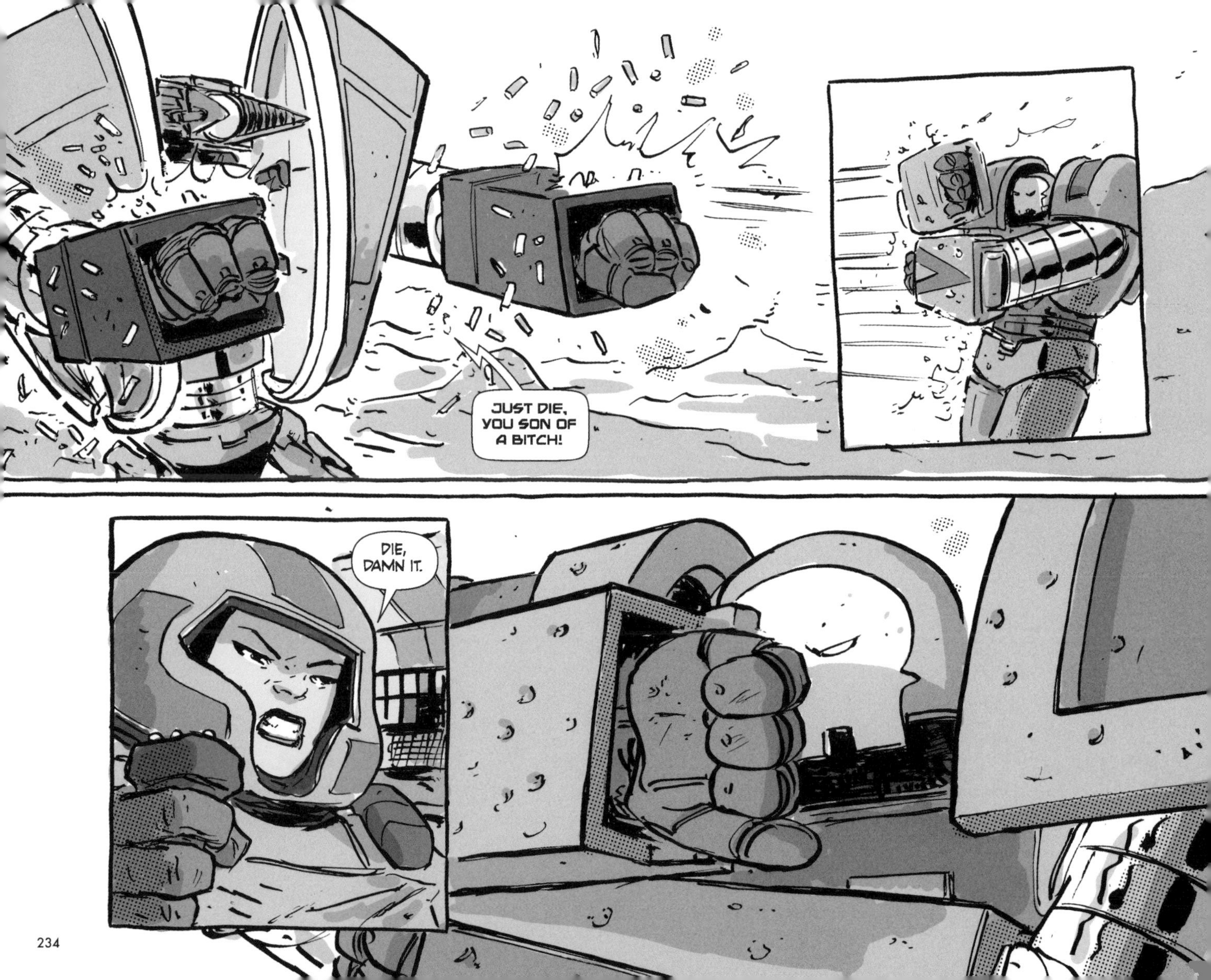
JUST DIE, YOU SON OF A BITCH!
DIE, DAMN IT.

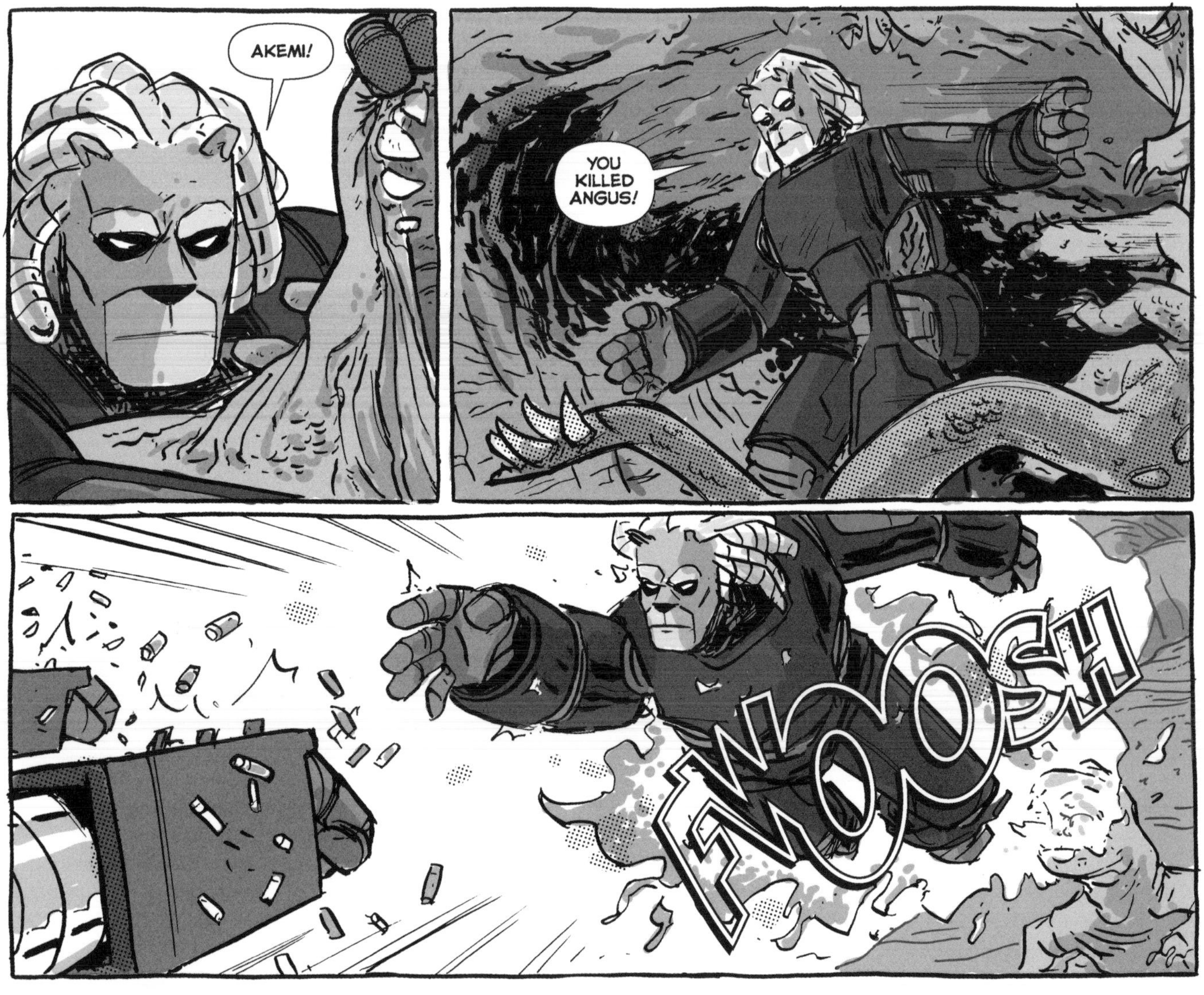
AKEMI!
YOU KILLED ANGUS!
WOOOSH

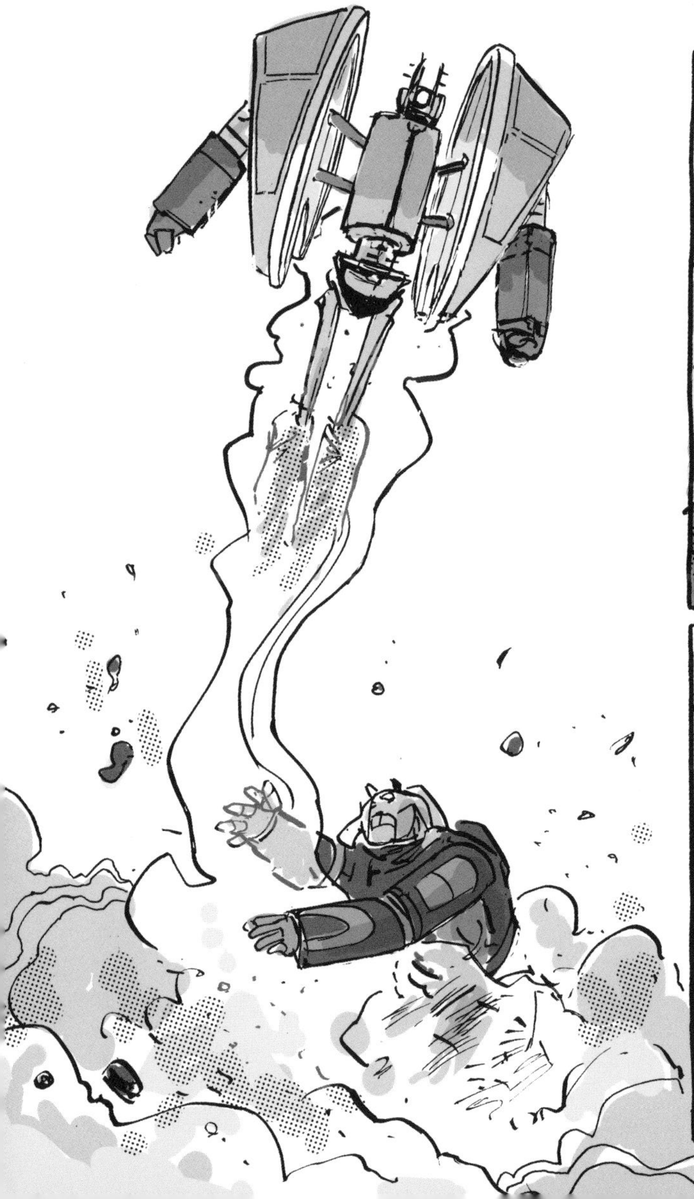

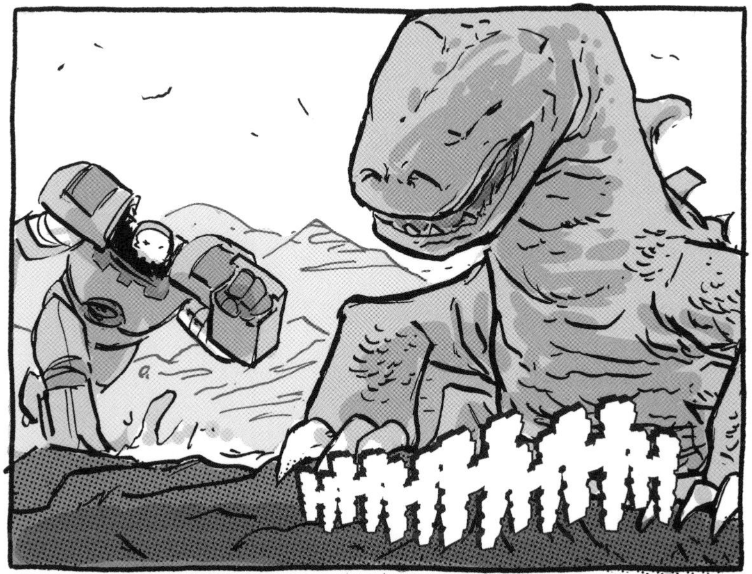
WHHHHHHH

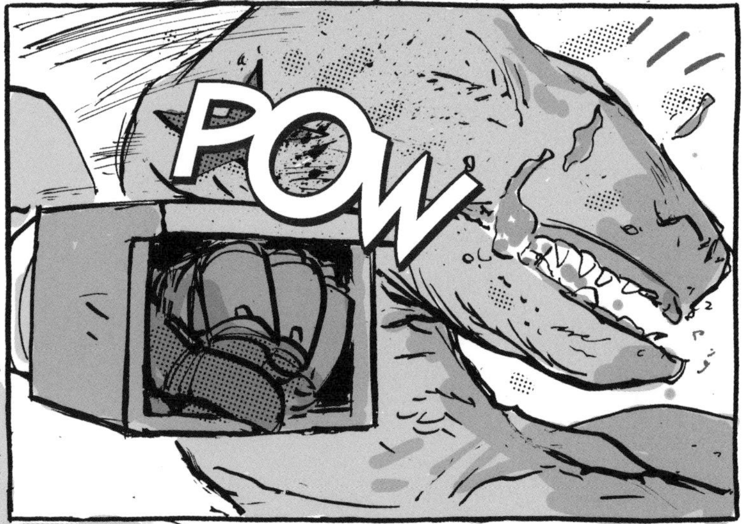
POW

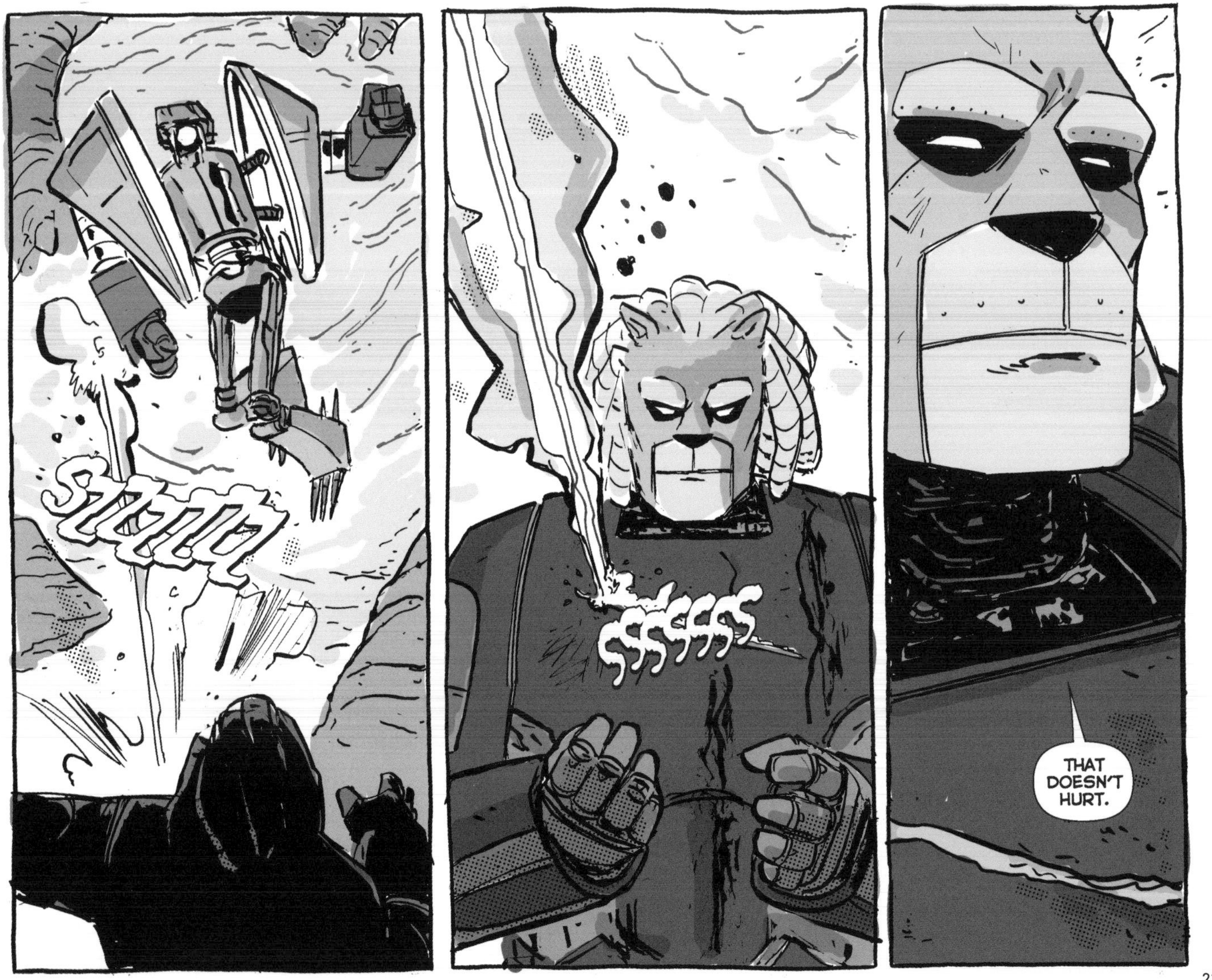
SSSSSS
THAT DOESN'T HURT.

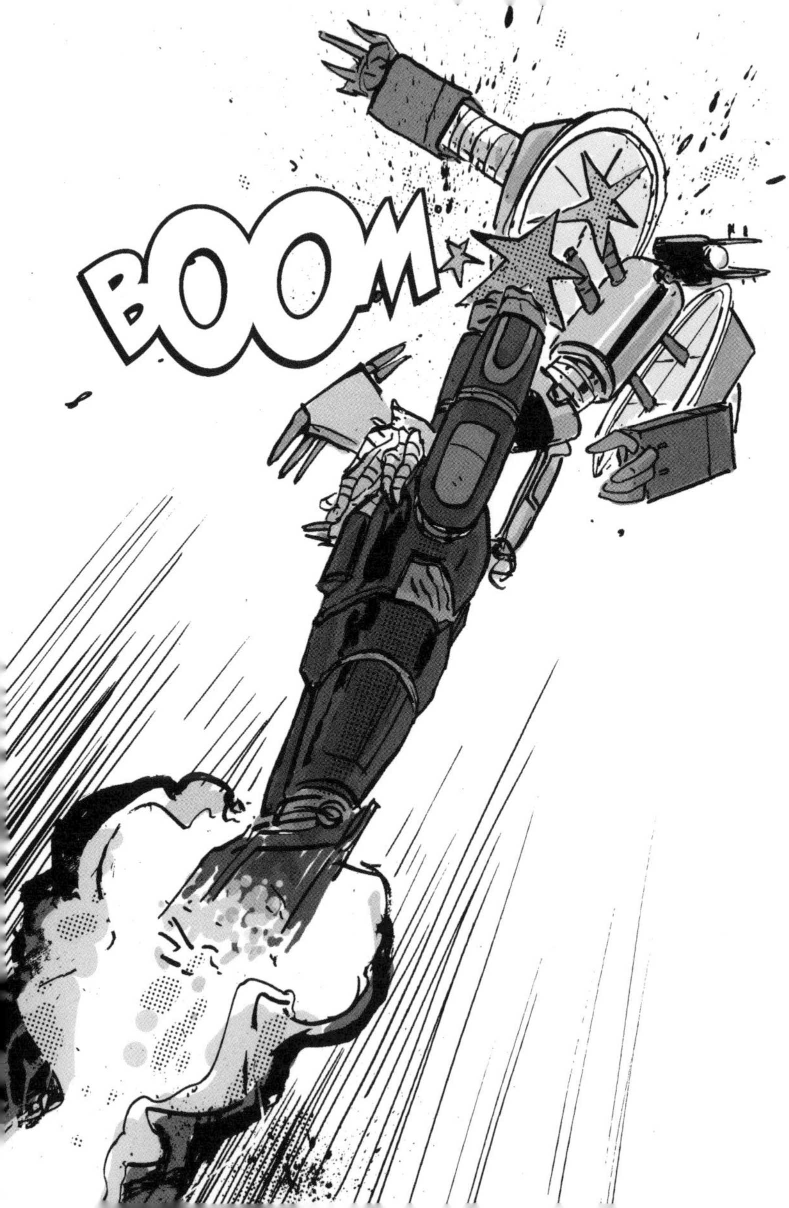
BOOM
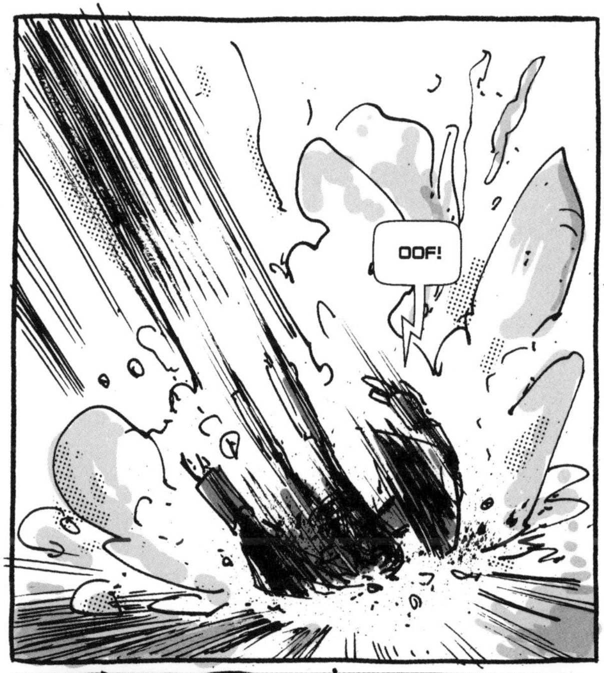
OOF!
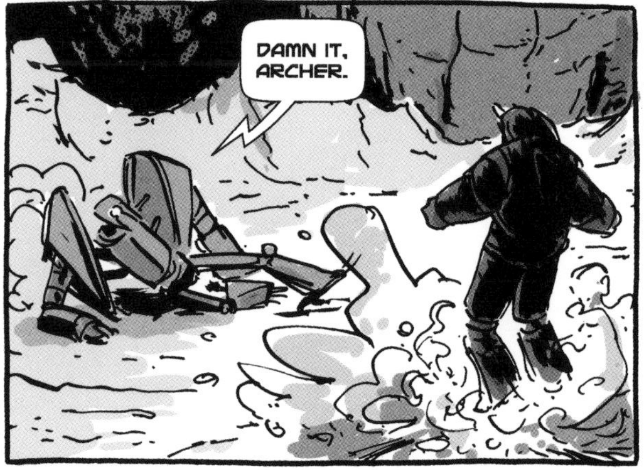
DAMN IT, ARCHER.

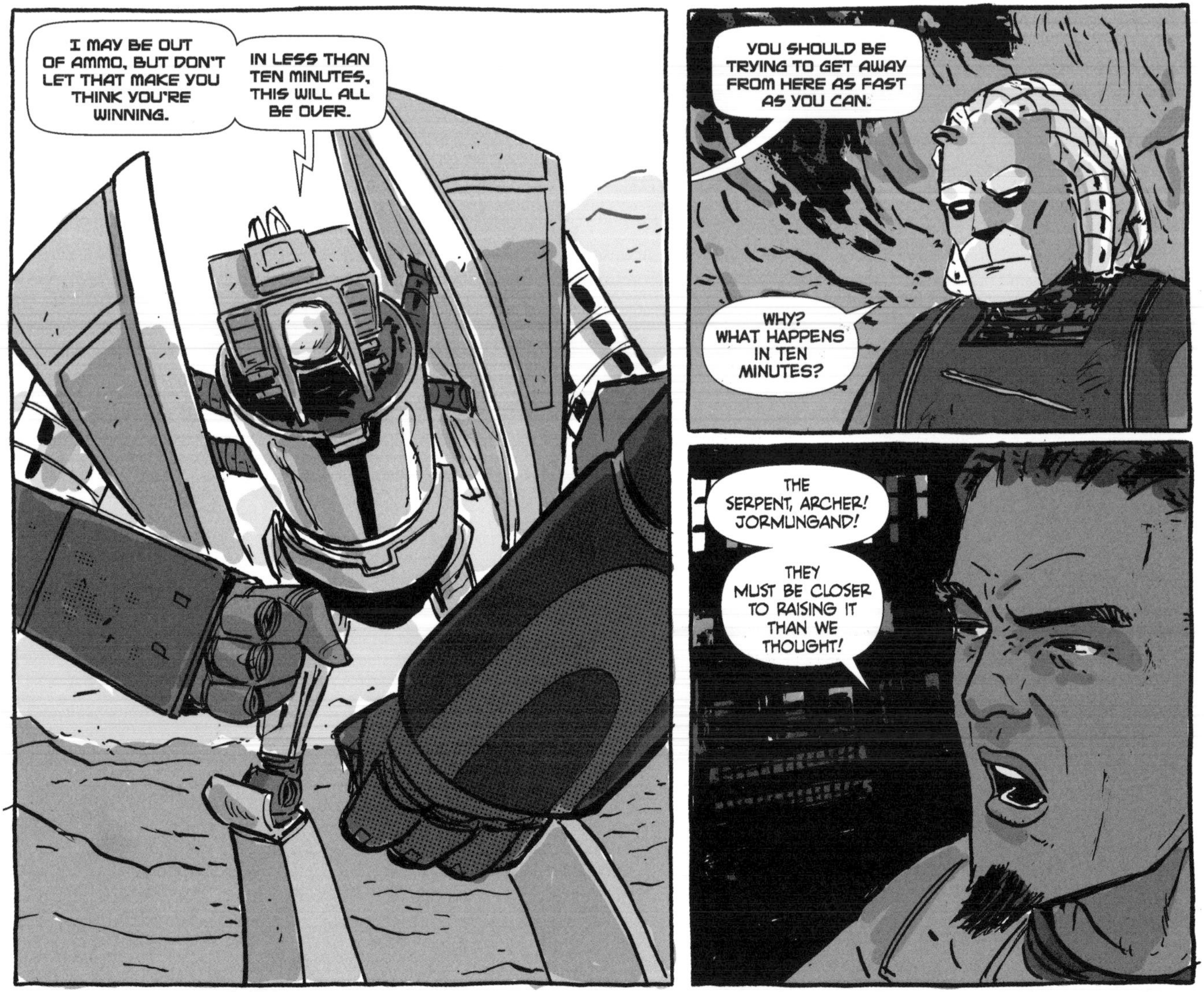
I MAY BE OUT OF AMMO, BUT DON'T LET THAT MAKE YOU THINK YOU'RE WINNING.
IN LESS THAN TEN MINUTES, THIS WILL ALL BE OVER.
YOU SHOULD BE TRYING TO GET AWAY FROM HERE AS FAST AS YOU CAN.
WHY? WHAT HAPPENS IN TEN MINUTES?
THE SERPENT, ARCHER! JORMUNGAND!
THEY MUST BE CLOSER TO RAISING IT THAN WE THOUGHT!

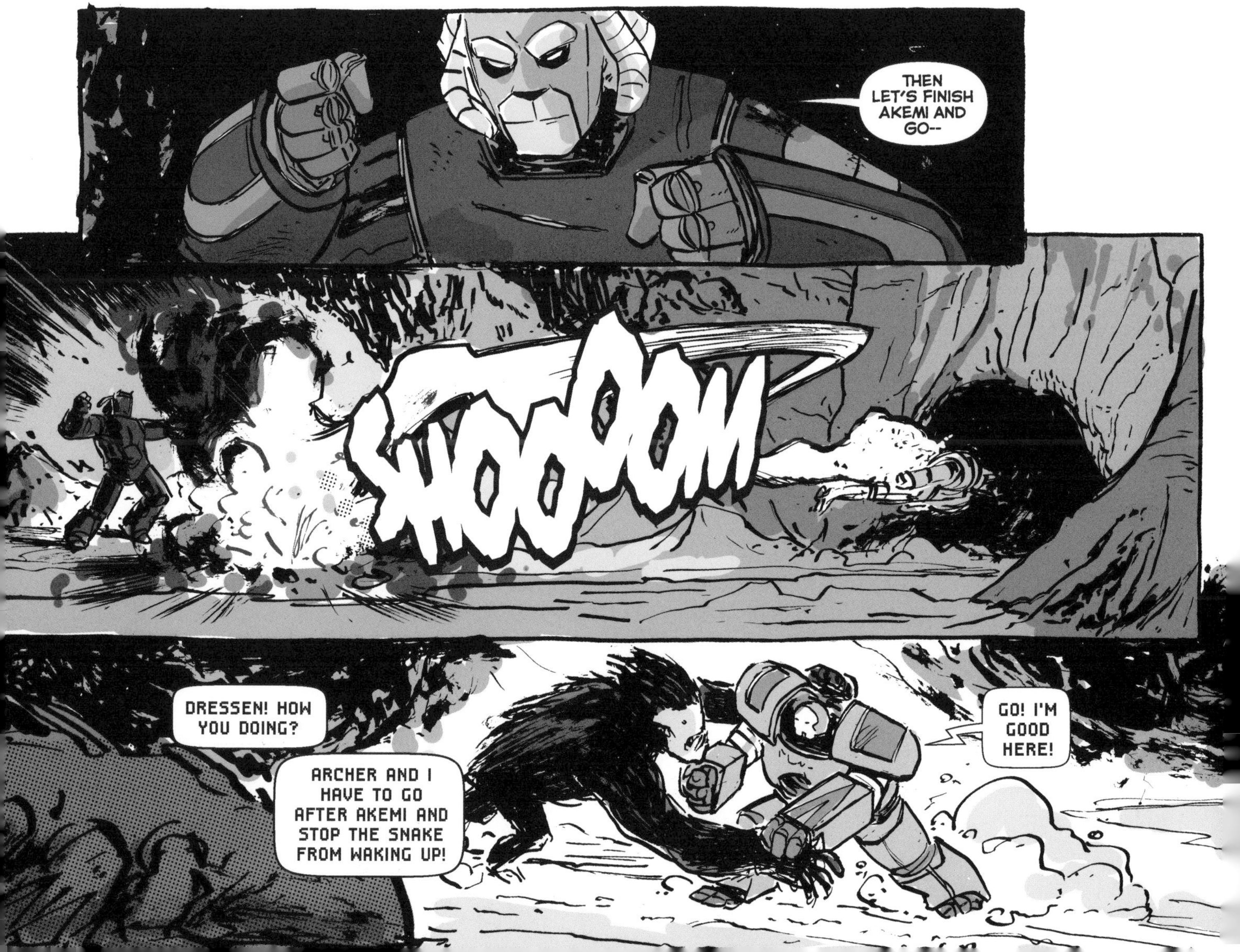
THEN LET'S FINISH AKEMI AND GO--
SHOOOOM
DRESSEN! HOW YOU DOING?
ARCHER AND I HAVE TO GO AFTER AKEMI AND STOP THE SNAKE FROM WAKING UP!
GO! I'M GOOD HERE!

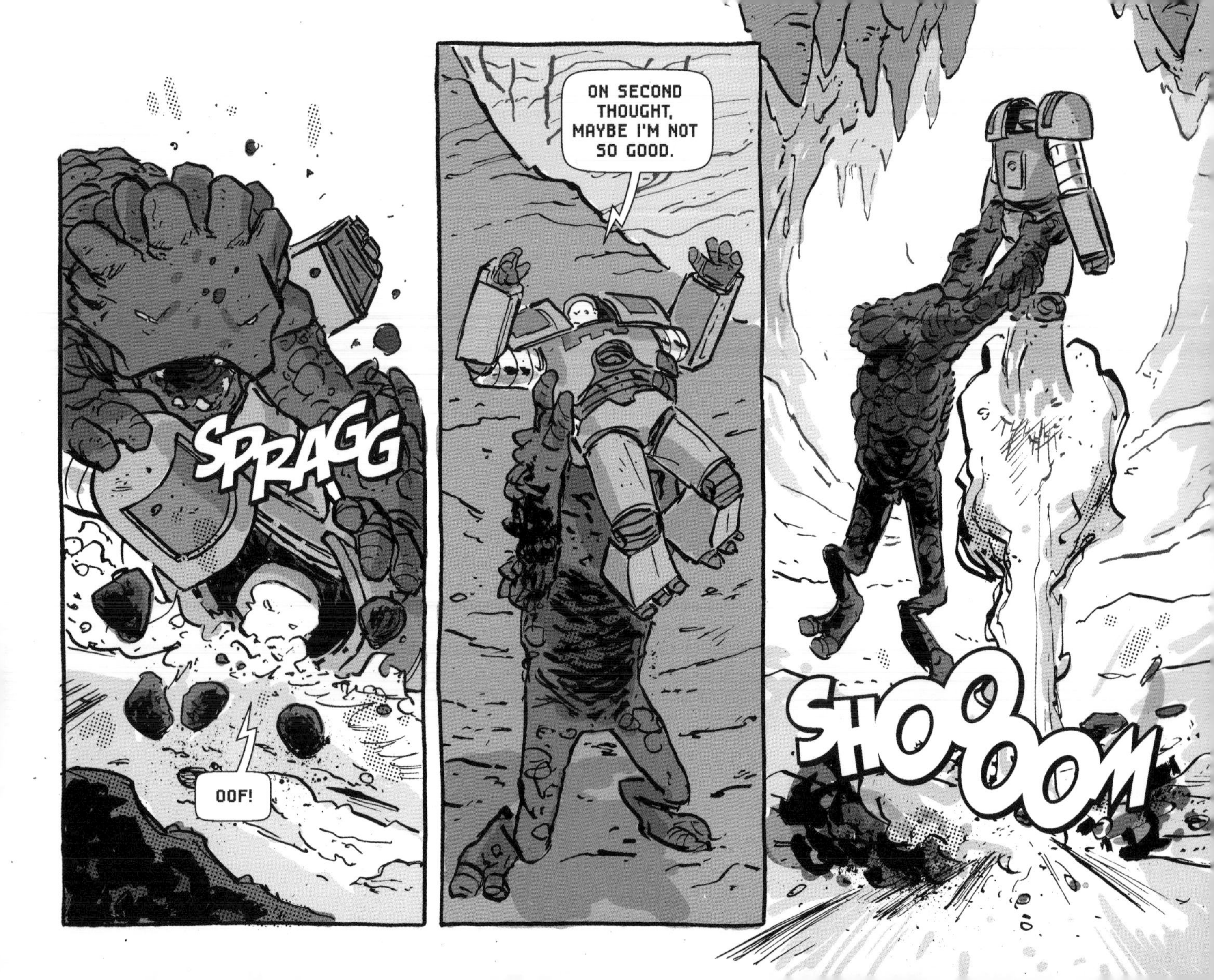
SPRAGG
OOF!
ON SECOND THOUGHT, MAYBE I'M NOT SO GOOD.
SHOOOOM

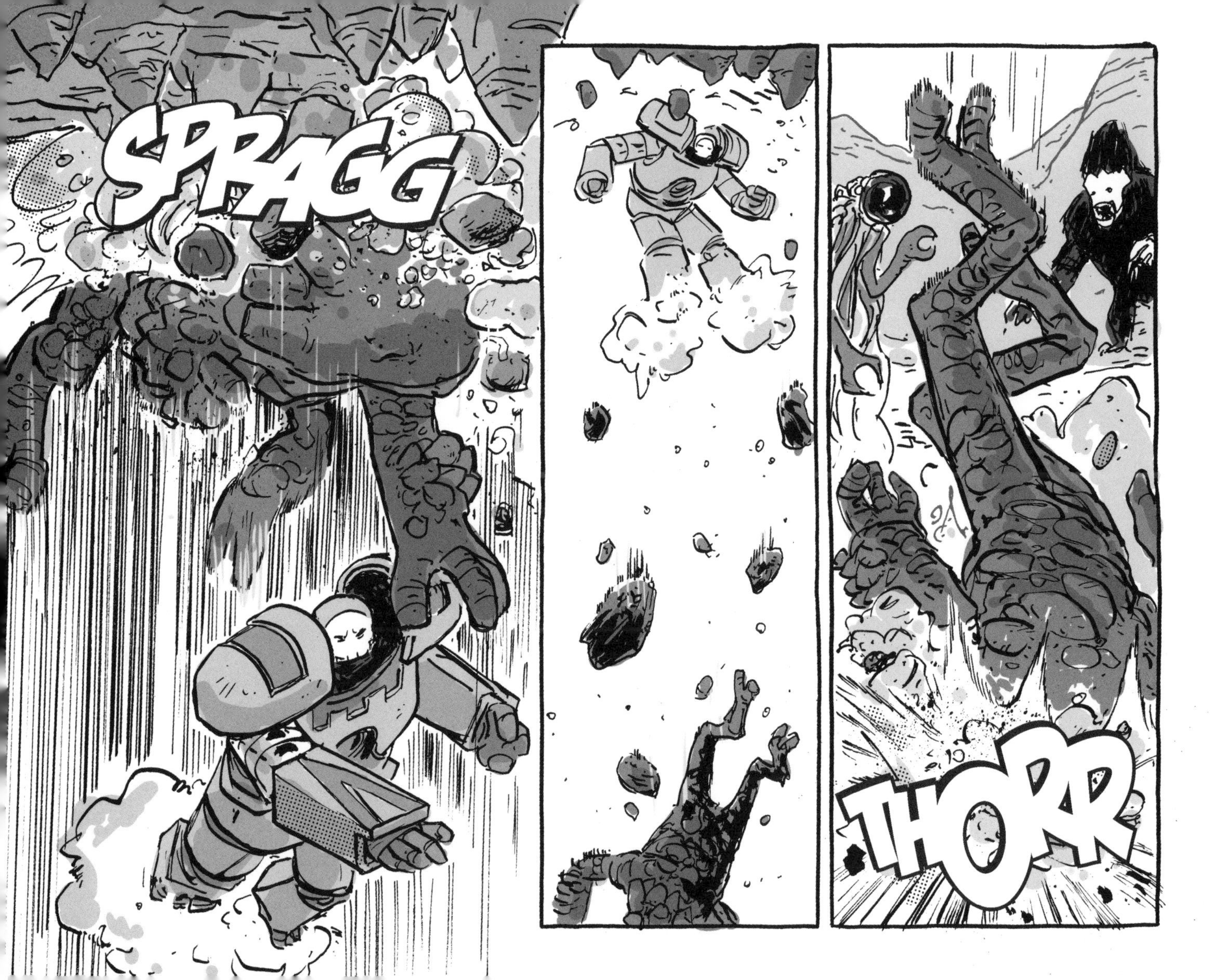
SPRAGG
THORR

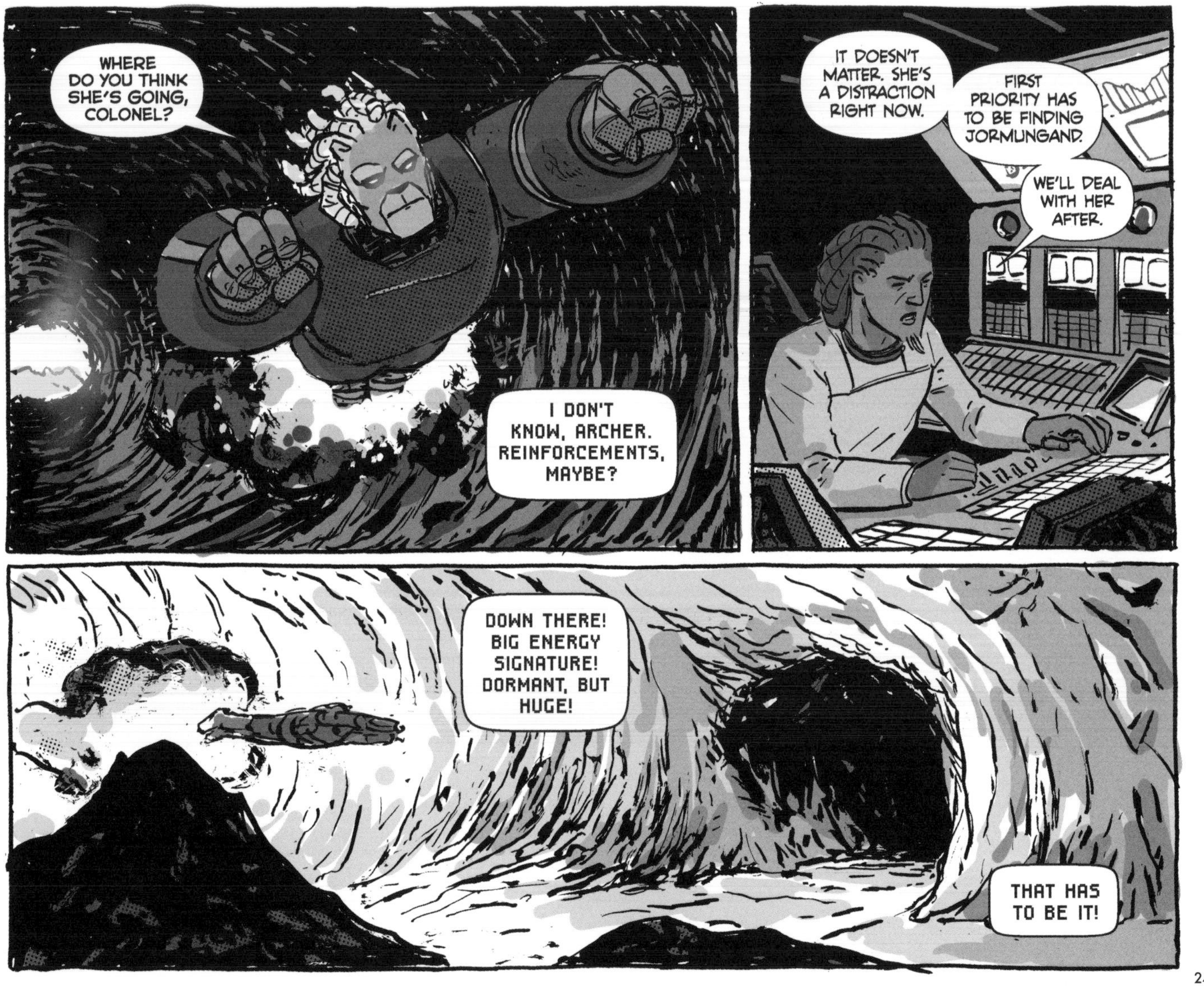
WHERE DO YOU THINK SHE'S GOING, COLONEL?
I DON'T KNOW, ARCHER. REINFORCEMENTS, MAYBE?
IT DOESN'T MATTER. SHE'S A DISTRACTION RIGHT NOW.
FIRST PRIORITY HAS TO BE FINDING JORMUNGAND.
WE'LL DEAL WITH HER AFTER.
DOWN THERE! BIG ENERGY SIGNATURE! DORMANT, BUT HUGE!
THAT HAS TO BE IT!

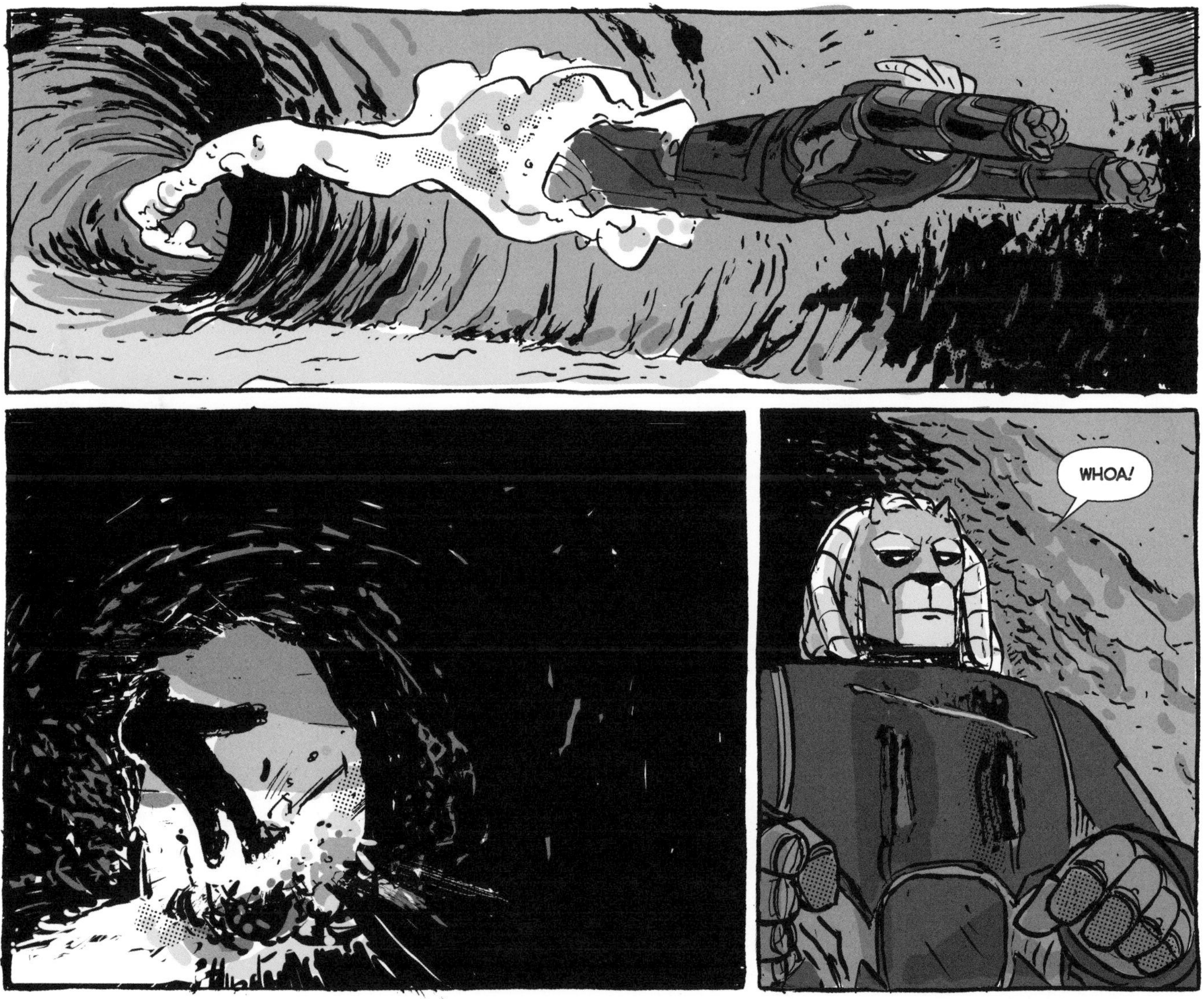
WHOA!

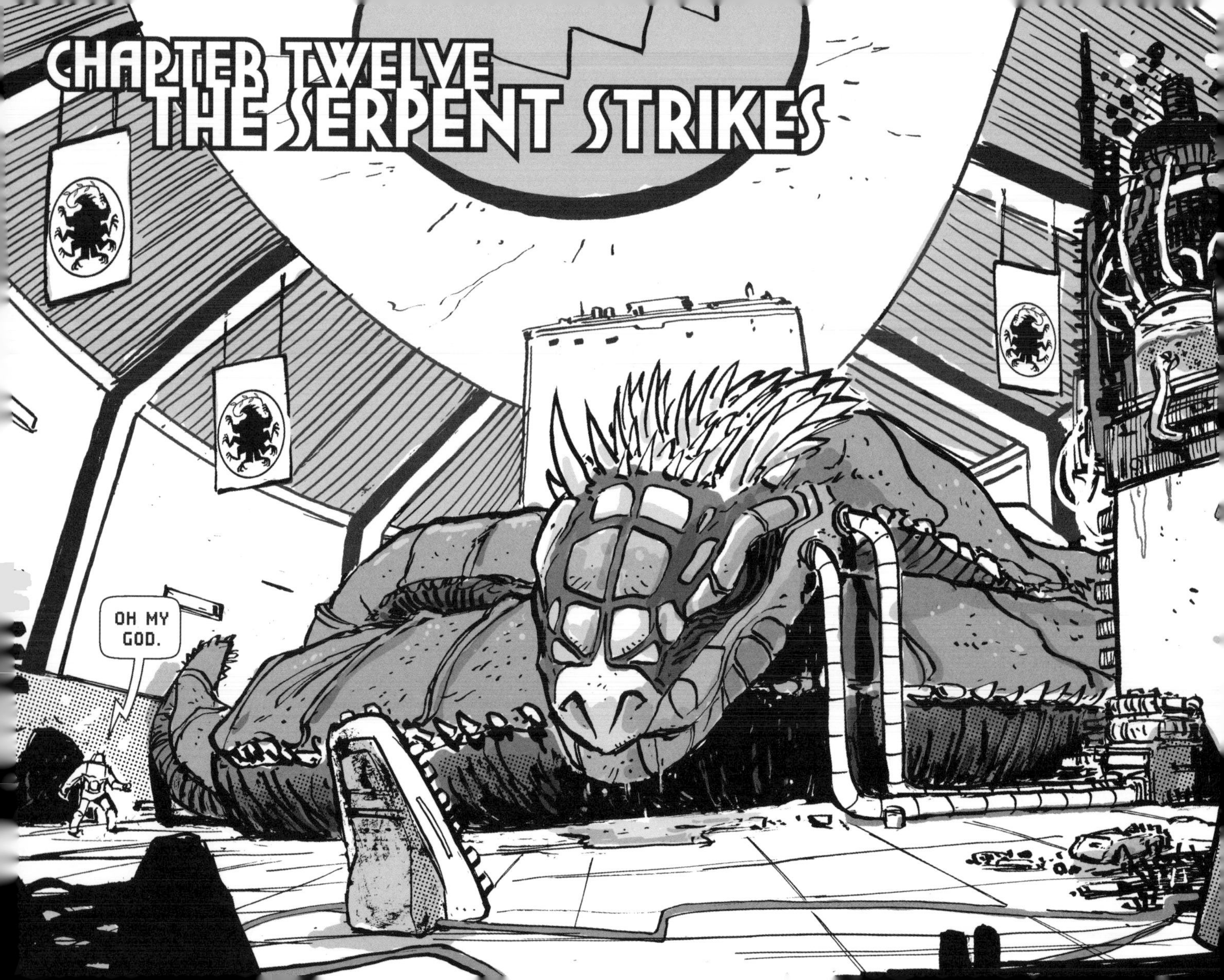
CHAPTER TWELVE
THE SERPENT STRIKES
OH MY GOD.

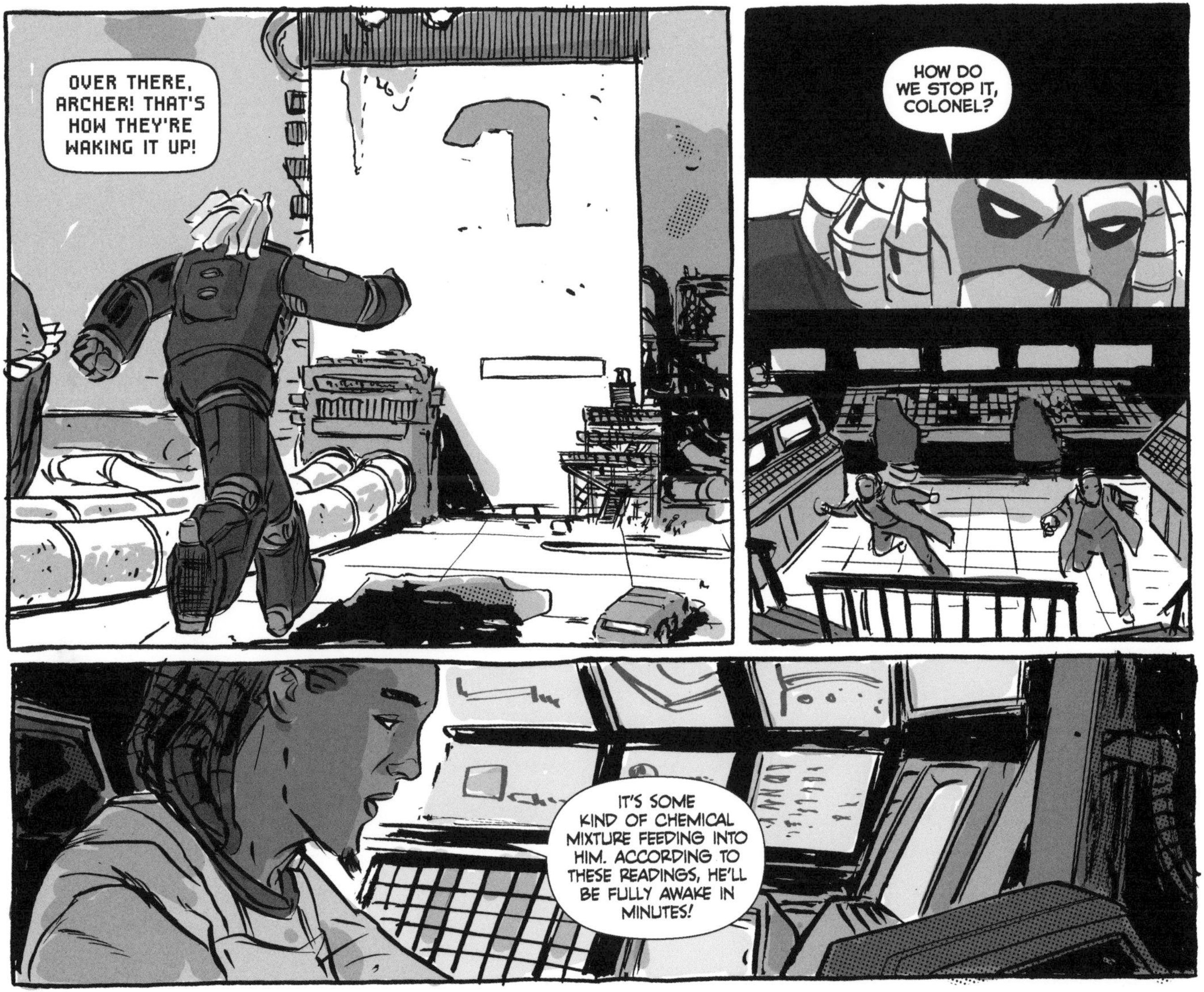
OVER THERE, ARCHER! THAT'S HOW THEY'RE WAKING IT UP!
HOW DO WE STOP IT, COLONEL?
IT'S SOME KIND OF CHEMICAL MIXTURE FEEDING INTO HIM. ACCORDING TO THESE READINGS, HE'LL BE FULLY AWAKE IN MINUTES!

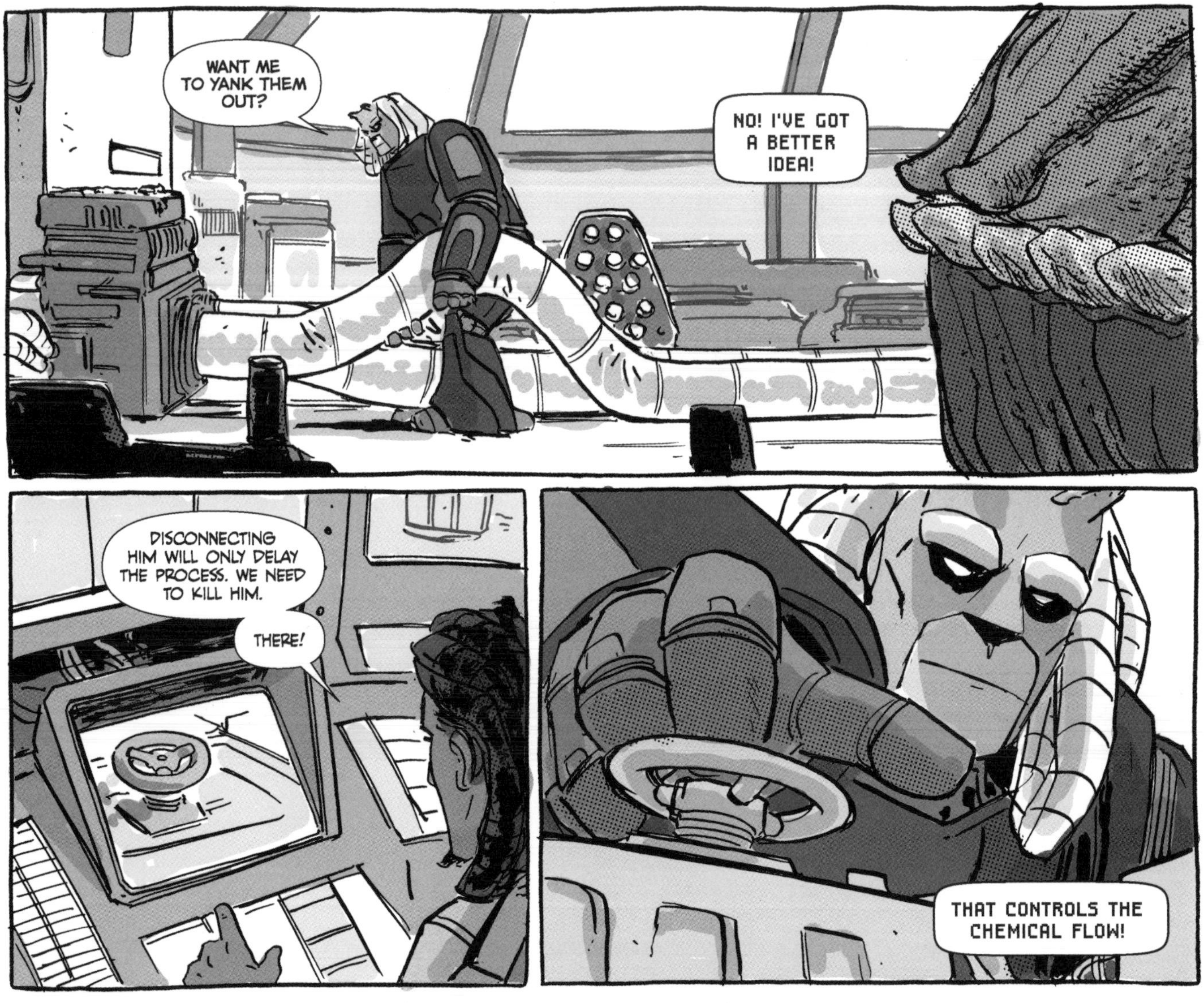
WANT ME TO YANK THEM OUT?
NO! I'VE GOT A BETTER IDEA!
DISCONNECTING HIM WILL ONLY DELAY THE PROCESS. WE NEED TO KILL HIM.
THERE!
THAT CONTROLS THE CHEMICAL FLOW!

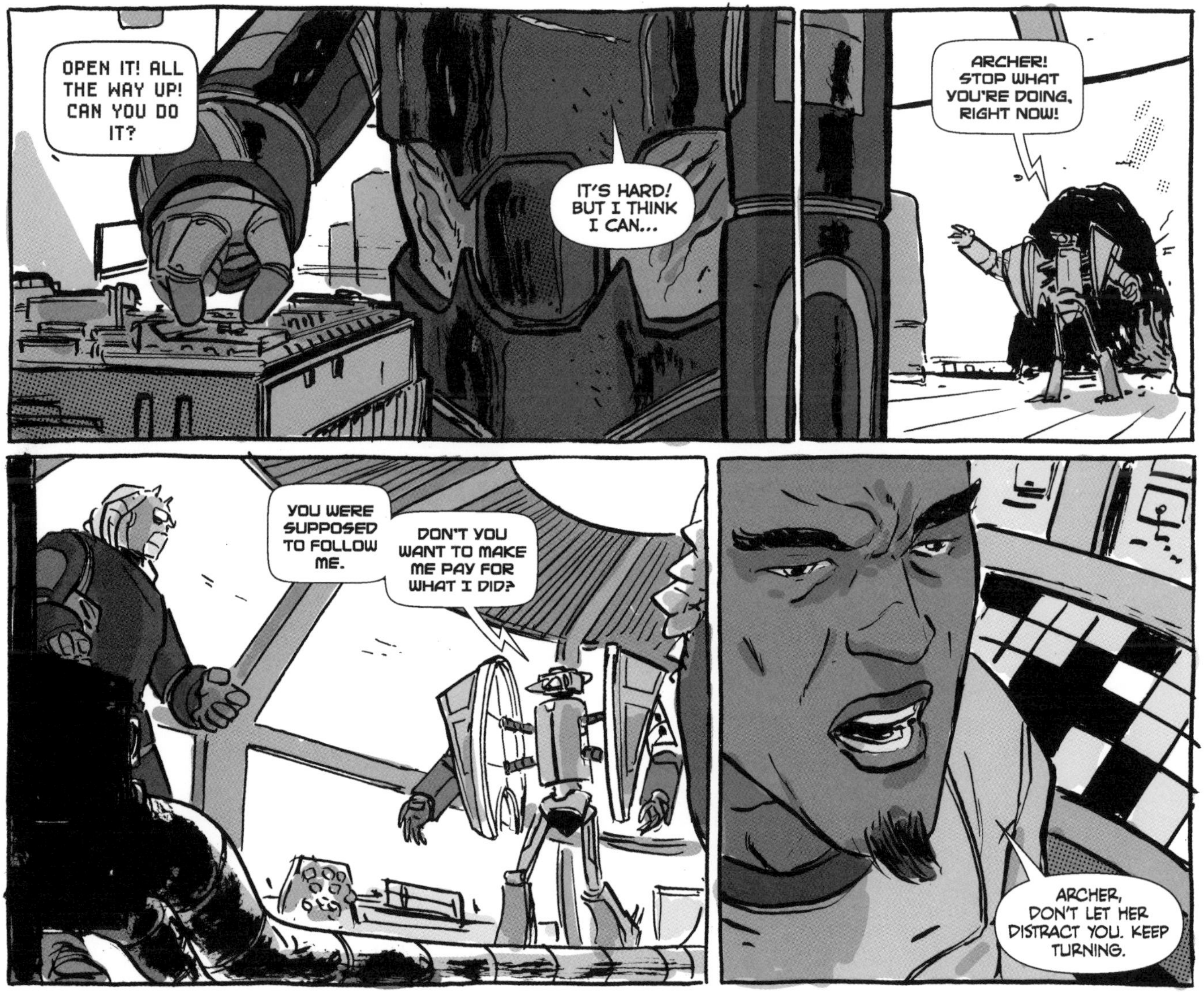
OPEN IT! ALL THE WAY UP! CAN YOU DO IT?
IT'S HARD! BUT I THINK I CAN...
ARCHER! STOP WHAT YOU'RE DOING, RIGHT NOW!
YOU WERE SUPPOSED TO FOLLOW ME.
DON'T YOU WANT TO MAKE ME PAY FOR WHAT I DID?
ARCHER, DON'T LET HER DISTRACT YOU. KEEP TURNING.

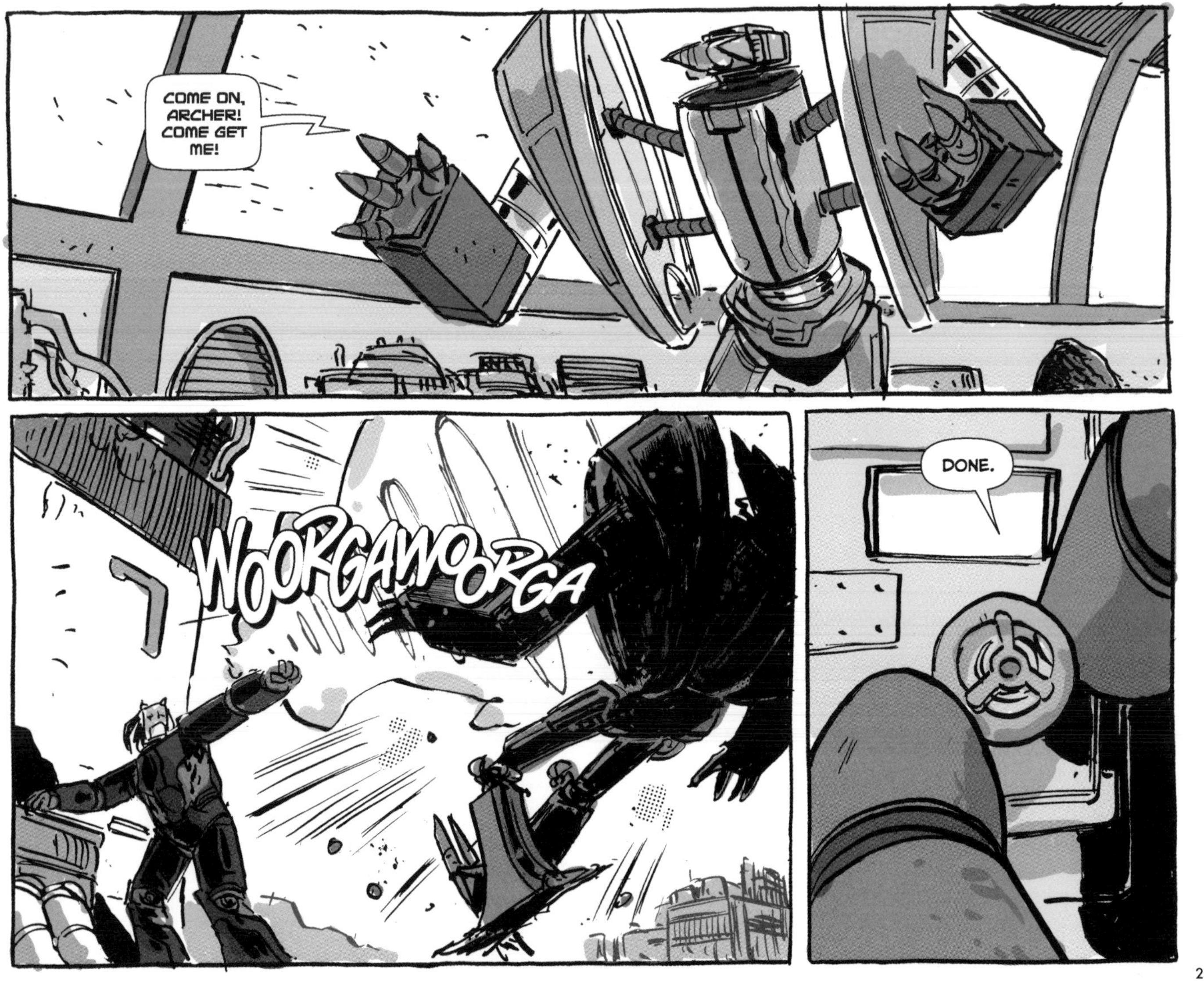
COME ON, ARCHER! COME GET ME!
WOORGAWOORGA
DONE.

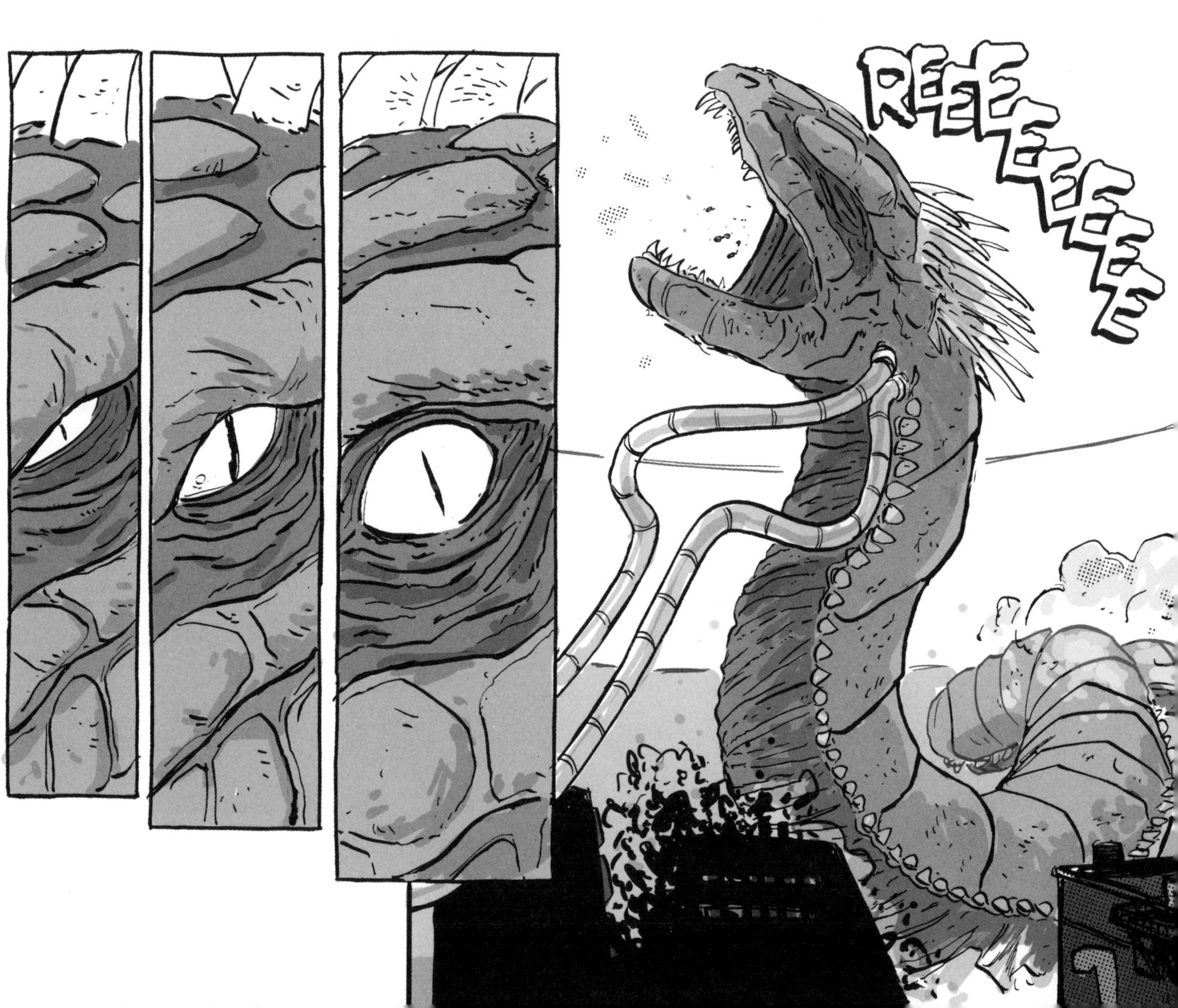
REEEEEEEE

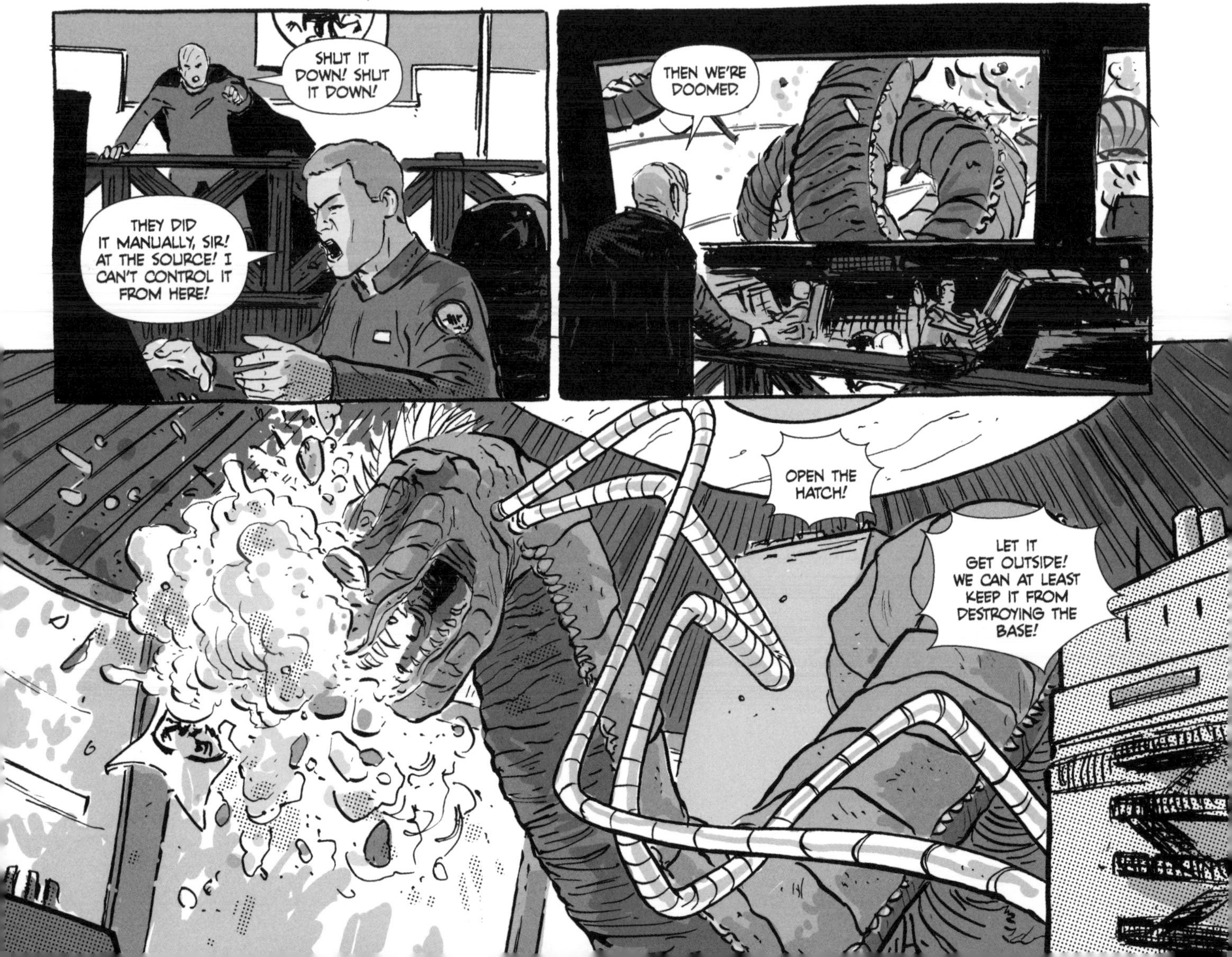
SHUT IT DOWN! SHUT IT DOWN!
THEY DID IT MANUALLY, SIR! AT THE SOURCE! I CAN'T CONTROL IT FROM HERE!
THEN WE'RE DOOMED.
OPEN THE HATCH!
LET IT GET OUTSIDE! WE CAN AT LEAST KEEP IT FROM DESTROYING THE BASE!

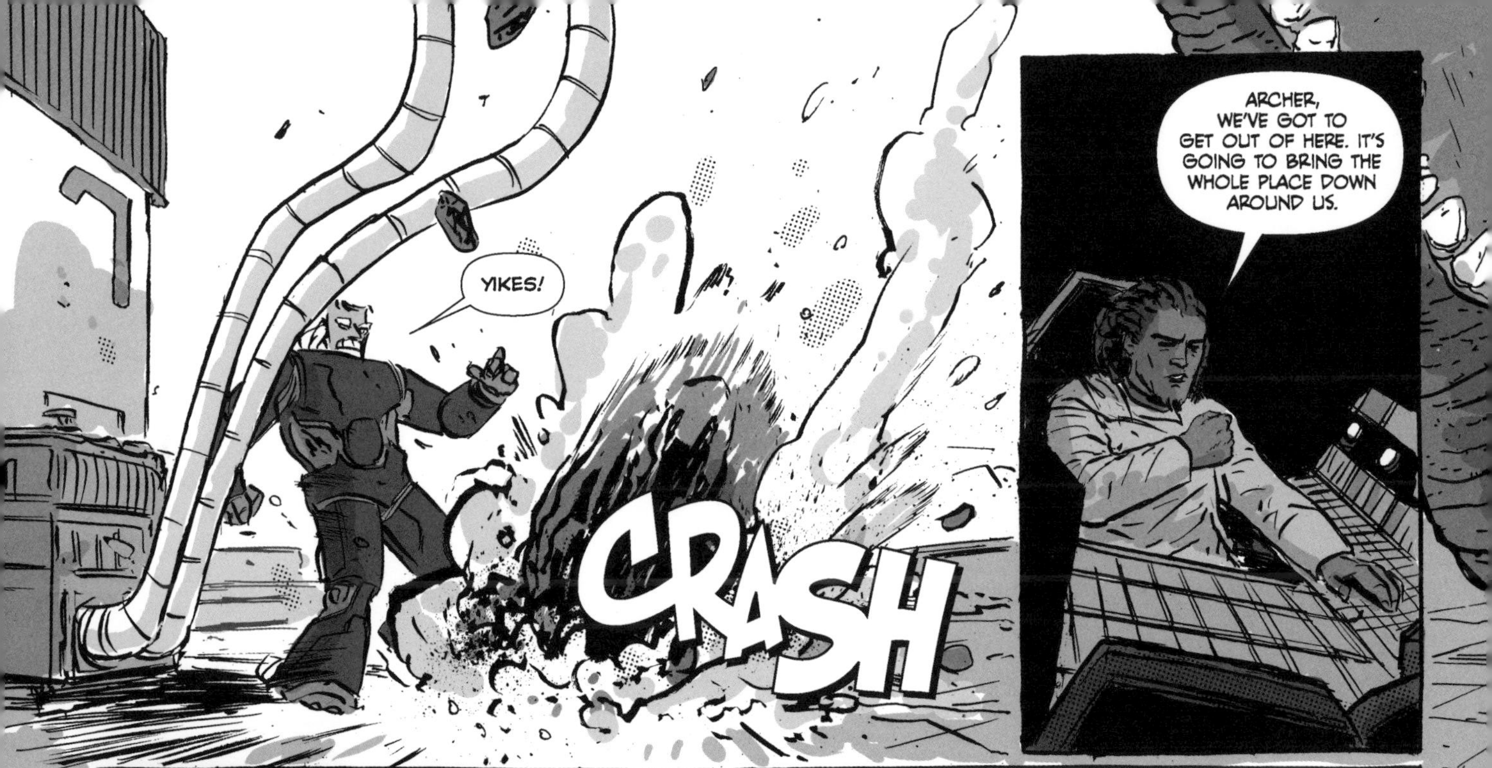
YIKES!
CRASH
ARCHER, WE'VE GOT TO GET OUT OF HERE. IT'S GOING TO BRING THE WHOLE PLACE DOWN AROUND US.

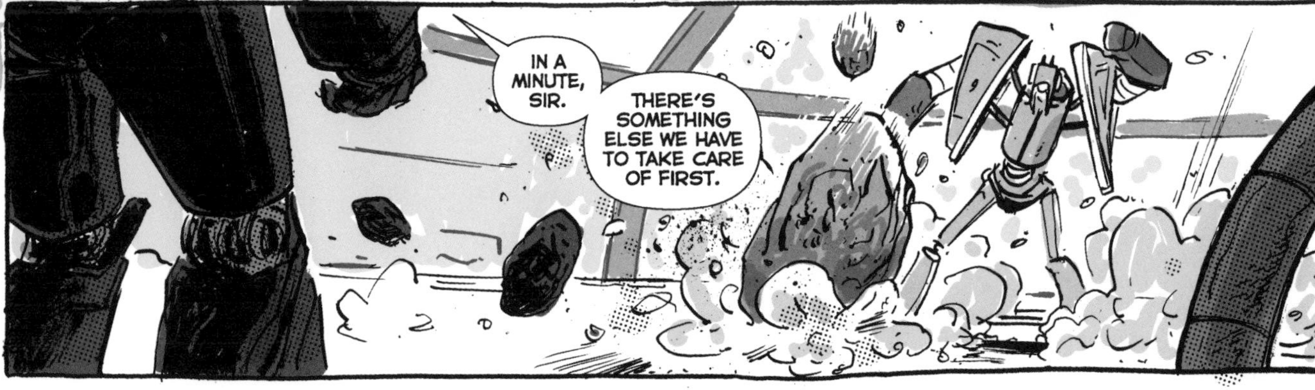
IN A MINUTE, SIR.
THERE'S SOMETHING ELSE WE HAVE TO TAKE CARE OF FIRST.

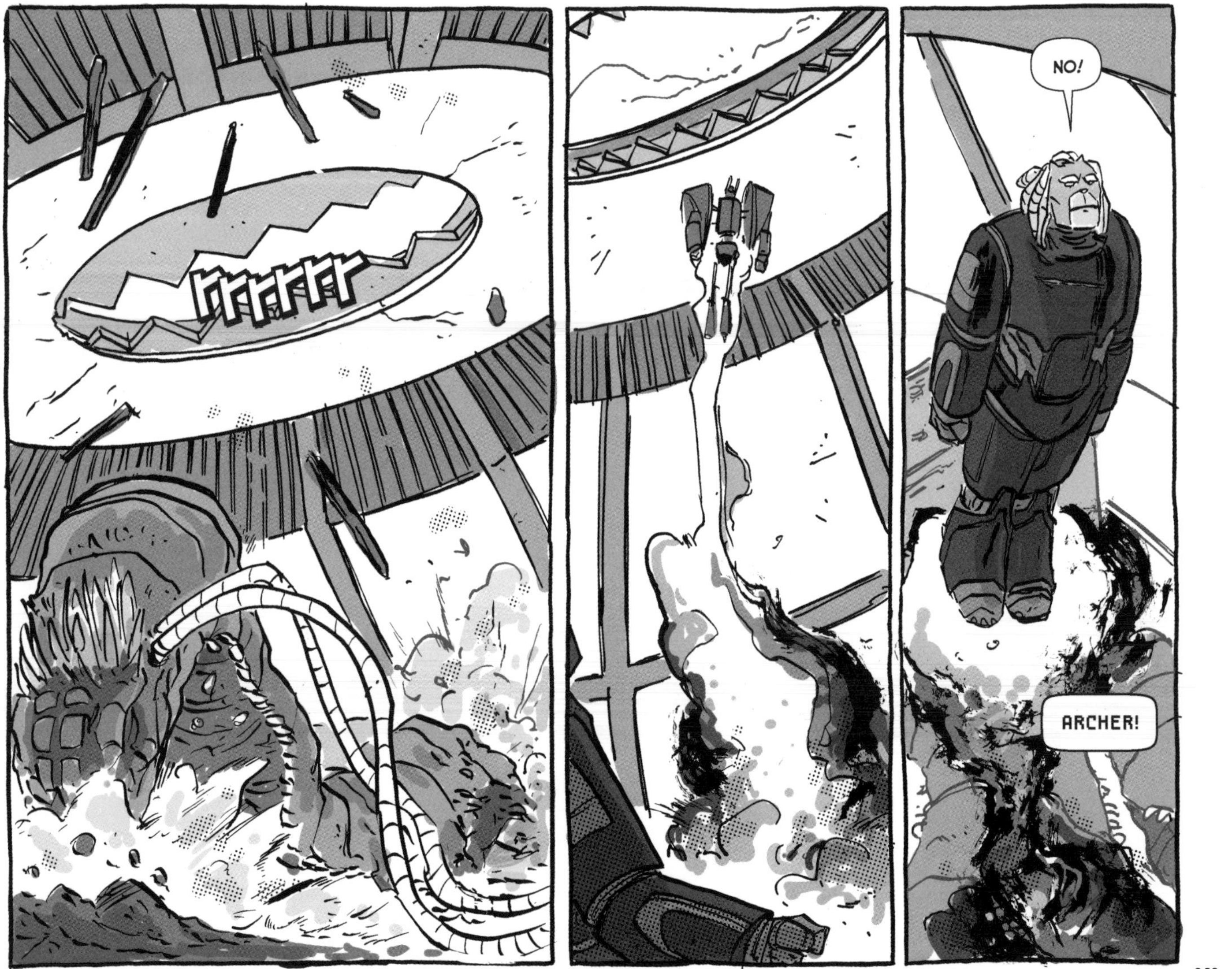
rrrrrr
NO!
ARCHER!

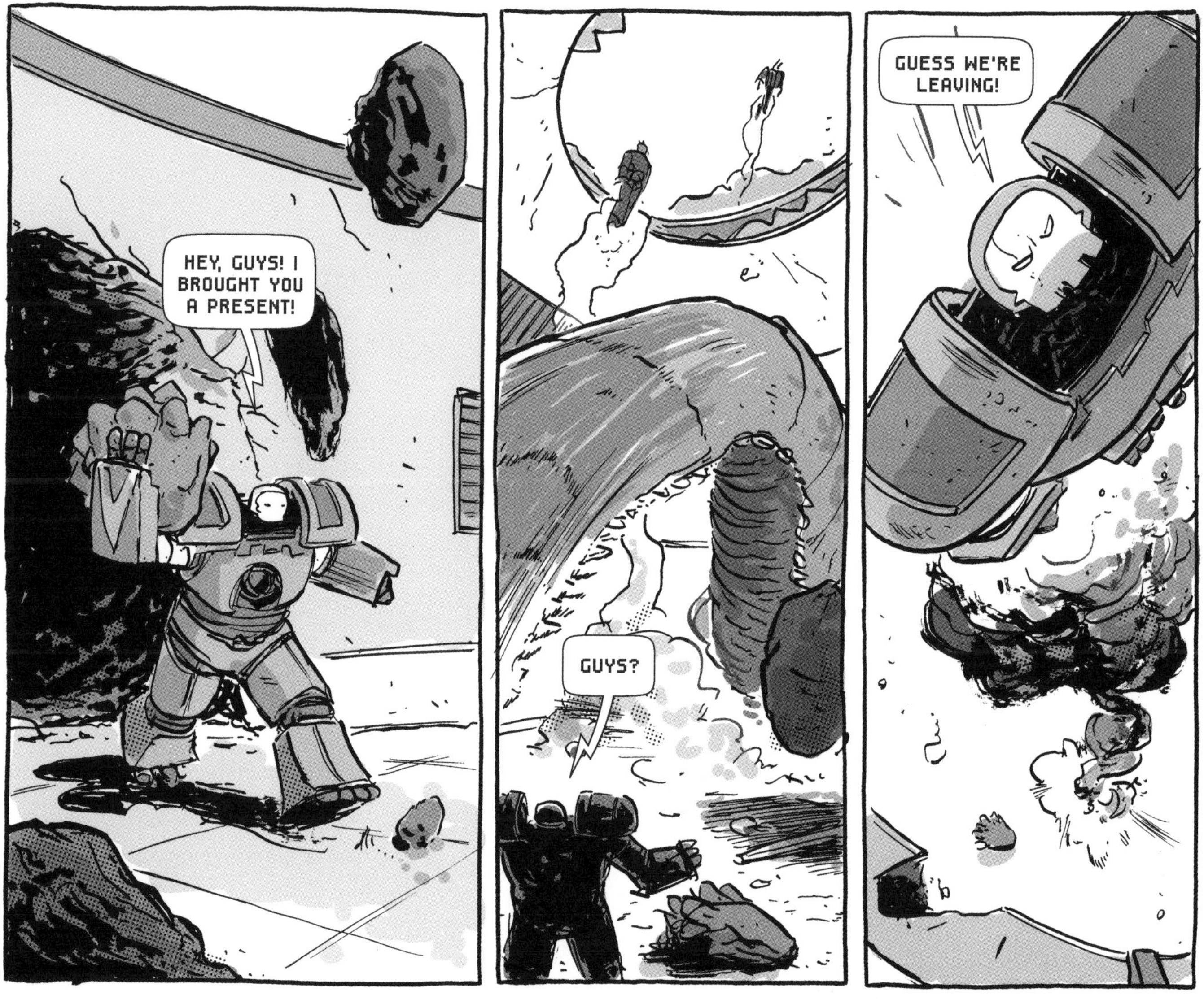
HEY, GUYS! I BROUGHT YOU A PRESENT!
GUYS?
GUESS WE'RE LEAVING!

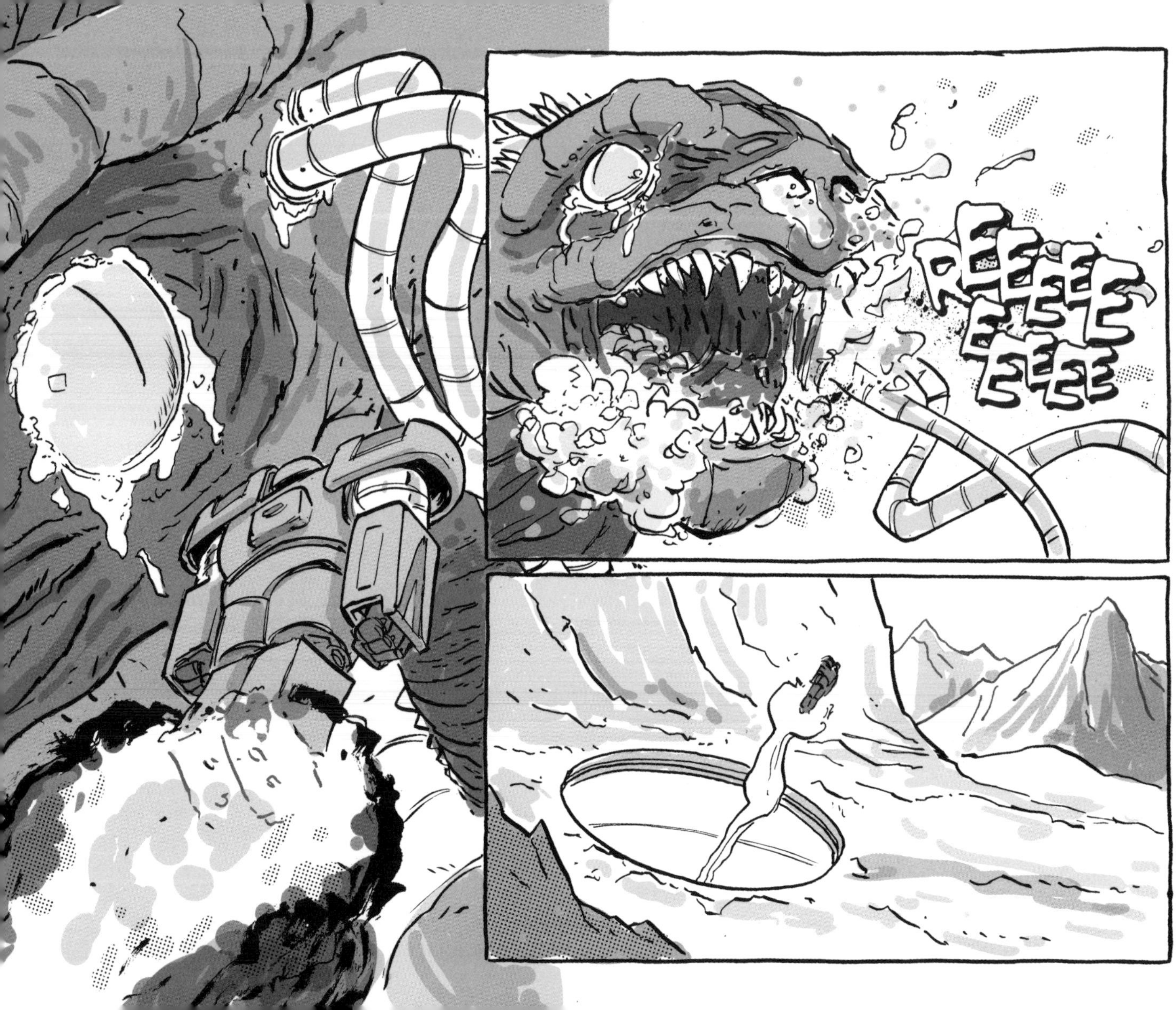
REEEEEEEEEEE

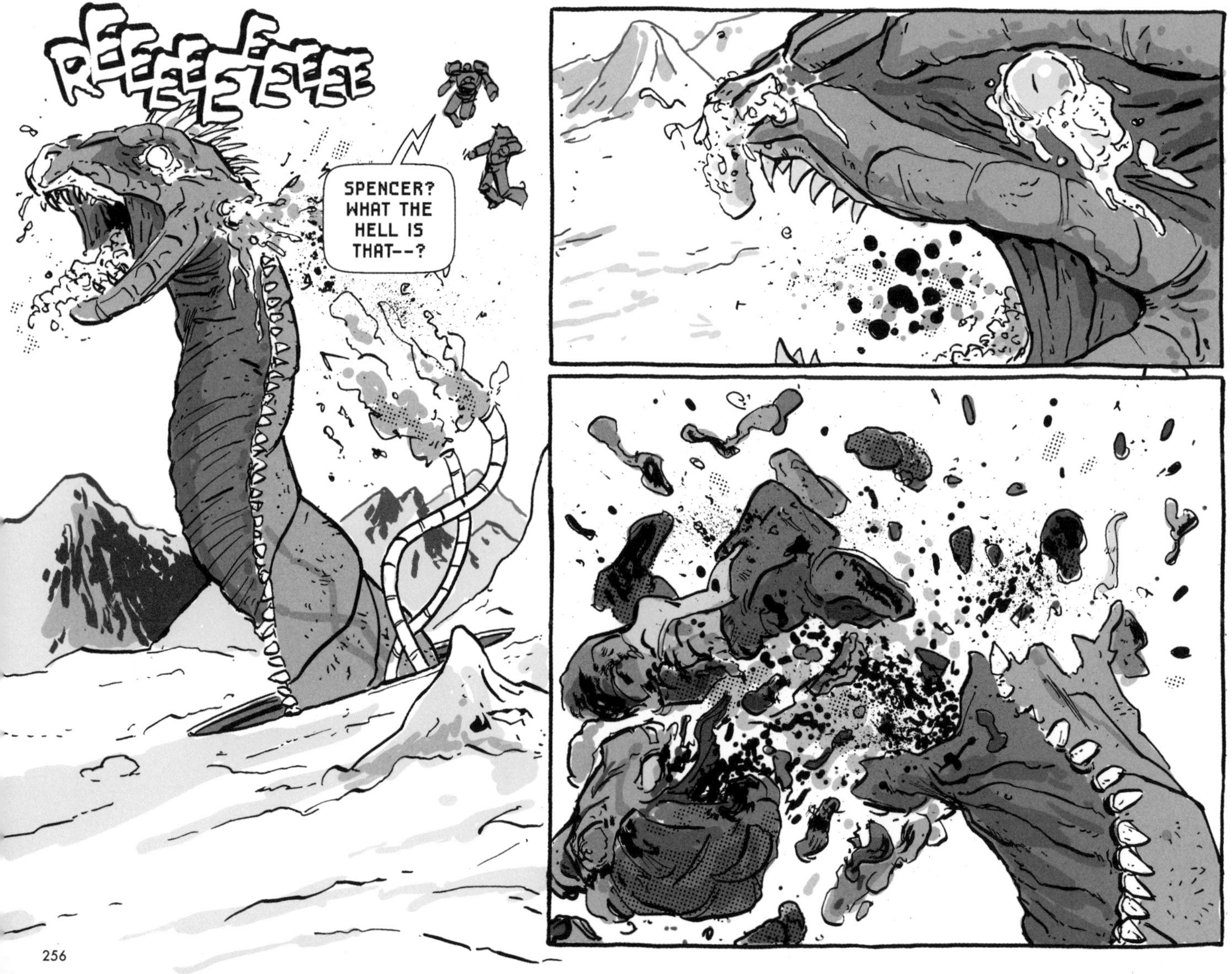
REEEEEEEEEE
SPENCER? WHAT THE HELL IS THAT--?

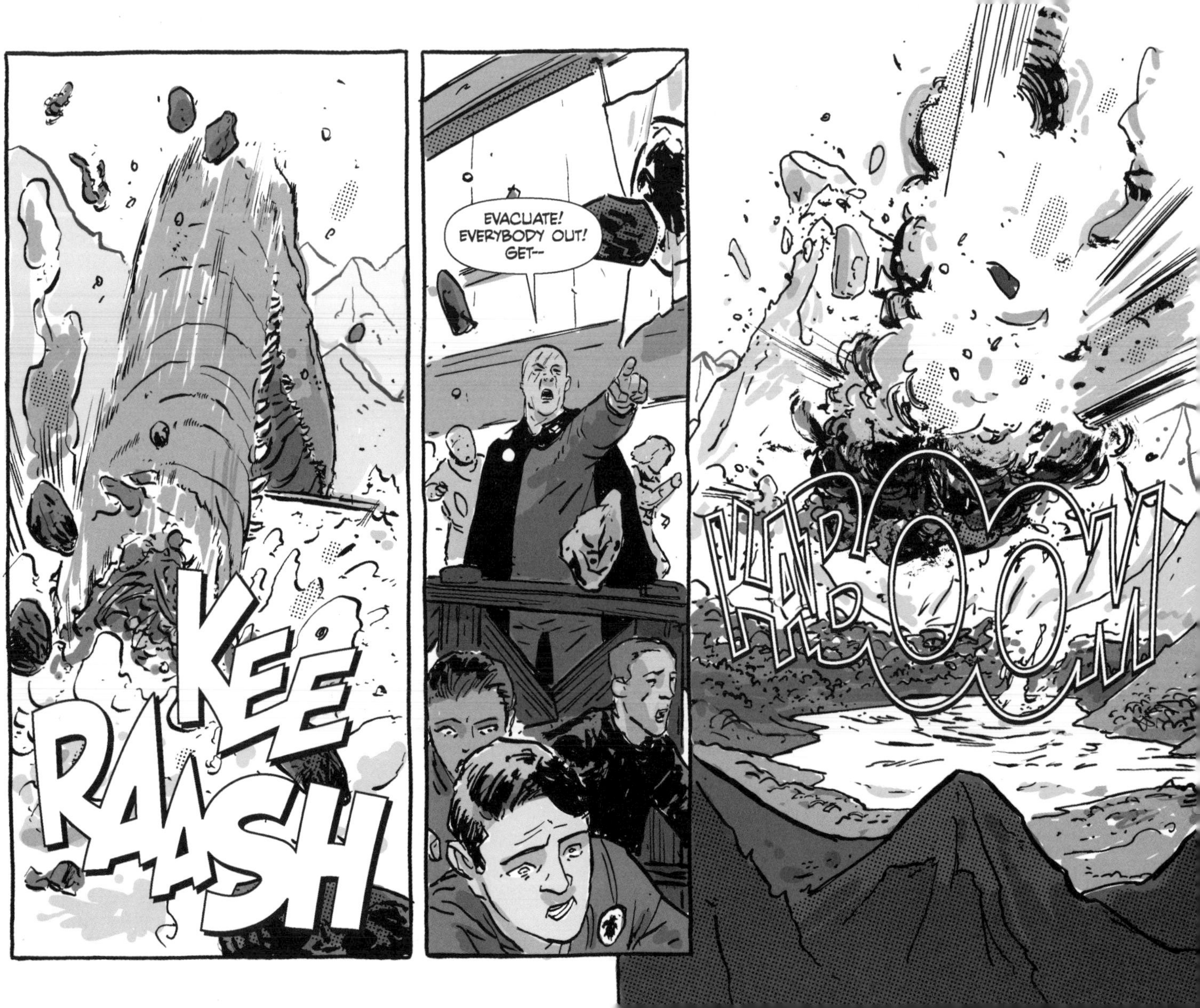
KEE RAASH
EVACUATE! EVERYBODY OUT! GET--
KABOOM

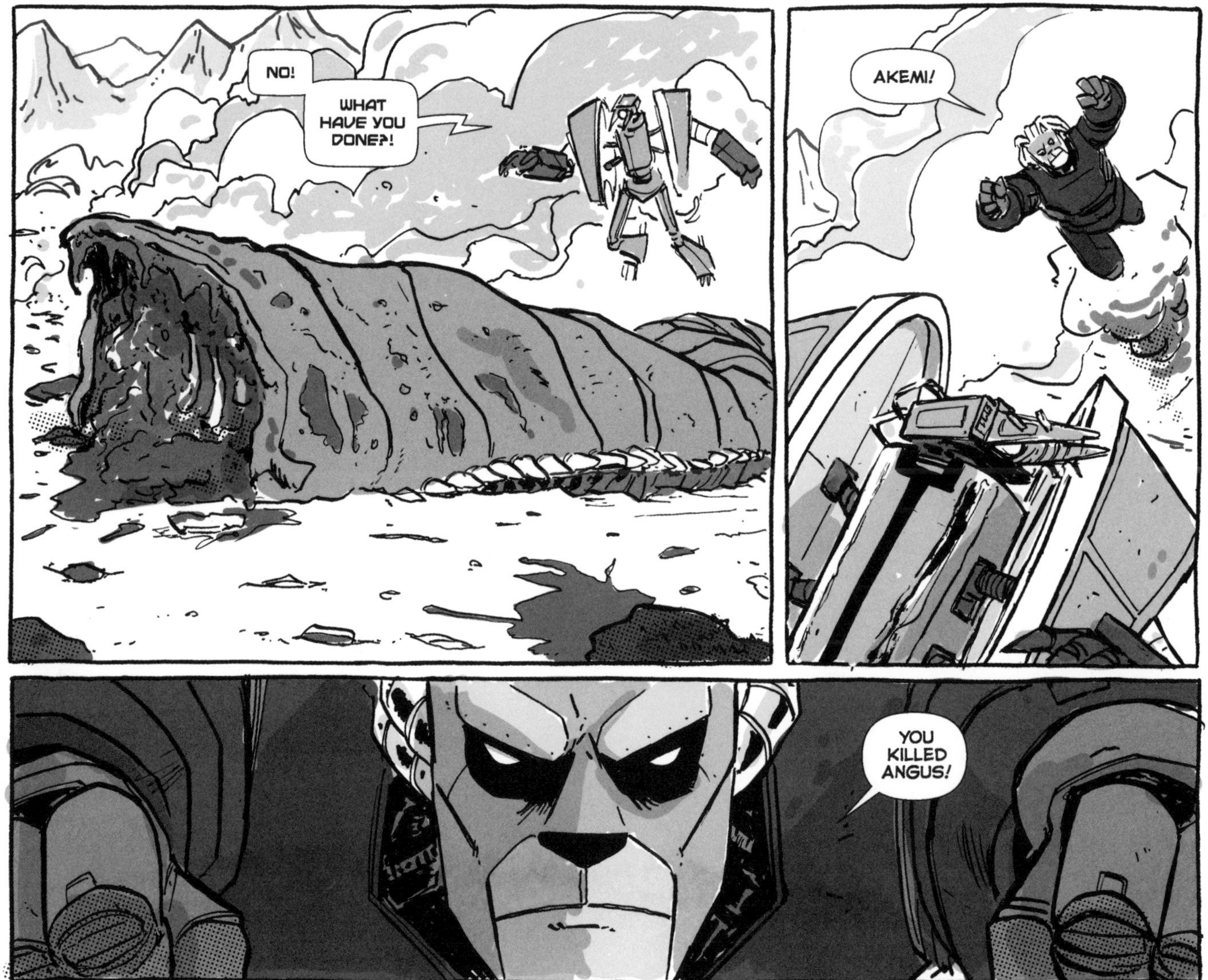
NO!
WHAT HAVE YOU DONE?!
AKEMI!
YOU KILLED ANGUS!

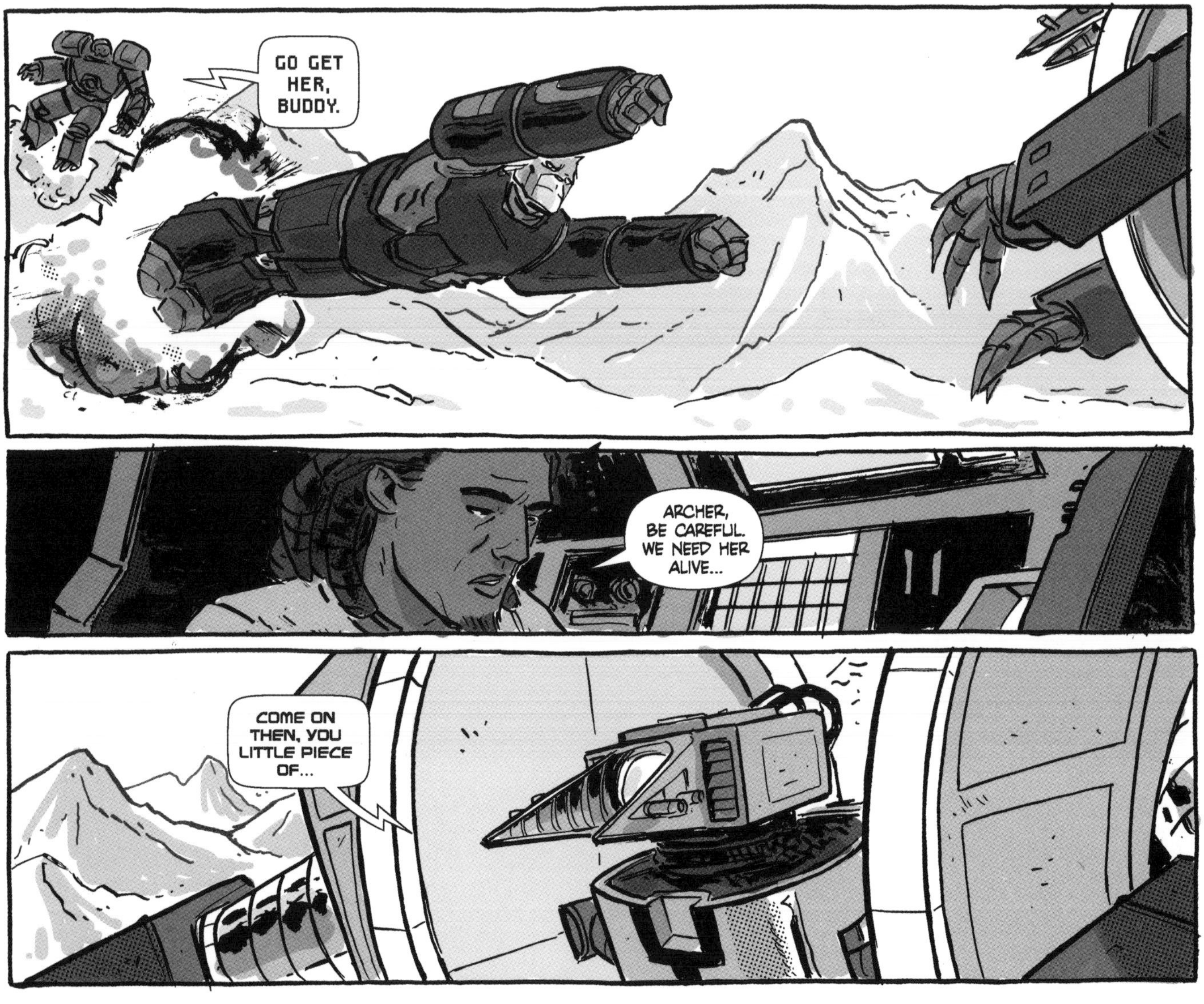
GO GET HER, BUDDY.
ARCHER, BE CAREFUL. WE NEED HER ALIVE...
COME ON THEN, YOU LITTLE PIECE OF...

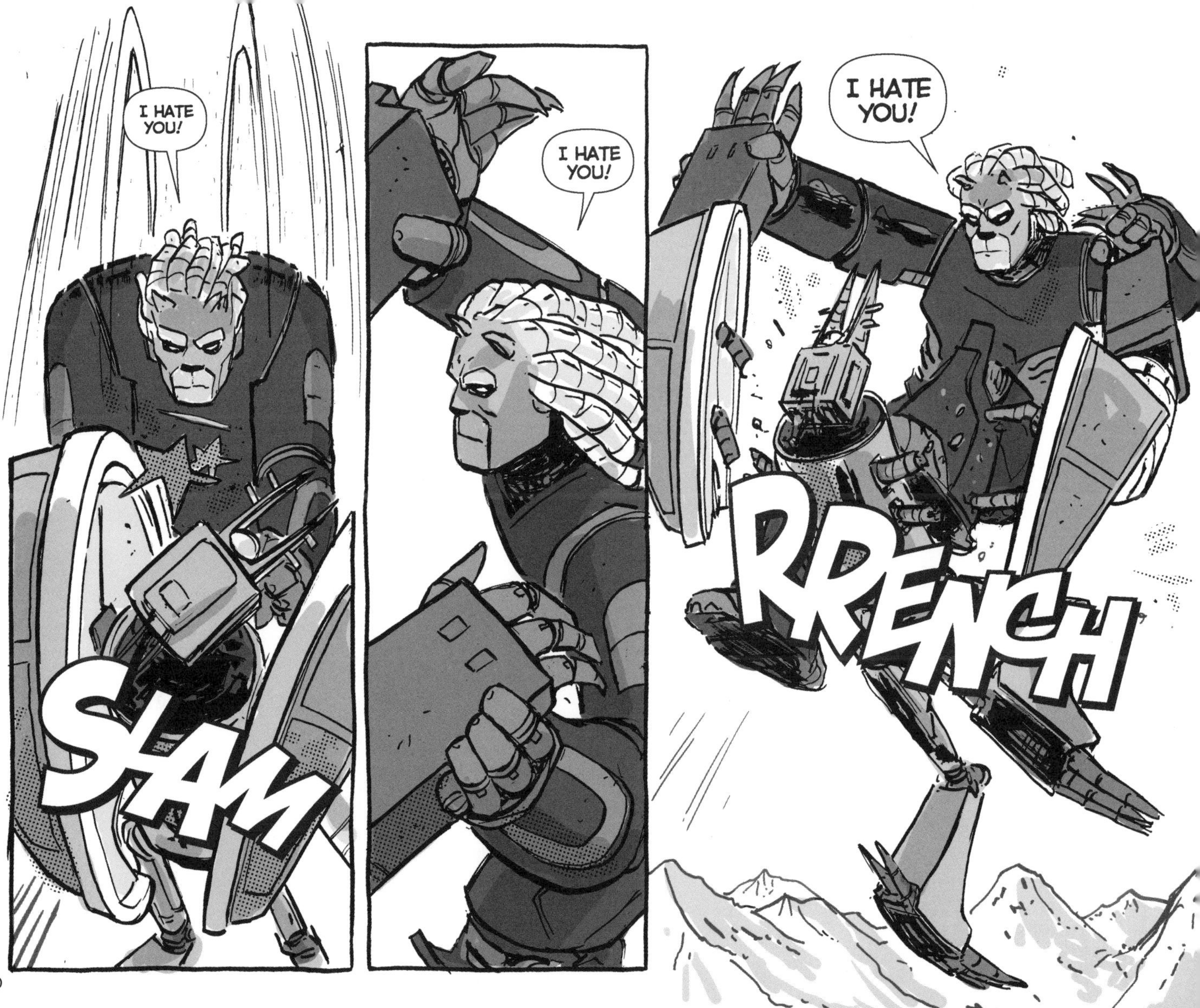
I HATE YOU!
SLAM
I HATE YOU!
I HATE YOU!
RRRENCH

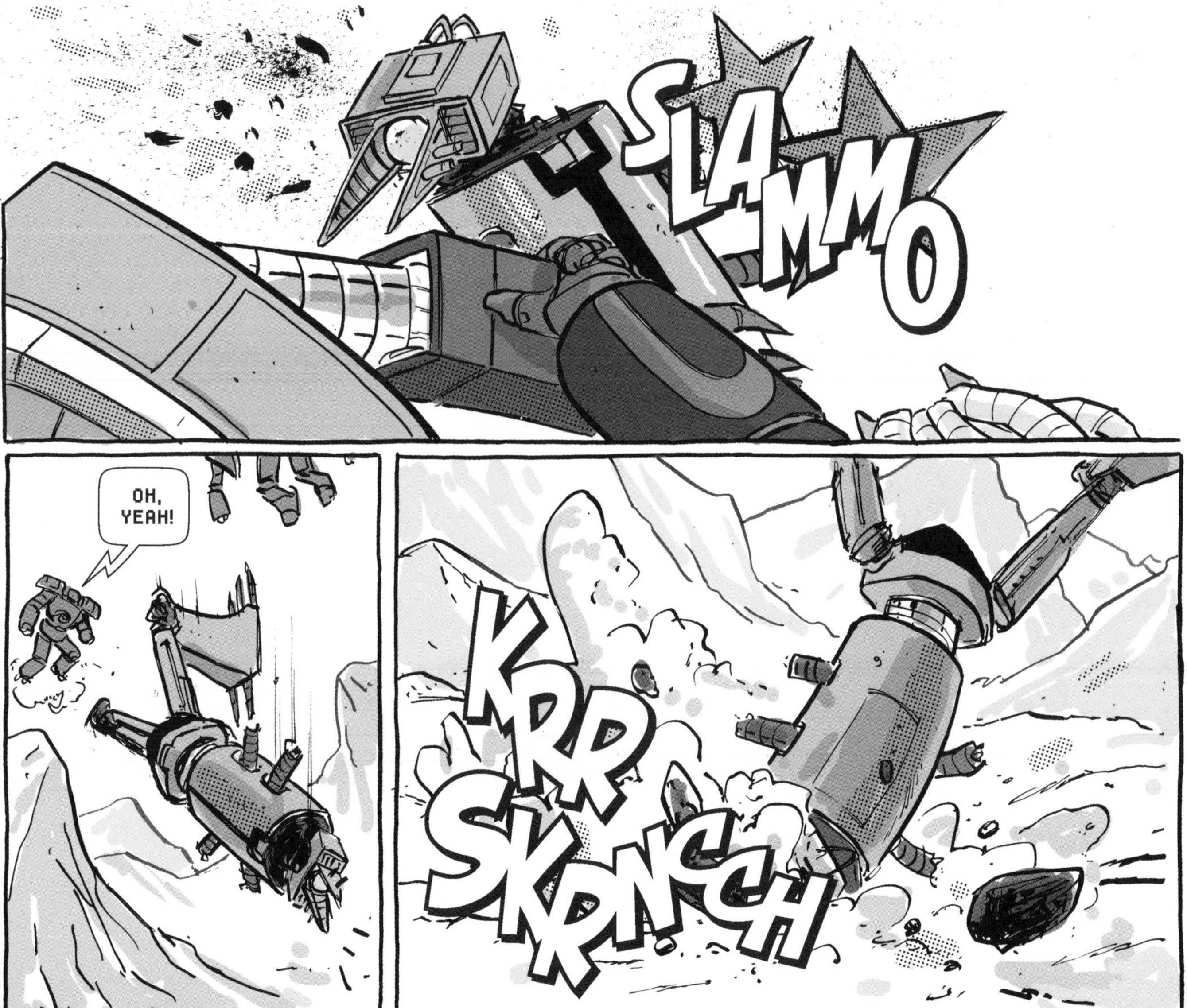
SLAMMO
OH, YEAH!
KRR SKRNCCH

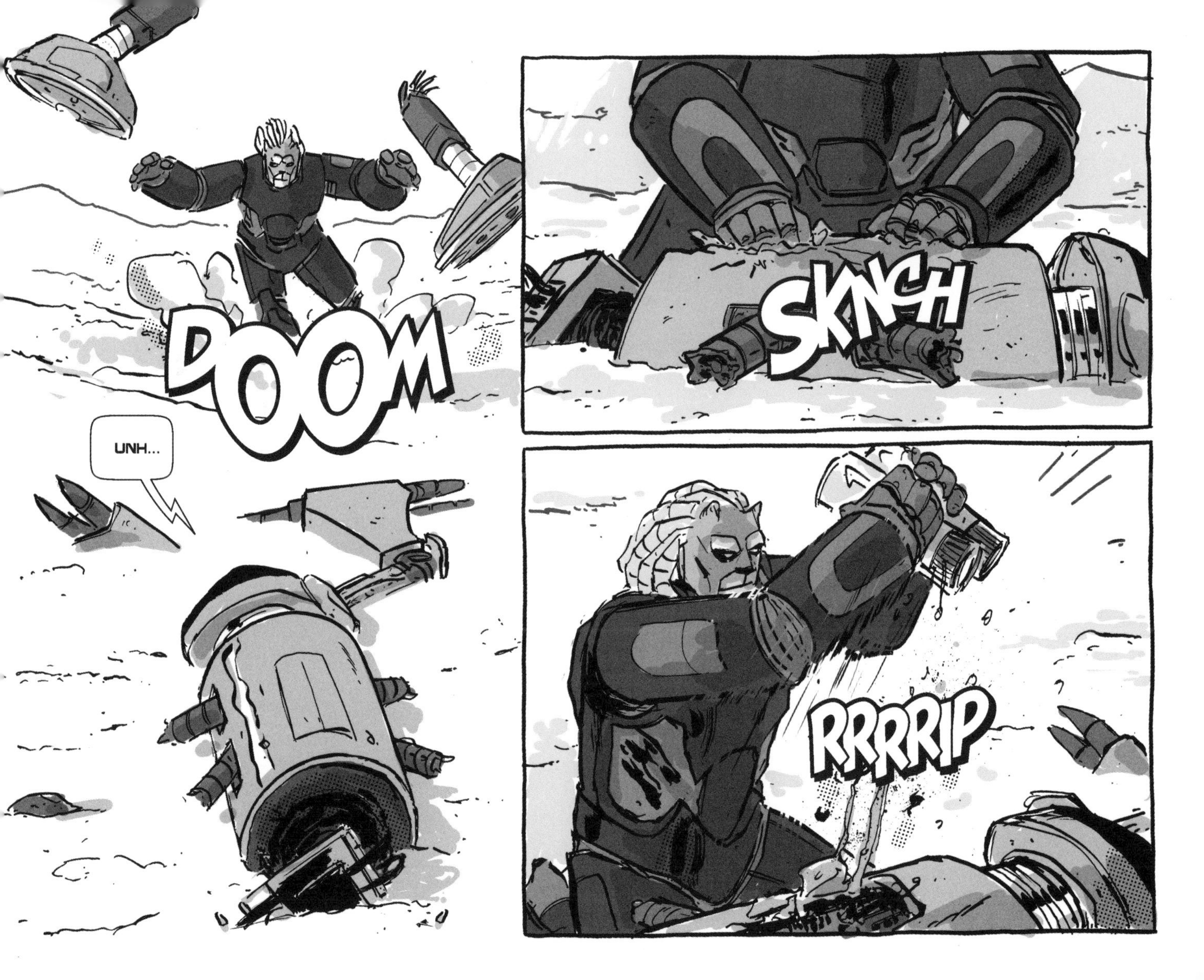
DOOM
UNH...
SKNCH
RRRRIP

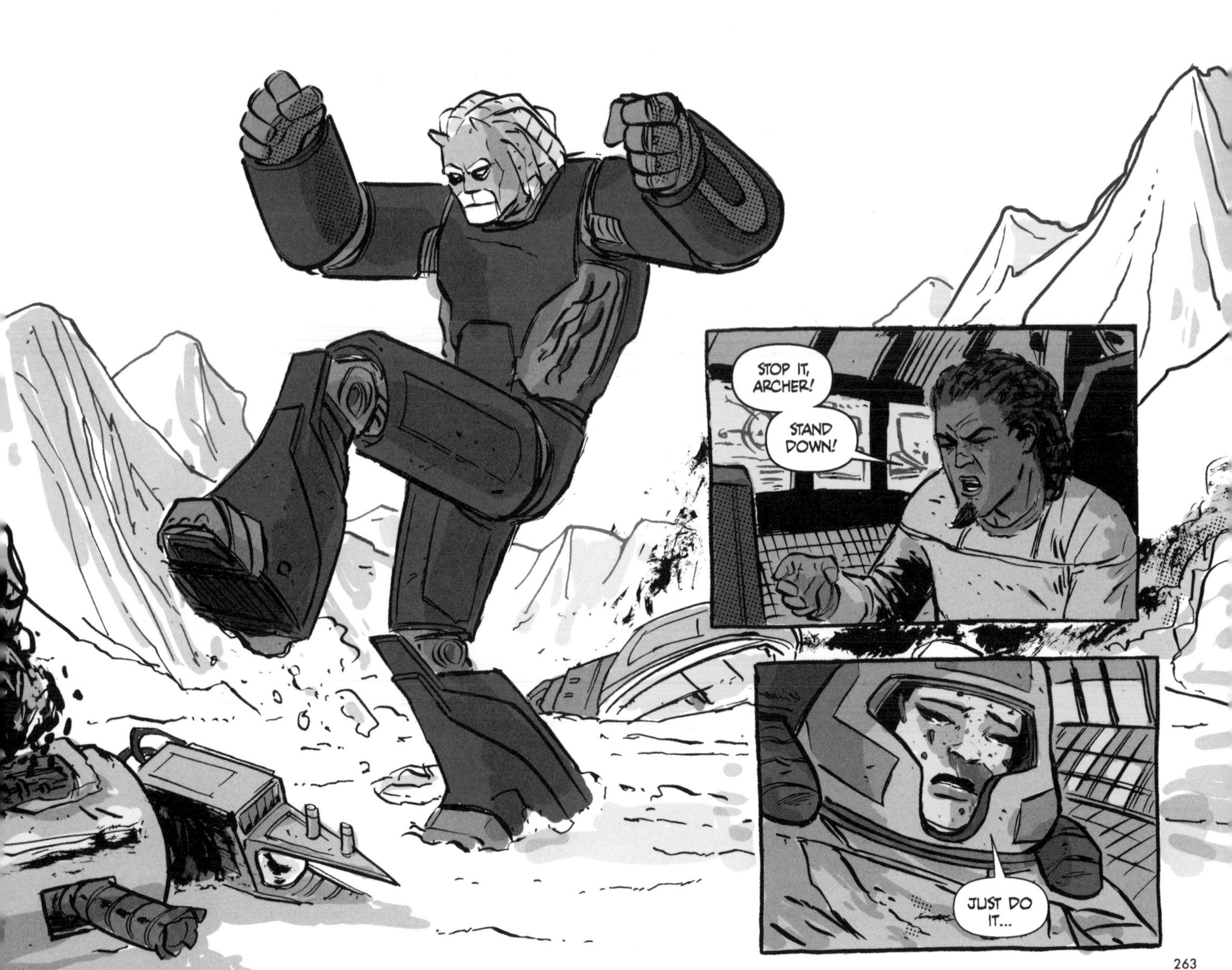
STOP IT, ARCHER!
STAND DOWN!
JUST DO IT...

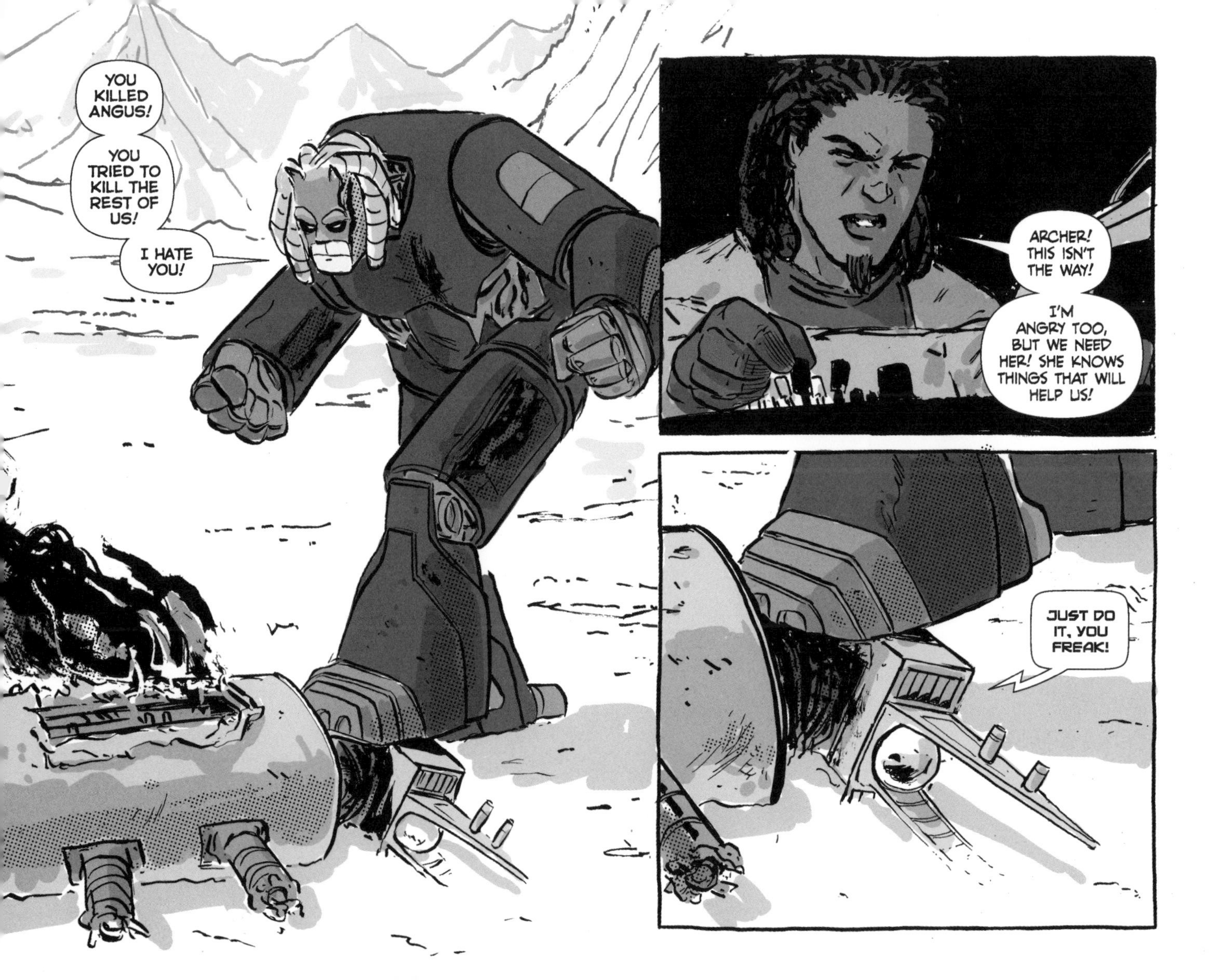
YOU KILLED ANGUS!
YOU TRIED TO KILL THE REST OF US!
I HATE YOU!
ARCHER! THIS ISN'T THE WAY!
I'M ANGRY TOO, BUT WE NEED HER! SHE KNOWS THINGS THAT WILL HELP US!
JUST DO IT, YOU FREAK!

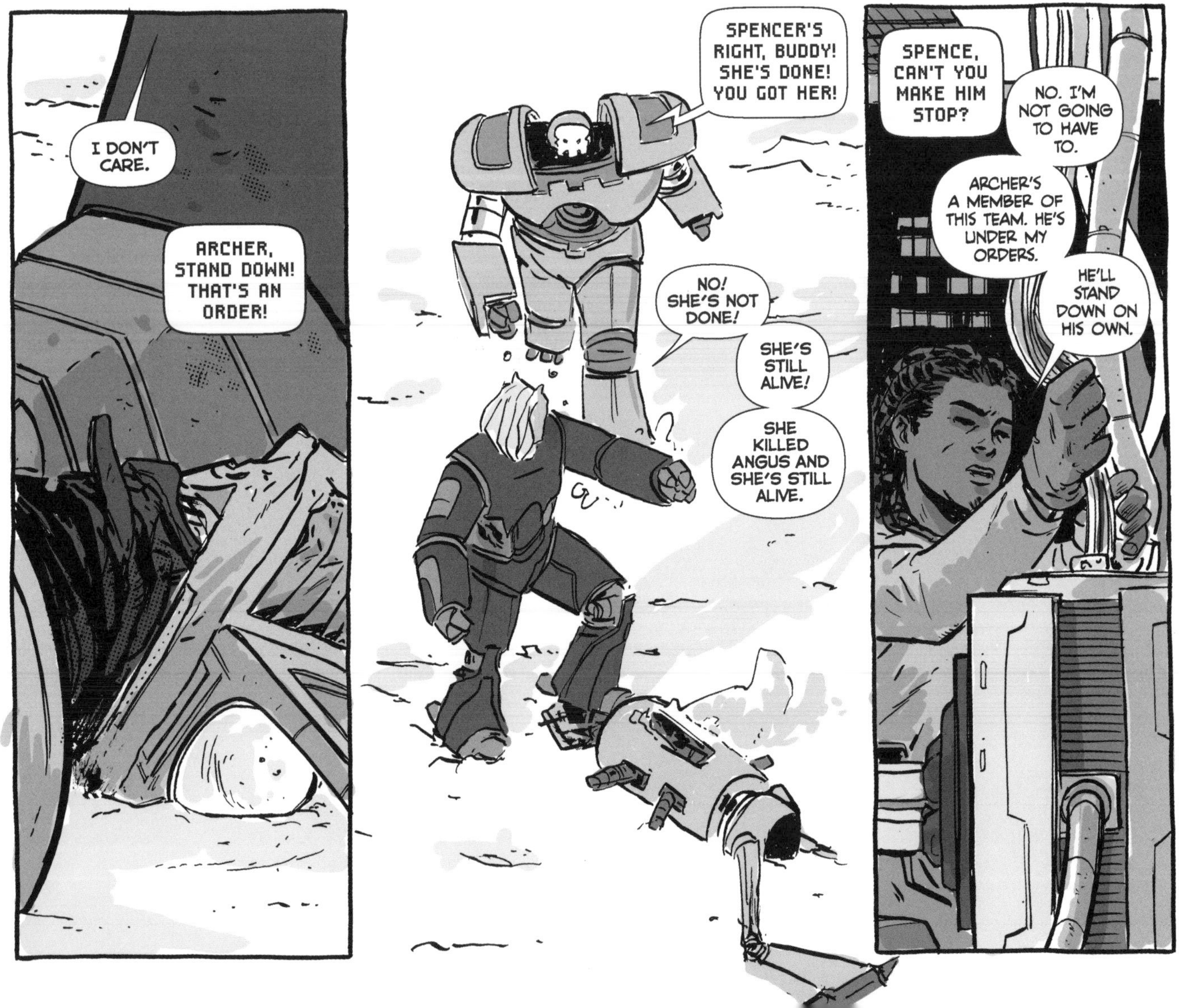
ARCHER, STAND DOWN! THAT'S AN ORDER!
I DON'T CARE.
SPENCER'S RIGHT, BUDDY! SHE'S DONE! YOU GOT HER!
NO! SHE'S NOT DONE!
SHE'S STILL ALIVE!
SHE KILLED ANGUS AND SHE'S STILL ALIVE.
SPENCE, CAN'T YOU MAKE HIM STOP?
NO. I'M NOT GOING TO HAVE TO.
ARCHER'S A MEMBER OF THIS TEAM. HE'S UNDER MY ORDERS.
HE'LL STAND DOWN ON HIS OWN.

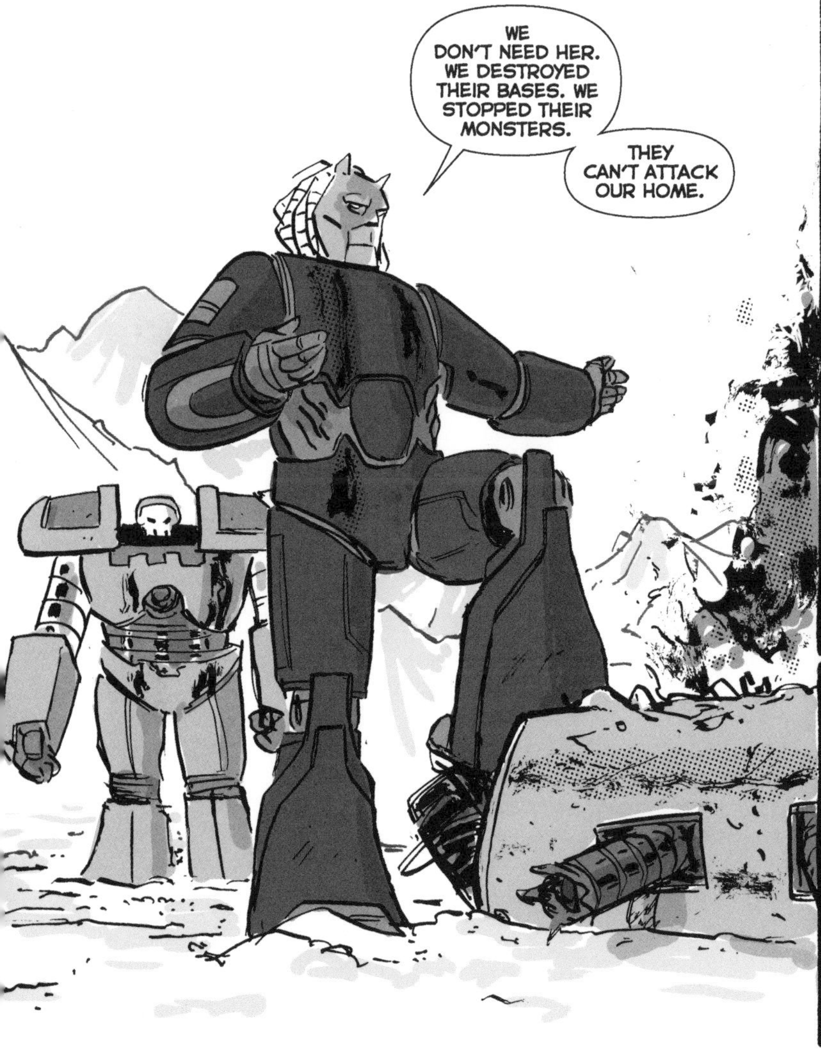
WE DON'T NEED HER. WE DESTROYED THEIR BASES. WE STOPPED THEIR MONSTERS.
THEY CAN'T ATTACK OUR HOME.

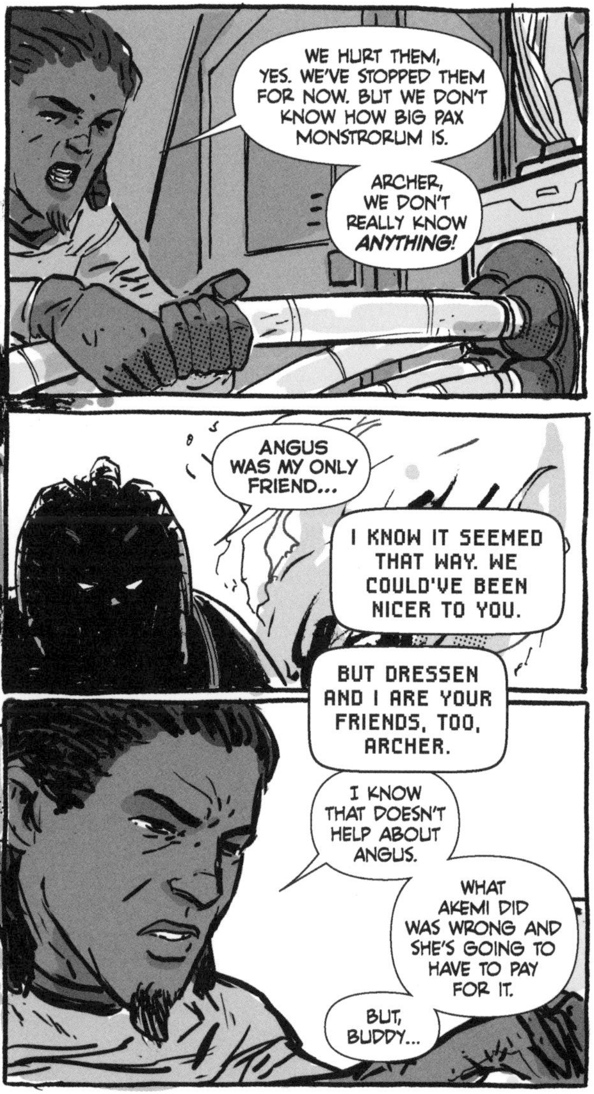
WE HURT THEM, YES. WE'VE STOPPED THEM FOR NOW. BUT WE DON'T KNOW HOW BIG PAX MONSTRORUM IS.
ARCHER, WE DON'T REALLY KNOW *ANYTHING!*
ANGUS WAS MY ONLY FRIEND...
I KNOW IT SEEMED THAT WAY. WE COULD'VE BEEN NICER TO YOU.
BUT DRESSEN AND I ARE YOUR FRIENDS, TOO, ARCHER.
I KNOW THAT DOESN'T HELP ABOUT ANGUS.
WHAT AKEMI DID WAS WRONG AND SHE'S GOING TO HAVE TO PAY FOR IT.
BUT, BUDDY...

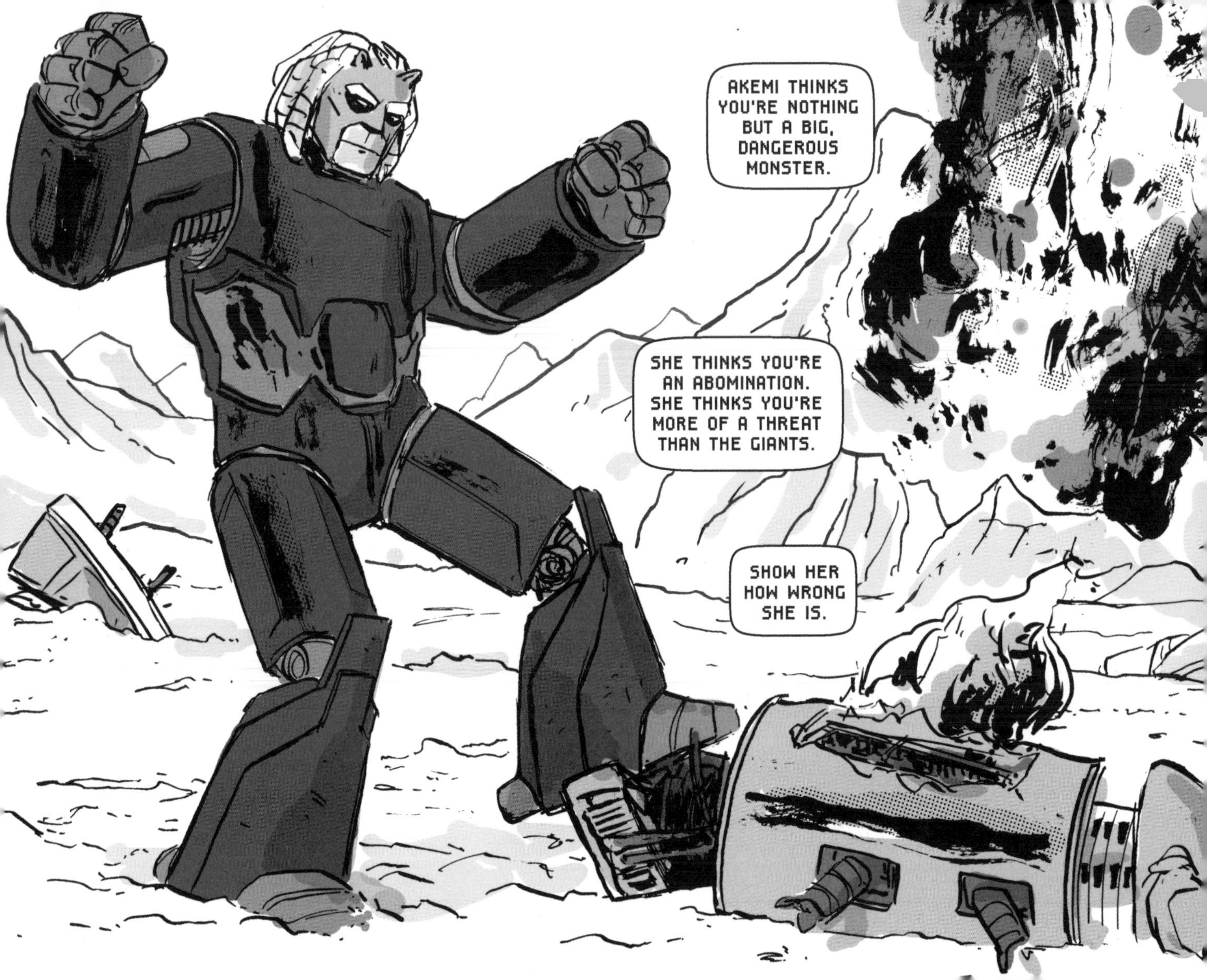
AKEMI THINKS YOU'RE NOTHING BUT A BIG, DANGEROUS MONSTER.
SHE THINKS YOU'RE AN ABOMINATION. SHE THINKS YOU'RE MORE OF A THREAT THAN THE GIANTS.
SHOW HER HOW WRONG SHE IS.

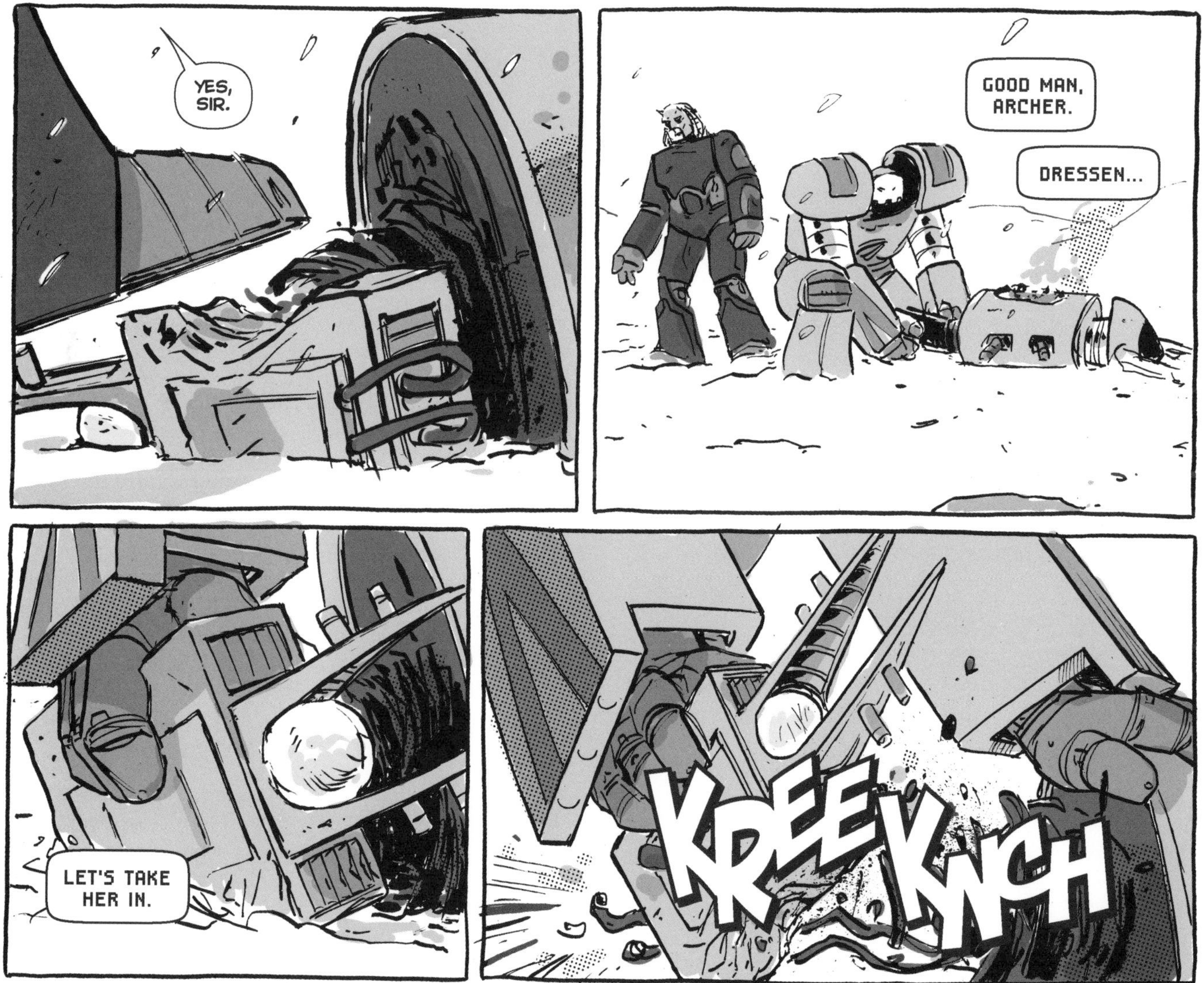
YES, SIR.
GOOD MAN, ARCHER.
DRESSEN...
LET'S TAKE HER IN.
KREE KNCH

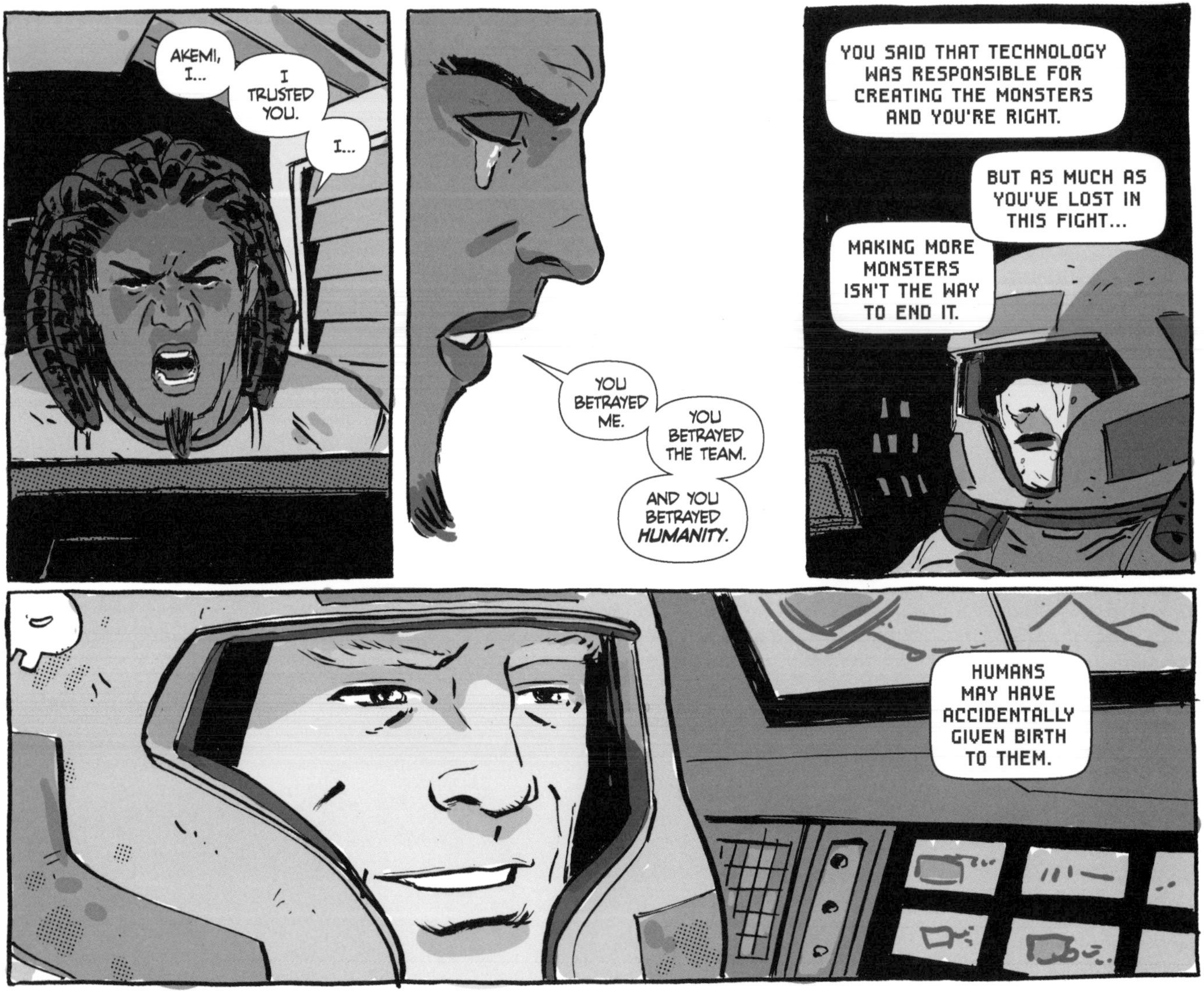
AKEMI, I...
I TRUSTED YOU.
I...
YOU BETRAYED ME.
YOU BETRAYED THE TEAM.
AND YOU BETRAYED *HUMANITY*.
YOU SAID THAT TECHNOLOGY WAS RESPONSIBLE FOR CREATING THE MONSTERS AND YOU'RE RIGHT.
BUT AS MUCH AS YOU'VE LOST IN THIS FIGHT...
MAKING MORE MONSTERS ISN'T THE WAY TO END IT.
HUMANS MAY HAVE ACCIDENTALLY GIVEN BIRTH TO THEM.

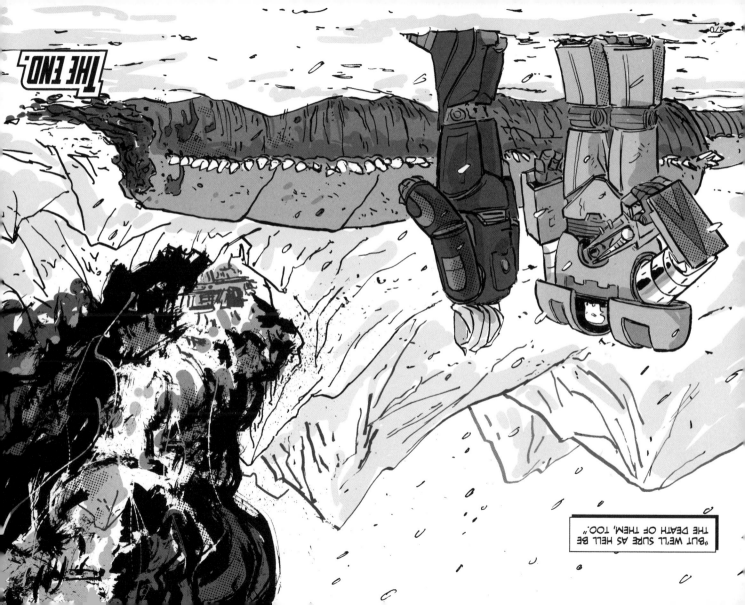

THE END.

"BUT WE'LL SURE AS HELL BE THE DEATH OF THEM, TOO."

THE MINISTRY OF ROBOTS

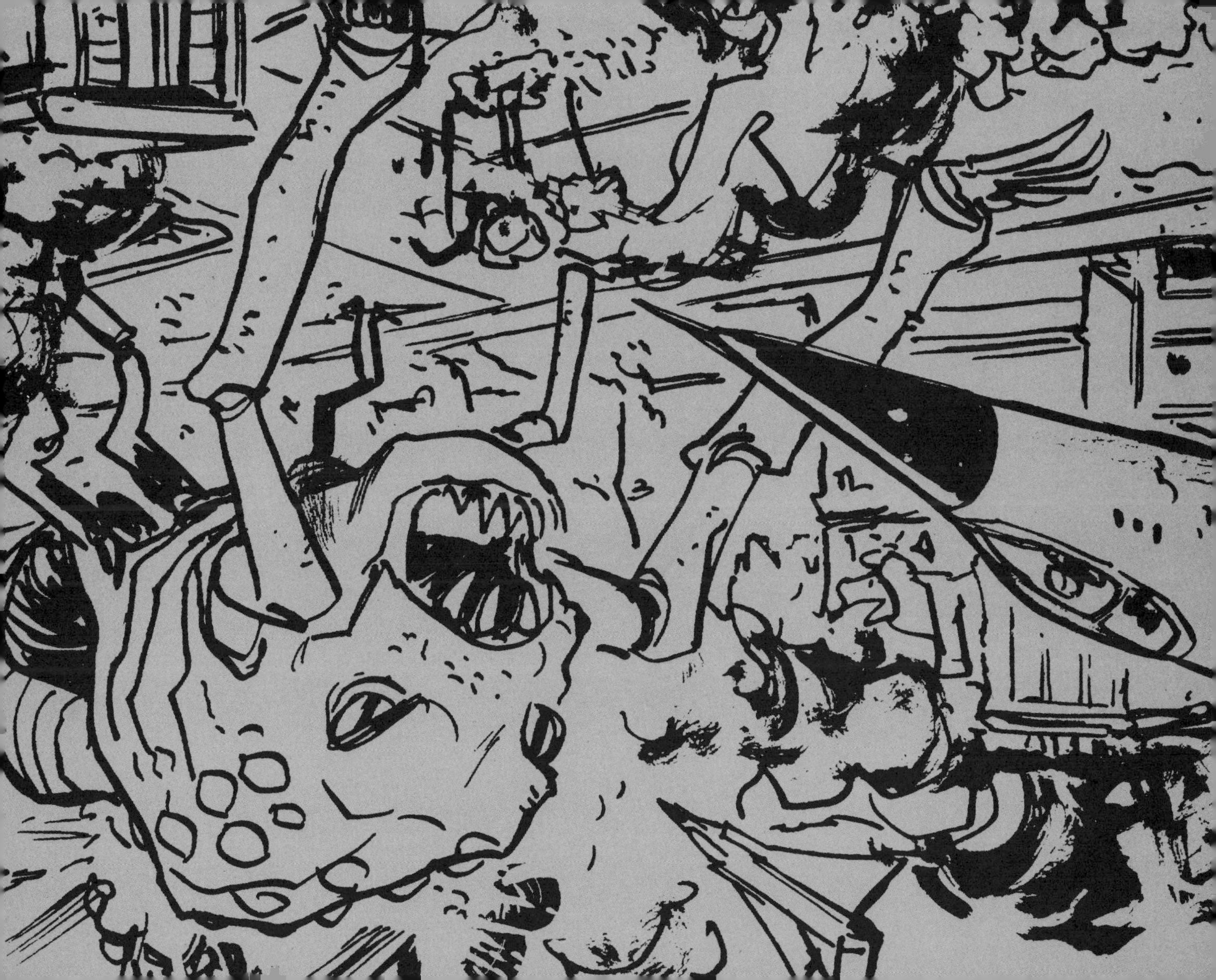

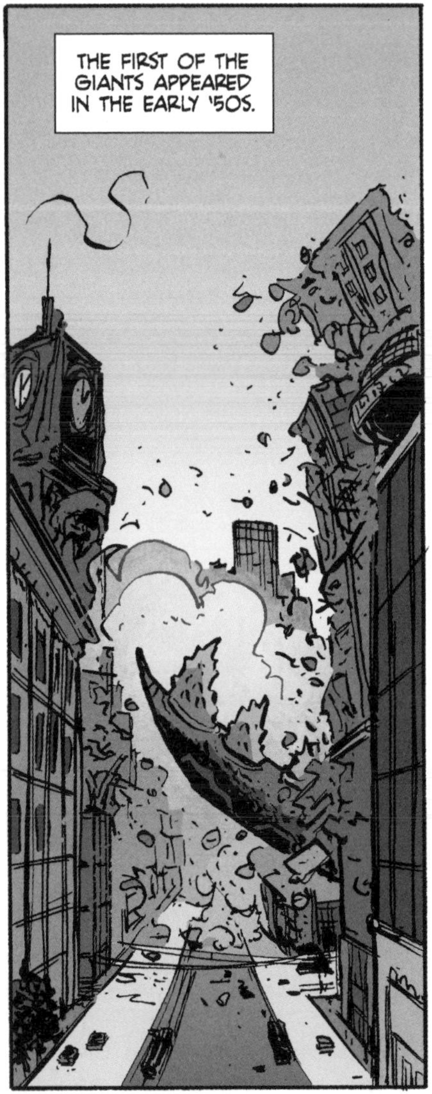
THE FIRST OF THE GIANTS APPEARED IN THE EARLY '50S.

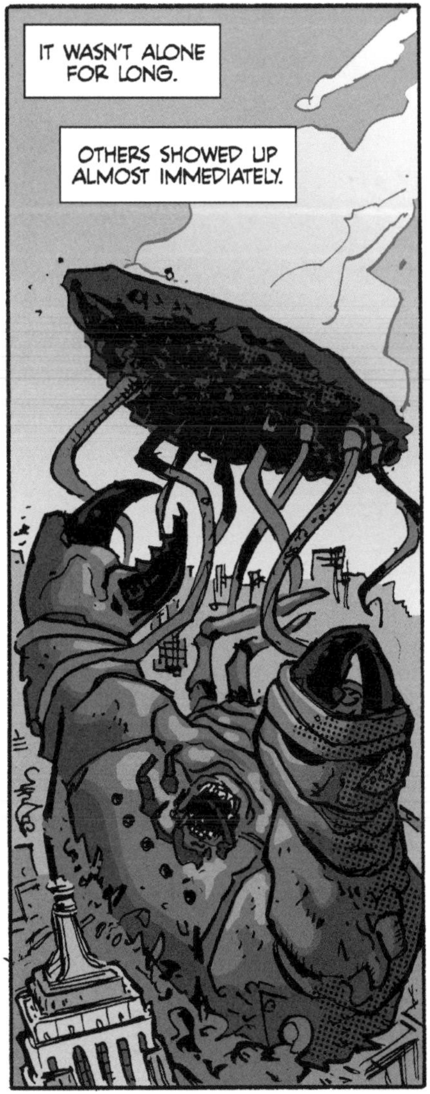
IT WASN'T ALONE FOR LONG.
OTHERS SHOWED UP ALMOST IMMEDIATELY.

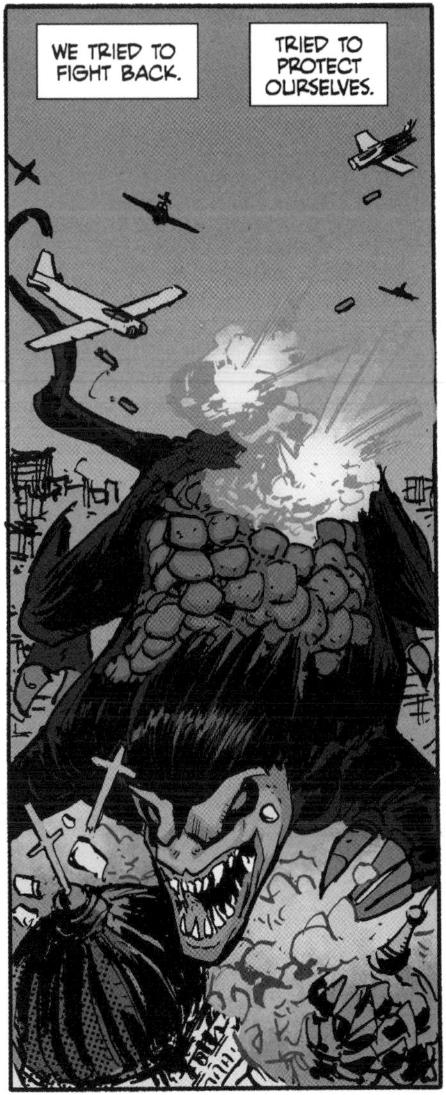
WE TRIED TO FIGHT BACK.
TRIED TO PROTECT OURSELVES.

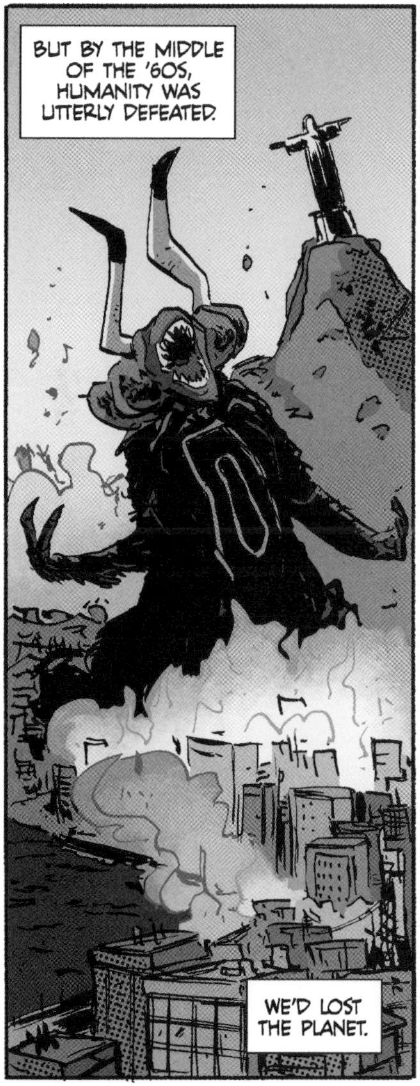
BUT BY THE MIDDLE OF THE '6OS, HUMANITY WAS UTTERLY DEFEATED.
WE'D LOST THE PLANET.

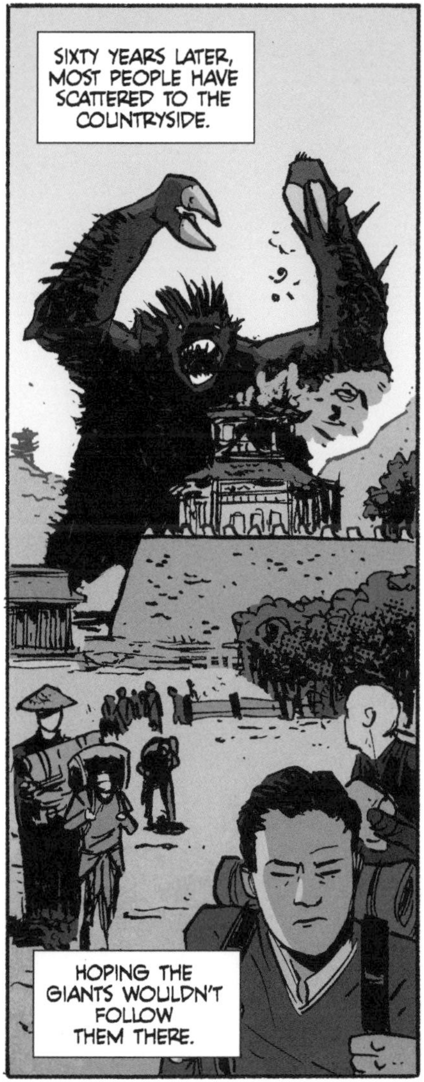
SIXTY YEARS LATER, MOST PEOPLE HAVE SCATTERED TO THE COUNTRYSIDE.
HOPING THE GIANTS WOULDN'T FOLLOW THEM THERE.

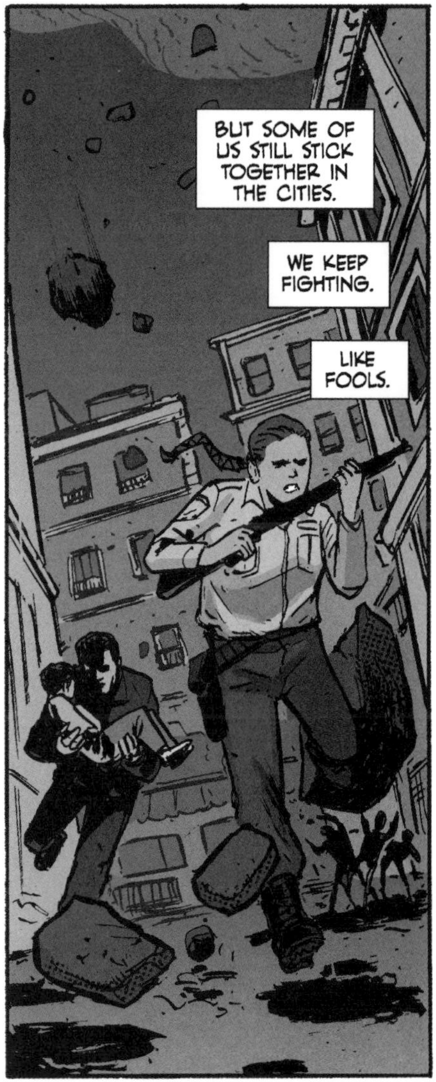
BUT SOME OF US STILL STICK TOGETHER IN THE CITIES.
WE KEEP FIGHTING.
LIKE FOOLS.

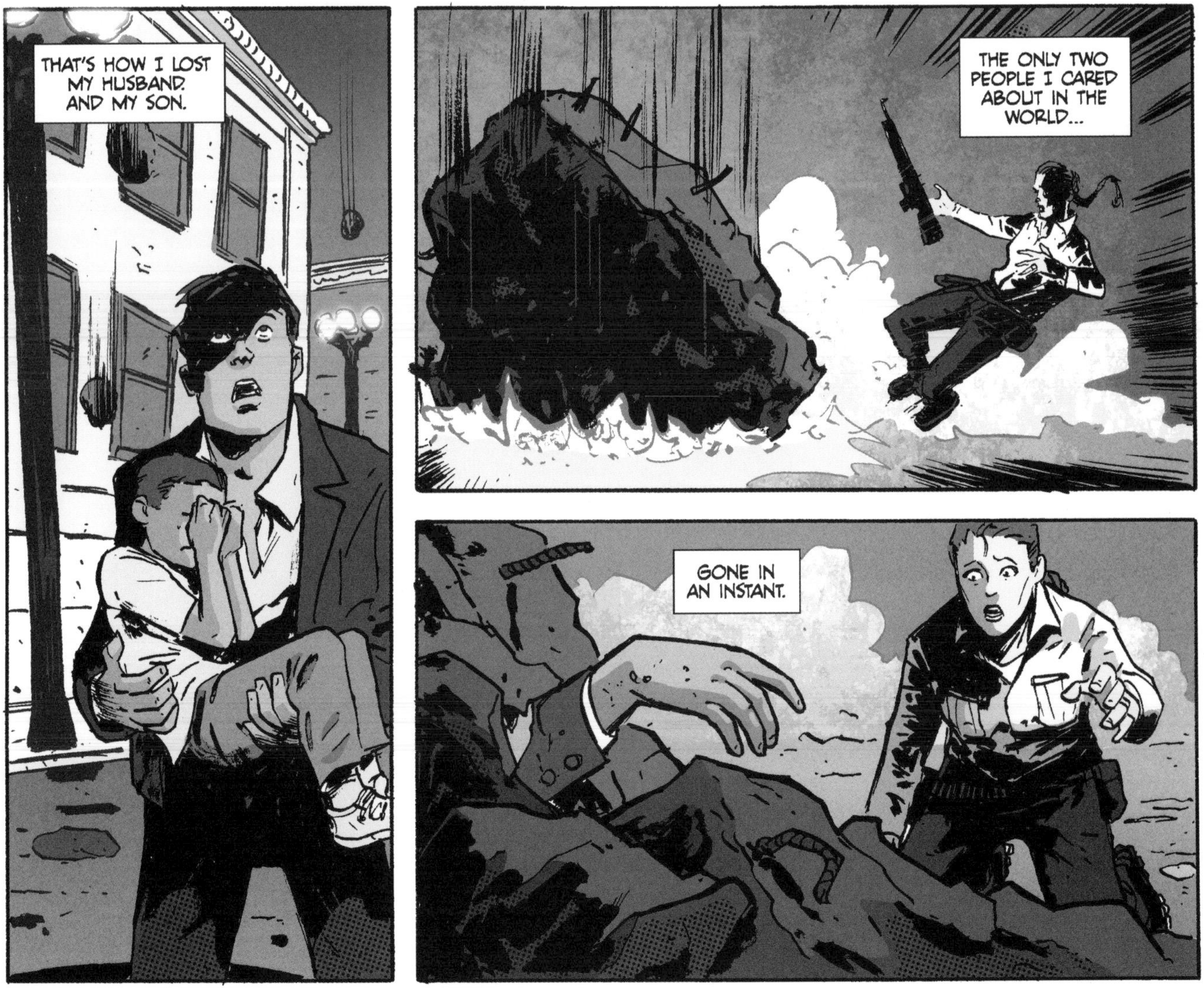
THAT'S HOW I LOST MY HUSBAND. AND MY SON.
THE ONLY TWO PEOPLE I CARED ABOUT IN THE WORLD...
GONE IN AN INSTANT.

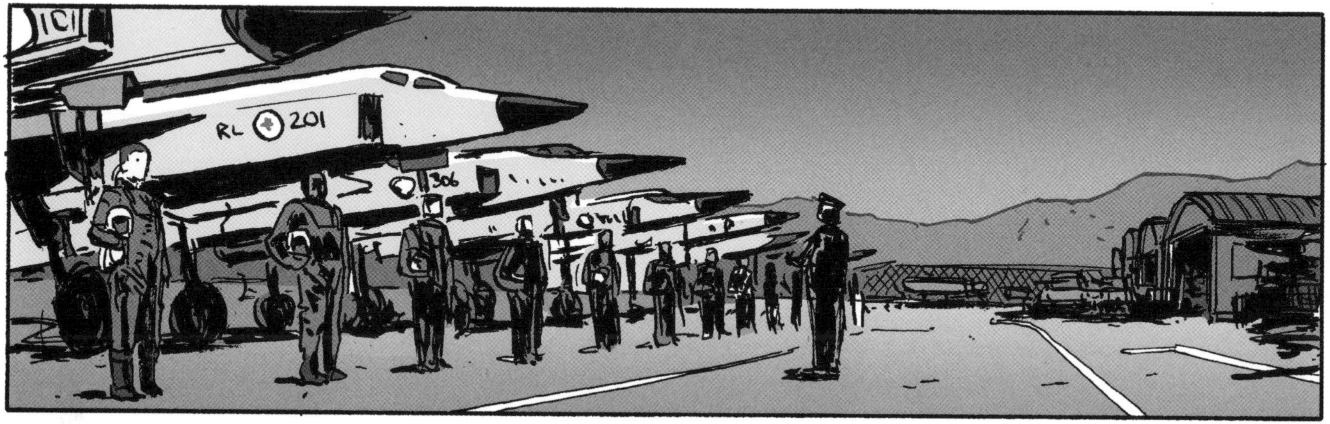
RL 201
306

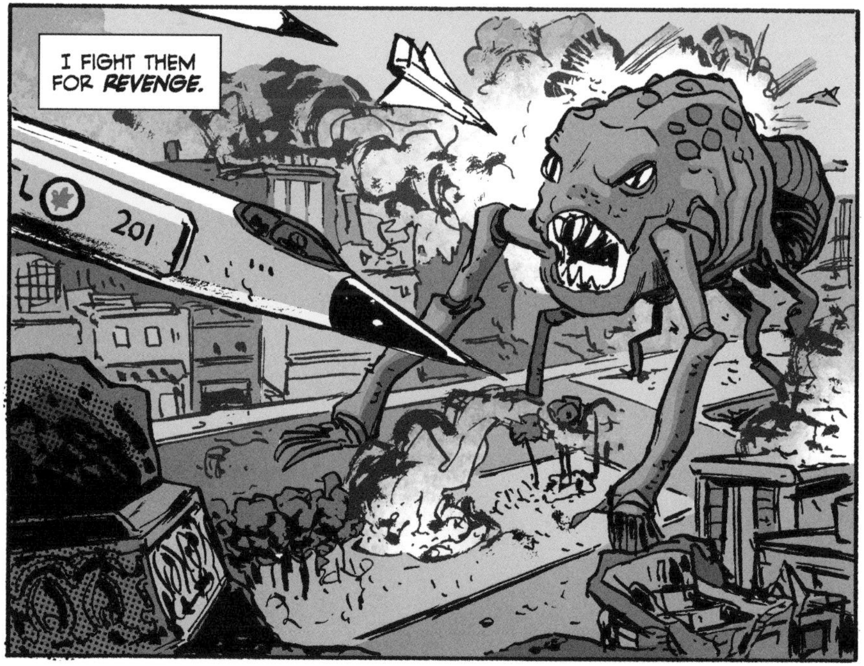
I FIGHT THEM FOR ***REVENGE.***
201

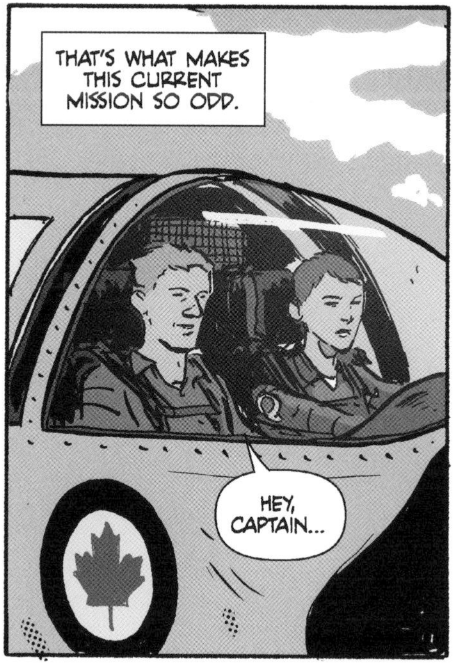
THAT'S WHAT MAKES THIS CURRENT MISSION SO ODD.
HEY, CAPTAIN...

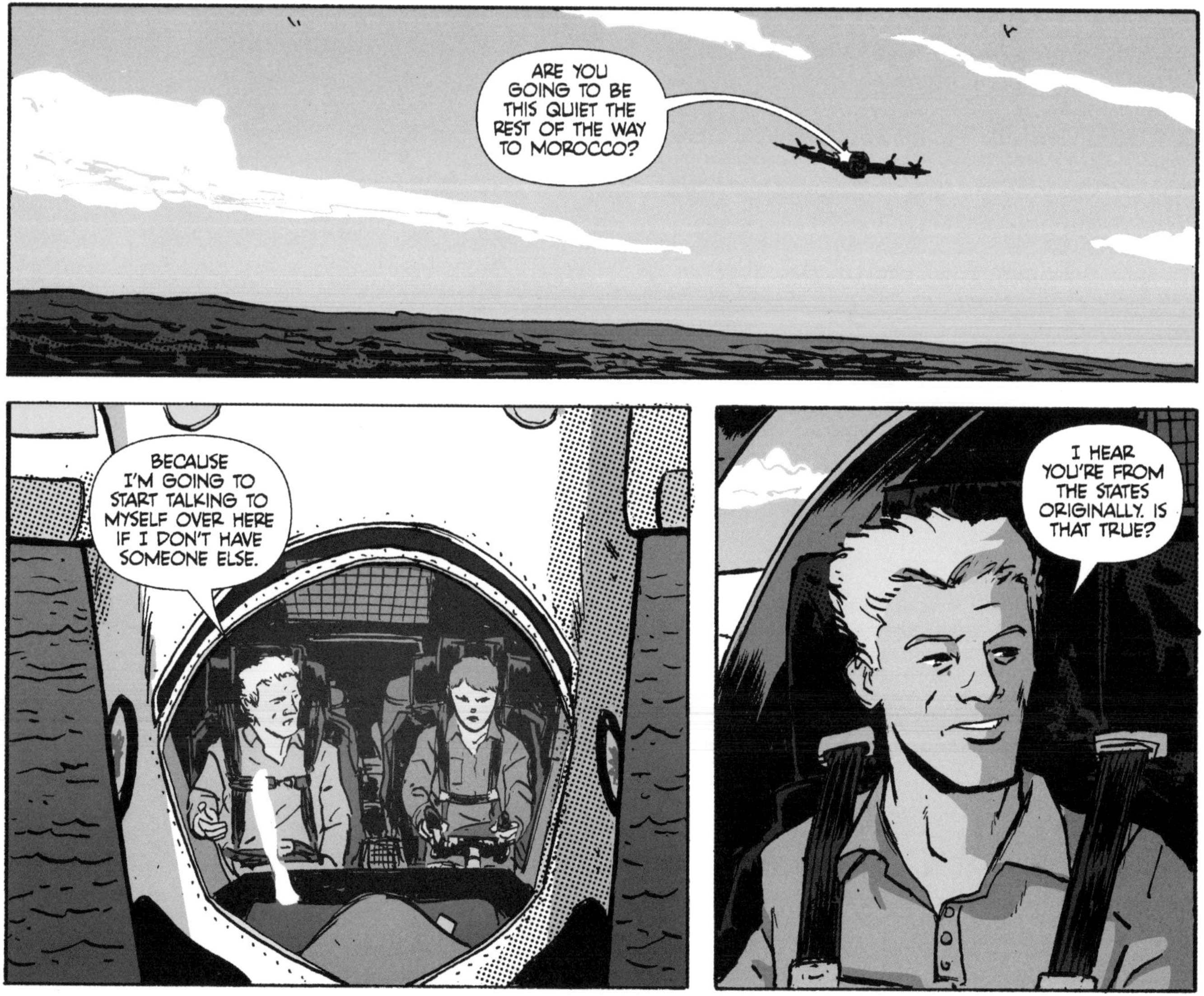
ARE YOU GOING TO BE THIS QUIET THE REST OF THE WAY TO MOROCCO?
BECAUSE I'M GOING TO START TALKING TO MYSELF OVER HERE IF I DON'T HAVE SOMEONE ELSE.
I HEAR YOU'RE FROM THE STATES ORIGINALLY. IS THAT TRUE?

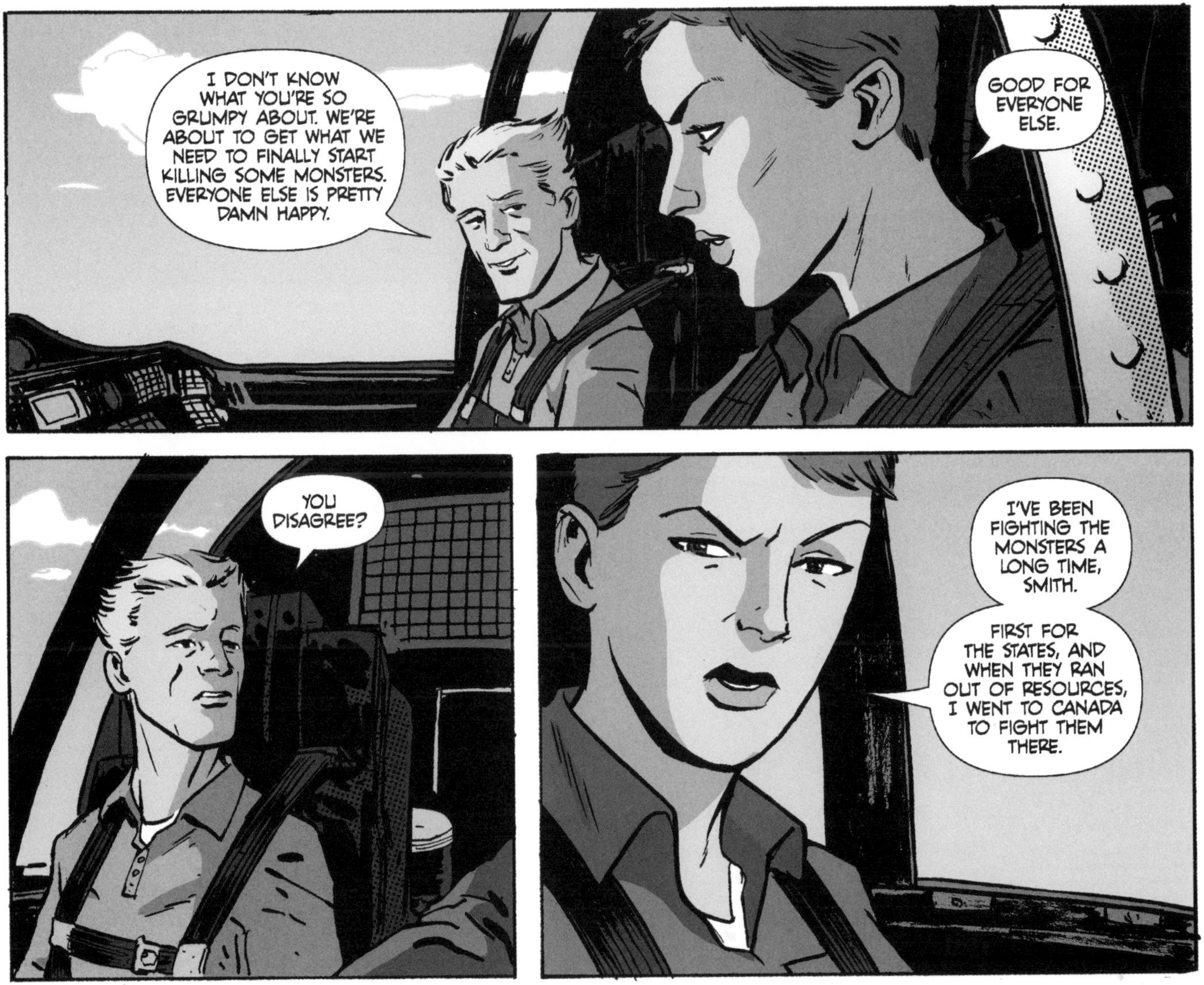
I DON'T KNOW WHAT YOU'RE SO GRUMPY ABOUT. WE'RE ABOUT TO GET WHAT WE NEED TO FINALLY START KILLING SOME MONSTERS. EVERYONE ELSE IS PRETTY DAMN HAPPY.
GOOD FOR EVERYONE ELSE.
YOU DISAGREE?
I'VE BEEN FIGHTING THE MONSTERS A LONG TIME, SMITH.
FIRST FOR THE STATES, AND WHEN THEY RAN OUT OF RESOURCES, I WENT TO CANADA TO FIGHT THEM THERE.

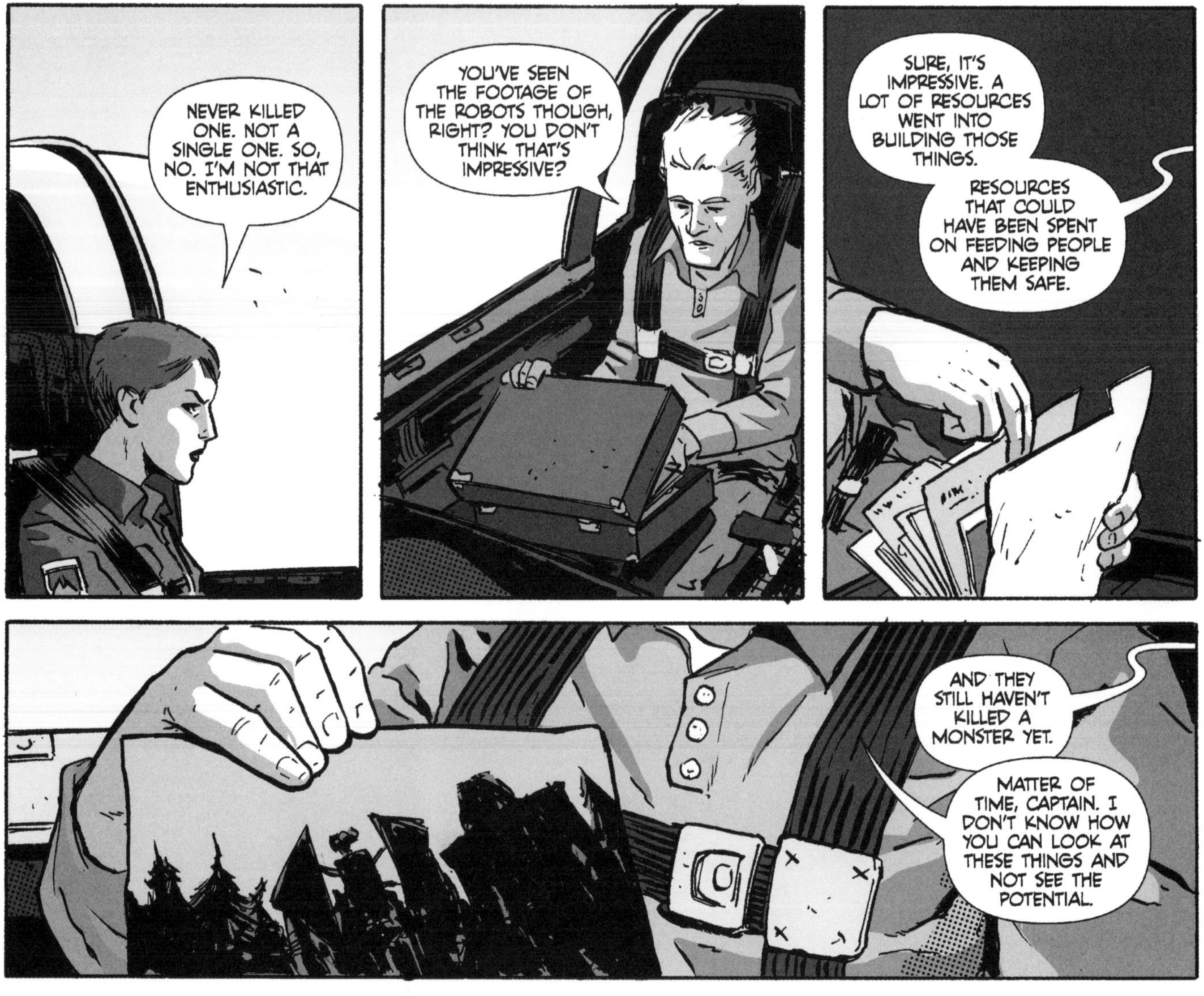
NEVER KILLED ONE. NOT A SINGLE ONE. SO, NO. I'M NOT THAT ENTHUSIASTIC.
YOU'VE SEEN THE FOOTAGE OF THE ROBOTS THOUGH, RIGHT? YOU DON'T THINK THAT'S IMPRESSIVE?
SURE, IT'S IMPRESSIVE. A LOT OF RESOURCES WENT INTO BUILDING THOSE THINGS.
RESOURCES THAT COULD HAVE BEEN SPENT ON FEEDING PEOPLE AND KEEPING THEM SAFE.
AND THEY STILL HAVEN'T KILLED A MONSTER YET.
MATTER OF TIME, CAPTAIN. I DON'T KNOW HOW YOU CAN LOOK AT THESE THINGS AND NOT SEE THE POTENTIAL.

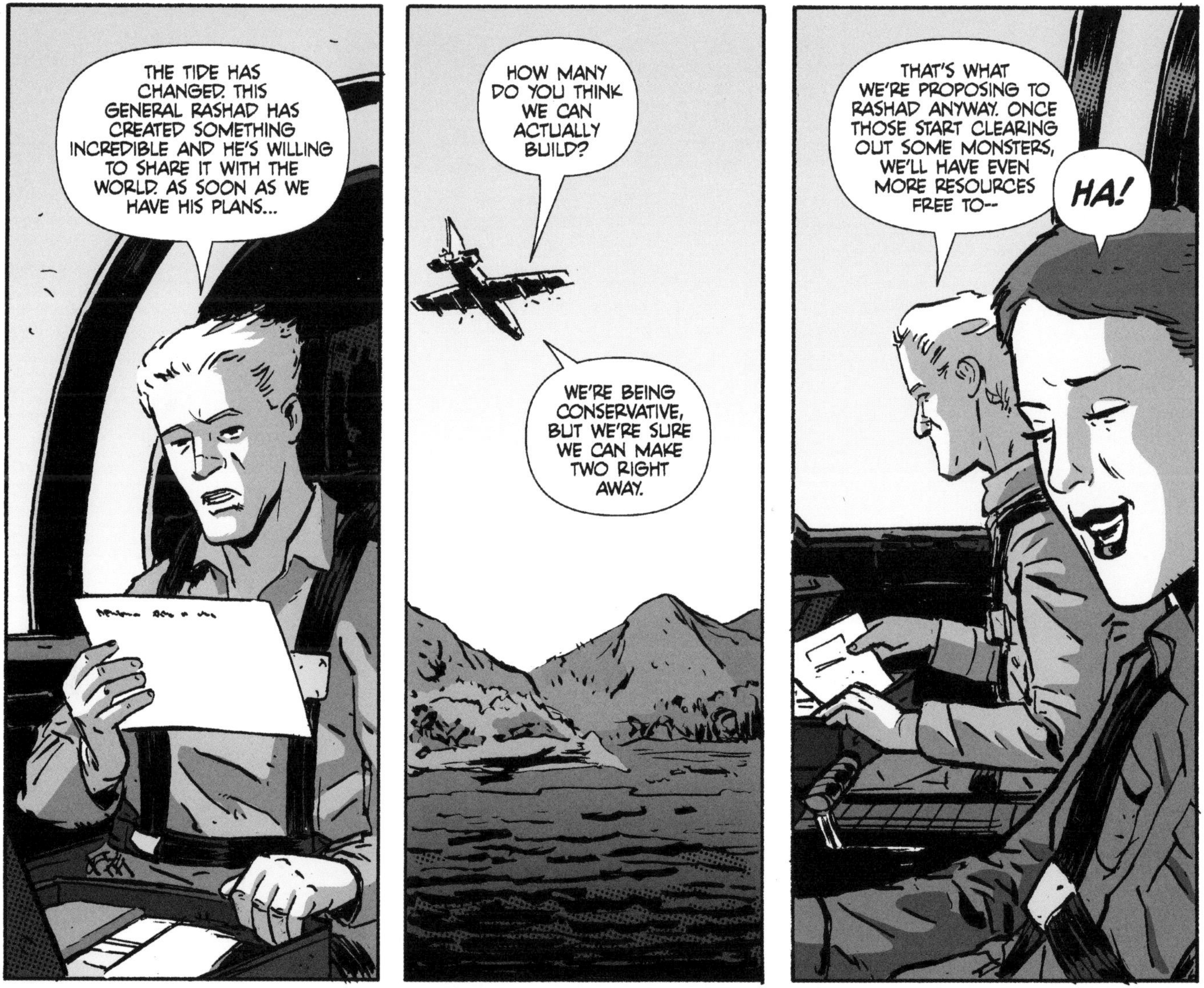
THE TIDE HAS CHANGED. THIS GENERAL RASHAD HAS CREATED SOMETHING INCREDIBLE AND HE'S WILLING TO SHARE IT WITH THE WORLD. AS SOON AS WE HAVE HIS PLANS...
HOW MANY DO YOU THINK WE CAN ACTUALLY BUILD?
WE'RE BEING CONSERVATIVE, BUT WE'RE SURE WE CAN MAKE TWO RIGHT AWAY.
THAT'S WHAT WE'RE PROPOSING TO RASHAD ANYWAY. ONCE THOSE START CLEARING OUT SOME MONSTERS, WE'LL HAVE EVEN MORE RESOURCES FREE TO--
HA!

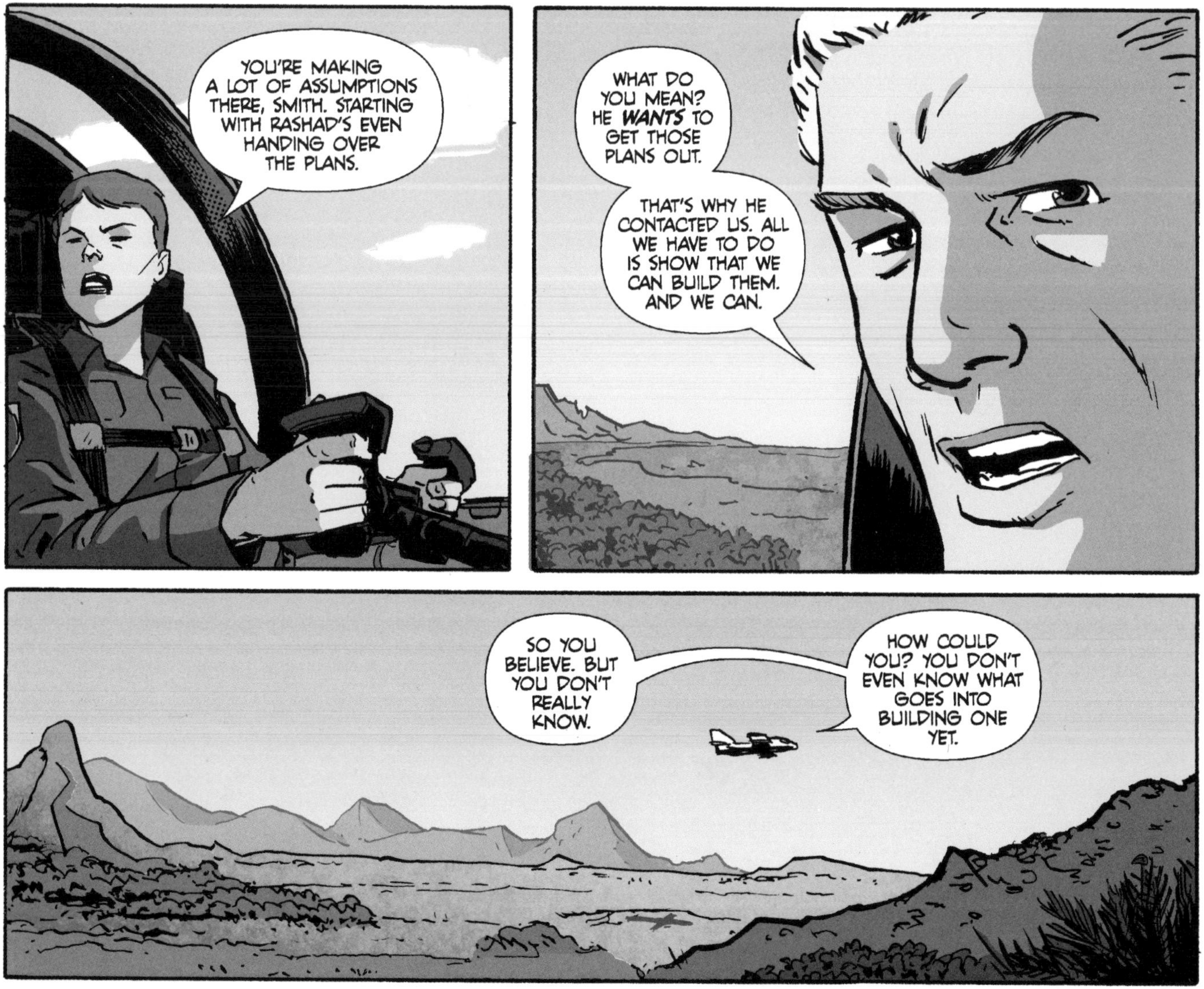
YOU'RE MAKING A LOT OF ASSUMPTIONS THERE, SMITH. STARTING WITH RASHAD'S EVEN HANDING OVER THE PLANS.
WHAT DO YOU MEAN? HE ***WANTS*** TO GET THOSE PLANS OUT.
THAT'S WHY HE CONTACTED US. ALL WE HAVE TO DO IS SHOW THAT WE CAN BUILD THEM. AND WE CAN.
SO YOU BELIEVE. BUT YOU DON'T REALLY KNOW.
HOW COULD YOU? YOU DON'T EVEN KNOW WHAT GOES INTO BUILDING ONE YET.

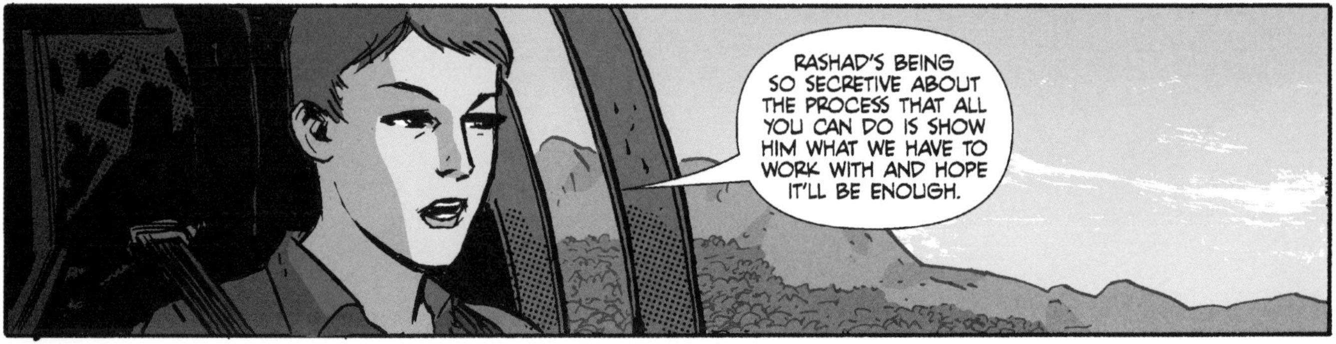
RASHAD'S BEING SO SECRETIVE ABOUT THE PROCESS THAT ALL YOU CAN DO IS SHOW HIM WHAT WE HAVE TO WORK WITH AND HOPE IT'LL BE ENOUGH.

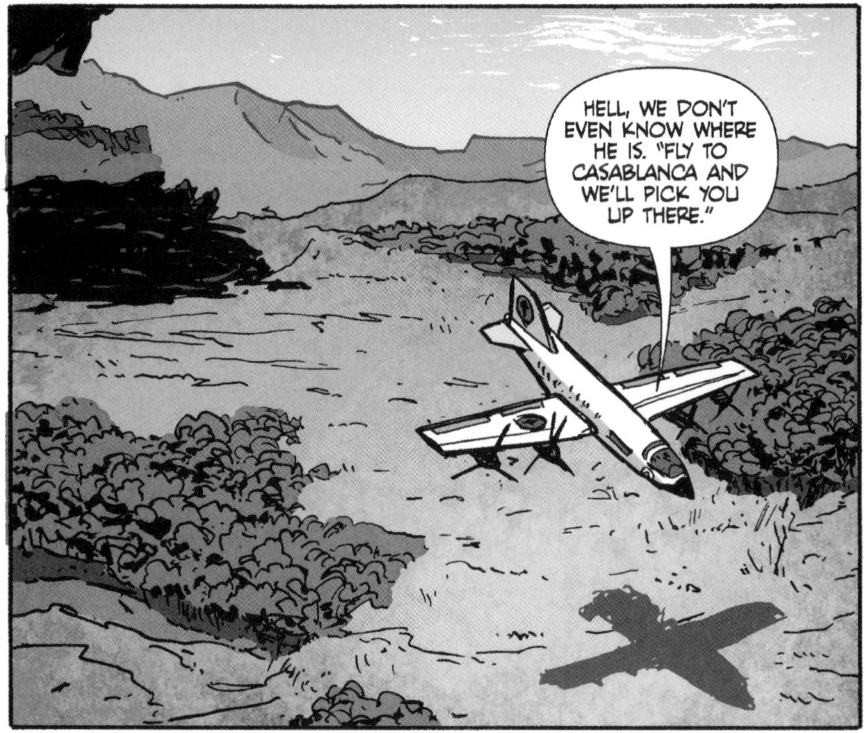
HELL, WE DON'T EVEN KNOW WHERE HE IS. "FLY TO CASABLANCA AND WE'LL PICK YOU UP THERE."

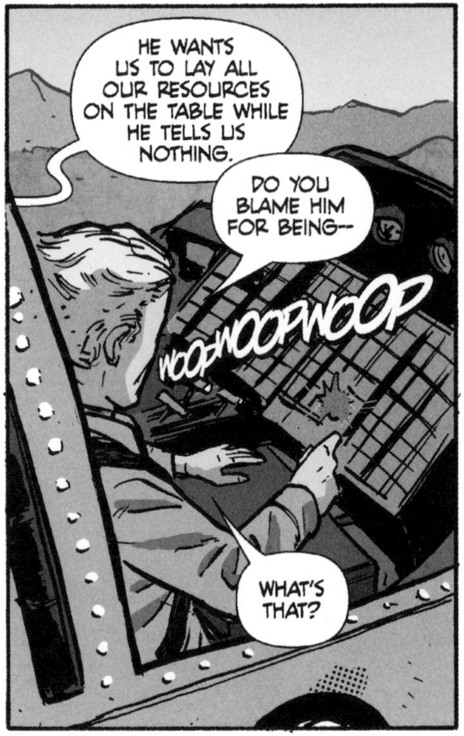
HE WANTS US TO LAY ALL OUR RESOURCES ON THE TABLE WHILE HE TELLS US NOTHING.
DO YOU BLAME HIM FOR BEING--
WOOPWOOPWOOP
WHAT'S THAT?

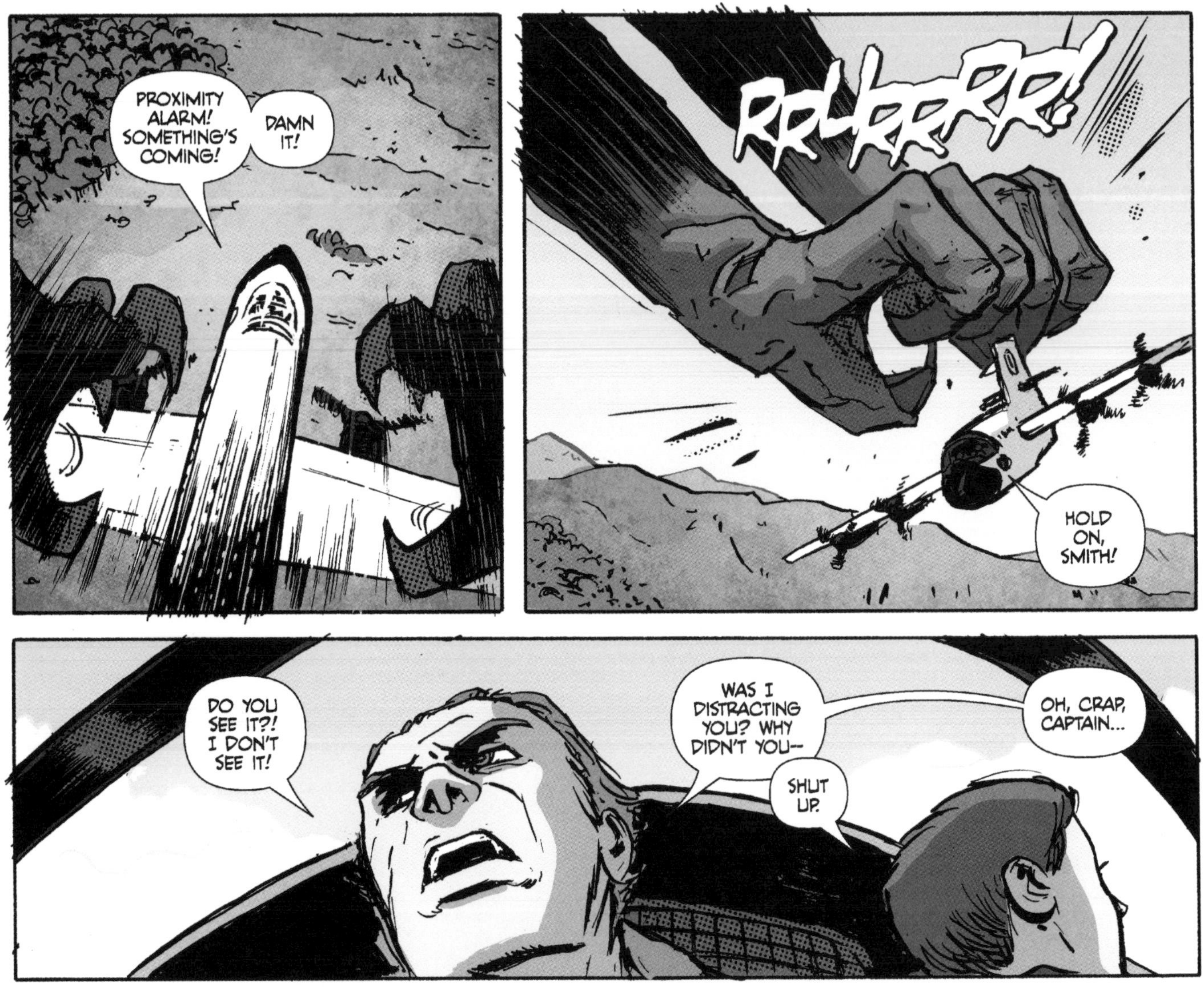
PROXIMITY ALARM! SOMETHING'S COMING!
DAMN IT!
RRLRRRRR!
HOLD ON, SMITH!
DO YOU SEE IT?! I DON'T SEE IT!
WAS I DISTRACTING YOU? WHY DIDN'T YOU--
SHUT UP.
OH, CRAP, CAPTAIN...

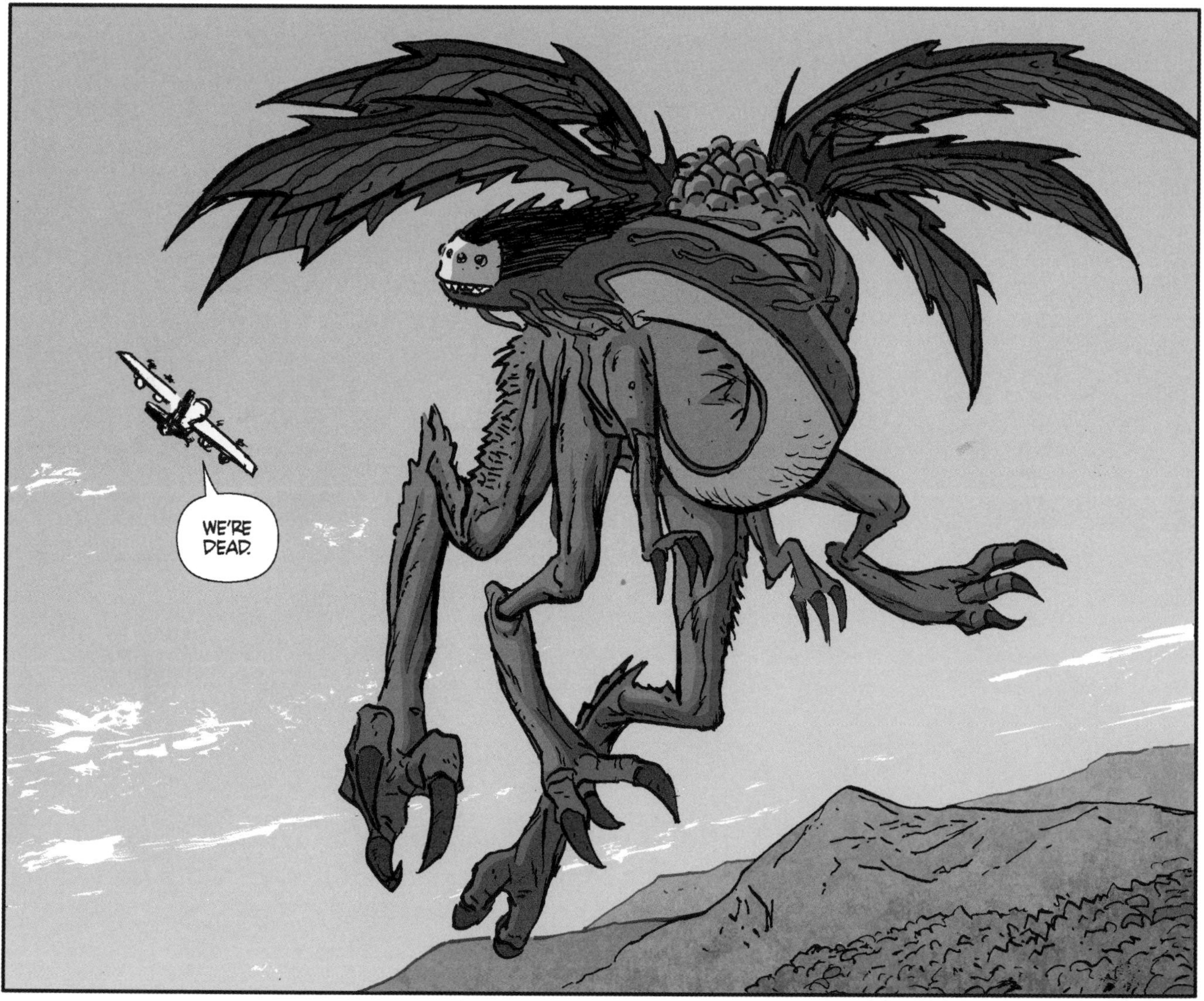
WE'RE DEAD.

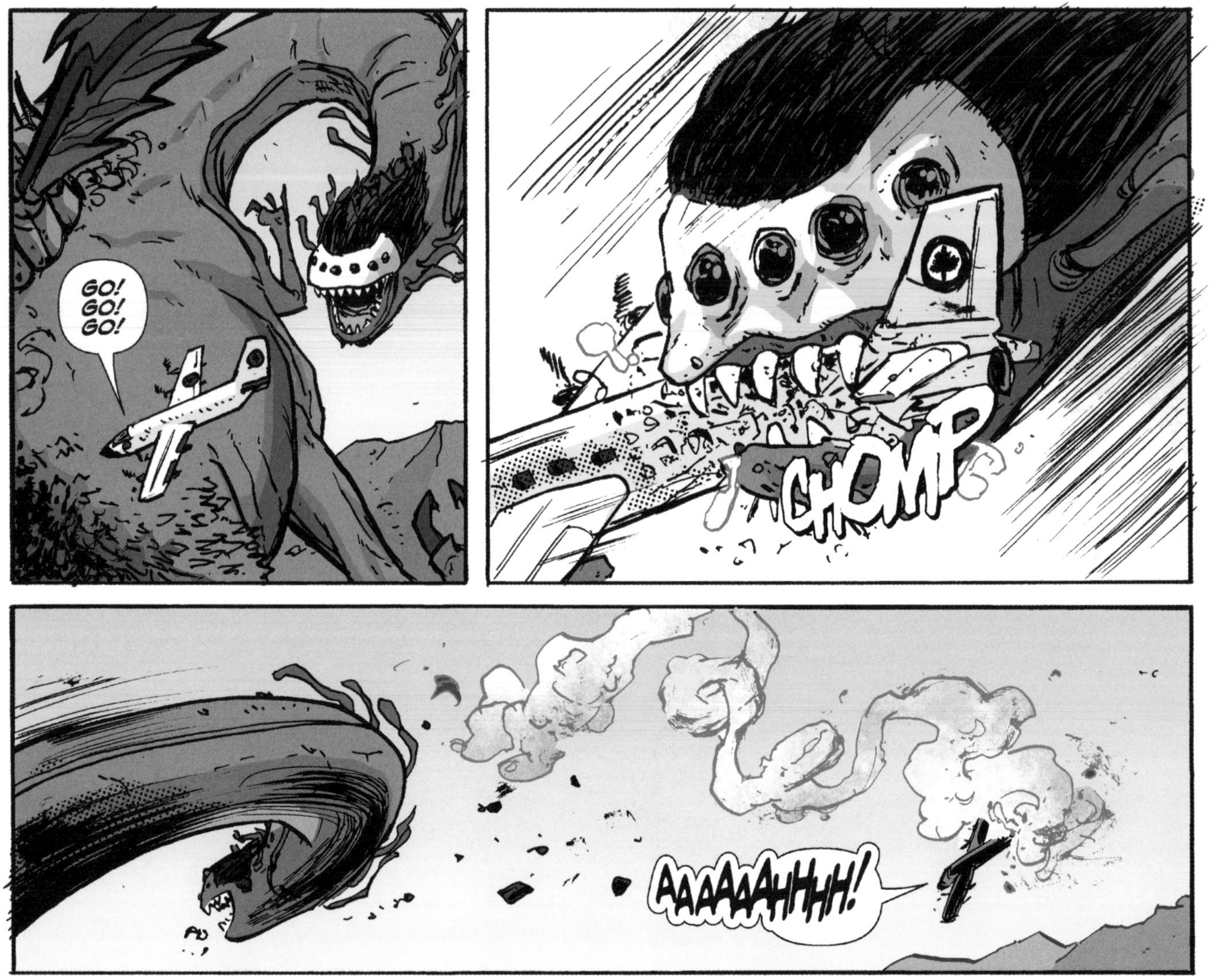
GO! GO! GO!
CHOMP
AAAAAAHHHH!

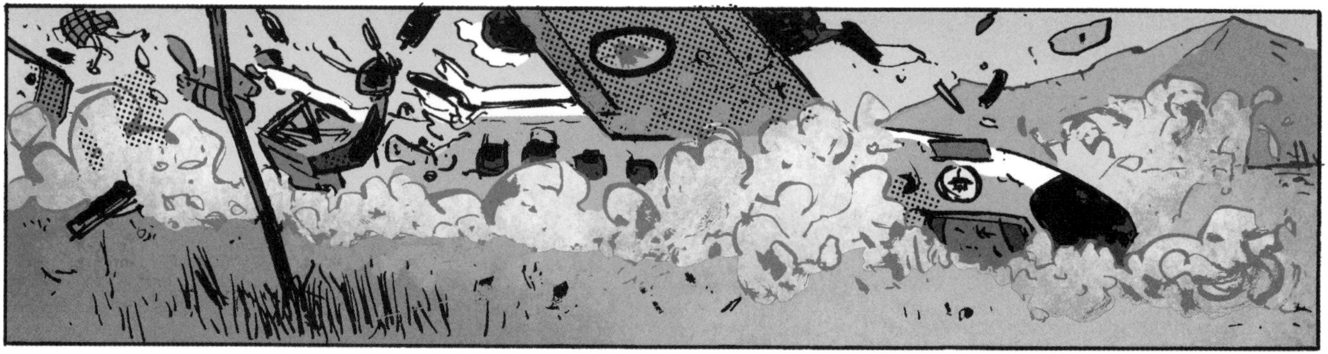

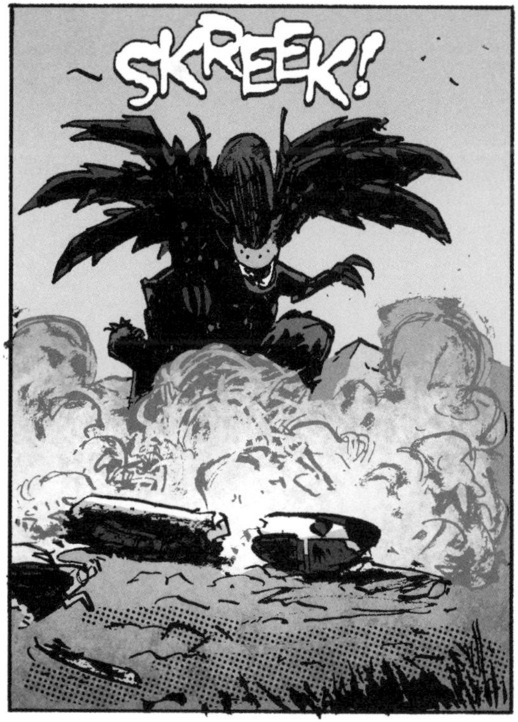
SKREEK!

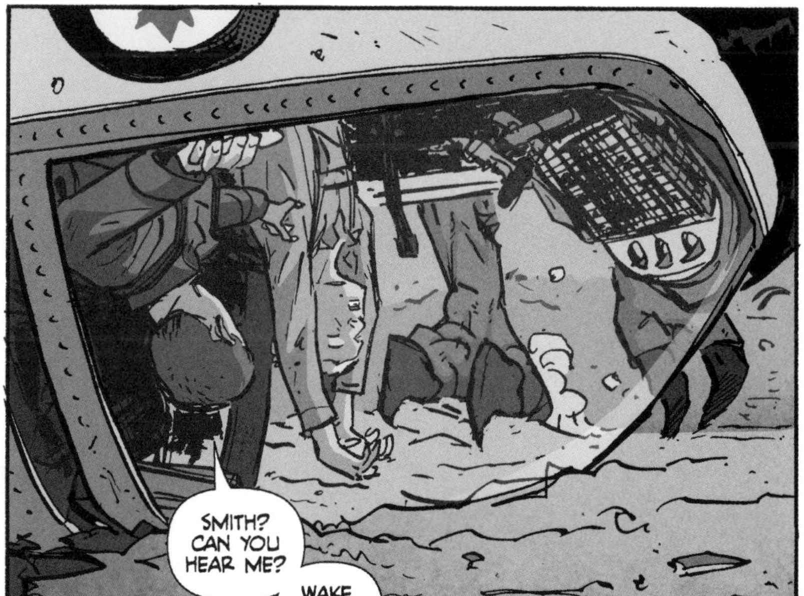
SMITH? CAN YOU HEAR ME?
WAKE UP, SMITH!

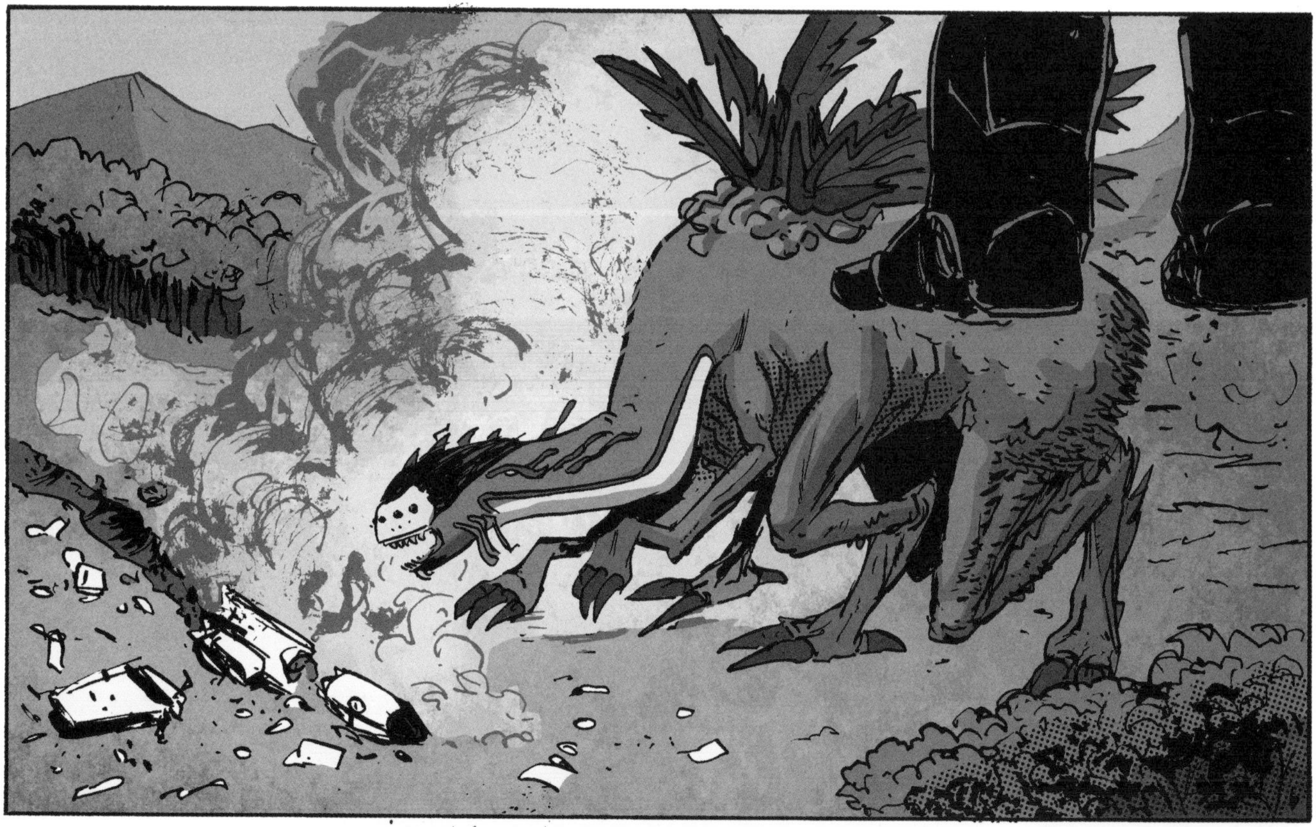

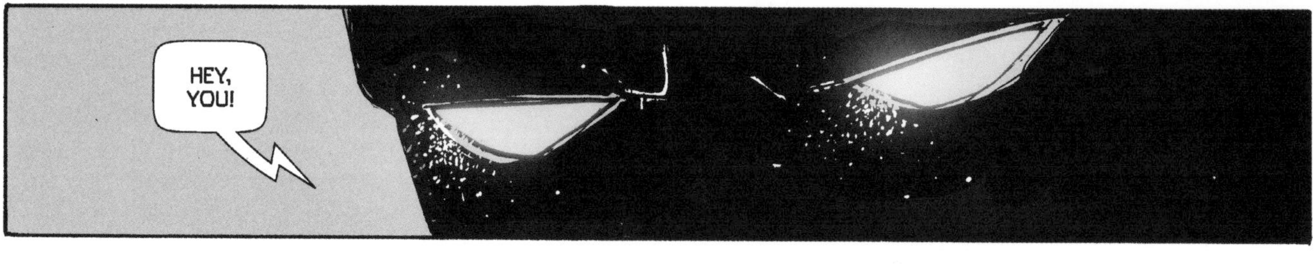
HEY, YOU!

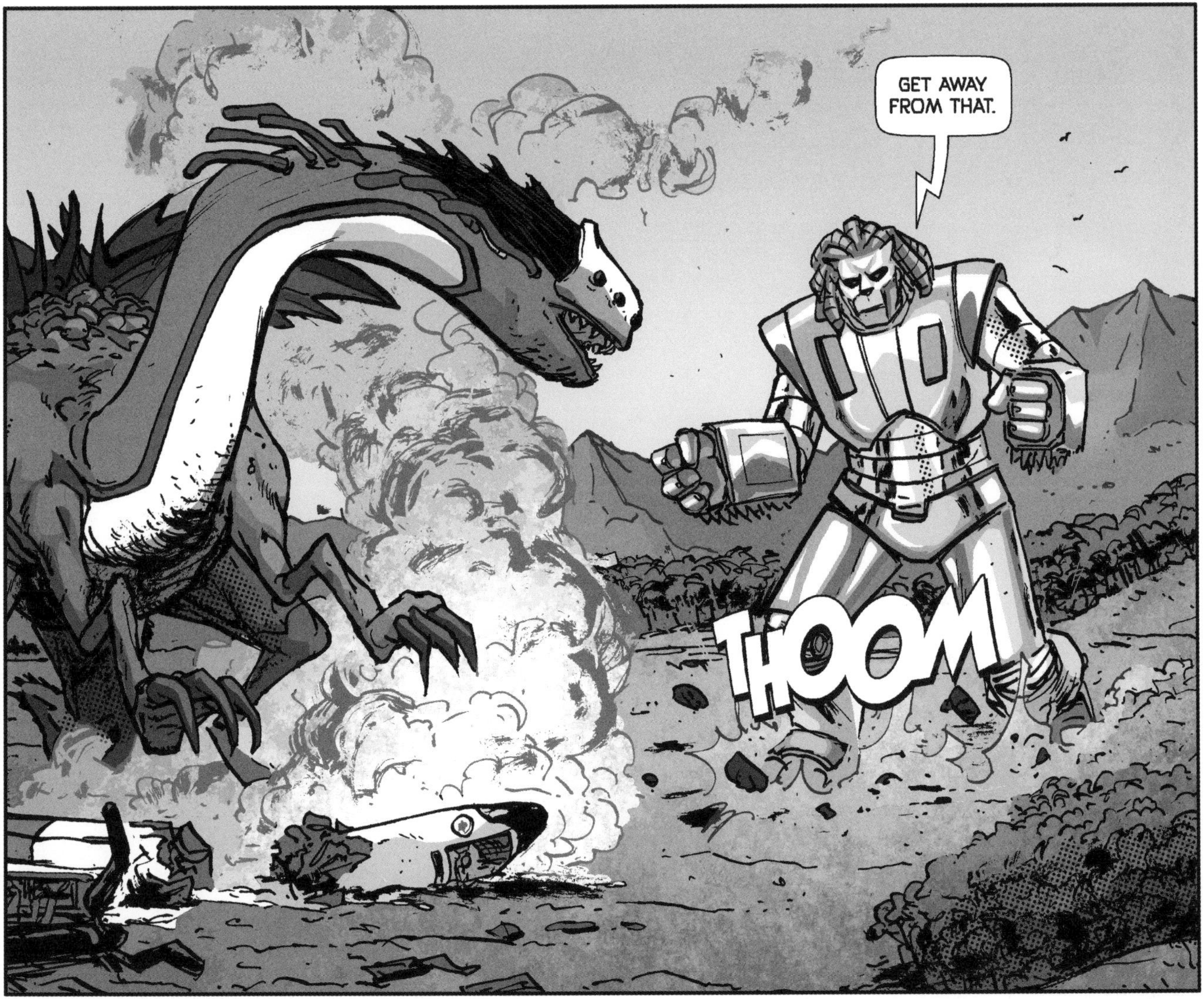
GET AWAY FROM THAT.
THOOM

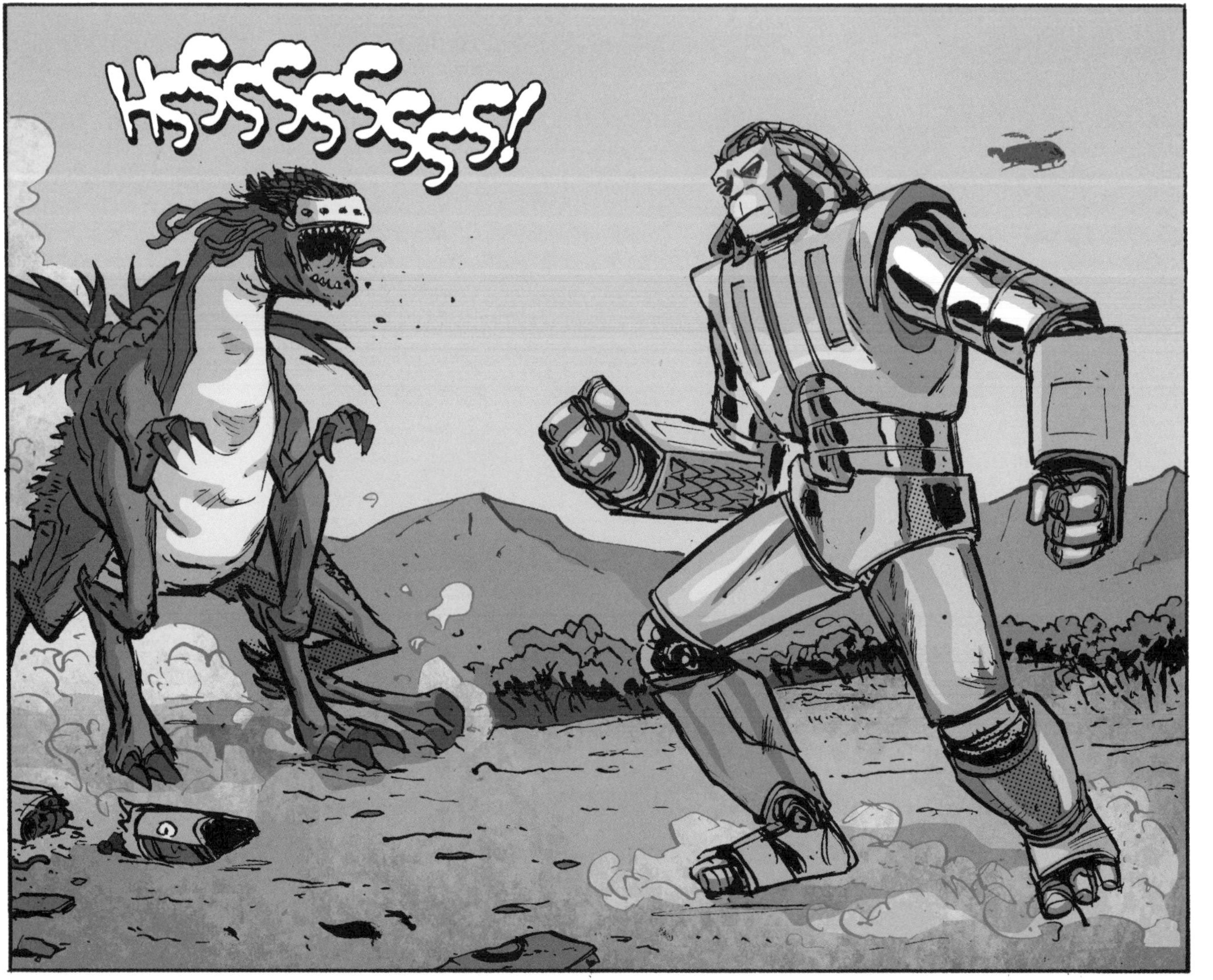
HSSSSSSSS!

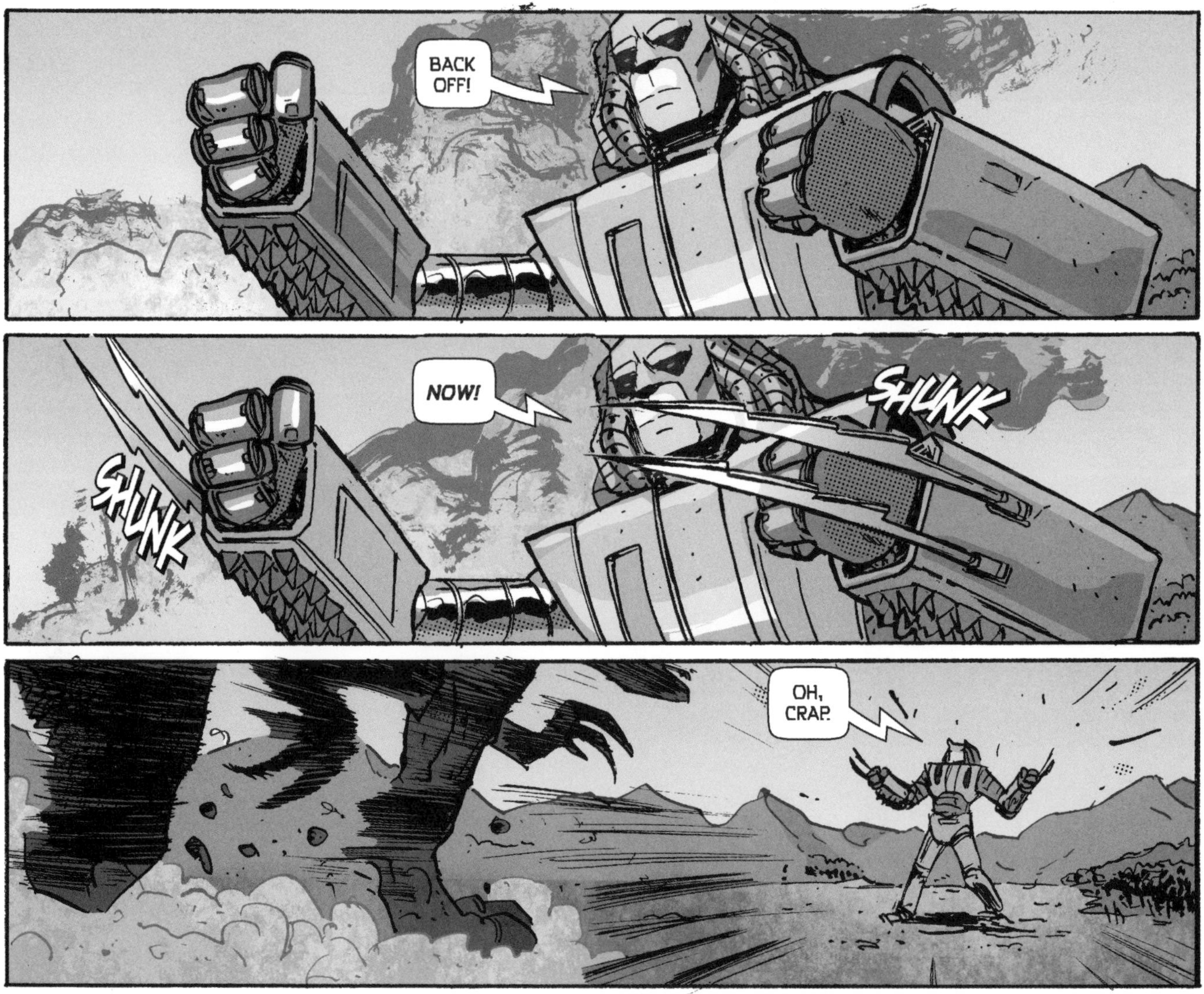
BACK OFF!
NOW!
SHUNK
SHUNK
OH, CRAP.

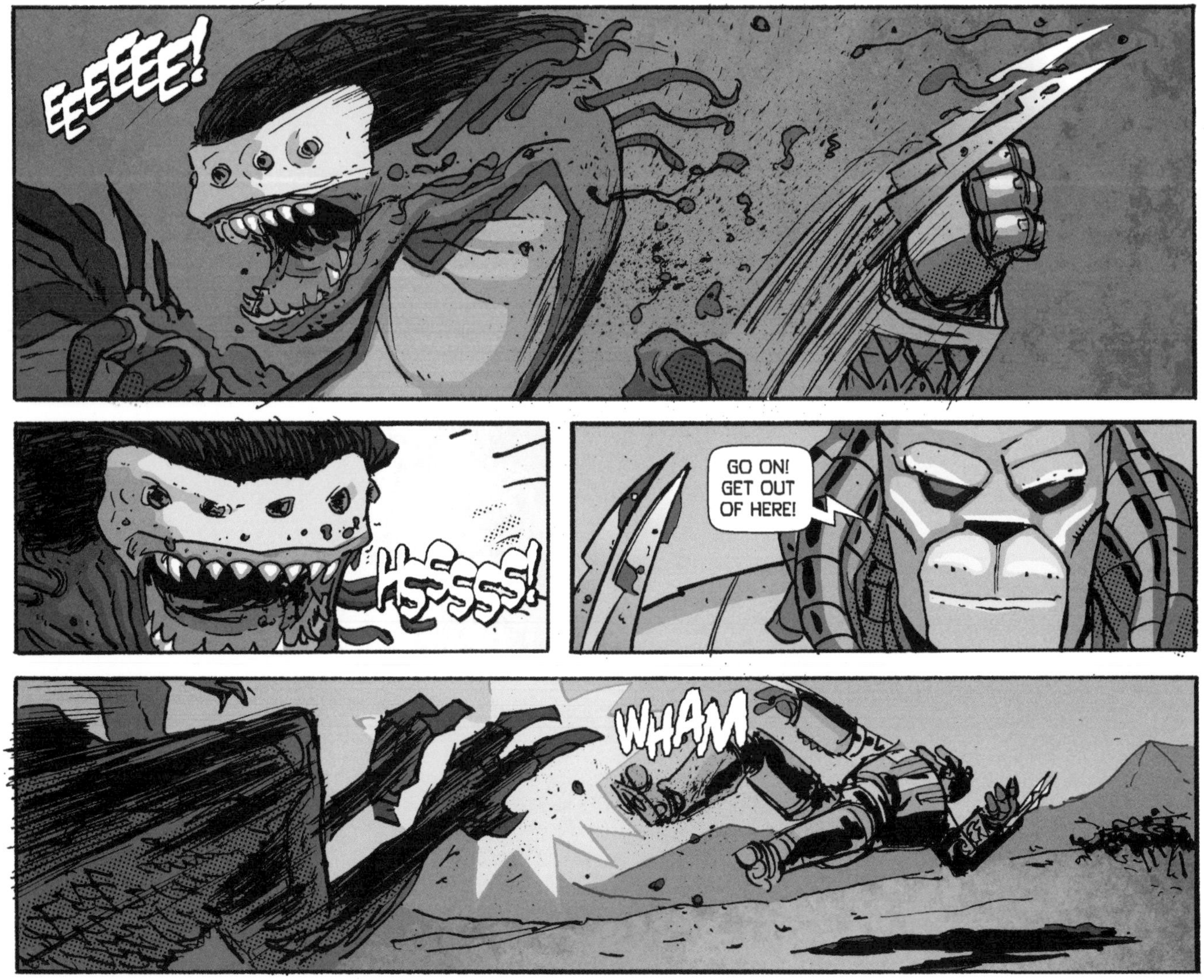
EEEEEE!
HSSSSS!
GO ON! GET OUT OF HERE!
WHAM

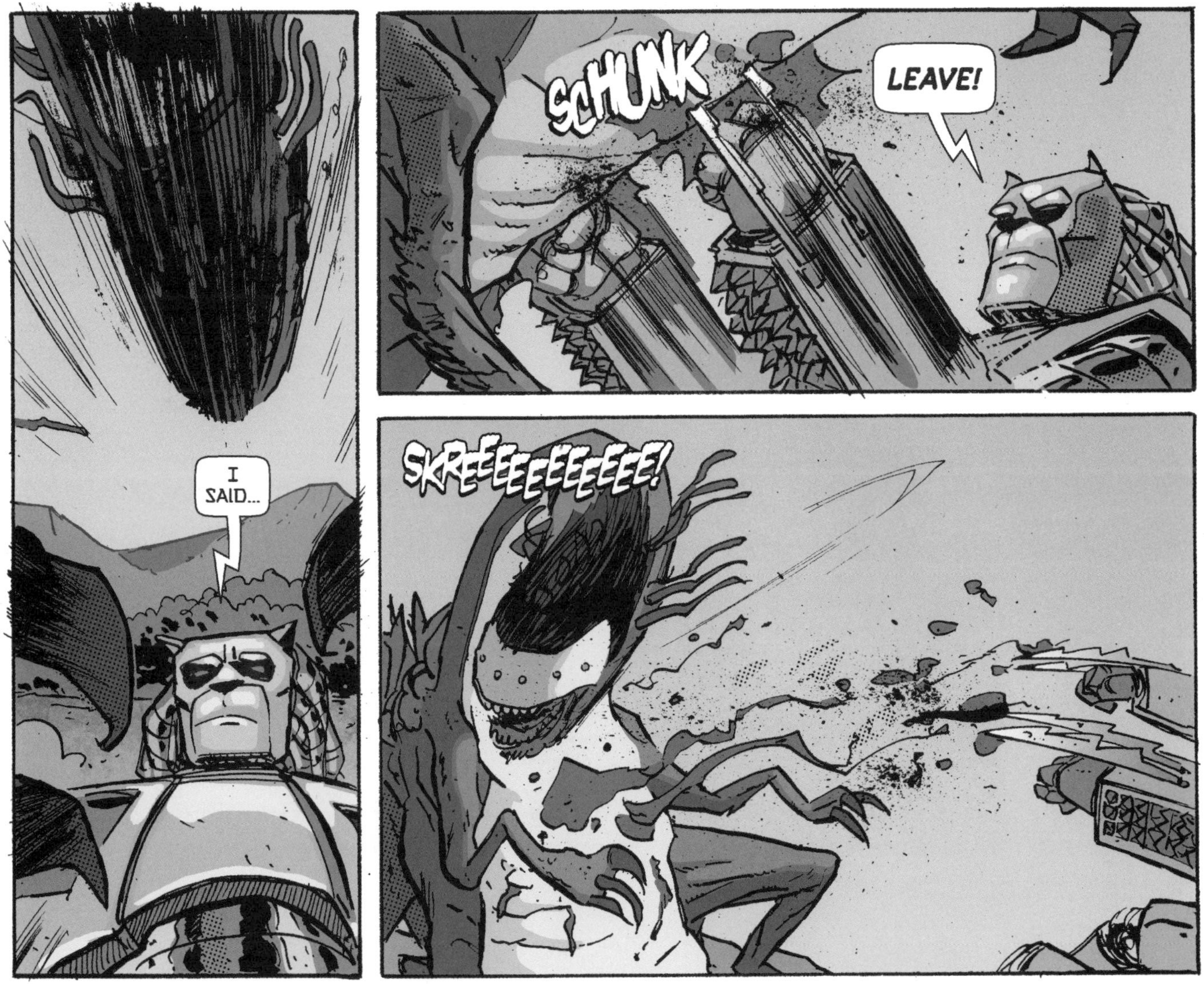
I SAID...
SCHUNK
LEAVE!
SKREEEEEEEEEEEE!

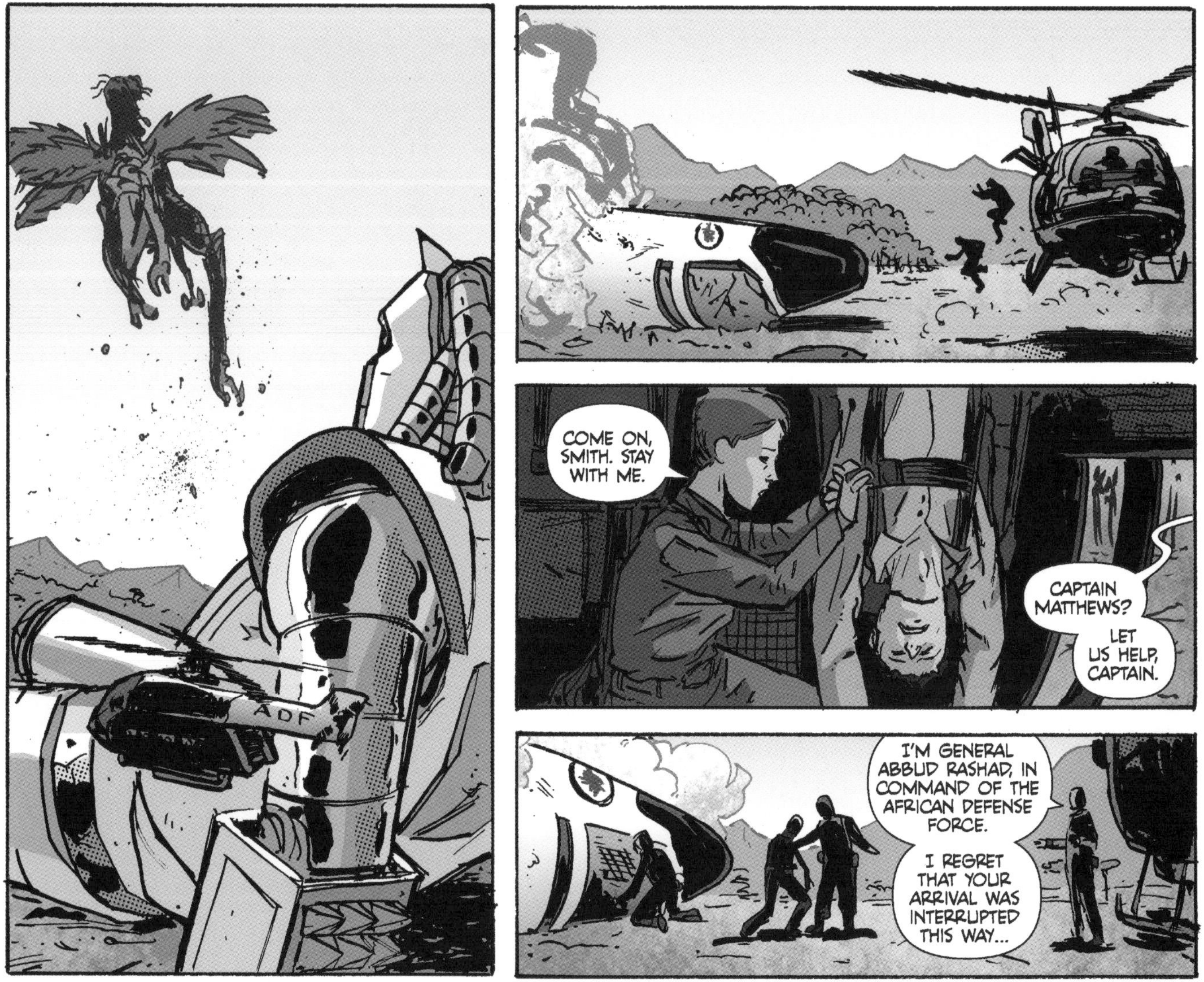
ADF
COME ON, SMITH. STAY WITH ME.
CAPTAIN MATTHEWS?
LET US HELP, CAPTAIN.
I'M GENERAL ABBUD RASHAD, IN COMMAND OF THE AFRICAN DEFENSE FORCE.
I REGRET THAT YOUR ARRIVAL WAS INTERRUPTED THIS WAY...

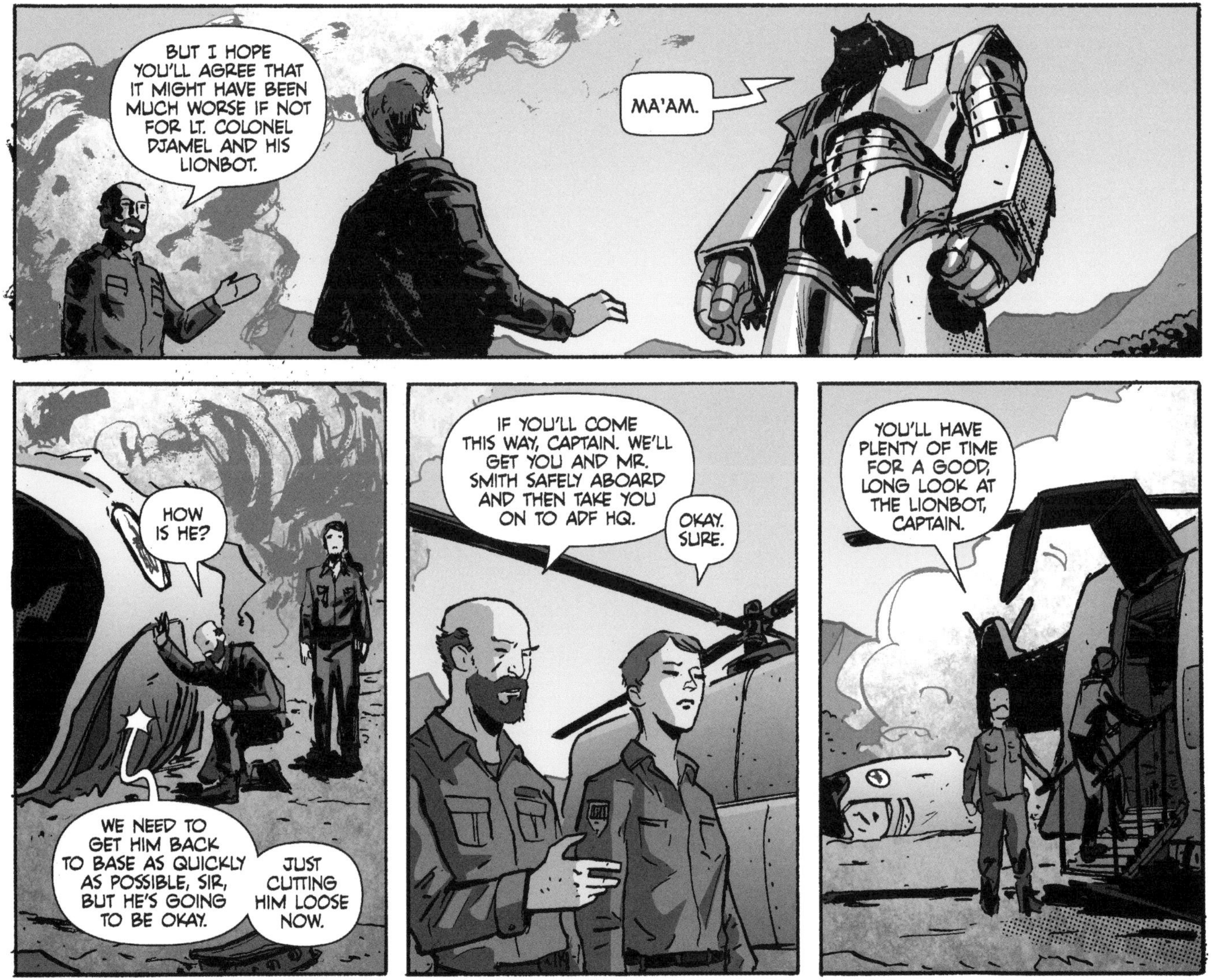
BUT I HOPE YOU'LL AGREE THAT IT MIGHT HAVE BEEN MUCH WORSE IF NOT FOR LT. COLONEL DJAMEL AND HIS LIONBOT.
MA'AM.
HOW IS HE?
WE NEED TO GET HIM BACK TO BASE AS QUICKLY AS POSSIBLE, SIR, BUT HE'S GOING TO BE OKAY.
JUST CUTTING HIM LOOSE NOW.
IF YOU'LL COME THIS WAY, CAPTAIN. WE'LL GET YOU AND MR. SMITH SAFELY ABOARD AND THEN TAKE YOU ON TO ADF HQ.
OKAY. SURE.
YOU'LL HAVE PLENTY OF TIME FOR A GOOD, LONG LOOK AT THE LIONBOT, CAPTAIN.

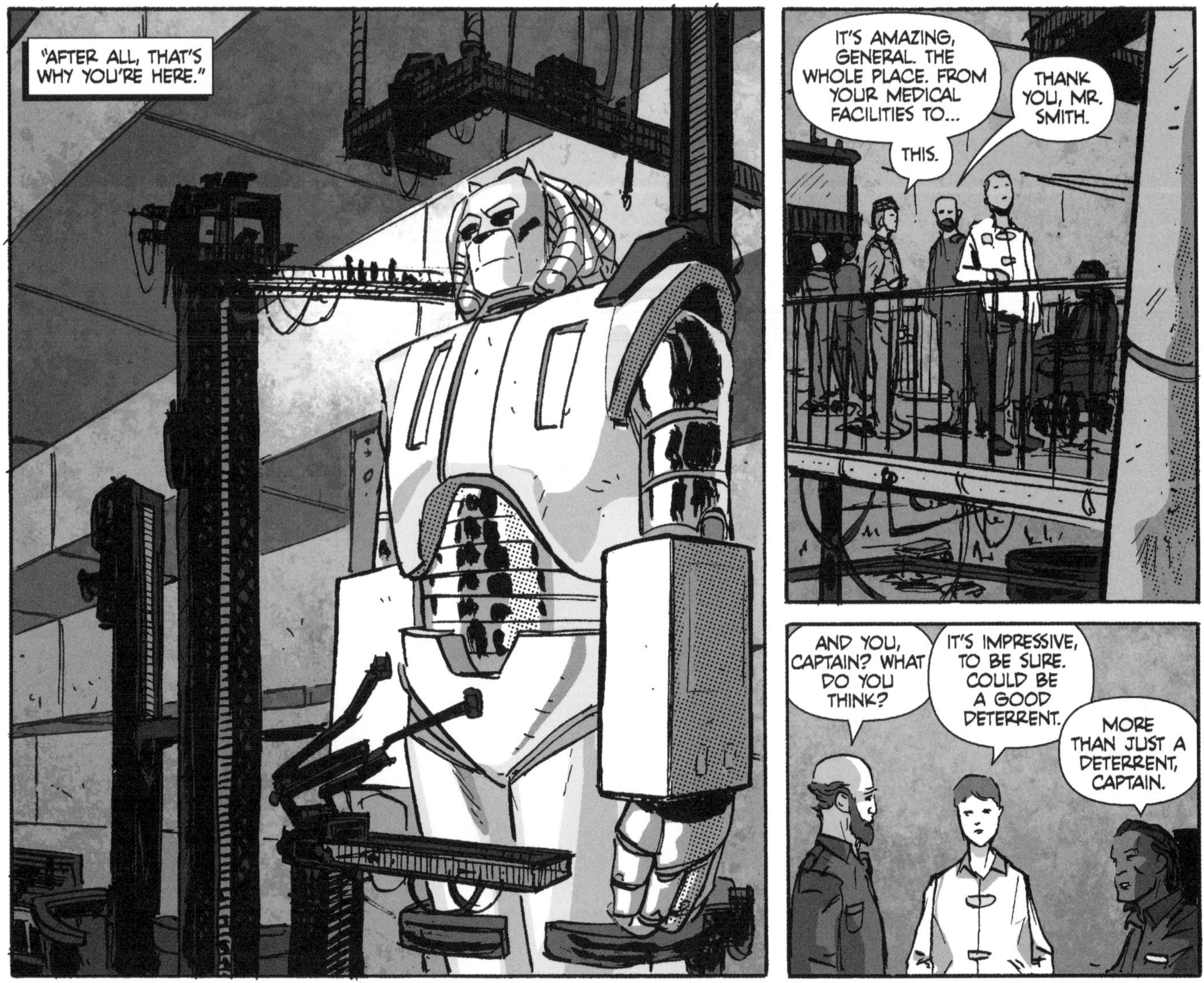
"AFTER ALL, THAT'S WHY YOU'RE HERE."
IT'S AMAZING, GENERAL. THE WHOLE PLACE. FROM YOUR MEDICAL FACILITIES TO...
THIS.
THANK YOU, MR. SMITH.
AND YOU, CAPTAIN? WHAT DO YOU THINK?
IT'S IMPRESSIVE, TO BE SURE. COULD BE A GOOD DETERRENT.
MORE THAN JUST A DETERRENT, CAPTAIN.

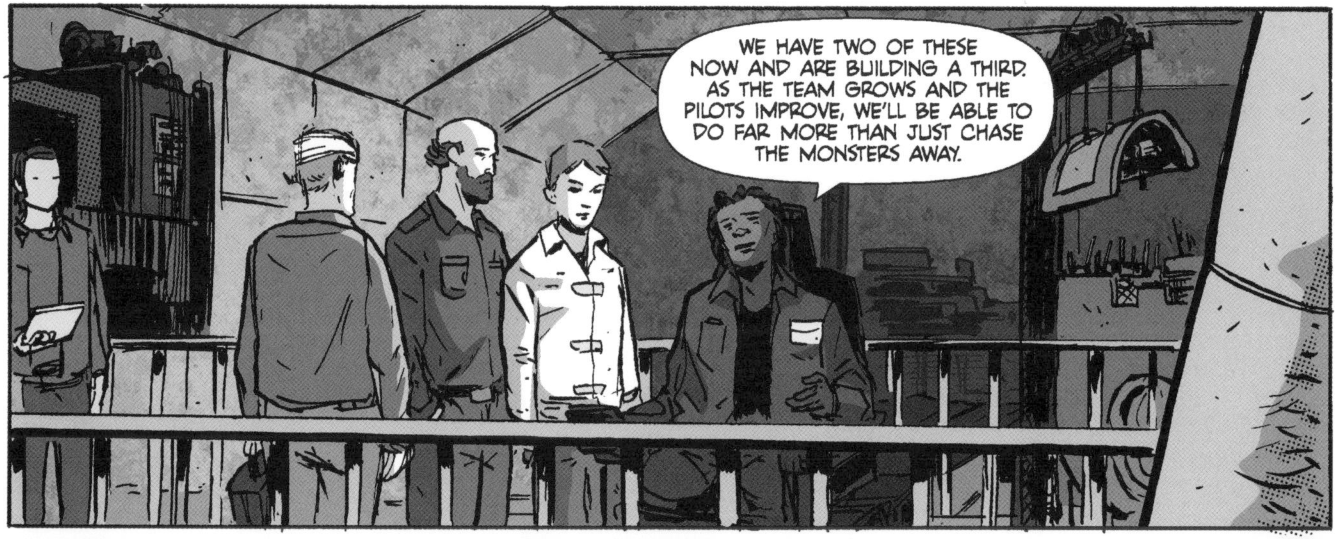
WE HAVE TWO OF THESE NOW AND ARE BUILDING A THIRD. AS THE TEAM GROWS AND THE PILOTS IMPROVE, WE'LL BE ABLE TO DO FAR MORE THAN JUST CHASE THE MONSTERS AWAY.

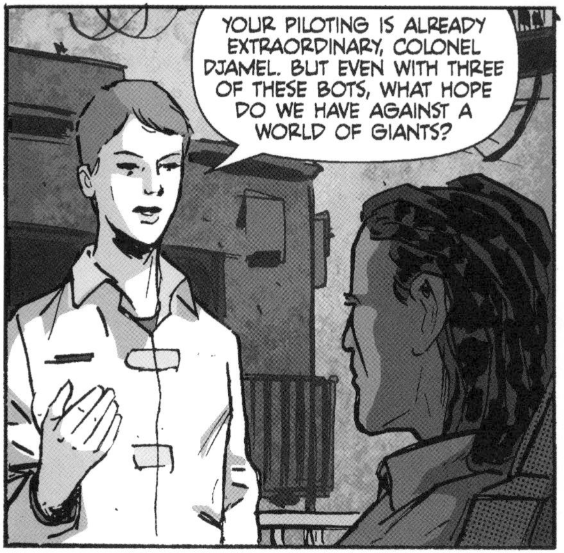
YOUR PILOTING IS ALREADY EXTRAORDINARY, COLONEL DJAMEL. BUT EVEN WITH THREE OF THESE BOTS, WHAT HOPE DO WE HAVE AGAINST A WORLD OF GIANTS?

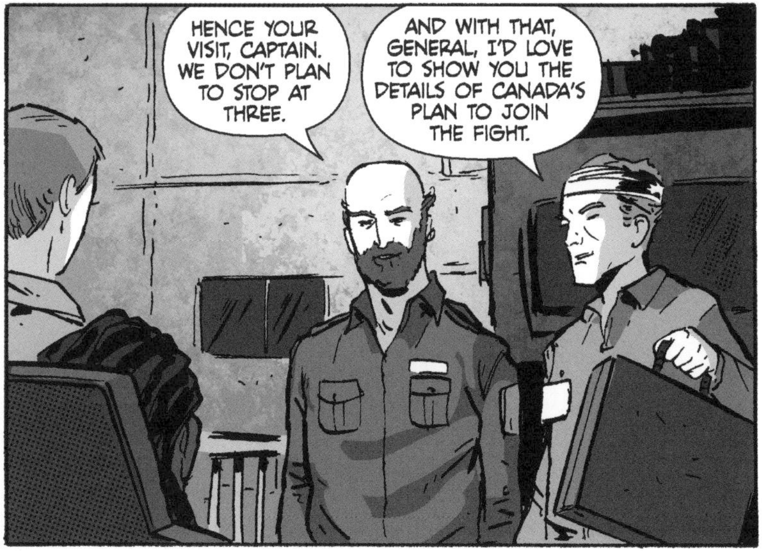
HENCE YOUR VISIT, CAPTAIN. WE DON'T PLAN TO STOP AT THREE.
AND WITH THAT, GENERAL, I'D LOVE TO SHOW YOU THE DETAILS OF CANADA'S PLAN TO JOIN THE FIGHT.

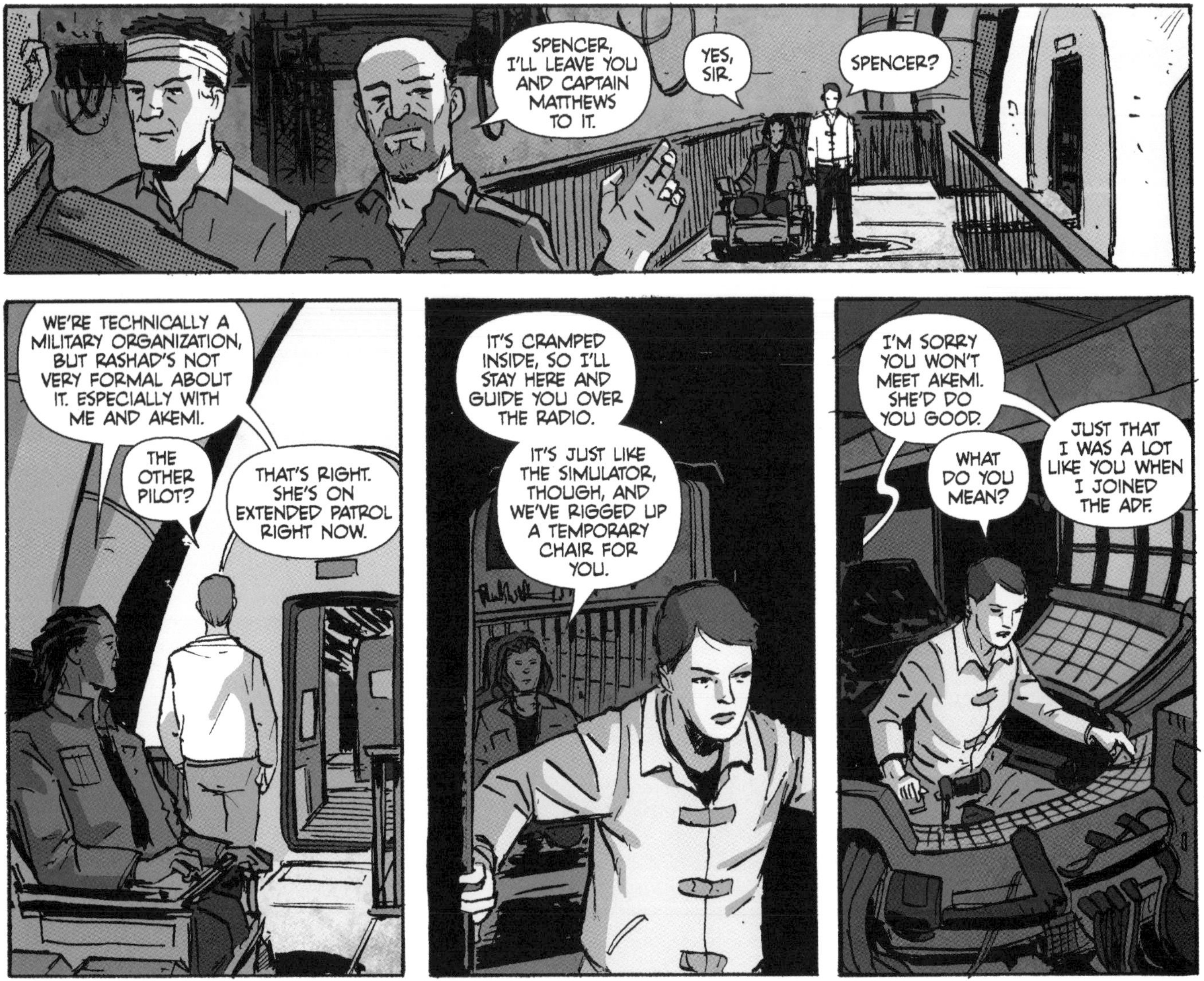

SPENCER, I'LL LEAVE YOU AND CAPTAIN MATTHEWS TO IT.
YES, SIR.
SPENCER?
WE'RE TECHNICALLY A MILITARY ORGANIZATION, BUT RASHAD'S NOT VERY FORMAL ABOUT IT. ESPECIALLY WITH ME AND AKEMI.
THE OTHER PILOT?
THAT'S RIGHT. SHE'S ON EXTENDED PATROL RIGHT NOW.
IT'S CRAMPED INSIDE, SO I'LL STAY HERE AND GUIDE YOU OVER THE RADIO.
IT'S JUST LIKE THE SIMULATOR, THOUGH, AND WE'VE RIGGED UP A TEMPORARY CHAIR FOR YOU.
I'M SORRY YOU WON'T MEET AKEMI. SHE'D DO YOU GOOD.
WHAT DO YOU MEAN?
JUST THAT I WAS A LOT LIKE YOU WHEN I JOINED THE ADF.

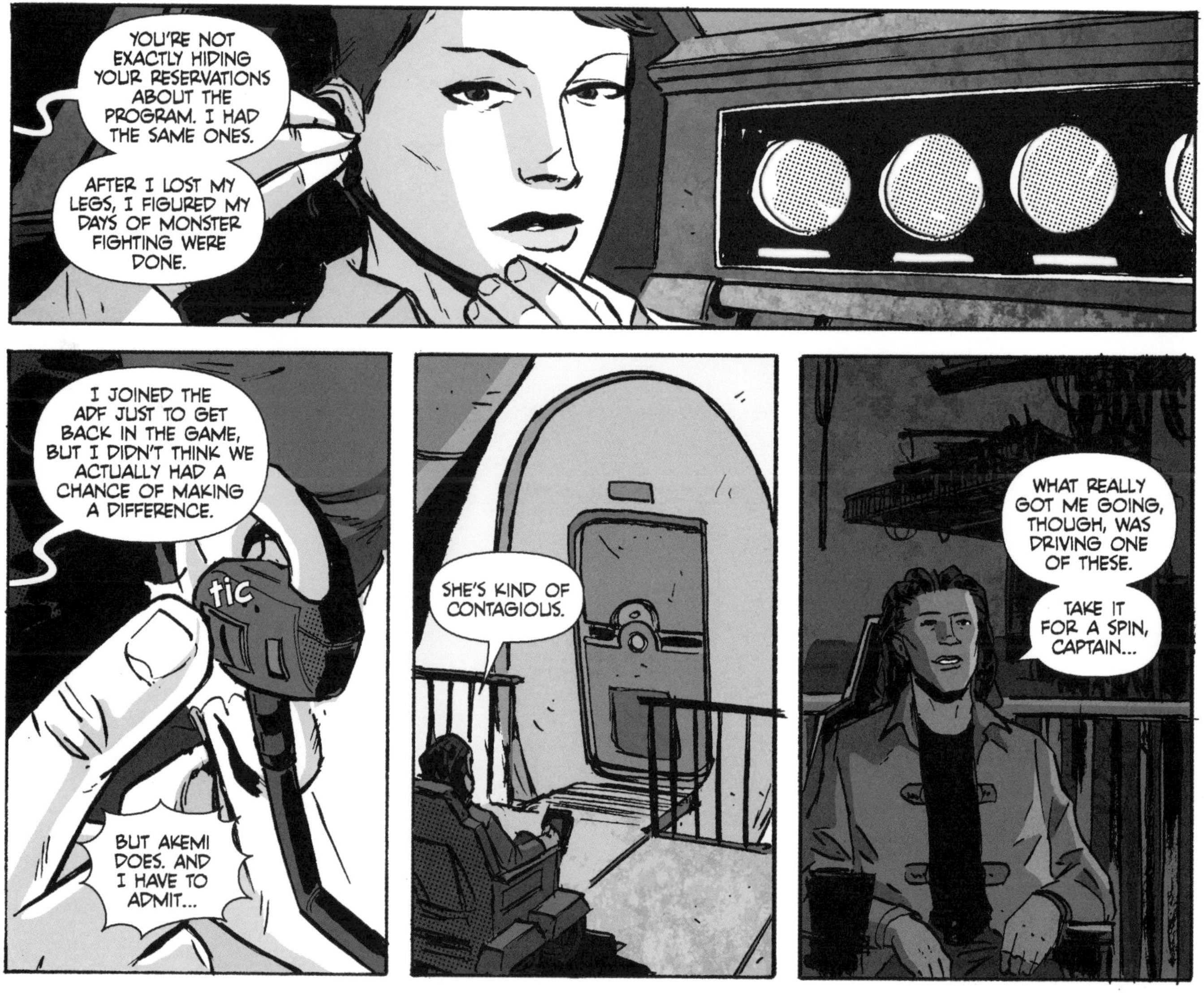
YOU'RE NOT EXACTLY HIDING YOUR RESERVATIONS ABOUT THE PROGRAM. I HAD THE SAME ONES.
AFTER I LOST MY LEGS, I FIGURED MY DAYS OF MONSTER FIGHTING WERE DONE.
I JOINED THE ADF JUST TO GET BACK IN THE GAME, BUT I DIDN'T THINK WE ACTUALLY HAD A CHANCE OF MAKING A DIFFERENCE.
tic
BUT AKEMI DOES. AND I HAVE TO ADMIT...
SHE'S KIND OF CONTAGIOUS.
WHAT REALLY GOT ME GOING, THOUGH, WAS DRIVING ONE OF THESE.
TAKE IT FOR A SPIN, CAPTAIN...

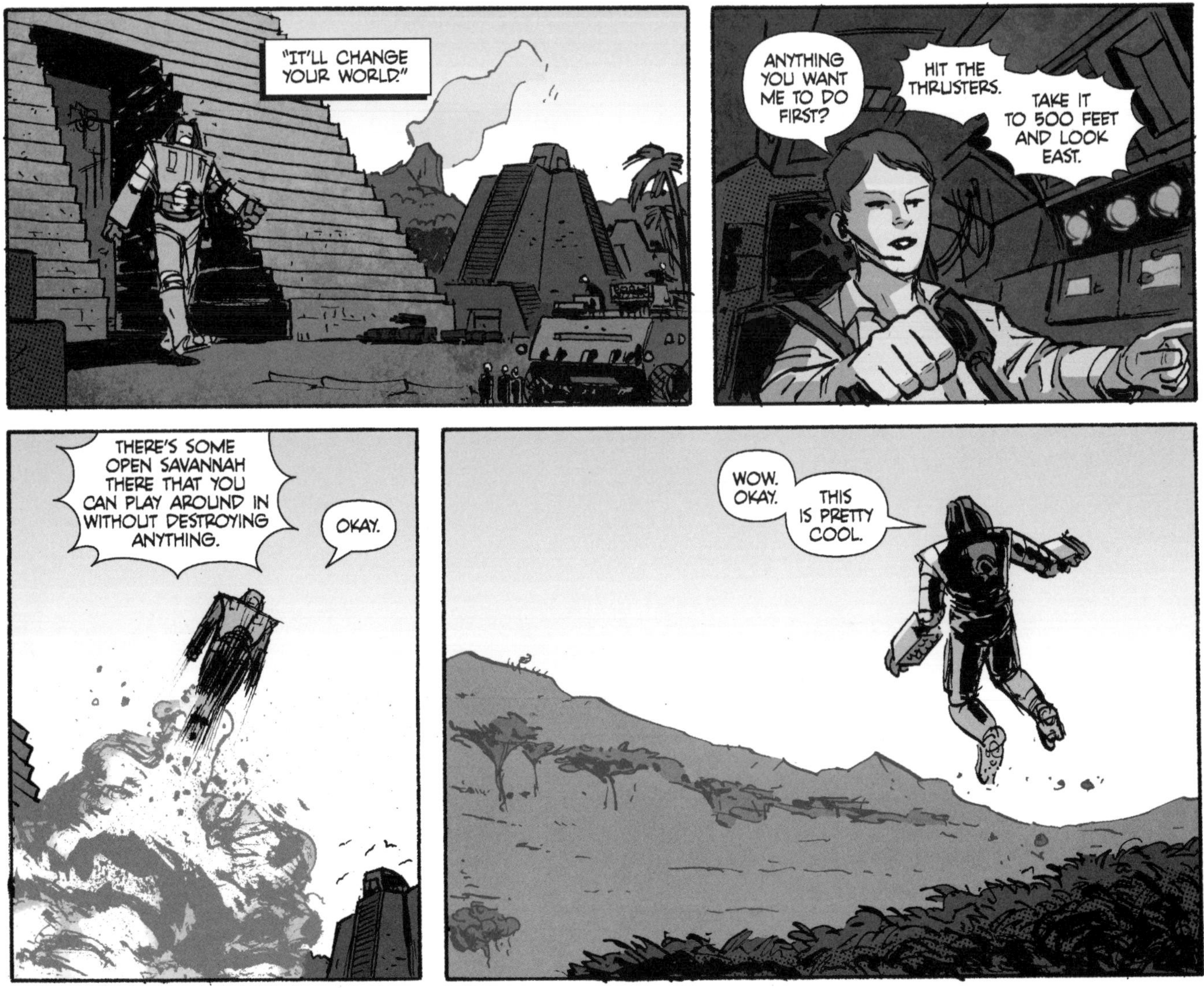
"IT'LL CHANGE YOUR WORLD."
ANYTHING YOU WANT ME TO DO FIRST?
HIT THE THRUSTERS.
TAKE IT TO 500 FEET AND LOOK EAST.
THERE'S SOME OPEN SAVANNAH THERE THAT YOU CAN PLAY AROUND IN WITHOUT DESTROYING ANYTHING.
OKAY.
WOW. OKAY.
THIS IS PRETTY COOL.

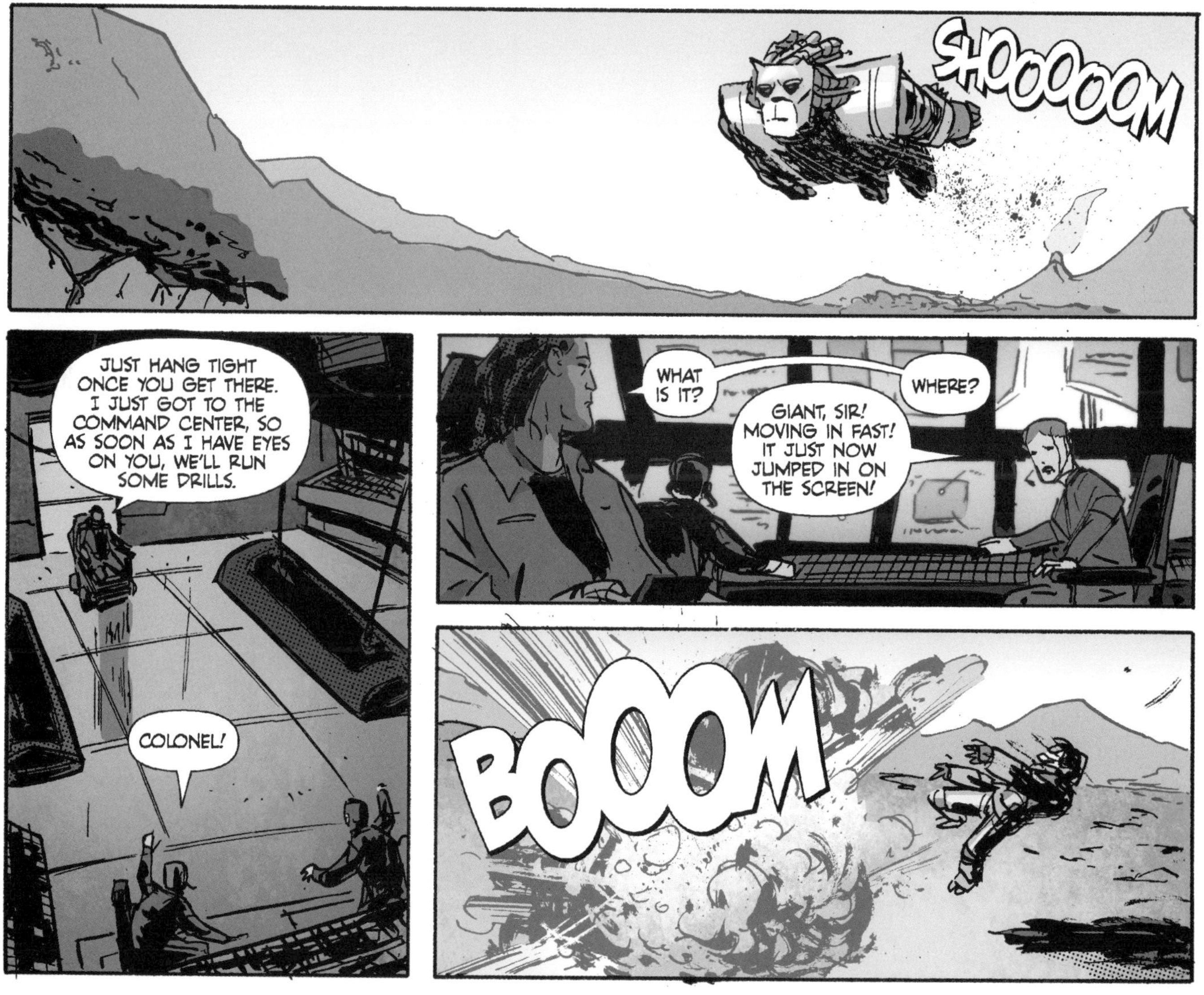
SHOOOOOM
JUST HANG TIGHT ONCE YOU GET THERE. I JUST GOT TO THE COMMAND CENTER, SO AS SOON AS I HAVE EYES ON YOU, WE'LL RUN SOME DRILLS.
COLONEL!
WHAT IS IT?
WHERE?
GIANT, SIR! MOVING IN FAST! IT JUST NOW JUMPED IN ON THE SCREEN!
BOOOOM

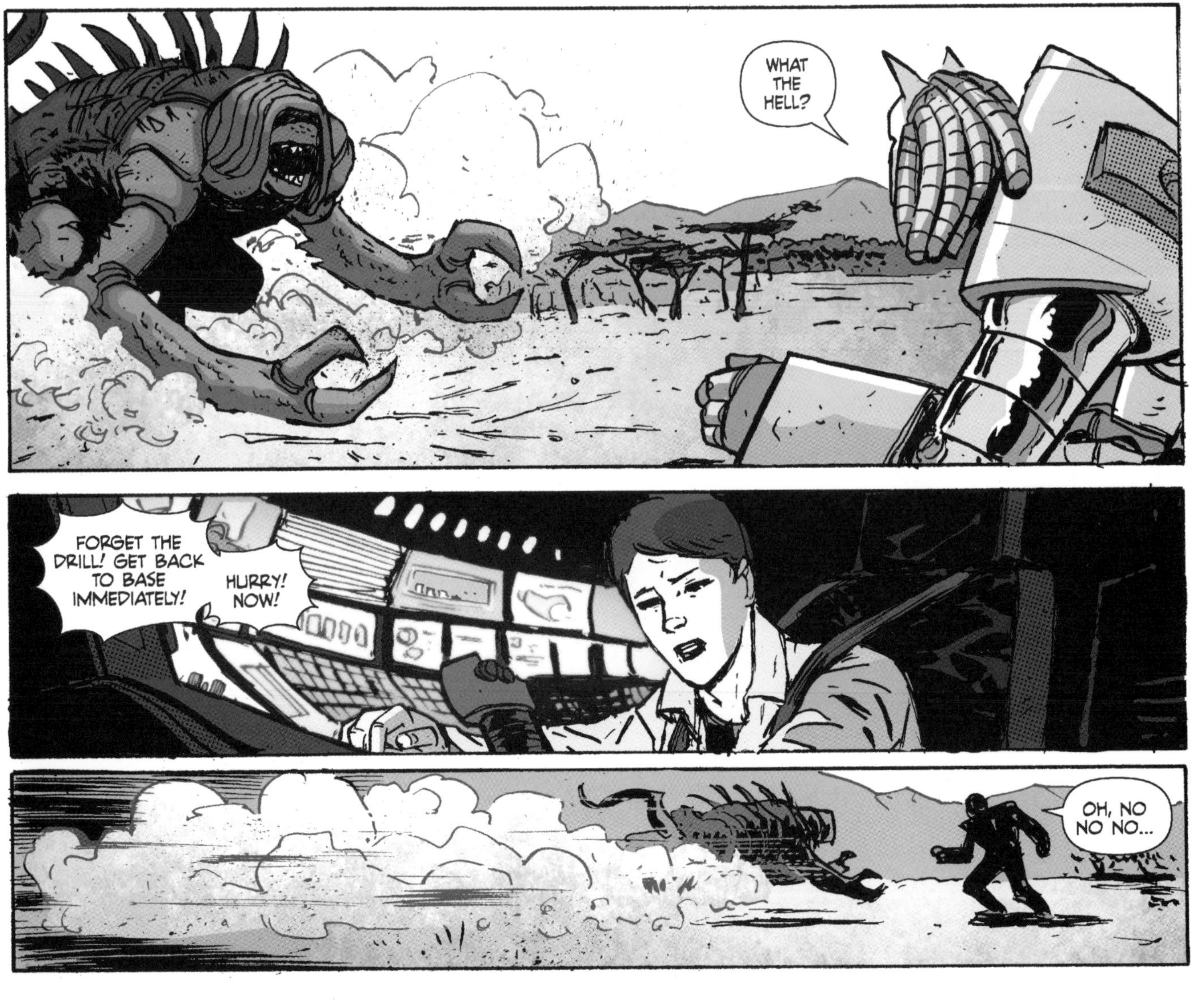
WHAT THE HELL?
FORGET THE DRILL! GET BACK TO BASE IMMEDIATELY!
HURRY! NOW!
OH, NO NO NO...

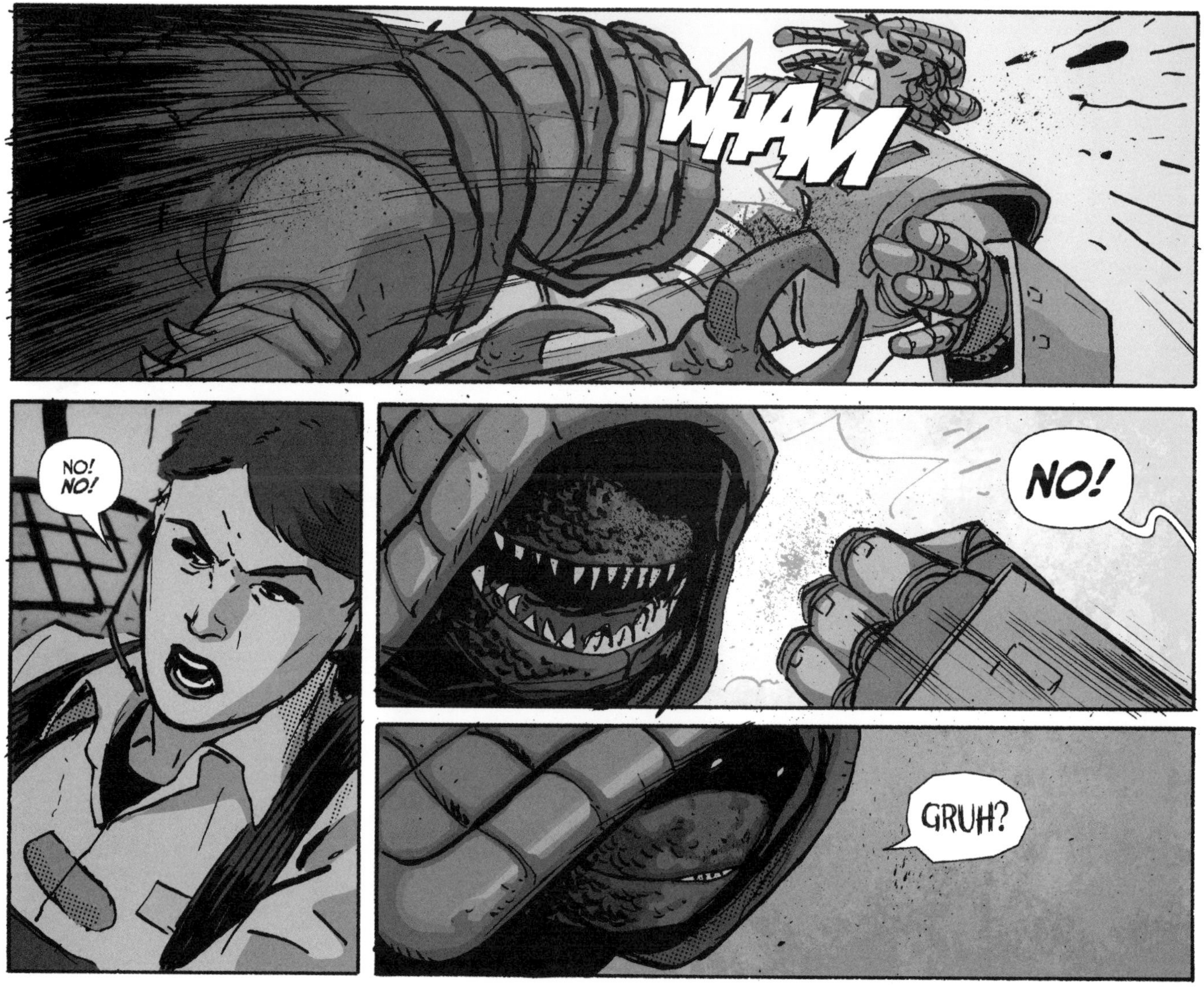
WHAM
NO! NO!
NO!
GRUH?

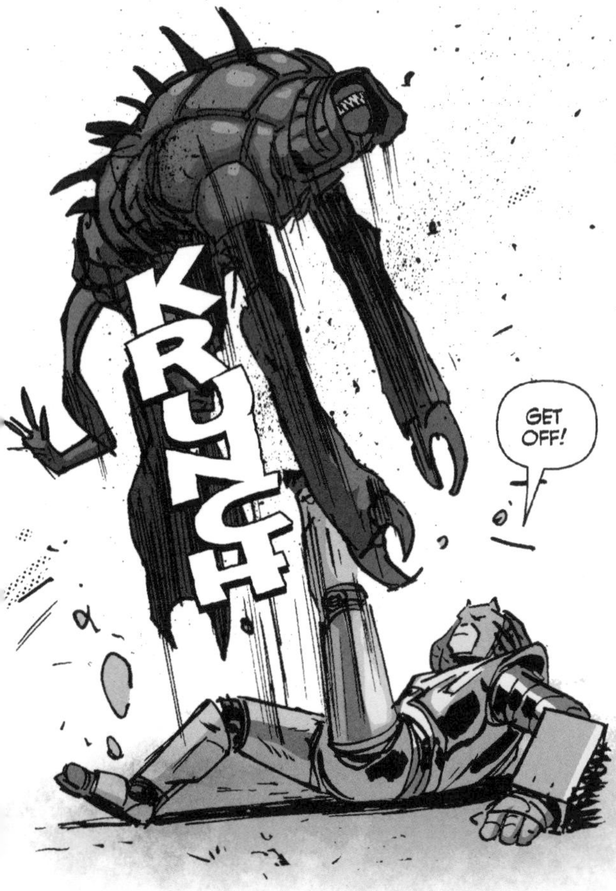
KRUNCH
GET OFF!

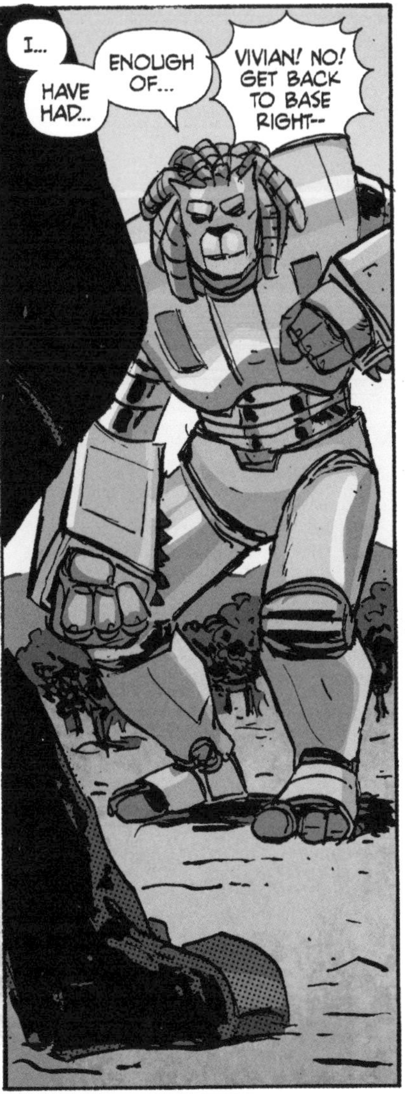
I...
HAVE HAD...
ENOUGH OF...
VIVIAN! NO! GET BACK TO BASE RIGHT--

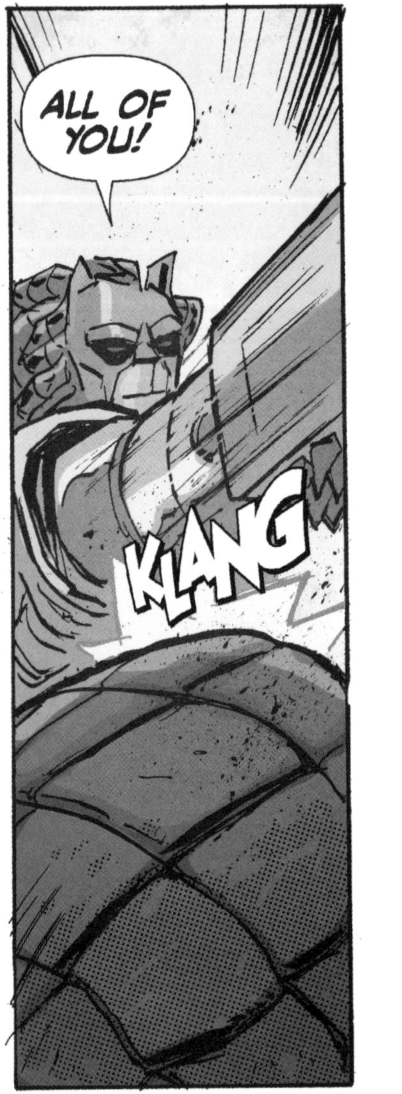
ALL OF YOU!
KLANG

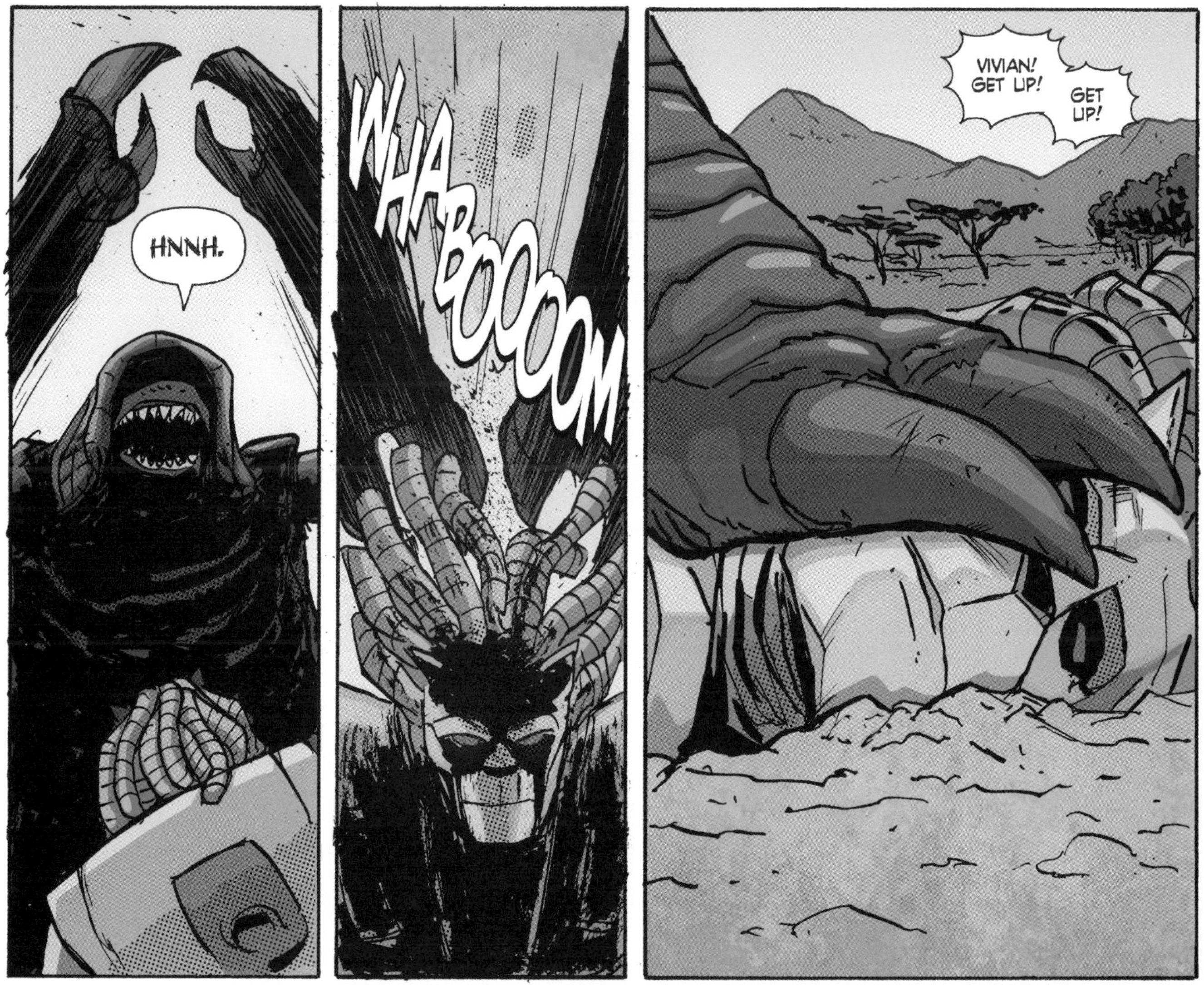
HNNH.
WHABOOOOM
VIVIAN! GET UP!
GET UP!

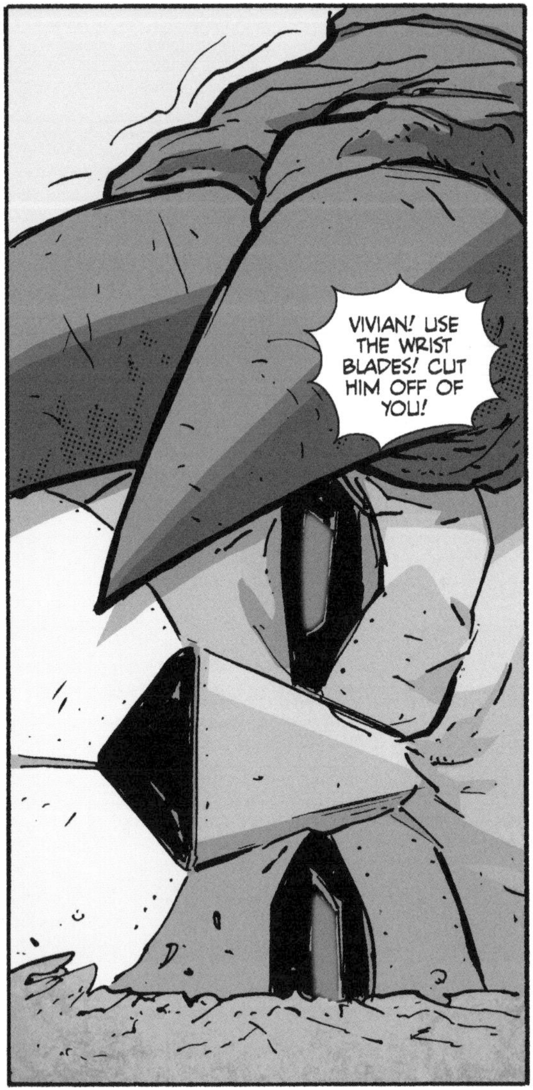
VIVIAN! USE THE WRIST BLADES! CUT HIM OFF OF YOU!

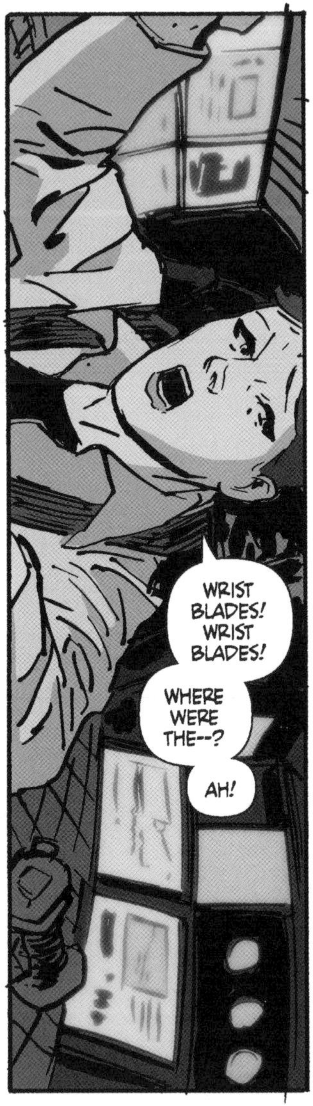
WRIST BLADES! WRIST BLADES!
WHERE WERE THE--?
AH!

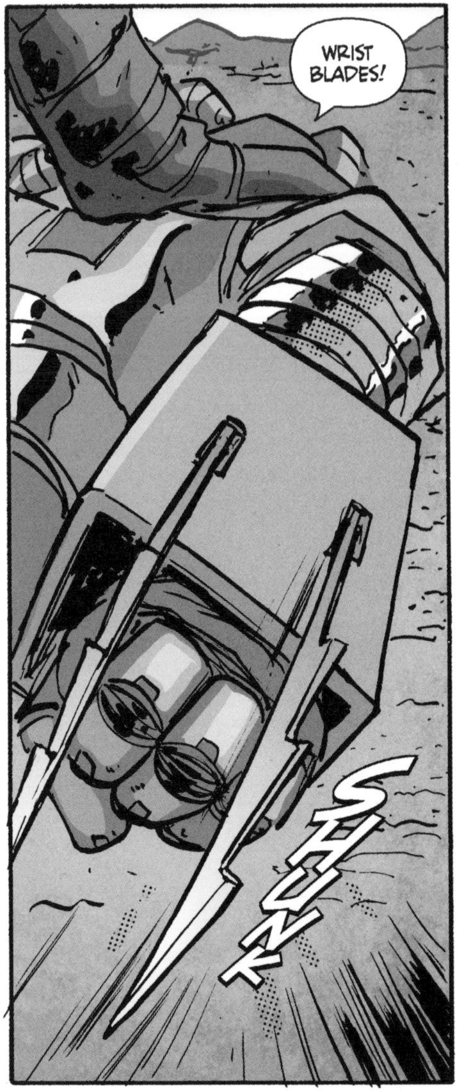
WRIST BLADES!
SHUNK

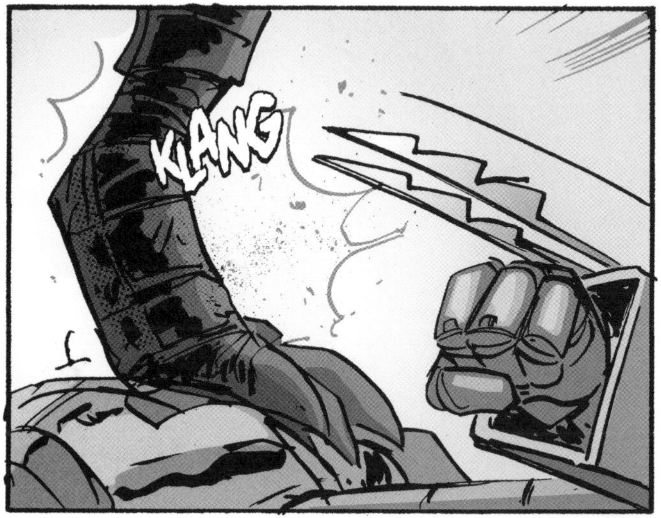
KLANG

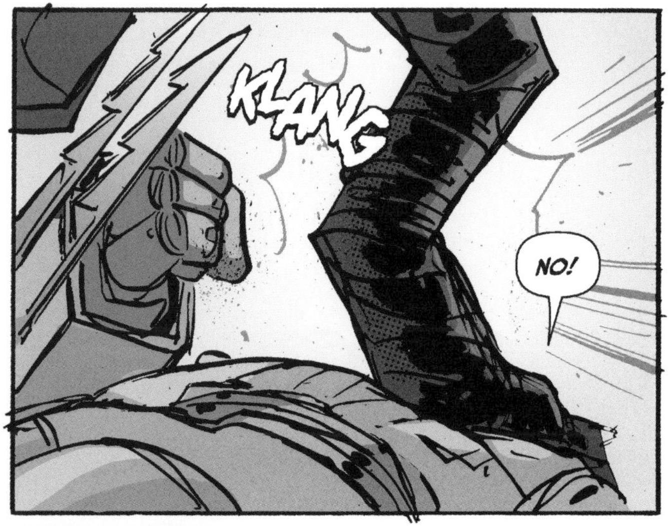
KLANG
NO!

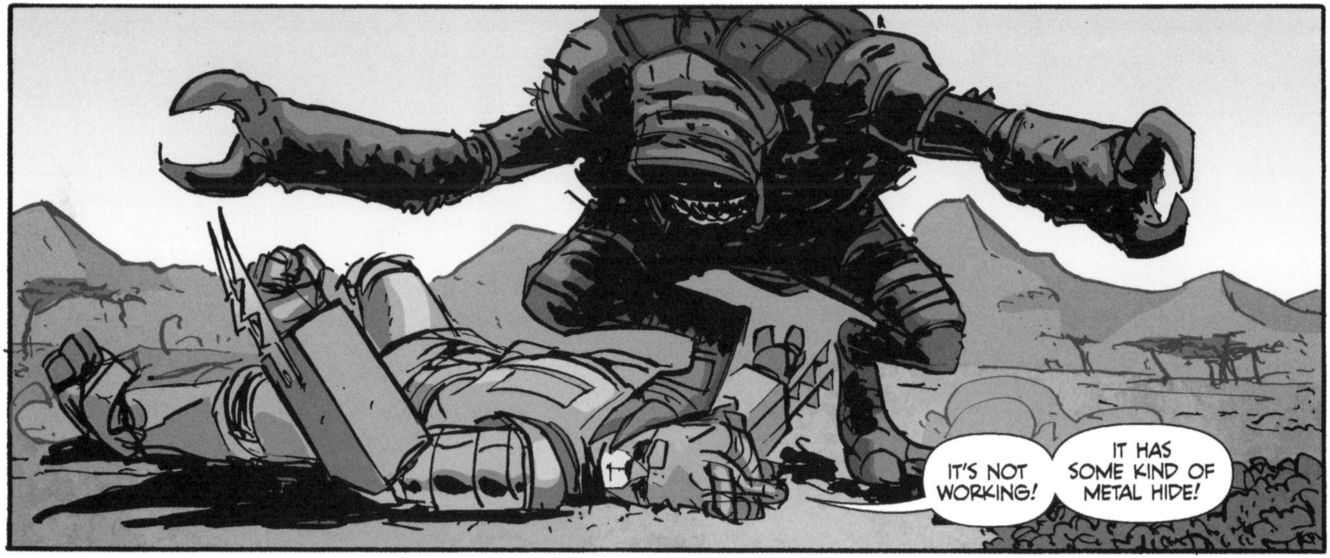
IT'S NOT WORKING!
IT HAS SOME KIND OF METAL HIDE!

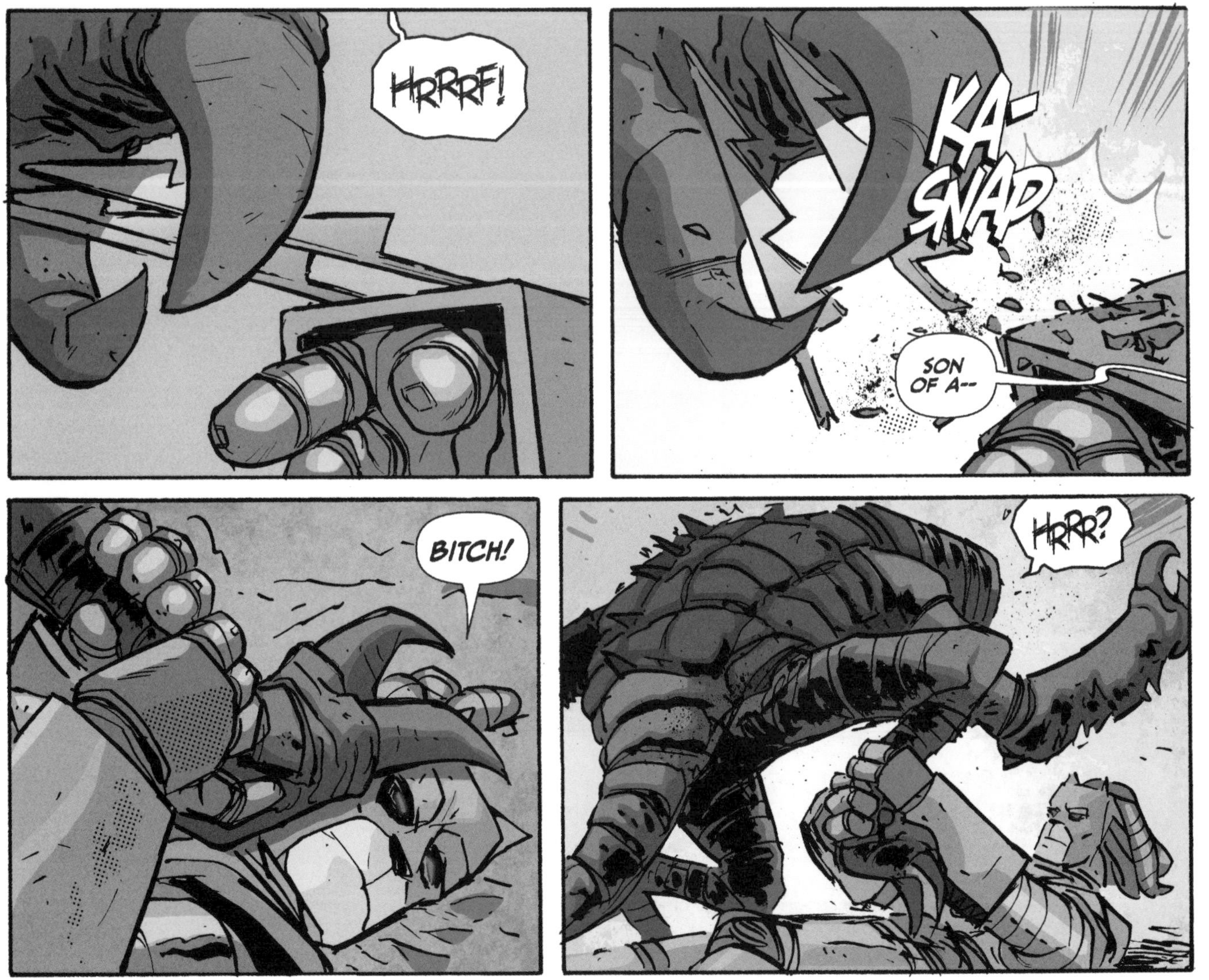
HRRRF!
KA-SNAP
SON OF A--
BITCH!
HRRR?

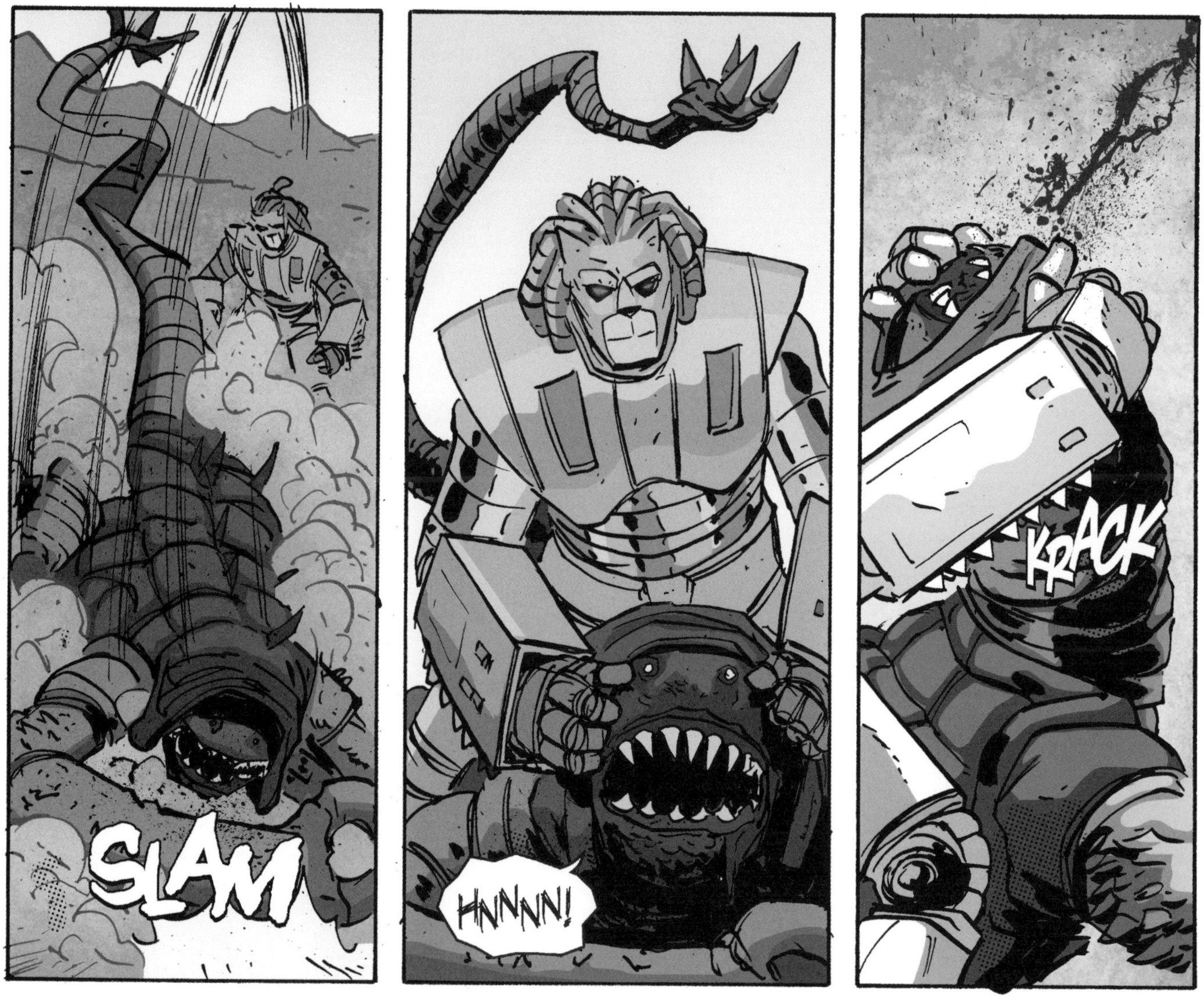
SLAM
HNNNN!
KRACK

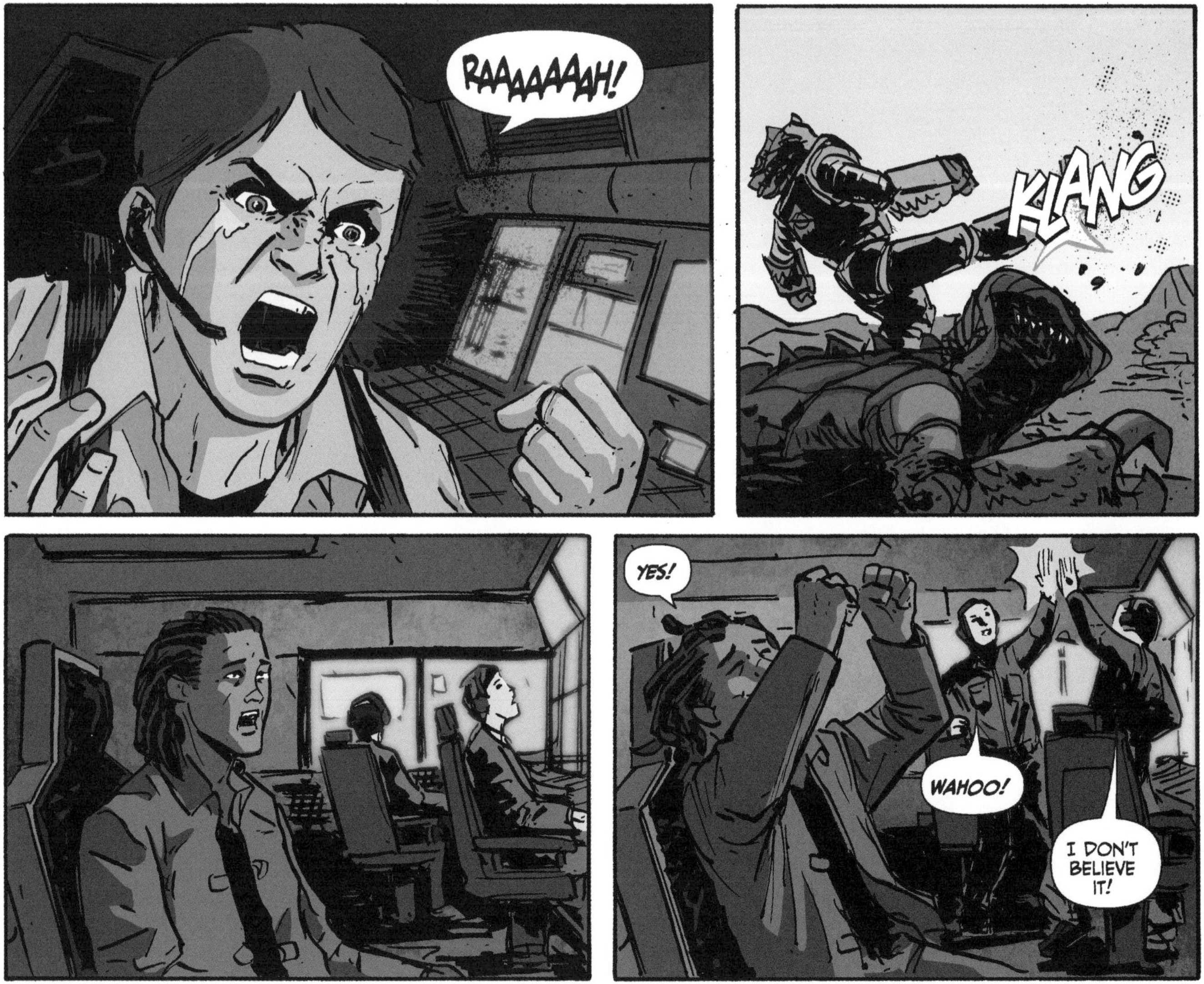
RAAAAAAAH!
KLANG
YES!
WAHOO!
I DON'T BELIEVE IT!

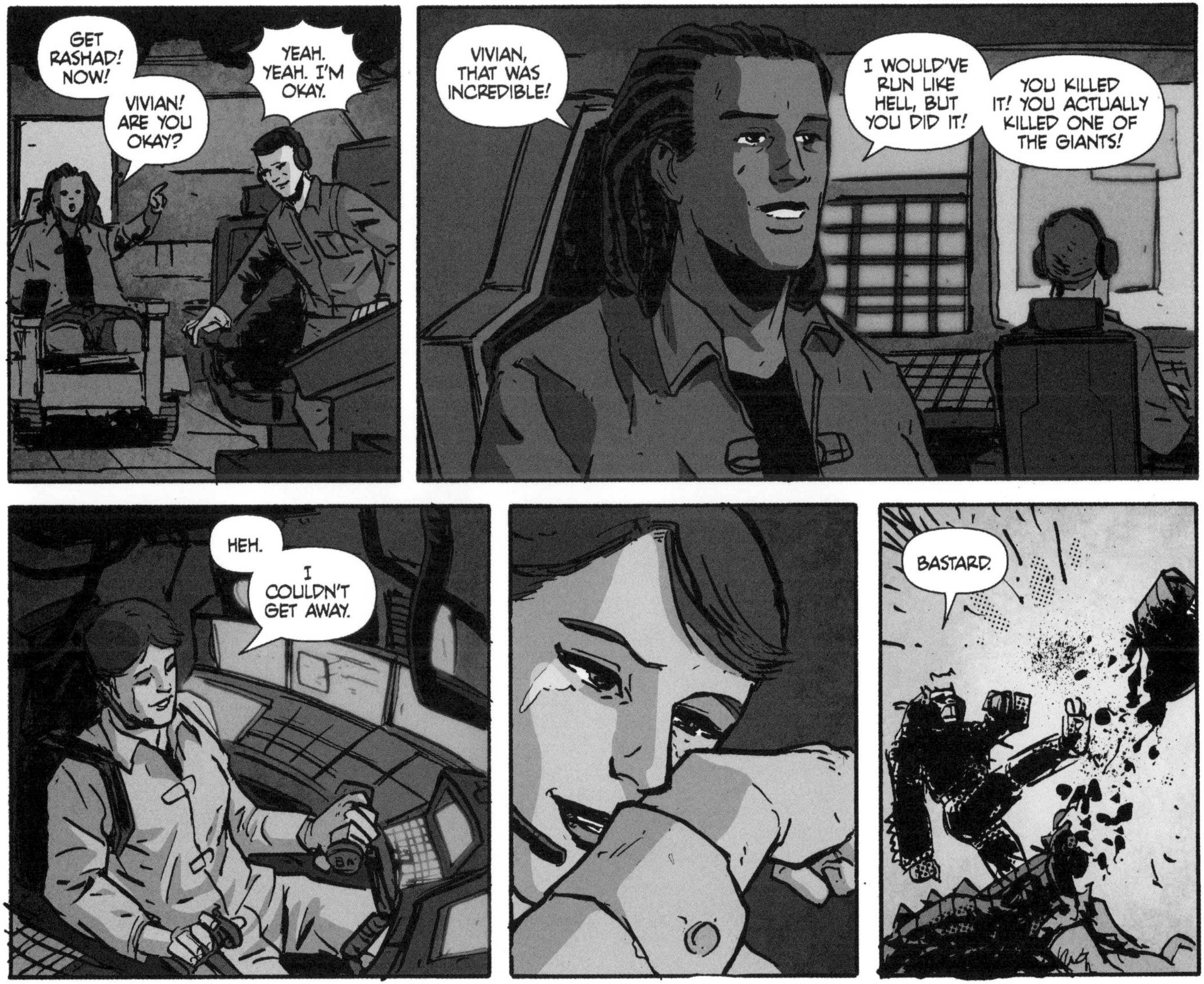
GET RASHAD! NOW!
VIVIAN! ARE YOU OKAY?
YEAH. YEAH. I'M OKAY.
VIVIAN, THAT WAS INCREDIBLE!
I WOULD'VE RUN LIKE HELL, BUT YOU DID IT!
YOU KILLED IT! YOU ACTUALLY KILLED ONE OF THE GIANTS!
HEH.
I COULDN'T GET AWAY.
BASTARD.

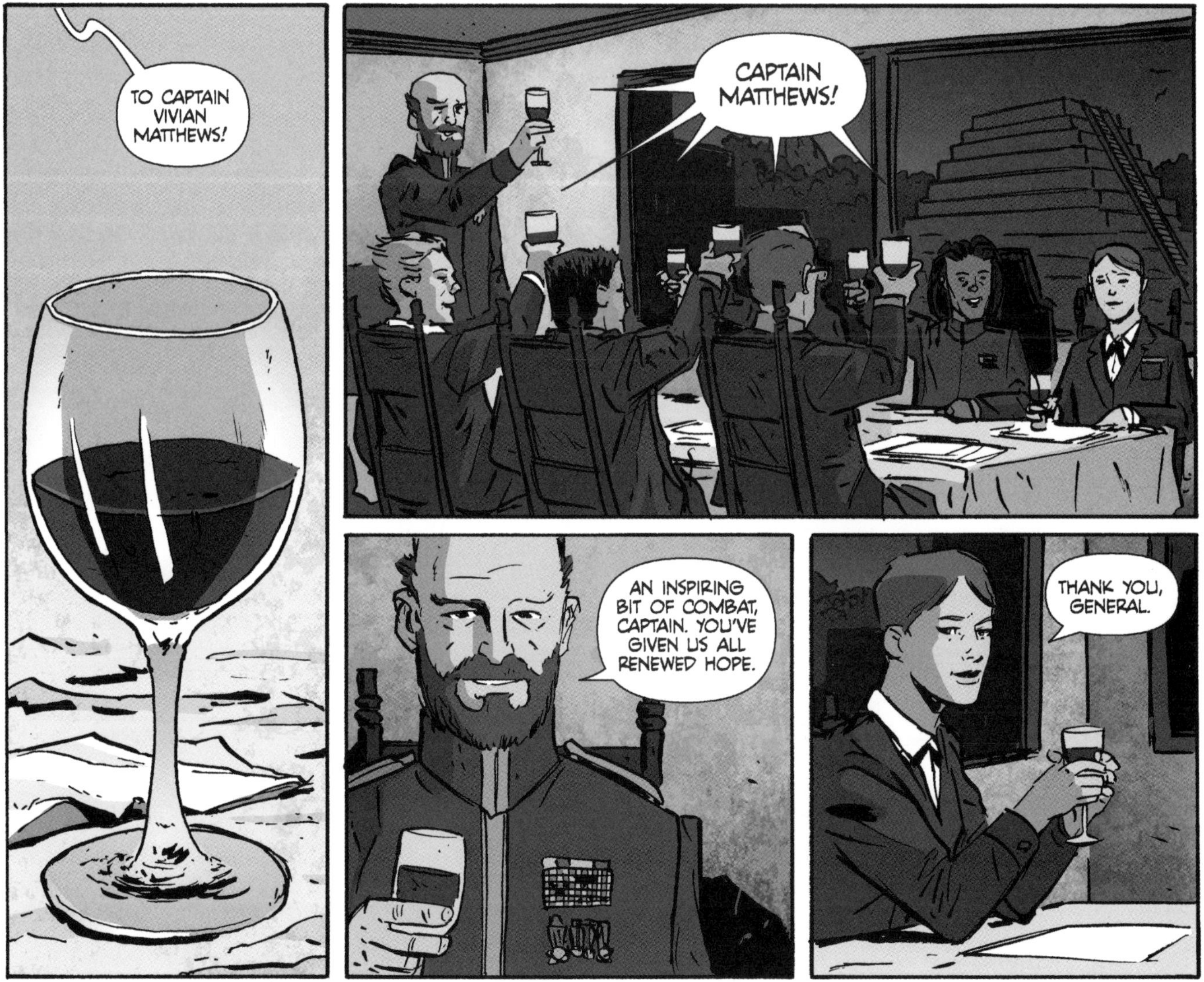
TO CAPTAIN VIVIAN MATTHEWS!
CAPTAIN MATTHEWS!
AN INSPIRING BIT OF COMBAT, CAPTAIN. YOU'VE GIVEN US ALL RENEWED HOPE.
THANK YOU, GENERAL.

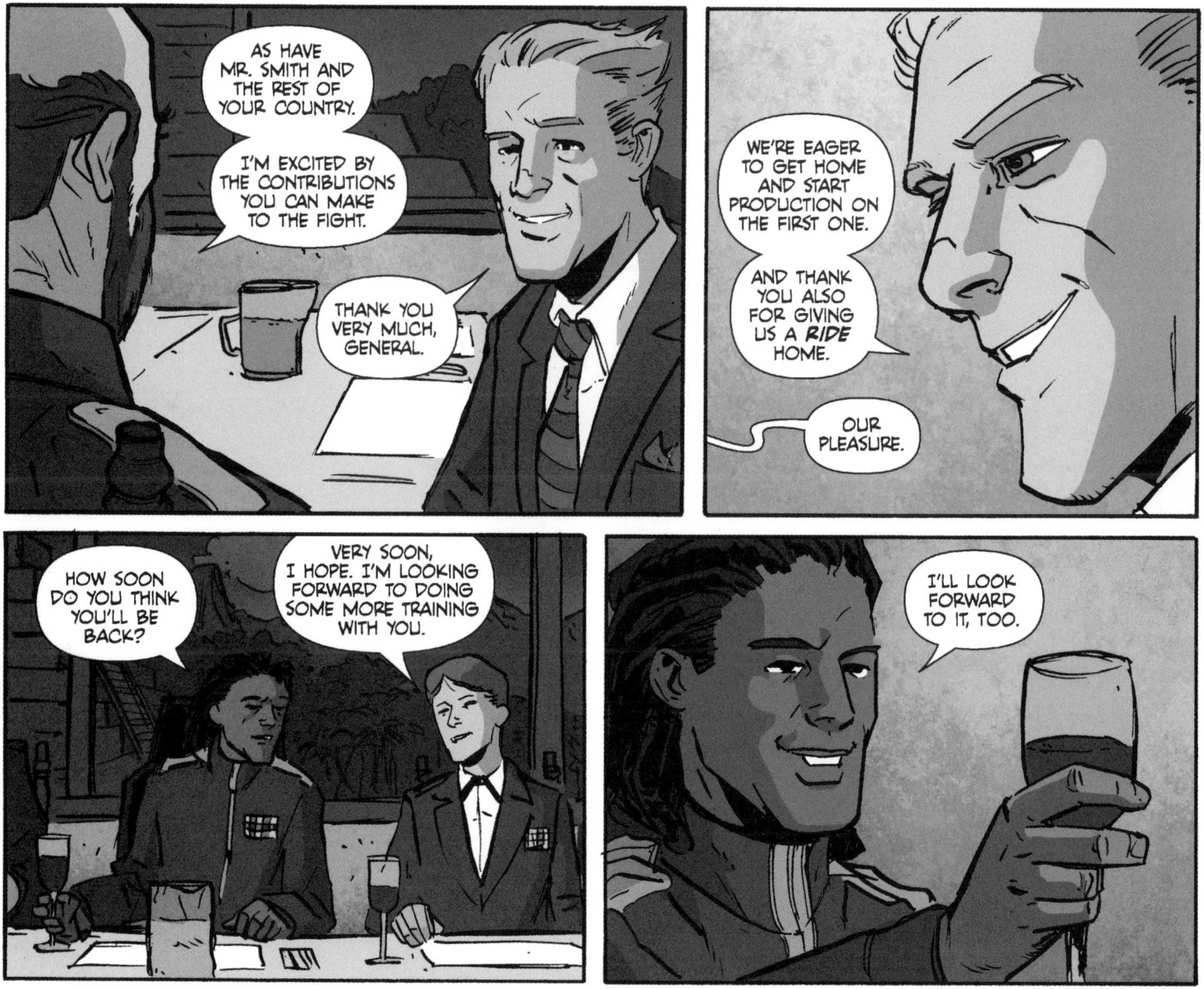
AS HAVE MR. SMITH AND THE REST OF YOUR COUNTRY.
I'M EXCITED BY THE CONTRIBUTIONS YOU CAN MAKE TO THE FIGHT.
THANK YOU VERY MUCH, GENERAL.
WE'RE EAGER TO GET HOME AND START PRODUCTION ON THE FIRST ONE.
AND THANK YOU ALSO FOR GIVING US A ***RIDE*** HOME.
OUR PLEASURE.
HOW SOON DO YOU THINK YOU'LL BE BACK?
VERY SOON, I HOPE. I'M LOOKING FORWARD TO DOING SOME MORE TRAINING WITH YOU.
I'LL LOOK FORWARD TO IT, TOO.

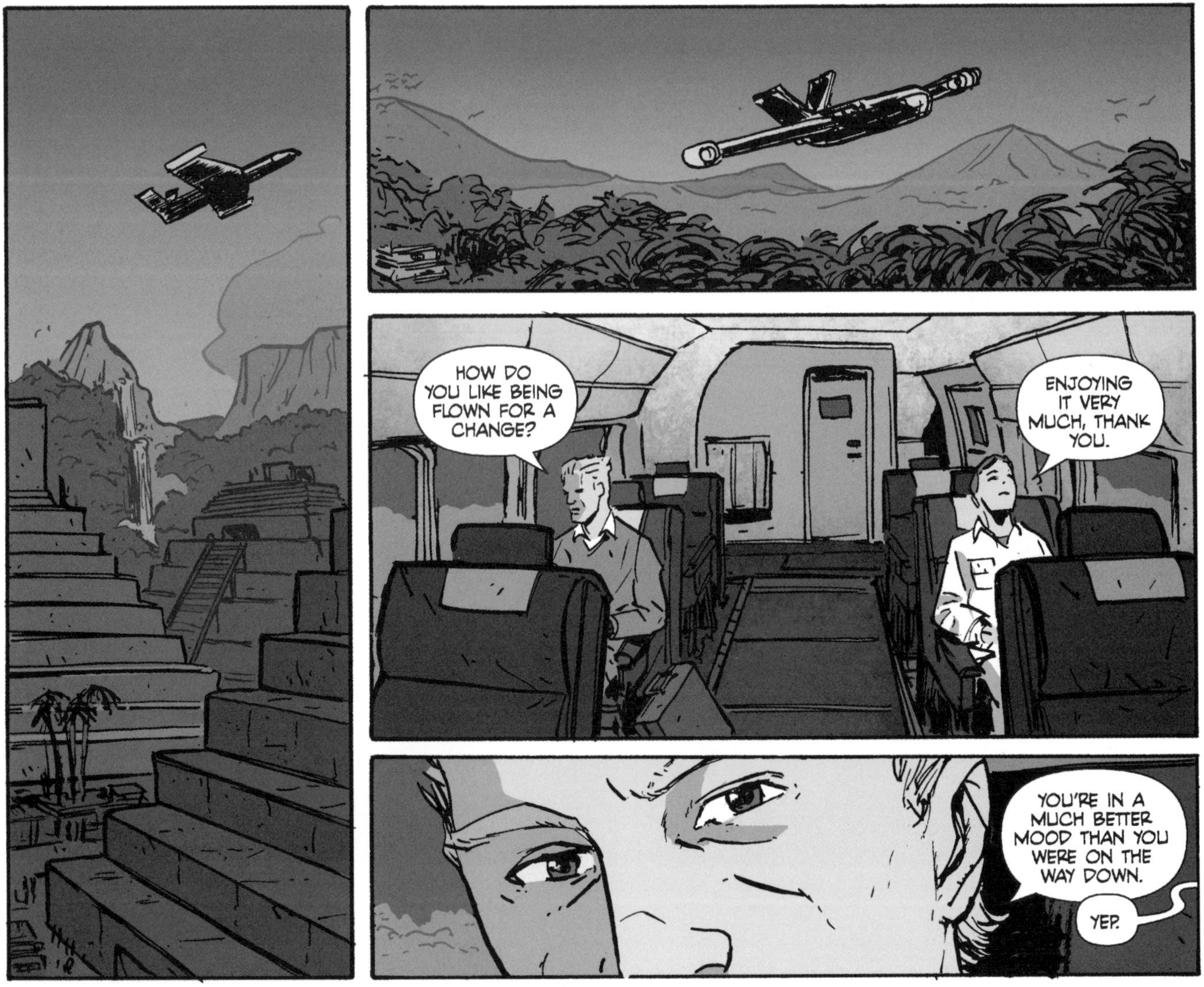
HOW DO YOU LIKE BEING FLOWN FOR A CHANGE?
ENJOYING IT VERY MUCH, THANK YOU.
YOU'RE IN A MUCH BETTER MOOD THAN YOU WERE ON THE WAY DOWN.
YEP.

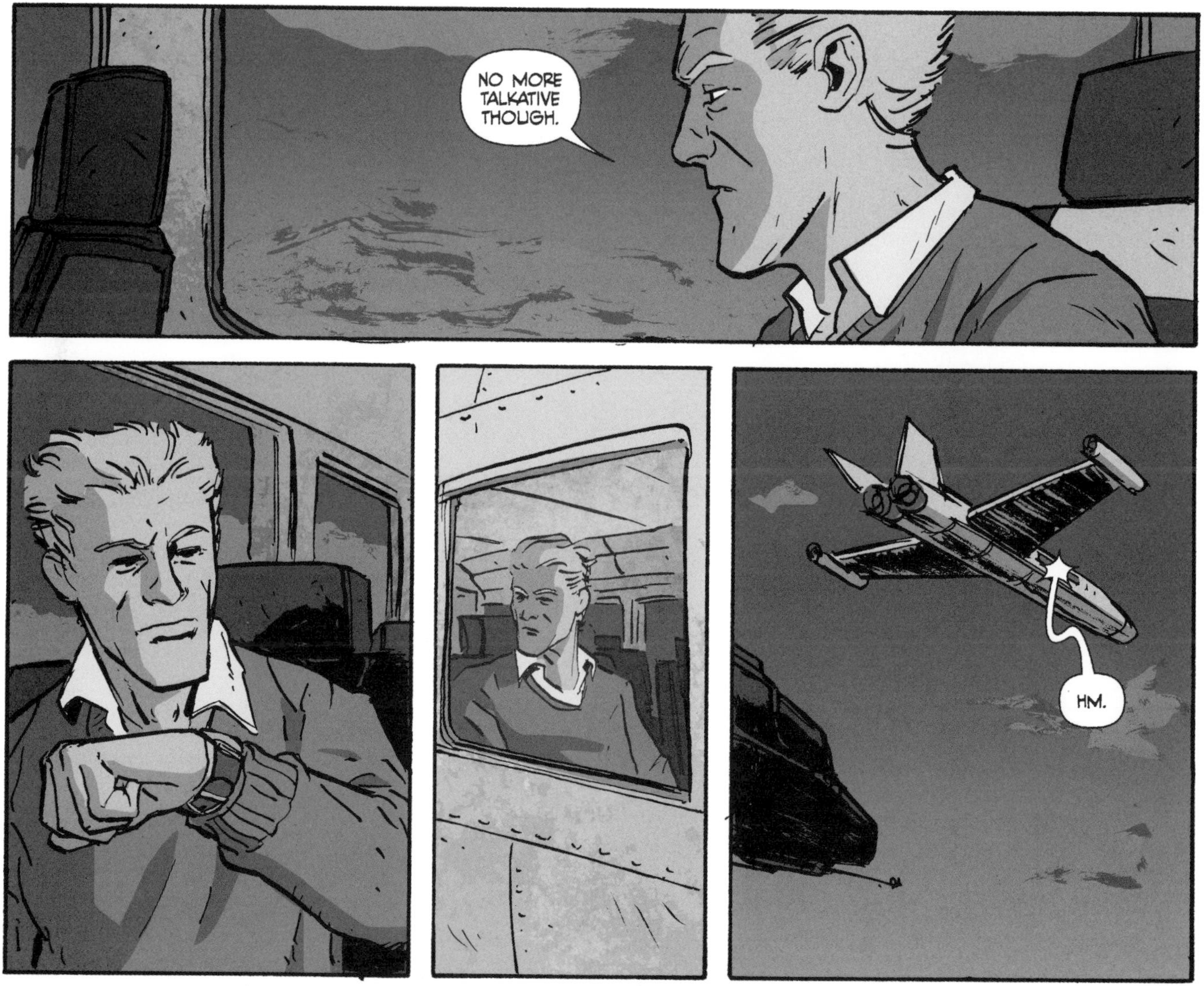
NO MORE TALKATIVE THOUGH.
HM.

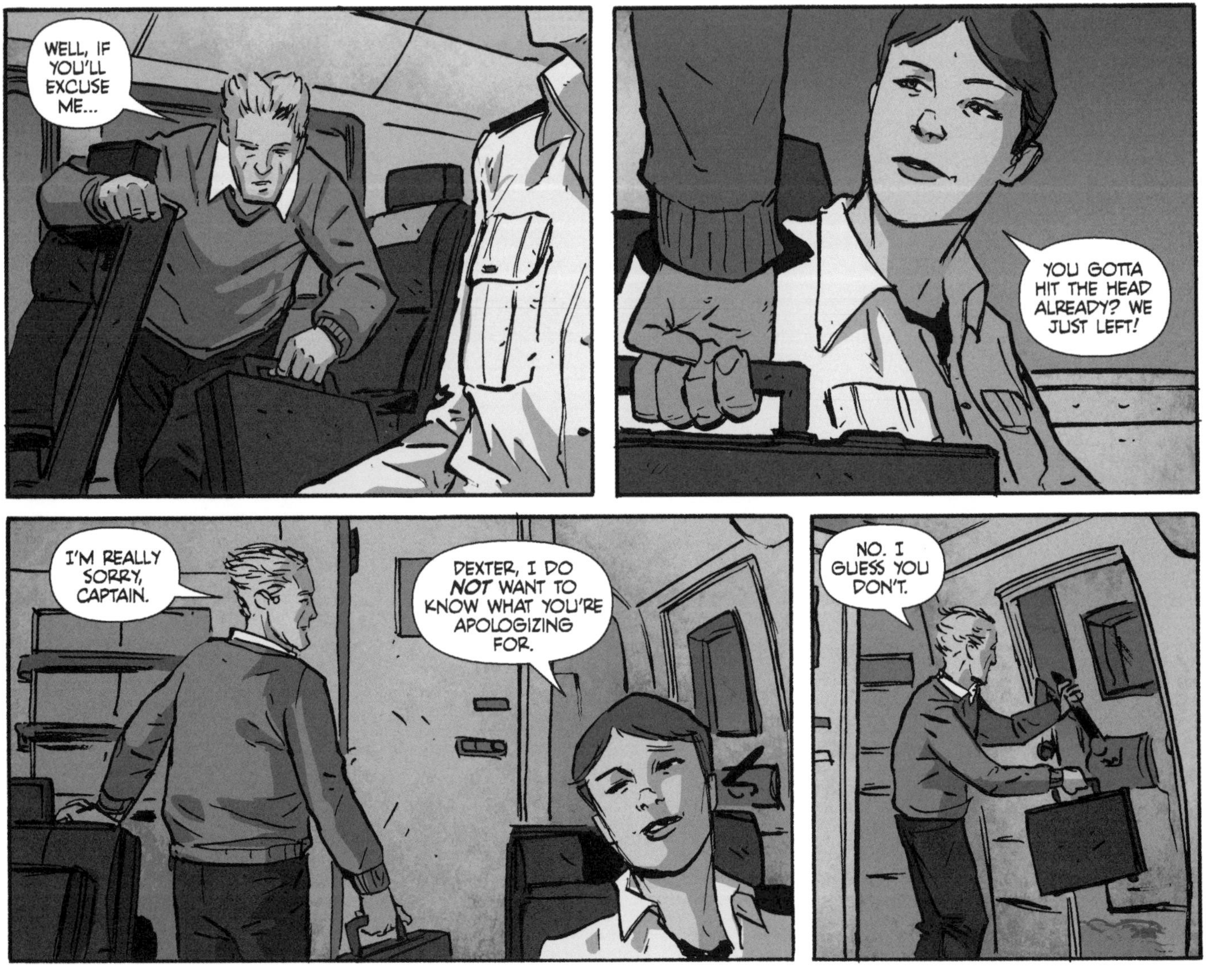
WELL, IF YOU'LL EXCUSE ME...
YOU GOTTA HIT THE HEAD ALREADY? WE JUST LEFT!
I'M REALLY SORRY, CAPTAIN.
DEXTER, I DO ***NOT*** WANT TO KNOW WHAT YOU'RE APOLOGIZING FOR.
NO. I GUESS YOU DON'T.

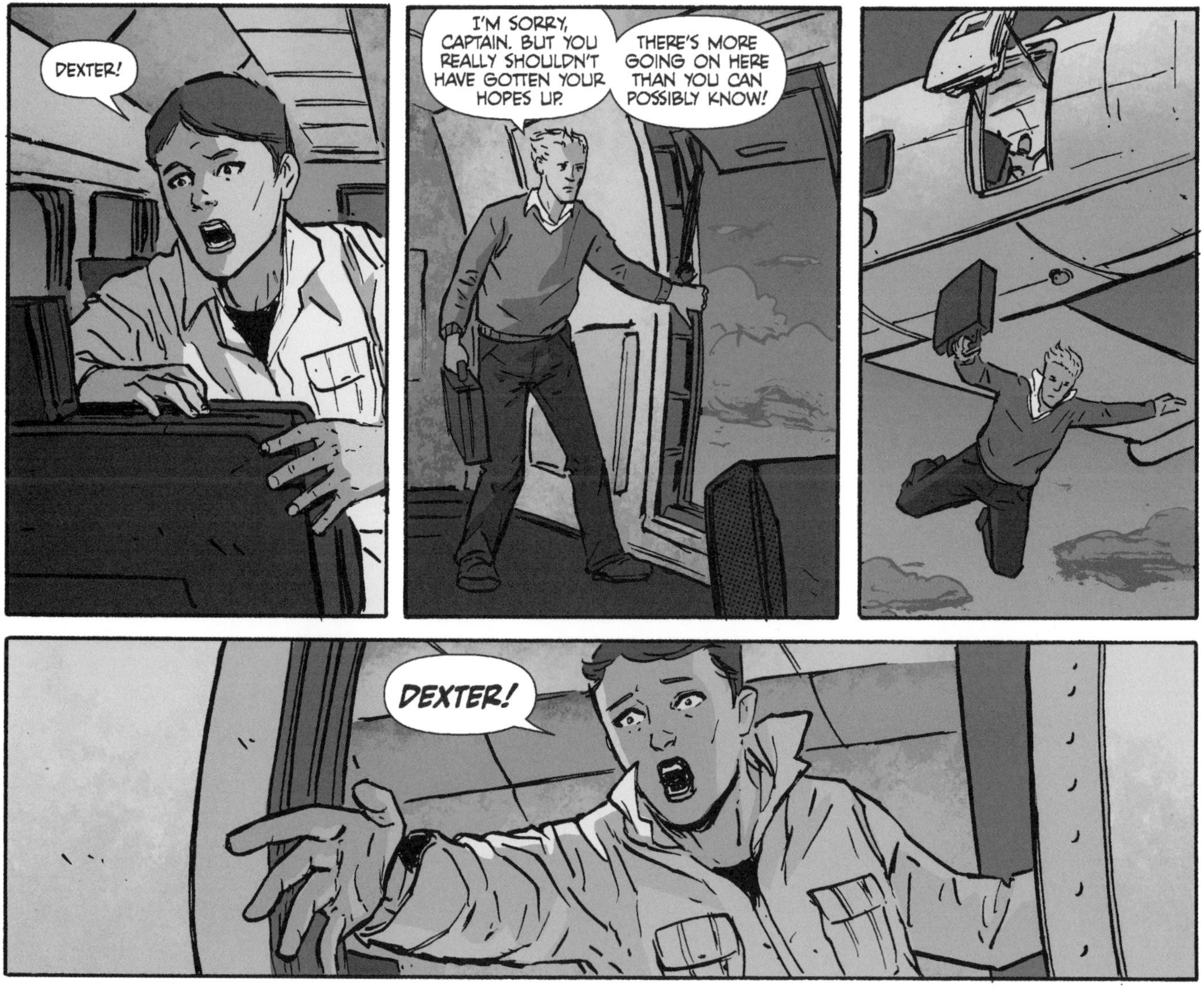
DEXTER!
I'M SORRY, CAPTAIN. BUT YOU REALLY SHOULDN'T HAVE GOTTEN YOUR HOPES UP.
THERE'S MORE GOING ON HERE THAN YOU CAN POSSIBLY KNOW!
DEXTER!

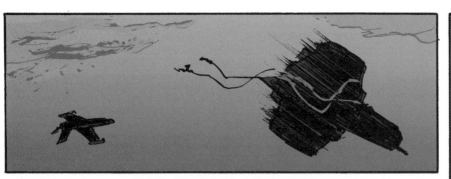
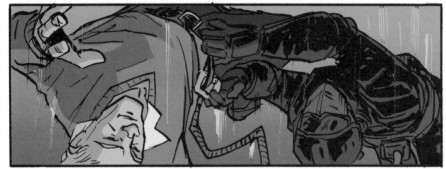
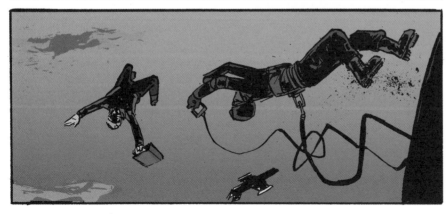
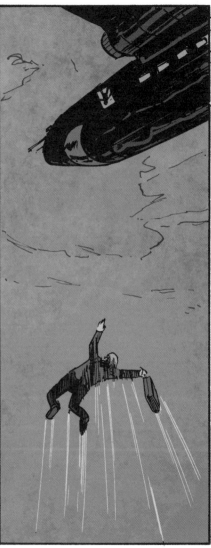

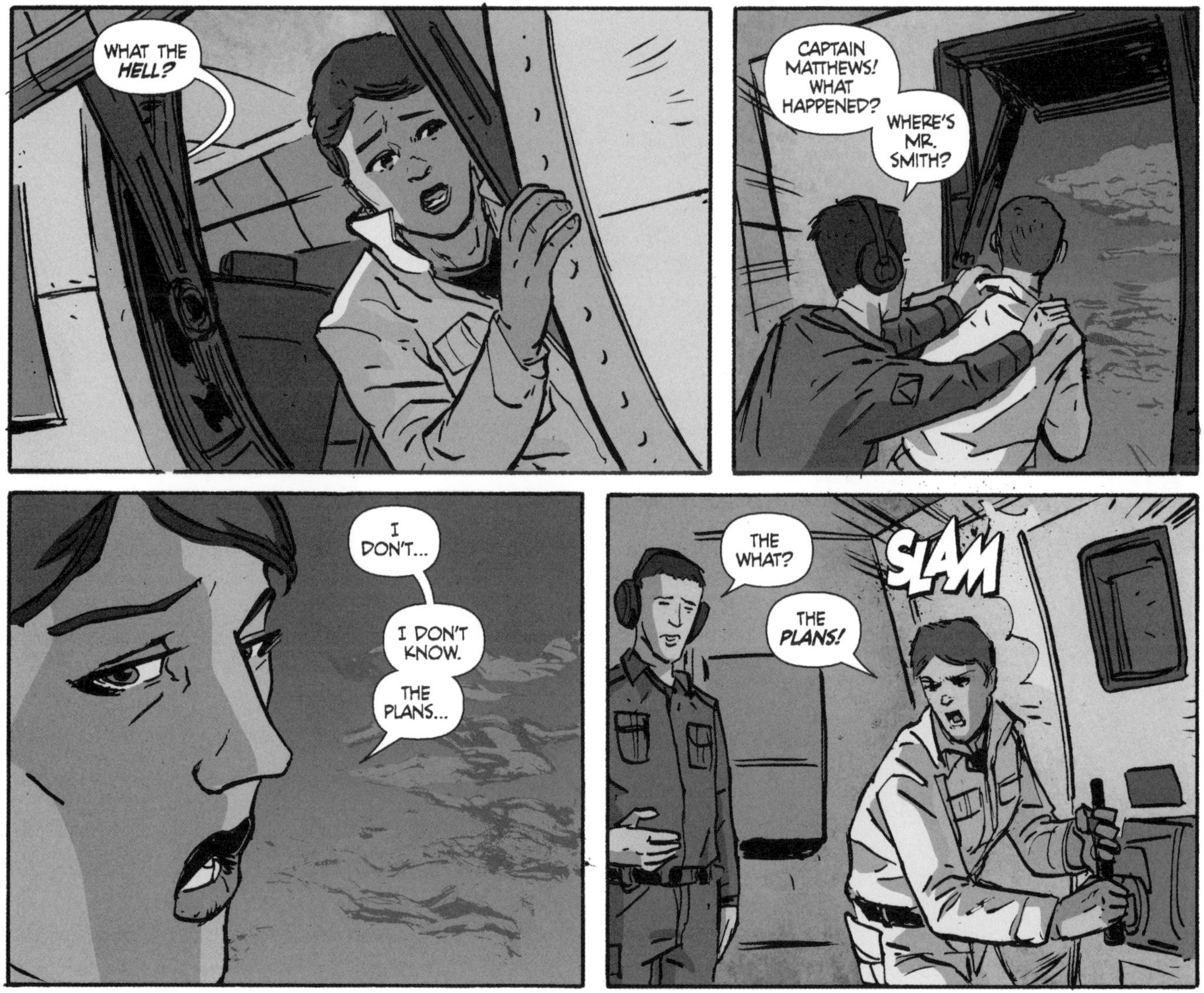
WHAT THE *HELL?*
CAPTAIN MATTHEWS! WHAT HAPPENED?
WHERE'S MR. SMITH?
I DON'T...
I DON'T KNOW.
THE PLANS...
THE WHAT?
SLAM
THE *PLANS!*

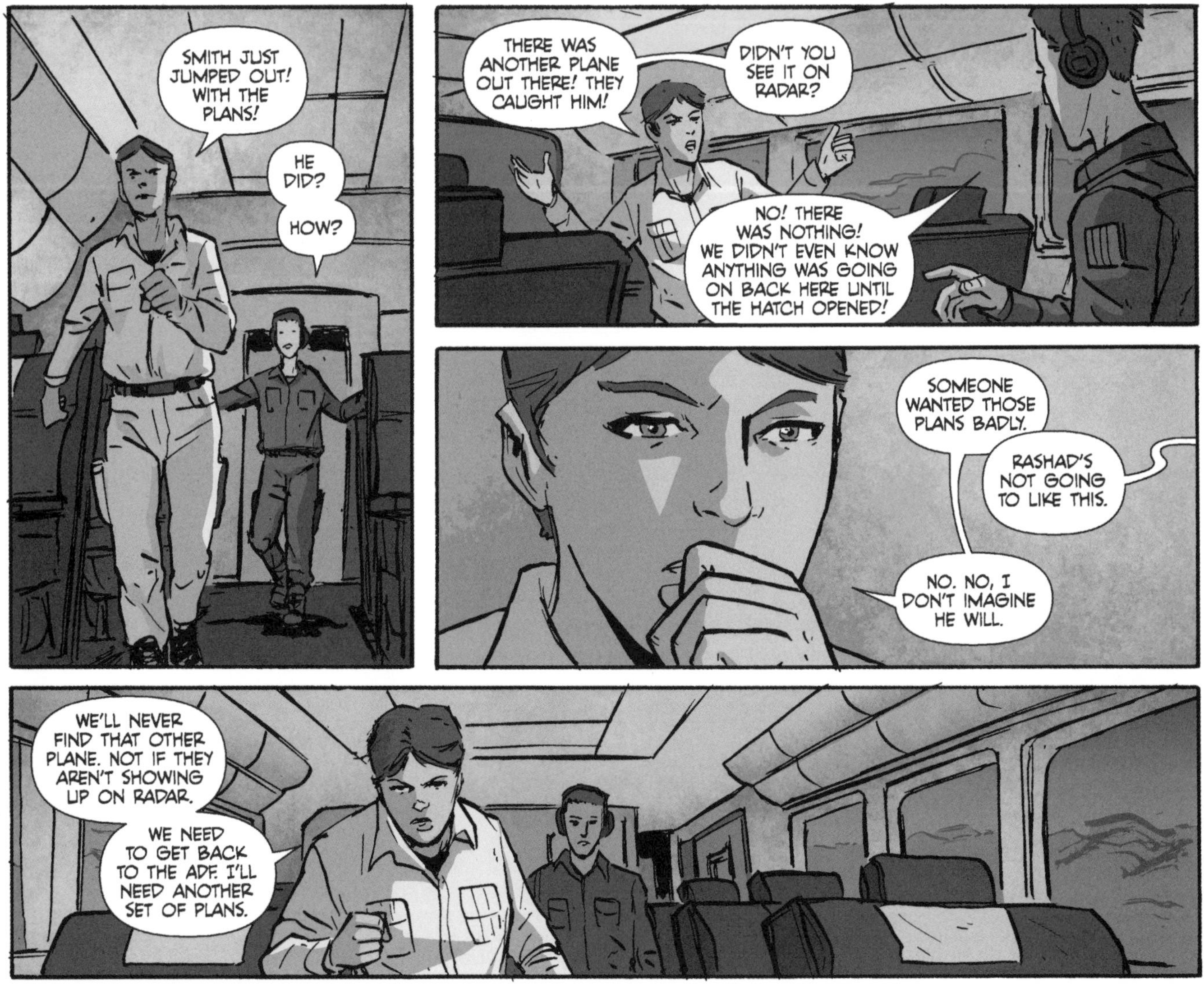
SMITH JUST JUMPED OUT! WITH THE PLANS!
HE DID?
HOW?
THERE WAS ANOTHER PLANE OUT THERE! THEY CAUGHT HIM!
DIDN'T YOU SEE IT ON RADAR?
NO! THERE WAS NOTHING! WE DIDN'T EVEN KNOW ANYTHING WAS GOING ON BACK HERE UNTIL THE HATCH OPENED!
SOMEONE WANTED THOSE PLANS BADLY.
RASHAD'S NOT GOING TO LIKE THIS.
NO. NO, I DON'T IMAGINE HE WILL.
WE'LL NEVER FIND THAT OTHER PLANE. NOT IF THEY AREN'T SHOWING UP ON RADAR.
WE NEED TO GET BACK TO THE ADF. I'LL NEED ANOTHER SET OF PLANS.

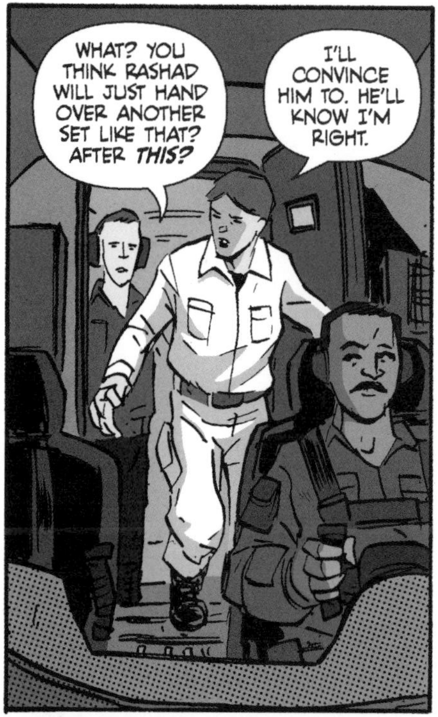
WHAT? YOU THINK RASHAD WILL JUST HAND OVER ANOTHER SET LIKE THAT? AFTER ***THIS?***
I'LL CONVINCE HIM TO. HE'LL KNOW I'M RIGHT.

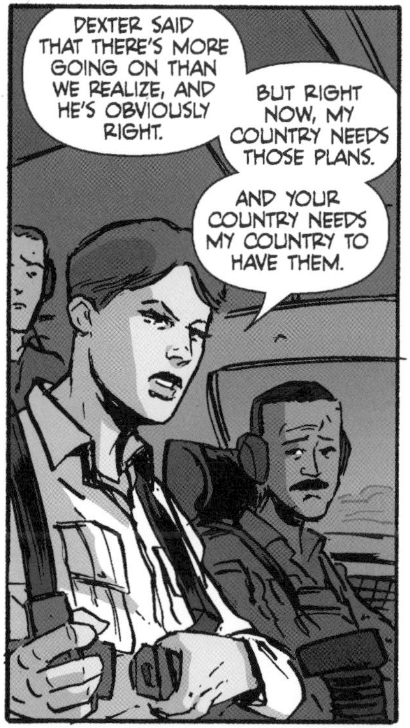
DEXTER SAID THAT THERE'S MORE GOING ON THAN WE REALIZE, AND HE'S OBVIOUSLY RIGHT.
BUT RIGHT NOW, MY COUNTRY NEEDS THOSE PLANS.
AND YOUR COUNTRY NEEDS MY COUNTRY TO HAVE THEM.

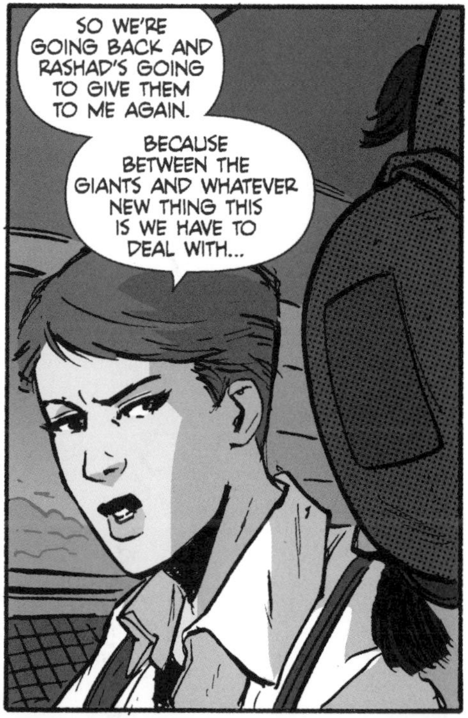
SO WE'RE GOING BACK AND RASHAD'S GOING TO GIVE THEM TO ME AGAIN.
BECAUSE BETWEEN THE GIANTS AND WHATEVER NEW THING THIS IS WE HAVE TO DEAL WITH...

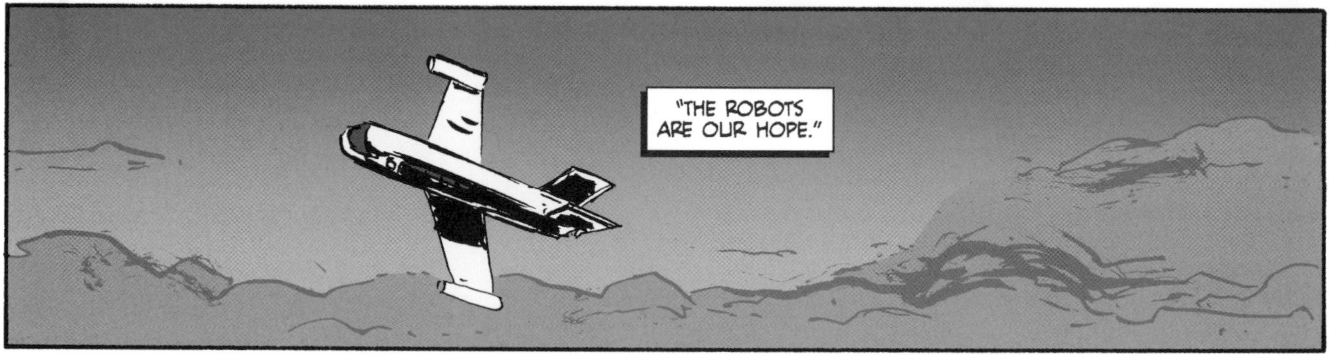
"THE ROBOTS ARE OUR HOPE."

ISLAND OF GIANTS

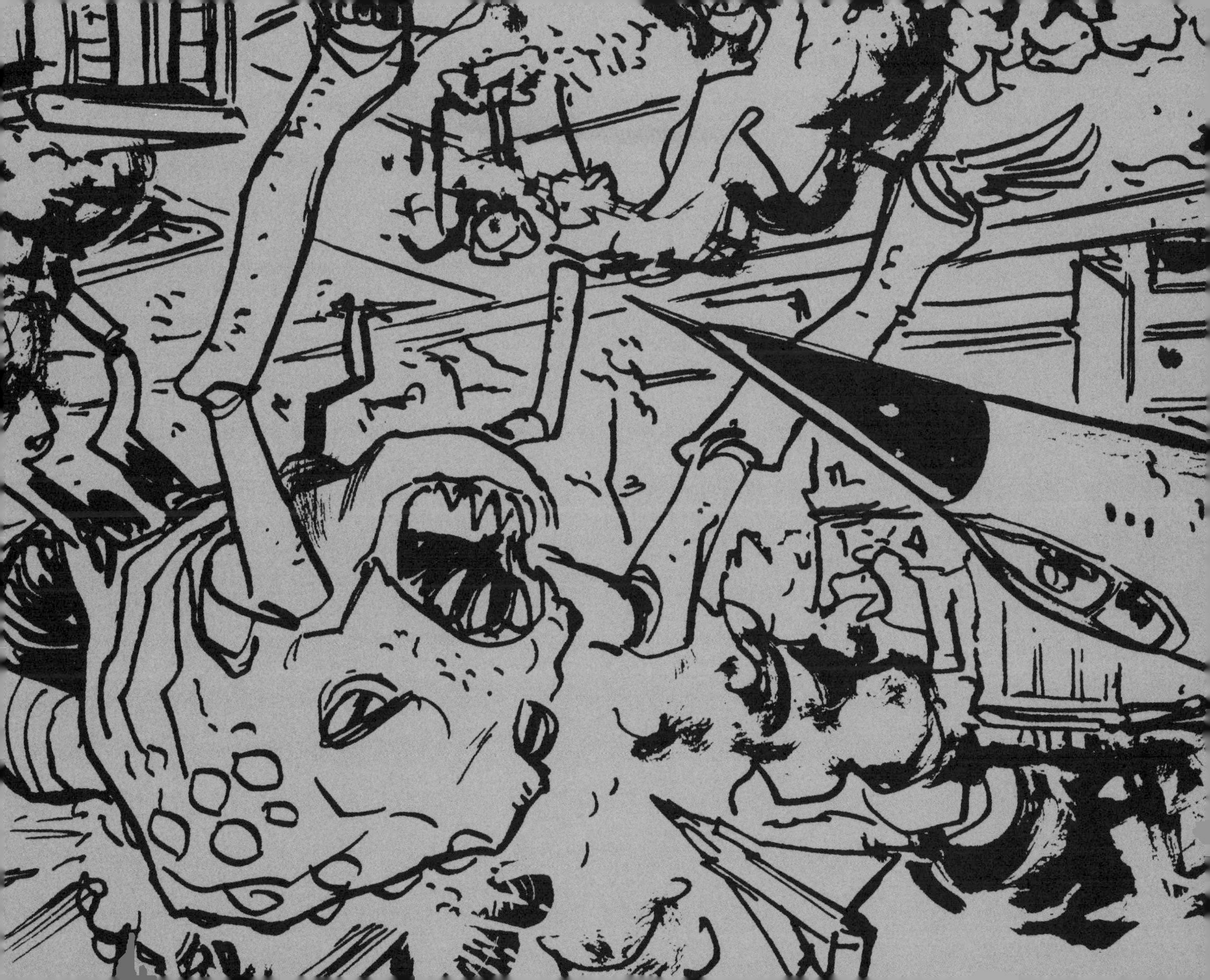

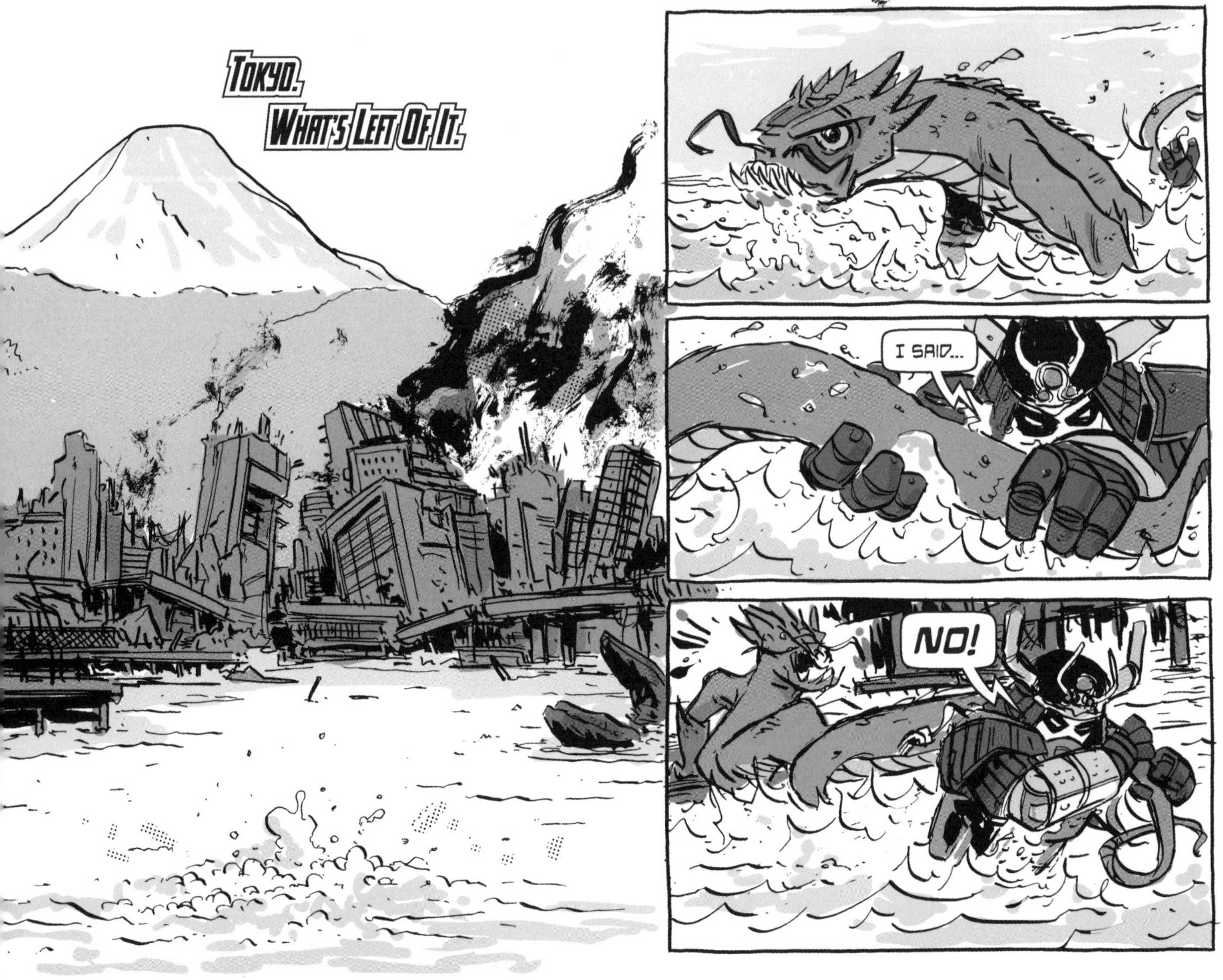
TOKYO.
WHAT'S LEFT OF IT.
I SAID...
NO!

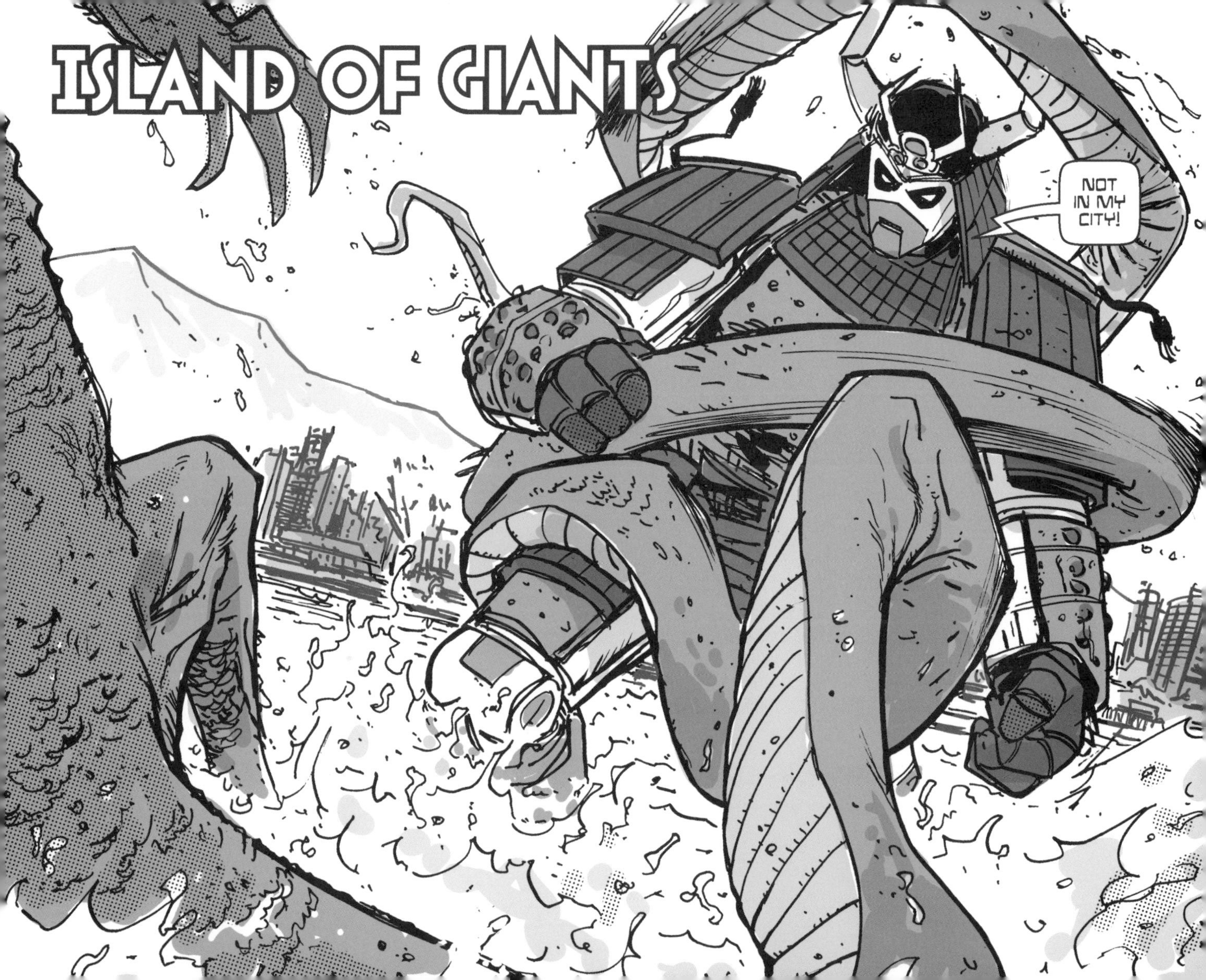
ISLAND OF GIANTS
NOT IN MY CITY!

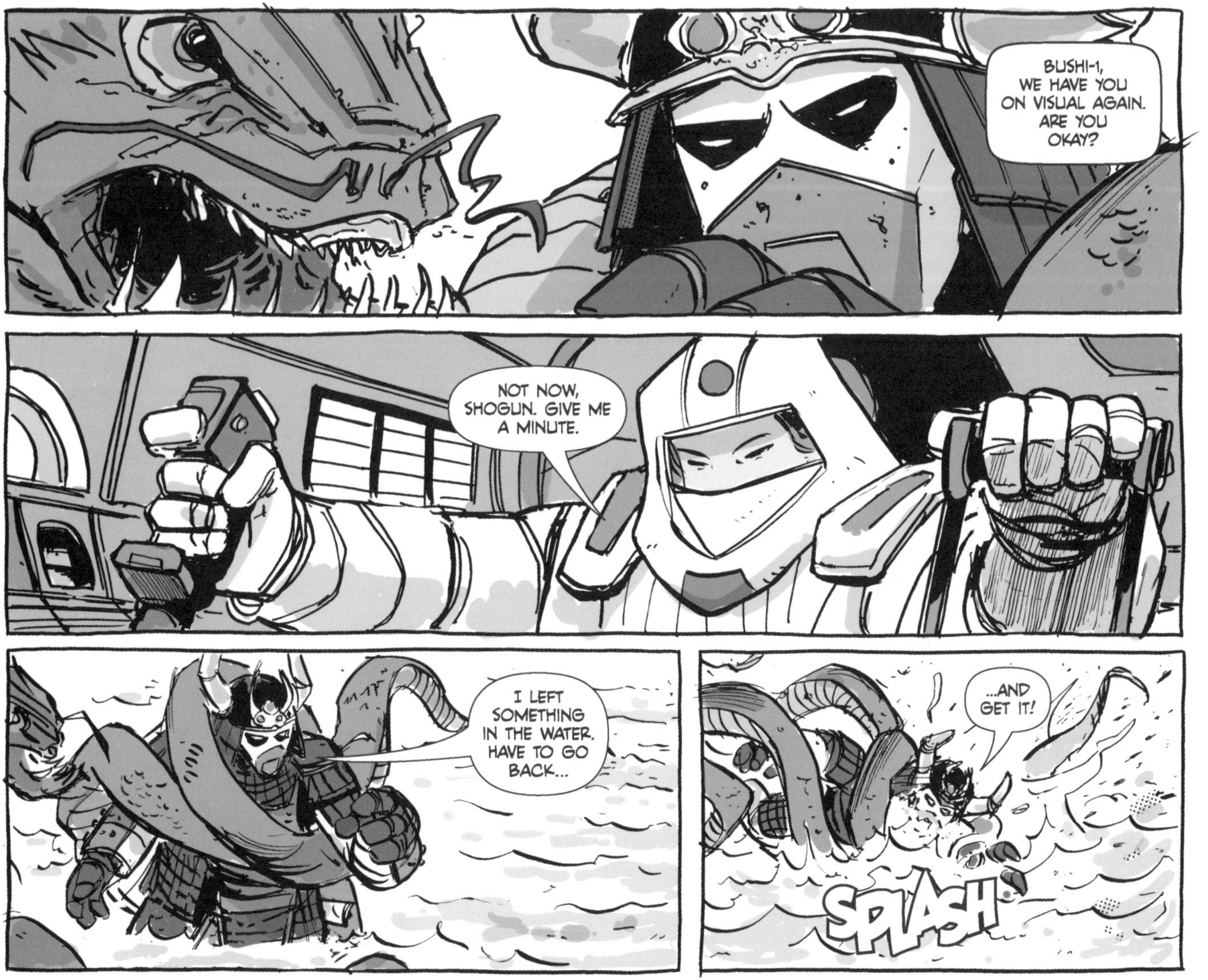
BUSHI-1, WE HAVE YOU ON VISUAL AGAIN. ARE YOU OKAY?
NOT NOW, SHOGUN. GIVE ME A MINUTE.
I LEFT SOMETHING IN THE WATER. HAVE TO GO BACK...
...AND GET IT!
SPLASH

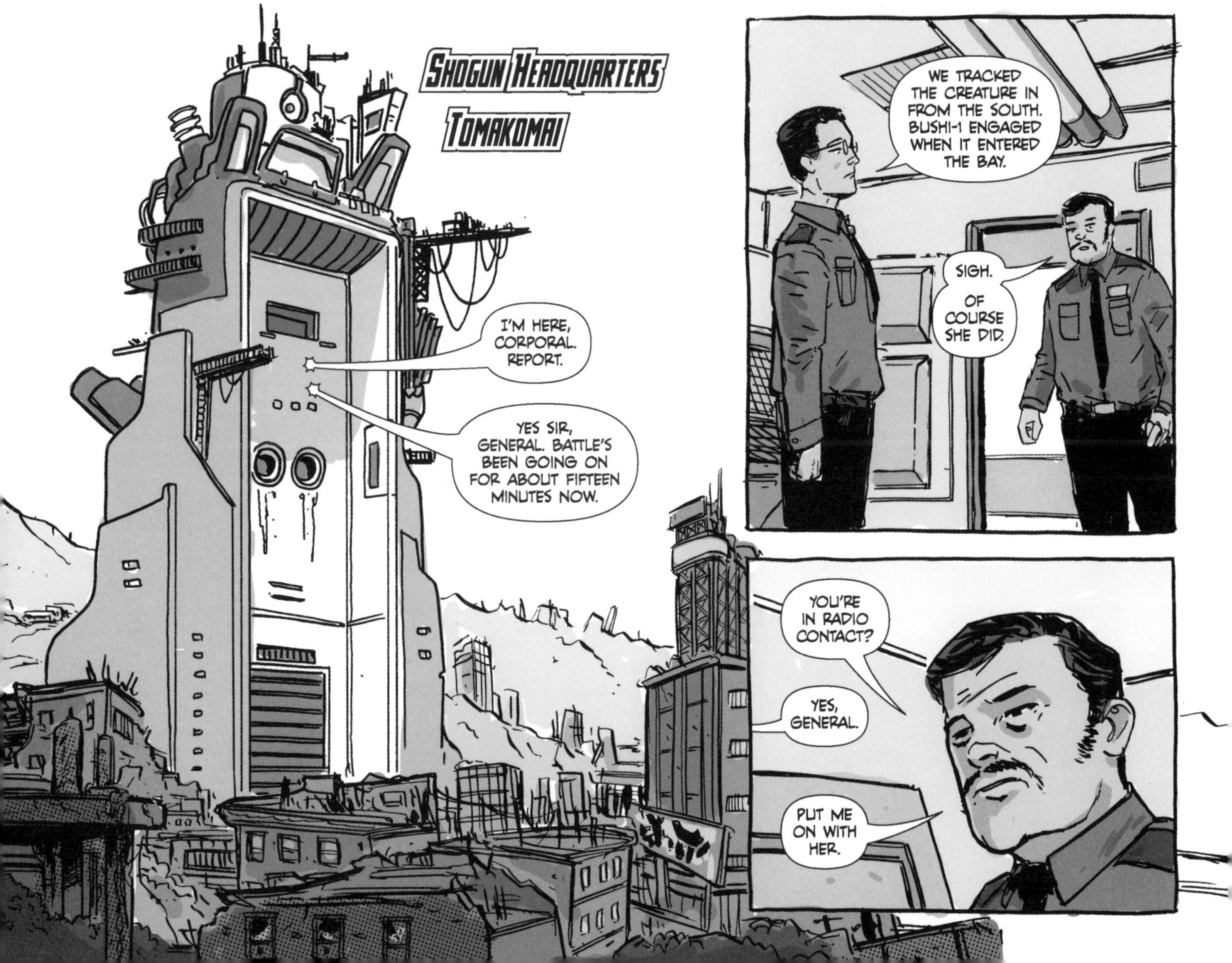
SHOGUN HEADQUARTERS
TOMAKOMAI
I'M HERE, CORPORAL. REPORT.
YES SIR, GENERAL. BATTLE'S BEEN GOING ON FOR ABOUT FIFTEEN MINUTES NOW.
WE TRACKED THE CREATURE IN FROM THE SOUTH. BUSHI-1 ENGAGED WHEN IT ENTERED THE BAY.
SIGH.
OF COURSE SHE DID.
YOU'RE IN RADIO CONTACT?
YES, GENERAL.
PUT ME ON WITH HER.

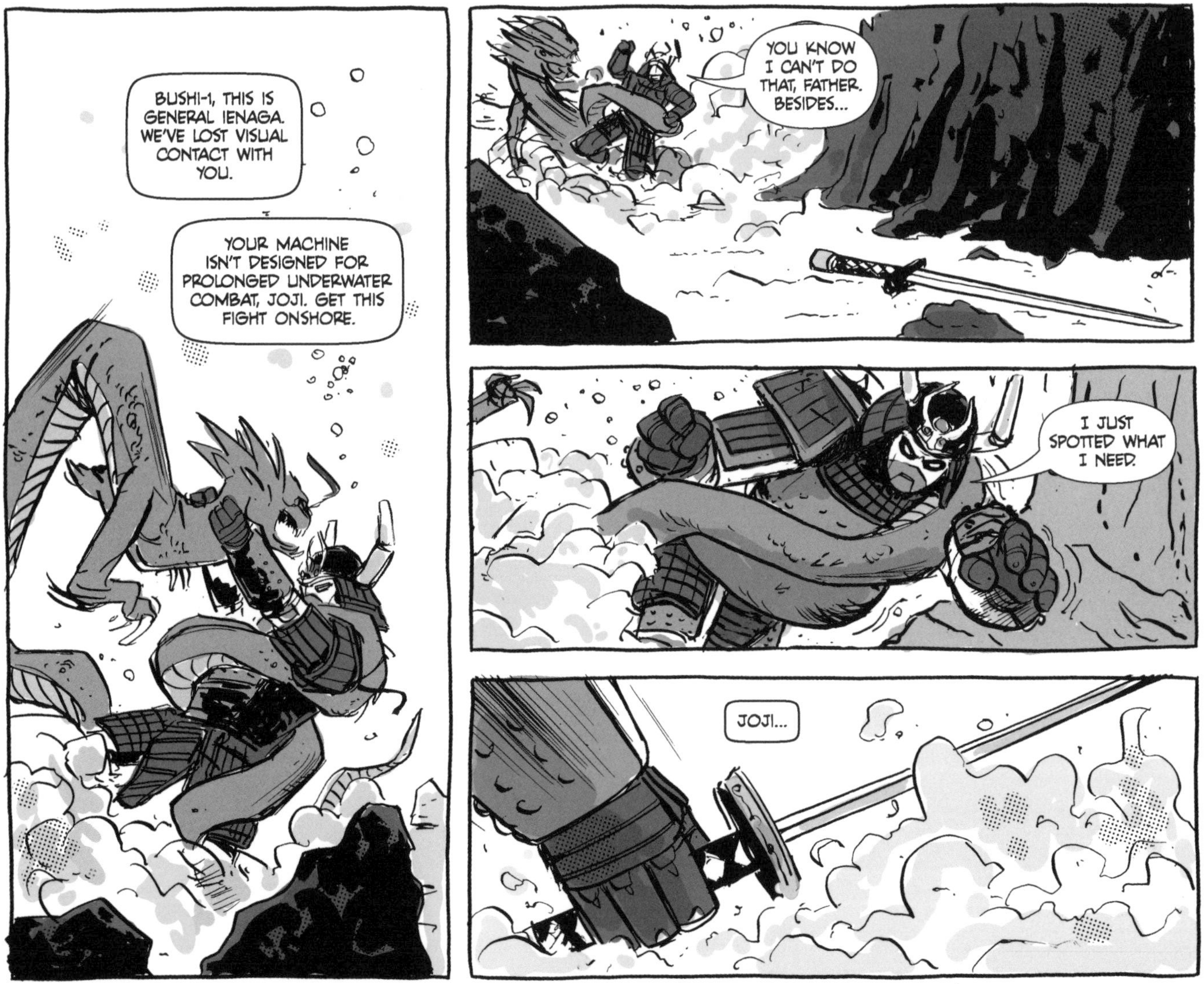
BUSHI-1, THIS IS GENERAL IENAGA. WE'VE LOST VISUAL CONTACT WITH YOU.
YOUR MACHINE ISN'T DESIGNED FOR PROLONGED UNDERWATER COMBAT, JOJI. GET THIS FIGHT ONSHORE.
YOU KNOW I CAN'T DO THAT, FATHER. BESIDES...
I JUST SPOTTED WHAT I NEED.
JOJI...

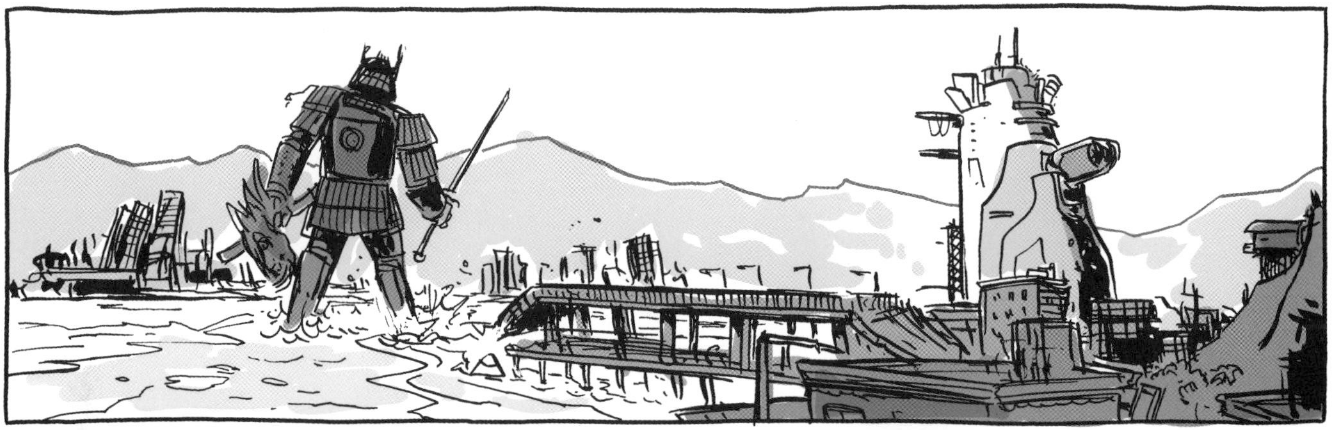

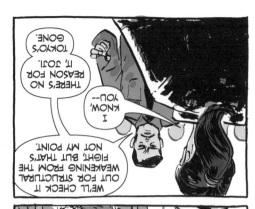

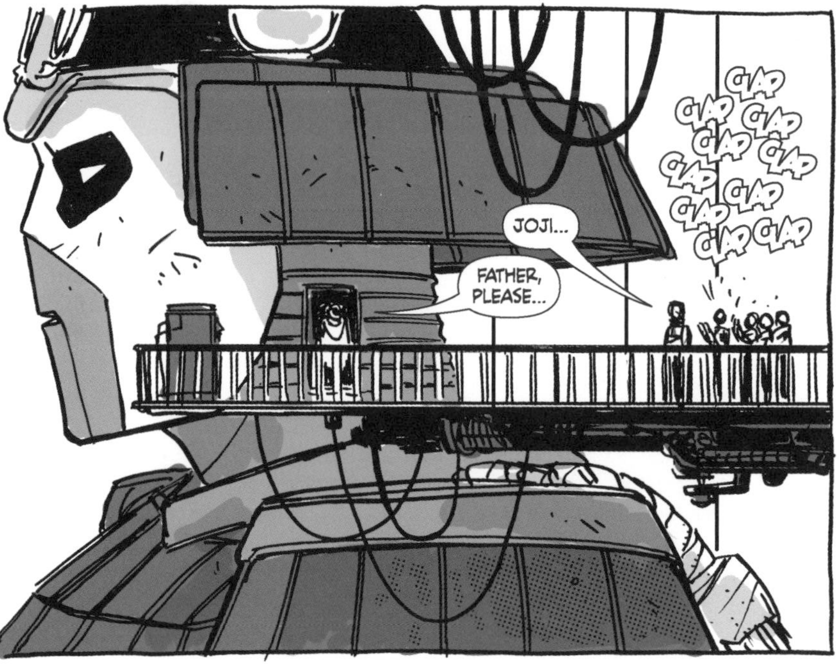
CLAP CLAP CLAP CLAP CLAP CLAP CLAP CLAP CLAP CLAP CLAP
JOJI...
FATHER, PLEASE...

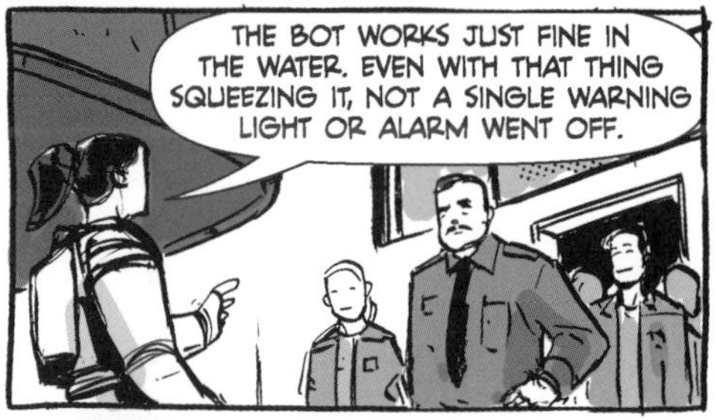
THE BOT WORKS JUST FINE IN THE WATER. EVEN WITH THAT THING SQUEEZING IT, NOT A SINGLE WARNING LIGHT OR ALARM WENT OFF.

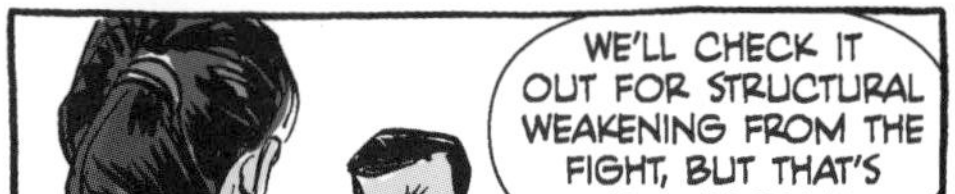
WE'LL CHECK IT OUT FOR STRUCTURAL WEAKENING FROM THE FIGHT, BUT THAT'S NOT MY POINT.
I KNOW, YOU--
THERE'S NO REASON FOR IT, JOJI.
TOKYO'S GONE.

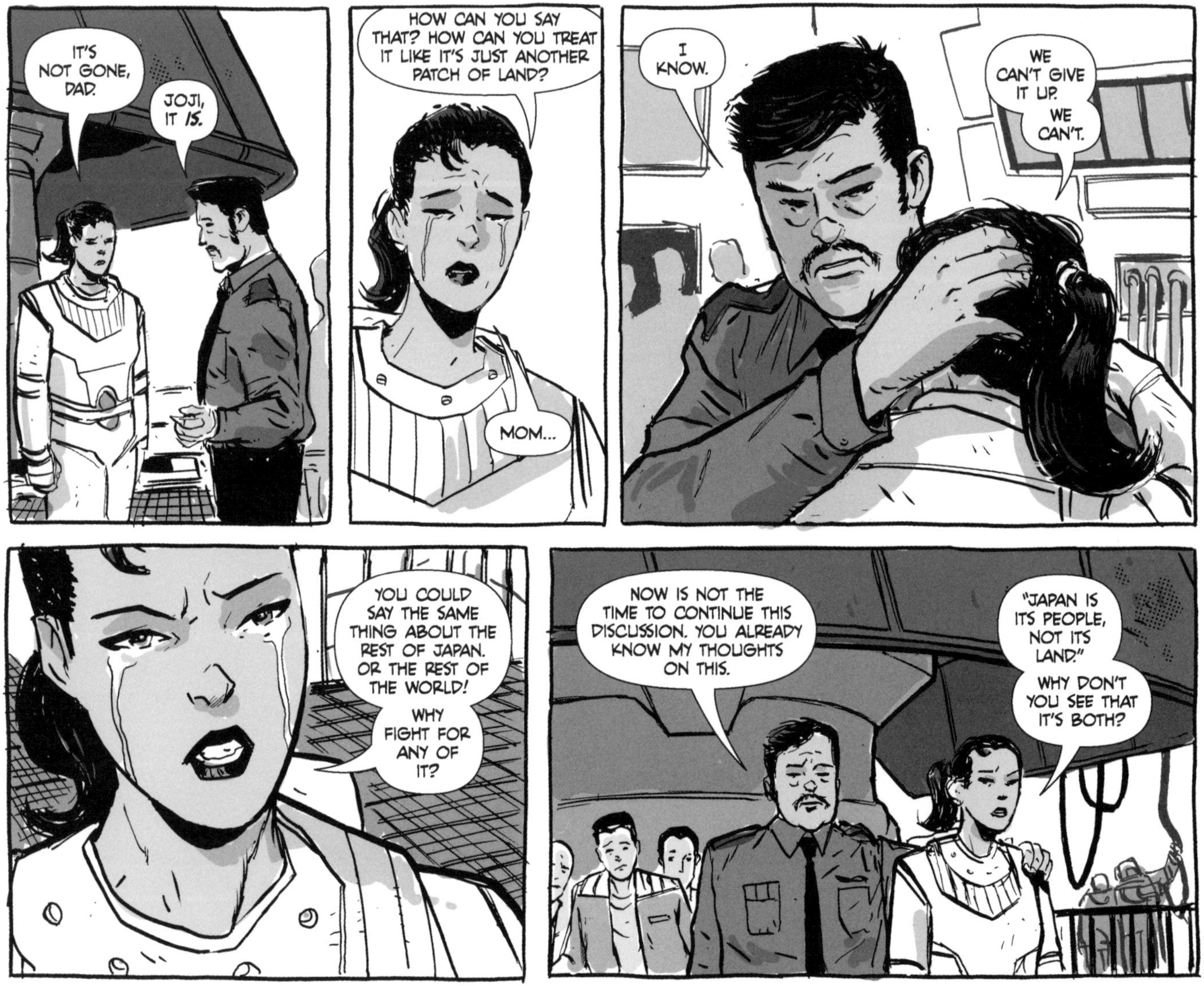

IT'S NOT GONE, DAD.
JOJI, IT IS.
HOW CAN YOU SAY THAT? HOW CAN YOU TREAT IT LIKE IT'S JUST ANOTHER PATCH OF LAND?
MOM...
I KNOW.
WE CAN'T GIVE IT UP.
WE CAN'T.
YOU COULD SAY THE SAME THING ABOUT THE REST OF JAPAN. OR THE REST OF THE WORLD!
WHY FIGHT FOR ANY OF IT?
NOW IS NOT THE TIME TO CONTINUE THIS DISCUSSION. YOU ALREADY KNOW MY THOUGHTS ON THIS.
"JAPAN IS ITS PEOPLE, NOT ITS LAND."
WHY DON'T YOU SEE THAT IT'S BOTH?

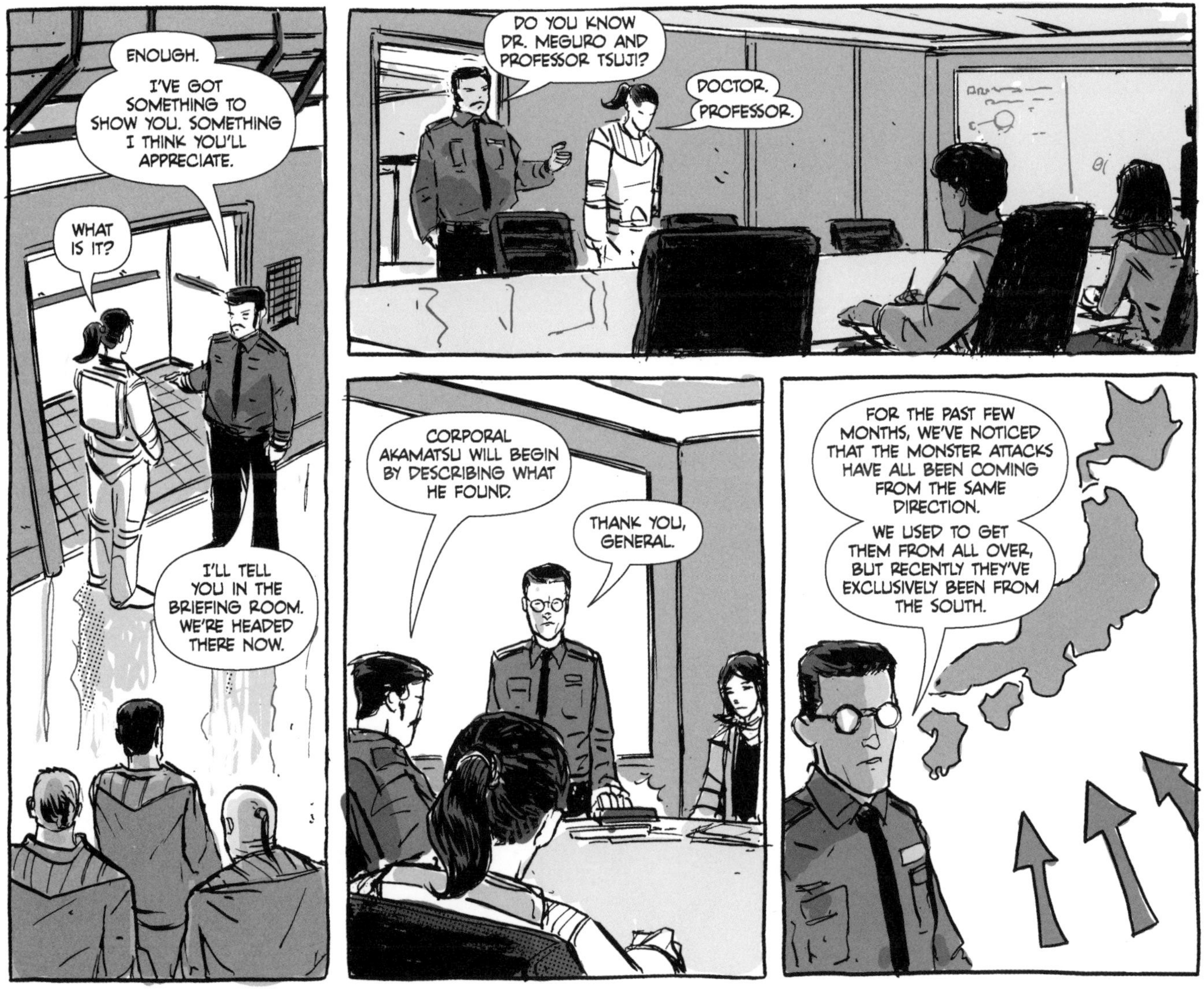
ENOUGH.
I'VE GOT SOMETHING TO SHOW YOU. SOMETHING I THINK YOU'LL APPRECIATE.
WHAT IS IT?
I'LL TELL YOU IN THE BRIEFING ROOM. WE'RE HEADED THERE NOW.
DO YOU KNOW DR. MEGURO AND PROFESSOR TSUJI?
DOCTOR. PROFESSOR.
CORPORAL AKAMATSU WILL BEGIN BY DESCRIBING WHAT HE FOUND.
THANK YOU, GENERAL.
FOR THE PAST FEW MONTHS, WE'VE NOTICED THAT THE MONSTER ATTACKS HAVE ALL BEEN COMING FROM THE SAME DIRECTION.
WE USED TO GET THEM FROM ALL OVER, BUT RECENTLY THEY'VE EXCLUSIVELY BEEN FROM THE SOUTH.

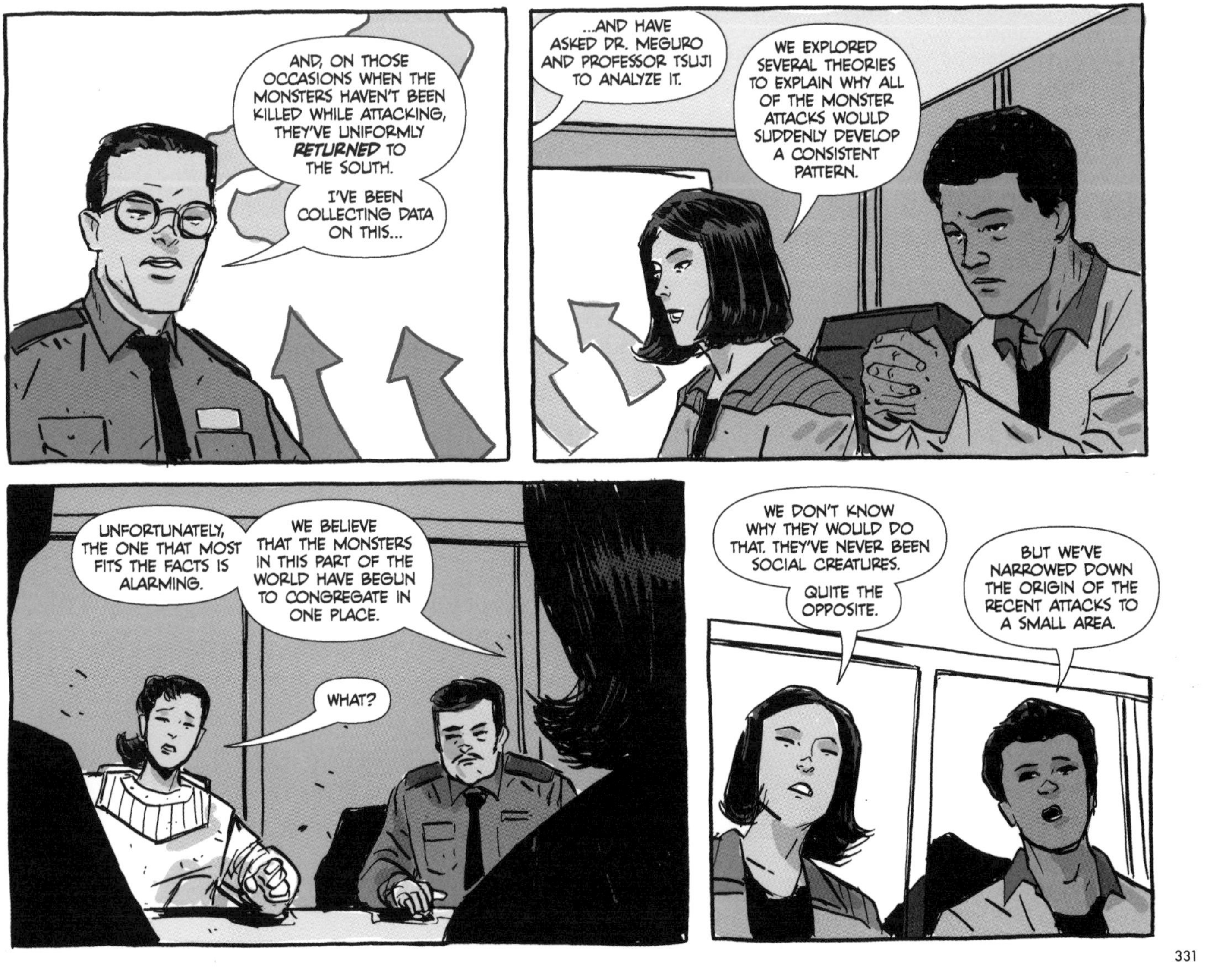
AND, ON THOSE OCCASIONS WHEN THE MONSTERS HAVEN'T BEEN KILLED WHILE ATTACKING, THEY'VE UNIFORMLY ***RETURNED*** TO THE SOUTH.
I'VE BEEN COLLECTING DATA ON THIS...
...AND HAVE ASKED DR. MEGURO AND PROFESSOR TSUJI TO ANALYZE IT.
WE EXPLORED SEVERAL THEORIES TO EXPLAIN WHY ALL OF THE MONSTER ATTACKS WOULD SUDDENLY DEVELOP A CONSISTENT PATTERN.
UNFORTUNATELY, THE ONE THAT MOST FITS THE FACTS IS ALARMING.
WE BELIEVE THAT THE MONSTERS IN THIS PART OF THE WORLD HAVE BEGUN TO CONGREGATE IN ONE PLACE.
WHAT?
WE DON'T KNOW WHY THEY WOULD DO THAT. THEY'VE NEVER BEEN SOCIAL CREATURES.
QUITE THE OPPOSITE.
BUT WE'VE NARROWED DOWN THE ORIGIN OF THE RECENT ATTACKS TO A SMALL AREA.

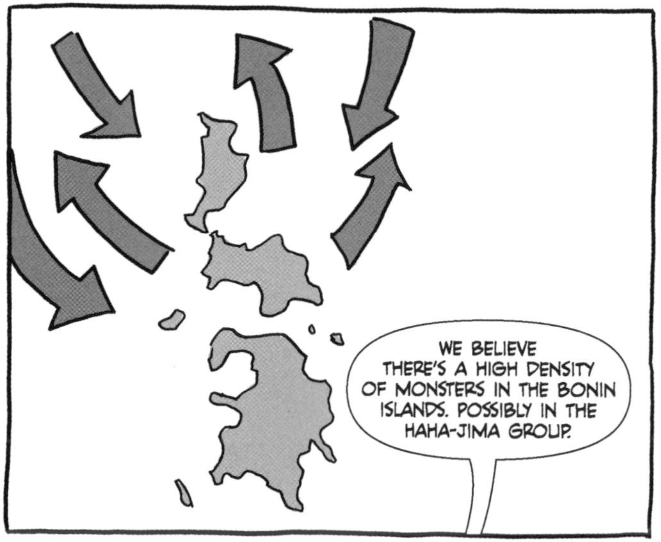
WE BELIEVE THERE'S A HIGH DENSITY OF MONSTERS IN THE BONIN ISLANDS. POSSIBLY IN THE HAHA-JIMA GROUP.

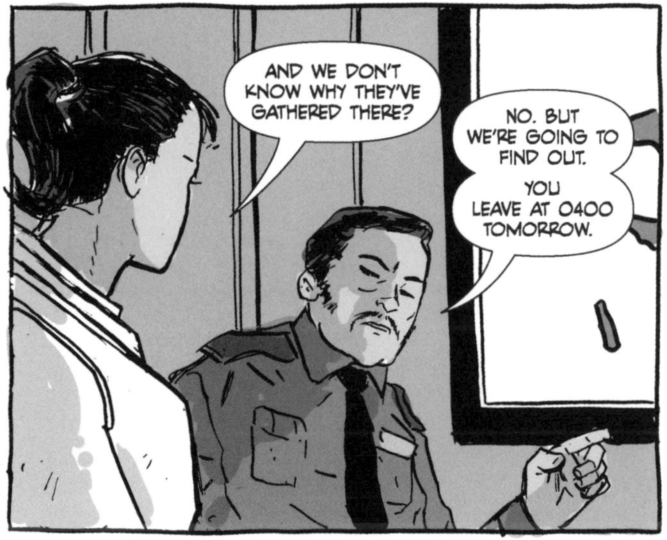
AND WE DON'T KNOW WHY THEY'VE GATHERED THERE?
NO. BUT WE'RE GOING TO FIND OUT.
YOU LEAVE AT 0400 TOMORROW.

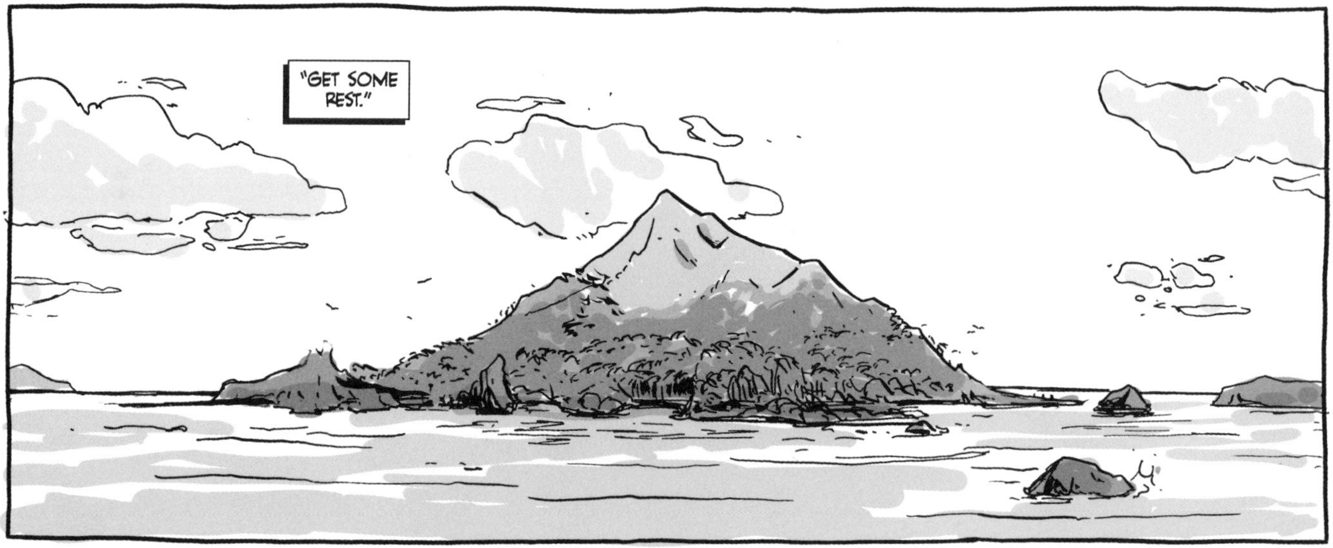
"GET SOME REST."

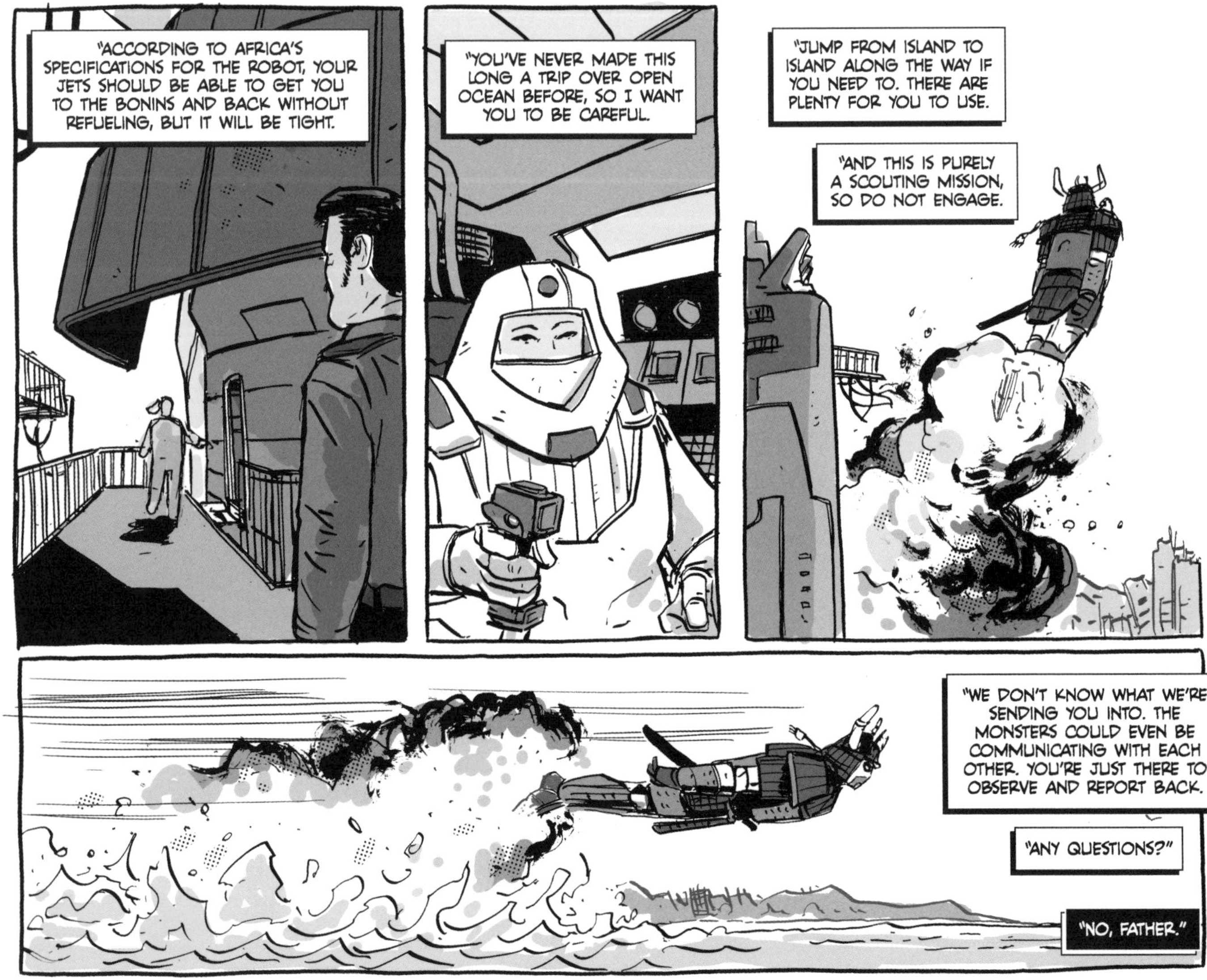
"ACCORDING TO AFRICA'S SPECIFICATIONS FOR THE ROBOT, YOUR JETS SHOULD BE ABLE TO GET YOU TO THE BONINS AND BACK WITHOUT REFUELING, BUT IT WILL BE TIGHT.
"YOU'VE NEVER MADE THIS LONG A TRIP OVER OPEN OCEAN BEFORE, SO I WANT YOU TO BE CAREFUL.
"JUMP FROM ISLAND TO ISLAND ALONG THE WAY IF YOU NEED TO. THERE ARE PLENTY FOR YOU TO USE.
"AND THIS IS PURELY A SCOUTING MISSION, SO DO NOT ENGAGE.
"WE DON'T KNOW WHAT WE'RE SENDING YOU INTO. THE MONSTERS COULD EVEN BE COMMUNICATING WITH EACH OTHER. YOU'RE JUST THERE TO OBSERVE AND REPORT BACK.
"ANY QUESTIONS?"
"NO, FATHER."

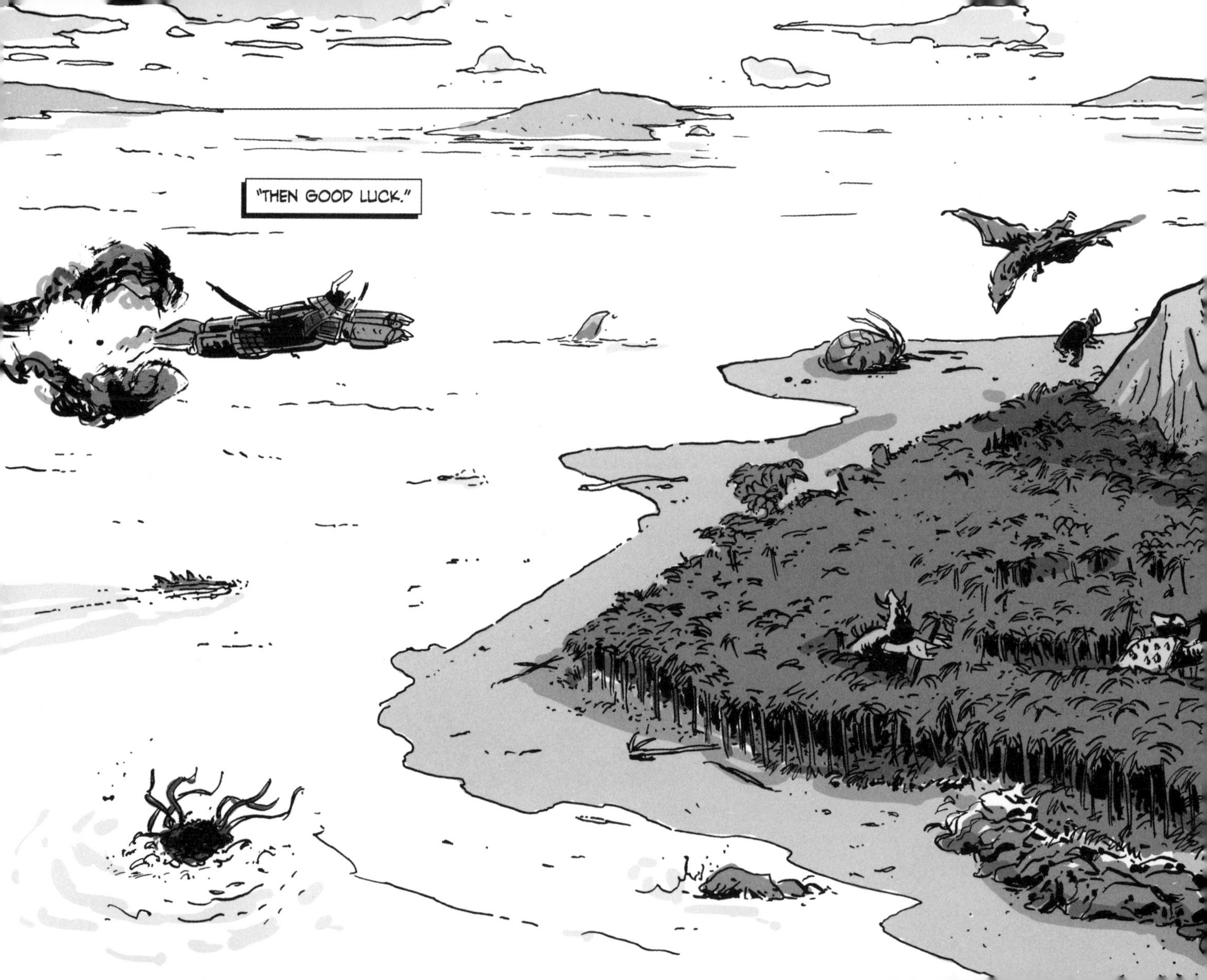
"THEN GOOD LUCK."

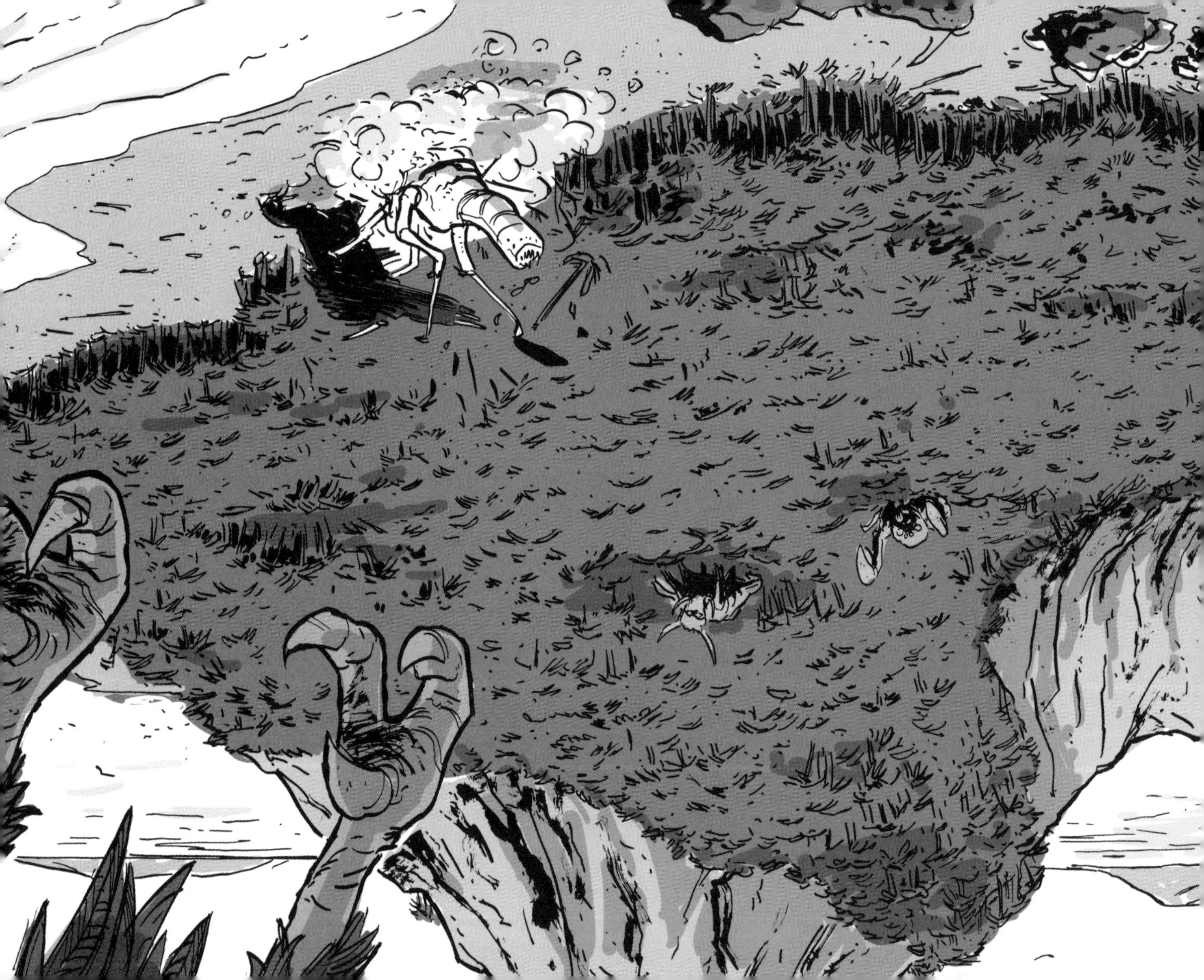

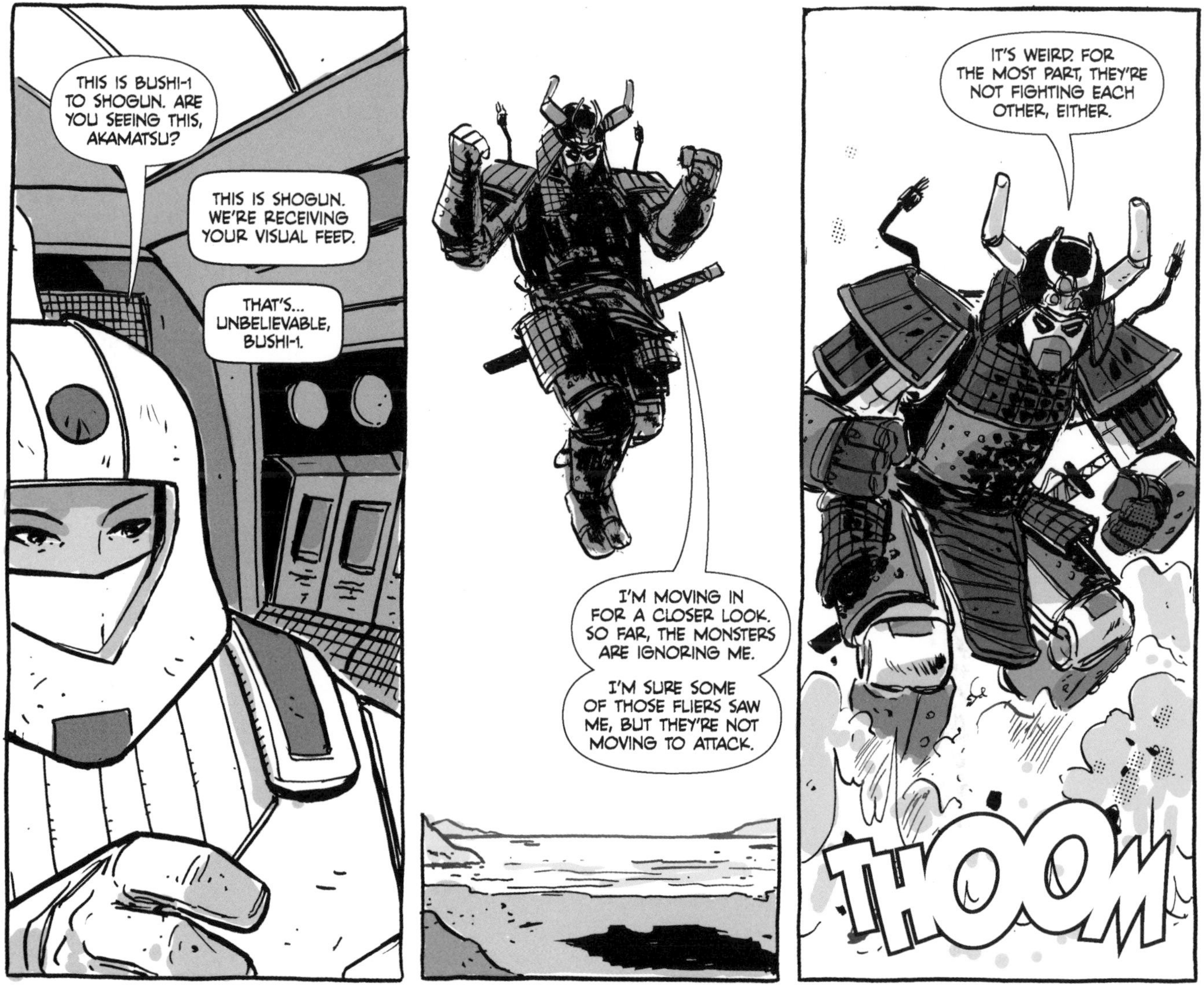
THIS IS BUSHI-1 TO SHOGUN. ARE YOU SEEING THIS, AKAMATSU?
THIS IS SHOGUN. WE'RE RECEIVING YOUR VISUAL FEED.
THAT'S... UNBELIEVABLE, BUSHI-1.
I'M MOVING IN FOR A CLOSER LOOK. SO FAR, THE MONSTERS ARE IGNORING ME.
I'M SURE SOME OF THOSE FLIERS SAW ME, BUT THEY'RE NOT MOVING TO ATTACK.
IT'S WEIRD. FOR THE MOST PART, THEY'RE NOT FIGHTING EACH OTHER, EITHER.
THOOM

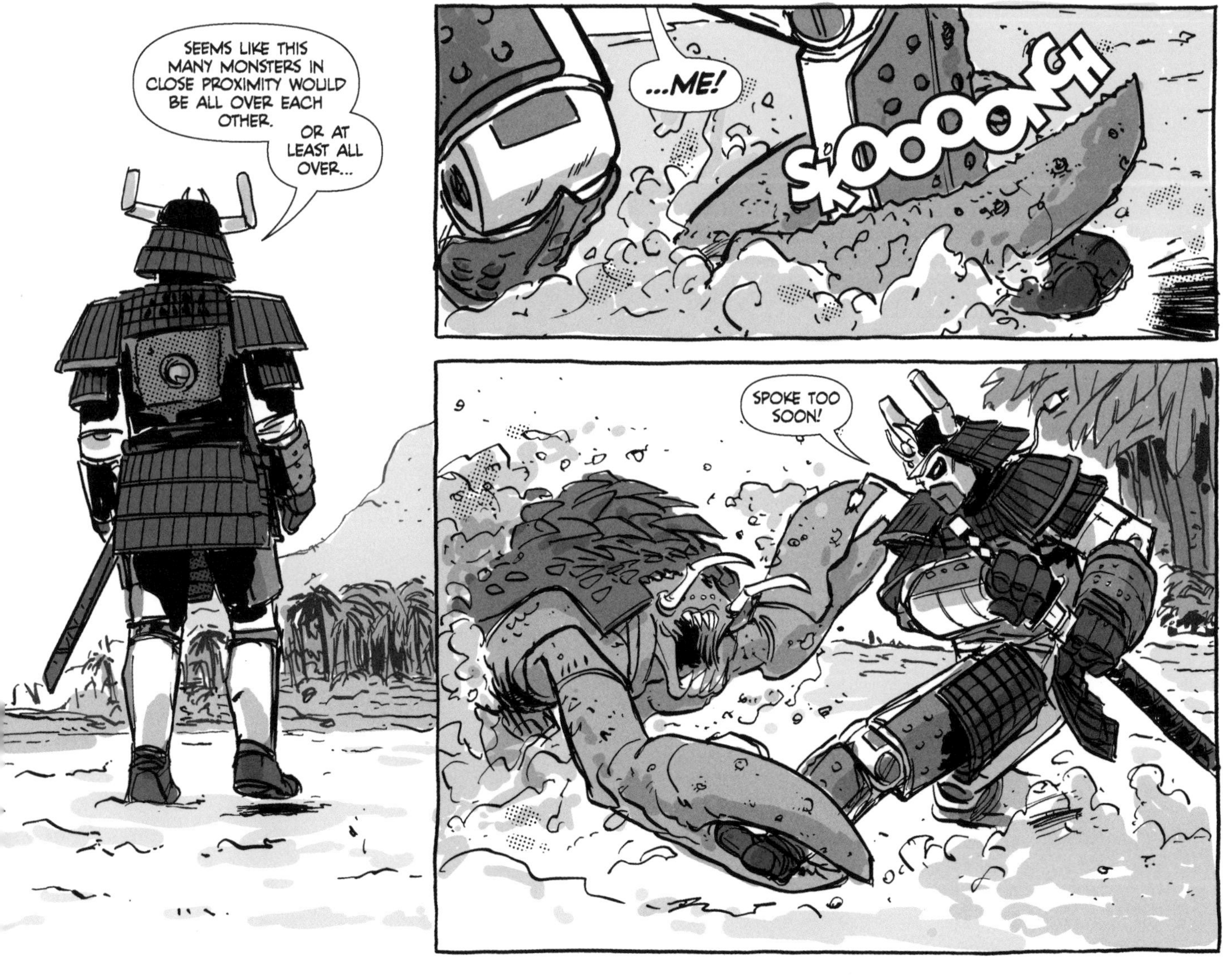
SEEMS LIKE THIS MANY MONSTERS IN CLOSE PROXIMITY WOULD BE ALL OVER EACH OTHER.
OR AT LEAST ALL OVER...
...ME!
SKOOOONCH
SPOKE TOO SOON!

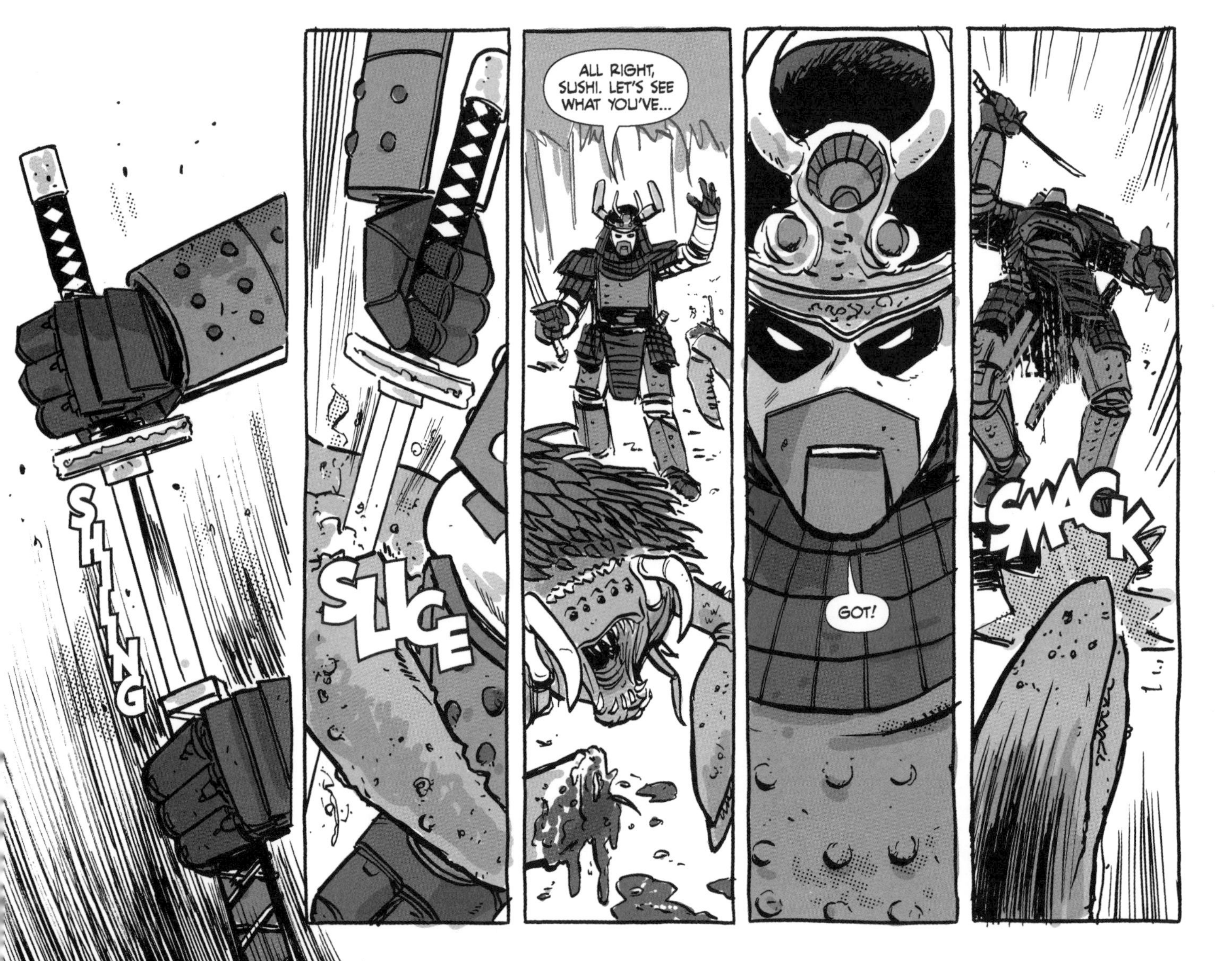
SHING
SLICE
ALL RIGHT, SUSHI. LET'S SEE WHAT YOU'VE...
GOT!
SMACK

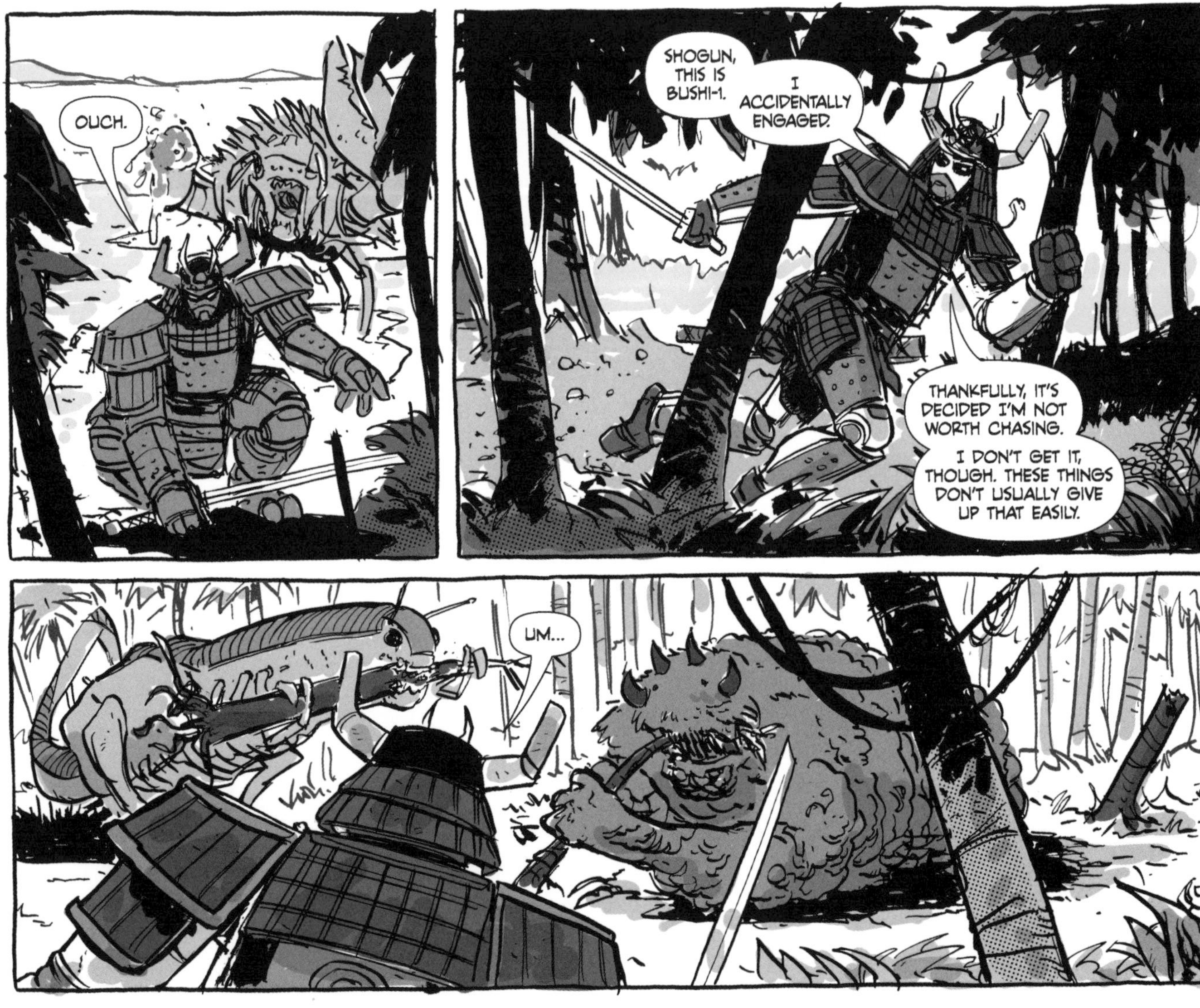
OUCH.
SHOGUN, THIS IS BUSHI-1.
I ACCIDENTALLY ENGAGED.
THANKFULLY, IT'S DECIDED I'M NOT WORTH CHASING.
I DON'T GET IT, THOUGH. THESE THINGS DON'T USUALLY GIVE UP THAT EASILY.
UM...

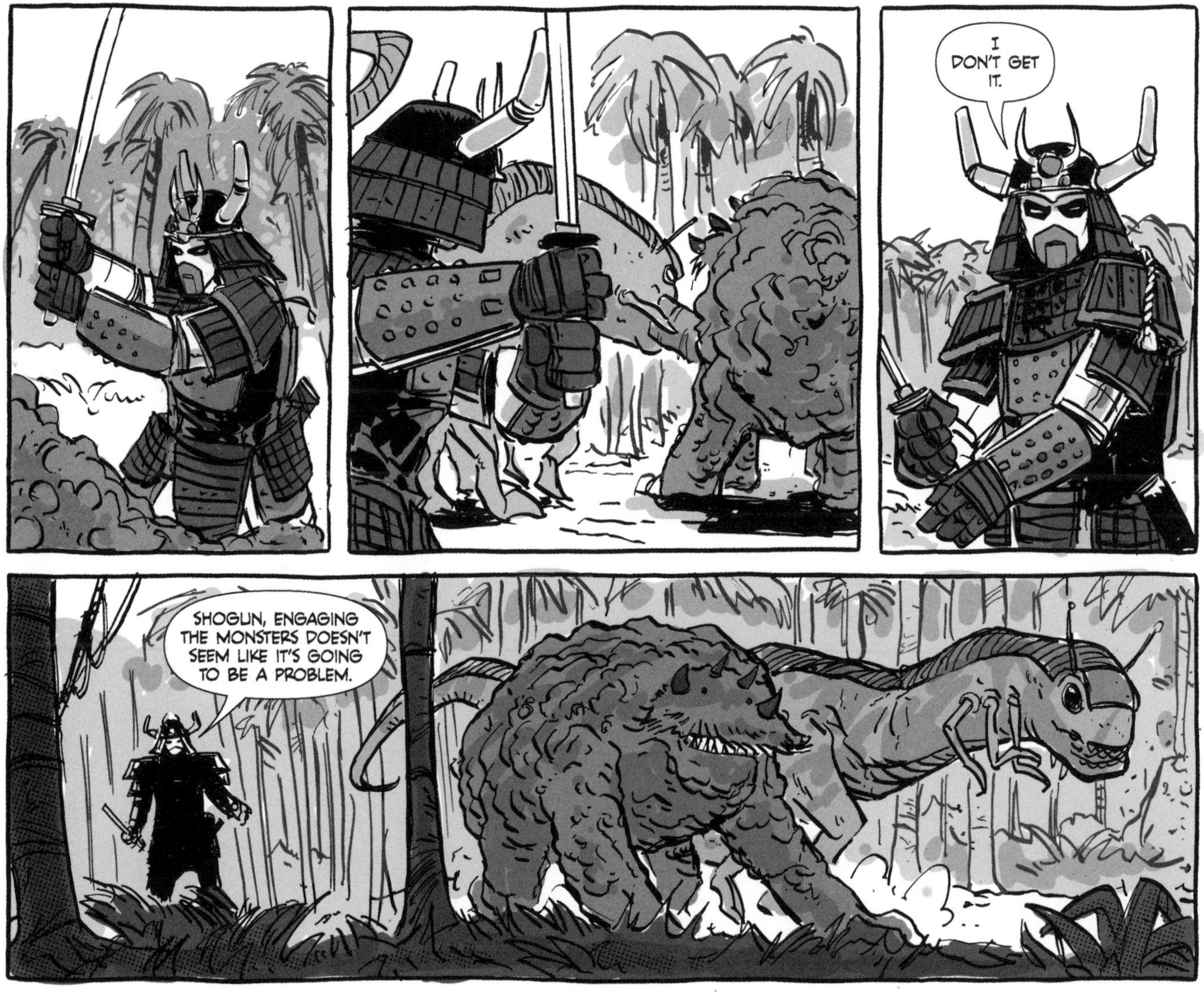
I DON'T GET IT.
SHOGUN, ENGAGING THE MONSTERS DOESN'T SEEM LIKE IT'S GOING TO BE A PROBLEM.

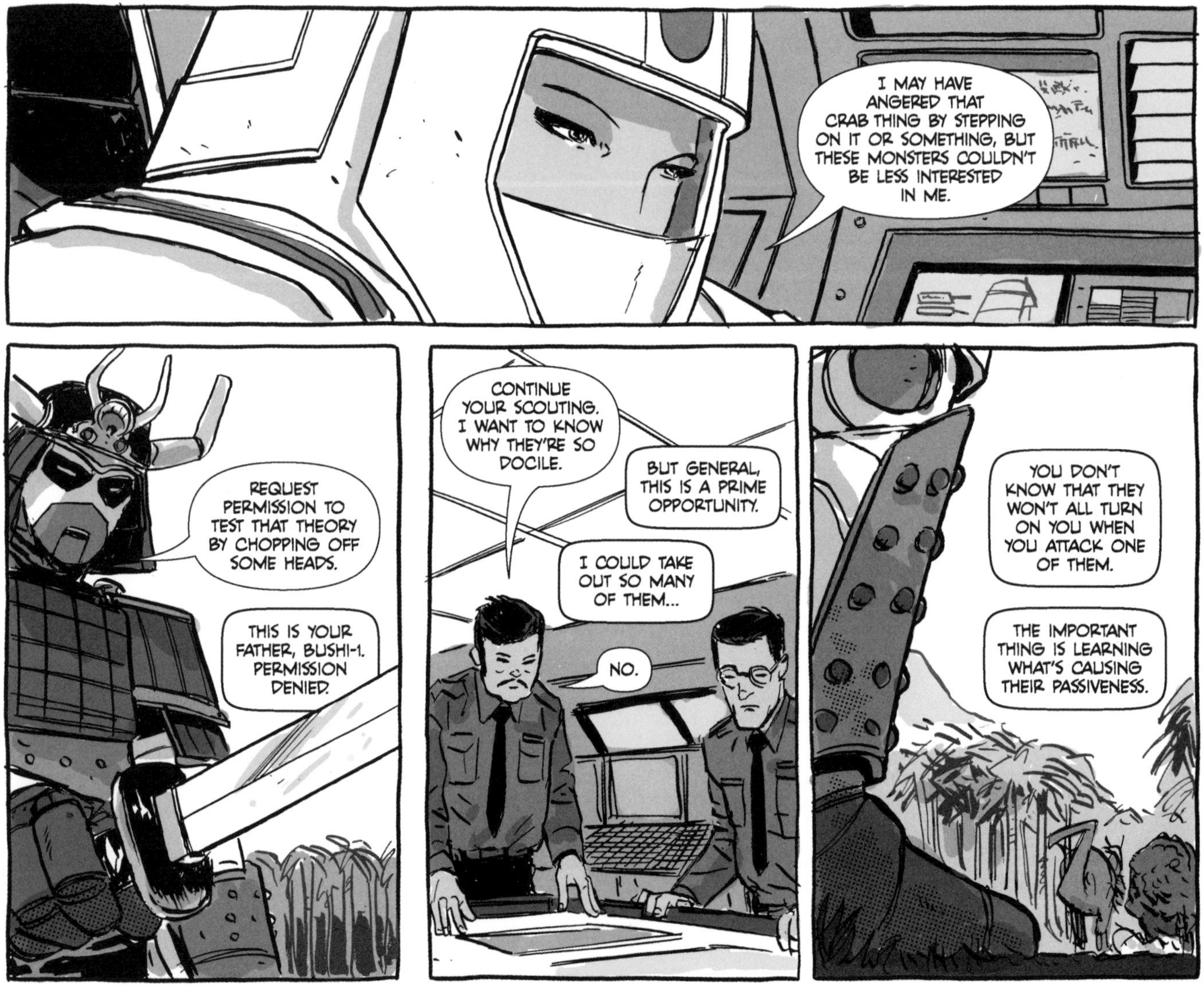
I MAY HAVE ANGERED THAT CRAB THING BY STEPPING ON IT OR SOMETHING, BUT THESE MONSTERS COULDN'T BE LESS INTERESTED IN ME.
REQUEST PERMISSION TO TEST THAT THEORY BY CHOPPING OFF SOME HEADS.
THIS IS YOUR FATHER, BUSHI-1. PERMISSION DENIED.
CONTINUE YOUR SCOUTING. I WANT TO KNOW WHY THEY'RE SO DOCILE.
BUT GENERAL, THIS IS A PRIME OPPORTUNITY.
I COULD TAKE OUT SO MANY OF THEM...
NO.
YOU DON'T KNOW THAT THEY WON'T ALL TURN ON YOU WHEN YOU ATTACK ONE OF THEM.
THE IMPORTANT THING IS LEARNING WHAT'S CAUSING THEIR PASSIVENESS.

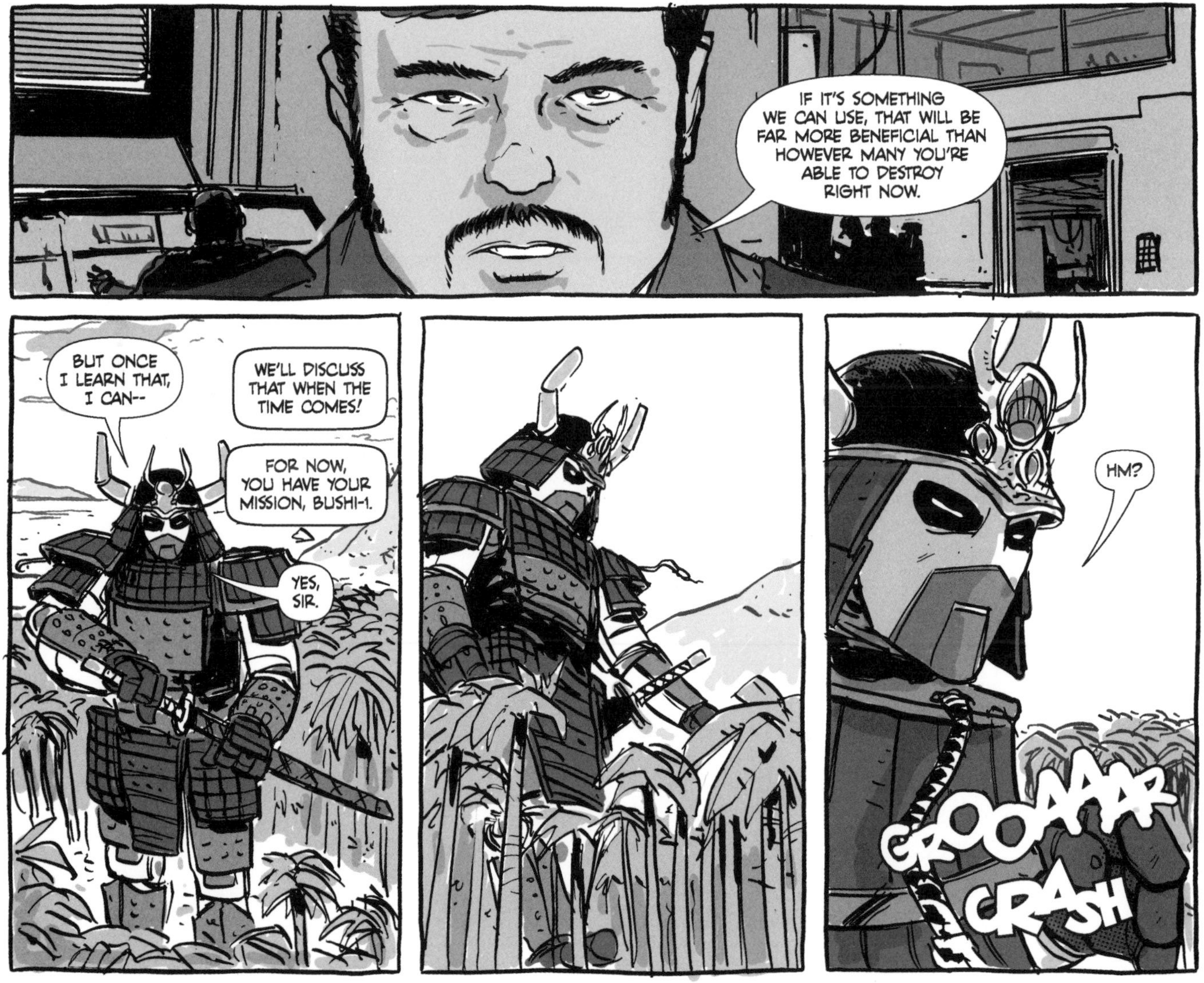
IF IT'S SOMETHING WE CAN USE, THAT WILL BE FAR MORE BENEFICIAL THAN HOWEVER MANY YOU'RE ABLE TO DESTROY RIGHT NOW.
BUT ONCE I LEARN THAT, I CAN--
WE'LL DISCUSS THAT WHEN THE TIME COMES!
FOR NOW, YOU HAVE YOUR MISSION, BUSHI-1.
YES, SIR.
HM?
GROOAAAR
CRASH

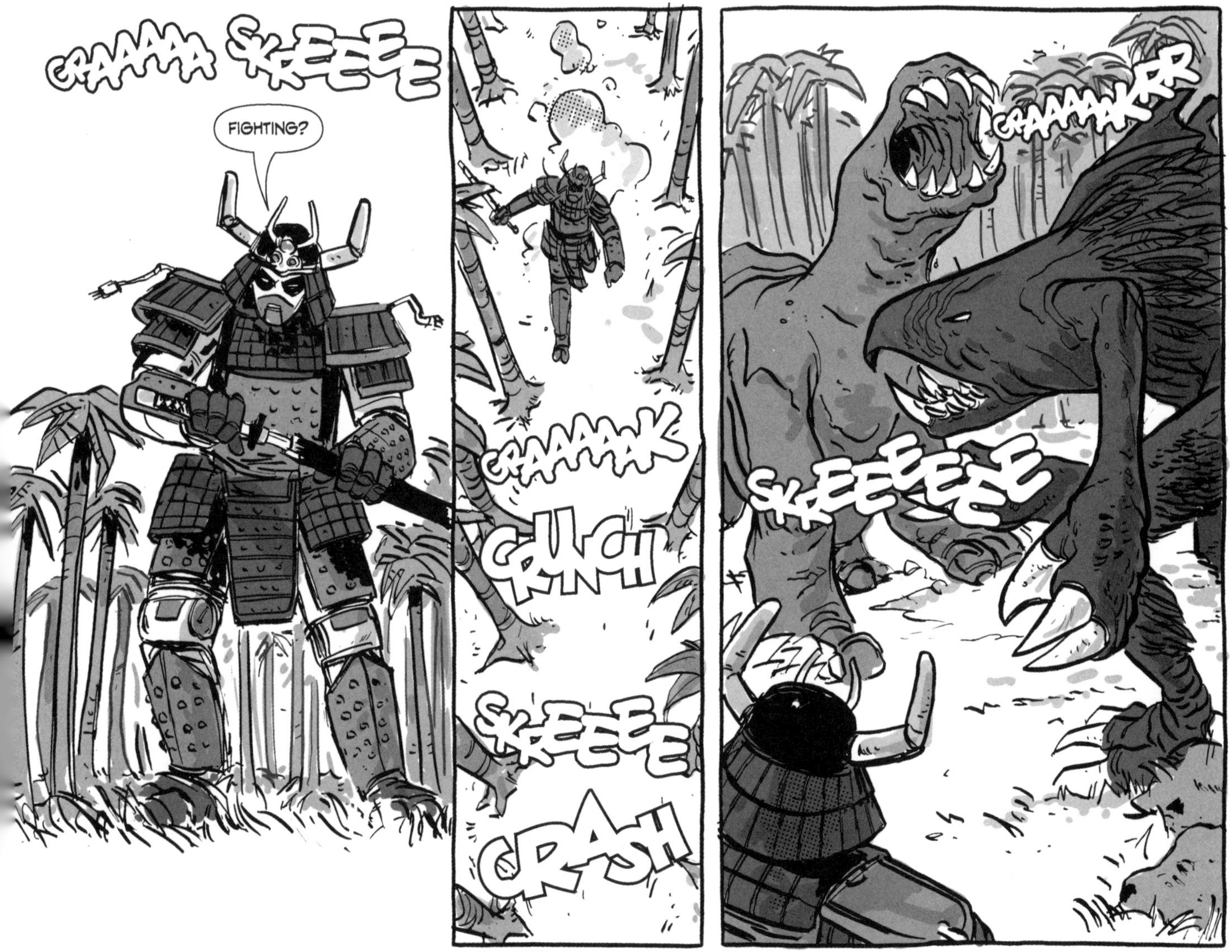
GRAAAAA SKREEEE
FIGHTING?
GRAAAAAK
CRUNCH
SKREEEE
CRASH
GRAAAAAKRR
SKREEEEEEE

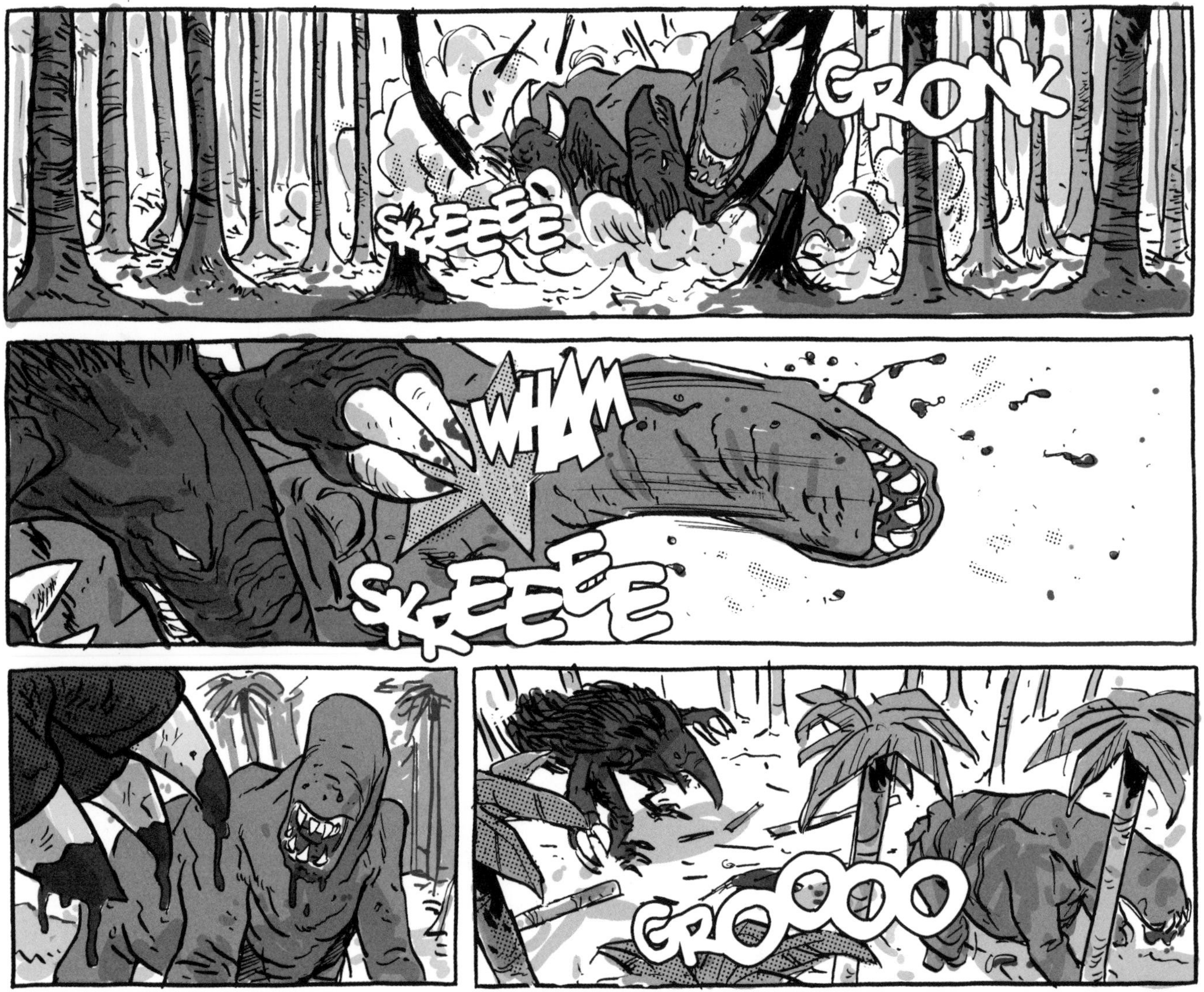
SKREEEE
GRONK
WHAM
SKREEEE
GROOOOO

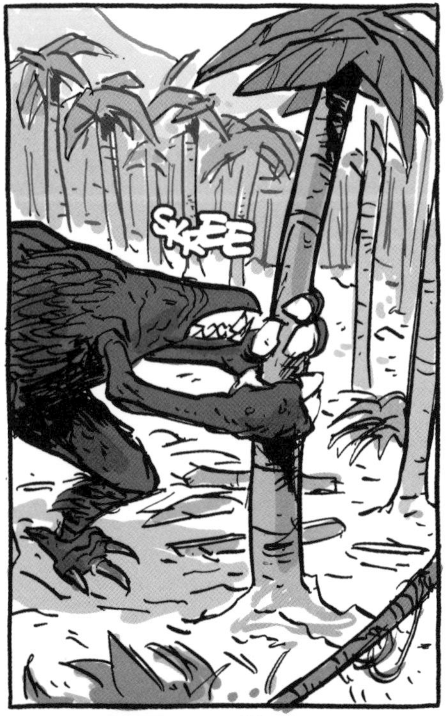
SKREE
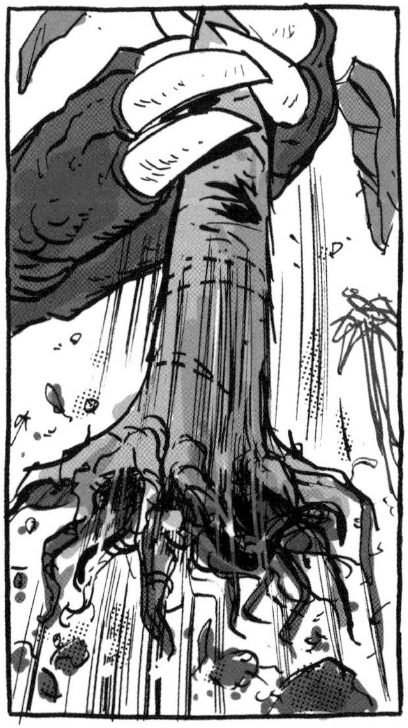
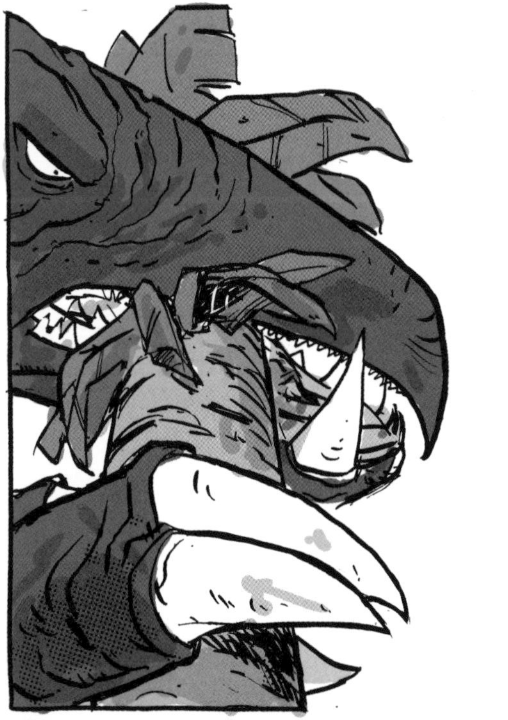
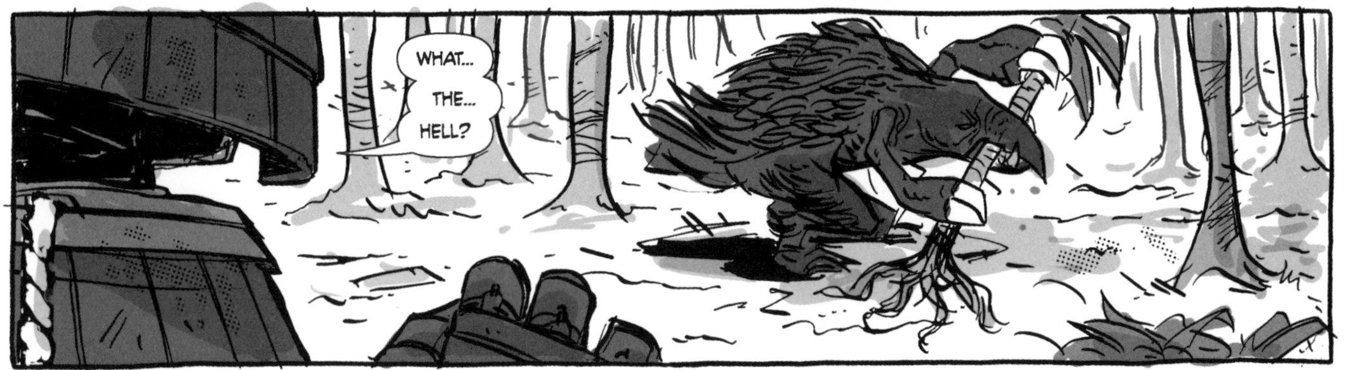
WHAT...
THE...
HELL?

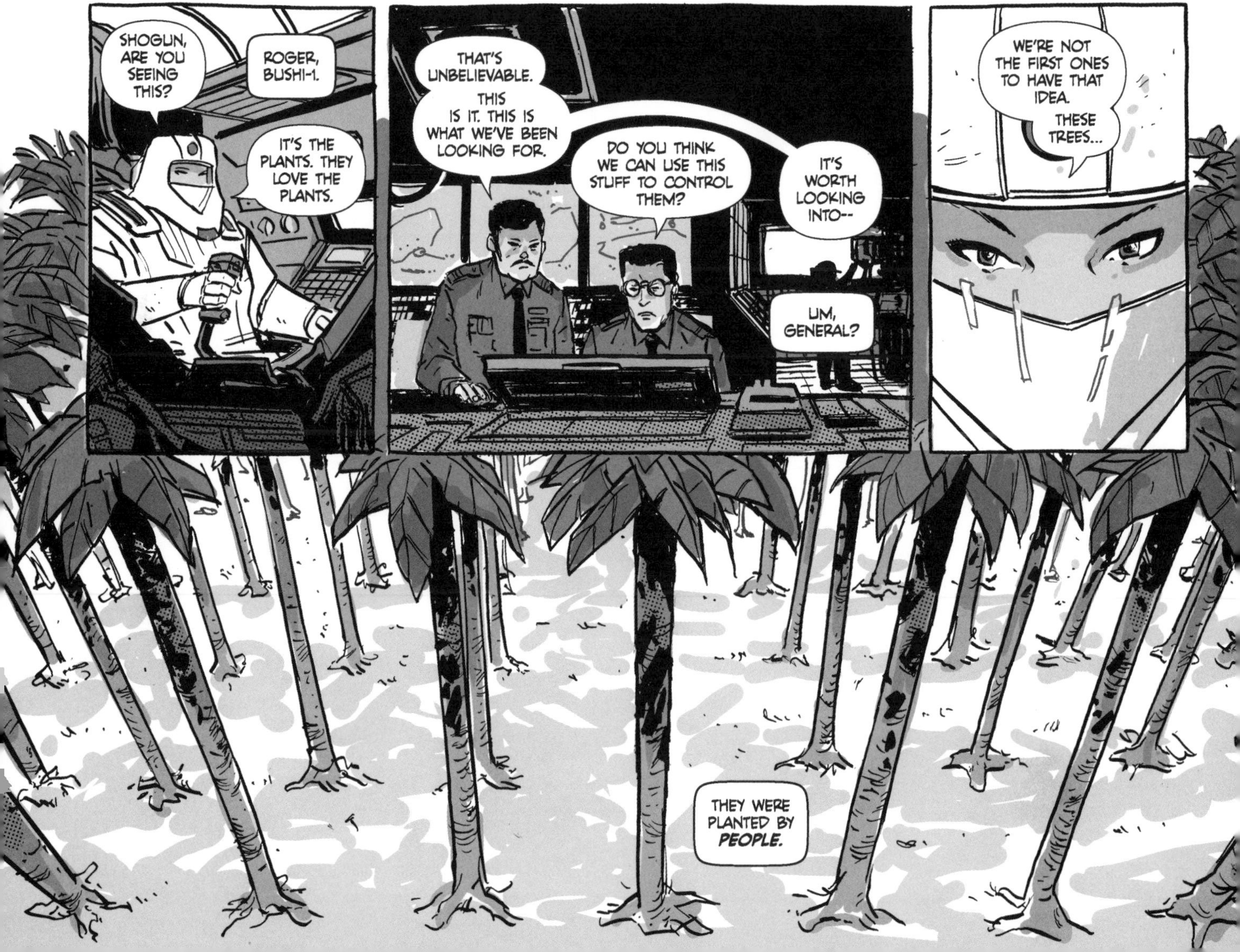
SHOGUN, ARE YOU SEEING THIS?
ROGER, BUSHI-1.
IT'S THE PLANTS. THEY LOVE THE PLANTS.
THAT'S UNBELIEVABLE.
THIS IS IT. THIS IS WHAT WE'VE BEEN LOOKING FOR.
DO YOU THINK WE CAN USE THIS STUFF TO CONTROL THEM?
IT'S WORTH LOOKING INTO--
UM, GENERAL?
WE'RE NOT THE FIRST ONES TO HAVE THAT IDEA.
THESE TREES...
THEY WERE PLANTED BY *PEOPLE.*

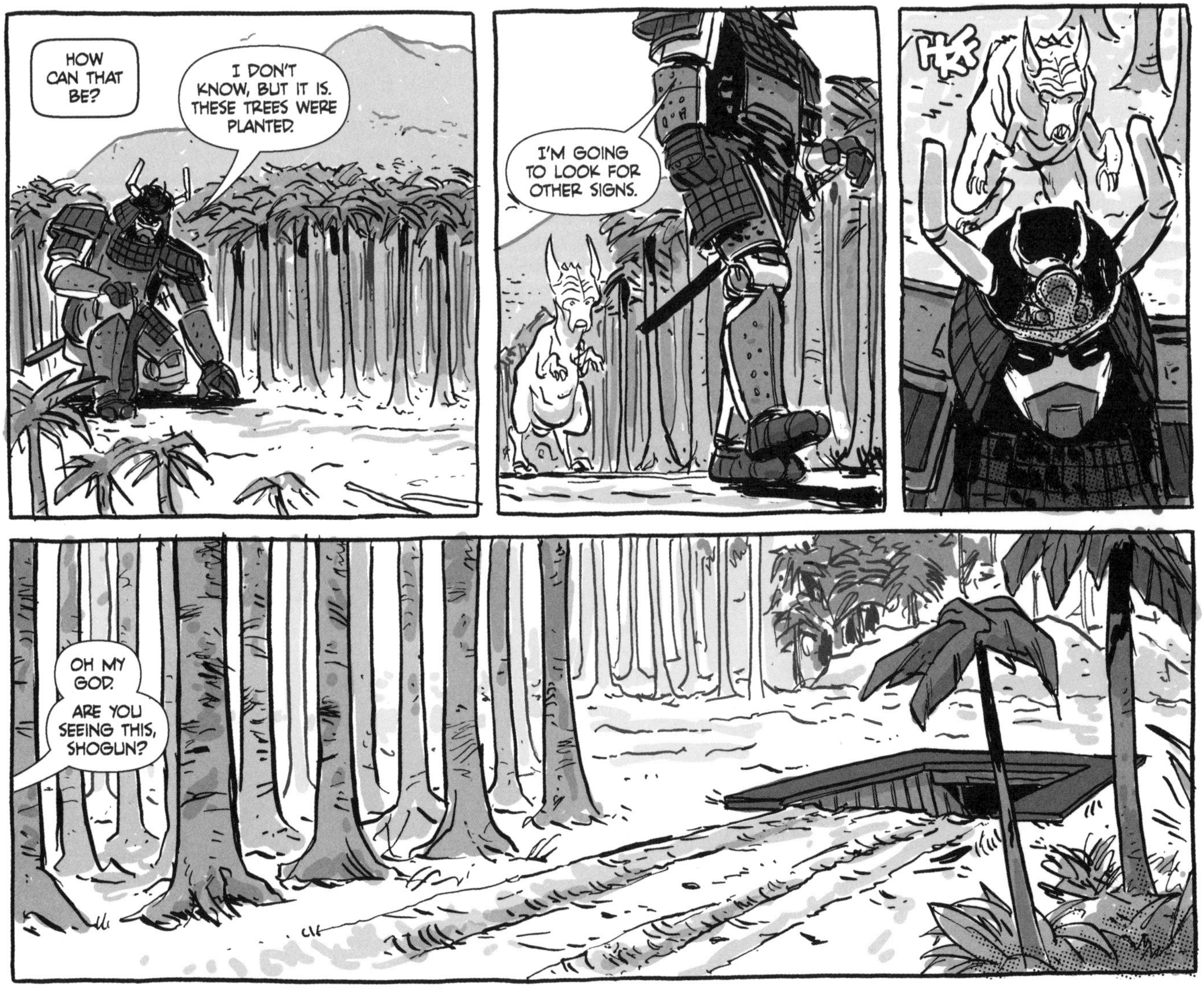
HOW CAN THAT BE?
I DON'T KNOW, BUT IT IS. THESE TREES WERE PLANTED.
I'M GOING TO LOOK FOR OTHER SIGNS.
OH MY GOD.
ARE YOU SEEING THIS, SHOGUN?

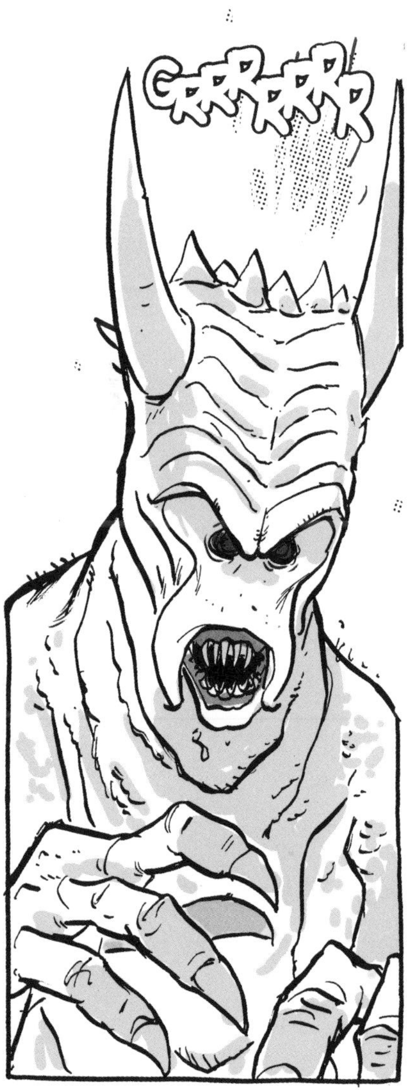
GRRRRRR
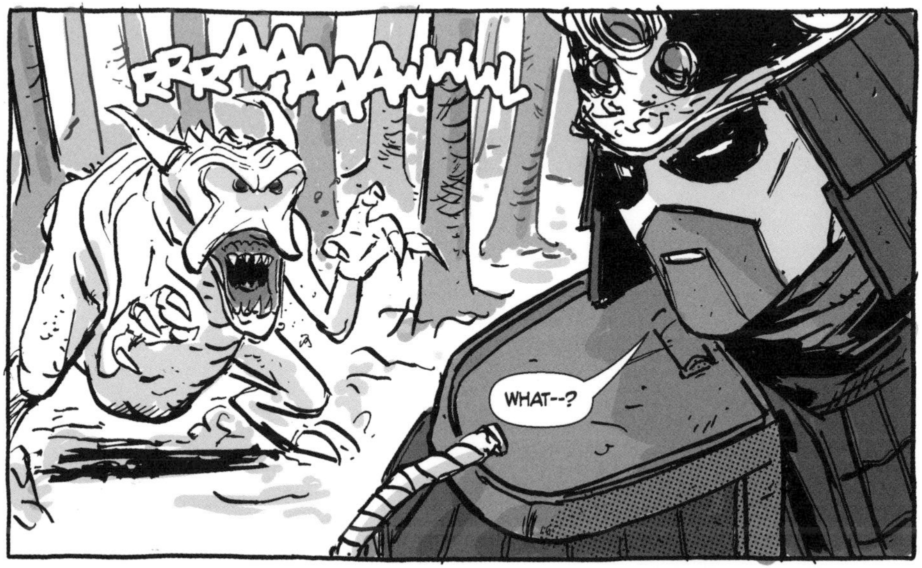
RRRAAAAAWWL
WHAT--?
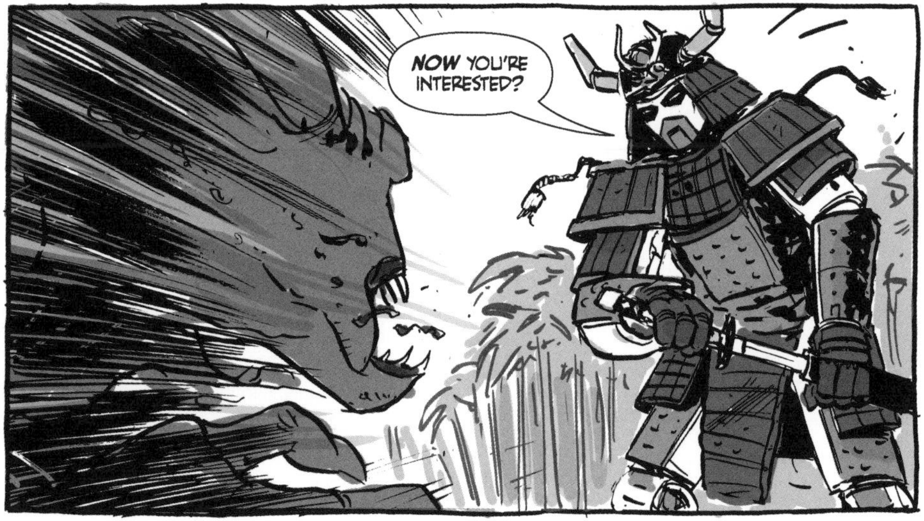
NOW YOU'RE INTERESTED?

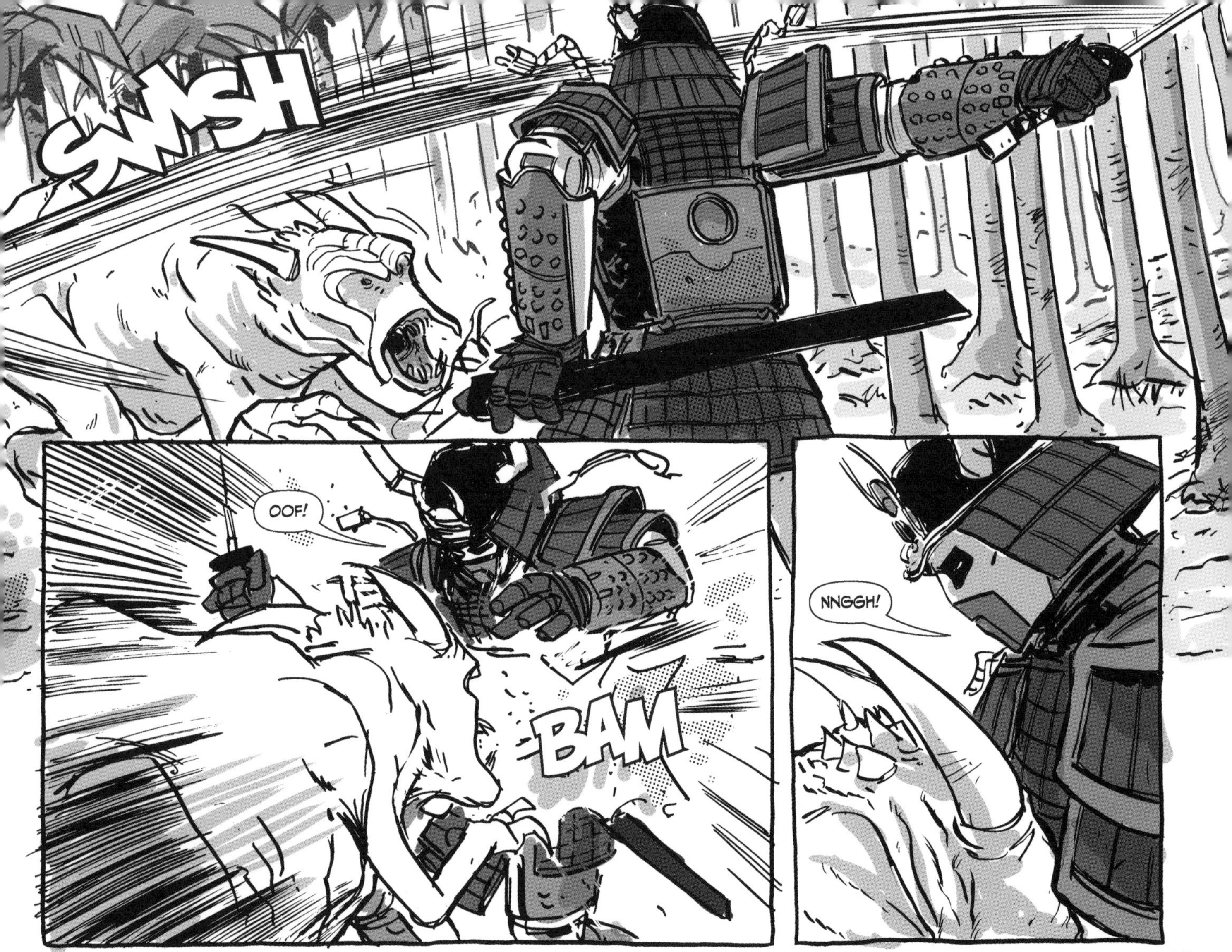
SWISH
OOF!
BAM
NNGGH!

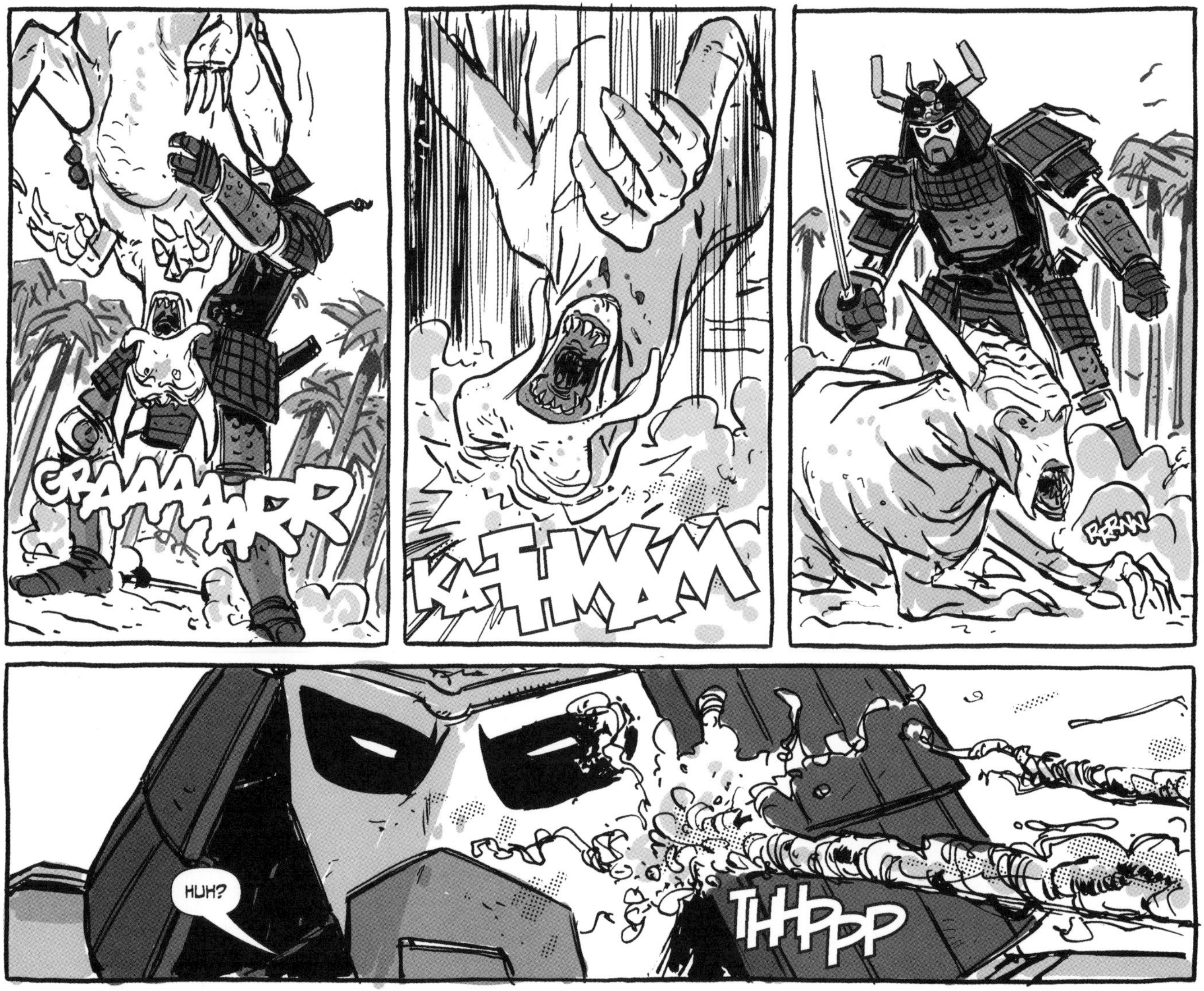
GRAAAARR
KA-THWAM
RRRNN
HUH?
THHPPP

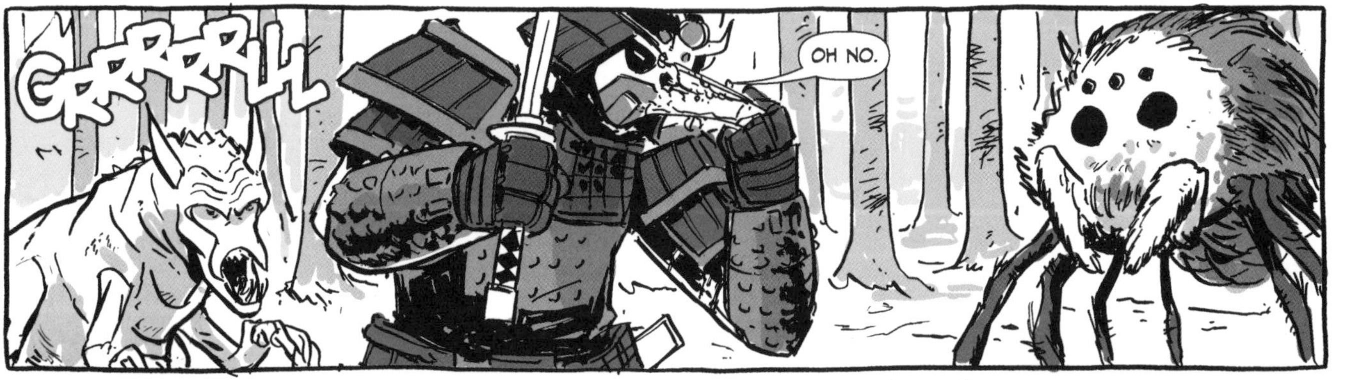
GRRRRLLL
OH NO.

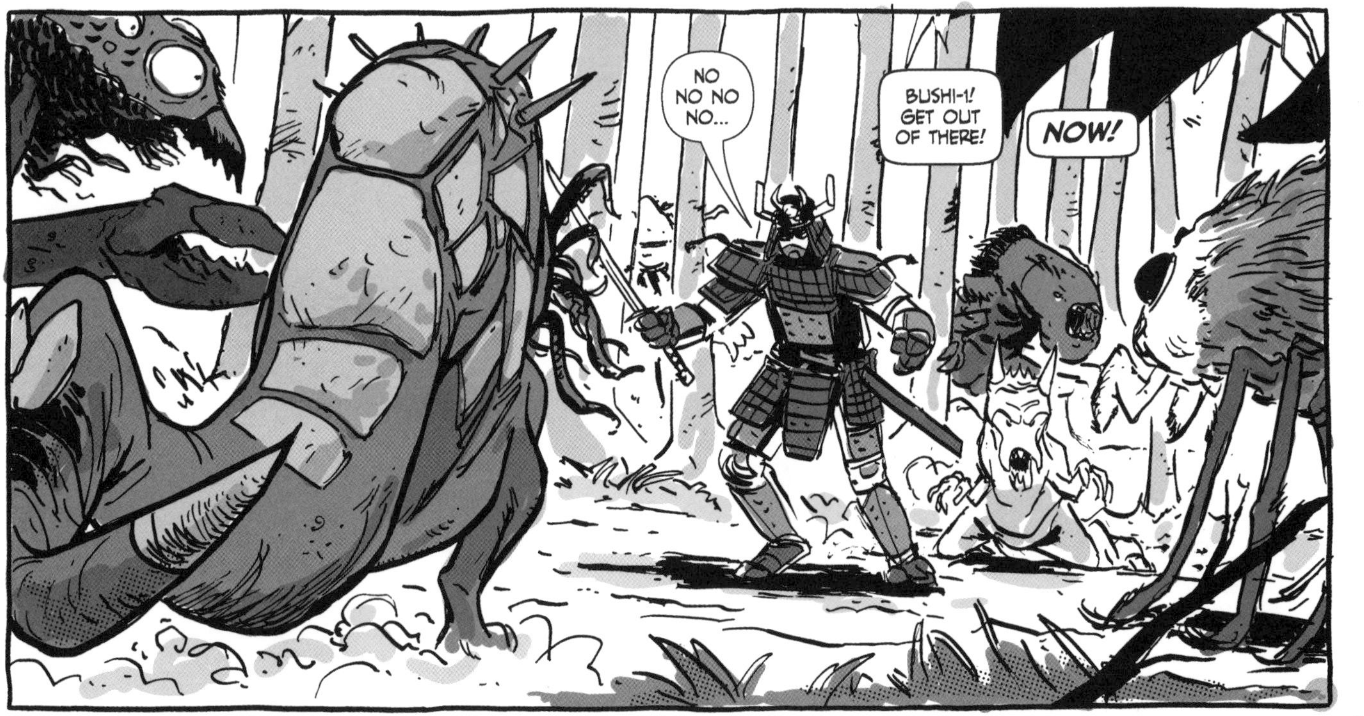
NO NO NO NO...
BUSHI-1! GET OUT OF THERE!
NOW!

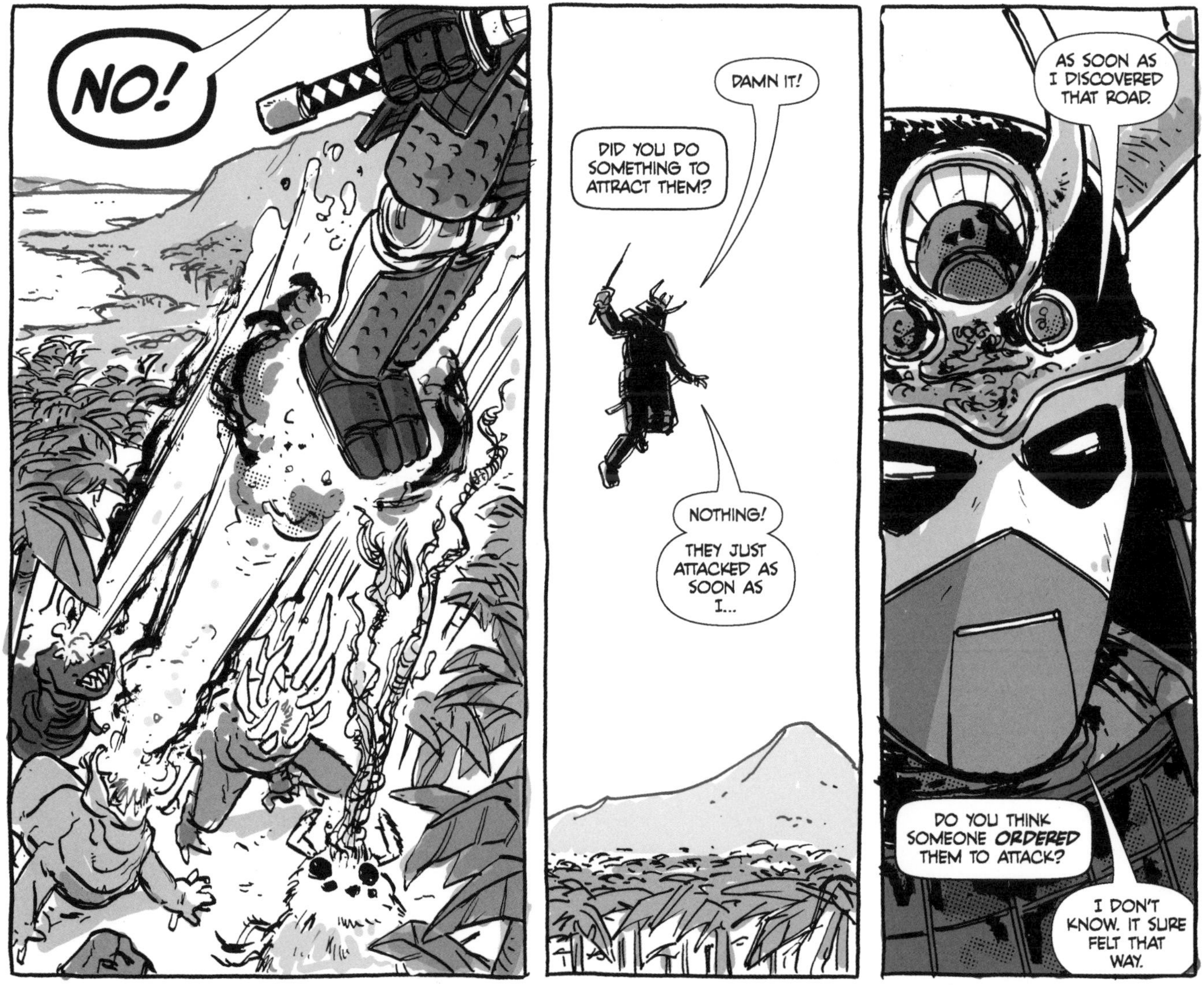
NO!
DID YOU DO SOMETHING TO ATTRACT THEM?
DAMN IT!
NOTHING!
THEY JUST ATTACKED AS SOON AS I...
AS SOON AS I DISCOVERED THAT ROAD.
DO YOU THINK SOMEONE ***ORDERED*** THEM TO ATTACK?
I DON'T KNOW. IT SURE FELT THAT WAY.

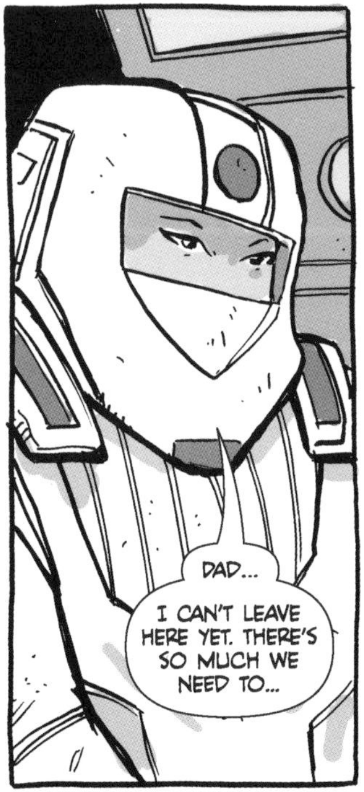
DAD...
I CAN'T LEAVE HERE YET. THERE'S SO MUCH WE NEED TO...

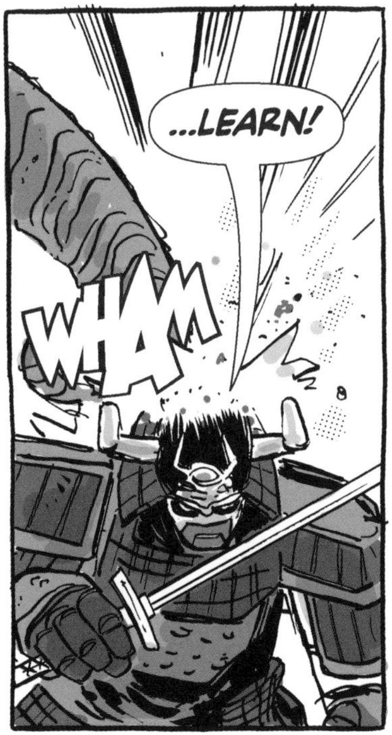
...LEARN!
WHAM

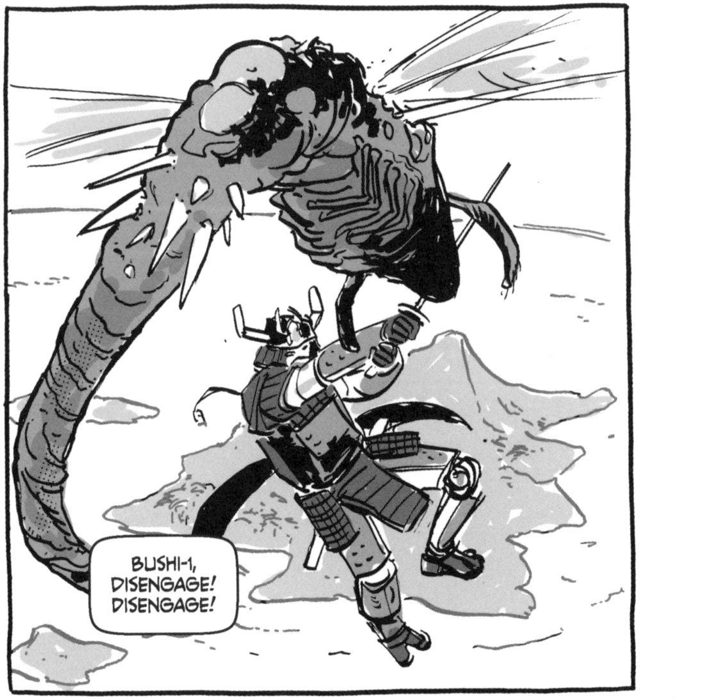
BUSHI-1, DISENGAGE! DISENGAGE!

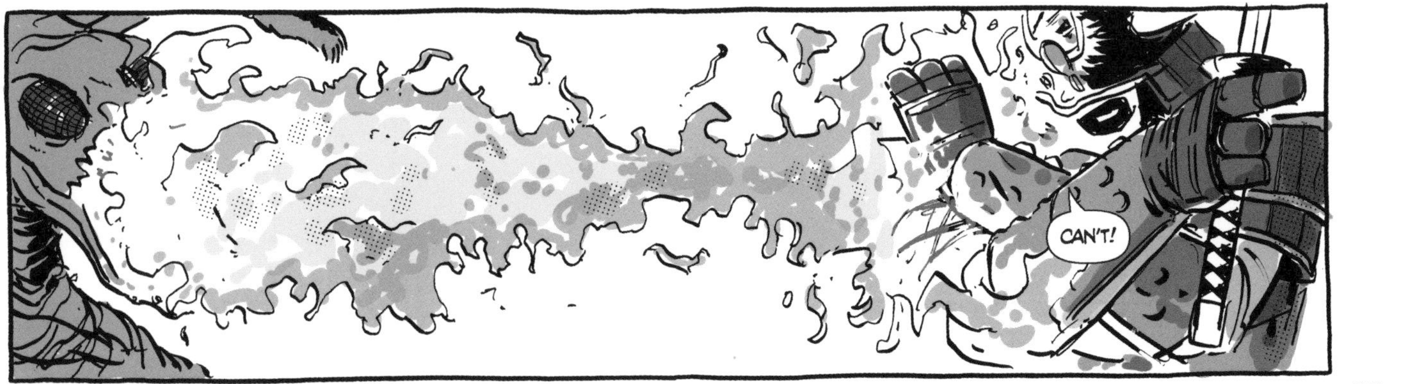
CAN'T!

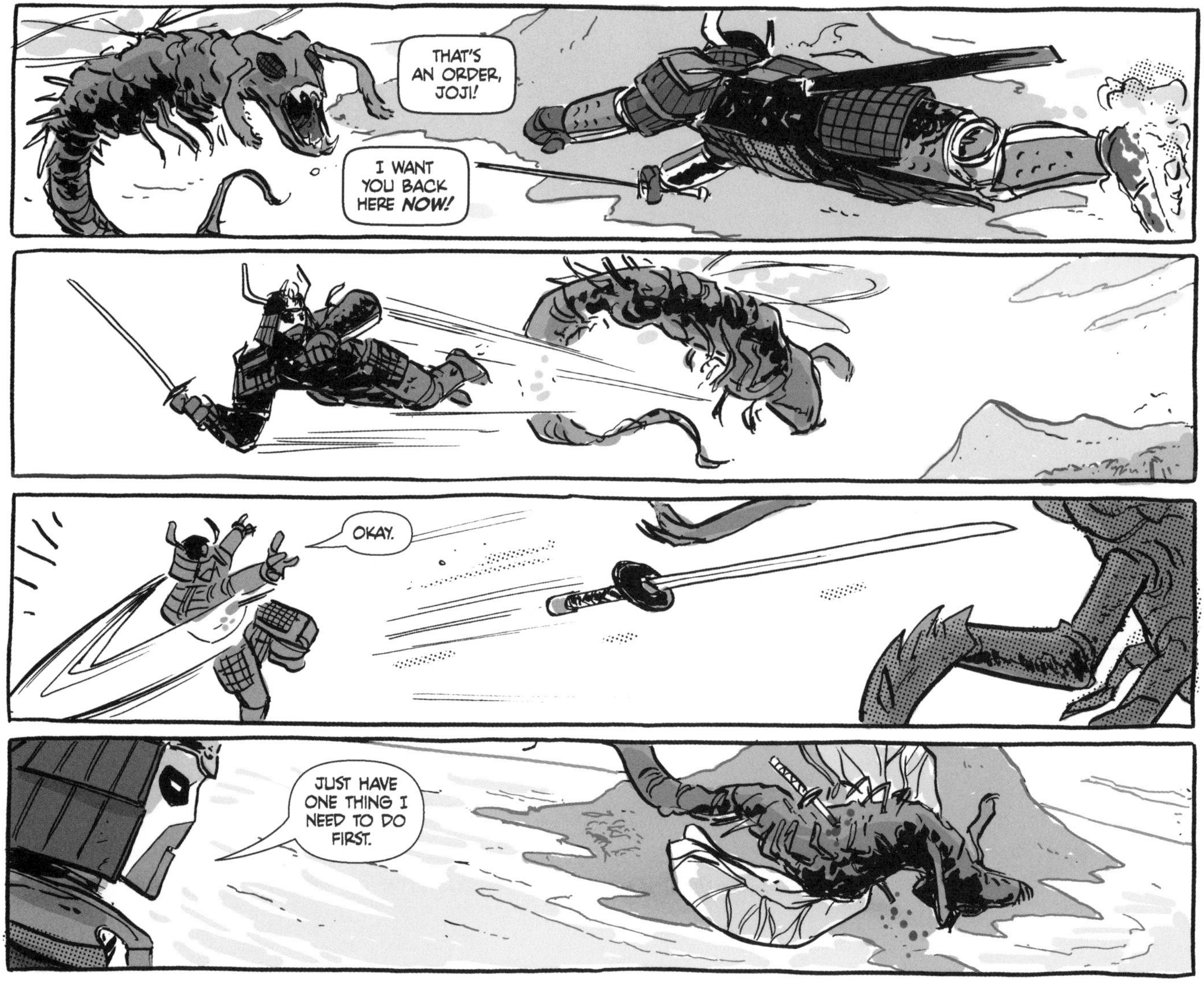
THAT'S AN ORDER, JOJI!
I WANT YOU BACK HERE **NOW!**
OKAY.
JUST HAVE ONE THING I NEED TO DO FIRST.

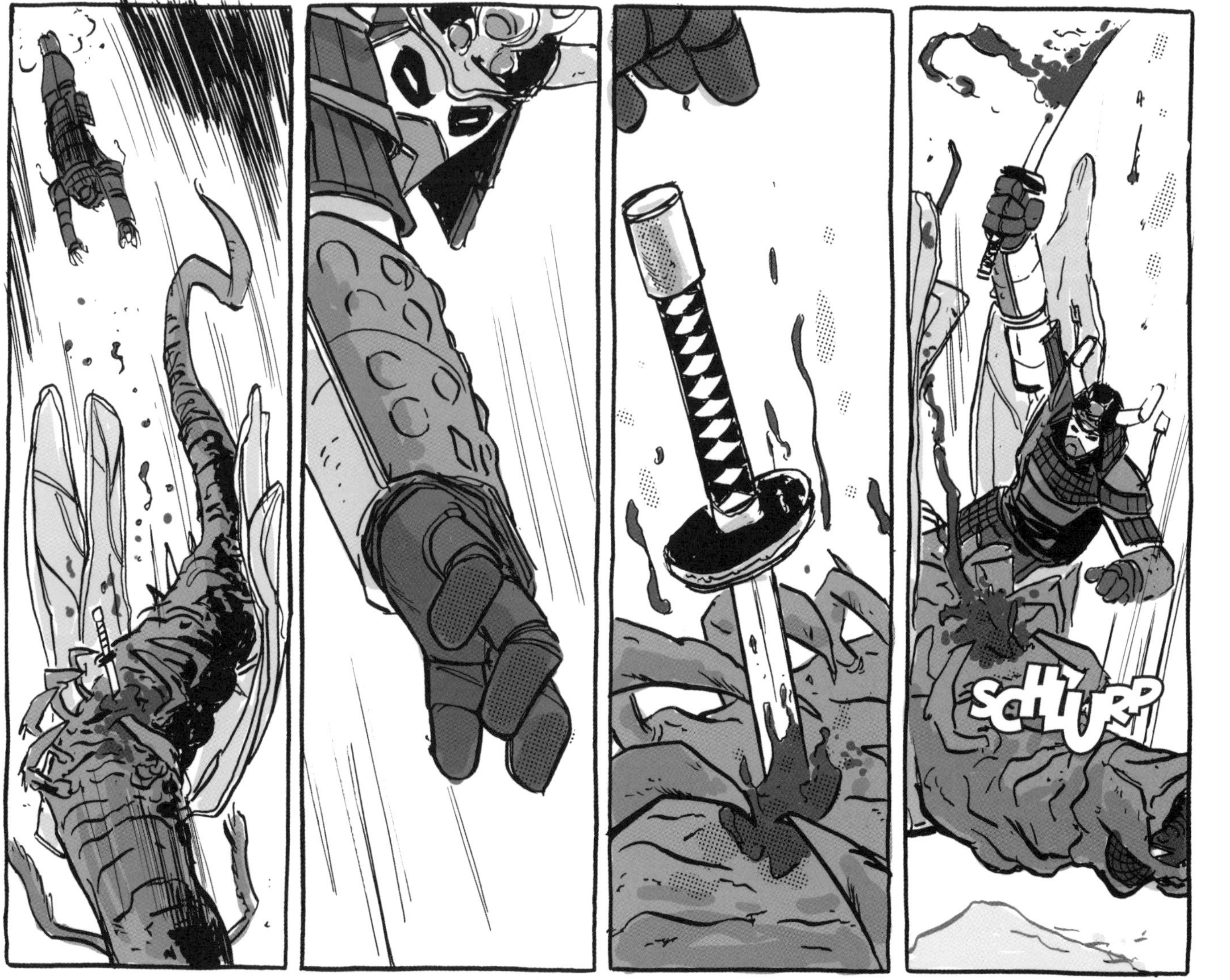
SCHLURP

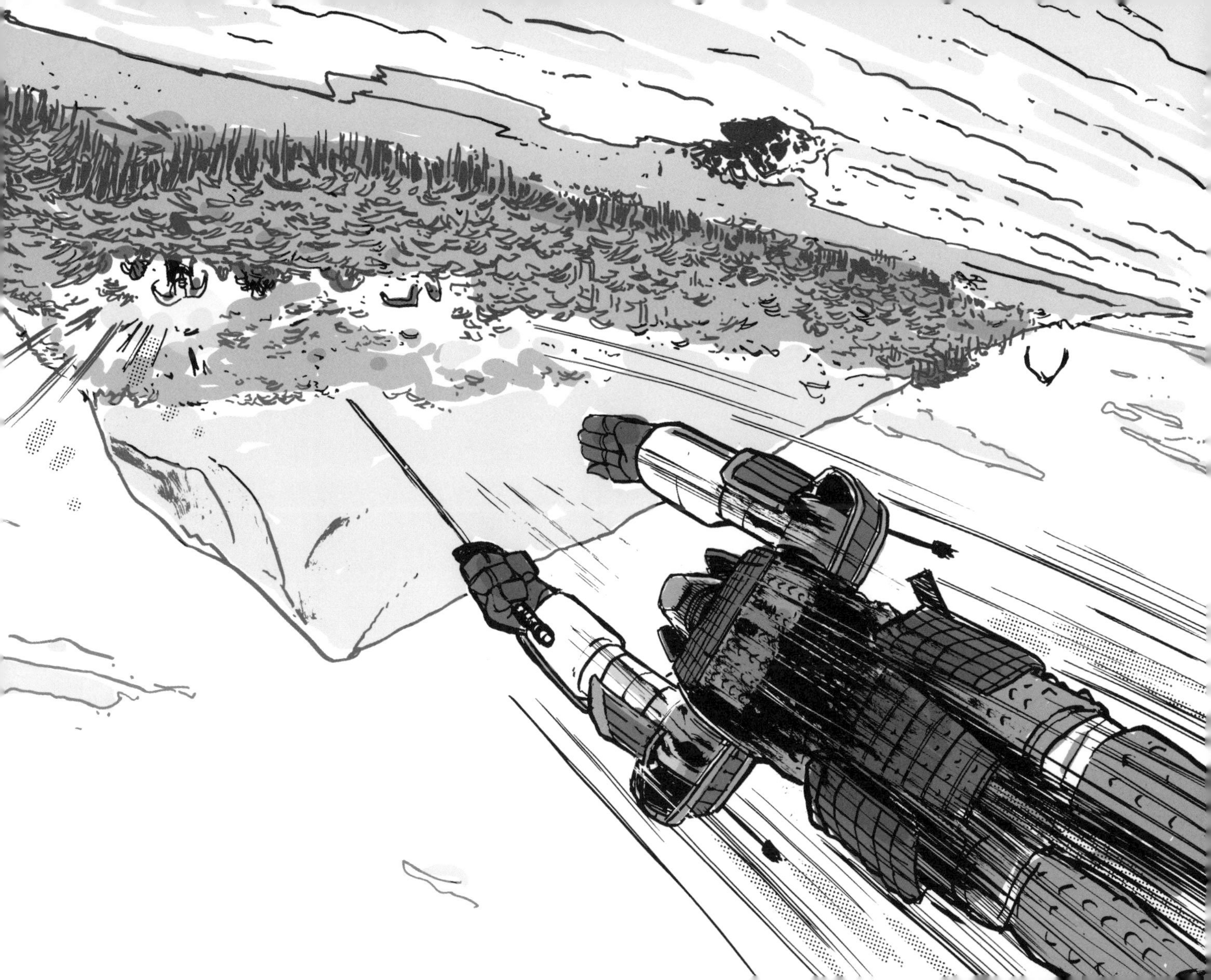

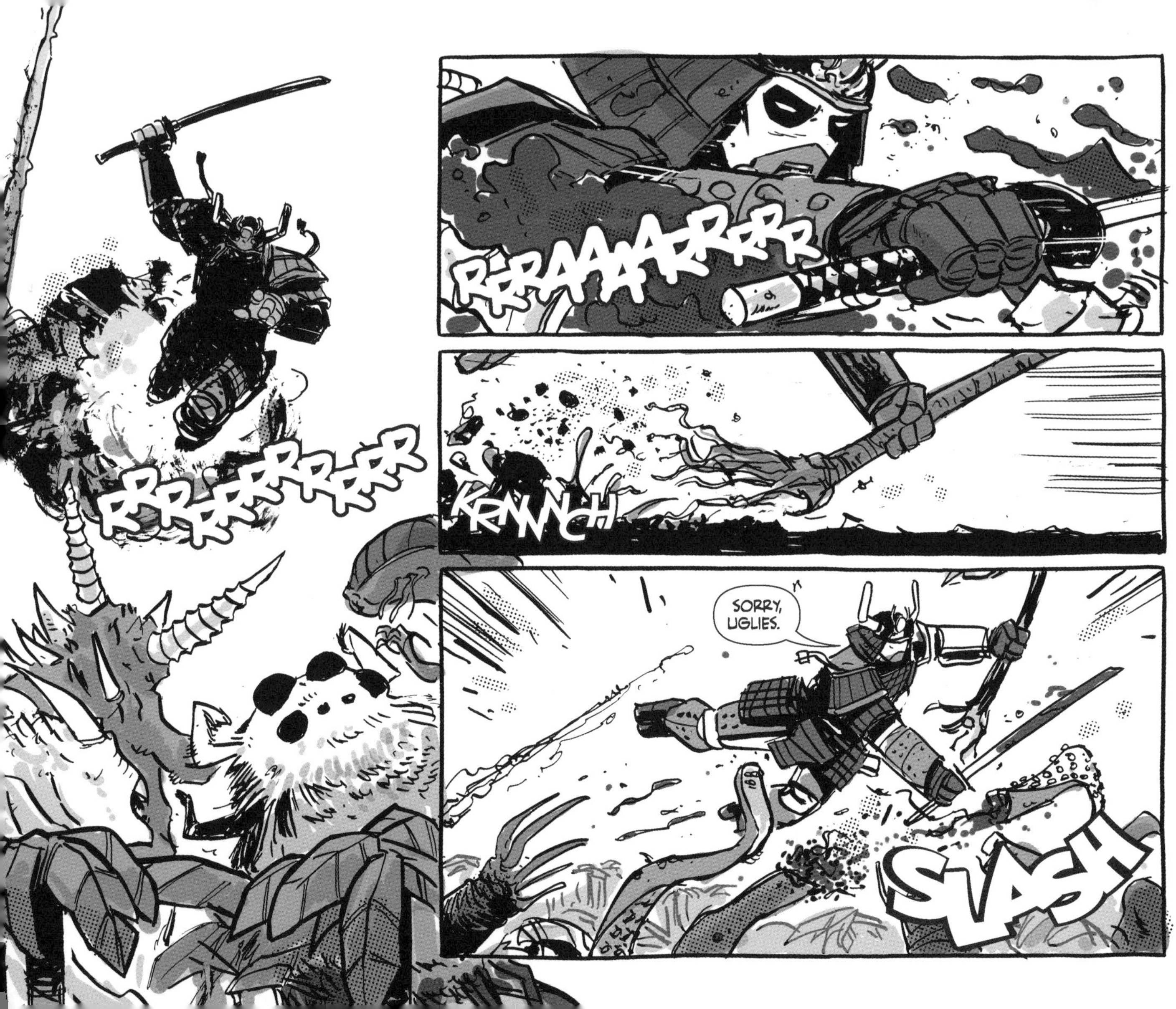
RRRRRRRRRR
RRRAAAARRRR
KRNNNCH
SORRY, UGLIES.
SLASH!

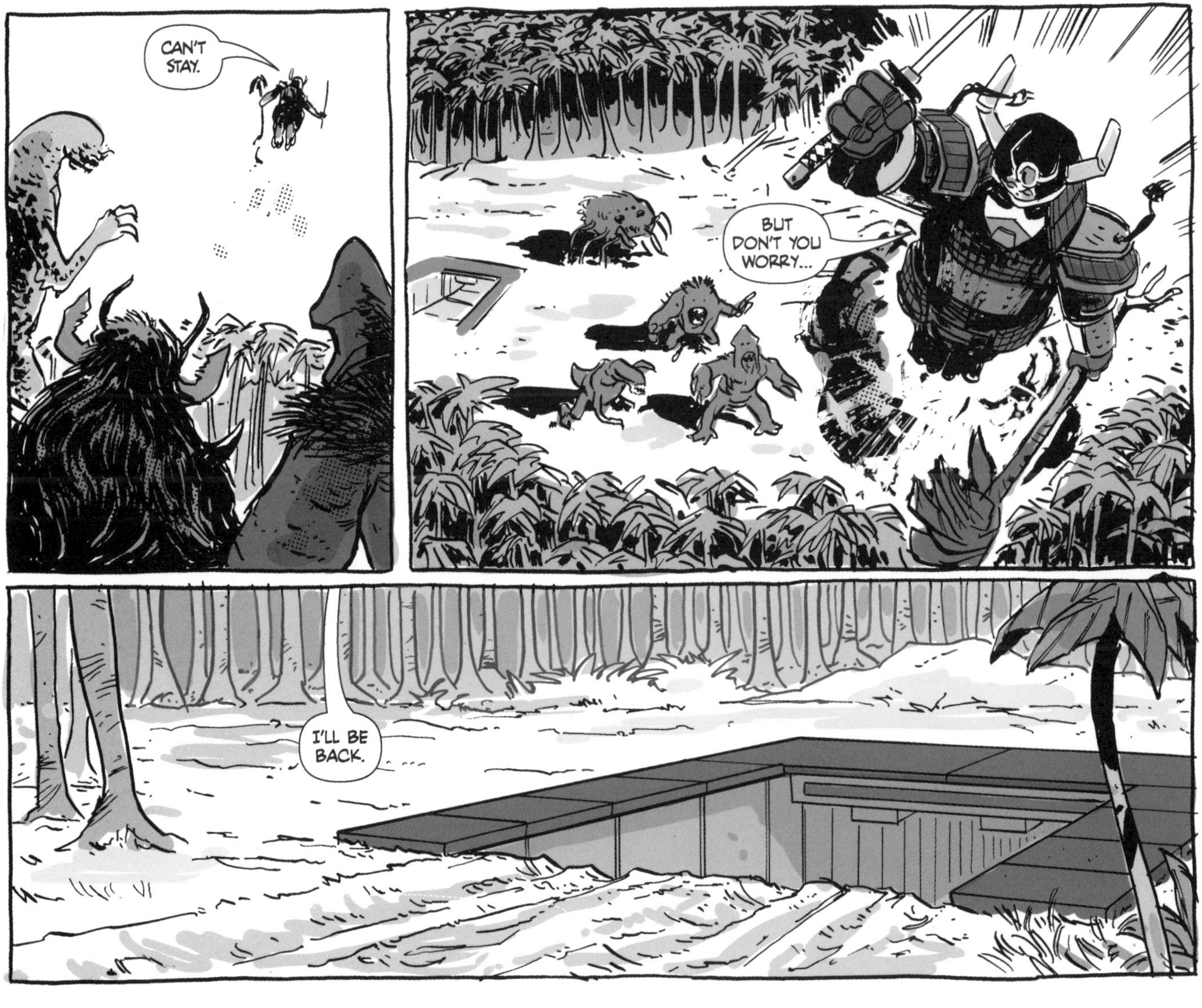
CAN'T STAY.
BUT DON'T YOU WORRY...
I'LL BE BACK.

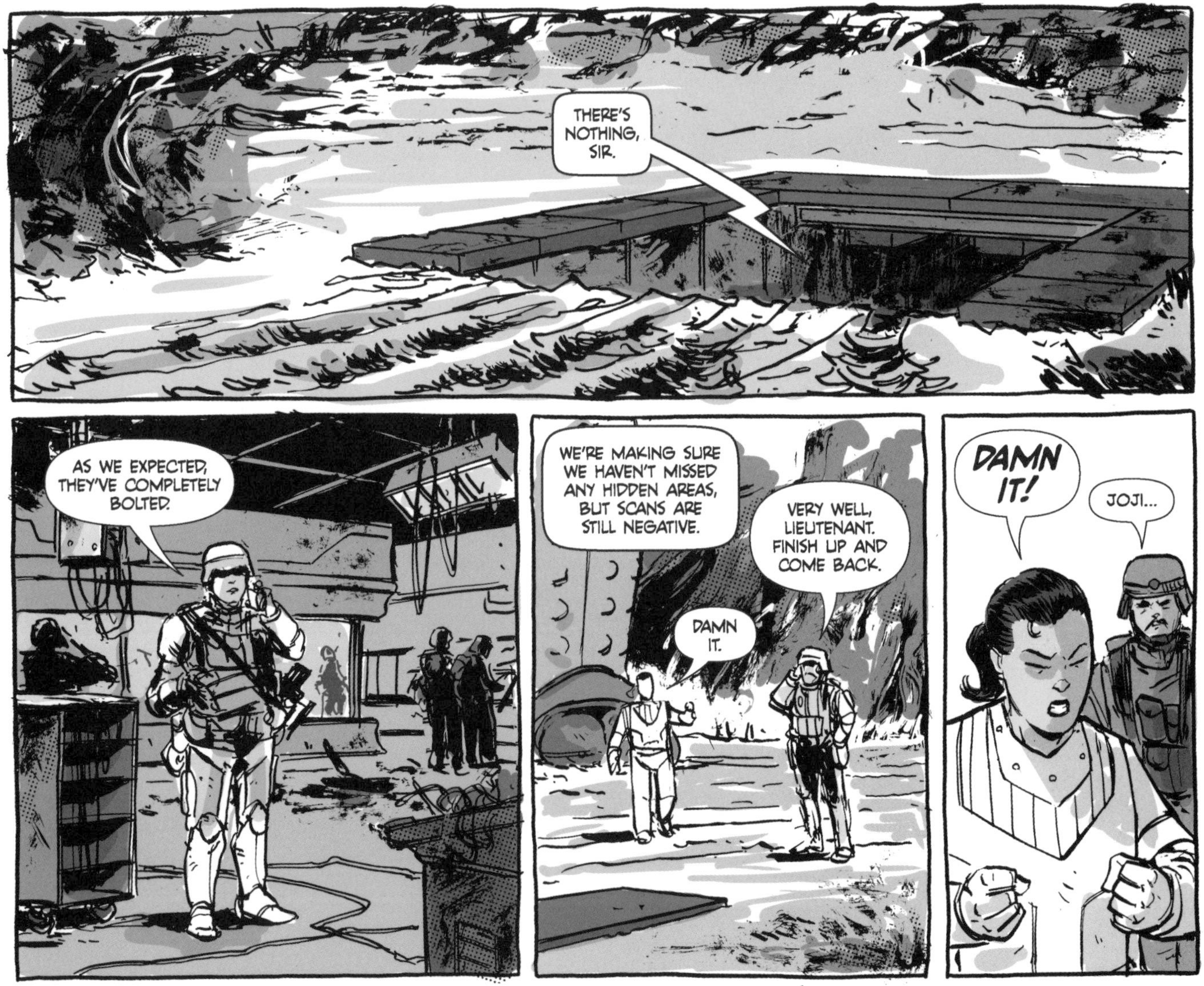
THERE'S NOTHING, SIR.
AS WE EXPECTED, THEY'VE COMPLETELY BOLTED.
WE'RE MAKING SURE WE HAVEN'T MISSED ANY HIDDEN AREAS, BUT SCANS ARE STILL NEGATIVE.
DAMN IT.
VERY WELL, LIEUTENANT. FINISH UP AND COME BACK.
DAMN IT!
JOJI...

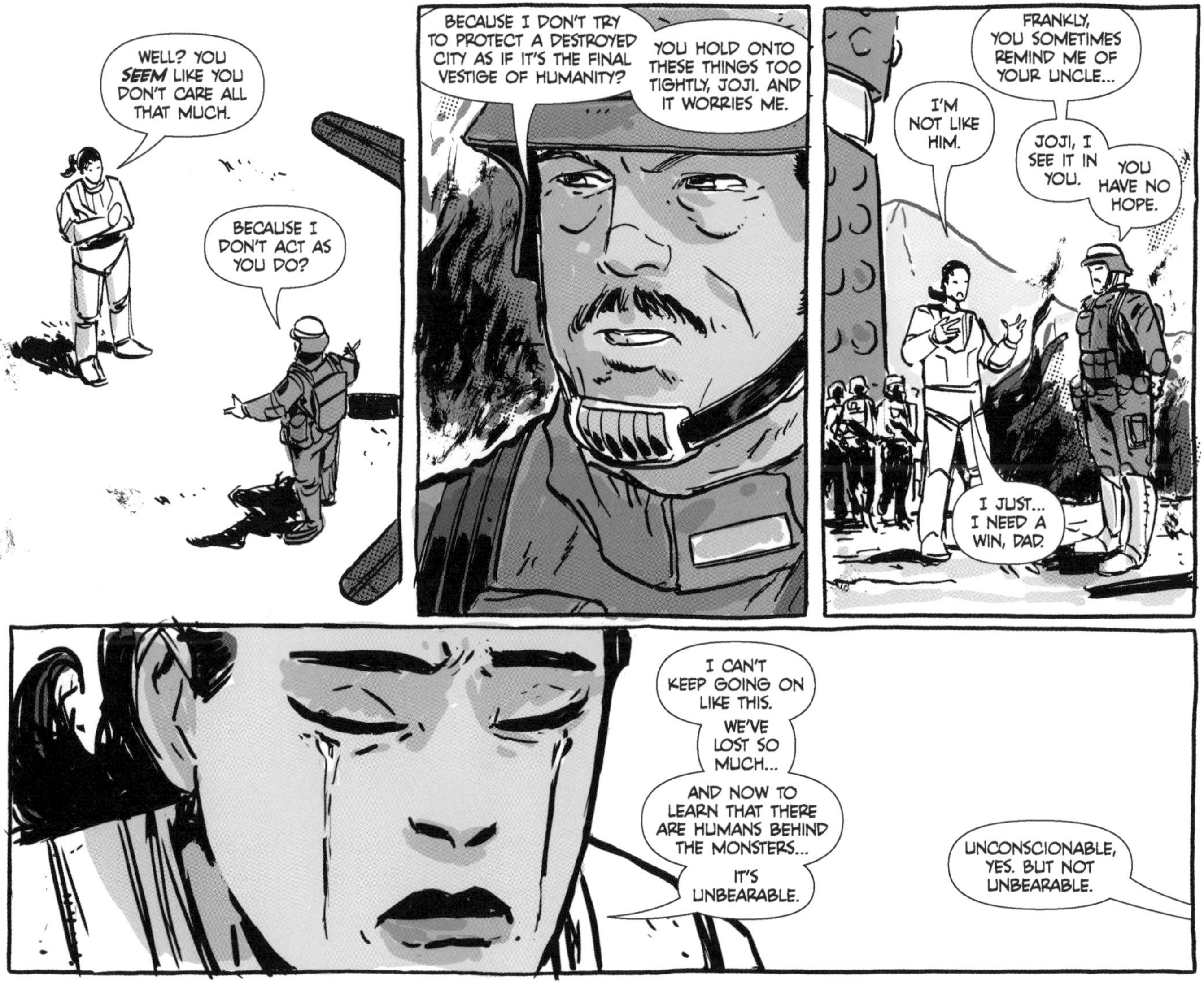
WELL? YOU **SEEM** LIKE YOU DON'T CARE ALL THAT MUCH.
BECAUSE I DON'T ACT AS YOU DO?
BECAUSE I DON'T TRY TO PROTECT A DESTROYED CITY AS IF IT'S THE FINAL VESTIGE OF HUMANITY?
YOU HOLD ONTO THESE THINGS TOO TIGHTLY, JOJI. AND IT WORRIES ME.
FRANKLY, YOU SOMETIMES REMIND ME OF YOUR UNCLE...
I'M NOT LIKE HIM.
JOJI, I SEE IT IN YOU.
YOU HAVE NO HOPE.
I JUST... I NEED A WIN, DAD.
I CAN'T KEEP GOING ON LIKE THIS.
WE'VE LOST SO MUCH...
AND NOW TO LEARN THAT THERE ARE HUMANS BEHIND THE MONSTERS...
IT'S UNBEARABLE.
UNCONSCIONABLE, YES. BUT NOT UNBEARABLE.

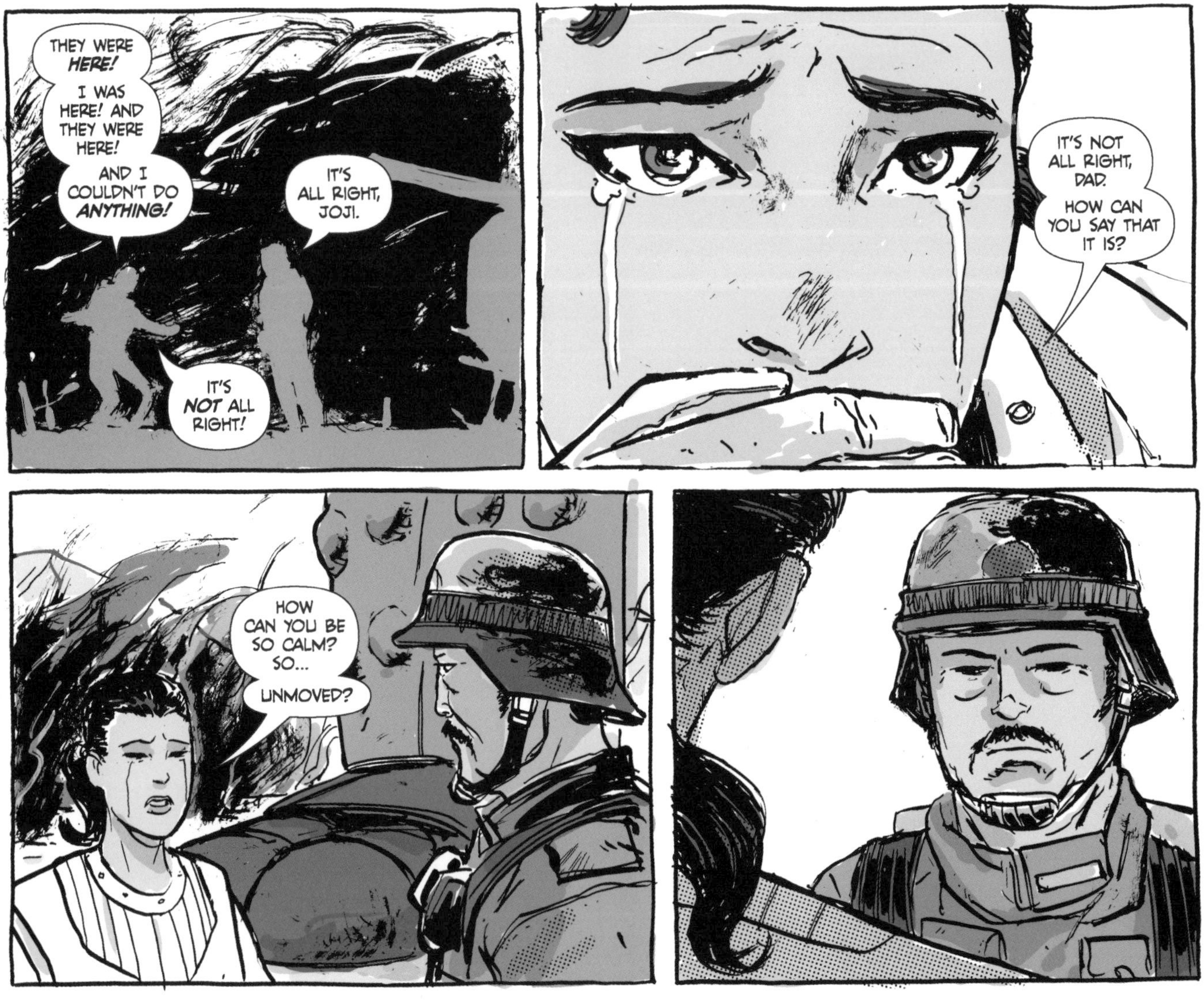
THEY WERE **HERE!**
I WAS HERE! AND THEY WERE HERE!
AND I COULDN'T DO **ANYTHING!**
IT'S ALL RIGHT, JOJI.
IT'S **NOT** ALL RIGHT!
IT'S NOT ALL RIGHT, DAD.
HOW CAN YOU SAY THAT IT IS?
HOW CAN YOU BE SO CALM? SO...
UNMOVED?

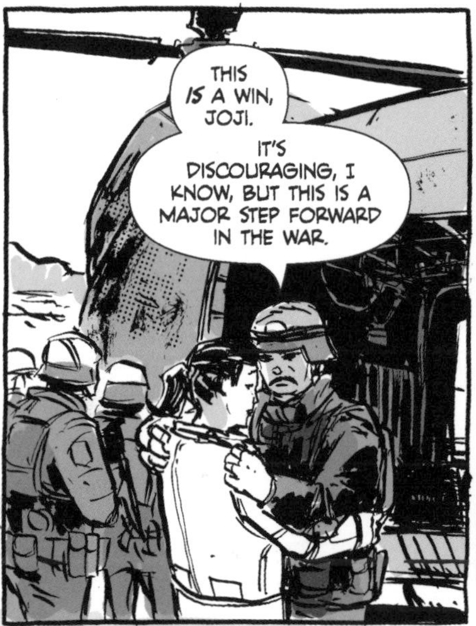
THIS *IS* A WIN, JOJI.
IT'S DISCOURAGING, I KNOW, BUT THIS IS A MAJOR STEP FORWARD IN THE WAR.
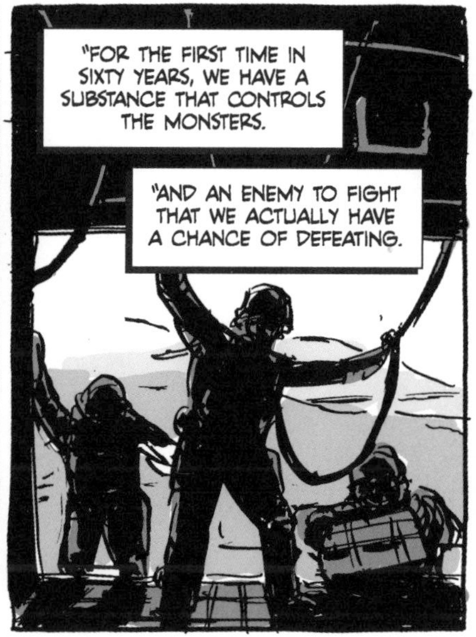
"FOR THE FIRST TIME IN SIXTY YEARS, WE HAVE A SUBSTANCE THAT CONTROLS THE MONSTERS.
"AND AN ENEMY TO FIGHT THAT WE ACTUALLY HAVE A CHANCE OF DEFEATING.
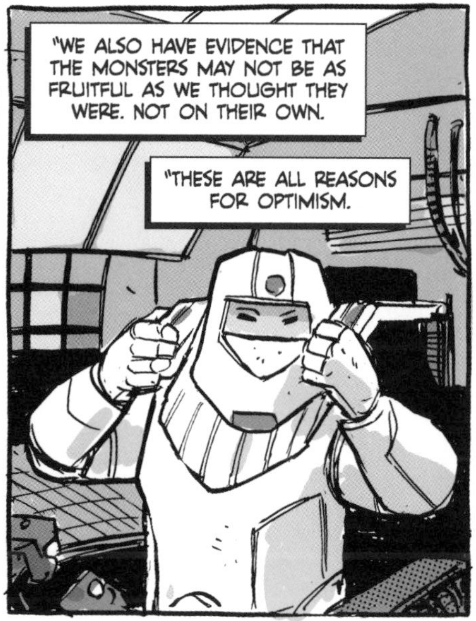
"WE ALSO HAVE EVIDENCE THAT THE MONSTERS MAY NOT BE AS FRUITFUL AS WE THOUGHT THEY WERE. NOT ON THEIR OWN.
"THESE ARE ALL REASONS FOR OPTIMISM.
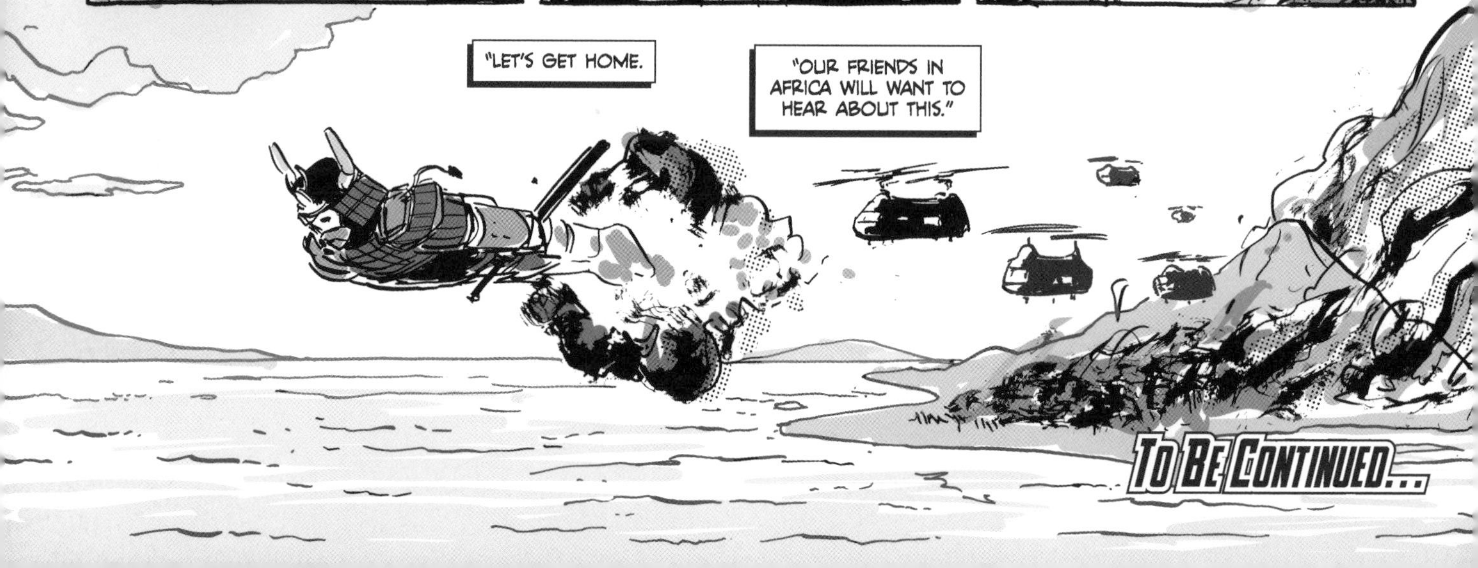
"LET'S GET HOME.
"OUR FRIENDS IN AFRICA WILL WANT TO HEAR ABOUT THIS."
TO BE CONTINUED...

PINUP GALLERY

ILLUSTRATIONS BY

BRIAN LEVEL
FRANKIE B. WASHINGTON
JEFF McCOMSEY
JOHNNIE CHRISTMAS
OTIS FRAMPTON

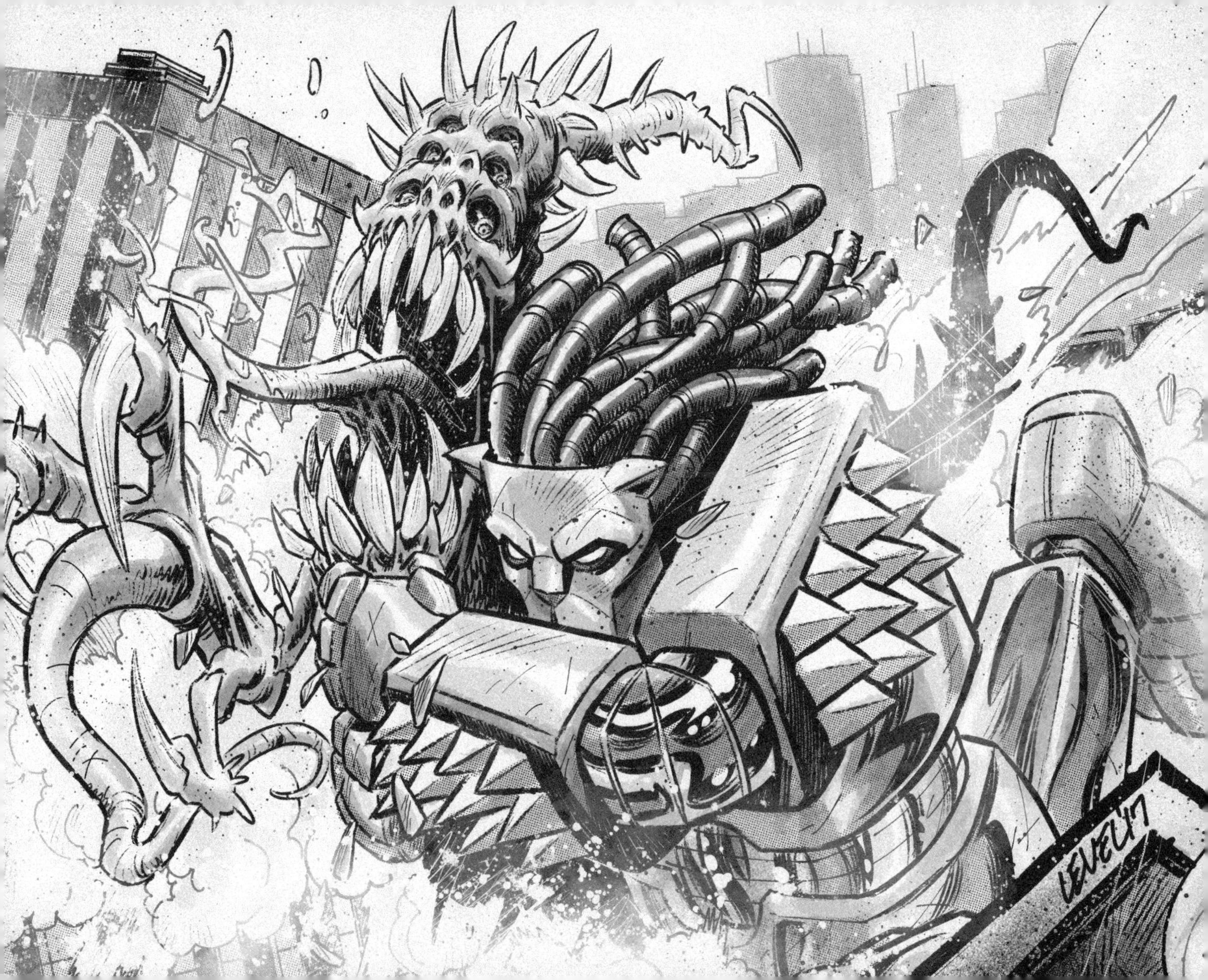
LEVEL'17

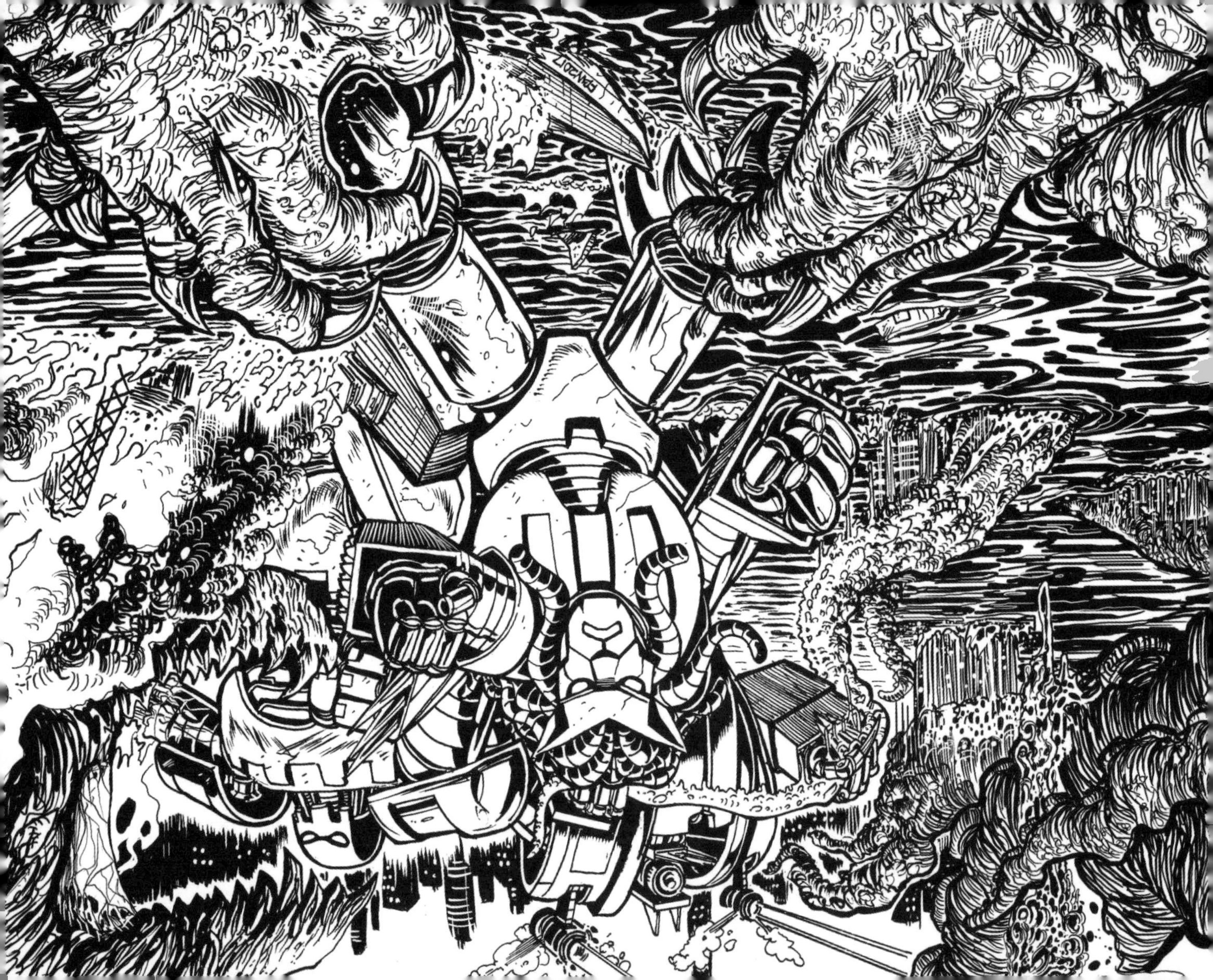

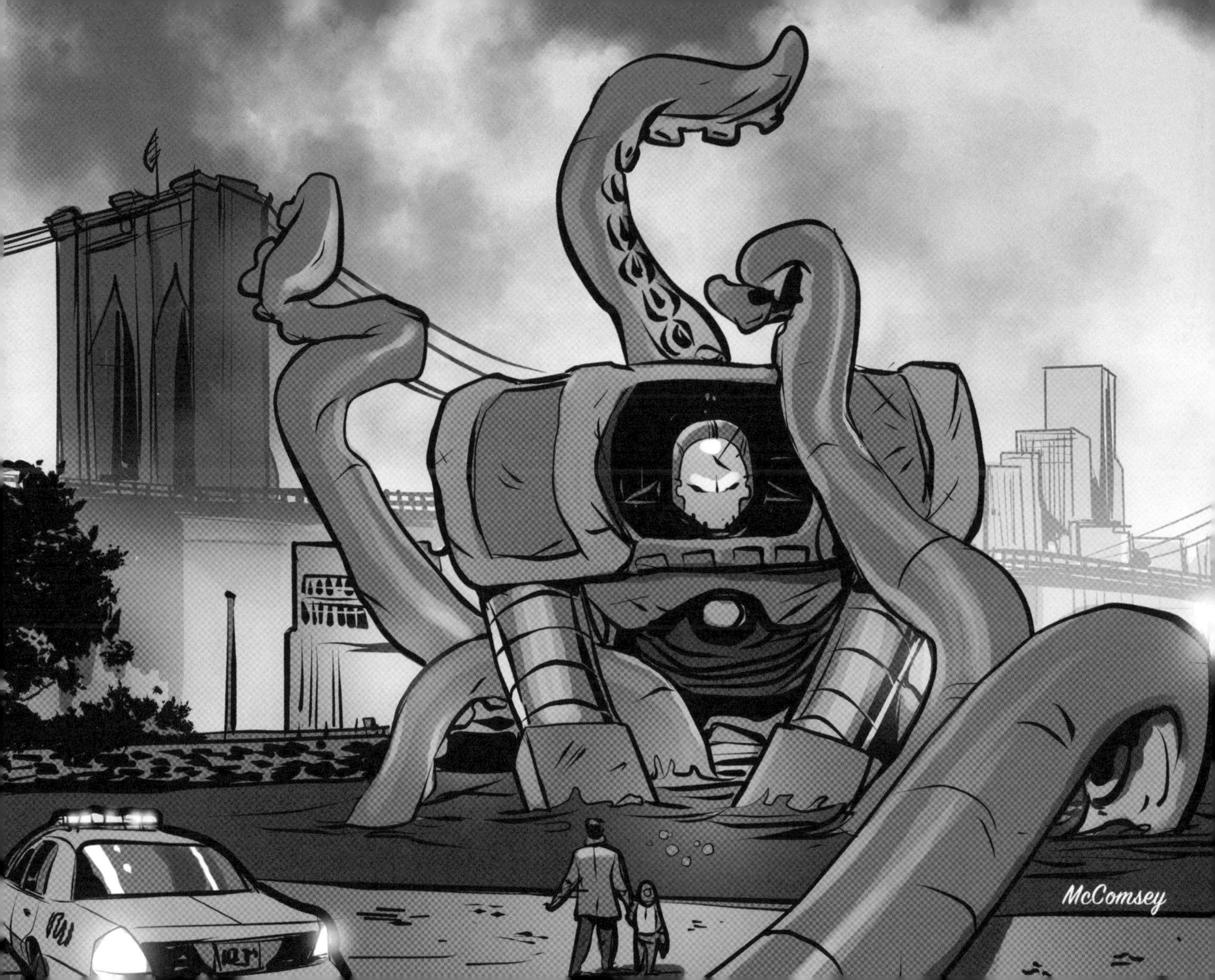
McComsey

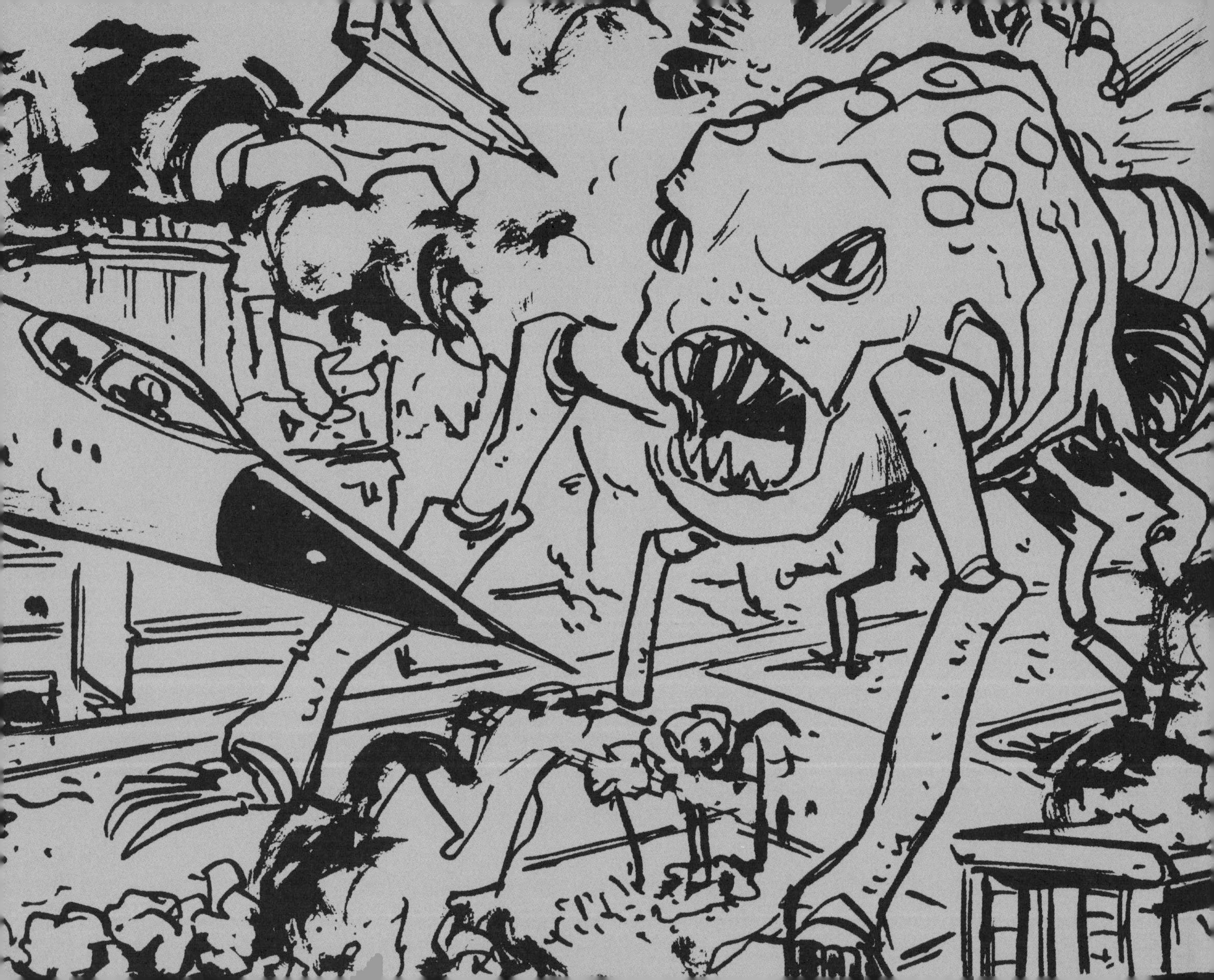

KILL ALL MONSTERS!™

W9-DCF-038